AN AGE
OF
TYRANTS

"On his progresses, Constantius went with downcast eyes and sullen countenance. He was a man with large eyes, long neck, and broad head, who bent far over toward the neck of the horse carrying him and glanced here and there out of the corners of his eyes so that he showed to all, as the saying goes, 'an appearance worthy of a tyrant.'"—Olympiodorus

CHRISTOPHER A. SNYDER

AN

AGE

OF

TYRANTS

BRITAIN AND THE BRITONS
A.D. 400–600

SUTTON PUBLISHING

First published in 1998 by Penn State Press

First published in the UK in 1998 by Sutton Publishing Limited
Phoenix Mill, Thrupp, Stroud, Gloucestershire, GL5 2BU

British Library Cataloguing in Publication Data

A catalogue record for this book is available from the
British Library

ISBN 0 7509 1928 0 (cased)
ISBN 0 7509 1929 9 (paperback)

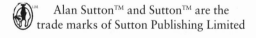 Alan Sutton™ and Sutton™ are the
trade marks of Sutton Publishing Limited

Printed in the United Stated of America.

CONTENTS

List of Illustrations   vii

Preface   ix

Introduction   xiii

Part I: THE TWILIGHT OF ROMAN BRITAIN

1 Roman Britain in the Fourth Century   3

2 Independent Britain, A.D. 406–10   17

Part II: SUB-ROMAN BRITAIN
The Written Record

3 Introduction to the Written Sources   29

4 *Britannia*   50

5 *Patria*   58

6 *Britanni*   66

7 *Cives*   73

8 *Reges*   81

9 *Tyranni*   90

10 Miscellaneous Terms   109

Part III: SUB-ROMAN BRITAIN
The Archaeological Record

11 Introduction to the Archaeological Evidence   131

12 Significant Sites   137

13 Continuity and Change   217

CONTENTS

Part IV: SYNTHESIS
Toward a Picture of Britain in the Fifth and Sixth Centuries

14 The Britons   225

    Conclusion   251

    Appendix A: Arthur and Merlin   253

    Appendix B: Chronology of Events   257

    List of Abbreviations   261

    Notes   263

    Bibliography   353

    Index   389

LIST OF ILLUSTRATIONS

1 Late Roman coinage featuring Britain and its usurpers

2 Map of the Diocese of the Britains

3 Late Roman bastion from the walls of York

4 Map of Hadrian's Wall

5 Map of coastal fortifications, Britain and northern Gaul

6 Map of conjectural locations of British kings and kingdoms

7 Map of significant sites in sub-Roman Britain

8 Map of major roads and towns of fourth-century Roman Britain

9 Map of Roman towns occupied in sub-Roman Britain

10 Part of the late Roman silver hoard found at Canterbury

11 Plan of a house from fifth-century London

12 The Balkerne Gate of Roman Colchester

13 Plan of a townhouse from sub-Roman Verulamium

14 Visible remains of the baths basilica, Wroxeter

15 The Newport Arch, Roman Lincoln's north gate

16 Map of Roman forts occupied in sub-Roman Britain

17 The barrack blocks at Roman Caerleon

18 The Roman amphitheater at Caerleon

19 Hadrian's Wall at Walltown Crags

20 Foundations of the granary at Birdoswald, Hadrian's Wall

21 Resurfaced main street at Corbridge, Northumbria

22 Corner tower of Burgh Castle, on the Saxon Shore

23 Map of rural sites in sub-Roman Britain

24 Plateau and ramparts of South Cadbury hillfort

25 Sub-Roman structures from the terraces on "Tintagel Island"

26 Degannwy Castle, Caernarvonshire

27 Plan of Dinas Powys contours and structures

28 Yeavering Bell, Northumberland

29 Holyhead Mountain and the Ty Mawr hut group

30 Map of excavated religious sites in sub-Roman Britain

31 Plans of churches in late and sub-Roman Britain

32 Foundations of the late Roman basilical "church" at Colchester

33 Excavations at Whithorn, Galloway

PREFACE

"An Age of Tyrants" is a slightly ironic—and certainly unusual—way of describing Britain in the fifth and sixth centuries A.D. Our modern notions of tyranny will undoubtedly conjure up images that are inappropriate for early medieval Britain. Nevertheless, "tyrants" appear again and again in contemporary written accounts from and about the island, so much so that in the waning years of the Roman Empire Britain was earning a special reputation as a "province fertile with tyrants." By looking closely at what these writers meant by the term "tyrant," we can uncover a variety of clues about the society that was producing these intriguing individuals.

The less ironic phrase "Britain and the Britons, A.D. 400–600" defines the chronological, geographic, and ethnic parameters of this study. Britain is here defined as the once-Roman area of the island of Britain, from the Forth-Clyde line to the Isles of Scilly. The period 400–600 is often labeled "sub-Roman." Technically, this label is used by archaeologists to describe pottery or other materials that show degeneracy from Roman forms. "Sub-Roman Britain" would then be the society that degenerated after the withdrawal of Roman troops c. 400. Many historians have adopted this term to describe the fifth- and sixth-century "interlude" between the Roman and Anglo-Saxon periods. "Sub-Roman" is for many reasons a regrettable label, but since it is generally accepted by scholars for lack of a better candidate, I have employed it as a convenient term for the present study. However, I use it here as purely a chronological indicator, not as an accurate description of the society. Sub-Roman Britain, then, is here defined as the period that began when Rome lost imperial control of the island (c. 410) and ended when Rome reestablished partial ecclesiastical control (c. 597) through the Anglo-Saxon kingdoms that had come to dominate lowland Britain.

If history is concerned with people, place, and time, then the people part needs some elucidation as well. Sub-Roman Britain was inhabited by different "peoples," defined ethnically, linguistically, or whatever way you like. This study is concerned primarily with the only group that has left us significant written testimony of their society during these two centuries. I call them "Britons" (because in Latin they called themselves *Britanni*) or, sometimes, "the British" (not to be confused with our modern notions of "British"). At least some Britons felt threatened by barbarian outsiders, whom they termed Picts (*Picti,* who inhabited most of Scotland), Scots (*Scotti,* from Ireland), and Saxons (*Saxones*). Of these terms, the last is the most oversimplistic, encompassing as it does several German-speaking groups from northwestern Europe. I will call them simply "Saxons" because the British writers used this shorthand, though "Anglo-Saxon" may also creep in here and there (despite not being historically attested until the writings of Paul the Deacon in the eighth century).

I need also to say a few words about my methodology and the conventions used in this study. Part II of the work is primarily concerned with written sources from the period, in particular their language and terminology. Thus, the transmission of these words over time is an important issue, and I have traced the manuscript tradition for key works such as the writings of Patrick and Gildas. In all cases, I have used the most recent or reputable editions, and when discrepancies regarding the orthography or form of a chosen term occur among the various manuscripts, I have discussed the variants in the notes. While the possibility of scribal intrusion or error always exists for such a study, the key terms on which I have chosen to focus are those which appear frequently and consistently in the manuscript tradition, although in some cases the variations themselves are the subject of my discussion. Furthermore, these terms have all been discussed (to a lesser extent) in modern critical works concerned with authors like Patrick and Gildas and have been judged genuine products of the period, not later additions. I have generally reproduced the Latin of the modern editions in its exact printed form, though I have capitalized proper nouns, inserted the consonantal *v* for consistency, and placed Latin nouns in the nominative case for clearer discussion of the terms. For inscriptions, I have simply replicated the epigraphic format of the source, followed either by a Latin reconstruction or English translation. Other conventions are described in the List of Abbreviations preceding the Notes.

In this study I have built upon the work of many fine historians and archaeologists, and I would now like to acknowledge my debt to their scholarship. I would especially like to thank Thomas S. Burns for his support of this project, my diligent editor Peter Potter, and the following individuals, who read and commented upon various parts of this study: Stephen D. White, David F. Bright, and Herbert Benario (Emory University); Steve

Fanning (University of Illinois at Chicago); Fred Suppe (Ball State University); Ralph Mathisen (University of South Carolina); Patrick Wormald (Oxford University); Michael Jones (Bates College); and W. R. McLeod (West Virginia University). I would also like to thank Chuck Spornick and Danielle Mokbel for their invaluable help, and the staff members at the following institutions for their assistance: the Woodruff Library, Emory University; the Swem Library, College of William and Mary; the Reinsch Library, Marymount University; the Institute for Historical Research and the British Library (London); the Ashmolean Museum Library (Oxford); the Cambridge University Library; the National Library of Wales (Aberystwyth); the University of Glasgow Library; and the Edinburgh University Library, the National Library of Scotland, and the Library of the Museum of Antiquities (Edinburgh). Financial support for study and travel was graciously provided by Emory University, Marymount University, the English Speaking Union of America (Atlanta Branch), the Frank Berry Memorial Trust, the St. Andrews Society of Washington, D.C., and the Council of Scottish Clans and Associates. Most appreciated of all was the sustaining love and support of my parents and my wife, Renée.

Dedicatum Deo.

INTRODUCTION

In the historical record of the island of Britain, two centuries have been lost. We know that the Romans, who introduced historical writing to Britain, made this island the westernmost province of their empire in A.D. 43. By the year 400, Roman Britannia had more than twenty walled cities, numerous temples and villas, and an extensive military network stretching from lowland Scotland to the southern coast of Wales. In the year 600, the Roman Empire was a fading memory in Britain—as it was in most of the West—and its legions, its Latin-speaking urban *cives* (citizens), and its villa economy were all gone from the island. When Romans returned to Britain in 597, they returned as Roman Catholic missionaries sent to convert a group of German-speaking newcomers who had settled outside the crumbling walls of a Roman town once called Durovernum Cantiacorum, henceforth Cantwara-byrig (Canterbury). In 600, the first archbishop of Canterbury dealt with local kings rather than imperial governors, and surveyed a Britannia whose "citizens" were peoples called Angles, Saxons, Welsh, Scots, and Picts.[1]

These two "lost centuries," from 400 to 600, are the beginning of what has been popularly termed the Dark Ages, that mysterious time between classical antiquity and the Middle Ages proper, when history becomes uncertain as myth and legend take center stage. King Arthur, Merlin, Saint Patrick, the hero Beowulf—these figures all have roots in the fifth and sixth centuries, either treading on British soil as real persons (Patrick certainly, Arthur and Merlin possibly)[2] or praised in songs (Beowulf) that filled the island's timber halls. The so-called Dark Ages also gave birth to Britain's first vernacular literatures, and witnessed a flourishing native artistic tradition that produced masterpieces in the form of sculpture, metalwork, and illuminated manuscripts.

Historians and archaeologists have never liked the label Dark Ages. For even though written records from this period are scarce and archaeological finds are difficult to date and interpret, there are numerous indicators that these centuries were neither "dark" nor "barbarous" in comparison with other eras. Latin learning survived in Christian monasteries; biblical and classical manuscripts were collected and copied; the first medieval penitentials were produced; commercial and ecclesiastical contacts with the Continent were reestablished; and, by 731, a substantive history of the "English" people in Britain was provided by the Northumbrian scholar Bede (673–735). Britain was back on the historical track.

But the fifth and sixth centuries still pose problems for scholars. Roman Britain can be understood through scattered references in imperial chronicles and through a wealth of excavated remains, much of it in metal and stone. This holds true up until about the year 410, when Rome officially recognizes its loss of Britain. Part I of the present study details these "twilight years" of Roman Britain by piecing together the written and archaeological evidence, providing a background for the crucial—but little understood—events following 410. For after that important year, historical references to Britain begin to dry up, coins are no longer minted, and construction switches to ephemeral materials, like earth and timber. At the other end of the period is Anglo-Saxon England, which can be traced backward historically as far as Bede's sources remain reliable, which is about the beginning of the seventh century. Additionally, there are rich archaeological finds from the early Anglo-Saxon kingdoms (like the regal Sutton Hoo ship burial), from the monasteries of Wales and the Western Isles, and from the forts of the Highland Picts. Thus, scholars have divided into camps where evidence is the richest, yielding Romanists, Anglo-Saxonists, and Celticists, many of whom have shied away from tackling the fifth and sixth centuries. Typically, scholars have treated the period as a mere "transition" from Roman Britain to Anglo-Saxon England;[3] at best, some have seen it as an enigmatic "interlude" between two better-understood eras,[4] a "dark age" of the Dark Ages.[5] Only recently has it been given a name: sub-Roman Britain.

This situation deserves remedying. Obviously, there must have been more than transition going on for two centuries, and calling a historical period an interlude is to provide an excuse for ignoring it. What happened between 410 and 597 is not easily discerned, but neither should it be easily dismissed. The written records that we do possess, along with numerous inscriptions and a growing corpus of archaeological evidence, speak of a vibrant civilization of kings and chariots, magistrates and imported wine, monks and villa chapels. These Britons devised complex military and political solutions to face a changing world, resuscitated their economy by trading mineral resources for Eastern luxury goods, and enjoyed a vigorous culture encompassing bardic songs and Latin schools. Just as the label "Dark Ages" was dismissed, so too must "sub-Roman" eventually be discarded. While it has become convenient (especially for archaeologists), it is not universally accepted, nor does it adequately describe contemporary British society. Moreover, "sub-Roman" implies both a continued connection to the Roman world and an inferiority of the British culture that survived. The validity of both of these implications is debatable.

Traditionally, there have been two methodological approaches to studying this period: historical and archaeological. These approaches are not, of course, mutually exclusive, although some have considered them so.[6] Bede was probably the first historian to gather the meager contemporary written evidence in order to write a history of the fifth and sixth centuries in Britain.[7] His chief source for this period was the British cleric Gildas, who lived in the first half of the sixth century. Gildas wrote a long sermon condemning the sinful activities of the kings and priests of his day.[8] While not a history, this work contains a historical preface (of sorts) and much detailed information concerning the political and ecclesiastical arrangements of the Britons. Using this work as a historical source presents problems;[9] nevertheless, historians from Bede to the present have acknowledged Gildas as our most important witness for sixth-century Britain.

For the fifth century, we have the writings of another British cleric, Saint Patrick. Born in the waning years of Roman Britain, Patrick was kidnapped as a youth and taken to Ireland. After returning years later to his family in Britain, Patrick trained to be a priest and sought to become a missionary to the Irish. Back in Ireland, Patrick corresponded with a British "tyrant" named Coroticus and penned a spiritual autobiography in which it is clear that he maintained contact with the British church.[10] Patrick's writings are, of course, invaluable sources for early Irish history. But they also provide precious clues about the activities of Britons, Picts, and Scots on mainland Britain in the fifth century.

Patrick and Gildas are of greatest use to historians because they are contemporary witnesses to the events of the fifth and sixth centuries, and because they are themselves Britons. Outsiders also composed a few contemporary writings, including Constantius of Lyon's *Life of St. Germanus* (Germanus paid two visits to Britain, in 429 and c. 445)[11] and two entries in the *Gallic Chronicles of 452 and 511*.[12] For the last years of Roman Britain, we have the reliable account of Ammianus Marcellinus,[13] a list of military and civilian posts known as the *Notitia Dignitatum*,[14] and the works of a host of imperial and church chroniclers (Olympiodorus, Sozomen, Orosius, Zosimus). Of later works, the collection known as the Llandaff Charters (pertaining to southern Wales in the mid–fifth to twelfth century),[15] Bede's *Ecclesiastical History,* a *History of the Britons* attributed to the Welsh monk Nennius (ninth century),[16] and the early entries in the *Anglo-Saxon Chronicle* (ninth to the twelfth century)[17] are of some limited use. Finally, tangential to the historical sources is the large corpus of Latin inscriptions from Britain, which yield some significant clues about personal names, religion, professions, burial, and political identity.[18]

While not insignificant, this body of historical sources is not overly impressive. Problems beset many of these sources. Accurate dating of the composition of the work and of the manuscript that contains it is often difficult. Scribal error must occasionally be taken into account, as must the biases and shortcomings of both author and copyist. Most distressing of all is the fact that, for Britain, there exists no narrative chronicle or history—contemporary or otherwise—covering these two centuries. For the modern historian, constructing a narrative history of sub-Roman Britain out of scattered references and clerical sermons remains extremely difficult if not impossible.

This is perhaps why so many have turned to an archaeological approach to studying the period. In the last twenty-five years, more than a dozen major works have been produced that examine the archaeology of fifth- and sixth-century Britain, while only a few purely historical works have appeared.[19] Some archaeologists have even studied the period as if it were prehistoric, ignoring all written sources and letting the archaeological remains speak for themselves.[20] These remains are diverse and attractive. Roman cities and forts have shown signs of continued occupation in the fifth century and beyond; Roman and Anglo-Saxon cemeteries have yielded clues about religious ritual and burial practices; native hillforts and other defensible enclosures have provided examples of timber halls and imported Mediterranean pottery. Artifacts range from the spectacular—multistoried townhouses, gold coins and rings, fine crafted silverware—to the mundane—coarse pottery, iron nails, butchered animal bones. While no comprehensive archaeological survey exists, the last two decades alone have produced several regional and thematic studies that have enhanced our knowledge of sub-Roman Britain enormously.[21]

But the archaeological approach has its problems as well. The end of occupation for most Roman towns in Britain remains uncertain, as does the beginning of occupation for native hillforts. Such uncertainty can be blamed on the difficulties in dating occupation of sites as well as individual artifacts. Archaeologists have, for this period, several aids to help them in ascertaining dates: historical sources, coins, pottery, typology, scientific analyses (predominantly radiocarbon estimates). As noted above, however, the written sources are of little help, and the minting of coins in Britain ended by 410. Comparisons of pottery and metalwork types can be quite useful, but, like radiocarbon estimates (when excavators are lucky enough to find organic material to test), they can give only chronological parameters, not precise dates. The interpretation of finds and settlements also poses difficulties and often tells us more about the preoccupations of the excavator than the object or site being examined. Archaeological models are notoriously idiosyncratic and sometimes simply cannot be reconciled with the historical sources.

The methodology of the present study follows both approaches, historical and archaeological.[22] That in itself is hardly innovative. But the emphasis, swimming against the tide of recent studies, is on the historical. My approach to the texts of sub-Roman Britain—which are not primarily "historical"—is to see them as "cultural products" of their age. That is to say, they cannot be used to reconstruct narrative history, but they can shed light on various aspects of British culture and the mental images of the writers composing them. Of particular interest—forming Part II of this study—is the sociopolitical language of contemporary writers, reflected in their use of such terms as *patria* (homeland), *cives, reges* (kings), *monachi* (monks), *servi* (slaves), and *tyranni* (tyrants).[23]

This last term is a good example of how we can learn from the changes taking place in the political vocabulary of late antiquity.[24] *Tyrannus* (Greek τυραννος) had long been recognized by Greeks and Romans as a political description—not necessarily negative—of a man who seizes power illegitimately, usually by military force, corresponding roughly to the English term "usurper." The weakened Roman Principate of the third century A.D. saw the rise of thirty consecutive military usurpers, and Britain itself spawned several of these *tyranni* in the fourth and fifth centuries. One such pretender, Constantine III, withdrew most (perhaps all) capable Roman troops from Britain in his bid for empire in 407, leaving the island independent but virtually defenseless. However, the sources continue to refer to Britain as "a province fertile with tyrants" who, after 410, wielded insular authority. Patrick writes a condemning letter to one "tyrant-like" British ruler, and Gildas complains that "Britain has kings, but they are tyrants."[25] It is clear from the British sources that the meaning of *tyrannus* in sub-Roman Britain had evolved dramatically since the appearance of the first tyrants in ancient Greece. I describe this evolution in Part II, showing how the concept of "tyrant" passed through successive political, philosophical, and religious "filters"—including Plato, Aristotle, and Augustine as well as the British witnesses—before being applied to British rulers. Surprisingly, indigenous beliefs about tyrants in the Celtic-speaking world are remarkably similar to the original Greek notion of local "strongman."

Similar evolution was occurring with many of the other aforementioned terms, as I believe can be demonstrated using this methodology of close examination of the language of the certain fifth- and sixth-century sources. Patrick and Gildas are particularly useful because they are literary bookends to the sub-Roman period, the former writing in the fifth century, with strong ties to the Roman world, the latter writing in the sixth century, with a disapproving eye cast on the Heroic Age that succeeded it. Focusing on their writings, indeed upon key words and concepts like *tyrannus*, enables us to judge how the cultural and political landscape was changing in this crucial period of British history. I hope in the present study to illustrate the complexity of this society by focusing attention on these terms, and to dispel any notion that the Britons were a marginal group waiting to be swept aside by the Germanic newcomers.

The second methodological approach taken here might best be termed "historical archaeology."[26] In Part III, I have surveyed over fifty British sites that have yielded strong evidence of sub-Roman occupation, and have described them in brief narratives according to settlement type. These narratives are in no way comprehensive, but they do include descriptions (and in some cases illustrations) of structures and of the artifacts used to date and interpret the sites. In using archaeology, the historian must constantly be aware of the problems of interpretation and dating. The findings herein are based on the original excavators' interpretations, supplemented by later criticisms or reevaluation and, of course, my own insights. The question of accuracy in dating all of these sites requires special attention,[27] as does the problem of "continuity" of occupation in both urban and rural settlements.[28]

There is currently a need for an in-depth assessment of the fifth-century survival of Roman towns in Britain, as well as a comparison of these urban settlements with the contemporary reoccupied hillforts. In Part IV, I synthesize the historical and archaeological evidence to address these and other issues. The society of the sub-Roman Britons is examined in many of its aspects: political, military, religious, economic, social.[29] I show that the political revolution of 410, when Britain gained its lasting independence from Rome, was an aristocratic *coup* that turned power over to local tyrants; that the military arrangements of the Britons owed much to both Roman and Celtic inspiration; that the spread of Christianity (and especially monasticism) after 400 was swift and unhindered by paganism; that the economy of Britain was not completely coinless and indeed, enjoying a revival of trade with Gaul and the Mediterranean, was seemingly vigorous; and that the growing cultural antagonism between the Britons and the Saxons would have far-reaching consequences. The written sources are used to affix names and personalities to the "dull dry bones" of archaeology,[30] and in turn the archaeological artifacts provide substance and texture to the flat written word. Finally, I place sub-Roman Britain in a wider historical context and propose a new label for the period.[31]

Merely to bring together what has already been done by archaeologists and historians working in the Roman and Celtic fields would be a major contribution. But this is not just a collection and assessment other scholars' findings. A study of the evolution of sociopolitical terminology in sub-Roman Britain, such as is begun here, has never been done before for any Western society in late antiquity. Such important terms as *patria, cives,* and *tyranni,* found throughout the literature, give us, as their meanings change, valuable insight on a society moving from the sphere of *Romanitas* to that of the Christian early Middle Ages.

Most important of all, this study is an attempt to establish an identity for a historical period that has suffered greatly from a lack thereof. The uniquity of sub-Roman Britain—both in the historical narrative and in the archaeological record—demands that a significant place be made for this era in the periodization of British history.

PART I

◆

THE TWILIGHT
OF ROMAN BRITAIN

1

◆

ROMAN BRITAIN IN THE FOURTH CENTURY

Roman Britain is the most obvious reference point for a discussion of sub-Roman Britain. For many scholars, sub-Roman Britain is measured by its degeneracy from the standards of Roman Britain: political degeneracy, military degeneracy, artistic degeneracy. I need not comment here on the validity of this perspective, but say merely that it rests on a presumed understanding of the period of Roman rule in Britain. Before looking in any detail at sub-Roman Britain, it is therefore necessary to examine Roman Britain at least in its later phases. We are fortunate (because the Romans were kind enough to leave behind extensive written and physical remains) in being able to piece together a narrative history of Roman Britain up to about A.D. 410, when the beleaguered emperor Honorius informed the Britons that they must defend themselves. Part I of the present study offers a brief survey of Roman Britain during the fourth century, followed by a closer look at the crucial events of the years 406–10. This provides the needed historical background for understanding both the written sources and the archaeological evidence of the sub-Roman period, which is the subject of Parts II and III of this book.

The conquest of Celtic Britain by the Roman legions had not been an easy one. In A.D. 43 the emperor Claudius rode triumphantly into the British capital of Colchester—with war elephants!—and celebrated his conquest of the island, claiming that it had cost few Roman lives. But he did not foresee that a handful of Roman military garrisons and treaties with a few native rulers would not be enough to make the island a stable part of the empire. The first century of the Roman occupation was marked as much by the bloody native revolts of Caratacus (c. 50) and Boudicca (60/61) as by the successes of the military governor Agricola in Scotland (78–84). Since the island was never completely conquered, military garrisons remained a permanent part of the Welsh landscape, and, of course, two fortified walls—the Hadrianic (begun in 122) and the Antonine (begun in 143)—were constructed across northern Britain to delineate Roman territory from barbarian. The northern barbarians promptly overran the Antonine Wall, while Roman troops in Britain elevated the first in a long series of imperial usurpers, Clodius Albinus (c. 192). Few legitimate emperors bothered to visit the distant and turbulent province (and those who did—Claudius, Hadrian, Septimius Severus and Caracalla, Constantius I and Constantine I, Constans—were there for purely military reasons), and Britain sent few of its native sons abroad for distinguished political careers in the imperial administration (though Britons did fill the lower ranks of the imperial army). In the third century Britain was even part of the breakaway Gallic Empire, and no sooner was it recovered by Rome than its coasts were strengthened by fortifications to fend off North Sea raiders. Native uprisings, military coups, and a continuing barbarian presence earned Britain a less than respectable reputation throughout the empire.

The Roman historian Tacitus wrote that imperial strategy in Britain, as in other distant provinces, rested upon the belief that simply transplanting Roman cities—the ultimate manifestation of Roman culture—would make the provincials want to become Romanized. Britain was therefore outfitted with two dozen major towns (though not comparable to the populous cities of the Mediterranean), as well as dozens of country estates—villas—which dominated large-scale agricultural production. Britain also sent off such exports as tin, lead, and grain to aid the imperial economy, though never in quantities comparable to the coin, food, and drink imported to sustain the province's large military presence. While the success of Romanization is currently a matter of vigorous scholarly debate,[1] no one can seriously doubt that the Roman army was the single most dominant aspect of the four-hundred-year occupation. Roman Britain had its periods of peace and prosperity, but they were overshadowed—at least in the written record—by military events. In this aspect, Roman Britain and sub-Roman Britain were much alike.

The fourth century is illustrative of this principle.[2] Just as the third century had opened with the death of a campaigning Roman emperor (Septimius Severus) on British soil, so too did the fourth. Constantius Chlorus came to Britain in 296 to put down the rebellion of Carausius and Allectus and died there ten years later, preparing for a northern campaign, in the city of Eburacum (York).[3] The rebel Carausius had distinguished himself by earning a maritime command from the Augustus, Maximianus, and by crushing the Frankish and Saxon pirates in the English Channel.[4] (The Roman Principate, rule of one emperor, had by this point given way to the Tetrarchy created by Diocletian, in which two emperors, each bearing the title Augustus, ruled together with two junior colleagues, who bore the title Caesar.) But after hints of collusion and treason, Carausius was forced to rebel openly by holding Britain and the Gallic coast with his fleet (the *classis Britannica*) and land base at Boulogne. Falling only sixteen years after the demise of the Empire of the Gauls, independence from Rome must have again become "an attractive memory" for the British troops who supported Carausius's regime.[5] There are signs, too, that Carausius actively sought British support by playing on native interests. In his coinage, he depicts himself as the *restitutor Britanniae* (restorer of Britain) welcomed by the *genius Britanniae*, the "guardian spirit" of the island (see Fig. 1).[6]

His support, however, was not enough to match the forces of Constantius. Carausius was assassinated and succeeded by his finance minister, Allectus, who fell in battle against Constantius's generals while the Caesar himself sailed triumphantly into London (see Fig. 1).[7] After rescuing the city from Frankish pirates, Constantius set about strengthening the defenses on the northern frontier. It was also at this time that Britain was exposed to Diocletian's administrative reforms, which had begun in the rest of the empire while Britain was under the control of Carausius. Britain had been divided by Severus into two provinces: Britannia Inferior and Britannia Superior. Now the "diocese of the Britains" consisted of four provinces: Britannia Prima, Britannia Secunda, Flavia Caesariensis, and Maxima

Fig. 1. Silver *denarius* of Carausius, with Britannia greeting Carausius on the reverse *(upper left)*; gold medallion of Constantius I, illustrating his relief of London *(upper right)*; gold solidus of Magnus Maximus *(lower left)*; silver *siliqua* of Constantine III *(lower right)*. (The coins of Constantius I and Magnus Maximus are reproduced courtesy of The British Museum)

Caesariensis (see Fig. 2). Each province had a capital city and a civilian governor (*praeses* or *rector*), who was responsible to the *vicarius Britanniarum* in London. He in turn reported to the praetorian prefect in Gaul, making Britain's inclusion in the "Prefecture of the Gauls" a clear sign that its future would from now on be linked with events happening across the Channel, militarily and otherwise.

Constantius returned to Britain in 306, accompanied by his son Constantine, and began a military campaign in the North. A victory is recorded over the Picts (*Picti*, "the painted men"), who make their first appearance (under this name) in the historical sources at this time and who

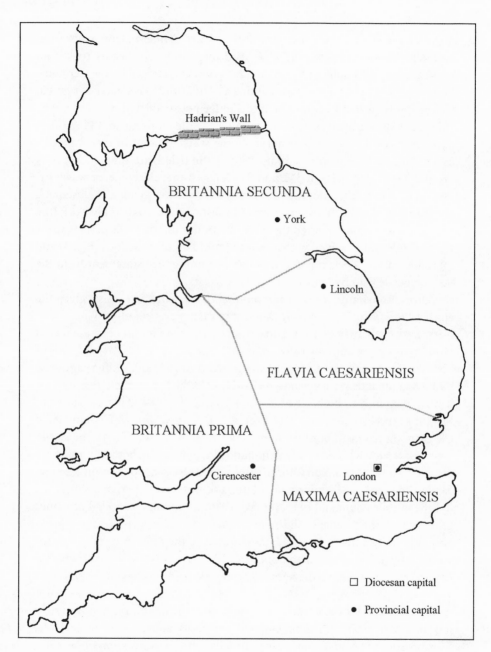

Hadrian's Wall

BRITANNIA SECUNDA

● York

● Lincoln

FLAVIA CAESARIENSIS

BRITANNIA PRIMA

●
Cirencester

London ▣

MAXIMA CAESARIENSIS

☐ Diocesan capital

● Provincial capital

Fig. 2. The Diocese of the Britains

are often linked, in these sources, with the "Irish" (*Hiberni,* later *Scotti* from an Irish verb meaning "to raid").[8] When Constantius returned to York from his victory, he died quite suddenly, and his army, encouraged by the Germanic "king" Crocus,[9] proclaimed Constantine as Augustus.[10] This unconstitutional succession launched Constantine into eighteen years of civil war and political maneuvering until he finally emerged as sole emperor in 324. Britain appears favorably in the panegyrics as the starting point of the emperor's ascension, and Constantine himself took the title Britannicus Maximus around 315. Gold coins of 312 and 314 suggest that the emperor was visiting Britain and that London was serving as a comitatensian mint.[11] Constantine also supported military reconstruction in Britain, and predictably York (the site of his accession) received the greatest attention. The walls of its fortress were rebuilt and provided with a series of multiangular bastions (Fig. 3) and a broader ditch. York stood as a grand and impressive statement from the new emperor who had emerged from the West.

Constantine (later, for his championing of the Christian cause, given the epithet "the Great") effectively completed the separation of provincial military and civil offices that had begun with Diocletian. He answered Diocletian's great administrative reforms with sweeping military reforms of his own. Stationary frontier generals were given the rank of *dux,* and new mobile commands were given to men who held the higher rank *and* title (for it was given also to high officials at his court) of *comes.* This translated in Britain as three major commands: the *dux Britanniarum,* who commanded the garrison troops (*limitanei*) along Hadrian's Wall (see Fig. 4); the *comes litoris Saxonici,* who probably commanded troops along both the southeast coast (the so-called Saxon Shore)[12] and northwest coast of Britain (see Fig. 5); and the *comes Britanniarum,* a later addition given (perhaps temporarily) the mobile command of crack cavalry units (*comitatenses*).[13] The Count of the Saxon Shore remains the most enigmatic of these posts. This was probably originally a *dux* who was later elevated to the rank of *comes,* perhaps with the inclusion of command of the Welsh coast. It is still debated whether *litus Saxonicum* means the shore was attacked *by* Saxons or settled *with* Saxons.[14]

As indicated by the evidence (villa construction and renovation, new mosaics, road repairs), Britain enjoyed prosperity under Constantine's rule. This prosperity began to slip only gradually with the succession of his sons, Constantine II, Constans, and Constantius II. The emperor Constans made an official visit to Britain in 343 (in midwinter) for some unknown reason, though victory over barbarians seems to have been one result.[15] Shortly after

Fig. 3. Exterior and interior of a late Roman bastion from the walls of York

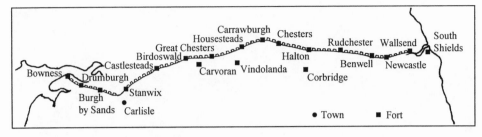

Fig. 4. Hadrian's Wall

this visit the elder Gratian, father of the emperor Valentinian I, was appointed to Britain with the command and status of *comes rei militaris*.[16] The reason again is obscure, but this is probably the first sign of unrest in the North. Constans had more serious trouble at home, however, for in 350 he fell victim to a palace plot, and rule in the West went to a usurper named Magnentius.[17] After three years of rule, Magnentius was defeated in battle by the eastern emperor Constantius II. Constantius then sent the imperial notary Paulus Catena (Paul "the Chain") to Britain to suppress the conspirators, and the savagery with which the supporters of Magnentius were hunted down in Britain suggests that they were loyal and many.[18]

Britain again appears in the sources with the Gallic campaigns of Julian, Constantius's Caesar and ultimately his challenger. In 359 Julian organized a fleet of six hundred ships to transport grain from Britain to support his army, seemingly an attempt to reopen an important supply route that had ceased to function.[19] A year later he was informed that the Picts and the Scots had broken a truce and were raiding the northern frontier lands of Britain.[20] This was spreading alarm throughout the British provinces, and the morale of the army was said to be very low. Julian decided not to go himself, but sent his *magister equitum* Lupicinus to Britain with four units of his field army.[21] Lupicinus waited out the winter in London, and was soon after recalled by Julian and arrested under trumped-up charges. While Julian was making his own play for power, the situation in Britain was growing steadily worse.

Ammianus Marcellinus records that in 364 Britain was constantly being harassed by four peoples: Picts, Saxons, Scots, and "Attacotti."[22] These last peoples, perhaps hailing from Ireland or the Western Isles, were described as cannibals by the credulous Saint Jerome.[23] We do not know what the Roman response was to these attacks, for they occurred shortly after the confusion surrounding Julian's death. But Ammianus gives a detailed account of the more serious attacks of 367, which he calls the "barbarian conspir-

Fig. 5.   Coastal fortifications in Britain and northern Gaul

acy."[24] The news reached the emperor Valentinian, while he was suffering from a serious illness, that several groups of barbarians had conspired together to launch a joint attack: Picts ("[who] were divided into two tribes, the Dicalydones and the Verturiones"), Attacotti, and Scots devastated much of Britain, while Franks and Saxons ravaged the coast of Gaul. Under promises of booty, the *areani*—frontier spies—had abandoned their duty and had allegedly allied themselves with the barbarians.[25] Thus the enemy attacked without warning and ambushed the *dux Britanniarum*, Fullofaudes,[26] who was taken prisoner. At the same time Nectaridus,[27] the "*comes* of the maritime region" (which probably included the Saxon Shore and the forts on the west coast of Britain, possibly those on the Gallic coast as well),[28] was killed. After these disasters, the barbarians split up into small bands and pillaged the provinces at will. Desertions from the army were numerous, and armed thugs roamed the land unchecked.

The presence of Franks and Saxons on the coast of Gaul may have delayed the news from Britain as well as the Roman response. The emperor did not come himself but sent his commander of the guard to assess the situation.[29] He was soon recalled, and four units of the field army were dispatched to Britain in 368 under the command of the *comes rei militaris* Theodosius,[30] the father of the future emperor of the same name. Count Theodosius landed at Richborough and advanced with his army to London, cutting down the bands of marauders laden with booty. At London he established a new *vicarius* (aptly named Civilis) over the diocese of Britain and issued a general pardon to those who had deserted from the British garrisons. When Theodosius took to the field, he routed the barbarians and even pursued them on the seas.[31] Subsequently, he had to deal with a serious revolt led by a rich exile named Valentinus, who may have been luring frontier troops away from their posts with promises of booty.[32] Theodosius quickly dealt with the rebellion (Valentinus was executed, his supporters pardoned), and the recovered lands were organized into a fifth British province, Valentia.[33]

Ammianus also tells us that Theodosius restored the cities and forts in the British provinces. Some have taken this to mean that the devastation of 367 was vast and that all of the refortification attested by archaeology should be attributed to a restoration program by Theodosius. But it is probably safer to say that the devastation was the result of successive barbarian raids and that Theodosius merely continued the refortification process that had been going on in Britain since Constantine.[34] One new area of construction took place on Britain's northeastern coastline, where a series of well-fortified watchtowers were built to warn nearby forts of seaborne Pictish raids (see Fig. 5). Similar stations built on the northwest coast had gone out of service in the second century, but there is archaeological evidence that some of the Cumbrian coastal forts were rebuilt at this time to protect against raids coming around the other side of Hadrian's Wall.[35]

One of Count Theodosius's lieutenants in Britain was a soldier from the Hispanic provinces named Magnus Maximus (see Fig. 1).[36] Maximus was sent back to Britain in the early 380s to organize defenses, whether as *dux Britanniarum* or *comes* is unclear.[37] He is credited with a victory over the

Picts and Scots in the north in 382, and a year later his British troops declared him emperor of the West.[38] The usurpation began with Maximus taking his army (perhaps from the garrisons in Wales, though certainly not all of the British troops, as Gildas states) into Gaul, where he defeated and killed the young emperor Gratian (whose troops had deserted him). Maximus established his court at Trier and was baptized a Catholic, securing the blessings of the Church and the western frontier at the same time.[39] The eastern emperor, Theodosius (son of the Count), was forced to offer some recognition of Maximus, now in control of the West. Not until five years later, after Maximus had crossed the Alps and occupied the imperial city of Milan, did Theodosius make a move against his rival (although his intention to do so was scarcely disguised in his coinage). Maximus was defeated twice in Pannonia and was finally seized and beheaded at Aquileia in 388.[40] Orosius wrote that "by the terror of his name alone [Maximus] exacted tribute and dues from the savage German tribes"; ironically, Maximus was brought down by Saxon troops employed by Theodosius, and his son, Victor, was killed by the Frankish count Arbogast.[41]

The effect Maximus's bid for power had on Britain is uncertain. Gildas states that Britain promised submission to Roman rule, and in exchange a "legion" was sent by sea to drive out the Scots and the Picts.[42] The panegyricist Claudian records that in 398, while Stilicho was busy suppressing revolt in Africa, Britain was suffering from "attacks" by Saxons, Scots, and Picts.[43] Stilicho, the Vandal-born *magister militum* (chief military commander) of the western emperor Honorius, is given credit for a victory over these barbarians, though he may not have been himself in Britain.[44] In 402 Claudian says that Stilicho withdrew from Britain "a legion, protector of the furthest Britons," an assumed reference to a garrison from Hadrian's Wall.[45] The last Roman coins that appear in Britain in large numbers also date to around 402, and it has been suggested that either Stilicho had stripped Britain of most of its garrison or the impoverished imperial government could no longer pay the troops.[46] Either situation could explain the insular unrest that led to the dramatic events of 406–10.

The historical narrative raises a couple of questions about the fourth century that remain problematic. First, how can we assess the effects of the barbarian raids on Britain? Second, did the fourth century result in the dramatic decline of urban life in Britain? The written sources—Ammianus, Claudian, Gildas—portray an island suffering from constant attack by the most savage of peoples, who forayed unhindered into the British countryside and terrorized the vulnerable cities. Some years are singled out (296, 367, 398) as worse than others, usually because of joint attacks, and Britain is only narrowly saved by the heroic efforts of an imperial general. Archaeologists have, in the past, taken these years as historical landmarks in their search for signs of destruction and decay. The result is an overly neat model for the collapse of Rome's westernmost province.

In recent years both historians and archaeologists have begun to question this picture. Peter Salway and Sheppard Frere have cautioned against automatically attributing all archaeological signs of fire, demolition, and reconstruction to these landmark dates (which, in any case, may be related to surviving imperial propaganda).[47] Precise archaeological dating is very difficult for late Roman Britain because of the scarcity of inscriptions, coinage, and written sources. "The ineffectiveness of Roman defensive arrangements was exposed not by a single disastrous raid," remarks Stephen Johnson, "but by the cumulative effect of a series of such raids,"[48] which overextended the system's recovery capacities.

A further problem is that a barbarian presence in Roman Britain did not always mean fire and destruction. In the early stages of the Roman occupation some British chieftains entered into client-king relationships with Rome, and the northern Votadini and Selgovae tribes perhaps maintained such peaceful relations through the fourth century. Maximus's organization of Britain's defenses may have included the resettlement of Irish or British tribes in Wales. Such mercenaries appear throughout the late Roman world as *laeti* or *foederati*. *Laeti* were barbarian warriors who were recruited—especially under Constantine and often *en bloc*—to serve in the Roman army as irregular soldiers (particularly as cavalry and other specialized units) under Roman commanders. The *foederati* were whole groups of barbarians who were invited inside the empire and given land and supplies (*annona, epimenia*) in exchange for fighting against hostile invaders. This was an attempt to strengthen the frontier (*limes*), and eventually federate status was extended to such groups as the Visigoths and the Ostrogoths.

Archaeologists have developed the theory that Germanic mercenaries began to be used extensively in Britain during the calamities of the fourth century, in particular to man city garrisons and protect rural estates. Inscriptions and the *Notitia* show that Germanic units were commonly part of the regular army stationed in Britain, while Ammianus records the transfer of an Alamannic king to Britain in 372, where he was given the rank of tribune.[49] The widespread occurrence in Britain of Germanic metalwork—particularly belt buckles and other military items—seems to correlate with the Germanic equipment used by the *laeti* stationed along the Gallic frontier. But there are problems with the identification of *laeti* in Britain. This equipment may not have been used exclusively by soldiers: it may have been sold as "army surplus" to civilians with "ethnic" tastes, or used as insignia by the new civil administration. Furthermore, even regular Roman soldiers along the *limes* were equipped with Germanic-style fittings; many of their colleagues were of Germanic origin, and it was becoming increasingly difficult to discern "Roman" from "barbarian" along the fourth-century frontier.[50] Not until the end of the fourth century and into the fifth was it at all likely that barbarian "federates" or allies enjoyed separate command in Britain, if at all.[51]

Another theory that has gained in popularity is that by about 350 the cities of Britain had been reduced to mere villages and all signs of urban life had disappeared.[52] This is based mainly on archaeological evidence, which shows a lack of expenditure on public buildings such as the forum and basilica in the fourth century. What we do see is a tremendous amount of military construction in and around the cities. Ditches were widened, and external towers were added to the city walls to provide fighting platforms, which could also support catapults and *ballistae*.[53] These improvements, most commonly attributed to Theodosius, actually helped the towns to outlive the forts, which were constantly being stripped of manpower.

The critics would say that these expenditures merely prove that the cities had ceased to be centers of urban activity and had become walled fortresses. The *Notitia* shows that even the civilian *vicarius* in London had command of some troops. Still, it would be closer to the truth to say, not that urban life had *ceased* in the fourth century, but that it had *changed*.

Martin Millet has provided a more complete model of this change, which may be summarized as follows:[54] The crisis of the third century led to radical changes in the structure of Roman Britain—the decline of the *civitas* capitals, the emergence of the small towns (*pagi*), and the decentralization of the economy to the periphery. The *pagi* came under the control of local magnates, or *possessores,* whose status was sanctioned in the laws. The *possessores* owned villas nearby and turned increasingly to these small towns as markets for their goods. The cities "were no longer principally economic foci but rather defended centres for their districts, which contained large private houses but comparatively little productive capacity."[55] These private residences in the cities were no doubt owned by the same magnates who, though maintaining their status as *decuriones* (town councillors), relied on the *pagi* as their personal power bases. Judging from excavated examples of the large *domus* in Romano-British cities, these powerful curial families increasingly spent money on their own properties and pursuits rather than their communities, perhaps leading to what appears in the archaeological record as the rapid collapse of orderly urban life in Britain after 400.[56]

The fourth century yields many signs of the emergence of a landed elite over and beyond the traditional farmers of the *villae rusticae*. These men no longer depended on the Roman government for advancement, and no longer saw the cities as the exclusive means to display their wealth and power. They turned increasingly to patron-client relationships to build a loyal body of supporters, with whom they eventually seized control of their districts.[57] In the fifth century they stepped out of the shadows to take the reins of government in independent Britain. The term used most often to describe them was *tyranni*, "tyrants," and after 410, according to Saint Jerome, the island "was fertile of tyrants."[58]

Then again, the fourth century had begun with a tyrant elevated on British soil. Constantine I, Christian emperor and military innovator, was himself an imperial usurper who made good his claim by wielding a mighty sword and showing favor to the Christians, who would chronicle his reign. While Roman cities in Britain may have been in decline throughout the century— and I believe the archaeological record does indeed show this to have been the case—Roman politics was no less so. Strong leaders with the backing of a client army could legitimately conceive the highest of political aspirations. From Britain, both Constantine and (for a shorter time) Magnus Maximus had come to rule the West, after displaying the might of Roman armies over barbarians on British soil. Who could blame the British tyrants of the early fifth century for following in such illustrious footsteps?

2

◆

INDEPENDENT BRITAIN,
A.D. 406–10

The historical narrative for Roman Britain comes to a dramatic halt in A.D. 410, for in that year the diocese was formally cut off from imperial protection and became increasingly alienated from the distant chroniclers of Rome's fall. Likewise, as payment ceased to reach the remnants of the imperial army stationed along the British *limes,* coinage ceased to enter the archaeological record, and we are left without that method of dating new structures and settlement. The tumultuous events of 406–10—the last in Britain to be detailed by imperial historians—therefore deserve close scrutiny, for they resulted in a Britain that is both remarkable for its bold initiatives for independent rule and self-defense and frustratingly elusive of the historian's grasp. This is also the period from which the British tyrants emerge, first as claimants to the western imperial title, later as more limited insular authorities. So frequent were British usurpations in this brief four-year period that the island earned a long-lasting reputation, throughout the once-Roman world, for political irregularity and vice. By 410, an age of tyrants had begun in Britannia.

Separation and independence, however, were unlikely to have been on the minds of Britons a decade earlier. At the turn of the fifth century, Britain seems to have played a part in the larger military strategy of the western imperial "partners," Honorius and Stilicho. Already exercising the chief military command in the West under Theodosius I, Stilicho maintained his position after Theodosius's death in 395 by claiming that the emperor had entrusted him with the guardianship of his two sons, Honorius and Arcadius. Arcadius, ruling in the East, balked at such a notion, and thus Stilicho's activities remained confined to the West, where he maneuvered between the young emperor Honorius and the powerful warlord Alaric. When containing Alaric's westward movements by armed confrontation proved ineffective, appeasing the Visigothic leader with regular subsidies and a Roman title became Stilicho's preferred option.[1] At first the emperor Honorius, who was Stilicho's son-in-law, passively sanctioned Stilicho's arrangements with Alaric, despite the growing indignation of the senatorial aristocracy. Indeed, until the end of the year 406 Stilicho seemed to have things in the western provinces well in hand.

Unfortunately, for much of Stilicho's activity in these years we must rely upon evidence from the poet Claudian, whose panegyrics give us only a vague notion of what was going on in Britain. Some successes against the Saxons at sea and the Picts in Scotland[2] were followed up by a full-scale war against the Picts in 398.[3] Claudian implies that Stilicho led the forces in Britain himself, but it may be that he only initiated the campaign as *magister militum* in the West. We cannot even be certain (despite Claudian's sycophantic verse) that Stilicho's campaign was a success, though Gildas seems to confirm this.[4] Regardless, problems in Italy warranted Stilicho's attention and necessitated the withdrawal of troops from Britain—according to Claudian, "a *legio*" from Hadrian's Wall.[5] This likely happened in 401 or 402,[6] and Gildas makes it (predictably) a dramatic event: "They [the Romans] then bade the Britons farewell, as if intending never to return."[7]

Though Britain was not left completely unprotected, its security was more than ever tied to the precarious defense of the western provinces, which was centered in Gaul. Disaster struck on the last day of December 406, when Alans, Vandals, and Sueves crossed the frozen Rhine and overran the provinces of Gaul.[8] Zosimus states that the invasion of Gaul terrorized the troops in Britain, who, fearing that the barbarians would cross the Channel next, responded by electing their own emperors to solve the frontier problems.[9] The first to be elected was a soldier named Marcus,[10] but he was soon put to death when he failed to please the soldiery.[11] Their second choice is more interesting. He was a civilian named Gratian,[12] described by Orosius as a *municeps* (civilian official).[13] According to Zosimus, the soldiers bestowed upon Gratian the imperial garb—purple robe and crown—and "formed a bodyguard for him as they would an emperor."[14] But the results of this usurpation were the same: failing to please his supporters, Gratian was killed after a four-month reign.[15]

The third candidate proved to be longer lived. Constantine[16]—who became Constantine III (see Fig. 1)—was chosen from the ranks of the military solely, we are told, on the basis of his name.[17] Cashing in on the reputation of Constantine the Great, who had also been declared emperor by the troops in Britain exactly one hundred years before, the new usurper carried the propaganda even further by renaming his sons Constans and Julian.[18] He then followed the example of that other British tyrant, Magnus Maximus, by taking British troops across to Gaul to secure the western frontier.

It is worth taking a closer look at the well-intentioned and partially successful plans of Constantine III, called "the Pretender." Zosimus tells us that his first official act was to name two generals, Justinianus and Nebiogastes, as *magistri militum* in Gaul,[19] an unusual act seemingly in imitation of Maximus.[20] He then crossed the Channel with his army and landed at *Bononia* (Boulogne, in northern Gaul), staying in the area a few days to gain the support of the local forces.[21] Stilicho responded to the pretender by dispatching his *magister,* Sarus, against Constantine's army. Sarus engaged Justinianus, "killing him and his troops and capturing a vast amount of booty."[22] Sarus then headed for Valentia, which Constantine considered a safe headquarters, and was approached by the remaining *magister* Nebiogastes. The two exchanged oaths of friendship, which Sarus immediately disregarded by slaying the general.[23] Constantine then appointed as his new *magistri* the Frank Edobinchus and the Briton Gerontius;[24] Sarus is said to have been so fearful of their military experience and bravery that he withdrew from Valentia after besieging it only seven days.[25]

With Sarus and his army no longer a threat, Constantine grew bolder in his initiatives. First, he reestablished garrisons along the Alpine passes to guard himself against another invasion from Italy.[26] Then he bestowed upon his eldest son, Constans, the title of Caesar, and sent him to Spain with Gerontius.[27] Zosimus says that Constantine feared the power of Honorius's "relatives" in Spain, who could launch an attack over the Pyrenees and, with the help of an Italian army, encircle Constantine's forces.[28] Constans arrived in Spain, having appointed various Gallic aristocrats to military posts there,[29] and suppressed the imperial loyalists.

After his initial successes, Constans returned to his father in Gaul, leaving his wife at his court in Saragossa and entrusting Spain to the *magister* Gerontius.[30] Constans brought with him as hostages two relatives of Honorius, Verenianus and Didymus, who were immediately put to death in Gaul.[31] At this time, probably 409, an embassy representing Constantine arrived at Honorius's court. They explained to Honorius that Constantine had not wished to become emperor, but that the title had been forced upon him by the army (by now a standard usurper's lament).[32] Honorius, presently distracted by the approach of Alaric's Visigothic army and fearing the safety of his relatives, pardoned Constantine's usurpation and began to explore the benefits of recognizing him as his colleague.[33] On hearing that his relatives had been murdered, however, Honorius withdrew his peace agreement. Another envoy was then sent by Constantine, a well-respected diplomat named Jovius. Jovius asked that the previous peace agreement be confirmed and that a pardon be granted for the murder of Didymus and Verenianus, who (he claimed) had been put to death against the wishes of Constantine. Seeing how this disturbed the emperor, Jovius promised that he himself would bring Constantine's army to aid in the defense of Italy. "On these terms," comments Zosimus, "Jovius was allowed to depart."[34]

According to Renatus Frigeridus, Constantine was pleased with the peace negotiations with Honorius and, freed from fear of an attack from Italy, sent his son Constans back to Spain, accompanied by a new *magister,* Justus, to replace Gerontius.[35] It is at this moment, late in the year 409, that everything began to fall apart for Constantine. Somehow Gerontius got wind of these developments and proclaimed one of his own dependents, a man ironically named Maximus, as emperor.[36] Zosimus states that Gerontius was able to win his soldiers' support for Maximus and even incited the barbarians in Gaul to revolt against Constantine, who, denuded of his Spanish troops, "allowed the barbarians over the Rhine to make unrestricted incursions."[37] These same "barbarians from beyond the Rhine" (though here the confused Zosimus likely means other trans-Rhine barbarians, such as the Saxons) also harassed the inhabitants of Britain and some of the Gallic peoples, forcing them to take up arms (illegally) and rebel against Rome.[38] "The revolt of the provinces of Britain and Gaul occurred during Constantine's tyranny," comments Zosimus, "because the barbarians took advantage of his careless government."[39]

Constantine responded to the crisis by making Constans his colleague, as Augustus, and appointing a new praetorian prefect, Decimus Rusticus.[40] These two he sent to subdue Spain, while Edobinchus was sent to recruit allies in Germany.[41] Constantine himself seems to have led an army across the Alps to meet Honorius in 410, perhaps to be defeated by Alaric (who had brought the Visigothic army into Italy in 408 to force Honorius to honor a treaty with his people) or else to have his supporters at Honorius's court eliminated in another palace revolt. At any rate, the pretender soon returned to Gaul.[42]

While Constantine's position in the West seemed to be slipping and Alaric's army hovered in northern Italy blocking (by default) any invasion force, the emperor Honorius felt safe and secure within the fortified confines of the new imperial capital of the West, Ravenna. His only real threat appeared to be the powerful Stilicho; this threat was eliminated by execution of the general along with his son and supporters in 409. After the death of his patron Stilicho, Alaric, desperate to receive the pay promised to his people, surrounded Rome with his troops and negotiated with Honorius and the Roman senate for a new treaty for his people and, for himself, the title of Master of the Soldiers. The besieged senate paid his price, but Honorius would not budge, and the Visigothic army sacked the Eternal City for three days in August 410. While the pillaging was rather mild by contemporary standards, it was nevertheless a sack heard round the world. Jerome, in far off Jerusalem, wrote of the event as if it signaled the end of the world.

Honorius hardly saw it that way, but for Constantine the end was indeed near. Constans and Rusticus were repulsed by Gerontius and his allies in Spain, and the pair returned to Constantine at Arelate along with Frankish and Alamannic recruits.[43] Constantine then sent his son, in 411, to Vienna, but Constans was intercepted and killed by Gerontius.[44] Gerontius then marched on Arelate and besieged Constantine there. Honorius finally decided to rid himself of the usurper, and sent an army to Gaul under the command of his new *magister militum*, Constantius (later the briefly reigning emperor Constantius III).[45] Upon seeing the imperial army, Gerontius fled to a friend's estate, where he was himself besieged by his own troops.[46] While Constantius continued the siege, Constantine received news that Edobinchus had been defeated and a new usurper, Jovinus, had been set up in northern Gaul.[47] The despairing Constantine then laid down his power and took refuge in a church, where he was hurriedly ordained a priest.[48] The city gates were then opened, and Constantine's troops turned the usurper and his young son Julian over to Constantius's army.[49] While the prisoners were being transported back to Italy, Honorius sent a band of assassins to meet them, and they were beheaded near the River Mincio.[50]

Constantine, Constans, Gerontius, and Maximus were all disposed of by 411, and Jovinus and Decimus Rusticus were soon to follow.[51] The sources are unequivocal in their judgment of Constantine and his ilk: they were "tyrants."[52] The sources are also quick to point out the negative impact that the actions of the tyrants (and their barbarian allies) had on Britain, Gaul, and Spain. Zosimus records that fear of barbarian invasions is what drove the Britons to support Constantine's ambitions in 406.[53] But according to the *Chronicle of 452*, while Constantine was busy "oppressing" Gaul, he left Britain defenseless against a devastating attack by the Saxons in 408 or 410.[54] Though there is some uncertainty about this date, R. W. Burgess reminds us that Saxon pirates were a constant threat in the Channel at this time.[55] Indeed, Zosimus records another Saxon attack on Britain in 409, which deserves quoting in full:

> [Constantine] allowed the barbarians over the Rhine to make unrestricted incursions. They reduced the inhabitants of Britain and some of the Gallic peoples to such straits that they revolted from the Roman empire, no longer submitted to Roman law, and reverted to their native customs. The Britons, therefore, armed themselves and ran many risks to ensure their own safety and free their cities from the attacking barbarians. The whole of Armorica and other Gallic provinces, in imitation of the Britons, freed themselves in the same way, by expelling the Roman magistrates and establishing the government they wanted.[56]

The actions taken by the Britons and Armoricans in successfully freeing themselves from the empire were revolutionary, illegal, and unprecedented in the annals of Roman history. Fortunately, we do not have to rely on Zosimus alone to verify what was happening in Britain. Procopius tells us that, after the revolt of Constantine III, "the Romans were no longer able to recover Britain, which from that time on continued to be ruled by tyrants."[57] A passage in the *Narratio de imperatoribus,* describing events in 410, confirms this: "The British provinces were removed from Roman authority forever."[58] Even later writers like Bede preserve the tradition that the year 410 marks the end of Roman rule in Britain.[59]

If it is clear that this revolution was significant, it is not so clear just who was revolting against whom. J.N.L. Myres suggests that Britain's independence was the result of a struggle between two powerful factions: a pro–Roman Catholic party and a pro–Celtic Pelagian party.[60] Though anti-Roman sentiment doubtless played a role in the revolt, this view has largely been discounted.[61] Equally provocative is E. A. Thompson's theory that *bacaudae*—dissident peasants—were the ones responsible for expelling the Roman magistrates in Britain and leading the counterattack against the barbarians.[62] This theory assumes that the revolutionaries in fifth-century Britain were the same as the *bacaudae* that had plagued Gaul since the third century.[63] There is no textual proof of *bacaudae* in Britain, though Ian Wood points out that there may be some truth in this theory if we widen our definition of fifth-century *bacaudae* to include failed local magistrates, dispossessed heirs, widows, and orphans.[64]

Can we be more precise about who were expelled by the revolutionaries? Zosimus says simply that the Britons (as well as those in Armorica and other parts of Gaul) expelled "the Roman magistrates."[65] Some have interpreted this to mean the civil and military officials of the faltering Constantine III.[66] Others have taken Zosimus at his literal word, believing the Britons to have expelled all Roman officials in 409—not just Constantine's men—in what appears to have been a resurgence of local (native) authority.[67] Zosimus speaks in very general terms throughout this passage, saying that the Britons "revolted from the Roman Empire, no longer submitted to Roman law, and reverted to their native customs."[68] Gildas similarly uses general terms, contrasting "Britons" and "Romans," chastising the former for "ungratefully rebelling" against "Roman kings" and failing in their "loyalty to the Roman Empire."[69] It appears thus that the Britons in 409 rejected the imperial infrastructure in Britain and the laws that had bound them to the sinking ship that was the western Roman Empire. In 407, those optimistic about recovery attached themselves to a military "emperor" with the auspicious name of Constantine, who took the bulk of the British army to Gaul to secure the West (including Britain) from barbarians. By 409, Constantine was besieged by both the legitimate western emperor and his own general, Gerontius, along with his barbarian allies; Burgundians were now settled inside the Rhine, while the first barbarians who had broached that frontier were plundering Spain as they had Gaul; and Britain was left alone to face Saxon devastation. To take up arms against the barbarians threatening their cities, the Britons would by necessity have had to disobey Roman law and those responsible for enforcing it: Constantine's officials. The senior civil officials were, in any case, likely to have been transient career men with little stake in the island's fortunes;[70] the military officials likewise may have been pulled away from Britain by various loyalties—to Constantine, to Gerontius, to Honorius, to their homeland, or to whomever was in the best position to pay them (much of the army in Britain had not received regular payment in coin since 402).[71] Those remaining to defend and govern Britain, who rejected Roman government and now truly saw themselves as Britons, were those with most at stake in the island: civic officials in their expansive town houses, major landholders with their rural estates, Christian bishops and their growing congregations, ordinary soldiers born in Britain or having land and families there. For these Britons, assuming power and responsibility was a local affair made easier by the removal of the costly and burdensome civil and military bureaucracy that had been controlled from Gaul and Italy.

One further piece of significant evidence that has been seen by many to signify the official end of Roman rule in Britain is the Rescript of Honorius. This survives in a passage in Zosimus, who, while describing Alaric's activities in Italy in 410, writes: "Honorius sent letters to the cities [πολεις] in Britain [βρεττανια], urging them to fend for themselves."[72] This may have been in response to an appeal for help from some party in Britain, and it is significant that Honorius addressed his letters to the cities in Britain. One would expect such letters to be sent to the *vicarius* or some such imperial representative; the implication is that the municipal authorities were the only officials to survive the tumultuous events of 406–10.[73]

Recently, this interpretation of Zosimus (6.10.2) has come under attack by some historians. It has been argued that, because the rest of Zosimus's chapter 10 deals with Alaric's campaigns in Italy, the term βρεττανια does not refer to Britain but rather to Bruttium (βρεττια), a province in southern Italy: let the cities of BRUTTIUM fend for themselves.[74] Thompson has argued powerfully against this "rewriting" of Zosimus.[75] No enemy, writes Thompson, was threatening Bruttium and southern Italy in early 410 (Alaric was in Liguria); and even if there were such an enemy, why would Honorius write not to the governor (*corector*) but to the cities of Bruttium—and not to the cities of the neighboring provinces as well?[76] Furthermore, a passage in Gildas—entirely independent of Zosimus (and Olympiodorus)—preserves the message of the Rescript of Honorius: "The Romans therefore informed our country that they could not go on being bothered with such troublesome expeditions. . . . Rather, the British should stand alone, get used to arms, fight bravely, and defend with all their powers their land."[77]

Though the "Bruttium" reading has been adopted by many commentators, it is possible that Thompson's defense will swing scholarly opinion back to Britain.[78] I find Thompson's arguments more compelling, and they prevent us from having to correct the diction of a medieval copyist when we have no other manuscript tradition for comparison. Michael Jones, also convinced by Thompson's arguments, offers an alternative chronology for the events of 406–10.[79] He believes that the rescript should *precede* the rebellion in Britain and reflects an attempt by the Britons to get military aid from Honorius to defend themselves against Saxon attacks. Failing to receive support, the Britons then expelled the remnants of Roman administration and took matters into their own hands.

A careful interpretation of the political and military events of 406–10 is crucial to an understanding of what kind of society emerged in Britain in the immediate post-Roman years. Who engineered Britain's independence from Rome and why are questions of great importance to historians in this field. Yet they cannot be answered with quick-and-easy theories based solely on the evidence given to us by Zosimus. Only by evaluating all relevant contemporary evidence, and comparing that with the testimony of Zosimus and Gildas, can a compelling case be made for Britain's "revolutionary" years. In Part IV, I offer such an interpretation of these events and a historical reconstruction of these first sub-Roman years. But before such a model can be proposed, a more careful examination of the language of the written sources must be undertaken. It is to such a study that I turn in Part II.

PART II

◆

SUB-ROMAN BRITAIN
The Written Record

3

◆

INTRODUCTION TO THE
WRITTEN SOURCES

The years 406–10 are among the best chronicled in the history of Roman Britain. After 410, however, there is silence. We hear nothing about independent Britain until Saint Germanus's first visit there in 429, described later by Constantius of Lyon. Apart from a brief mention in the *Chronicle of 511*, Britain appears in no real histories again until the age of Bede. Thus, 410 marks the end of narrative history as far as the Britons are concerned.

This does not mean, however, that the independent Britons have no history. What we sacrifice in terms of historical narrative we make up for by having, for the first time, the voices of the Britons themselves. These voices—of which Patrick and Gildas are the most prominent—are not the voices of classical historians, but they are products of their age. Their writings therefore betray a great deal about the social, political, and religious climate in which they lived. In Part II of this study, I identify which of the written sources for Britain were produced in the sub-Roman period, and concentrate on the language used by these writers to describe contemporary ethnic, geographical, sociopolitical, and religious concepts. This terminology, which has never before been the subject of such close scrutiny, will illuminate our understanding of the period and, I hope, open up many areas for future investigation.

Fifth- and sixth-century history in the British Isles is dependent upon much difficult and unconventional written evidence. In this chapter I examine this unconventional evidence, sorting out what should and what should not be used to write a history of sub-Roman Britain. Fortunately, there is a long tradition of textual criticism dealing with most of these sources. Much of this scholarship, however, has focused on the clues for a historical King Arthur.[1] David Dumville, in writing a critique of these "Arthurian" works, set down new criteria for evaluating the disparate sources for the sub-Roman period. While affirming the reliability of Patrick and Gildas, Dumville calls on the work of other textual scholars to discredit the later "Celtic" material (poetry, genealogies, hagiography) that has traditionally been used to write fifth- and sixth-century history.[2] Both historians and archaeologists have taken Dumville's cautionary remarks to heart.[3]

Dumville's essay leaves one with the impression that only the writings of Patrick and Gildas are permissible as historical evidence for this period. Recent work, however, may be opening up new avenues of research for those investigating the history of sub-Roman Britain. The credibility of the Gallic Chronicles has been somewhat restored,[4] and they are about to be published in a much-needed new edition;[5] Constantius's *Life of St. Germanus* has been resuscitated as a historical source for fifth-century Britain;[6] and the publication of the Llandaff Charters has led to new studies that question traditional assumptions about early medieval Wales.[7] If these and other sources are approached with the same caution used by critics like Dumville, historians of the period might, after all, avoid the negative "reductionism" that has ensnared so many archaeologists.

Ammianus Marcellinus

The most reliable source of information about Britain in the fourth century is the late-imperial historian Ammianus Marcellinus. Born A.D. 330 to a

Greek family in Syrian Antioch, Ammianus was selected at an early age to become a member of the *protectores domestici*, which had become the imperial bodyguard after Constantine disbanded the praetorian guard in 312.[8] He was then assigned, by the emperor's orders, to serve under Ursicinus, the *magister militum* of the East, and was stationed in Nisibis in Mesopotamia.[9] Ammianus was very close to Ursicinus, and followed his commander on various missions to Antioch, Gaul, and Pannonia. Most of his military career was spent on campaigns against the Persians, including that of Julian in 363. After this last campaign, Ammianus appears to have settled in his native Antioch, making occasional trips to Egypt.[10] In Antioch he began reading in preparation for writing a history, and later traveled through Thrace and Italy, collecting material for this project. By 383 he had settled in Rome, acquired some position there, and made friends with Symmachus and other literati. He died there sometime after 393, probably around 397.

Ammianus set out to write a comprehensive history in the style of Tacitus, which would cover the period from the accession of Nerva in 96 to the death of Valens in 378. Divided into thirty-one books (the first thirteen of which are lost), it bore the simple title *Res Gestae*. Published in installments, the first books appeared probably in 390 or 391. The only books that survive deal with a twenty-five-year period, from 353 to 78, in which Britain plays a somewhat prominent role. Ammianus thus provides information about the island as it figured in the lives of Magnentius, Julian, and Theodosius the Elder, recounting as well the *barbarica conspiratio* of 367 and naming Britain as a place of exile. Ammianus is also a chief source of information about Valentia, the alleged fifth British province, whose creation he ascribes to Theodosius.[11] His detailed account of the campaign of Theodosius provides important information about the military in late Roman Britain[12] and has helped archaeologists to determine the dating of defensive construction in various British towns in the fourth century. Finally, Ammianus stands as an example of secular historical writing in the late empire, and his language can thus be compared and contrasted with that of the Christian "historical" writers whose accounts dominate the fifth and sixth centuries.

The *Notitia Dignitatum*

Our earliest written evidence for fifth-century Britain is an enigmatic document known as the *Notitia Dignitatum Occidentis*.[13] Literally "a register of offices of the West," it is a list of military and civil offices in the western empire (there is also an eastern half), which originated in the office of the *primicerius notariorum* of the West. The date and purpose of the *Notitia* are much disputed, but generally historians have followed A.H.M. Jones in regarding the surviving text as based on an official list composed between 395 and 408, with later revisions (perhaps by an ill-informed clerk) made up to about 425.[14]

The *Notitia* is indeed a vast (though incomplete) survey of the administrative bureaucracy of the late empire, including detailed information about imperial finance, mints, and industries as well as lists of military posts and the units that garrisoned them.[15] For Britain, the military evidence amounts to a list of forts associated with two *limitaneus* commands—the *dux Britanniarum* (along Hadrian's Wall) and the *comes litoris Saxonici per Britannias* (along the southeast coast)—and a list of units under one *comitatensis* command—the *comes Britanniarum*. The term *litoris Saxonici*, "Saxon Shore," exists only in the *Notitia*, which gives us no further clue to its meaning.[16] As for the civil administration in Britain, the *Notitia* lists the governors of the five British provinces—Valentia being the fifth—as well as the staff of the *vicarius* in London.

It is still a matter of debate how up-to-date the British sections of the *Notitia* were kept. It is unlikely that these officials survived the expulsion of the Roman administration in 409, with the possible exception of the military commanders (that is, those who were not taken to Gaul with Constantine III). While it is encouraging that studies of the *Notitia* continue to proliferate, for now the British sections can tell us little about the state of politics and the military in Britain after Stilicho's Pictish wars c. 400. The *Notitia* is most useful, however, in helping archaeologists determine which forts were manned up to 400 and which may have survived afterward as private strongholds or civilian settlements.[17]

The Imperial Chroniclers

In the previous chapter, the narrative of the events of 406–10 was reconstructed from the accounts of a diverse group of fifth-century chroniclers. These men, whether they were in the service of church or state, lived and traveled in the Mediterranean world and were unlikely to have had any firsthand knowledge of the British Isles. Their knowledge of the affairs of Britain, therefore, may represent what was more or less common knowledge of the fate of the far-western provinces in the fifth century. Were it not for the threat of Constantine III, which drew the chroniclers' attention temporarily to the west, Britain may not have appeared in these works at all.

The earliest of these works is the lost history of OLYMPIODORUS.[18] A native of Egyptian Thebes, Olympiodorus was a pagan who described himself as primarily a poet. But he was also an active politician, "the first of a distinctive profession—of Byzantine diplomats."[19] His diplomatic missions included several embassies to the Huns and other barbarian peoples, who held him in great esteem.

Olympiodorus describes his work, not as a history, but as source materials for a history. Indeed, it survives as fragments summarized and preserved by Photius in the ninth century and as reflected in later Byzantine manuals.[20] Photius tells us that Olympiodorus's history covered the years 407 to 425, in twenty books. We know that it was dedicated to Theodosius II and published not long after 425. It was composed in annalistic fashion, using consular years for dating events. John Matthews points out the great precision that Olympiodorus used in technical matters, accurately transliterating Latin bureaucratic passages directly into Greek.[21] If anything is lacking, it is Olympiodorus's own judgment of the events he describes.[22] For commentary we must turn to the lesser writers who drew on Olympiodorus's work, such as Sozomen and Zosimus.

Next we come to OROSIUS.[23] A native of Spain, possibly Bracara, Orosius was both priest and historian. In his *Adversum Paganos,* Orosius provides many details about the usurpation and death of Constantine.[24] Writing in 417, he unfortunately never refers to Britain after Constantine leaves for Gaul in 407.[25]

The most enigmatic figure is RENATUS PROFUTURUS FRIGERIDUS.[26] His *Historia* is known only through the passages preserved by Gregory of Tours in the *History of the Franks*.[27] Gregory quotes Frigeridus, along with Sulpicius Alexander, in describing the events leading up to the sack of Rome in 410. While mostly discussing the role of the Franks in the early fifth century, Gregory turns to Frigeridus to relate the activities of Constantine III and Constans.[28] Frigeridus was probably writing in the middle years of the fifth century; unfortunately we know nothing more about him.

Also writing in the mid–fifth century was SOZOMEN.[29] With family origins near Gaza, Sozomen became an *advocatus* at Constantinople c. 440. At this time he began writing his *Ecclesiastical History,* which spans the years 324 to 439 and is dedicated to Theodosius II.[30] "The narrative of the ecclesiastical historian Sozomen is disappointing," laments Thompson.[31] Sozomen relies heavily on the work of Olympiodorus in describing the activities of the British usurpers. He adds little to the earlier accounts.

Also heavily reliant upon Olympiodorus is ZOSIMUS.[32] He was perhaps, by profession, an *advocatus fisci* in one of the prefectorial courts in the East. An avowed pagan who did not hide his animosity toward the Church, Zosimus wrote an incomplete Roman history that terminates just before Alaric's sack of Rome in 410.[33] Because of his pagan attitudes, Zosimus's *New History* was all but neglected by the medieval scribes.[34]

Zosimus does not enjoy the best of reputations among the historians of the late empire.[35] In piecing together his sources—mostly Olympiodorus and Eunapius—Zosimus makes numerous chronological and geographic blunders and sometimes confuses minor characters. Writing probably at the turn of the sixth century, Zosimus's separation in time and space from Britain would seem to make him a poor witness to events there in the early fifth century. This is indeed problematic, for he is our primary source for two very important events: the revolts in Britain and Gaul, and the Rescript of Honorius.[36] He is likely relying on Olympiodorus for these accounts, but we have no way of knowing how accurately he is relaying the information. These cautionary remarks do not invalidate the evidence, however, contrary to what some skeptics (and many archaeologists) have written. "Modern historians . . . tend to dismiss Zosimus as a mere copyist of his sources," comments R. T. Ridley, "which is simply to say that he was an ancient historian, and also ignores his own special contributions."[37] If anything, the skepticism surrounding Zosimus warns us of the dangers in constructing a strictly narrative, or chronological, history for fifth-century Britain.

Finally, we have the observations of another Byzantine writer, PROCOPIUS of Caesarea.[38] Procopius came from the landowning provincial upper class, and like Zosimus entered into a career as a civil servant, though his service to Belisarius gave him intimate knowledge of Byzantine military affairs. He also, of course, had intimate knowledge of the imperial court at Constantinople. So, while Procopius has long been respected as a historian of Justinian's wars, he has also earned a reputation as a scandalous writer of court intrigue.

Procopius offers a few scattered bits of information concerning Britain. In the *Secret History,* he describes how Justinian distributed diplomatic payments to various "barbarian" peoples, including the inhabitants of Britain.[39] In the *Wars,* he states that Britain was ruled by "tyrants" after 409, includes confusing geographic details about two distinct lands he calls Brettania and

Brittia, describes Britain as the Isle of the Dead, mentions a Sibyl who fore-tells the misfortunes of the Britons, and claims that Belisarius offered the whole of Britain to the Goths in exchange for Sicily.[40] The inconsistencies and myths in Procopius's information about Britain are not easy to explain. Admittedly he was writing far from Britain and had no firsthand knowledge. However, he did have access to both Belisarius and Justinian on matters of diplomacy. J. O. Ward has argued that Justinian did indeed believe he had a claim to Britain, perhaps through diplomatic relations with the British princes who were importing goods from the East and aping Byzantine styles in their memorial inscriptions.[41] Similarly, Averil Cameron envisions some informa-tion about Britain—distorted though it may be—reaching sixth-century Constantinople via Angles accompanying a Frankish embassy.[42] Thompson further argues that Procopius is not being contradictory with his terminol-ogy, but rather trying to distinguish the island of Britain (Brittia) from Brittany (Britannia).[43] Cameron admits this as a good possibility (if true, it is the earliest suggestion of the name Brittany), but advises caution in using Procopius as a source for Britain: "There is just enough plausible detail, among the hearsay and personal comment, to qualify as serious evidence, with sufficient distortion to make its interpretation highly problematic."[44]

The Gallic Chronicles

The so-called Gallic Chronicles have attracted much scholarly attention of late, mainly because they offer something extremely rare for this period: dates. There are actually two collections—the *Chronica Gallica a CCCCLII* (*Gallic Chronicle of 452*) and the *Chronica Gallica a DXI* (*Gallic Chronicle of 511*)—named after the years of their final entries.[45] The Gallic Chronicles are pertinent to this study not only because they are crucial to anyone try-ing to construct a chronology for fifth-century Britain, but also because their language describing British events can be compared to contemporary usage on the Continent.

Britain features prominently in three fifth-century entries. The first two are from the *Chronicle of 452*:

> Honorius, XVI: Britanniae Saxonum incursione devastatae. (In the sixteenth year of the reign of Honorius, the Britains were devastated by an incursion of Saxons.)

> Theodosius II, XVIII–XVIIII: Britanniae usque ad hoc tempus variis cladibus eventibusque latae in dicionem Saxonum rediguntur. (In the eighteenth and nineteenth years of the reign of Theodosius II, the Britains, which to this time had suffered from various disasters and misfortunes, are reduced by the power of the Saxons.)

The third entry is from the *Chronicle of 511:*

> Theodosius II and Valentinian III, XVI: Britanniae a Romanis amissae in dicionem Saxonum cedunt. (In the sixteenth year of the reign of Theodosius II and Valentinian III, the Britains, lost to the Romans, yield to the power of the Saxons.)

Here, seemingly, is straightforward evidence for dating the Saxon devastation and eventual takeover of Britain. If these entries are authentic, we have a contemporary Gallic witness to British events who provides not only dates but terms for political geography and peoples as well.

Textual scholarship in the last twenty years began by questioning the authenticity of this evidence, but has now swung in favor of cautious acceptance. The chronicles survive in a number of manuscripts, all of which seem to derive from a ninth- or tenth-century Carolingian copy now in the British Library.[46] Though the authors are anonymous, they appear—from internal references—to be products of a monastic establishment in southern Gaul.[47] The *Chronicle of 452* also includes attacks on both Augustine and Pelagius, pointing to semi-Pelagian authorship and a date of pre-530, when semi-Pelagianism was flourishing in Gaul.[48] Skeptics have pointed out some erroneous dates given by the chronicles and the general confusion caused by multiple dating schemes. Both chronicles record secular and ecclesiastical events accompanied by the corresponding imperial regnal years. However, the *Chronicle of 452* has two additional dating schemes: Olympiads (every four years) and years numbered from the birth of Abraham (every ten years). Ian Wood has pointed out that dating by Olympiads is uncommon in later annalistic texts.[49] Furthermore, Michael Jones and John Casey have shown that the regnal years given by the *Chronicle of 452* are quite accurate when compared with outside evidence, and that Carolingian editing was limited to a few attempts to combine the Gallic Chronicles with those of Jerome and others to make a continuous history.[50]

Though many historians have been willing to accept the authenticity of the Gallic Chronicles, this has not resulted in agreement upon the dates for the British entries.[51] Jones and Casey have tried to make sense of these diverse arguments in their recent attempt to authenticate the *Chronicle of 452*. By defending (and recalculating) the regnal years, they have come up with hard-and-fast dates for the British entries.[52] Their reading of these passages can be summarized as follows:

A.D. 410: Britain is devastated by Saxon incursions.

A.D. 441: Britain, which had suffered from many misfortunes, passes into the power of the Saxons.

Jones and Casey assert strongly that the *Chronicle of 452* is proof that the "Saxon invasion which led to the British revolt against Roman authority took place in A.D. 410," and that the *Chronicle of 511* confirms that, to "contemporary observers in Gaul, some significant portion of Britain passed into Saxon control in A.D. 441."[53] R. W. Burgess, however, in preparing his own edition of the chronicles, has criticized Jones and Casey's study.[54] His remarks are aimed not solely at dating schemes, but more specifically at the reliability of the Gallic Chronicles as an accurate witness to fifth-century events in Britain.[55]

While Burgess's comments rightly caution us against putting too much faith in precise dates for fifth-century events, they do not undermine the position of the Gallic Chronicles as a document contemporary to the events they describe. "Despite these [chronological] difficulties," writes Wood, "there are indications in both the earliest manuscript of the *Chronicle* [*of 452*] and the *Chronicle*'s contents to suggest that the work belongs to the fifth or early sixth century."[56] Since it is believed that both chronicles derive from a common (fifth-century) source,[57] both are indeed legitimate witnesses to fifth-century events. That does not mean, however, that they are always accurate witnesses. The chronological problems notwithstanding, the Gallic Chronicles remain a valuable historical source that can and should be used, if not to construct a chronology or narrative, then at least as a biased opinion from Gaul on what was happening across the Channel.

Constantius of Lyon

Another Gallic perspective on British affairs comes from Constantius's *Life of St. Germanus*.[58] Of noble birth, Constantius was an effective orator as well as a distinguished poet.[59] This we know from Sidonius Apollinaris, for the two corresponded frequently (Constantius encouraged his friend to publish his *belles lettres*). We also know that Constantius became a priest at Lyon, and c. 480—when he was old and infirm—he began researching and writing a biography of the soldier-saint Germanus of Auxerre. The finished work was dedicated to Patiens, bishop of Lyon.[60]

Constantius tells us that Germanus made two visits to Britain to fight the Pelagian heresy. The first visit can be dated with certainty to the year 429, for we have the independent evidence of Prosper of Aquitaine:

> A.D. 429: The Pelagian Agricola, son of the Pelagian bishop Severianus, corrupted the churches of Britain through his underhanded ways, but, on the initiative of the deacon Palladius, Pope Celestine sent Germanus, bishop of Auxerre, as his representative to confound the heretics and guide the Britons to the Catholic faith.[61]

While Prosper states that Germanus's first visit was prompted by Palladius in Rome, Constantius records that it was the Britons themselves who requested the bishop's presence: "About this time a deputation from Britain came to tell the bishops of Gaul that the heresy of Pelagius had taken hold of the people over a great part of the country and help ought to be brought to the Catholic faith as soon as possible. A large number of bishops gathered in synod to consider the matter and all turned for help to the two who in everybody's judgement were the leading lights of religion, namely Germanus and Lupus, apostolic priests who through their merits were citizens of heaven, though their bodies were on earth."[62] Although Constantius's language here is unfortunately vague,[63] it is clear that both he and Prosper agree that Pelagianism was the primary reason for Germanus's visit.

When Germanus arrived in Britain, a meeting was arranged for the bishop and the Pelagian leaders to debate. The Pelagians are described as richly adorned (*conspicui divitiis, veste fulgentes*), which betrays their vanity, but which also may suggest that their ranks included members of the secular urban aristocracy.[64] After the Pelagians are (predictably) defeated in debate, Constantius's narrative proceeds to a series of miracles that prove the sanctity of Germanus and his cause. First, the saint heals a blind girl who is the daughter of a "man of tribunician power."[65] Then, Germanus and his companion, Lupus, decide to visit the shrine of St. Alban, presumably—but not definitely—at Verulamium, where they pay homage to the saint and help promote his cult.[66] During Lent of that year, Germanus and Lupus are called on by the troops in Britain to help against the attacks of the Saxons and the Picts. Again Constantius is vague, for he does not describe these troops or tell us what part of Britain was being attacked. He does relate that the bishops preached to the troops, many of whom were baptized, and then organized them in an ambush against the enemy, in which they surrounded the barbarians and shouted "Alleluia!" until they fled. It is tempting here to see Germanus, who may have had some prior military training (à la Martin of Tours),[67] as serving in a supportive role to beleaguered troops much in the same manner as Saint Severinus did in Noricum. The details of the battle itself, however, must remain shrouded in the allegory.

Constantius records a second visit to Britain by Germanus, who is this time accompanied by Severus. Some have questioned the authenticity of this part of Constantius's account, seeing the second visit as a mere doublet of the first.[68] Recent writers have not followed this skepticism,[69] but on the contrary have debated vigorously over the proper date of the second visit. Most scholars place the return visit in the early 440s, and Ralph Mathisen constructs a chronological scheme for Germanus's later years that suggests 445 for the second trip to Britain.[70] Thompson originally suggested 444, but has recently argued, against the tide of opinion, for the year 437.[71] Wood takes a similarly iconoclastic stance, though arguing on different grounds for a date c. 435.[72]

The second visit was prompted by news that Pelagianism was once more spreading in Britain: "Meanwhile news came from Britain that a few promoters of the Pelagian heresy were once more spreading it; and again all the bishops joined in urging the man of blessings to defend the cause of God for which he had previously won such a victory."[73] Germanus returned to Britain (this time accompanied by Severus) to find that most of the flock had remained faithful. One Elafius, who was the chief man of his region (regionis illius primus) and who had great political support (Elafium provincia tota subsequitur),[74] greeted the bishop and asked him to heal his crippled son. Germanus succeeded, and was rewarded by delivery of the few remaining Pelagian heretics, whom he condemned to exile. To this day, writes Constantius, the faith "in those parts" remains unimpaired.[75] Constantius's phrase "in those parts" is typically vague, and subsequent references to Pelagius and Pelagianism in the British Isles have led some to question Germanus's success.[76] But regardless of Constantius's claims for Germanus, this Gallic witness to British affairs is valuable because of his chronological nearness to the events he is describing. Though not providing firsthand knowledge of these events, the language of Constantius can be usefully compared to that of contemporary writings from Britain.

Patrick

The first member of the British church whom we get to hear—not just hear about—is a contemporary of Constantius with links (in the hagiographic tradition at least) to Germanus himself. The Briton Patrick, though he spent most of his life in Ireland, produced two works that are somewhat concerned with political and ecclesiastical happenings in his native land.[77] The first—the *Epistola*—is a letter written to the soldiers of a British ruler named Coroticus, who was killing and enslaving Patrick's Irish converts. The *Confessio*, written somewhat later, is a spiritual autobiography that follows Patrick's enigmatic career from his boyhood in Britain to his successful mission in the land that had once enslaved him.

Medieval hagiography and legend have somewhat obscured our attempts to piece together the life of the historical Patrick.[78] Fortunately, Patrick's own writings supply enough evidence to allow us at least to construct an outline. In the *Confessio* (1), Patrick states that he was raised on a small estate (*villula*) outside the town of Bannavem Taburniae (*vico bannavem taberniae*). We know nothing of this town other than that it existed in Britain, perhaps in the form Banna Venta Bernia.[79] The *villula* was owned by his father, Calpornius, who was both a decurion and a deacon in the church; Calpornius's father, Potitus, had been a priest.

At the age of sixteen Patrick was captured, along with others from his father's estate, and taken to Ireland, where he was sold into slavery.[80] Some six years later he escaped from his master, walked a long distance to the coast, and sailed with some pirates back to Britain. At some point he was reunited with his parents and underwent formal ecclesiastical training, becoming first a deacon and eventually a bishop. Inspired by a vision, Patrick returned to Ireland on a mission to convert the Irish people. At this he was extremely successful, and it appears that he never left Ireland again, despite appeals from his family and an enigmatic scandal involving him and members of the British church.[81]

More serious were the violent actions of Coroticus and his soldiers, which caused Patrick to respond with two harsh letters (of which only the second has survived). That Coroticus was a Briton there is no doubt; his locus and status, however, are open to debate.[82] Patrick attacks the *tyrannidem*— "despotic rule," "unjust rule," or "tyranny"—of Coroticus, but does not give him a title.[83] This should not surprise us, for Patrick is concerned more with spiritual than with temporal matters. Thus, toward the end of his life, Patrick composed a spiritual autobiography, or *Confessio*. From the unpolished Latin of both this work and the *Epistola*, we catch only glimpses of the social and political order of Britain and Ireland in the fifth century. The most significant of these terms, which I discuss in the following chapters, are those such as *cives* and *patria*, which Patrick repeats with a confidence that his audience will understand their meaning in context.

The use of such terminological evidence rests on the historian's ability to reconstruct Patrick's "context" and chronology. Unfortunately, Patrick's dates have been a matter of disagreement since the seventh century. There are no dates at all in Patrick's own writings, which has sent scholars in all sorts of directions looking for outside clues with which to date him. However, as Dumville has recently argued, any reconstruction of Patrick's career must begin, at least, on the "common ground" of clues that the saint himself gives.[84] These clues, which place Patrick securely in the fifth century, can be summarized as follows:

1. Patrick refers (*Epistola*, 14) to the Franks as heathens who capture Christians. This reference must, therefore, predate Clovis's famous conversion to Catholicism in 497.[85]
2. Ludwig Bieler has shown, from Patrick's biblical quotations, that he was familiar with *both* the Old Latin text of the Old Testament and Revelation *and* the Vulgate text of Acts.[86] This places Patrick after 383–404, the period in which Jerome published the Vulgate.
3. Patrick enthusiastically encouraged monasticism in Ireland (*Confessio*, 41, 42, and 49; *Epistola*, 12). This could only have occurred so far west a good time after the career of Saint Martin (d. 397).

From these clues, we can confidently place Patrick's writings between 404 and 496. This is the most we can say from the internal evidence.

Others have turned to external sources to be more precise. Various early medieval (though not contemporary) Irish annals agree that Patrick came to Ireland as bishop in 432,[87] but give two conflicting dates for Patrick's death— 461 and 492. The "orthodox" dating scheme for Patrick was laid out in 1905 by J. B. Bury, who maintained two of the "traditional" dates in calculating 389 for Patrick's birth, 432 for the year he became bishop, and 461 for the year of his death.[88] Bury's scheme differs from the "traditional" scheme only in the *obit* year of the latter, which had preferred an ancient Patrick dying in 492. Subsequent Irish scholars have attempted to clear up this confusion of two death dates by turning to the theory that there were actually *two* Patricks. T. F. O'Rahilly claimed that the first Patrick was actually Palladius, the Roman deacon who (according to Prosper) was sent by Pope Celestine to Ireland in 431;[89] James Carney followed a similar line by stating that the first Patrick was actually a Gallic bishop who had accompanied Palladius.[90] Either way, this first Patrick is said to have died in 461 and was much later confused with the second (British) Patrick, who died in 492. Unconvinced, both John Morris and R.P.C. Hanson prefer to see the earlier Patrick as authentic, confirming (on different grounds) Bury's "orthodox" dates.[91] Charles Thomas rightly points out that the "orthodox" dates rely on the problematic British genealogies, which give the *floruit* of Coroticus of Strathclyde (c. 420–70), and the equally problematic association of Patrick with Germanus and Auxerre (c. 418–31); he then argues for an alternative "late" dating scheme—a birth date of c. 415 and a death date of c. 492.[92] Dumville, in the most thorough analysis of the external evidence to date, rejects all of the precise dates put forward for Patrick's *floruit*, concluding that the most we can say is that it "lasted through much of the second half of the fifth century."[93] Finally Thompson, after critiquing the various dating schemes, urges us all (perhaps sagely) to "turn our backs to them and walk away, looking neither to right nor to left."[94]

If an absolute dating scheme for Patrick is beyond the realm of possibility, we are back, then, to the internal evidence, which places Patrick firmly, albeit unspecifically, in the fifth century. From here we can move in a positive direction: constructing a "relative" chronology of Patrick's life and career from (and only from) his own words. Patrick tells us that he was sixteen when he was taken as a captive to Ireland, and six years later he escaped. We can deduce that he must have been around thirty to thirty-five when he was made a bishop, and must have been in Ireland at least twenty years before he composed the *Epistola*, because he tells us therein that he had trained the Irish priest carrying the first letter to Coroticus "from childhood" (*ex infantia*). This path too is fraught with difficulties, but at least it allows us to stick closely to the texts written by Patrick, as opposed to later Irish tradition (which is often entangled in ecclesiastical politics) or the ever-changing opinions of Patrician scholars.

While the last fifty years have witnessed raging debate over the dating of

Patrick, relatively little has been written about the language he employs or the literary and historical merit of his works.[95] Christine Mohrmann has produced the only significant study of Patrick's Latin,[96] but it is now dated and in need of revision.[97] David Howlett has done a more recent study of Patrick's biblical style,[98] which places him in the company of more respected insular writers like Gildas and Columbanus.[99] Of utmost importance—at least to the present study—is the identification of the sources used by Patrick. Bieler believed that, as well as the Old Latin and Vulgate Bibles, Patrick had read Cyprian, Augustine's *Confessions,* and the *Corpus Martinianum.* Dronke, in a more detailed study of sources, substantiated much of Bieler's findings, seeing traces of the *Confessions,* Cyprian's writings, and the *Pastor Hermas* in Patrick.[100] I show, in the following chapters, where Patrick fits among such Christian authors of late antiquity.

Gildas

Gildas provides a second British voice for historians. But if his writings are slightly more substantial than Patrick's, he tells us less about himself. He says that he was born the year of the battle of Badon Hill, and that he was writing in the forty-fourth year after that battle. The date of Badon Hill, however, is a subject of much debate, and suggestions have ranged from 490 to 520.[101] Although Gildas "Sapiens" enjoyed a respectable reputation in the early Middle Ages,[102] hagiographic details of his life were rather late in coming.[103] Unreliable and seldom used by modern historians, the *Vitae* have nevertheless preserved a persistent tradition that Gildas came from northwestern Britain and studied in a monastic school in Wales. It is unclear from Gildas's own writings whether he was a monk or a member of the secular clergy,[104] though Welsh hagiographic tradition honored him as a monastic saint and his Breton cult considered him the founder of the monastery of St. Gildas de Rhuys in Brittany.[105]

Gildas's reputation—then and today—rests mainly on his work *De excidio Britanniae* (On the ruin of Britain).[106] The *De excidio* is an epistle[107] that consists implicitly of three parts: a "historical" preface (chaps. 1–26), a "Complaint" against the British kings (27–65), and a "Complaint" against the British clergy (66–110).[108] Though it is the preface that has captured the attention of most historians, it is the Complaint sections that betray the purpose of their author and (presumably) the interests of the original readers.

Unfortunately, the "historical" preface is not historical at all, but rather a selective recounting of events during the Roman occupation and subsequent withdrawal of Britain whose purpose is to illustrate the "wicked" behavior of the Britons. Robert Hanning and others have rightly identified Gildas's use of the Old Testament "jeremiad" to rebuke his fellow countrymen, following a convention of Christian historiography (used most notably by Jerome and Salvian) that explains earthly calamities (among them barbarian invasions) as God's punishment for the sins of "His people" (Israelites/Romans/Britons).[109]

The preface, then, is a narrative of past British "sins" and "calamities" that foreshadow the even greater sins of Gildas's own day. The worst of the calamities are the invasions of the Picts and the Scots, which cause the Britons to appeal "to Aetius, thrice consul" (*Agitio ter consuli*).[110] When the Romans fail to respond, "all the members of the [British] council [*omnes consiliarii*], together with the proud tyrant [*una cum superbo tyranno*]," decide to hire Saxons "to beat back the peoples of the North."[111] Soon the Saxons turn against their employers, inflicting an even more deadly "plague": many towns are destroyed, and most of the survivors are either "butchered in the mountains" or flee to "lands beyond the sea." The remnant mount a resistance, led by a gentleman (*viro modesto*) named Ambrosius Aurelianus, "the last of the Romans [*solus . . . Romanae gentis*]": "From then on victory went now to our countrymen, now to their enemies. . . . This lasted right up to the year of the siege of Badon Hill, pretty much the last defeat of the villains, and certainly not the least."[112]

The period between the victory of Badon Hill and Gildas's writing is a time of respite from the barbarian menace, but it is a peace that breeds corruption. "Britain has kings [*reges*], but they are tyrants [*tyrannos*]; she has judges [*judices*], but they are wicked." Gildas's Complaint against the kings is a specific denunciation of five British rulers: "Constantine, tyrant [*tyrannicus*] whelp of the filthy lioness of Dumnonia"; "Aurelius Caninus, lion-whelp"; "Vortipor, tyrant [*tyranne*] of the Demetae"; "Cuneglasus, in Latin 'red butcher'"; and "Maglocunus . . . dragon of the island."[113] His Complaint against the clergy is not as specific but equally as colorful: "Britain has priests [*sacerdotes*], but they are fools; very many ministers [*ministros*], but they are shameless; clerics [*clericos*], but they are treacherous grabbers." Though most of the Complaint sections is biblical sermonizing, beneath the prejudices are rare sociological glimpses. As Leslie Alcock reminds us, Gildas "tells us a great deal about both the political arrangements and ecclesiastical organization of western Britain in the sixth century,"[114] a fact often overlooked by historians trying to make sense of Gildas's confused historical narrative.

Also frequently overlooked are Gildas's other writings, the *Fragmenta* and the *Poenitentia*.[115] The *Fragmenta* are fragments of lost letters, reportedly written by Gildas, dealing with various ecclesiastical affairs.[116] We know from the writings of Columbanus that Gildas *auctor* did correspond with British (and possibly Irish) clergy and that he was considered an authority on asceticism.[117] The *Fragmenta* cover such subjects as excommunication, abstinence, overzealous monks, and the roles of bishops and abbots.[118] Both regular and secular clergy, in their various ranks, are dealt with in the *Poenitentia*.[119] This penitential, along with those ascribed to "Vinnian" and Columbanus, are the oldest known to us,[120] and had a profound influence on the famous Irish penitentials that became the norm for the entire western church. The "Penitential of Gildas" is a brief collection of very simple and practical rules for a British church that was becoming increasingly stratified and monastic.

While more work needs to be done on these last two works, the *De excidio* has certainly not lacked modern historical commentary.[121] But as with Patrick, we run into difficulty when discussing absolute dates for Gildas and his location when writing the *De excidio*. Regarding internal dating evidence, Gildas provides no absolute dates, but he does give some chronological indicators:[122] the rebellion of Magnus Maximus (383–88),[123] the Rescript of Honorius (410),[124] the letter to *Agitio ter consuli* (446–54),[125] the siege of Badon Hill (?), and the reigns of the British rulers whom he denounces (the dating of which rests on shaky genealogical evidence). In assessing these scraps of internal evidence, Dumville has constructed a relative chronology that places Gildas's birth at c. 500 and his writings c. 545, which is essentially the "orthodox" scheme.[126] External evidence, from later annals and hagiography, also gives Gildas a *floruit* in the mid–sixth century.[127] Some scholars have suggested earlier dating schemes,[128] noting, for example, that Gildas does not seem to show familiarity with Christian writers of the late fifth or early sixth centuries.[129] These arguments, however, have not been as strong as Dumville's assertion of the orthodox scheme.[130] Later hagiographic tradition makes Gildas a product of northwestern Britain, and some scholars have argued at length for a northern perspective in the *De excidio*.[131] Recently, however, Nick Higham and Ken Dark have argued more persuasively for a West Country location for Gildas, perhaps in Dorset.[132] As is shown in subsequent chapters of this study, Gildas's geographic perspective in the *De excidio* is quite broad, encompassing all of the once-Roman territory on the island of Britain.

There is more of a consensus concerning the sources that Gildas used in writing the *De excidio*. François Kerlouégan has produced a major study of Gildas's language, which should be supplemented with the articles by Michael Lapidge and Neil Wright in the *Gildas: New Approaches* collection.[133] To many readers, Gildas's writing has appeared peculiar and pedantic, a raving sermon issued from a land of barbarians. However, the above-mentioned scholars have demonstrated that, despite his dependence on biblical themes, Gildas's prose style is more akin to that of fifth-century rhetoricians like Sidonius and Ennodius. It is now evident that Gildas was familiar with most of the books of the bible (in both the *Vetus Latina* version and Jerome's newer Vulgate edition) in addition to works by Virgil (especially the *Aeneid*), Rufinus, Orosius, Sulpicius Severus, Jerome, John Cassian, and Prudentius.[134] Such wide reading, accompanied by impeccable grammar and syntax (according to Late Latin standards, with no vulgarisms), suggests that Gildas was the recipient of a superior classical education in an insular school.[135] In the present study, I attempt to show, through the examination of a few key terms, how Gildas came out of this classical rhetorical school but presented his social and political views in an insular and wholly Christian scheme.

The Llandaff Charters

Another written source that reflects both British ecclesiastical and political organization in the post-Roman period is the *Liber Landavensis*.[136] This book contains a collection of 158 charters, commonly referred to as the Llandaff Charters, which record grants given to the bishopric of Llandaff in southeast Wales. These grants span a period of time from the mid–fifth century to the twelfth, and the charters that record them were copied many times in the same period. Each charter consists of two parts: diplomatic formulas and witness lists. Despite its problems (see below), this corpus is the largest and most valuable body of historical evidence for preconquest Wales.

Wendy Davies has thoroughly evaluated these charters and shown that their primary value lies in identifying the location and administration of early medieval estates in southeast Wales, especially in the turbulent eighth century.[137] However, if the information recorded in the earliest charters is accurate, they may also provide information about the continuity between Romano-British villa estates and the post-Roman estates documented around

Llandaff.[138] The question of continuity/discontinuity, as critics have pointed out,[139] hinges on the accurate transmission of information in the earliest recorded charters. Davies also recognizes the problems: "This [early material] is difficult to use because the chronological problems cannot be definitively resolved, because the Latin is often bad and *the meaning of each word really needs detailed and separate consideration,* and because the material is fragmentary and sometimes obscure" (italics added).[140] Though the chronology of the Llandaff Charters may remain imprecise, a detailed (and comparative) study of the language of the charters—which include an abundance of late Roman terms—would indeed add to our knowledge of political and ecclesiastical conditions in post-Roman western Britain.[141] Although the present study is not such an ambitious undertaking, I attempt at least to examine some of the key political and ecclesiastical terms for the light they may shed on western Britain in the latter part of the sub-Roman period.

Inscriptions

There is a body of seldom-used evidence that falls, in definition, between the written and the archaeological material: inscriptions. Epigraphic evidence from Roman Britain is rather meager compared to other Roman provinces.[142] However, the number of soldiers' tombstones and other military inscriptions (now scattered in various museums, especially those along Hadrian's Wall) is large, and they tell us a great deal about veterans and life along the frontier.[143] These inscriptions have been and continue to be published in illustrated catalogues.[144] Regrettably, few of the inscriptions can be dated accurately to the late Roman period.[145]

There is an abundance of inscriptional evidence, however, on the early Christian monuments found, primarily, in the "Celtic fringe." These have been published in near comprehensive editions for southwestern Britain, for Wales, and for Scotland.[146] Examples from the fifth and sixth centuries are usually classified as "simple inscribed stones," that is, natural or rough-hewn slabs and pillar stones with inscriptions in Latin, Irish, Ogam (an early insular script),[147] or a combination of these.[148] Most were set up as tombstones, memorials, or boundary markers, and some are reused Roman monuments. The language used in these inscriptions is extremely valuable for historians, for along with personal names (of both Celtic and Mediterranean origin), we find titles (*rex, protector*), tribal allegiance (*Venedotis cives*), and occupations both secular (*magistratus, medicus*) and ecclesiastical (*sacerdos, presbyter*). Though precise dating is not always possible,[149] epigraphic evidence can be very useful for comparative studies of language, artistic styles, and funerary customs. Together with the written evidence, it can make a compelling case for social and political diversity in sub-Roman Britain.

Later Sources

Finally, there are several early medieval written sources that, though post-dating the sub-Roman period, include significant accounts of Britain in the fifth and sixth centuries. The most important of these can be summarized as follows: the early Welsh and Irish penitentials, the oldest of which may date to the sixth century;[150] the bardic poetry of Aneirin and Taliesin, thought to have been composed in northern Britain at the end of the sixth century but not written down until much later;[151] the writings of Bede, especially his *Ecclesiastical History;* the *Anglo-Saxon Chronicle,* most of which was composed in Wessex beginning in the ninth century, heavily reliant upon Bede but including traditional English accounts of battles against the Britons in the fifth and sixth centuries; the *Historia Brittonum* (History of the Britons), attributed (perhaps wrongly) to the Welsh monk Nennius, compiled in the early ninth century;[152] the *Annales Cambriae* (Welsh annals), written down from the eighth to the tenth centuries but possibly drawing on some contemporary records from the late sixth century onward;[153] and a vast body of Welsh genealogies and saints' lives.[154]

Many scholars have used these works as primary sources in writing their histories of the period, overlooking the chronological difficulties altogether. Others have used these sources to supplement Patrick and Gildas, believing that although they were written down later, they drew upon contemporary accounts or oral tradition. Dumville's thorough critique of these later sources has left few brave souls willing to sort through their chronological and methodological problems to find a way to incorporate them into studies of the sub-Roman period.[155] For the purpose of the present study, these problematic materials are used primarily to show how language and ideas either changed or remained constant in Britain after the sixth century.

In this chapter, I have distinguished which written sources can and cannot be used for a terminological study of sub-Roman Britain. In the following chapters, I look at the evolution of individual terms by moving, chronologically, through their use by both secular and Christian authors in the fourth, fifth, and sixth centuries. Since the terms themselves reveal details about the social, political, and religious arrangements of the sub-Roman Britons, changes in their usage also reveal wider developments taking place in the early medieval world.

4

◆

BRITANNIA

The last chapter was, more or less, a discussion of which written sources may be used legitimately to construct a history of sub-Roman Britain. Most historians who have used these sources have tried to construct narrative histories complete with names, battles, and (approximate) dates.[1] This course inevitably leads to chronological confusion and to such problematic figures as Arthur, Vortigern, Hengest, and Horsa. Other scholars have attempted to construct broad historical models with few (or no) names or dates.[2] These models, however, often strain the "historical" material in the writings of non-historians like Constantius and Gildas in attempting to establish relative chronology and geographical focus. Finally, some historically minded archaeologists have put forward their own models, which either downplay the written evidence or use it sparingly, whenever it serves to illustrate an archaeological point.[3]

This chapter—and those following in Part II—diverges from these three approaches by studying the contemporary written sources while temporarily ignoring the archaeological evidence. The chapters in Part III deal with the archaeology on its own. While this study attempts to avoid problematic dates and historical figures, it is neither a narrative nor a construction of a historical model. Rather, it is a detailed study of the language of the source material, particularly of the sociopolitical terminology used by the writers. I first trace such terminology—*patria, cives, tyranni*—in its classical Latin context, then trace it as it evolves in the late Roman (secular) and Christian traditions. Finally, I indicate whether and how these traditions affected Patrick and Gildas, the two chief British witnesses. From a comparison of their use of these terms—as well as the appearance of the terms in insular charters and inscriptions—I hope that we can come to a better understanding of the social, political, and religious arrangements of the peoples inhabiting Britain in the fifth and sixth centuries.

A good place to start is with a large concept like "Britain." In the ancient world, this term was used to describe an island, a Roman province, a Roman diocese, and lastly a region of the island that had once been part of the Roman Empire. When a British Latin writer like Gildas uses the term *Britannia,* he thus has several classical precedents that exert influence over him. But these Greek and Latin traditions are only part of the story, for the native Britons must have had non-Mediterranean concepts of their island as well. In order to understand what terms like *Britannia* and *tyranni* mean when they occur in a sub-Roman source, we must come to terms with all of these traditions and weigh their varying influence on the author or authors.

The terms "Britain" and "Britons" have a long, and somewhat inconsistent, linguistic history. The first word used to describe the island was that romantic epithet "Albion," used by the earliest Greek geographers.[4] This was soon replaced in normal Greek usage by Ρρεττανια, and later by the form βρεττανια, which became the most common.[5] Regular Greek forms include βρεττανια (Britain), βρεττανος (a Briton), βρεττανικος (adj., British), and αι βρεττανιαι (the British Isles [including Ireland]).[6] The early Latin writers used the form *Britannia,* which became standardized after Caesar's description of the island.[7] Subsequent Latin writers, influenced by Greek forms, sometimes preferred the spelling *Brittania.* The standard Latin forms, then, became *Britannia* (Britain), *Britannus* (a Briton), and *Britannicus* (adj., British).[8]

To this point, all of the Greek and classical Latin forms of "Britain" carried with them a purely geographic definition. Although this geographic notion never goes away, after A.D. 43 a competing political definition emerges. *Britannia* then becomes the name of the Roman province (excluding the non-Romanized highland zones) created by the emperor Claudius. Sometime between 197 and 213, Britain was divided into two provinces—Britannia Superior and Britannia Inferior.[9] Within a century, the emperor Diocletian introduced more radical administrative reforms that divided the empire into prefectures, dioceses, and provinces. Britain was divided into four provinces—Britannia Prima, Britannia Secunda, Flavia Caesariensis, and Maxima Caesariensis—which together formed the "diocese of the Britains" (see Fig. 1) and which in turn became part of the "prefecture of the Gauls."[10] The plural *Britanniae* then begins to appear in the Latin sources to refer to the political diocese. Thus we find two nominative forms for "Britain," *Britannia* and *Britanniae* (along with variant spellings), and three definitions—the island, the old province, and the diocese—from which Latin writers could choose in the fourth and fifth centuries.[11]

Technically, the official form used by Latin writers should have been the plural *Britanniae* from the inception of Diocletian's reforms to at least 410. The so-called Verona List (A.D. 312–14) does give the plural *Britanniae* in reference to the diocese, with the variant spelling *Brittaniae*.[12] The *Theodosian Code* also gives the plural form *Brittaniae* in the one occurrence of Britain in the laws.[13] In the provincial list of Polemius Silvius (c. 385), however, it is *Brittania* that contains five provinces.[14] Clearly, geographical notions of Britain continued to circulate in the fourth century, as can be seen in the numerous references to the *insula Britannia* in the Latin *Geographi*.[15] The Latin panegyrics of this period prefer the geographic notion of Britain to the political, and thus the singular over the plural.[16] Claudian, for example, uses the singular *Britannia* to personify the beleaguered island.[17] Poets certainly had matters of form and meter to consider, but it also seems that they were engaging in the typical Roman habit of territorializing peoples into geographic personifications. This practice is obvious in classical writers like Caesar and Tacitus, but it can also be seen in the language of.imperial coinage.[18]

Ammianus Marcellinus frequently refers to the barbarian raids on Britain in the years 364–68, and in doing so he consistently uses the plural *Britanniae* to refer to the diocese.[19] Ammianus also names *Britanniae* as a place of exile,[20] and describes one Alypius as *"ex vicario Britanniarum."*[21] In all his references to Britain, Ammianus uses the plural nine times, the singular only twice. In the first of these two instances, he uses the singular for both Britain and Spain: Paulus, "a native of Spain" (*ortus in Hispania*), is "sent to Britain" (*in Britanniam missus*).²² In the second instance, he is clearly speaking geographically of the entire island, for he describes "the flow of the ocean" and the origins of the Picts, who inhabited an area outside of the diocese.²³

We would expect the *Notitia Dignitatum* to maintain the official, plural usage in describing the various military and civilian officials assigned to Britain in the late fourth and early fifth centuries. But the *Notitia* is, at best, inconsistent in this regard. For example, in chapter 1—an index of all the highest ranking officials in the West—the list includes the *vicarius Britanniarum* (pl.), the *comes Britanniarum* (pl.), the *comes litoris Saxonici per Britannias* (pl.), and the *dux Britanniae* (s.). Elsewhere, however, we find *comes Britanniae . . . Provincia Britannia* (s.), *comes litoris Saxonici per Britanniam* (s.), and *dux Britanniarum* (pl.).²⁴ To add to the confusion, the illustration of the island under the command of the *comes Britanniae* is itself labeled *Britannia*.²⁵ The plural is used more often than the singular in the *Notitia*, and Frere has suggested that at least one of the headings giving the singular is an error.²⁶ Still, this official document shows some confusion about which form of Britain to use, and probably at least two different hands or renditions.

A brief survey of both secular historians and ecclesiastical authors writing in the late fourth and early fifth centuries shows a similar inconsistency. Aurelius Victor (fl. 360–90) describes a *vicus* of *Britannia* (s.), and consistently uses the singular throughout his works.²⁷ Eutropius (fl. 365) refers to Britain frequently (some twelve times) in his work, but displays no understandable pattern in his use of both the singular and the plural.²⁸ The *Historia Augusta* also uses (indiscriminately) both singular and plural along with the variant spellings *Brittania, Brittaniae, Brittannia*, and *Brittanniae*, leading A.L.F. Rivet and Colin Smith to comment that this variation is either careless copying or a deliberate attempt of the author(s) at archaism.²⁹ A signatory of the Council of Arles (A.D. 314) claims that he is from *provincia Britania* (variants *Britannia* and *Brittinia*).³⁰ Orosius begins his great work by describing the island called *Britannia* (variants *Brittania, Britania*), but later states that Gratian was *apud Britannias* when he was declared emperor.³¹ Victricius of Rouen (d. 407) writes that he kept himself busy *intra Britannias* (pl.),³² while Prosper of Aquitaine believes that the *ecclesias Brittaniae*, "the churches of Britain," were infected with the Pelagian heresy in 429.³³ Sulpicius Severus (c. 360–420) uses both the plural and singular in his *Chronica*.³⁴ Finally, in the voluminous writings of Jerome, we find nearly every conceivable form of "Britain" used: *Britannia, Britanni . . . provincia, Brittannia*, and *Brittaniae*.³⁵

This marked inconsistency in the sources calls for some explanation. Scribal error may account for some, though not all, of the orthographic variation. Again, there are at least three different traditions that are influencing these writers: Britannia as an island (geographic), Britannia as a Roman province within an island, and Britanniae as a Roman diocese encompassing several provinces within an island. One problem is that the sources are not always clear whether they are referring to a geographic area or a political one. For example, a Roman general sailing to Britain is coming both to an island and to a diocese, and a *civitas* belongs—at the same time—to the island, to a province, and to the diocese. Another problem is that some fourth- and fifth-century writers are describing events that happened both before and after the political divisions within Britain; their choice of singular or plural may then depend on their own style and/or their sources, and consistency is perhaps too much to hope for.

We should, then, expect this pattern of inconsistency to continue into the early part of the fifth century. But what of those writing after 410, who were well aware that Britain was no longer (politically) a Roman province or a diocese? The three British entries in the Gallic Chronicles are consistent in their use of the nominative plural *Britanniae*.[36] Both times that Constantius of Lyon refers to the island, he uses the plural: *ex Brittaniis*.[37] Patrick only refers (specifically) to Britain three times, all in the *Confessio,* and he also uses only the plural:

> chap. 23: And again a few years later I was in Britain [*in Britaniis*] with my family.

> chap. 32: [The] defense of my case, at which I was not present, for I was not in Britain [*in Britanniis*].

> chap. 43: And so even if I wanted to part from them and head for Britain (*in Brittanniis*] . . .

Again the spelling is inconsistent, but the form is always the ablative plural.[38] Muirchu, while writing his *Life of Patrick* in the seventh century, seems to have been confused by Patrick's use of the plural. He uses both forms, misspelling the plural twice.[39]

What are we to make of these fifth-century writers? Patrick, Constantius, and the authors of the Gallic Chronicles all follow the tradition of referring to Britain in diocesan terms, "the Britains," though spelling often varies.

Comparing this usage to that of preceding Latin authors tells us nothing more than that these fifth-century writers thought the plural *Britanniae* was still an acceptable (and understandable) form to use in the later fifth century. However, Muirchu, writing much later and adapting Patrick's text, seems a bit confused by the use (and spelling) of the plural form, but nevertheless appropriates it from his source (Patrick) to use along with the more familiar (by his time) singular.

Turning to the sixth century, the situation is markedly different. Gildas consistently uses the singular *Britannia* throughout the *De excidio,* even when he is referring to the time when Britain was a Roman diocese. "Habet Britannia rectores" (Britain has governors), remarks Gildas in his first reference to Britain.[40] This begs the question, What does he mean by Britain? Almost in reply to this, Gildas begins his narrative proper with "Brittania insula . . . octingentorum in longo milium" (The island of Britain . . . [is] eight hundred miles long).[41] After describing Britain geographically, he moves on to history. "Since it was first inhabited, [Britain] has been ungratefully rebelling," which Gildas says has led Porphyry (read Jerome) to comment that "'Britannia is a province fertile of tyrants.'"[42] Jerome actually said this, and he used the form *Britanni;* Gildas corrects it to make it consistent with his usage elsewhere.

This usage continues when he speaks of the Roman era in Britain. The Romans endeavored to conquer Britain and put it in servitude, "such that its name should be regarded not as *Britannia, sed Romania.*"[43] During this time, God "acted to save *Britannia*" from darkness by introducing the worship of Christ.[44] As "the tyrant thickets increased . . . the *insula* was still Roman in name, but not by law and custom," and soon "*Britannia* was despoiled of her whole army."[45] Gildas has thus gone through his entire discussion of Roman Britain without lapsing into diocesan terminology. As Britain appears thereafter in post-Roman contexts, the singular *Britannia* is consistently maintained.

When Gildas speaks of Britain—before, during, and after the Romans—he is clearly speaking of the entire island. This does not mean, however, that he is concerned only with geography; *Britannia* is also used by Gildas when he is thinking in political terms, be it of the Roman province (as in his quote from Jerome) or of the *patria* of his own day.[46] Neil Wright has done a detailed study of Gildas's geographical terminology.[47] He points out that Gildas uses the terms *Britannia* and *insula* interchangeably, never modifying his definition of Britain as later commentators do.[48] Wright then concludes:

> At the very outset, . . . Gildas sets his account in its geographical per-
> spective—the island of Britain in its entirety. Throughout the narra-
> tive Britain is variously referred to as *Britannia, insula,* and *patria.*
> Indeed, Gildas's frequent personification of *Britannia* is indicative of
> his attitude to his *patria* as a single entity. He similarly terms its
> inhabitants *cives* ("fellow-citizens"): he does not think of them in
> terms of various successor-states. In short, Gildas's view of British
> history is of one *Britannia—Britannia insula.*[49]

Patrick Sims-Williams, Nick Higham, and Michael Jones have reached similar conclusions.[50] Gildas's consistent use of the singular *Britannia* is especially significant placed in context with the traditional usage of *Britannia*
and *Britanniae* discussed earlier. It sets him apart from both the late imperial writers, who could not decide on which form (the traditional/singular or
the technical/plural) to use, and the fifth-century writers like Patrick and
Constantius, who still viewed Britain in diocesan terms.

Unfortunately, there is no mention of "Britain" in contemporary epigraphy or charters to which we could compare Gildas's testimony. However, we
can put Gildas's use of *Britannia* in the context of contemporary and later
Latin writers. Aponius (fifth/sixth century) describes the island of *Britannia*
(s.) in his work.[51] Cassiodorus (fl. 519) refers once to *Brittannia* (s., variant
Brittania) in his chronicle.[52] Jordanes lists *Britannia* five times in the singular, and only once in the plural (that in a clearly Roman context).[53] Venantius
Fortunatus (c. 540–600) records *Britannia* (s., variants *Britinia, Brittania,
Brittania*) once.[54] Pope Gregory the Great writes of the *lingua Britanniae* (s.),
the *fratres in Brittannia* (s.), and *omnes Brittaniae sacerdotes* (s.).[55] Isidore
of Seville (fl. 620) mentions Britain several times, mostly in geographical contexts, consistently using the singular.[56] Indeed, most of these writers speak of
Britain in geographic, not political, terms. By the sixth century, they know
that there are no Roman provinces or diocese on the island, and are little
interested in Britain politically. Roman political language has become foreign to them, and they are able to speak only of Britain in broad terms. The
exception to this is Bede, writing in the eighth century but consciously trying to recall both the content and style of his sources. He too speaks mostly
of Britain in a geographic way, using the singular form most often in the
Ecclesiastical History (with the variant spellings *Britannia* and *Brittania*).[57]
However, when specifically discussing Roman Britain, unlike Gildas he
switches to the plural form, then back to the singular again for post-Roman
Britain.[58] Clearly, the venerable historian is trying to follow his sources

closely.[59] However, in his nonhistorical works and when he is not relying on older accounts, he overwhelmingly prefers the singular *Britannia*.[60]

It must be admitted that there were no clearly defined rules for Latin writers of the fourth through sixth centuries using the term *Britannia*. Nor, it would seem, was there a clearly defined spelling. What Patrick and Gildas did have at their disposal, however, was literary precedent and contemporary usage. Patrick was consistent with most of the writers in the second half of the fifth century in consciously using the diocesan plural form. Similarly, Gildas was consistent with later writers who abandoned the diocesan terminology in favor of the geographic singular (with the exception of Bede, who maintained consistency with his sources). What this meant to these British writers in terms of their social and political conception of their island can only be answered by comparing their use of *Britannia/Britanniae* with the oft-used synonym patria.

5

♦

PATRIA

Patria is another Latin term whose meaning was evolving in late antiquity along political, geographic, as well as Christian lines. It is often used by Latin writers to express something intimate, for it is a word that connotes belonging, be it to a land, to a people, or even to a religion. We might expect, then, that those writing in Britannia (or who originated there) might use this term to refer to their "homeland." Fortunately, Patrick and Gildas both use *patria;* but what exactly do they mean by this term? To what *patria* are they referring? to the British Isles? to Britain alone? to the "Romanized" portion of Britain? to a specific province or *civitas*? or merely to their own native region or village?

The roots of this word be can traced back to the classical Latin term *patrius,* "belonging to the father," "hereditary," or "native." The feminine noun *patria(e)* (Greek πατρις) is thus related—in its primary meaning, that of "fatherland"—to such words as *pater, paternus,* and *patricius.* However, its classical and later applications were often more varied and specific.[1] As a noun, *patria* usually signifies the place where one lives, resides, or originates, but this can mean many different things: a *domus* (Naev. com. 93); "the army" (Livy, 44.39.5); a *civitas* (Cicero, *Flac.,* 99); the *res publica* (Tacitus, *Annals,* 4.43.5); "Rome" (Cicero, *Tusc.,* 5.106); "Italy" (Cicero, *Verr.,* 2.5.170); the *imperium Romanum* (Pliny, *Naturalis Historia,* 7.99); a *regio, terra,* or *provincia* (Virgil, *Aeneid,* 1.540; Commodianus, *Apol.,* 1031; *HF,* 3.11); or even "the world" (Cicero, *Rep.,* 1.19; Seneca, *Ep.,* 102.21). In a more figurative sense, *patria* can also refer to one's "race" or "family" (biblical); *parentes* (Plautus, *Amph.,* 650); *libertas* (Plautus, Capt., 300); *leges* (Seneca the Elder, *Controversiae,* 1.8.1); *dei or penates* (Cicero, *Pis.,* 50); or "fatherhood" (biblical; Jerome). Finally, to Christian writers, *patria* can also signify *paradisus* (Augustine, *De civitate Dei,* 5.17); the "heavenly city, the New Jerusalem" (Augustine, *Confessio,* 10.35.56); even God (Augustine, *Soliloquia,* 1.1.4).

Suzanne Teillet has studied the term *patria* as part of the sociopolitical terminology used to describe Visigothic Spain.[2] Beginning with the authors of the republic, Teillet distinguishes several different types of *patriae* and traces the evolution of these terms up to the seventh century. In Cicero and Martial there is apposition between Rome, *la patrie spirituelle et universelle* (*patria communis*), and *la terre natale* (*terra patria*). The latter is commonly referred to by Teillet as *la petite patrie,* a more familiar term (often accompanied in the Latin sources by *meus or noster*) denoting *"simplicité et le caractere particulier,"* as opposed to *"la majesté et . . . l'universalité de la patrie romaine,"* which is a concept borrowed from the Stoics.[3] This is essentially a difference between an abstract *patria* and a concrete *patria.*

In Ammianus we see both traditions: an abstract or universal *patria* that stands for Rome and empire, and a concrete *patria* that stands for native land.[4] As Ammianus waxes sentimental about the Eternal City and its Caesars, he declares that happiness is "above all else to have a *patria gloriosa.*"[5] Similarly, when discussing Pompey he says that "none was more valiant or circumspect with regard to his *patria.*"[6] More often, however, *patria* in Ammianus refers to the place where one is born. That place can be a city—Constantinople is Julian's *patria* (22.9.2), Ephesus is the *patria* of the philosopher Maximus (29.1.42), Maiozamalcha and Nisibis are *patriae* of the Persians (24.4.11 and 25.9.1), and the besieged inhabitants of Miletus die in the flames of their *patria* (28.1.3)—or a broader geographic entity—

the Sarmatians see their *patria* perishing by the sword (17.12.5), Codrus sacrificed himself for his *patria* in the Dorian War (22.8.12 and 28.1.4), the Armenian king Papa gathers together companions from his *patria* (30.1.5), and Serenianus and Valens share a common *genitalis patria* (26.10.1).

Teillet believes that, by the end of the fourth century, a *conscience provinciale* is emerging among many writers in the western part of the empire.[7] We see this first, perhaps, in the writings of Ausonius (d. 395).[8] The Romano-Gallic aristocrat Ausonius was a native of Bordeaux (Burdigala) in Aquitania, and he frequently expresses both his veneration for Rome and his love for his native city—*"diligo Burdigalum, Romam colo"*—proudly declaring that he is a *civis* in both.[9] Bordeaux *est natale solum* for Ausonius, and he addresses it poetically as *o patria*.[10] Finally, he places his duel loyalties in context: "Burdigala ancipiti confirmet vertice sedem. Haec patria est, sed patrias Roma supervenit omnes." (Let Bordeaux establish her place, leaving the precedence unsettled. This is my own country, but Rome stands above all countries.)[11] Teillet points out the important subtleties in Ausonius's language; intimacy and sentimentality are attached to Bordeaux, his *petite patrie*, while due loyalty and respect are paid to Rome (Ausonius was, after all, mindful of his political career).[12]

Teillet also points out that it is Bordeaux, not Gaul, that Ausonius addresses as *patria; Galliae* is significantly represented in the plural, and its diversity, not unity, are stressed by the poet.[13] Though he does not use the term *patria,* Ausonius does refer frequently and with affection to Aquitania and Gallia Aquitanica, perhaps representing an intermediary step toward a *conscience provenciale*.[14] A similar step is taken in Spain by the *poeta rusticus* Prudentius (348–c. 405), who, though usually reserving the term *patria* for Rome (*urbs patria*) and religion (*patriae nam gloria christus*), nevertheless speaks with great sentimentality both for his native city, Caligurris, and for all of Hispania.[15] The martyrs about whom Prudentius writes are from *terra Hibera* (i.e., Spain), and each is a *patriae martyr*.[16] Returning to Gaul, we see further use of this intimate language in the writing of Rutilius Namatianus.[17] In his poem *De Reditu* (c. 417), Rutilius says of Rome, "Fecisti patriam diversis gentibus unam" (You made one *patria* from diverse nations).[18] But Rutilius contrasts this abstract *patria* with his native *patria,* Gaul, to which he often refers in possessive terms (*patrius, avitus*) or describes with evocative intimacy (*Gallica rura, arbuta, arua, tecta*).[19] In contrast with Ausonius, Rutilius does not refer to a particular Gallic city or province, but rather to the whole of Gaul, in both adjectival (*Gallica*) and diocesan (*Gallorum* [sic]) terms.[20] This extension is further carried out in the writings of Sidonius Apollinaris (430–c. 490). Teillet shows that Sidonius differentiates *republica* and *patria* in his letters, the latter expressed as *patria nostra* and clearly encompassing not just Auvergne or Aquitaine but all of Gaul.[21] Like Ausonius, Sidonius uses both the singular and plural forms for Gaul; but even when he is using the plural diocesan form, it is in the manner of personification.[22] Sidonius frequently personifies *Gallia* and *Africa* in this manner, as Hydatius does with *Hispania* and Claudian does with *Britannia*.[23]

This pattern signals a return to older literary conventions concerning the "province." At the same time that this was going on in the West, Christian writers throughout the empire were also helping to redefine *patria* based on still older Greco-Roman and biblical traditions. The word *patria* appears thirty times in the Vulgate, twenty-two times in the Old Testament, and eight times in the New Testament. Many of the Old Testament examples refer vaguely to some person's tribal land, often accompanied by the words *populus* or *gens,* while the majority (fifteen) of references occur in one book, 2 Maccabees, where *patria* takes on a more concrete political meaning. All but one of the references in the New Testament are in connection with Jesus' statement, "A prophet has no honor in his own *patria,*" which in this case means the specific region of Galilee. Interestingly, the last occurrence, Hebrews 11.14, follows none of these traditions, but rather speaks of the virtuous Jews who died while seeking a *patria* that, to this Christian writer, was "a heavenly one."

These biblical *patriae* are further developed by writers like Ambrose, Jerome, and Augustine in their own scriptural commentaries. Here we find Bethlehem as "patria domini"; Christ as an "exul . . . patriae, cuius est mundi"; a "patriae Gothorum"; "non sola Iudaea, sed omnes patriae gentium"; the Lord promising "aliam patriam aeternam"; "Samaria patria"; "patria est vita christi and patria est mansio christi"; "beatam patriam"; "paradisum patriam . . . sanctorum"; and "patriam caelestem angelicam."[24] What these Christian writers appear to be saying in the commentaries and in their other theological works is that many people (*omnes gentium, multi genti, universae*) have concrete "homelands," but we all share one *patria* that is eternal and is of Christ. Here, as in the secular sources, the concrete *patria* encompasses a wide range of geographic notions: a city (Bethlehem, Jerusalem), a territory (Israel, the land of Abraham), an ethnic group (the Goths). Often, *patria* appears as the geographic destination—in the broad sense of "homeland" or "country"—of someone who has been on a long journey, away on a military campaign, in exile, or on a pilgrimage.[25] In this context, *patria* is frequently associated with words like *desiderium* to express intimate longing or desire.[26]

If an individual in late antiquity could express a longing or desire for his or her earthly *patria*, should not Christians express such desire for their heavenly *patria*? It is this *patria* with which the ecclesiastical writers are most concerned. The abstract *patria* of the secular writers, *Roma aeterna,* is transformed into *la patrie chrétienne* (as Teillet calls it) by writers like Ambrose and Augustine in an effort to keep the universal or philosophic concept alive. Thus, accompanying *patria* we often find words like *aeterna, beatifica,* and *anima*, as well as the possessives (*sua, tua*) and active verbs (*desiderare, abdicare, suscitare,* and *amare*) that the secular writings had used to convey intimacy and affection. Jerome begins one correspondence, "You wander in your *patria*, rather it is not your *patria*, for you have lost your *patria*," then continues to extol the way of the Cross.[27] In the *Confessions,* Augustine shouts from his heart, "Jerusalem my *patria*, Jerusalem my mother."[28] These two great rhetoricians are using a standard literary device—the expression of feeling for one's homeland—and transforming it for their purpose: to get fifth-century Christians to feel the same way about the *patria* of Christ.

When *patria* first appears in connection with Britain, then, three literary traditions are in current use: *patria* as Rome or the Roman Empire, quickly going out of use; *patria* as God's homeland, that is, Heaven; and *patria* as a term used to refer intimately and affectionately to one's earthly homeland, increasingly becoming specific (at least in Gaul and Spain) to the old Roman provincial entities. Constantius uses *patria* in his *Life of St. Germanus,* but unfortunately not in the context of Britain. He describes the dying Germanus assuring his companions in Ravenna that God has revealed that his body will be returned *ad patriam*, which in this case is the city of Auxerre.[29] Contemporary Gallic historiography is more inexact. In the *Life of St. Honoratus, patria* seems to refer to some vague region of Gaul,[30] while in the *Life of St. Maximus* the heroes wander through *diversae patriae.*[31]

Can we be more specific for fifth-century Britain? Patrick is our only source, and he is seldom specific. In the *Epistola* (1), he says that he has given up *patria et parentes* to proselytize among the Irish. Patrick uses the phrase *patria et parentes* three times in his writings, likely choosing it for its alliteration,[32] but this says nothing more than that he was equally fond of his "home" (whatever that entails) and his family. The only other occurrence of *patria* in the *Epistola* is in a biblical paraphrase: "And if my own people (*mei*) do not recognize me, well, a prophet does not have honor *in patria sua.*"[33] We can only infer that, since Patrick is speaking of Coroticus's soldiers (*mei,* from his *patria,* therefore Britons), *patria* here must mean something broader than his father's estate.[34]

Patrick describes in the *Confessio* a dream he had in Ireland in which a voice tells him, "You do well to fast, since you will soon be going *ad patriam tuam.*"[35] Though still unspecific, the adjectives *sua* and *tua* that accompany *patria* in these last two examples suggest the familiar language used by Ausonius and Rutilius when describing their *petites patries.* The remaining two incidents of *patria* are again in the phrase *patria et parentes;*[36] but in the latter case, *Brittanniae* appears in the same sentence: "And so even if I wanted to part with them and head for *Brittanniae*—and I would have been only too glad to do so, to see my *patria et parentes. . . .* God knows that I longed to." Though Patrick seems here to be equating *Brittanniae* with *patria* (and once again uses terms of intimacy and affection), it is not certain that he is doing so. Unfortunately, Patrick does not develop his thoughts far enough for us to be any more specific about his *patria.*[37]

Whereas Patrick's narrative is personal and spiritual, Gildas's is broad and political. Gildas writes about the problems of *Britannia,* which he identifies unequivocally as his *patria.* As Wright has noted, the terms *Britannia, insula,* and *patria* are clearly synonymous and used interchangeably throughout Gildas's narrative.[38] This is made evident in the very beginning of the preface to the *De excidio.* Chapter 1 begins with Gildas stating that his sympathies are with his homeland (*condolentis patriae*), while chapter 2 is one long sentence ending with "the final victory of the *patria.*"[39] Then the very next words, which begin chapter 3, are *Brittannia insula.* In chapter 4, *Britannia* is used once and *patria* twice in the same sentence: "I shall not enumerate the devilish monstrosities of my *patria. . . .* [Porphyry said,] '*Britannia* is a province fertile of tyrants.'. . . I shall do as well as I can, using not so much literary remains from this *patria* (which . . . have been burnt by the enemies or removed by the *cives* when they went into exile)."[40] Clearly, this *patria,* which has *cives, scripti,* and *victoriae,* is no *villa* or *regio.* Gildas says that the *cives* went into exile "across the sea" (*transmarina*), implying that the *patria* must be reached by sea. Again, he says that the Roman army "crossed the ocean to the *patria* by ship," and that British priests who "sail across the seas" to attain church offices return in pomp *ad patriam.*[41] *Patria* here can be nothing other than the *insula.* For Gildas, *patria* is the island and former Roman province of Britannia.[42]

Gildas then goes on to say that after the Scots and Picts devastated Britain, the Britons "prayed that the *misera patria* should not be wiped out."[43] After the Romans "informed the *patria*" that they could no longer protect it, a council was convened that decided to hire Saxons "as a guard [*praesidium*] for the *patria*."[44] The Saxons settled "in the eastern part of the island [*in orientali parte insulae*] . . . seemingly to fight for the *patria*," in reality to slaughter the "frightened inhabitants who stayed in the *patria*."[45] Despite the great victory of Badon Hill, in Gildas's time "the cities of the *patria* are depopulated"; "the *cives* conceal [their own crimes] . . . while surrounding nations [*in circuitu nationes*] are aware and reprove them"; "*Britannia* has kings, but [they are] tyrants . . . who chase some thieves across the *patria* but love the thieves that sit at their tables"; such tyrants "hate peace in the *patria*"; Gildas chastises them—the *regibus patriae* and the *patriae duces*—as well as the *sacerdoti . . . patriae*.[46] In every instance, Gildas uses *patria* in a broad and general sense, and if territorial limits could be set to his notion of homeland, they would be those of the island itself.[47] "Pour Gildas," writes Kerlouégan, "la Bretagne forme une unité, qui se distingue d'autres unités: c'est une patrie et . . . c'est toute la terre occupée par les Bretons: soit la Bretagne de l'indépendance, soit la Bretagne reduite par l'invasion saxonne" (Britannia constitutes a unity, which is distinct from other unities: it is a *patria* and . . . it is all of the land occupied by the Britons, whether it be independent Britannia or the Britannia reduced by the Saxon invasion).[48]

Unfortunately, Gildas is the only writer to describe a British *patria* in the sixth century. We might expect the term to appear in the epigraphic evidence, perhaps in an inscription on some patriotic Briton's tombstone. There is one inscription, if the date and interpretation stand, that could provide powerful testimony to such patriotism. A fragmentary slab found in Cynwyl Gaeo, Carmarthenshire, bears a damaged Latin inscription in five horizontal lines: SERVATVR FIDAEI / PATRI (a) EQ (ue) SEMPER / AMATOR HIC PAVLIN/VS IACIT CVL [T]OR PIENT []/(s) SIM [VS AEQVI], "Preserver of the Faith, constant lover of his *patria*, here lies Paulinus, the devoted champion of righteousness."[49] Though to generalize from this one example would be incautious, this "constant lover of his *patria*" would appear to share the sympathies (*condolentis patriae*) of his fellow Briton Gildas. Did Paulinus also have such a broad, insular definition of *patria*?

Patria was, in any case, a concept that held meaning only for the surviving *Latin* writers from this period who chose to express their feelings about their British homeland. They did so in the late Roman fashion of expressing sentiment through the use of the term *patria* accompanied by personal terms like *parentes* (Patrick) and *condolentis* (Gildas), just as Sidonius and Augustine had described their *patriae* using personal possessives like *nostra* and *mea*. That contemporary church writers were also using *patria* to denote the Christian homeland could only have strengthened the rhetorical impact of these writings. Patrick "longed" to see his earthly *patria*, Britain, just as he longed to please God. Gildas parallels the sins plaguing his island *patria* with those which God unleashed on ancient Israel. Both writers use strong and personal language to describe their *patria*, following the precedent of Ausonius and Rutilius. "Nationalism" is too strong a word to use for this *patria* sentimentalism.[50] Still, one has only to look at the works of later Brittonic writers (e.g., the author of *Armes Prydein Vawr,* Nennius, and Geoffrey of Monmouth) to see the impact of this nascent "patriotic" sentiment in Britain.[51]

6

◆

BRITANNI

A good question to ask when investigating any society, ancient or modern, would be, By what name are they called? or, even better, What do they call themselves? Too often in antiquity we can only answer the first question, especially in the nonliterate world of northern Europe. The Greeks and the Romans—who were at least somewhat introspective and self-identifying— practiced their amateur enthnography on their barbarian neighbors like the Celts and the Germans, but what the barbarians called themselves is much harder to determine.[1] In the case of fifth- and sixth-century Britain, we have a Celtic-speaking population with an elite Latin-writing element, both of which seem for the first time to be trying to express their ethnic or political identity.[2] The word most commonly, but not exclusively, used to identify the inhabitants of Roman and sub-Roman Britain is *Britanni,* "Britons." How it was used in the fifth and sixth centuries may give a rare clue to this enigmatic society's view of itself and of its relationship to others.

As noted previously, in the discussion of *Britannia,* the first Greeks to mention the inhabitants of Britain called them *Albiones.*[3] This term was soon replaced by Ρρεττανος, more commonly spelled βρεττανος, which later became in Latin *Britannus,* first appearing at about the time of Caesar's campaigns.[4] The noun *Brit(t)annus(i)* is the most common classical Latin term used to describe the inhabitants of *Britannia,* and (due mainly to the influence of Caesar) it dominates in the literature, inscriptions, and military records of the early empire.[5] An alternative form for Briton, *Brit(t)o(nis),* first appears in Martial and in contemporary inscriptions, becoming quite popular by the fourth century and appearing in Bede (and thereafter) as *Bretto.*[6]

The form *Britanni* is most common in the writings of the secular historians, from Caesar and Tacitus on. Ammianus uses it exclusively: Theodosius the Elder rendered aid "to the fortunes of the *Britanni*" in 369; Frontinus was sent in exile *ad Britannos* c. 371–72.[7] So, too, does the *Historia Augusta,* where it appears eight times spelled *Brittanni.*[8] In these historical works, the *Britanni* are portrayed as a people who are harassed by *hostes,* who receive political exiles, who rebel, and who are among the remote peoples of the world.[9]

Britanni also seems to be the form preferred by the ecclesiastical writers of the fourth and fifth centuries. Jerome mentions the *Britanni* five times, mostly in the context of *extremi homines.*[10] Orosius uses *Britanni,* with the variant *Brittani,* again in a "geographic" sense.[11] Sulpicius Severus uses *Britanni* to describe bishops at the Council of Ariminum, then mentions Britain in the context of exile.[12] Prudentius remarks that Christ has reached the furthest peoples, even the *Britanni.*[13] Sidonius calls the remote Caledonians of Scotland *Britanni.*[14] Augustine and Arnobius prefer the form *Brit(t)o,* while Prosper uses both forms.[15] Most of those Christian writers using the form *Britto,* however, are influenced by its association with the heresiarch Pelagius; indeed Augustine says that *Britto* has become his cognomen. To round out our picture with this ecclesiastical evidence, then, the Britons appear as remote and foreign, harboring exiles, and giving birth to heretics.

By the middle of the fifth century, the term *Britanni* takes on an alternative geographic meaning. In Gallic contexts, it often refers to those British refugees living in the Armorican peninsula.[16] Sidonius, our chief Gallic witness, says that *Britanni* had settled north of the Liger, and that the *Britanni* answerable to the warleader Riothamus were enticing slaves away from a Gallic estate.[17] Gregory of Tours and Jordanes later discuss the activities of this Riothamus and his *Britanni*.[18] However, the nature of the "British" settlement in Armorica is not clearly understood.[19] The only contemporary description of British migration is Gildas's enigmatic statement that, because of the Saxon threat to Britain in the fifth century, some Britons "made for lands beyond the sea; beneath the swelling sails they loudly wailed, singing a psalm that took the place of a sea shanty."[20] Procopius claims that it was overpopulation that was, in his day, leading people from Britain to migrate to Francia,[21] and some scholars have accepted his term *Britannia* as the first description of Armorica as "Brittany."[22] Later, migration traditions gave way to myth, such as Magnus Maximus's planting a British colony in Armorica during his Gallic campaigns.[23] Inscriptions show that Britons were traveling (and settling) throughout the western provinces in the Roman period, and given the ethnic and linguistic similarities between Britons and Armoricans (described first by Tacitus), it should not be surprising to find traces of Britons in Armorica in both the archaeological and historical records; the trans-Channel *Litus Saxonicum* (and its offshoot, the *Tractus Armoricanus et Nervicanus*) may provide another common link (see Fig. 3).

Still, it is nearly impossible to be precise in describing the increasingly large influx of Britons to the Continent in the late fifth and sixth centuries. References in the historical sources are too few,[24] and fuller accounts are found mainly in the hagiography produced in the ninth century and later. Though late in date, these Breton saints' lives do testify to a large and active British Christian community in western Gaul. The bishops of this community are addressed in the proceedings of the Second Council of Tours held in A.D. 567: "We add also that, in Armorica, neither Briton nor Roman shall be consecrated bishop without the consent of the metropolitan and his provincial colleagues."[25] This passage suggests that there was a clear distinction, at least in the eyes of the Church, between Britons (*Brittani*) and Romans (*Romani*) in sixth-century Armorica.[26] Given the later linguistic demarcation between Breton and French speakers in Brittany, the *Brittani* referred to here are likely the immigrants from Britain, who spoke a Brittonic language, while the *Romani* are likely indigenous Romanized Gauls, who spoke the Vulgar Latin that would become French.

No such distinction is recorded for Britain. The written sources for the fifth and sixth centuries do not speak in terms of Britons and Romans, but rather *Britanni* and *cives,* and here the two terms are often synonymous. Constantius tells us that during Germanus's first visit to Britain, the *Brittani* were fighting a war against the *Saxones* and the *Picti*.[27] Constantius, when speaking of Gaul and Italy, describes the people as *populus* or *plebs* belonging to a city (Auxerre, Milan) or a province (*Armoricanae, Augustudense*); only in Britain are the inhabitants given ethnolinguistic labels (*Brittani, Saxones, Picti*).[28] This serves to separate himself from the people of Britain, who are too remote (like the Alans) to speak of in the same terms of familiarity that he applies to the people of Gaul.[29] Patrick, on the other hand, describes Britain in the same period but from an insider's point of view. Like Constantius, he does not feel it necessary to describe in ethnolinguistic terms the people to whom he is writing.[30] They are simply *cives* or *mei*,[31] while the outsiders (*extranei*), the foreign people (*genti exterae*), are described as *Scotti, Picti,* and *Franci*.[32] Just as Constantius was able to describe Germanus's activities in Galliae without specifying that the people were Gauls, so too can Patrick talk about his friends and family in Britanniae without mentioning that they were Britons.[33]

We might expect Gildas similarly to imply Britons without explicitly naming them, and indeed he does use the term *cives* for this purpose just as Patrick had.[34] However, the *De excidio* is different from Patrick's works in both style and purpose. Gildas tries, at least, to distance himself as he chronicles past events, acting as an omniscient (though not objective) observer of the various peoples struggling for control of the island of Britain. In doing this, Gildas provides a great deal of information about the Britons. He says that it has become a proverb that "the *Britanni* are cowardly in war and faithless in peace," and that the Britons sent a letter to Aetius entitled "The Groans of the Britons" (*gemitus Britannorum*).[35] Throughout the narrative of the *De excidio,* the Britons (more often the *cives*) are contrasted with the Romans: the Britons are obstinate and rebellious, the Romans brave and stern. Furthermore, when Gildas speaks of *Romani,* it is as if he were speaking about a people ancient and foreign to him, thus producing awkward phrases like "the kings of the Romans" (*reges Romanorum*), "our worthy [Roman] allies" (*auxiliares egregii*), and "Ambrosius . . . the last of the Roman people" (*Ambrosio . . . quo solus . . . Romanae gentis*).[36] Romans were, to Gildas, an alien people of the past.[37] "Despite [his] Roman cultural trappings," remarks Michael Jones, "Gildas perceived himself and his countrymen to be Britons, distinct from the foreign Romans."[38]

More than one commentator has suggested that in Gildas's day *Romani* and *Britanni* were "antipathetic parties" that divided the loyalties of independent Britain.[39] Such division is undoubtedly an oversimplification, for there were other loyalties competing in Britain. *Christianus* must certainly have been a strong identifier, though we do not know the precise relation (or ratio) between Christians and pagans in Britain.[40] Tribal loyalties—sentimental or real—were undoubtedly strong at this time, as indeed they had been even under Roman rule.[41] Gildas denounces "Constantine, tyrant of Dumnonia [*Damnoniae tyrannicus*]," and "Vortipor, tyrant of the Demetae [*Demetarum tyranne*]."[42] Such tribal names, many of which predate the Roman conquest, appear as well in post-Roman inscriptions. Three early inscribed stones from Wales (dating from the fifth to the early sixth centuries) commemorate an "Elmetian" (*Elmetiacos*, i.e., a native of the kingdom of Elmet in Yorkshire), an "Ordovician" (*Ordous*, i.e., a native of north-central Wales), and a "citizen of Gwynedd" (*Venedotis cives*).[43] The Llandaff Charters and Welsh vernacular literature as well show that such territorial associations were quite common among the Britons in Wales especially.[44]

To proclaim oneself (or be proclaimed) a Briton or an Ordovician in stone, especially given the brevity (and probably expense) of most inscriptions, is a good indicator of the importance of such ethnic labels. Britons appear sporadically in Roman inscriptions, both in Britain and throughout the Continent.[45] *Brit(t)o* is the preferred form in these inscriptions, often appearing as an epithet or even a cognomen. From the epigraphic evidence, it is clear that in the Roman period many people, both in Britain and abroad, took pride in calling themselves Britons.[46] Unfortunately, there are no such examples from fifth- and sixth-century Britain. However, there are some cases, literary and epigraphic, of fifth-century expatriates who still considered themselves Britons.[47] At Arles, the lid of a sarcophagus bears the epitaph (dated c. 420–60) of Tolosanus *Britannus Natione*.[48] Mansuetus, a signatory to the Council of Tours in 461, styled himself *episcopus Britannorum,* though it is not known whether he was a British pilgrim traveling through Gaul or the pastor of a resident Breton community.[49] Another bishop, the Pelagian author Fastidius, is called *Britto* by the late-fifth-century writer Gennadius of Marseilles.[50] Sidonius's friend Faustus of Riez ministered to the Britons and is very likely to have been a Briton himself.[51] A tombstone found at Mertola, in southern Portugal, records the death of a *Britto presbyter* in A.D. 546.[52] Then, of course, there is Pelagius, who, though he himself did not leave us a statement of his background, was called (derisively) Briton by several of his opponents.[53]

The most curious example comes from the Gallic poet Ausonius. In an epigram written by Ausonius c. 382, an otherwise unknown British poet named Silvius Bonus is made infamous:

DE QUODAM SILVIO BONO QUI ERAT BRITO
Silvius ille Bonus, qui carmina nostra lacessit,
nostra magis meruit disticha, Brito bonus.
Silvius hic Bonus est. "Quis Silvius?" Iste
Britannus.
"Aut Brito hic non est Silvius, aut malus est."
Silvius esse Bonus fertur ferturque Britannus:
quis credat civem degenerasse bonum?
Nemo bonus Brito est. Si simplex Silvius esse
incipiat, simplex desinat esse bonus.
Silvius hic Bonus est, sed Brito est Silvius idem:
simplicior res est, credite, Brito malus.
Silvi, Brito Bonus: quamvis homo non bonus esse
ferris nec <se quit> iungere Brito Bono.

(ON ONE SILVIUS "GOOD" WHO WAS A BRITON

That Silvius "Good" who attacks my verse, has the more fully earned my
lampoon, being a good Briton.
"This is Silvius 'Good.'" "Who is Silvius?" "He is a Briton." "Either this
Silvius is no Briton, or he is Silvius 'Bad.'"
Silvius is called Good and called a Briton: who would believe a good citizen
had sunk so low?
No good man is a Briton. If he should begin to be plain Silvius, let the plain
man cease to be good.
This is Silvius Good, but the same Silvius is a Briton: a plainer thing—believe
me—is a bad Briton.
Thou Silvius art Good, a Briton: yet 'tis said thou art no good man, nor can
a Briton link himself with Good.)[54]

"Apparently 'a good man' and 'a Briton' were regarded as a contradiction
in terms," observes Hugh White, "and a Briton surnamed Bonus as something extremely humorous."[55] This snide attitude is echoed in the remarks
of a fellow Gallic aristocrat, Rutilius Namatianus, who wrote c. 417 that the
virtues of his friend Victorinus were known even by "the wild Briton."[56]
Compare these comments with the remark of Jerome's—that Britain is a
province fertile with tyrants—and it is clear to see that the barbarous reputation of the Britons had changed little since Caesar's day.[57] Note also that
Ausonius uses both forms for Briton, *Brito* and *Britannus*, in his poem, probably for metrical reasons. In this context, however, *Brito* again seems to have

an epithetical purpose, perhaps colloquially, while *Britannus* has a longer-standing formal literary tradition.

When Pelagius started causing trouble in the early fifth century, Jerome and Prosper had Ausonius's precedent with which they could sting the heretic by simply calling him *Britto*. This did not, however, prevent subsequent churchmen from declaring themselves Britons on paper and stone. Most of these examples (mentioned above) come from the Continent, identifying wayfaring Britons who were out of context and whose place of origin was thus not so obvious. The term "Briton," therefore, was commonly used as an identifier in noninsular contexts, and it would have made perfect sense to an audience familiar with the Britons of Caesar and Tacitus. If an individual on the Continent was calling himself a Briton, *Britto* or *Britannus,* it simply meant to his new neighbors that he was from the island of Britain, whether he was a *Britto bonus* or a *Britto malus*.

If "Briton" was used as a geographic identifier abroad, what purpose did it serve in insular contexts? Patrick and Gildas were in the best position to judge whether "Briton" was a legitimate label in Britain itself. Patrick remains silent, while Gildas both bears witness to the tribal division that had occurred in sub-Roman Britain and, at the same time, shows through his language that *Britanni* and *cives* were still unifying words that could describe many of the inhabitants of the island. Contemporary insular inscriptions, however, show that Gildas's fellow countrymen preferred to identify themselves with local/tribal terms. Gildas and Patrick are, of course, churchmen writing in Latin and looking to classical and biblical authors for inspiration. When Gildas uses the term *Britanni,* he is influenced by the formal literary tradition used by "outsiders" to describe the inhabitants of Britain. Would non-Latin-writing and speaking peoples in Britain have thought of themselves as *Britanni?*

For the sub-Roman period, this may be an unanswerable question. We do know that in the earliest vernacular poetry the term *Brython* (or *Brythoniaid*) was widely used to describe Britons living in northern Britain, Wales, Dumnonia, and Armorica.[58] However, while Latin-writing Britons (like Geoffrey of Monmouth and Gerald of Wales) continued to use the term *Britones* (or the English version, *Wallenses*) in the Middle Ages, other Britons came to prefer another Latin term for themselves, *cives,* which they found useful because of its similarity to a vernacular term that would, to this day, give identity to their descendants, the Cymry of Wales.[59]

7

$\blacklozenge$

CIVES

In the early years of the Roman Empire, the "citizens" (*cives*) were distinguished from the "natives" (*populi*) in the provinces. After the Edict of Caracalla in 212 no such distinction existed, as virtually all free peoples living within the borders of the empire became *cives* (the sole exception being barbarians who had recently submitted themselves to Rome through surrender). But what happened when these borders changed in the fifth century? Writers in Britain as well as on the Continent continued to use the term *cives* for several centuries. What, then, did it mean to be a "citizen" in Britain when the imperial apparatus was long gone?

Like the term *patria, cives* has a long linguistic history, and its meaning evolved as it passed successively through the Greek, Roman, and Christian worlds.[1] The Latin noun *civis* (m. and f.) is used at the outset to refer to a participant in a *civitas*.[2] Since the primary *civitas* is Rome, "citizenship" changed as Rome grew from a Latin community to a republic and eventually to an empire. By the late empire, the term *civis* carried with it a diversity of associations, political and otherwise. Political participation or identification could be expressed in a variety of ways: *civis Romanus* (Caesar, *BCiv.*, 2.20.5; Ammianus, 27.9.9; throughout the laws); *civis Latinus* (*CIL*, VII.879); *civis Italia* (Seneca, *Dial.*, 6.3.1); *civis patriae* (Seneca the Elder, *Controversiae*, 7.1.2); *civis* of an *urbs, civitas,* or *municipium* (Plautus, *Amph.*, 376 [Thebes]; *CIL*, V.1658 [Aquileia]; Ausonius, *Ordo*, 298.39 [Bordeaux]); and *civis* of a *provincia* (Pliny, *Naturalis Historia*, 12.5 [*Galliarum*]). One could also be a *civis mundi* (Cicero, *Leg.*, 1.61); a *civis saeculi* (Augustine, *De civitate Dei*, 15.1); a *civis sanctorum* (Vulg. Eph. 2.19); a *civis supernae patriae* (Eugippius, *Epis.*, 9); even a *civis bestiae* (Ovid, *Hal.*, 18).

In the fourth-century secular tradition this variety continues. Ioannes Viansino has shown that Ammianus describes three different types of *civis* in his writings.[3] First is the *civis Romae,* which means an inhabitant of the city.[4] Second, the *cives aliarum urbium* are inhabitants of various other cities.[5] Last, the *concives,* that is, *civis* used in conjunction with a possessive pronoun, is used inclusively of a group of *cives*.[6] It seems to me, however, that these three categories in Ammianus are all variations on one theme: the classical idea of the *civis* as a participant in the *civitas*. Ammianus is interested in the specific political unit of the "city," and does not speak in general of imperial citizenship.

The late imperial idea of "dual citizenship"—in secular terms—is expressed by Ausonius of Bordeaux.[7] In *The Order of Famous Cities*, written c. 388, Ausonius saves his warmest praise for his native city:

> Haec patria est: patrias sed Roma supervenit omnes.
> Diligo Burdigalam, Romam colo;
> Civis in hac sum, consul in ambabus;
> Cunae hic, ibi sella curulis.

> (This is my own country; but Rome stands above all countries.
> I love Bordeaux, Rome I venerate;
> In this I am a citizen, in both a consul;
> Here was my cradle, there my curule chair.)[8]

Ausonius indicates, through the structure of this poem, that he sees himself first as a *civis* of his *patria*, the city of Bordeaux. However, allegiance to

Rome takes precedence over his instinctual love for his *patria,* and he has to remind himself that, as consul, he serves both Bordeaux and Rome. In this sentence, citizenship in Bordeaux is explicit, while Roman citizenship is implied by the fact that he is a consul and by his "veneration" of Rome.[9] By the end of the fourth century, the secular tradition had clearly developed a complexity of political identifications and loyalties.

The situation became even more complex when Christian authors began adopting the concept of "citizenship" for their own purposes. *Civis* was deemed a useful term by the ecclesiastical writers of the fourth and fifth centuries. Forms of *civis* appear thirty-two times in the Vulgate Bible, twenty-seven in the Old Testament, and five in the New Testament. Interestingly, all but one of these references follow the secular tradition of "citizenship." That is to say, the biblical *civis* most often refers to political association—be it formal or informal—and is used to contrast "neighbor" (*propinquus*) with "stranger" (*peregrinus, advena*).[10] The sole exception, Eph. 2.19, refers to "heavenly citizenship" by transforming the secular phrasing: "So you are no longer strangers (*hospites*) and sojourners (*advenae*), but you are fellow citizens of the saints (*cives sanctorum*) and members of the household of God (*domestici Dei*)" (my translation).

This transformation of secular citizenship, begun by Paul (who was himself proud of his status as a Roman citizen), is fully completed in the works of the fourth-century church fathers. Ambrose, elaborating on Paul's words, makes "heavenly citizenship" attractive to the average Roman by linking it with the Roman values of family and companionship: one could be a *civis* of the greatest city (the New Jerusalem), a member of the household of God, a child of the Church, a companion of the saints.[11] This idea achieves its finest statement in the metaphors of Augustine. In the *City of God,* Augustine consciously parallels the *civitas superna* with the *civitas terrestris,* frequently associating the latter with the *imperium Romanorum* and discussing the metaphor with technical terms like *cives* and *munera.*[12] Augustine's regard for order and unity is expressed in his view of one (earthly) *civitas,* of many *gentes,* under Rome: "[F]ieret, . . . ut omnes ad Romanorum im-perium pertinentes societatem acciperent civi-tatis et Romani cives essent, ac sic esset omnium quod erat ante paucorum" (It came about that all subjects of the Roman Empire received the bond of citizenship and became Roman citizens, so that the privilege of the few was given to all).[13] Elsewhere, Augustine recognizes the classical meaning of *civis* as participant of a *civitas,* and even extends citizenship to the provincial level.[14] His language is most intimate and forceful, however, when he speaks of the citizens of the City of God:

they are "my *cives*."[15] Again, this "heavenly citizenship" is often framed in the mundane expressions of the secular tradition ("that Jerusalem, of which the holy angels are *cives*"), betraying Augustine as the seminal transitional figure—in this area, as in many others—between the classical and Christian worlds.[16]

Teillet has shown that with the barbarian incursions of the fifth century, writers on the Continent began distinguishing *cives* (usually meaning the inhabitants of a *civitas*) from *hostes* or a particular *gens* (e.g., *gens Francorum, gens Gothorum*).[17] Thus, in the western provinces at least, writers after 410 seem to have noted the diversity in the population by their choice of terms. If one were to judge by the language of Constantius, there would seem to be a great difference between the populations of Gaul and Britain in the fifth century. As Thompson has pointed out, Constantius refers to the people of Gaul as *plebs, provinciales,* and *cives,* while the Britons are always *populus* or *populi*.[18] This undoubtedly has to do with Constantius's better familiarity with Gaul (he names Gallic cities, whereas in Britain he speaks only of vague *regiones*). Still, it may reflect his uncertainty whether the Britons are still *cives*.

The Briton Patrick, on the other hand, has no doubts. In writing his *Letter to the soldiers of Coroticus,* written probably in the middle of the fifth century, Patrick attempts a level of familiarity with these men in order to justify his disgust over their murderous activities. Thus, he identifies himself as a bishop living "among barbarian peoples" (*Inter barbaras . . . gentes*), having given up *patria et parentes* for the sake of God: "With my own hand I have written and composed these words to be given, delivered and sent to the soldiers of Coroticus—I do not say to my fellow-citizens [*civibus meis*] nor to fellow-citizens of the holy Romans [*civibus sanctorum Romanorum*], but to fellow-citizens of the demons [*civibus daemoniorum*], because of their evil actions. Like the enemy they live in death, as allies of Irish and of Picts and apostates."[19] The assumption from this rhetorical phrasing is that Patrick should be addressing the soldiers as *cives meorum* and *cives sanctorum Romanorum,* but he cannot because of their bloodthirsty actions (killing the neophytes). Patrick has clearly moved beyond a limited secular meaning of *civis* to one in which "citizenship" is contingent upon moral behavior.

The phrase *cives meorum* is usually translated simply as "my fellow citizens,"[20] but scholars dispute whether Patrick means "fellow Roman citizens" or "fellow countrymen," that is, Britons.[21] The problem is that those who favor "Romans" for the first clause also interpret the second clause, "*civibus sanctorum Romanorum*," as "Romans";[22] but this sets up an unnecessary repetition and weakens Patrick's rhetorical purpose. The more likely meaning of *cives meorum,* which is consistent with Patrick's language elsewhere, is "my fellow Britons." A little later he says, referring to the soldiers, "And if my own people [*mei*] do not recognize me, well, a prophet does not have honor in *patria sua.*"[23] As Hanson puts it, "Patrick here makes it crystal clear that Coroticus and his men were British."[24] Since Patrick himself is from Britain[25] and Coroticus's men are of the same *patria,* the latter can only be Britons, Saxons, Picts, or Scots. But the name Coroticus is clearly not Anglo-Saxon, and the *milites* are explicitly distinguished by Patrick from the Picts and Scots.[26] This leaves Britons as the only possibility, and in a passage in the *Confessio,* Patrick even speaks of "our nationality" (*genere nostro*) in a context that has been taken to mean Britons.[27]

More difficult to understand is the second clause, *cives sanctorum Romanorum.* As one scholar commented wryly, "Since when are the Romans 'blessed' or 'sanctified'?"[28] Most commentators, as I have noted, have taken this phrase to mean "Romans" or "Roman citizens."[29] If, however, Coroticus was a "king" or "tyrant" living in Strathclyde—beyond the imperial border—Patrick would hardly have considered him a Roman citizen.[30] Michael Jones has put forward another suggestion, that *cives sanctorum Romanorum* means "fellow Christians," in contrast with the "demons" and the "apostates."[31] Other references by Patrick to "the Roman Christians of Gaul" (*Romanorum Gallorum Christianorum*), "the brethren in Gaul" (*Gallias . . . fratres*), and "the church of the Irish, or rather of the Romans; in order to be Christians like the Romans" (*Aeclessia Scotorum immo Romanorum; ut Christiani ita ut Romani*) would seem to support this interpretation.[32] Coroticus and his men were certainly Christians, at least in name, or Patrick would not be threatening them with excommunication.[33] Though Patrick's language is typically awkward here, I agree that *cives sanctorum Romanorum* most likely signifies "Christians," as an alternative to *cives meorum*—"citizens of my *patria,*" that is, Britons—and in contrast to *cives daemoniorum.*

As well as being Christians, those addressed in Patrick's letter were also clearly able to understand Latin.[34] Patrick asks that the letter be read aloud before the people and in the presence of Coroticus.[35] His audience must also have been familiar with the Latin terminology he uses to impress them: "I was free-born according to the flesh [*Ingenuus fui secundum carnem*]; my father was a decurion [*decorione*]. I sold my good birth [*nobilitatem meam*] . . . in the interest of others."[36] These Roman "status symbols" meant something to Coroticus and his followers, whether or not they were ever technically Roman citizens. Patrick's use of the possessive pronouns establishes a familiarity with the audience of the *Epistola*,[37] who share his *patria*, his religion, and his culture; they are not referred to in the same terms (*barbarae, genti exterae*) with which he addresses "outsiders" like the Picts and Scots.

As Hanson implies, Patrick's understanding of *civis* is a complex one that encompasses both secular and Christian traditions.[38] The best parallel is Augustine, whose *Confessio* Patrick is likely to have read.[39] Augustine uses the phrase *civis noster* in a context where it is clear that he is describing a fellow African,[40] just as Patrick uses *cives meorum* to describe the *milites* who Patrick implies are from his *patria*. Yet Augustine also uses this secular phrase in a spiritual metaphor—*cives meorum in aeterna hierusalem*—where he clearly means Christians.[41] Thus Patrick's rhetoric, although awkward in comparison to Augustine's, similarly uses a metaphor that balances secular (*cives meorum*), religious (*cives sanctorum*), and moral (*cives daemoniorum*) "citizenship."

Gildas uses the term *cives* on numerous occasions, often in opposition to both *Romani* and *hostes*. There were, he claims, *cives* in Britain even before the Romans got there: "Since it was first inhabited, Britain has been ungratefully rebelling . . . against [its own] *cives*."[42] After conquering Britain, the Romans left "some of their own people [*suorum*] in charge"; later, they "instructed the *cives* to build a wall across the island . . . to scare away the *hostes*."[43] When this failed, "the *cives* abandoned the towns and the high wall" until "the *hostes* retreated from the *cives*, but the *cives* did not retreat from their own sins."[44] "After . . . the cruel plunderers had gone home, . . . the wretched *cives*" banded together behind "Ambrosius Aurelianus, perhaps the last of the Roman people [*solus . . . Romanae gentis*]" to survive the storm.[45] "From then on victory went now to the *cives*, now to the *hostes*," until the age of peace in Gildas's time, when tyrants like Constantine "work their wiles on the *cives*."[46]

In the *De excidio,* there are "good citizens" (*bonis civibus*), "exiled citizens" (*civium exilii*), "wretched citizens" (*miserrimi cives*), and "pitiable citizens" (*deflendi cives*).[47] Gildas also has other synonyms at his disposal: *Britanni, populus, gens, homines,* and *reliquiae*. Yet he sets *cives* apart from these other words; for example, when he is chastising Cuneglasus, he asks, "Why do you wage such a war . . . against *homines*, that is *cives*?"[48] *Homines,* after all, could refer to any men, but the point here is that Cuneglasus is waging war against his own people, fellow Britons. *Cives* remains Gildas's most often used general term for, as Wright puts it, the inhabitants of his *patria,* his fellow citizens.[49] In this respect Patrick and Gildas are much alike.[50] Unlike Patrick, however, Gildas never links the words *cives* and *Romani.* In Gildas, there are no lingering sentiments about Britons as Roman citizens or Christians as heirs to the Romans. Neither is there any hint of provincial or civic loyalties. Whereas Augustine had constructed a sophisticated metaphor to contrast earthly and terrestrial *cives,* Gildas simply contrasts the *cives* with the *hostes.* Gildas's audience did not need to decipher rhetoric to understand that *cives* meant fellow Britons.

Civis is a term quite commonly used in Roman inscriptions, both pagan and Christian, and in Britain it is often found on the tombstones of foreign-born men stationed along the frontier. There is one very interesting post-Roman (fifth- or early-sixth-century) example found on a pillar stone in Penmachno, Caernarvonshire, Wales. The inscription reads: CANTIORI(x) HIC IACIT / [V]ENEDOTIS CIVE (s) FVIT / [C]ONSOBRINO (s) // MA[G]LI / MAGISTRAT, "Cantiorix lies here. He was a citizen of Gwynedd (and) cousin of Maglos the Magistrate."[51] In a similar vein, a pillar stone from Llantrisant in Anglesey (later sixth century) commemorates the wife of "Bivatigirnus, . . . priest [*sacerdos*] and an example to all his fellow citizens [*civium*]."[52] Though these are the only known instances in Britain of the term *cives* in early Christian inscriptions, there is a comparable example from Salonae in Dalmatia (dated A.D. 425) commemorating *Clarissima femina, civis Dunnonia,* that is, a member of the Dumnonii of Devon and Cornwall.[53]

Clearly, tribal loyalties mattered in fifth-century Britain, at least to some. Yet Patricks makes no mention of tribes at all, and Gildas names only two (the Dumnonii and the Demetae), in order better to identify his *tyranni.* The identification of a person's "citizenship" was, it seems, still a subjective matter in post-Roman Britain. Patrick and Gildas may have used the term *cives* for all Britons because of a desire for unity in Britain, a political and religious unity appropriate for God's chosen people.

However, it should be admitted in closing that Latin-writing clerics were not the only ones keeping alive the concept of *civis* in post-Roman Britain. A similar sense of "citizenship" survived in the vernacular, first as the British word *combrogi* ("men from the same *bro*"), later as the Welsh *cymry* or *cumbri,* which mean "fellow countrymen."[54] This survival is most vivid in British place-names. In both Wales and northern Britain there are numerous places with either *cumbri* or *cumber* (the English form) as part of their names.[55] This is strong evidence that the Britons were using this term of self-identification before they were split by the encroaching invaders (both the Welsh and the northern Britons called themselves *Combrogi*),[56] and that the

English as well knew the Britons by this term and used it when they named British settlements throughout the island. Just as both Gildas and "Nennius" used *cives* as a synonym for *Britanni/Brittones,* so too did the authors of early Welsh poetry and chronicles use *cymry* as a synonym for *Brythoniaid.*[57] Although the empire may have receded from British political consciousness, observes Dumville, "*patria* (in the shape of Britain) and *cives* (the Cymry *combrogi, 'fellow-countrymen,' Britons) were still prominent and were forces which might occasionally encourage cooperative action" against the English invaders.[58]

The "British" perspective on insular history, from Gildas to Geoffrey of Monmouth, remains remarkably consistent: The island of Britain was once occupied by Britons, who ruled it all, from sea to sea, before the foreigners arrived and scattered the *cives,* who, if they could win back God's favor, would expel the foreigners and win back the land of the Britons.[59] "The Britons (the *Cymry,* our people) will rise again!" is, literally, the cry of these prophets,[60] and they will be led by the great *reges*—Arthur, Cynan, and Cadwaladr—of the Heroic Age.

8

◆

REGES

"Britain has kings, but they are tyrants." Gildas's words are an open invitation for the eager historian to delve into the problem of political organization in sub-Roman Britain. A political historian would soon be disappointed, however, because Gildas does not give precise information about these kings and tyrants, and because the written sources in general supply few names of rulers and the territory/people over which they ruled. Still, if we concern ourselves for the moment, not with prosopography, but only with the ways in which the terms for "king" were used by sub-Roman authors, we can then formulate a definition of "kingship" within which the few names that we do possess can be placed.

Both Latin and Celtic languages developed similar terms to describe "tribal" rulers in their societies. Common Celtic *rix* (king) spawned the Irish *ri* and the Brittonic *rig,* while Latin evolved *rex/regis* (king), and *regnum(i)* (kingship, kingdom).[1] After the Romans expelled the Etruscan kings and established the republic, most Latin authors considered kingship an inferior political system and applied the term *rex* indiscriminately to rulers of "outsiders."[2] However, when the empire absorbed many of these "outsiders"—along with their cultural and political systems—neither kings nor the concept of "kingship" immediately disappeared. Steve Fanning has shown that, even though Roman rulers after Julius Caesar avoided association with "the name and office" of king, writers of the late empire frequently applied the term *rex* to Roman emperors (and conversely used imperial terminology to describe the barbarians).[3]

The question of the survival of kingship in Roman and sub-Roman Britain has perplexed many scholars. It is well-attested that Britain had a military aristocracy of kings *and* queens before the Roman conquest: Caesar and the *Res Gestae* provide written evidence of named British *reges,* while native coinage and inscriptions show that British rulers had adopted the Latin term *rex* to describe themselves.[4] Some of these individuals—Cogidubnus, Prasutagus, Cartimandua—became client rulers after Claudius's invasion.[5] Others—Caratacus, Boudicca, Calgacus—continued the resistance up to the time of Agricola's governorship, after which there is no more mention of the native aristocracy in the historical or epigraphic sources. Since at least some of the pre-Roman tribal nomenclature survives into the post-Roman period, especially in the upland regions, it remains a possibility—but only a possibility at this point—that kings survived in the military zones and along the frontiers.[6]

The *reges* of Britain reappear in the literary and epigraphic sources of the fifth century. Constantius does not mention any British kings, but a friend of his does. Sidonius Apollinaris corresponded c. 470 with a man named Riothamus, complaining to him that certain Britons (*Britanni*)—"a crowd of noisy, armed, and disorderly men"— were enticing slaves away from a friend.[7] Jordanes provides further information about this individual: "Now Euric, king of the Visigoths, perceived the frequent changes of Roman emperors and strove to hold Gaul in his own right. The [western] emperor Anthemius heard of it and asked the Britons [*Brittones*] for aid. Their king Riotimus came with twelve thousand men into the state of the Bituriges by the way of Ocean, and was received as he disembarked from his ships."[8] This military arrangement is thought to have taken place c. 468. Jordanes adds: "Euric, king of the Visigoths, came against them with an innumerable army, and after a long fight he routed Riotimus, king of the Britons, before the

Romans could join him."[9] After his defeat, Riothamus fled with his follow-
ers to the district of Lyon and sought refuge among the Burgundians.
Gregory of Tours confirms that these "Britons [*Brittani*] were expelled from
Bourges by the Goths and many were killed at Bourg-de-Deols."[10]

Riothamus and Riotimus are both Latinized forms of *Rigotamos,* a Celtic
name and/or title meaning either "most kingly" or "supreme king."[11] Some
historians have seen Riothamus as a shadowy chieftain leading a group of
Breton (i.e., Britons settled in Armorica) mercenaries in a minor (and unsuccessful) skirmish.[12] Others, however, have chosen to interpret "by way of
Ocean" literally to mean that Riothamus brought his warband from Britain
to fight in Gaul.[13] Though Jordanes is certainly exaggerating the number of
his forces at twelve thousand, he confirms the information of Sidonius that
Riothamus was the leader (only Jordanes uses the title *rex*) of a warlike
group of Britons officially engaged by the emperor Anthemius to protect
Gaul from Euric. I believe it is quite probable that Riothamus was a king,
either in name or in deed,[14] and possible that he brought his warband from
Britain to fight against the barbarians in the tradition of Maximus and
Constantine III.[15] Sidonius's intimate greeting (*Sidonius Riothamo suo*) and
assessment of Riothamus's character ("I am a direct witness of the consci-
entiousness which weighs on you so heavily" [*Epistolae,* 3.9, my transla-
tion]) reveal a surprising level of both respect and familiarity between this
Briton and the Gallic aristocracy, perhaps due to family connections or previous communications (had Sidonius—or an associate—carried messages
between Anthemius and Riothamus?).[16] Whatever his place of origin or motivation for campaigning in Gaul, the enigmatic Riothamus remains the first
British king to appear in written sources since Tacitus.

A second candidate for a fifth-century British king might be Coroticus,
but we lack indisputable proof. Patrick does not call him king but refers to
his "unjust rule" (*tyrannidem*).[17] The only time Patrick mentions kings is
when he is talking about the converts he has made among the sons and
daughters of the Irish chieftains (*reguli,* "petty kings").[18] Most historians,
however, consider Coroticus a king. Their case rests mainly on two later
pieces of evidence: Muirchu's seventh-century *Life of Patrick,* which calls
Coroticus both *rex Britannicus* and *tyrannus,* and Welsh genealogies that
mention two kings named Coroticus, one in Cardigan and one in
Strathclyde.[19] Because the evidence is not contemporary, any discussion of
Coroticus's status must deal first with Patrick's assessment, that he "ruled
like a tyrant."[20]

Gildas, on the other hand, leaves no doubt that there were kings in Britain in his time. After the Romans left Britain for good, and after the Britons won their first victory against the Scots and Picts, Gildas writes: "Kings were anointed [*Ungebantur reges*] not in God's name, but as being crueller than the rest; before long, they would be killed, with no enquiry into the truth, by those who had anointed them, and others still crueller chosen to replace them. Any king who seemed gentler and rather more inclined to the truth was regarded as the downfall of Britain [*Britanniae subversorem*]; everyone directed their hatred and their weapons at him, with no respect."[21] This occurred in the interim period between the Roman withdrawal and the Saxon invasions, a time Gildas describes as an era of luxury and abundance.[22] Then a council (*consilium*) convened and brought in the Saxons, who rebelled and were finally halted at Badon Hill. In the ensuing period of peace, "kings [*reges*], public and private persons, priests and churchmen, kept to their own stations."[23]

But that age passed and left a people who were ignorant of the calamities of the past. Now, writes Gildas,

> Britain has kings [*reges*], but they are tyrants [*tyrannos*]; she has judges [*iudices*], but they are wicked. They often plunder and terrorize the innocent; they defend and protect the guilty and thieving; they have many wives, whores and adulteresses; they constantly swear false oaths; they make vows, but almost at once tell lies; they wage wars, civil and unjust; they chase thieves energetically all over the country [*patriam*], but love and even reward the thieves who sit with them at table; they distribute alms profusely, but pile up an immense mountain of crime for all to see; they take their seats as judges [*arbitraturi*], but rarely seek out the rules of right judgement [*iudicii regulam*]; they despise the harmless and humble, but exalt to the stars, so far as they can, their military companions [*commanipulares*], bloody, proud and murderous men, adulterers and enemies of God—if chance, as they say, so allows: men who should have been rooted out vigorously, name and all; they keep many prisoners in their jails [*in carceribus*], who are more often loaded with chafing chains because of intrigue than because they deserve punishment. They hang around the altars swearing oaths, then shortly afterwards scorn them as though they were dirty stones.[24]

Here we see clearly that, for Gildas, the qualities and functions of British kingship are to be tested against the moral and ethical behavior of the individuals. This is what is most important to Gildas, and the rest of the details about the kings that he gives us are mere by-products from his recounting of royal sins. Of the five tyrants whom he denounces, Gildas calls Vortipor, who sits on a "throne" (*throno*), "bad son of a good king" (*boni regis nequam fili*); Maglocunus has a "king's neck" (*regiae cervici*), a "kingdom" (*regno*), and a "royal uncle" (*avunculum regem*).²⁵ There are also "sons of kings" (*regiorum puerorum*), "a ring of kings" (*regium anulum*), "royal gold and silver" (*regni auri argenti*), and "kings of the homeland" (*regibus patriae*).²⁶ The terms *tyrannus* and *princeps* also appear in this section of the *De excidio*, primarily because Gildas is searching for appropriate synonyms to keep his sermon from getting too repetitive.²⁷

Gildas gives us a surprising amount of information about British kings. First of all, he gives us five personal names—in their Latin forms Constantinus, Aurelius Caninus, Vortipor, Cuneglasus, and Maglocunus—along with vivid descriptions of their "bestial" behavior.²⁸ As Paul Schaffner has shown, in the above-quoted lengthy passage Gildas is using *tyranni* and *iudices* rhetorically as interchangeable epithets for *reges*.²⁹ Thus, he is likely describing here the various (mostly condemnable) activities of the typical British *rex:* acting as judge, policing the kingdom, publicly professing to serve God, waging war, giving gifts, and even maintaining jails. We can also infer from other information given by Gildas that these kings practiced hereditary succession, exhibited outward symbols of their power (thrones, rings, cloaks), maintained (and distributed) a treasury based on gold and silver, were anointed and swore Christian oaths, and sometimes sold church offices.³⁰

It is a surprising fact that Gildas does not accuse any of his contemporary rulers of being pagans; rather, they are simply bad Christians. For Gildas, being bad Christians is inextricably tied to their being bad kings. This theocratic political philosophy is, of course, derived from Old Testament kingship, and Gildas was not the first writer in late antiquity to subscribe to it. Secular historians like Ammianus, not surprisingly, cared too little to judge barbarian kings (except in terms of their military abilities), whereas emperors (sometimes referred to as *rex*) were held up to classical Greco-Roman moral standards.³¹ After Constantine the Great, however, Christian writers began to judge emperors not just by the standard of their successful predecessors, but by a new theocratic model of the ideal ruler. This model drew from the portraits of Old Testament kings, above all David and Solomon, as well as some New Testament attributes of the King of Kings, especially from Revelation. The scriptural commentaries of Ambrose, Augustine, and Jerome were perhaps the most influential in the construction of this model, though its fullest expression is in Augustine's *City of God*. Unlike secular historians such as Tacitus and Ammianus, these Christian writers were concerned not so much with military valor or political hierarchies as with the moral qualities of rulership.[32] The Old Testament *reges* were warleaders, but they were instruments of God, and their successes and failures depended upon their behavior off the battlefield.[33]

Apocalyptic undertones made this model attractive to many ecclesiastical writers in the fifth century, as *imperator* steadily gave ground to *rex* in the West. The best example is the moralist Salvian of Marseilles, who attributed fifth-century disasters to the sins of wicked judges.[34] Patrick also subscribes to this model, even though his purpose is not political reform. He is dismissive of the *milites* of Coroticus, who fight and plunder "for the sake of a miserable temporal kingdom [*miserum regnum temporale*] which will in any case pass away in a moment," concerning himself instead with "the righteous . . . [who] shall judge the nations (*nationes*) and hold sway over wicked kings [*regibus iniquis*]."[35]

Gildas, however, does not just want restitution from the *reges iniquus:* he wants them to change their ways. His critique of British rulers, running some forty chapters, is an impassioned sermon aimed at exposing all the public and private sins of five ruling dynasties (family members are not spared). More than one scholar has commented that Gildas's moralizing is modeled after the Old Testament book of Jeremiah and parallels the tone of Salvian's writing.[36] Like many Old Testament kings, Gildas's *reges* are "anointed" (*ungebantur*), but they do not live up to their vows to God.[37] Patrick and Gildas both show concern about rulers swearing false oaths.[38] For Gildas, Christian kingship—to which his *reges* at least give lip service—means that the ruler is responsible both to God and to his people. Because these British *reges* have lied to God and are behaving immorally, their irresponsible sins are bringing punishment—plague, famine, civil wars, and barbarian raids— upon the Britons. This idea is not far removed from those of Salvian, and it will have a great impact on the moralizing histories of Bede, "Nennius," and Geoffrey of Monmouth.[39]

Gildas's description of the functions of British kings can be compared with evidence from the Llandaff Charters. Gildas names only five kings and does not give precise information about the location of their kingdoms (see, however, Fig. 6).[40] The charters, on the other hand, provide the names and locations of several dynasties in southern Wales from the mid–sixth century onward.[41] Davies has observed from this data that "the kings of the sixth and early seventh century are only to be found in small, distinct areas. . . . Their kingdoms appear to be minute and self-contained."[42] Around 600 there was some change, as victories over the Saxons began to be recorded and the major dynasty of the southeast (that of Meurig) came to dominate the whole area. This evidence neither confirms nor contradicts that of Gildas, who is unconcerned with territorial kingship and speaks of kingdoms only in vague terms. In general, the Llandaff Charters show that the activities of sixth-century kings (at least in southern Wales) included donating land to the church (in particular to bishops, archbishops, and "saints"), guaranteeing other people's gifts, and waging war.[43] This roughly corresponds to Gildas's remarks that the *reges* distributed alms and church offices, sat as judges, and waged civil wars.[44] The charters also show—and Gildas seems to imply—that royal succession normally passed from father to son (or uncle to nephew), and that brothers could share kingship.[45] The emphasis in Gildas and in the charters on the military activity of kings is further supported by the portraits of the warrior-kings painted by the vernacular poets.[46]

The term *rex* also appears frequently on inscribed stones, perhaps as early as the fifth century, though most occurrences date from the eighth to the twelfth. The earliest example from Wales is a memorial stone found in Llangadwaldr in Anglesey, which reads: CATAMANUS / REX SAPIENTIS (s) I/MUS OPINATIS (s) IM/US OMNIUM REG/UM, "King Catamanus, wisest [and] most renowned of all kings, [lies here]."[47] This inscription commemorates the Welsh king Cadfan of Gwynedd (c. 565–c. 625)[48] in formal Byzantine style,[49] seemingly making claims of superiority for the rulers of Gwynedd.[50] Other examples commemorate individuals—such as Vortipor[51] and Cunomorus (King Mark of Cornwall)[52]—who are thought to be kings, though the inscriptions themselves do not state that. A sixth-century stone from Stourton, west Devon, reads PRINCIPI / IURIUCI / AUDETI, "[Stone of the] *Princeps* Iuriucus, [son of] Audetus," seemingly a reference to a ruler of Dumnonia.[53] Alternatively, British inscriptions may indicate aristocratic status through the Celtic element -*rix* or -*rig* ("king") found in many insular names.[54] Sub-Roman examples include the memorial stone of Cunorix (late fifth century), found just outside the Roman defenses at Wroxeter;[55] the Mens Scryfys ("Written Stone"), from Land's End, naming a man called Ri(g)alobranus, which name contains the Brittonic element *rigalo,* "kingly, royal";[56] and the inscribed stone from Barmouth (fifth or early sixth century) which reads CAELEXTI (s) / MONEDO/RIGI (s), "[The Stone] of Caelextis Monedorix."[57]

The epigraphic evidence is admittedly sparse on detail, but it does speak

Fig. 6. Conjectural locations of British kings and kingdoms, based on textual and epigraphic evidence

to a proliferation of kings and individuals bearing regal names in at least parts of Britain from the fifth century onward. It is difficult to say exactly what, if any, relationship these dynasties had with the native aristocracy who faded into the shadows with the coming of the Roman legions and four centuries of *Romanitas*. We have no native British voice from the Roman period to tell us about the survival of British tribes and their customs. What we can say securely is that kings do reappear in the written record at least by the end of the fifth century, probably earlier, and by the sixth century they were abundant. These kings soon took on legendary stature in the vernacular poetry, but thanks to the sober evidence provided by Gildas and the Llandaff Charters, we can begin to perceive the more mundane characteristics of governing in the British Heroic Age.[58]

9

◆

TYRANNI

Saint Jerome, writing at the beginning of the fifth century, complained that "Britain is a province fertile of tyrants [*tyrannorum*]." Gildas, writing a century later (in a work condemning such tyrants), repeats this quote as if it were already a tired axiom. From the perspective of these and other contemporary writers, Britain was truly experiencing an age of tyrants. The word "tyrant" is loaded with pejorative meaning for modern readers, yet it began life as a neutral political term in ancient Greece. By the time it was being applied to rulers in Britain, however, it had undergone centuries of evolution influenced by the political and religious changes taking place in the Roman Empire. Failed usurpers, local despots, and wicked kings played on the minds of writers from the sub-Roman period to the present day, who, meanwhile, settled on a strictly moral, condemnatory use of the term. We see this development perhaps most clearly in sub-Roman Britain, though we still must explain why the "tyrant" was so prevalent on the island, and so characteristic of this age.

Our English term "tyrant" derives from the Greek τυραννος, which in turn spawned the Latin nouns *tyrannus(i)*, "tyrant" or "usurper," and *tyrannis (idis or idos)*, "tyranny" or "usurpation." Other late Latin and medieval forms include: *tyranna(ae)* (noun), a "female tyrant" (Trebellius Pollio, *Scriptores Historiae Augustae*, 2.31.10); *tyrannia* (noun), "tyranny"; *tyrannis* (noun), "destructive power" (Cassiodorus [*MGH*, vol. 12], 10.29.2); *tyrannis* and *tyrannicus* (adj.), "tyrannical" (*Scriptores Historiae Augustae*, 1.28.18); *in tyrannizo* (verb), "tyrannize over" (Jordanes [*MGH*, vol. 5, chap. 1], line 308); *tyrannicida(ae)* (noun), "tyrannicide" (*Scriptores Historiae Augustae*, 1.17.34); and *tyrannopolita[nus](ae)* (noun), "citizen under a tyranny" (Sidonius, *Epistolae*, 5.8.3).¹ *Tyran(n)us* even came to be used as a *cognomen*.² The only common variant spelling is with two *rs*, as in *tyrannus, tyrrannicum,* and *tyrrannidem* (*Passio Sancti Leodegarii*, 6.1 and 7.1). Greek forms developed along the same lines as the Latin forms in late antiquity; thus we find τυραννια, τυραννις, and τυραννικος in authors such as Olympiodorus, Sozomen, and Zosimus.

The word τυραννος was introduced into Greece by the middle of the seventh century B.C., possibly from Lydia, where it appears to have been simply a title meaning something like "king."³ At first it seems to have been used by the Greeks merely as a synonym for βασιλευς, "king," and continued to be used as such by the dramatists of the classical age.⁴ By the sixth century, however, τυραννος had become associated with a particular type of ruler, distinguished from the kings who had dominated the Greek Dark Ages as well as the aristocrats who succeeded them. This τυραννος was a revolutionary who seized control by force from the legitimate ruler(s)—the basis of what we might call the Greco-Roman "political" definition of tyrant (see Diag. 1).⁵ So prevalent was this type of ruler in the Greek city-states that the period 650–510 B.C. is often called the Age of Tyrants in Greek history. Some of these tyrants were beneficial to the *polis,* but others were so unrestrained in their appetites and abusive in their exercise of power that the term τυραννος began to take on negative connotations. After the Spartans helped Athens to expel its tyrants in 510 and establish a democracy, subsequent Greek political theorists began to describe all monarchies as bad, and tyrannies as particularly wicked. Plato, who championed monarchical rule (in the guise of "philosopher-kings"), rescued somewhat the reputation of kings, ascribing all monarchical crimes to tyrants; Xenophon, Aristotle, and later philosophers followed his lead, viewing kingship as the good form of monarchy, tyranny as the bad.[6] This, which me might label the "philosophical" definition of tyrant (see Diag. 1), would have perhaps the greatest impact on later Roman and Christian writers.

Diagram 1. Definitions of "Tyrant"

Political:	Greco-Roman	One who seizes political power, often by military force, from the legitimate ruler(s). Synonyms: emperor, king, usurper, brigand.
Political:	Celtic(?)	The term for a "local ruler" (lord, *seigneur*) given by those in the district he/she rules. Synonyms: king, lord, prince.
Philosophical		A monarch whose interests are directed toward ruler rather than ruled. An unjust ruler, one driven by his/her appetites.
Religious		A wicked or sinful monarch.

The Greek tyrant first became well known in Rome as a stock character in the theater.[7] These theatrical tyrants exhibited the lack of restraint—especially arrogance (*superbia*), cruelty (*crudelitas*), and sexual license (*libido*)—characteristic of Plato's tyrants, and it is from these characters that Latin historians like Sallust, Livy, and Tacitus later constructed their rhetorical tyrants. Rome had early on expelled its kings (sometimes—but only retrospectively—called "tyrants"), and rose to power as a republic while the many kingdoms of the Hellenistic East were still being ruled by tyrants. Republican authors most often used the Latin term *tyrannus* to refer to these rulers, and saw "monarchy" (*rex, regnare,* and *regnum*) as a sufficiently serious accusation to use against power-hungry Romans like Tiberius Gracchus, Sulla, and Julius Caesar. This situation changed with the revolution of Octavius Caesar, who established a veiled dynastic monarchy for those future emperors who would bear his honorific, "Augustus." As monarchy returned to Rome, *rex* and *regnum* also returned in the literature of the empire, now no longer used with such disapprobation.[8] Roman authors who then wished to reprove wicked emperors accused them of behaving like *tyranni*—as illustrated on stage and in the higher sphere of Hellenic philosophy—even if such an accusation might cost them their lives.[9]

The influence of Greek political philosophy on Roman literati is obvious from this brief discussion of rhetorical tyrants in the republic and the early empire. But this is not the only Greek view of tyrants adopted by Roman writers. The older "political" definition of tyrant—a usurper who seizes power by force—was revived by Roman writers of the late empire, showing that Solon, Herodotus, and Thucydides were not to be overshadowed in this matter by Plato and Aristotle. That this should happen is a reflection of the political turmoil of the third century, as viewed (albeit retrospectively) in the late-fourth-century *Historia Augusta*. The author of this section of the *Historia* based his account of the "Thirty Tyrants" during the reign of Gallienus and Valerian admittedly on the Athenian τυραννοι.[10] These short-lived pretenders are depicted as obscure men (*tanta obscuritas*) who came from diverse parts of the empire (*ex diversis orbis partibus*) to seize power, after which followed cruel tyranny (*aspera tyrannis*) and luxurious excesses (*summa luxuria*); yet many of them are praised for being valiant in war (*in bello fortissimus*), for being loved by the provincials (*amor . . . in Gallicanorum mente populorum*), and for doing public works (*rei publicae profuit*); indeed, one, Victorinus, is even hailed as an excellent emperor (*optimus imperator*).[11] The authors of the *Historia Augusta* give us a complex portrait of the Roman *tyrannus* in the military crisis of the third century, a crisis that gave the tyrant both the opportunity to seize power and the ability to obtain acceptance (albeit temporary) of his *imperium*. For Alan Wardman, in his study of fourth-century usurpers, the tyrant emerges from the *Historia Augusta* as a "super-brigand . . . but also as a version of the [legitimate] emperor himself."[12]

The usurper of the *Historia* is closest to the earlier, "political" definition of tyrant, though the excesses of the "philosophical" tyrant are occasionally glimpsed. Ammianus Marcellinus gives us a similar description of fourth-century usurpers.[13] He uses the term *tyrannis* twice in his history to describe the act of usurpation: the suppression of the usurpation (*de tyrannide*) of Silvanus in 355, and Rusticus Julianus's "fears [concerning] the usurpation" (*metuens tyrannidis*) of Magnus Maximus c. 383.[14] The form *tyrannus* is used five times by Ammianus. Two references are to ancient Greek tyrants: the *tyrannus* Dionysius of Syracuse and the (two mythical) tyrants (*tyrannorum*) destroyed by Hercules.[15] The other three references are concerned with Roman usurpers: the "rebellious tyrants" (*rebellium tyrannorum*) of the third century and the *tyranno* Procopius, who had waged "civil war" (*civilia bella*) against "the legitimate emperors" (*princibus legitimis*).[16] Viansino points out the similarities between Ammianus and the *Historia Augusta* in depicting third-century usurpers. Ammianus also uses this shared "political" definition of *tyrannus* to describe such fourth-century usurpers as Procopius and Maximus, with little sign here of the "philosophical" condemnations.

The revival of this "political" definition of tyrant occurred at the same time as a new definition was being formulated by Christian writers in the empire. Shared somewhat by contemporary Jewish writers like Josephus, and heavily influenced by Hellenistic philosophy, this might be called the Judeo-Christian or "religious" definition (see Diag. 1). Beginning at least with Tertullian, ecclesiastical authors often discussed examples of "wicked" rulers in both the Greco-Roman and Judaic traditions.[17] The Vulgate Bible has some twenty explicit references to tyrants (*tyranni*) and tyranny (*tyrannis*), all but one from the Old Testament.[18] The term *tyrannis* always carries with it in these scriptural passages the negative connotations of tyranny, and is associated with words like *insidiarum, terroris,* and *interitum*.[19] The term *tyrannus,* on the other hand, is often used in a neutral sense as a synonym for *princeps* and is found in lists of rulers,[20] perhaps recalling the political variety in the Hellenistic East in the days before Pompey's conquests.

In late antiquity, Christian authors like Jerome and Augustine found *tyrannus* a convenient term with which they could comment upon the failings of secular authorities in an apocalyptic age. In this, as in so many ways, they are indebted to Plato. Most often, these were general discussions of the qualities of good and bad rulers that sprang from scriptural commentary, as in the commentaries of Ambrose and Jerome.[21] Elsewhere, Jerome speaks of Greek and Oriental tyrants and applies the label to such Roman usurpers as Procopius and Maximus.[22] In a British context, Jerome says that Valentinian put down the "tyranny" that was oppressing Britain in the mid–fourth century, and names Britain—"a province fertile of tyrants"—among the uncivilized nations of the world.[23]

Augustine also speaks of "tyrants" and "tyranny" in a very general sense—using such adjectives as wicked, unjust (*iniustus*), and cruel (*crudelis*)—throughout his sermons, commentaries, and theological treatises.[24] In the *City of God,* however, Augustine speaks with more precision about specific tyrants in Roman history. After discussing Scipio's views on lawful government, Augustine writes: "When, however, the monarch is unlawful [*iniustus est rex*]—(Scipio) used the usual Greek term 'tyrant' [*tyrannum*] for such a monarch—or (when) the nobles are unlawful—he

called their mutual agreement a faction—or (when) the people itself is unlawful—for this he found no current term if he were not to call it too a tyrant
[*tyrannum*]—then the state is no longer merely defective, . . . but . . . does
not exist at all."[25] Here is an interesting case in which Augustine, who elsewhere uses *tyrannus* in a general moral sense, is trying to arrive at a political definition by citing a Roman Stoic tradition derived ultimately from
Aristotle's "philosophical" definition of "the unjust tyrant." Augustine is
also capable of recognizing the "political" definition of "tyrant as usurper,"
which he applies to Tarquin, Maximus, and Eugenius.[26] Most frequently,
however, he expresses a Christian worldview that can encompass both definitions: "Through Me kings reign, and through Me tyrants hold the earth."[27]

If Plato was most influential in the formulation of a "philosophical" definition of tyrant, Augustine certainly held this position in the creation of the
"religious" definition. Patrick and Gildas both had some familiarity with the
writings of the bishop of Hippo, as did most of the fifth-century ecclesiastical writers who discussed the British tyrants. Christian authors like Augustine
would have gone through a long process in the formulation of the "religious"
definition of tyrant, a process that recognized and built upon previous definitions. Simplified, it could be illustrated thus: A tyrant is a ruler who usurps
power from a legitimate authority (POLITICAL); unrestrained by traditional
limits to his authority, he becomes "lustful" (PHILOSOPHICAL), which makes
him a wicked ruler in God's eyes (RELIGIOUS). Most Christian writers would
have been guided by this transitional view of tyrants in the fifth and sixth
centuries. After that, when Greco-Roman political entities and philosophy
had all but faded in the medieval West, the "religious" definition would have
evolved to the final stage of the process, where "tyrant" became simply the
measure of "wicked kings."[28]

It remains to test this hypothesis against the written evidence from the
fifth and sixth centuries, with emphasis on British contexts. In the years
between Augustine's arrival in Rome and his departure in the wake of
Alaric's invasion, the City of Man was engulfed in a series of military crises
made worse by the ambitions of usurpers. Britain plays an important role in
this series of events, first with the successful tyrant Magnus Maximus, and
later with the shorter-lived Marcus, Gratian, and Constantine III. The careers
of these British tyrants were chronicled, as I have noted, by contemporaries
such as Eunapius, Olympiodorus, Orosius, Sulpicius Severus, and Renatus
Frigeridus, and by later writers who drew largely from their accounts, such
as Sozomen, Prosper, Zosimus, Procopius, and Gregory of Tours.[29] Of these
writers, Eunapius, Olympiodorus, Renatus, Zosimus, and Procopius are

representatives of the secular tradition, while Orosius, Sulpicius, Sozomen, and Prosper represent the ecclesiastical; Gregory of Tours, perhaps, has one foot in each camp.

We begin to see the divergence of secular and ecclesiastical witnesses over the representation of tyrants at about the time of Magnus Maximus's usurpation in Britain. Maximus's rise to power closely parallels the example of many of the *tyranni* in the *Historia Augusta*. A native of Hispania, Maximus served under Count Theodosius in Britain c. 368 (as well as in Africa in 375 and, possibly, on the Danubian frontier in 376) and later returned to the island to organize defenses along its frontiers.[30] Maximus is credited with a victory over the Picts and Scots in 382, and the next year he was proclaimed emperor by his troops in Britain and took them to the Continent to make good his bid for the *imperium*.[31] Sozomen states that Maximus "gathered a very large army of Britons, neighboring Gauls, Celts and the tribes thereabouts,"[32] and Gildas (mistakenly) makes him a British-born usurper.[33]

Despite his initial military successes, political recognition, and championing of the Church,[34] Maximus is consistently portrayed in the sources— both secular and ecclesiastical—as a *tyrannus*.[35] The secular writers and the chroniclers are mostly nonjudgmental about Maximus, while contemporary ecclesiastical writers are somewhat ambivalent. Sulpicius Severus, describing Maximus's attempts to woo Martin of Tours, calls him *imperator, princeps,* and *rex,* but never *tyrannus*.[36] This is somewhat surprising, considering that elsewhere Severus calls the Caesar (and future Augustus) Julian *tyrannus* when the latter mistook Martin's Christian pacifism for cowardice.[37] Presumably, Julian deserved the label *tyrannus* because he was a wicked pagan, while Maximus—despite his usurpation—was a Catholic who sought the favor of Bishop Martin, and Martin was not wholly unsympathetic to Maximus's interest in the Gallic church. Indeed, Severus has some positive things to say about Maximus (and, elsewhere, of the empress): "The Emperor Maximus then ruled the state, a man whose whole life would have been praiseworthy if he could have refused the crown illegally thrust upon him by a mutinous army and refrained from waging civil war. But a great Empire cannot be refused without risk or retained without fighting."[38] Orosius speaks of Maximus in similar terms, calling him "a man vigorous in action, upright, and worthy of imperial honors had he not risen to prominence by breaking his oath of loyalty and an illegal assumption of power [*tyrannidem*]."[39] And the anonymous author of the *Gallic Chronicle of 452* gives extensive *and* positive treatment to Maximus, which, taken with Severus's treatment, is perhaps evidence of a sympathetic Gallic tradition.[40]

In any case, these ecclesiastical writers recognize the illegality of Maximus's usurpation, his *tyrannis,* but are hesitant (in Severus's case, unwilling) to label him a *tyrannus,* because of his moral character and, perhaps, partisan support.

Later church writers, however, are more harsh than their sources in judging Maximus. As Hagith Sivan comments, the deceased Maximus was a much safer target for writers than the live usurper, especially for those writing in Gaul.[41] Accepting Orosius's statement that Maximus had Gratian murdered, these writers portray Maximus as a pretender who lies about both his religious and political claims. Ausonius, writing just after the usurper's death, calls Maximus "a camp follower posing as a warrior" and "the brigand of Rutipiae [Richborough, in Britain]."[42] Sozomen says that Maximus's championing of the Gallic church "was to clear himself of the imputation of usurpation [τυραννου]."[43] The author of the *Life of St. Ambrose* claims that Ambrose withheld communion from Maximus and warned him that "he must do penance for shedding the blood of one who was his master and . . . an innocent man." Maximus refused, "and he laid down in fear, like a woman, the realm [*regnum*] that he had wickedly usurped [*male arripuerat*], thereby acknowledging that he had been merely the administrator, not the sovereign, of the state [*ut procuratorem se reipublicae, non imperatorem fuisse*]."[44] It is this Christian tradition concerning Maximus, unabashedly judgmental and moralistic, that will have the greatest influence on Gildas.

The year 406 saw the elevation of no less than three imperial usurpers in Britain, though unfortunately these events are not as thoroughly chronicled as those surrounding Maximus. Zosimus believes that the barbarians crossing the frozen Rhine in that year "inspired terror even among the forces in Britain, who were then forced through fear the barbarians might move against them into electing tyrants [τυραννου], namely Marcus, Gratian, and Constantine."[45] (Here, as in his discussion of Maximus, Zosimus is using the "political" definition of "tyrant as usurper.") The army's first choice, a soldier named Marcus, was put to death when he disagreed with their plans.[46] Their second choice was Gratian, whom Orosius calls a "civilian official on the island" (*municeps eiusdem insulae*) and who was also "illegally made emperor."[47] According to Zosimus, the mutinous British troops gave Gratian "a purple robe, a crown and a body-guard, just like an emperor."[48] He too was killed, "after no longer than four months," when he fell out of favor with the army.[49]

His successor took the name Constantine III in an effort to gain confidence in his leadership ability.[50] Constantine, though basically following the same path as Magnus Maximus, emerges from the sources as a less clearly defined figure. Zosimus, drawing upon Olympiodorus, provides the most information about Constantine; both writers give a fairly neutral assessment of his usurpation. Orosius's comments are wholly negative: Constantine was chosen from the lowest ranks of the military, had no personal valor, was frequently tricked by the barbarians, and was a great harm to the state.[51] Renatus Frigeridus adds that Constantine indulged in "daily rounds of over-drinking and over-eating."[52] Constantine is constantly referred to as *tyrannus,* as is his son Constans.[53] Even one Decimus Rusticus is called "prefect of the tyrants," *praefectus tyrannorum.*[54] Though Constantine "had become a tyrant" (*adsumpta tyrannide*), he names one son his Caesar (later co-Augustus) and calls the other *nobilissimus,* appoints *magistri militum* in Gaul, asks to be made consul and joint colleague in the West, and even has himself ordained as *presbyter.*[55] All of these actions are, of course, typical of the Roman usurper's pleas for legitimacy. For the legitimate emperors, however, these *tyranni*—by 411 their number included Constantine, Constans, and Gerontius's dependent Maximus—were simply a nuisance. Orosius writes that "the Emperor Honorius, seeing that no action could be taken against the barbarians with so many *tyranni* rising up against him, ordered that the *tyranni* themselves be disposed of as a first move."[56] They were ruthlessly disposed of, and Honorius soon after ordered that the rule of law be reestablished in the war-torn western provinces.[57]

The judgments of the written sources are, of course, *post factum,* and thus they cast Constantine in the light of his failure to secure both the throne and the Gallic frontier. For the fifth- and sixth-century secular historians, the character of Maximus and Constantine was irrelevant, because their illegal coups made them tyrants; their ecclesiastical counterparts, on the other hand, were influenced by the usurpers' failures—as well as by tyrant stereotypes—and thus cast aspersions on their character. As the fifth century progressed, the voices of the clerics and their "religious" definition of tyrant would drown out the few remaining secular historians with their "political" definition.

After Constantine's unsuccessful usurpation, no subsequent attempts for empire (that we know of) were launched from Britain. However, the term "tyrant" continued to be used to describe men in Britain who seemingly held only insular authority. Jerome, writing shortly after the events of 406–10, describes Britain as "a province fertile of tyrants" (*fertilis provincia tyrannorum*).[58] Procopius, writing in the sixth century but basing this part of his work also on Olympiodorus, believed that tyrants had ruled Britain since

410: "And the island of Britain revolted from the Romans, and the soldiers there chose as their king Constantinus [Constantine III], a man of no mean station . . . and Constantinus, defeated in battle, died with his sons. However, the Romans never succeeded in recovering Britain, but it remained from that time on under tyrants [τυραννου]."[59] Neither of these men had direct information about rulers in Britain after 410, so it is hard to believe that they are commenting specifically on the character of such individuals. Jerome may have had Marcus, Gratian, and Constantine in mind when he made his statement; but he must also have believed that similar men ruled in Britain after 410. Procopius states specifically that he is speaking about post-410, independent Britain.[60]

Who were these *tyranni* who came to power in Britain after Constantine's departure? Which definition (or definitions)—political, philosophical, or religious—was most important to Patrick and Gildas when they described contemporary British rulers as tyrants? When Patrick introduces Coroticus in his *Letter,* he does not give him a specific title. Rather, he says that he is addressing his letter "to the *milites* of Coroticus," who are "allies of Scots and of Picts and of apostates" (*socii Scottorum atque Pictorum apostatarumque*).[61] Later, Patrick says "the enemy shows his resentment through the tyranny of Coroticus [*per tyrannidem Corotici*], who does not fear God or His priests."[62] *Tyrannis* can refer to the rule of a specific *tyrannus* or to any oppressive rule. The question, then, is whether Patrick is using the term *tyrannis* in a technical sense (i.e., calling Coroticus a *tyrannus*) or speaking in a general way about Coroticus's tyranny.[63] Is Patrick following the late Roman secular tradition by using this term, or is he mimicking the moral condemnation of ecclesiastical writers like Augustine and Jerome?

I believe that Patrick is, in a roundabout way, providing specific information about Coroticus's regime. Coroticus is described as a man who gives orders, who has soldiers to do his dirty work, and who has dealings with neighboring peoples such as the Scots and the Picts.[64] He also has people who are (apparently) his subjects, engages in the slave trade "for the sake of a miserable temporal kingdom [*regnum*]," and faces God's judgment over "wicked kings" (*regibus iniquis*).[65] Was, then, Coroticus a king? John Morris, A.B.E. Hood, and Charles Thomas believe so, but their belief is influenced by the Dumbarton Coroticus of the genealogies.[66] E. A. Thompson and Michael Jones are less specific, preferring the terms "irregular ruler" and "British warlord" respectively.[67]

R.P.C. Hanson, however, is quite sure that Patrick used a specific technical term to describe the status of Coroticus: "The 'despotic rule' of Coroticus is a phrase translating a term in Latin which probably echoes the title taken by rulers of the successor kingdoms into which Britain broke up after the end of Roman rule—*tyrannus* (tyrant). In Latin it meant someone who ruled illegally or irregularly, but it may have become almost a technical term by now; it may have even looked and sounded like a British word meaning 'lord of territory,' and if this were so it would assist in the process of making the term in common use."[68] What Hanson suggests is that Patrick used *tyrannis* in the tradition of the secular writers, who used the "political" definition of tyrant when referring to the tyrannies of Maximus and Constantine. As noted, the Latin term *tyrannus* was not always used in a technical way, nor did it always describe an illegal or irregular ruler. Nevertheless, it is possible, as Hanson suggests, that *tyrannus* survived as a political description in sub-Roman Britain. But what kind of ruler would call himself *tyrannus*? Morris has suggested that Coroticus was the grandson of a *praefectus* planted by the Romans among the hostile tribes north of Hadrian's Wall.[69] Again, this is based on unreliable genealogical material, but the installation of such *praefecti* is not without precedent. Coroticus may have been claiming that his authority was based on some remnant of imperial jurisdiction, for Patrick tells him that he is not acting like an heir to the Romans and the Christians.[70] But was he also claiming to be a king? The answer to this question could only come from the discovery of an inscription or written reference that blatantly states what Patrick does not. That Coroticus had the authority of a king, that he was seen as a king by later writers and genealogists, are safer inferences.

Patrick's use of such words as *tyrannis, cives,* and *mei*—as well as his inclusive Christian sermonizing—signal that Coroticus was an "insider" to him. There is no Latin tradition of calling barbarians *tyranni*[71] or reason that Patrick would have been concerned about an outsider's "unjust rule" of his people.[72] Whether or not Coroticus called himself *tyrannus,* what better Latin term could Patrick apply to his political status? Coroticus was a British ruler, and no ruler in Britain after 410 was officially recognized by Rome, so legally (for those who cared) Coroticus was a usurper. Patrick's language regarding Coroticus shows familiarity, and for an "internal" term (as opposed to "external" terms used to describe pagan barbarian rulers), *tyrannis* seemed most appropriate. Coroticus the irregular ruler (at least in Patrick's eyes) was behaving unjustly, and certainly committed a grave sin in killing and enslaving Christians. Patrick need have looked no further than the Bible or Augustine for the precedent of referring to the *tyrannis* of "internal" rulers who behave wickedly. Patrick seems thus to be in the transition phase as far as *tyrannus* is concerned. He is aware of the "political" definition (he had his own father as an example of legitimate secular authority to contrast with Coroticus), but, like contemporary ecclesiastical authors, is more influenced by the "philosophical" disapprobations in arriving at a "religious" definition of Coroticus's tyranny.

There is less ambiguity in Gildas, who describes a Britain that is ruled by both kings *and* tyrants. Have these two entities become, once again, synonymous by the time Gildas was writing, probably in the early sixth century? In his long list of historical events, which he summarizes at the beginning of the *De excidio*, Gildas writes that he will say a little "about tyrants" (*de tyrannis*).[73] It does not take him long to get there: "I shall be silent on the long past years when dreadful tyrants [*immanium tyrannorum*] reigned, tyrants who were spoken of in other distant parts: in fact Porphyry, the 'mad dog' of the east who vents his fury on the church, has this to add to his crazy and meaningless writings: 'Britain is a province fertile of tyrants [*tyrannorum*].' I shall simply try to bring to light the ills she suffered in the time of the Roman emperors."[74] Gildas wrongly attributes this quote of Jerome's to the neo-Platonist Porphyry, and, interestingly, corrects Jerome's *Britanni* to *Britannia* to remain consistent in his own use of the singular. Here, Gildas clearly believes that the word *tyrannus* could describe many of those who ruled in Britain even *before* the Romans arrived (though he regrets that this has given "mad dogs" like Porphyry ammunition to deride Britain). Therefore, Gildas makes it immediately obvious that he is not using the precise technical definition of *tyrannus*—illegal *Roman* ruler—employed by Ammianus and Olympiodorus.

The first named tyrant whom we encounter in the *De excidio* is, surprisingly, the emperor Diocletian. Gildas describes "the persecution of the tyrant Diocletian" (*persecutionem Diocletiani tyranni*) as a background to his discussion of the British martyrs.[75] Again, Diocletian was not a usurper, so it is his wicked behavior that has made him a tyrant in Gildas's eyes.[76] Gildas then casts Magnus Maximus, whom he makes a homegrown tyrant, in a similarly sinister light: "At length the tyrant thickets [*tyrannorum virgultis*] increased and were all but bursting into a savage forest. The island . . . cast forth a sprig of its own bitter planting, and sent Maximus to Gaul with a great retinue of hangers-on and even the imperial insignia, which he was never fit to bear: he had no legal claim to the title, but was raised to it like a tyrant [*ritu tyrannico*] by rebellious soldiery."[77] According to Gildas, Maximus, once raised to the title, establishes "his wicked empire" at Trier and rages madly against his masters (the two legitimate emperors), "driving one emperor from

Rome, the other from his life—which was a holy one."[78]

Gildas bases much of his portrayal of Maximus on his sources, probably Prosper and Orosius.[79] It is thus unsurprising that his definition of "tyrant" up to this point is primarily a religious one. It is curious, however, that he has nothing to say about Marcus, Gratian, Constantine, and Constans, who feature in Orosius but whose memory had perhaps faded from Britain by the sixth century.[80] Gildas is content to blame the ruin of Britain on Maximus, stating that the army "followed in the tyrant's footsteps [*vestigiis . . . tyranni*], never to return home."[81] Also enigmatic is Gildas's use of Sulpicius Severus's *Life of St. Martin*. As Wright has shown, Gildas's phrase *"ut duos imperatores legitimos, unum Roma, alium religiosissima vita pelleret"* is an obvious parallel to Severus's *"qui imperatores, unum regno, alterum vita expulisset,"* and both are describing Maximus.[82] However, the venom that Gildas heaps upon Maximus is not in Severus's account.[83] Severus calls Maximus *imperator,* but to Gildas he is a *tyrannus* who is not "fit to bear" "the imperial insignia." The only explanation for this divergence is that, in the century that separates these two ecclesiastical authors, the usage of the term *tyrannus* was changing even among Christian writers. The vigorous general whom Severus saw as an aspiring emperor fallen from grace is, for Gildas, simply a wicked ruler like many who had emerged from his native land. Maximus is wicked, a *tyrannus,* because of his bloodthirsty actions— dispatching two *imperatores*—just as Diocletian is a *tyrannus* because he killed Christians.

Maximus is the first but not the worst of Gildas's British tyrants. "Then all the members of the council," he writes, "together with the proud tyrant [*superbo tyranno*]," devised a means to guard the country against the barbarians.[84] "On the orders of the ill-fated tyrant [*infausto tyranno*]," the Saxons came to fight for Britain.[85] Who is this *tyrannus, superbus* but *infaustus?* In two manuscripts of the *De excidio* he is given a name: Vortigern.[86] This is also the name Bede equates with the *superbus tyrannus,* as do "Nennius" and the *Anglo-Saxon Chronicle.*[87] Vortigern is remembered by the English as part of their settlement myth, and by the Welsh as the progenitor of two Powysian dynasties.[88] For Gildas, "Nennius," and Geoffrey of Monmouth, however, Vortigern is the wicked and foolish king who brought the plague of Saxons into Britain, ensuring his place in infamy.

Gildas says that the *superbus tyrannus* and the *consiliarii* acted together to hire the Saxons.[89] There are several varying inferences historians have made about this political arrangement:

1. The *superbus tyrannus* was the high king of Britain and presided over a council of subkings.
2. The *superbus tyrannus* was simply "the most powerful or wealthy" (most haughty?) of the *tyranni* in Britain, and called together a council of kings and/or *civitas* leaders.
3. The *superbus tyrannus* controlled only one kingdom or region in Britain and called a meeting of his own advisors.

Since Gildas nowhere calls this *tyrannus* "king," his work provides little support for the first explanation, though it is not outside the realm of possibility.[90] If it is true that, when Gildas speaks of his *patria,* he is speaking of all of Britain, then the third explanation is even more unlikely. Gildas does not mention any geographic region in connection with the *tyrannus,* though he does say that the *tyrannus* ordered the Saxons to settle "on the east side of the island,"[91] implying that at the very least the *tyrannus* held authority over an area spanning several kingdoms or *civitates.*[92] Furthermore, Gildas states that the Britons "convened a council" (*Initur . . . consilium*) that, "together with" (*una cum*) the *tyrannus,* "devised a guard [*praesidium*]" for the *patria;* the language does not suggest that these were mere advisors or ministers of a local chieftain.[93]

The second explanation, therefore, is the most appealing. Gildas uses similar language to describe both the *superbus tyrannus* and Magnus Maximus, and the military activities of the *superbus tyrannus*—hiring Saxons to protect the British coasts—cast him in the same tradition as Maximus and Constantine, who likewise used barbarian support to protect the western provinces against other barbarians. However, Gildas is not concerned with the political status of Maximus, but rather with the moral ramifications of his usurpation; this is likely the case with the *superbus tyrannus* as well. The words *superbus* and *infaustus* are moral qualifiers that a Christian writer might find convenient to use in judging a secular ruler.[94] Augustine, in the *City of God,* similarly labels Tarquinius Superbus *tyrannus.*[95] For Gildas, then, this individual was the most prominent of the British rulers because of his behavior. He was, then, an "arrogant (or haughty) usurper" (perhaps a better translation than "proud tyrant") who grabbed the reins of the military and government in the absence of a more powerful candidate. Whether or not this *tyrannus* personally claimed authority on the basis of civic status, ancestry,[96] or even military position,[97] Gildas had the hindsight of his proven folly to aid in casting aspersions on his legitimacy.

As Alcock puts it, the question we should be asking is, how did such

tyranni emerge out of the framework of the Roman civil administration that
(seemingly) collapsed in 410?[98] This is a difficult question to answer, because
no clear or logical pattern presents itself in the written sources. Gildas says
that soon after the Romans left Britain, kings were anointed (*ungebantur*),
ruled cruelly (*crudeliores*), and were killed by those who had anointed (*unctoribus*) them.[99] This failure led to the convening of the council and the
actions of the *superbus tyrannus*. When this political arrangement also
proved detrimental to Britain, the *cives* turned for leadership to "Ambrosius
Aurelianus, a gentleman and perhaps the last of the Romans."[100] The results
this time were victory and peace, during which Britain still had *reges*, *publici*, and *privati*.[101]

    That generation passed away, and Gildas describes the following age—
his own—with a succinct phrase: "Reges habet Britannia, sed tyrannos."[102]
He then denounces five contemporary rulers, two of whom (Constantine and
Vortipor) he calls *tyrannus*, one (Maglocunus) he accuses of "rule by force"
(*violenti regni*).[103] He also writes that the clergy are suffering under the
"shock of the tyrants" (*in concussione tyrannorum*).[104] It is clear in this section of the *De excidio* that the *tyranni* are also kings, and that Gildas is using
the terms (along with *princeps*) as synonyms. Does this mean that *tyrannus*
equals *rex* throughout Gildas's narrative? There is no clear distinction in the
De excidio, though this does not mean that Gildas always intended the two
terms to be equated.[105] Nicholas Higham believes that Gildas was trying to
show that the role of kingship was evolving slowly in post-Roman Britain,
"with the 'anointers'—probably the war-bands—making and unmaking
kings almost at will."[106] Given that *tyranni* like Maximus are often regarded
as kings by later British sources, it is likely that the *tyranni* of the fifth century—however they regarded themselves—were considered to be kings by
those unfamiliar with (or uninterested in) the "political" definition of *tyrannus*.[107] Gildas surely falls into this category, for he shows no familiarity with
the "political" definition of the term used only sparingly in the late empire
by secular historians like Ammianus. Pre-Roman British kings, legitimate
Roman emperors, Roman usurpers, sub-Roman rulers—even priests[108]—are
all *tyranni* to Gildas if they behave wickedly or are detrimental to the
patria.[109]

    Because the term *tyrannus* appeared most frequently in the works of eccle-
siasts like Orosius, Patrick, and Gildas, "tyrant" quickly became an entirely
pejorative moral label. Where the *tyranni* appear in later insular Latin
sources, according to Wendy Davies, they "are always presented as wicked,"
as they are in Gildas.[110] The inscriptional evidence in Britain suggests that

the rulers were not styling themselves or their forebears as *tyranni*.[111] This is not surprising, considering that the label *tyrannus* has historically said more about the views and background of the writer than the actual claims and perceptions of the ruler to whom it is being applied. The condemnatory overtones that had become attached to this Latin term by ecclesiastical writers from Augustine on would not have made *tyrannus* an attractive title for a Christian ruler to proclaim on his monument. Besides, "tyrant" was never any man's formal title. Or was it?

There is plenty of ancient Greek evidence that τυραννος was used, in some circumstances, both formally and with no negative connotations. I mentioned earlier that some Greek dramatists, notably Aeschylus and Sophocles, employ τυραννος interchangeably with βασιλευς in situations where nothing derogatory is implied. Antony Andrewes has pointed out that in certain Greek religious cults, τυραννος is even used as the epithet of a god.[112] Archedice, daughter of the Athenian tyrant Hippias, boasted on her epitaph that she was the daughter, wife, sister, and mother of tyrants.[113] Andrewes believes that the original Greek (and probably Lydian) use of τυραννος was as a simple equivalent for king, and within certain monarchs' courts the term might have retained its original innocence even after Plato's defamations.[114] Both Pindar and Isocrates wrote praise poems for Greek tyrants in which they used τυραννος as a synonym for king and in which they actually praised tyranny; in writings for other audiences, however, both writers condemned tyranny as an inferior political institution. As Andrewes points out, calling these rulers τυραννου to their faces would not have been taken as an insult, but rather as a recognition of their power and prestige: "[T]he tyrant did not try to conceal the fact of his power, knowing that the ordinary man would at least half admire him for it."[115]

Sub-Roman Britain is admittedly far removed from the Greek Age of Tyrants. Was there, however, a vernacular tradition concerning tyrants in Britain that was older than the imported Greco-Roman definitions, a Celtic term that, like its Indo-European cousin, originally had no negative connotations? Some historians have hinted at this. Hanson believed that *tyrannus* "may have even looked and sounded like a British word meaning 'lord of territory.'"[116] Dark has suggested that it was the sub-Roman vernacular term for "king."[117] More compelling is the fact that Gildas seems to have recognized a vernacular equivalent to *tyrannus,* and that written charters from early medieval Brittany explicitly link the two. Like the term *civis, tyrannus* may have survived in fifth-century Britain because it had a cognate in the British language: *tigernos.*

Gildas, as I have noted, believed that *tyranni* reigned in Britain before the Romans came.[118] How can this be, if the Romans brought their Greek-derived concept(s) of tyrant with them when they conquered and Romanized the island? Celticists have long recognized the element *tigernos*, "lord," commonly found in aristocratic names in Britain and Gaul. It is readily apparent, as Kenneth Jackson has shown, in such early medieval examples as *Cuno-tigernos* (Saint Kentigern), Cattegirn, Bivatigirnus, Tigernmaglus, Ritigern, and, of course, Vortigern.[119] The name Vortigern (Brittonic *Wertigernos* or *Wortigernos,* Old Welsh *Gwrytheyrn*) is a compound of the Brittonic elements *wor,* "on," "over," and *tigernos,* thus giving the meaning "overlord." Historians still debate whether this is a name and/or a title.[120] What we can be more certain about, however, is that Gildas recognized the vernacular element *tigernos* within this tyrant's name, and that he knew precisely what it stood for. As Jackson has demonstrated, Gildas's rhetorical skills allowed him to turn the name Vortigern, "Overlord," into the near equivalent (but derogatory) Latin phrase *superbus tyrannus,* "arrogant usurper," "playing on the literal meaning of the name," as Jackson puts it, "with a sneer."[121] That is, Gildas was making a vicious pun at Vortigern's expense, just as he did with the *tyranni* of his day.[122]

Gildas was not just commenting on an isolated case.[123] The element *tiger-nos* is Common Celtic, and spawned the Welsh term *teyrn* (or *theyrn*), the Irish *thigern,* and the Breton *tiern,* all of which translate in a general sense as "lord." These terms could, of course, be used more specifically in the proper context, or modified to give a more specific meaning as in *Wortigernos.* *Teyrn* (pl. *tëyrnedd*), for example, is the most common term for a "king" in the Taliesin poems,[124] but is used in the more general sense of "prince" in the *Gododdin* and the *Armes Prydein.*[125] Examples of compounds include the Old Irish *macthigern,* which again meant something like "overlord"; Welsh *mechdeyrn* and Cornish *myghtern,* both connected with viceregal authority; and the common Breton term *machtiern,* which designated a local lord over other local lords.[126]

Surprisingly, it is this last term, the *machtiern* of Brittany, that holds the key to our understanding of tyrants in sub-Roman Britain. Semantically, a machtiern—*mach-* (fine, great), *tiern* (lord)—was a "powerful lord," the *primus inter pares.*[127] Its frequent appearance in medieval Breton charters has allowed historians a rare glimpse into the social and political arrangements of Lesser Britain.[128] J.G.T. Sheringham has done a study of the origins of the machtierns that illustrates a plausible link between Roman provincial administrators, sub-Roman *tyranni,* and their Breton descendants.[129] Sheringham explains that the persistent medieval notion, throughout the "Celtic fringe," of *tigern/tiern* as "local lord" can be traced back to the very basic Celtic element *tigos,* "house"; thus these various kinds of *tierns* are each, in essence, a "master of the house," a *seigneur.*[130] This explains why Breton machtierns are associated with courts (*aulae*), sureties, and local disputes (*lites*) in the charters, just as the Welsh *teyrn* is usually associated with his hall (*llys*) in the vernacular poetry. What if, Sheringham then asks, Roman local administration in the Celtic-speaking provinces was conducted, not in Latin, but in the vernacular? What would the provincials of Britain and Armorica have called these local lords, these decurions, or *curiales,* who had their own *aulae* and settled *lites,* if not by the familiar term *tiern?*[131] If this had been so, there would have been no negative connotations for the Britons and Armoricans who used this term with reference to their local magistrates. Salvian, who certainly disapproved of the activities of "tyrants" in fifth-century Gaul, nevertheless seems to confirm this link: "What towns, as well as what municipalities and villages are there in which there are not as many *tyranni* as *curiales.* Perhaps they glory in this name of *tyrannus* because it seems to be considered powerful and honored."[132] Clearly Salvian has in mind the "religious" definition of "tyrant," with its negative connotations, in the first sentence. Still, he is puzzled in the second sentence because these decurions actually *like* being called tyrants, for the term seems to carry with it notions of power and prestige. Someone must be bestowing these upon the local aristocrats, and it makes the most sense that this would be done by their clients and retainers.[133]

There remains one more piece of strong evidence linking decurions, *tyranni,* and machtierns. Sheringham points out that much of the Breton cartulary material preserves *"vocabulaire administratif brittonique"* of the sub-Roman period,[134] and the machtierns themselves may date back to the British settlement of Armorica.[135] But it is one particular collection of charters, from the abbey of Saint-Sauveur de Redon and dating from the ninth to eleventh centuries, that makes the connection so explicitly. Throughout the Redon cartulary the machtiern appears occasionally under a Latinized guise as *tiarnus* or *tirannus.*[136] One charter, dated to the period between 814 and 825, seems to be echoing Gildas's word play when it describes one "Iarnhitin [of Ruffiac]" as both *machtiern* and *tyrannus.*[137] Here we have a medieval monastic author recognizing both the local "political" definition of tyrant (*machtiern*)—an honorable state—and the long-standing "religious" definition (itself derived from the "philosophical") with its derogatory implications (*tyrannus*). We can even carry this one step further, linking the machtierns of Brittany with the kings who ruled over their Brittonic kin in Cornwall and Wales. Like these kings, who were often termed *teyrn*, the machtierns' status was hereditary, they possessed considerable landed wealth, and they too were sometimes termed *princeps*.[138] While the Carolingians may have forbade the Bretons to have kings, clearly many of the "tierns" who stayed in Britain were associated with "kingdoms" and were called *reges* in Latin writings and inscriptions.[139]

We have come full circle, and it seems that there were two "political" definitions of tyrant, one from the Mediterranean world and the other from the Celtic-speaking lands, both of which could have been used—in the proper context—without moral opprobrium (see Diag. 1). Indeed, we know that some Britons of the sub-Roman period bore the term as a personal name (though perhaps some were simply remembered by their titles instead of their birth names),[140] while their counterparts in Gaul held the title of tyrant in great esteem and passed it down from generation to generation.[141] When clerics like Patrick, Salvian, and Gildas disapproved of the actions of these rulers, they used the Latin term *tyrannus* because it had long been associated with condemnation. Either way, Jerome was right: Britain was truly a land fertile with tyrants in the fifth and sixth centuries.

10

◆

MISCELLANEOUS TERMS

The preceding terms merited individual discussion because they feature prominently and frequently in several of the written sources for sub-Roman Britain. In these cases, I have traced the development of definition and application through late imperial, Christian, and early medieval usage. Many other terms, however, appear in only one or two sources, or indeed occur only once. Though often these cannot be studied in terms of change and development, they can nonetheless be considered together to reflect more upon the social and political arrangements of the Britons.

I have divided these miscellaneous terms into two categories: secular and ecclesiastical. Within these categories, I have grouped related terms to discuss such topics as the military, the professions, and monasticism. It will be obvious that I have concentrated on the top of the social scale. The historical sources were written by and for elites, and therefore the terminology is more precise and accessible for this segment of the population. It will also be apparent that the sources (especially the inscriptions) provide numerous personal names, of the famous and of the obscure, yet I devote little discussion here to particular personalities. Someday this material will be organized into a prosopography for early medieval Britain. The following study, however, is only a brief excursion into uncharted territory, an attempt to broaden our picture of British society in the fifth and sixth centuries by looking beyond kings and tyrants.

Secular

Focusing on *reges* and *tyranni* is admittedly only seeing the tip of the social pyramid. Fortunately, the written and epigraphic sources provide information about other types of secular status, both political and professional. Such information about soldiers, judges, and bards in sub-Roman Britain has never been fully explored, yet it is accessible and can be easily checked against what we know of these terms from late Roman usage outside of Britain.

This was in large part a military society. The difficulty is in gauging the long transition from a frontier society of Roman legions and comitatensian troops to a "heroic age" of disparate warbands and mounted warriors. The *Notitia Dignitatum* provides detailed information about the state of the Roman army in Britain at the opening of the fifth century. It lists the following commands: the *comes litoris Saxonici per Britannias* (commander of the troops stationed in forts along the southeast coast) and his staff; the *comes Britanniarum* (commander of the comitatensian troops) and his staff; and the *dux Britanniarum* (commander of the troops stationed in forts along and near Hadrian's Wall) and his staff. Ammianus mentions a *comes maritimi tracti* and a frontier *dux* (probably the *comes litoris Saxonici* and *dux Britanniarum,* respectively), and describes the *arcani* or *areani* who acted as spies among the tribes north of the Wall.[1] The only other clues about the last Roman forces in Britain come from archaeology.[2]

But there are problems with both the literary and archaeological sources. The accuracy of the information in the *Notitia* as it pertains to Britain cannot be extended far beyond 410. Archaeologists have also had difficulty identifying comitatensian burials and determining whether certain grave goods can be used to gauge the extent of Germanic recruitment. The last reorganization of Roman defenses in Britain is likely the work of Stilicho, c. 400. Our source is Claudian, who says rather vaguely that Stilicho withdrew from Britain a *legio,* "protector of the furthest Britons."[3] We do not know precisely what Claudian meant by *legio,* or whether the *legio* was ever replaced by Stilicho. Similarly, the withdrawal of troops by Constantine III in 407 is imprecisely recorded. Olympiodorus, Orosius, and Zosimus state merely that Constantine left Britain with his forces, and appointed his highest generals to commands in Gaul and Spain.[4] Though no mention is made of leaving military officers in command in Britain, Zosimus says that the beleaguered Britons expelled "the Roman magistrates" (ρωμαιων αρχουτας) in 409.[5] These men were probably Constantine's civilian officials; it is unlikely that the army (what was left of it) was expelled.

When Germanus visited Britain in 429, it appears that the British troops (*exercitus*) were in such a disarray that they needed a Gallic bishop to organize them against marauding Picts and Saxons.[6] Constantius describes Bishop Germanus, in this military role, as *dux proelii,* "leader for this battle."[7] Thompson, however, has rendered a credible reading of Constantius's text that shows the British army to have efficient reconnaissance scouts, both light and heavily armed troops, and some tactical expertise.[8] Still, the "Alleluia Victory" was probably only a regional skirmish, and tells us little about the overall defense of Britain.[9] Patrick provides a little more information about the fifth century, but it too is of a regional nature. His *Letter* is sent to the *milites* of Coroticus, whom he describes as "bloodthirsty men," "ravening wolves," "brigands" (*latrunculis*), "wretches," "villains," and so forth.[10] From Patrick's language, the *milites* appear to be nothing more than pirates.[11] We cannot tell how Coroticus organized his soldiers, and they appear more concerned with making a profit from the slave trade than with defending their portion of the island. However, the very fact that Patrick calls Coroticus's men *milites* (and that they considered themselves *cives*) may mean that they were once truly soldiers in a Roman or sub-Roman military defense of the north.[12]

Gildas claims that, after Maximus's escapades, "Britain was despoiled of her whole army [*omni armato milite*], her military resources [*militaribus copiis*], her governors [*rectoribus*], . . . and her sturdy youth, who had followed in the tyrant's footsteps."[13] The Romans informed the Britons "that they could not go on being bothered with . . . wandering thieves [*latrunculos*]," that the Britons should "get used to arms" and man their walls, and left them "manuals on weapons training" (*exemplaria instituendorum armorum*), but "the force [*acies*] stationed on the high towers" was too lazy to fight and fell to invaders from the North.[14] (If these *exemplaria* were formal manuals, this implies a Latin-reading officer corps in sub-Roman Britain.) Then came the decision to hire the Saxons, who asked for *annonae* and "falsely represented themselves as *milites*."[15] Supplies were given to them, but soon they "complained that their *epimenia* was insufficient," and threatened to "break the *foedus* and plunder the whole island unless more *munificentia* were heaped upon them."[16] These terms—*annona, epimenia, munificentia*—are all very traditional rewards for federates of Rome, even the monthly withdrawal of rations.[17] The technical language seems to be a strong indicator that Roman fiscal machinery was still operating—at least in the immediate post-Roman years described here by Gildas—in conjunction with some sort of military pay-and-requisition system.[18]

The Saxons kept their promise and put the Britons to flight, some holding out in "the high hills, steep menacing and fortified [*vallatis*], the densest forests, and the cliffs of the sea coasts."[19] The "wretched survivors [*reliquiae*]" were led by Ambrosius, "under whom our people regained their strength"; "victory went now to the *cives,* now to the *hostes* . . . [until] the *obsessio* of Badon Hill, pretty well the last but not the least defeat of the *furciferi*."[20] As for the soldiers in Gildas's time, they were "military companions, bloody, proud and murderous men" (*sanguinarios superbos parricidas commanipulares*)—a noted change in terminology from earlier military operations.[21] Their kings use "swords and spears" (*ensibus hastis*), ride in "chariots" (*currus*), have "personal arms" (*armis specialibus*), consider themselves "generals" (*Brittanniae ducibus*), and kill their "bravest soldiers" (*fortissimis . . . militibus*).[22]

Gildas's portrayal of the military situation in Britain is a complicated one. At first the Britons do not know how to fight, and have to be instructed by the Romans. Then the *consilium* and the *superbus tyrannus* decide to follow standard imperial practice and hire Saxon *foederati* to fight for them. When this fails, they turn to "the last of the Romans," Ambrosius, and finally gain the upper hand against the invaders. In the peace that follows Badon, however, tyrants and their personal warbands wage civil war, and no attention is given to national defense. In fact, to judge solely by Gildas's perception of his own time, the Saxons no longer appear to be a threat to the Britons.[23]

We know that by the close of the sixth century the Saxons were indeed a serious threat to the Britons. The Llandaff Charters mention lands won by Welsh kings who had defeated Saxon armies.[24] The vernacular poetry of Wales and northern Britain, some of which was composed c. 600 but not written down till much later, depicts a society dominated by "heroic"-style warfare. Kings transformed the Roman patron-client relationship by turning clients into warbands and bestowing lavish gifts upon them; this is apparent already in Gildas's time,[25] and is integral to the society described in the poems of Taliesin and Aneirin.[26] "The ruler was himself a fighter," reminds Davies, "not merely a launcher of armies or patron of champions. We should not lose sight of this for it has a significant bearing on our understanding of lifestyle and of administrative machinery too."[27]

Civil administration is less easy to discern in a society dominated by military crises. The *Notitia Dignitatum* illustrates the growing separation of civil and military authority in the fourth-century imperial infrastructure.[28] However, we do not know if the civilian officials the *Notitia* assigns to Britain—the three *praesides,* two *consulares,* and one *vicarius*—survived the tumult of 406–10. The usurper Gratian is described by Orosius as "a *municeps* on the island."[29] A *municeps* usually describes either a citizen of a *municipium* or (more specifically) an officer (*magistratus, decurio, curialis*) of a *municipium,* though it can sometimes refer to an inhabitant of a less specific *regio.*[30] Orosius does not associate Gratian with a specific city, but rather with the *insula* of the *Britanniae.* This could betray Orosius's ignorance of British geography, or it could mean that he knew Gratian held a civil office of more than local import, but did not know the specific title. Considering that Gratian had the support of (at least) a large portion of the army stationed in Britain, I believe that he must have held a major diocesan office, perhaps as *vicarius* or else as a *praeses* or *consularis* residing in a *municipium.*

Zosimus claims that, in 409, the Britons expelled the Roman magistrates and established "their own government [πολιτευμα]."[31] Our first glimpse of this new government comes perhaps from Germanus's visits to Britain in 429 and c. 445. On his first visit he debates the Pelagians, who are described by Constantius as "men of obvious wealth, resplendent in their attire," perhaps implying that the heretics were members of the secular aristocracy rather than the clergy.[32] After the debate, Germanus is approached by a *vir tribuniciae potestatis.*[33] This apparently specific piece of information is ambiguous compared to Constantius's precision in Gallic matters: was this man a military tribune? an administrative one? or both? Ian Wood points out that Constantius's friend and contemporary Sidonius identifies several men in Gaul as *vir tribunicius.*[34] Since Constantius uses the phrase *vir tribuniciae potestatis,* presumably he is trying to describe for his Gallic audience a man in Britain who exercised the "power" that a tribune would in Gaul. Thompson believes that Constantius is trying to be precise here, but that he can only give an equivalent to describe this man's local importance.[35] Unfortunately, Constantius provides no other information about this man that would allow us to categorize his authority as either civil or military. (The word TRIBVNI appears on an Early Christian inscribed stone from southwest Britain, but it is uncertain whether this *Tribunus* is a name or a title.[36])

It should be pointed out that this man did not take part in the public debate, only that he was present and wished Germanus to heal his daughter. A similar incident occurs during Germanus's second visit, when a man named Elafius asks the bishops to cure his withered son. This Elafius is described as *regionis illius primus,* and was supported by the *provincia tota.*[37] The phrase *regionis illius primus* is even less precise than *vir tribuniciae potestatis,* perhaps revealing Constantius's lack of information about the second visit. (It does, however, compare with the "chief man of the town" who meets the ship's captain arriving in late sixth-century Britain, recorded in *The Life of St. John the Almsgiver.*[38]) Again, the most we can assume is that Elafius was the richest or most powerful figure in that *regio* (or *provincia,* if Constantius is trying to be precise), and that Constantius did not know his title or office.[39]

Patrick is a more valuable witness to the Britain he grew up in than to the Britain he exiled himself from later in life. In describing his childhood he gives precise information about his family's social and religious status. He writes in his autobiography that his father, Calpornius, belonged to the town of Bannavem Taburniae and owned a *villulam* nearby.[40] In the *Letter to Coroticus* he adds, "I was free-born according to the flesh; my father was a decurion [*decorione*]."[41] Calpornius later implored him to stay at home and undertake *munera,* "public office."[42] The decurion status of Patrick's father has triggered much discussion.[43] Like *municeps, decurio* was a term that had both technical and general usage in late antiquity. Used technically, it could refer to an officer in the army, in local government, in a guild, or at court, while generally it was sometimes applied to wealthy members of a town.[44] In Britain, both military and civilian *decuriones* left frequent testimonies on inscribed stones from the Roman period.[45] Ammianus mentions both a *palatii decurio* and local *decuriones.*[46] The latter decurions (also called *curiales*) were, in the late imperial administrative system, officials in a town council (*ordo*) who were responsible for the maintenance of civic amenities, which they paid for with collected taxes or with their own money if the locals were not forthcoming. This became a great burden for the local aristocracy, who sought to avoid it sometimes by being ordained deacon or presbyter in the church, holy orders that were exempt from these curule duties. Since Patrick's father was also a deacon, many have concluded that Calpornius was obviously shirking his duties.[47] The decurions could, as well, become oppressive in their tax collecting. Thus, Salvian could write of Marseilles in the 440s that "there are as many tyrants as there are decurions," and that Romans were actually fleeing *to* the barbarians in order to avoid these corrupt tax gatherers.[48]

We need not speculate whether Calpornius was a good deacon or a corrupt decurion. More important is the fact that he held both positions—deacon and decurion—after the expulsion of the Roman magistrates from Britain in 409. "No longer submitting to Roman law," as Zosimus phrases it,[49] the British *possessores* were freed from the prohibition against holding both offices. Why, then, would Calpornius want to be a decurion? Probably for the lingering prestige the title must have held, possibly because he wanted to retain the traditional authority to collect taxes. Though there was no longer the need to forward revenues to imperial authorities, we need not go so far as Thompson in believing that Calpornius simply pocketed all the money.[50] More likely he used the funds to maintain the crumbling cities, or to hire soldiers to protect his interests (as Gildas's terminology—*annonae, foedus,* and the like—suggests others were doing in the fifth century).[51]

Gildas does not mention decurions in Britain, nor is he as precise in describing other civilian officials. However, his language does indicate that there was some variety in the government of the fifth and sixth centuries. "Britain has her governors [*rectores*], she has her investigators [*speculatores*]. . . . If not more than she needs, at least not fewer."[52] In Winterbottom's translation, *rector* is not just a general term for ruler, but a specific late Roman technical term for governor.[53] Ammianus uses *rector* in this technical sense, but he also frequently uses the term in a more general way.[54] A good illustration of this dual usage is the inscription on a column from Roman Cirencester, erected by a man who identifies himself as both the *praeses* of Britannia Prima and the *primae provinciae rector,* which clearly mean the same thing.[55] Christian writers also employ *rector* in a general sense to mean "ruler," and indeed God is sometimes addressed as such.[56] Gildas uses *rectores* twice when referring to the Roman period: the rebellious Britons "butchered the [*rectores*] . . . of Roman rule," and after Maximus "Britain was despoiled . . . of her [*rectores*]."[57] These references should be taken in the general sense, fitting Gildas's rhetorical purpose. Clearly he does not know the precise terms of Roman administration—*vicarius, praeses*—or, if he does, he has chosen a more general term. Gildas simply means to say that Britain has many "rulers," indeed, more than he deems necessary. If this is not a statement of precision, nor is it an admission of insular anarchy. Gildas's complaint is that Britain has competent rulers in place, but they are too burdened to speak out against corruption. Likewise the *speculatores,* and here again Gildas has chosen a term that has both technical and general associations. Ammianus employs *speculator* solely in a military context to mean "scout."[58] That Roman Britain had such military *speculatores* is attested in the epigraphic evidence.[59] The ecclesiastical writers, however, use *speculator* in a general sense to mean "watchman" or "guardian" (or even "one who speculates"), in contexts describing both God and the office of bishop.[60] Again, Gildas is more likely to fall into the latter camp.[61] He has chosen two terms—*rectores* and *speculatores*—that could have technical meanings, but he has chosen them not for precision but for reasons of rhyme and meter, to strengthen the rhetoric of his argument. A formal education in rhetoric and law would have provided Gildas with both the terms and the means with which to adapt them to his Christian purpose.

Even more intriguing is the appearance in the *De excidio* of the term *consilium,* "council." Gildas uses the form *consilium* twice (2.1 and 22.3) and *consiliarii,* "members of the council," once (23.1). He says that "they"— presumably the surviving Britons whom he has just described—convened a council to decide the best way to counter the raids of the Scots and the Picts. The members of the council, together with the *superbus tyrannus,* devised a plan to hire Saxon federates. As stated before, Gildas describes the convening of the council twice before he even mentions the *tyrannus,* so it is unlikely that the *tyrannus* is calling a meeting of his advisors.[62] Rather, the *consilium* seems to be a cooperative effort that functions together with—and with the same authority as—the *superbus tyrannus.*

Who attended this council is a matter of conjecture. The term *consilium* had, by late antiquity, taken on a myriad of meanings.[63] In the Latin West, a *concilium* was an assembly of aristocratic representatives within a province (*concilium provinciae*); there were also diocesan assemblies, though we only have information concerning one Gallic example.[64] In Ammianus, *consilium* usually means a military council or, less specifically, a "plan."[65] Sidonius refers frequently to the *concilium* of the praetorian prefect of Gaul, and to his friends who ranked among its members (*consiliarii*).[66] In the ecclesiastical tradition, *consilium* is used in a general way to refer to "counsel," while the form *concilia* was usually employed to describe church councils. The problem is that Gildas does not use the form *concilium,* but rather uses *consilium* in both the general sense, "counsel" or "advice,"[67] and in the formal sense, "a council was convened."[68] If *decuriones* like Patrick's father could survive the purge of 409, it is not impossible that they and other provincial representatives were the *consiliarii* whom Gildas describes.[69] More likely, it was a diverse gathering of men—*tyranni*, kings, forgotten Roman officials, and large-estate owners—who still had an interest in keeping property and commerce safe from roaming brigands. Gildas's *consilium* must be seen as an amazing cooperative effort for the times, regardless of its unfortunate decision.

Lapidge has commented that one of the chief concerns of Gildas's work is with law and the judicial process.[70] But here too his choice of words is problematic. "Britain has kings [*reges*], but they are tyrants [*tyrannos*]; she has judges [*iudices*], but they are wicked [*impios*]."[71] Later in this same sentence, Gildas says that these men "take their seats as judges [*arbitraturi*], but rarely seek out the rules of right judgement [*iudicii*]." It is tempting to see these as references either to still-functioning Roman courts or to the professional judges and jurors that are prevalent in early medieval Ireland and Wales. In the Roman secular tradition, a *iudex* was an individual appointed ad hoc to judge a criminal or civil proceeding, for which he would receive financial compensation.[72] Since *iudices* could also be provincial governors, military commanders, minor magistrates, or even (after Constantine I) bishops, the term came to have a wide range of meaning in the late empire.[73] Ammianus shows this diversity, using *iudex* to describe, for example, a *magister equitum*, a Prefect of the City (Rome), and the Alamannic king Ursicinus.[74] Schaffner has shown that this range of meanings for *iudex* found in the secular sources (Aurelius Victor and the *Codex Iustinianus* in addition to Ammianus) is found in biblical Latin as well.[75] Thus, *rex, tyrannus,* and *iudex* are Gildas's "rhetorical variations" (to use Schaffner's phrase) for "ruler," and the kings and judges of the Old Testament are his models. However, while Gildas is apparently not describing separate "offices," he is without a doubt describing distinct "functions" of these rulers, an important one being judiciary. Gildas emphasizes this by his use of the term *arbitraturi* to describe further the activities of the *reges/tyranni,* and by his frequent use elsewhere of biblical condemnations of bad judges: "[Y]ou did not judge [*iudicastis*] aright, or keep the law of justice [*legem iustitiae*]."[76]

The Llandaff Charters also show some diversity in government. The witness lists of several charters name men described as *meliores* (better men), *principes,* and *legiti viri* (lawful men), all terms that seem to signify "elders."[77] Davies sees these elders as groups of leading men who had the power to witness and legitimize the transfer of property, a power separate from but not impinging upon the power of the Welsh kings.[78] There is also evidence in the charters of a landowning aristocracy (*sodales*) and tenants (*heredes* and *hereditarii*).[79]

The most peculiar official title comes from the epigraphic evidence. A pillar stone found in the churchyard of Castell Dwyran in Carmarthenshire (southwest Wales), dated c. 540–50, contains a ring-cross and two inscriptions.[80] One, in Ogam, reads VOTECORIGAS, "[The stone] of Votecorix"; the other, in Latin, reads MEMORIA / VOTEPORIGIS / PROTICTORIS, "The memorial of Voteporix the Protector." The suffixes *rigas* and *rix* both mean "king," hence the identification with Gildas's Vortipor, king/tyrant of the Demetae in southwest Wales.[81] Why did Vortipor style himself "Protector"? The Latin title *protector* originally applied to members of the imperial bodyguard (*protectores domestici*), with the rank of officer, who were sometimes sent to the provinces (with their own troops) to perform various public services.[82] Ammianus mentions these imperial bodyguards several times, and once refers to the bodyguard of a provincial governor as *protector*.[83] Ammianus makes a particularly reliable witness, for he himself was made *protector* and sent abroad to serve under the *magister militum*.[84] The *protectores* were normally promoted from the ranks of young, promising soldiers and had to appear in person before the emperor to receive this honor, though A.H.M. Jones has also suggested that the title was later bestowed as an honorific upon senior officers and veterans as well.[85] There are two theories explaining Vortipor's use of the title: either he inherited and cherished the honorific because one of his relatives had actually been a Roman *protector*,[86] or *protictoris* is a Latin translation of a British term that carried the same connotations.[87] Though without precedent in Britain, the title *protector* appears on early Christian monuments in Gaul (Toulouse) and in the Rhineland.[88] Thus, it seems more likely that Vortipor was recalling a Roman title than a purely British one. Although it is highly unlikely that Vortipor of Dyfed (Demetae) received his title directly from the emperor, it is not too far-fetched to see Maximus, Constantine III, or even Ambrosius bestowing such an honor upon one of Vortipor's forebears.[89]

In a similar vein is the inscription on the Penmachno stone.[90] It commemorates "Cantiorix . . . citizen [*cive*] of Gwynedd (and) cousin of Maglos the Magistrate [*magistrat*]," and dates to the fifth or early sixth century. The term *magistratus* is otherwise unknown to early Christian British epigraphy, though civic antecedents can be found on contemporary inscriptions from Gaul and the Mediterranean.[91] Problematic is the fact that Cantiorix is claiming to be a "citizen" of Venedos, which is not a city but rather the region (and later kingdom) of Gwynedd. Nash-Williams sees this as evidence of "an

ordered system of government in northwest Wales in sub-Roman times . . .
an administrative district . . . centering on the Roman station of Caernarvon
[*Segontium*]."[92] Similarly, Alcock believes that "magistrate" refers to the surviving *civitas* leaders to whom Honorius sent his rescript in 410.[93] Once
again, *magistratus* is a term that has assumed both formal and informal
meanings.[94] Ammianus usually uses *magistratus* to denote the "magistracy"
of consulship, though once he refers to a *civitatis magistratus* (of
Hadrianopolis).[95] Zosimus used the Greek form in a very general sense of
"leaders" when describing the purge of Roman officials from Britain in
409.[96] The Christian authors follow this usage, imprecisely naming civic leaders, foreign potentates, temple guards, and city officials alike *magistratus*.[97]
We should assume, however, that the family of Maglos the Magistrate were
not using a generic label but did know precisely what *magistratus* meant, or
else they would not have chosen to include the term on his cousin's memorial. Their pride in a family member's civic status should remind us of
Patrick's boasting that his father was a *decorione*.[98] Perhaps we should see
this *magistratus* as belonging to the same surviving curial class that produced
the decurion Calpornius.[99]

The governing class is certainly better represented in the writings and
inscriptions than is the professional class. Gildas reminds Maglocunus,
"[Y]ou have had as your teacher [*praeceptorem*] the most refined master
[*magistrum elegantem*] of almost all Britain."[100] This "teacher" could have
been a priest or monk, but Lapidge has persuasively argued that this *magister elegans* was a professional "*rhetor* who accepted students for private
tuition."[101] Furthermore, it appears that Gildas himself was a product of such
a classical education—first by a *grammaticus* and then by a *rhetor*—which
included a good deal of legal training.[102] Patrick, whose own education was
interrupted by his captivity, nevertheless testifies to the presence of classically educated individuals (*dominicati rethorici*), well versed in law and oratory, in the British church of the fifth century.[103] Surprisingly, we hear very
little about vernacular education in Britain, which had (before *Romanitas*)
been the domain of the "bards." The existence of bards in sixth-century
Britain has been inferred from several passages in the *De excidio*, most
notably when Gildas chides Maglocunus for listening not to God's praises
but to his own, recited by "criers" (*praecones*) and "flatterers" (*parasiti*) at
his court.[104] Finally, a *medicus* makes himself known to us through his
inscribed memorial, found in Llangian, Wales, dating to the fifth or early
sixth century.[105] It reads MELI MEDICI / FILI MARTINI / I[A]CIT, "[The stone
or the body] of Melus the Doctor, son of Martinus, lies [here]." The mention

of secular profession is unusual for an early Christian monument, though again examples can be found on the Continent.[106]

There are, of course, innumerable peasants and laborers who go unnoticed in the written sources. Some may have left their mark on the many small inscribed monuments that bear only names and parentage. Most, however, remain anonymous. Issues such as patronage, tenancy, and slavery are harder to get at in the sources, and await an adept social historian to construct the appropriate methodology to excavate them.

Ecclesiastical

Given that the majority of evidence for this period comes from the works of Christian writers, it is not surprising that we should find a great deal of information about ecclesiastical organization in Britain. This was a crucial age for the spread and development of the Christian religion in the British Isles. At the end of the fourth century, Christianity was the religion of an affluent few, dominated by urban bishops and divided by theological controversy.[107] Two centuries later, it was a religion of monasteries and missionaries, wandering saints and anointed kings. What do the legitimate contemporary sources have to say about this era, which later hagiography dubbed the Age of the Saints? What specific terms did they use to describe the British church?

Starting, once again, at the top of the hierarchy, we find that "bishops" appear frequently in the sources. Scholars have concluded from scraps of information in various sources (especially the *acta* of the Council of Arles in 314) that the four provincial capitals of Roman Britain—York, London, Lincoln, and Cirencester—each had a metropolitan bishop (*episcopus de civitate*) by the fourth century (see Fig. 6).[108] If Britain followed suit with the plans for the Church in the West (backed by Constantine and all his successors, with the exception of Julian), by the end of the fourth century every *civitas* capital was likely to have had its own bishop.[109] Bishops would also have been present in other large urban centers—and perhaps major military installations—in Britain.

The earliest reference to British bishops, apart from the *acta* of the fourth-century Church councils, is a letter written c. 396 by Victricius of Rouen.[110] He excuses himself for going to Britain: "The bishops, my brothers in the priesthood, called on me to make peace there."[111] Dissent among the British bishops in the early fifth century is a well-attested fact, centering around debates over Pelagian doctrine. At least three well-known men of this period are called British bishops: Fastidius, who was involved with Pelagians in Gaul; Faustus, the semi-Pelagian bishop of Riez; and Mansuetus, a signatory to the Council of Tours in 461.[112] The activities of these men, however, are more telling of the situation in contemporary Gaul.

Prosper of Aquitaine writes, in 429, that "Agricola, a Pelagian, son of the Pelagian *episcopus* Severianus, by his underhanded ways, corrupts the churches of Britain."[113] Though it is not explicitly stated that Agricola and Severianus are Britons,[114] Agricola at least must have had some influence in the British church, for Prosper attributes Germanus's first visit to Britain to Agricola's activities: "[A]t the instance of Palladius the deacon, Pope Celestine sent Germanus, bishop of Auxerre, to act on his behalf; and having put the heretics to route he guided the British [*Britannos*] back to the Catholic faith."[115] Constantius, however, says merely that a *legatio* from Britain invited Germanus;[116] there is no mention here, or anywhere in the *Life,* of British bishops. The absence of British bishops here is more a sloppy omission of Constantius's than a historical fact.[117] Constantius's intent was to glorify Germanus, not to mention other bishops who—in the case of Britain—were likely to include a number of Pelagians.

Prosper elsewhere attests to the success of Celestine and Germanus, writing in 433 that the British provinces were freed from heresy, and that in 431 an *episcopus* was even sent to "the Irish [*Scotti*] believing in Christ."[118] The bishop in question was Palladius, but he quickly disappears from history.[119] His successor was Patrick, who was consecrated bishop, not by the pope, but by the British church.[120] Patrick leaves us no doubt about his own status: "I, Patrick, . . . put on record that I am a bishop [*episcopum*]."[121] Patrick also makes several references to the activities of his ecclesiastical *seniores* in Britain, some of whom objected to his mission and later tried to recall him.[122] He says that a number of these *seniores* "came and brought up my sins against my arduous episcopate [*episcopatum*]," implying that a delegation of British clerics came to Ireland to make their allegations against him.[123] Though Patrick never refers to the British *seniores* as bishops, he depicts them elsewhere as "the Lord's rhetors" (*dominicati rethorici*),[124] recalling the learned Pelagian and semi-Pelagian bishops who, as I have noted, were associated with Britain in the early fifth century.

Gildas testifies to the continuing presence of bishops in Britain into the sixth century. Although there is no mention of archbishops or metropolitans, Gildas uses the terms *episcopus, episcopatus,* and *pontifices* several times in the *De excidio.*[125] Bishops also appear in the *Fragmenta* and the *De*

Poenitentia.[126] Gildas implies that bishops and priests are normally elected by their parishes (*parochiae*), while some ambitious and undeserving clerics travel overseas to obtain their offices or simply buy them from corrupt rulers.[127] That Rome had knowledge of these sixth-century British bishops is attested by a piece of contemporary evidence preserved by Bede. He relates a correspondence of Pope Gregory the Great with Augustine (c. 597) in which Gregory alludes to "all the bishops of Britain" (*Brittaniarum . . . omnes episcopos*).[128] Bede records later that Augustine met with these "bishops and religious teachers of the neighboring province of the Britons" (*episcopos sive doctores proximae Brettonum provincae*).[129] In this famous episode, it should be remembered, the British bishops convened and decided to disregard Gregory's orders that they should be subordinate to the new archbishop of Canterbury.

The *Liber Landavensis* (which contains the Llandaff Charters) tells us a great deal about British bishops, including some of the names of those active in southern Wales. Two of the earliest, Dyfrig (*obit* 612) and Teilo (fl. c. 600), are called *archiepiscopus*, not because they were metropolitans but because they were highly honored or chief bishops.[130] In both the *Liber Landavensis* and the "Lives" of the early Welsh saints, the episcopal see is commonly referred to as *civitas*, occasionally as *episcopalis sedes*.[131] Davies points out that the terminology used to describe the bishops of southern Wales bears a closer relation to the episcopal-based Roman system than to the monastic-based Irish church. The sixth-century Welsh bishops, like Dyfrig, visit and inspect monasteries, where they perform ordinations and consecrations, activities that are the domain of the abbots and monastic bishops in Ireland and Scotland.[132]

Surprisingly, the term *episcopus* appears rarely in the epigraphic evidence. A fourth-century pewter bowl found on the Isle of Ely contains a partly legible inscription that has been read as *supectili epi(scopi) clerique*, "For the furnishings of the bishop and clergy."[133] A sixth-century inscription found at Peebles (Tweed), though now lost, read *Locus Sancti Nicolae Episcopi*, "The tomb of the saintly bishop Nicolas."[134] This scarcity of evidence may follow from the frequent use of the term *sacerdos* at this time as a synonym for *episcopus*, especially where it occurs together with *presbyter*, the latter signifying "priest." Examples of British *sacerdotes* can be found among the inscribed stones of Wales and Scotland.[135] One from Llantrisant, mentioned above, commemorates the wife of *Bivatig(irnus) . . . sacerdos et vasso Paulini*, "Bivatigirnus . . . bishop (or priest) and disciple of Paulinus."[136] Another, from Bodafon, Caernarvonshire (fifth to early sixth century), reads

SANCT/INUS / SACER (dos) / I[N] P (ace), "Sanctinus the Bishop (or Priest) [lies here] in peace."[137] Among the many early Christian memorials found in and around Whithorn is the Kirkmadrine stone (c. 500), whose inscription names Viventius and Mavorius as *sancti et praecipui sacerdotes*, "holy and distinguished bishops (or priests)."[138]

Given that bishops also perform the functions of a priest, and sometimes vice versa, it may be hard to distinguish the two offices in some sources. Gildas makes distinctions between these offices on some occasions, while on others he means to make general condemnations of the clergy when he speaks of *sacerdotes*. The best example of this is his long speech—the "Complaint Against the Clergy"—which parallels that which I have already examined against the tyrants:

> Britain has priests [*Sacerdotes habet Britannia*], but they are fools, very many ministers [*ministros*], but they are shameless; clerics [*clericos*], but they are treacherous grabbers. They are called shepherds [*pastores*], but they are wolves. . . . They have church buildings [*ecclesiae domus*], but go to them for the sake of base profit. They teach people—but by giving them the worst of examples, vice and bad character. Rarely do they sacrifice and never do they stand with pure heart amid the altars. . . . They canvass posts in the church [*ecclesiasticos*] more vigorously than the kingdom of heaven; they get them and keep them like tyrants [*tyrannico*]. . . . There, they remain in the same old unhappy slime of intolerable sin even after they have obtained the priestly seat [*sacerdotalem . . . sedem*] of bishop or priest [*episcopatus vel presbyterii*]. . . . They have grabbed merely the name of priest [*sacerdotali nomine*]—not the priestly way of life.[139]

Here, as in his denunciation of the tyrants, Gildas attaches moral and ethical conduct to officeholding, and both secular and ecclesiastical leaders are supposed to work for God and His people. Gildas's denunciation is overflowing with valuable information about the British clergy. However, one must keep in mind that this is, to say the least, a biased account, and we see only the corrupt side of the church. Davies has done a thorough analysis of the roles of British clerics as depicted by Gildas, identifying the following characteristics: the clergy have *parochiae* (parishes) and *greges* (flocks); bishops engage in politics and worldly affairs and are of importance to their rulers; celibacy is not obligatory; priests minister in churches (*domus ecclesiae*), where the Eucharist is celebrated and oaths are confirmed at the altars; ritual and belief remain orthodox, with perhaps a slight lingering of Pelagianism; there are unbelievers (*increduli*) within the church, but no mention is made of pagans; simony is prevalent; clerics often travel overseas, probably to Gaul; and some indulge in secular literature (including, probably, bardic tales) and entertainments (*ludicra*, games or shows).[140]

Gildas's ecclesiastical vocabulary is quite extensive. Terms he applies to the British secular clergy include *episcopus* (also *episcopatus*), *presbyter* (also *praesbiter*), *sacerdos* (also *sacerdotal*), *diaconus*, *clerici*, *ecclesiastici*, *ecclesiae filii*, *pastores*, *doctores*, and *ministri*; the regular clergy are designated as *abbas*, *monachus*, *meliores*, *sancti*, *fratres*, and *ordo*; there are also "a religious mother or sisters" (*religiosam . . . matrem seu sorores*) and "chaste widows" (*viduitatis castimoniam*). As Davies points out, Gildas also employs the terms *parochiae* and *greges* to describe the broader Christian community.[141] The forms *parochia* and *paroecia* appear first in fourth-century Christian writings (though there may be some relation to the republican secular term *parochus*).[142] In the fourth and fifth centuries, the term (in both forms) is clearly synonymous with "diocese," for it is usually linked with an *episcopus* or *presbyter* and encompasses *ecclesiae* and monasteries.[143] For Gildas's meaning, however, it might be better to look to his contemporary Caesarius of Arles, who links *parochiae* with *pastor, simplices, rustices,* and *sermo*.[144] Gildas and Caesarius may then have been living in a transition period in which small urban dioceses were being broadened to include smaller rural parishes. The origins of parishes are notoriously obscure, although historians and archaeologists are together finding pieces to the puzzle.[145]

In contrast to Gildas, Patrick is far less descriptive of the British church and clergy. He does tell us that his father, Calpornius, was a *diaconus*, "deacon," and that his grandfather, Potitus, was a *presbyter,* "priest."[146] Here again are two examples of married clergy in Britain; though clerical celibacy was at the time being promoted by influential churchmen, like Augustine and Jerome, it was certainly not the norm outside of the higher church offices. Apart from this, Patrick says nothing more about specific church offices and practices in his native land (his information about Ireland is a bit stronger). Constantius is even less forthcoming than Patrick. Unfortunately (for our knowledge of the transitional fifth century), the purpose of neither Patrick nor Constantius was to describe the British church, not even to criticize it, as did Gildas.

For the sixth and early seventh centuries, we have some evidence from the *Liber Landavensis* to add to that of Gildas. The term *sacerdos* appears in witness lists of charters dated c. 610 and 615, and *presbyter* occurs in charters of c. 585 and 650; both are more frequently used in charters of the tenth century and later.[147] Davies explains that the scarcity of priests is due to the prevalence of bishops and abbot-priests in the early religious communities, whereas later *sacerdotes* begin to replace abbots as community leaders and witnesses.[148] Again, it is possible that the *sacerdotes* that do appear in the charters and inscriptions are in fact bishops.

The early penitential literature contains much evidence of the classification of ecclesiastical offices in the British church. Along with those offices mentioned by Gildas, we can add readers (*lectores*) and subdeacons (*subdiaconi*) to the list.[149] The epigraphic evidence, though more slight, mirrors the written sources. The term *presbyter* appears on at least two inscribed stones, both from Caernarvonshire, dated stylistically to the fifth or early sixth century. The first reads VERACIVS / PBR (*presbyter*) / HIC / IACIT, "Veracius the Priest lies here."[150] The second reads SENACVS / PRSB (*presbyter*) / HIC IACIT / CVM MULTITV/D (i) NEM / FRATRVM // PRESB[IT]E[R] : "Senacus the Priest lies here with the multitude of the brethren. Priest."[151] The phrase *cum multitudinem fratrum* implies that Senacus lies in a monastic cemetery.

We should expect an abundance of information about monasticism in Britain, if it was indeed the birthplace and training ground of the "Age of the Saints" that insular hagiography claims it to be. The first recorded British monk is perhaps Constans, son of Constantine III, who left the monastic life to follow his father to Gaul.[152] The Briton Pelagius may also have been a monk—Jerome seems to have thought so—but he himself writes, "I do not wish to be called a monk."[153] Constantius gives no mention of monks in Britain. Patrick speaks admiringly of the *fratres* of Gaul (two of whom, Faustus and Riochatus, were likely Britons), and did himself encourage monasticism in Ireland.[154] But there is no indication in his writings that monasticism was extant in Britain.

Not until the writings of Gildas do we find conclusive evidence of British monasticism. In the *De excidio* references to monasticism are not scarce, though they are somewhat oblique. Gildas speaks of "the true sons" who lead "worthy lives"; "the habit of a holy abbot" (*sancti abbatis amphibalo*); Maglocunus pondering "the Godly life and rule of the monks" (*de deifico tenore monachorumque decritis*) and vowing "to be a monk [*monachum*] forever"; "the caves of the saints"; "bishops and other priests and clerics in our order [*in nostro . . . ordine*]"; and of his own desires to be one of the *sancti* before he dies.[155] Considering that the *De excidio* is intended to be a denunciation of the corrupt British clergy, it is not surprising that Gildas seldom directly mentions the *monachi* whom he seems to admire so much.

Gildas was himself considered to be an expert on monastic practices. Columbanus writes, c. 600, that a certain *Vennianus auctor* consulted Gildas on the subject of monks (*de monachis*) who leave their monastery to seek a stricter discipline, and that Gildas wrote a "most polished" (*elegantissime*) reply.[156] It seems likely that the *Fragmenta* (1 and 7) are remnants of the letter Gildas wrote in reply to this "Vinnian." They display the same sort of moderate asceticism that characterizes the "Penitential of Gildas."[157] The *Fragmenta* deal with such subjects as excommunication, fasting, the Apocalypse, ascetic monks, weak abbots, and the judgments of and relationship between bishops and abbots. Richard Sharpe sees the "Fragments" as our most important source for British monasticism in the sixth century, and considers them to be a response to "an increasing asceticism" in the British church, which came about, in part, because of Gildas's preaching against ecclesiastical corruption in the *De excidio*.[158] The "Penitential" expands upon the themes of the "Fragments" and provides interesting details about the daily life of the monk, including what kinds of food and drinks were being consumed.[159]

The Llandaff Charters, along with the earliest penitentials and saints' lives, testify to the growth of monasticism in the sixth century, at least in Wales. Monasteries named in sixth-century grants include Welsh Bicknor, Llandinabo, Llan-Arth, Llanddowror, Llandeilo Fawr, and Penally, and the list grows in the seventh century.[160] Many of the sites designated *ecclesia* and those place-names beginning with *Llan-* may also have originated as monasteries.[161] Terms for monastic offices occur rarely in witness lists of the early (sixth-century) charters, although by the seventh century *abbates, principes, magistri,* and "monastic virgins" begin to appear.[162] Likewise, monks and abbots are absent from the earliest inscriptions from Wales. A possible exception is the inference of a monastery from the inscription *cum multitudinem fratrem* on the Aberdaron stone discussed above.[163] It is thought by many that the religious community founded at Whithorn by Saint Ninian (Nynia) was a monastic one,[164] but the Whithorn inscribed stones tell us only that it was Christian. The early penitentials are full of references to monks, virgins, abbots, and brethren.[165] One interesting entry applies to "a man who has made the vow of perfection," perhaps another example of lingering Pelagianism in Britain.[166] Overall, these sixth- and seventh-century penitentials present a balanced picture of secular and regular clergy, along with examples of mixed communities.

From the historical evidence alone, we should agree with Charles Thomas

that the pre-Gildas British church was still dominated by the Roman episcopal model, and only in the sixth century did monasticism play a leading
role.[167] Prosper, Constantius, and Patrick paint a picture of *episcopi*—though
not all of them native—operating in the British Isles in the fifth century,
learned men involved in theological disputes. In the sixth-century sources,
particularly Gildas, we find a more diverse church in which theological controversy has died down, while both monasticism and pastoral care have
become more prominent. The interaction between church and state is also
vividly portrayed in both centuries, with accounts of simony, excommunication, and the like.[168] Close study of the terminology employed by these
writers brings us much nearer to being able to construct, with confidence, a
history of this murky era. Archaeology must now take us the rest of the way.

PART III

◆

SUB-ROMAN BRITAIN
The Archaeological Record

11

◆

INTRODUCTION TO THE ARCHAEOLOGICAL EVIDENCE

In examining the written evidence for sub-Roman Britain, one gets a clear impression that the historian must unravel the "facts" from the many biases and shortcomings of the few (mostly ecclesiastical) authors whose works have survived. Although their testimony should be the first avenue of any inquiry into this period, their words can describe only part of the social fabric and topography of Britain. This is why archaeological evidence is increasingly used to broaden the historical picture to include the many towns, forts, and farmsteads that excavation has for the first time uncovered, and to reveal something of those manifold anonymous Britons who have escaped written notice.

It must be said that archaeology, like history, is not without its own biases and shortcomings. Problems such as imprecise dating, unrestrained interpretation, and reliance upon controversial historical evidence have long beset archaeology. Despite the limits of our historical traditions, archaeology of historic eras works best when balanced by written evidence. The most recent trend, however, is to divorce written history from archaeology so that the latter can grow as an independent discipline. Archaeologists have complained (with cause) that historians often provide imprecise or inaccurate dates for periods and events, which in turn destroys the credibility of subsequent archaeological models. Even if the date is accurate, it can act as a "red herring" to distract archaeological inquiry and influence results that may not be tied to that particular event. A good example of this for Roman Britain is the "barbarian conspiracy" of 367 described by Ammianus, which led archaeologists to look for signs of destruction and—if found—credit all of them to this recorded event. There would, of course, have been many ravages in Britain that were not associated with this one datable event.

Archaeological studies of Roman and early medieval Britain have also shifted focus according to prevailing ideologies. Those broad surveys that have become standards and classics—by such as R. G. Collingwood and J.N.L. Myres, John Wacher, Sheppard Frere, and Leslie Alcock—have generally had a healthy respect for written history and historical dates and events.[1] Critics have charged that this breed of archaeologist is too trusting of historical sources. More recently a school of reductionists, whose work is typified by C. J. Arnold's *Roman Britain to Saxon England* (1984), have (in Alcock's words) wished "to treat the archaeology of the fifth to eighth centuries in Britain as though it were prehistoric, or more correctly preliterate."[2] Their complete exclusion of written evidence has regrettably led to even less illumination of this murky period of Britain's past. Others, however, continue the tradition of balancing the written word with archaeological finds to build their models, two recent examples of which are Nicholas Higham's *Rome, Britain, and the Anglo-Saxons* (1992) and Kenneth Dark's *Civitas to Kingdom* (1994). Still, nearly all the models proposed by archaeologists in these surveys have barely scratched the surface of the accumulated evidence.

The approach taken in the following chapter is to avoid speculative models, both positivist and reductionist. Rather, it is hoped that by discussing at length particular sites in Britain where sub-Roman activity is thought to have occurred, conclusions can then be drawn—in Part IV—by comparing the archaeological data from these sites with the evidence previously drawn from the study of the vocabulary of the written sources. In one respect this is a "rescue operation," an attempt to salvage the scattered excavation reports of fifth- and sixth-century sites that have been "lost" in the end pages of surveys concentrating on the more prosperous centuries of Roman Britain. Only by isolating the evidence of sub-Roman activity can we avoid, on the one hand, the inevitable judgment of sub-Roman Britain as "in decay" compared to the "splendor of Roman Britain" and, on the other, the tendency to overlook what does remain in the quest for the first signs of Anglo-Saxon England.

This brings us to our first problem, how to identify "ethnicity" in the archaeological record.[3] Structures, coins, pottery, jewelry, and military equipment have all traditionally been used by archaeologists to identify settlements and graves as Romano-British, Celtic, Germanic, and so forth. Yet, as F. T. Wainwright so wittily mused, "[The archaeologist] can stare at brooches as long as he likes but they will never speak Celtic to him and they will never tell him what language their wearers spoke."[4] All of the items listed above can, of course, be used or reused by groups of people not necessarily responsible for their design. For example, a "Roman" structure could be inhabited by "Germanic" squatters, and a "Romano-Briton" could wear "Germanic" jewelry. This has resulted in the questioning of several traditional assumptions. "Germanic" belt buckles used to be taken for a sure sign of the presence of barbarian *foederati* in Roman Britain; now they may not even indicate a military presence. In fact, the widespread findings of "Germanic" jewelry and pottery have suggested to some scholars that the majority Britons were simply adopting the tastes of the minority Saxons, indicating a change of culture more than a change of population.[5]

Rare, then, is the archaeological artifact that can unquestionably define the ethnicity of a burial or settlement. However, some stylistic terms are widely accepted and used by archaeologists for descriptive purposes (e.g., "Romano-Celtic temple," "Germanic pottery"), and these will be used in the present survey.[6] Here archaeology must work with written evidence to "suggest" the continuity of a Romano-British settlement, the "reemergence" of a native British community, or the appearance of a new population of barbarian settlers, be it Irish or Germanic. Imported Mediterranean pottery, penannular brooches, and Germanic *Grubenhäuser* (sunken-floored huts) are all strong indicators of ethnicity, but their importance here rests in their ability to help date a particular site. It is preferable, for this archaeological discussion, to build a picture of what people wore and how and where they lived in sub-Roman Britain, than to label them with total confidence "Roman," "Briton," or "Saxon."[7]

Dating is the most crucial problem that faces such a study. For this survey, I have focused on the fifth and sixth centuries A.D., roughly from the Rescript of Honorius to the arrival Saint Augustine in Canterbury. The two most important archaeological means of dating settlements within this period are coinage and pottery. Radiocarbon estimates, when available, are helpful as supportive evidence, particularly those tests conducted quite recently, which offer significantly enhanced precision. Glass, bonework, and jewelry are also helpful when and if they are of an identifiable design.

In the fourth century, currency entered Britain in the form of precious-metal coins, bullion (usually plate), and (silver) ingots.[8] Up to 326, the mint at London also issued bronze coinage for insular use, and for a brief period, 312 and 314, it issued some gold.[9] Again, from 383 to 388, London minted some gold coinage for Magnus Maximus (see Fig. 1); but at some subsequent date the London mint ceased to operate, and coinage was sent to Britain from Continental mints, usually from Gaul.[10] Numismatic experts tell us that new bronze issues ceased to be sent to Britain after 402, and the last issues of gold and silver to reach the island were those of the emperors Arcadius and Honorius minted in the first decade of the fifth century, along with those of Constantine III minted between 407 and 411.[11] Individual finds in Britain dating later than 411 tend to be copies or counterfeit, not official issue.[12]

Thus, the picture one gets is that the Roman state was no longer providing coins to the diocese of the Britains after the Rescript of Honorius. Does this mean, then, that coins went out of use soon after 410? The standard answer is yes, and that the Britons must therefore have engaged only in barter economy subsequent to this date. However, some numismatists are now suggesting that older-issue coins circulated in Britain throughout the fifth century (and perhaps later) along with more recent counterfeits, and that those that were lost are noticeably worn because of their continued use.[13] This seems to have been the case for many areas of the sub-Roman West, resulting in a "hotchpotch" coinage (to borrow Kenneth Dark's phrase), based on shape and weight rather than denomination, that continued well into the medieval period.[14] Some clues from the written evidence corroborate this picture of continued coin use in sub-Roman Britain.[15]

As an alternative to coin and bullion, foodstuffs could be used in making official payments. For example, the Roman army along the frontier needed to be supplied with grain (*annona*), which was transported over long distances in large ceramic containers called amphoras. Commercial trade in luxury goods, including ceramic table wares, often followed these same official trade routes. Britain also had thriving commercial kilns making a variety of regional wares.[16] Thus pottery is ubiquitous in Roman Britain, as indeed it is in most periods, for without it there could have been no civilized life. Pottery also has a remarkable ability to survive in the archaeological record. From the first centuries of Roman rule, excavators have found fine table wares—both locally made and imported Samian varieties—along with the imported amphoras. There is little doubt, however, that commercial British pottery-manufacturing centers ceased operating after 410. Late Roman fine wares found in fifth-century British settlements like Wroxeter and Verulamium appear to be purely residual.[17] The only locally made pottery in fifth-century Britain is "grass-tempered" ware and similar varieties, which, admittedly, appear crude in comparison with the earlier commercially made pottery. This decline is seen to parallel the decline of a money economy (that is, the absence of new coins) in Britain, and to have been influenced by the absence of both the military and urban markets.

However, this picture of decline and collapse is misleading. Like coins, pottery could have circulated for many years after the state production centers had closed. As for imported pottery, excavation is revealing an actual *revival* of fine wares and amphoras carrying luxury items. These imports include not only Gaulish products coming to Britain from the old river routes of Gaul, but also goods produced in such diverse Mediterranean centers as Byzacena, Phocaea, Cyprus, Gaza, and the Aegean, coming to Britain *directly* from such ports as Carthage and Alexandria in the fifth and sixth centuries.

These imports were first discovered during the excavations of C. A. Ralegh Radford at Tintagel, Cornwall in the 1930s.[18] Termed colloquially "Tintagel ware," the imports soon began turning up at other excavated sites in western Britain and Ireland, though the Tintagel collection remains the largest and most diverse.[19] Since the initial Tintagel excavations, major studies of these pottery types have appeared,[20] and the British finds have been labeled and cataloged.[21] Because they can be approximately dated, these imports have become one of the most valuable tools for identifying sub-Roman sites in Britain. How and why this pottery came to Britain is discussed in the next chapter under the specific sites on which it occurs, as well as in the discussion of the economy of sub-Roman Britain in Part IV.

Finally, a few words must be said about the precision of the archaeological evidence for this period. The scientific cataloging and analysis of finds like coins, pottery, and jewelry is a relatively recent phenomenon, with inexact reports more typical for those sites excavated several decades ago. Even when more recent analysis could be exact, as in the case of numismatic evidence, it is seldom accomplished in excavation reports, many of which remain only in preliminary form. Given these drawbacks, the purpose of the present study is not to offer precise dates for Roman and sub-Roman occupation at particular sites. Rather, I use coins and pottery only to help place activity in the fifth and sixth centuries, the period contemporaneous with the written evidence previously discussed. If *this* can be done with some confidence, discussion of the sub-Roman Britons in terms of their structures, weapons, jewelry, pottery, and other surviving artifacts may follow. Once the scholarly community agrees upon at least *some* definite sub-Roman sites,[22] the artifactual and written evidence combined will provide plenty of material for discussion of the politics, economy, and culture of the enigmatic Britons.

12

◆

SIGNIFICANT SITES

The recent archaeological studies of sub-Roman Britain have produced some intriguing models and daring interpretations of the evidence.[1] These studies have bravely tackled the big questions—when and why did Roman Britain end? when did the Saxons arrive in Britain? when and how did they wrest control of the island from the Britons?—with a firm awareness and grasp of the data from excavated sites. The theories presented by these archaeologists will likely challenge historians entering the field for years to come.

Yet there is something noticeably missing from these studies. Individual sites are cursorily discussed and in a random fashion, brought into the narrative if and when they strengthen the model being proposed. Little or no time is spent describing the physical nature of a specific site or the character of its occupation. Unlike the Roman period, sub-Roman Britain has yet to inspire a single general survey of its settlements.

This chapter is a modest attempt to remedy the situation.[2] I have chosen here excavated sites that have yielded the strongest evidence for occupation in the fifth and/or sixth centuries (see Fig. 7), and whose remains inspire the most compelling vignettes of life in sub-Roman Britain. These sites I have grouped into four broad categories: towns, forts, rural sites, and religious sites. (Note that some sites appear under two categories—for example, towns that also have a substantial religious component—while other multifaceted sites will be discussed only under their predominant descriptor). While there are some noticeable omissions, I believe these examples provide an archaeological picture of sub-Roman Britain sufficient for a comparison with the written evidence.

Towns

An obvious place to start this survey would be with the large urban centers in Britain (Figs. 8 and 9). The vexing problem of urban survival and continuity in sub-Roman Britain is specifically addressed in the next chapter. It should be noted at the outset, however, that "cities" are a phenomenon of the Mediterranean world imported to Britain with the Roman invasion of A.D. 43, and that these Roman towns (the preferred term) in Britain are small in comparison with their counterparts elsewhere in the empire. "Indigenous" settlement in Britain from the Stone Age to the late pre-Roman Iron Age (LPRIA) is not classified as urban, though Celtic-speaking immigrants from Gaul were developing prototowns—which Julius Caesar called *oppida*—in the southeast on the eve of the Roman invasion.[3] St. Albans, Colchester, Silchester, Winchester, and Canterbury are all examples of towns with LPRIA *oppida* whose populations became the basis of later Roman towns. When the Romans conquered an *oppidum* or a rural hillfort, the surviving population was usually settled outside of the defenses in a nearby low-lying area. This settlement, if it grew into a Roman town, would have streets and buildings laid out in the typical gridlike plan and would eventually be surrounded by a defensive wall. Of course, not all Roman towns were walled, and many grew up strictly from military or commercial beginnings.

LONDON is an example of the latter. Among European capitals, London has a most ancient yet enigmatic history.[4] Britons in the Bronze and Iron Ages gathered along the banks of the Thames for ceremony and trade, yet no significant settlement was established until the coming of the Romans. Although

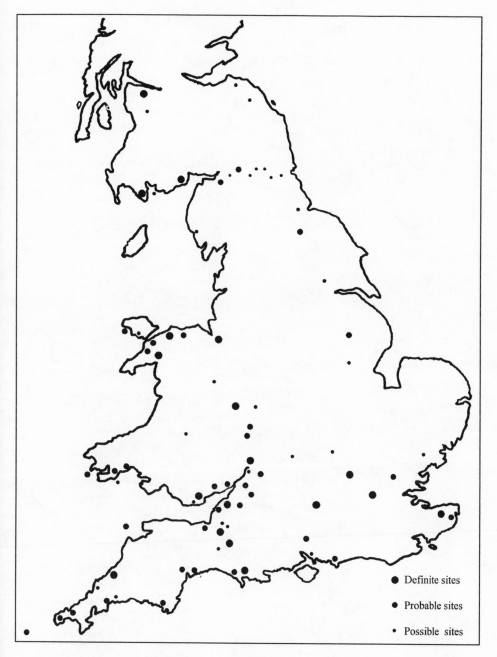

Fig. 7. Significant sites in sub-Roman Britain (after Snyder, *Sub-Roman Britain*, 12)

Fig. 8.   Major roads and towns of fourth-century Roman Britain

Fig. 9. Roman towns occupied in sub-Roman Britain

Claudius's legions gained control of the river banks in the invasion of A.D. 43, the emperor decided to establish the capital of the new province further northeast at Colchester (the site of the British fortress Camulodunum). A bridge was built over the Thames to provide an overland route to Colchester from the channel ports in Kent, and this site became a focal point for the newly constructed Roman road system. Soon a settlement grew up on the north bank, and military defenses were added. The Romans named this new small town and port Londinium, perhaps after its original British name.[5]

This Londinium was destroyed in the native revolt led by Boudicca in A.D. 60/61, along with Colchester and St. Albans (Verulamium). London was soon rebuilt, however, and became the new capital of the province of Britannia. As such it was the home of the civilian *procurator*, the headquarters of the Provincial Council, and the winter residence of the military governor. When Britain was divided into two provinces, c. 200, London remained the capital of Britannia Superior, and after Diocletian's administrative reforms it became the capital of the province of Maxima Caesariensis. Not only did London have its own provincial governor, but it was also the seat of the new *vicarius* of the diocese of the Britains. Honored with the title Augusta, London remained throughout the financial center of Roman Britain, and housed an imperial mint beginning in 288.

Settlement continued in London into the fifth and sixth centuries, but its character changed dramatically from its once-lofty status as administrative center of the province and diocese. London's great basilica was carefully demolished at the start of the fourth century, though its apse was left standing and became part of some new structure standing alone on the now-vacant forum.[6]

The London waterfront, on the other hand, showed signs of revival in the late fourth century.[7] Urban occupation continued there until the sixth century, and there is some evidence—scattered finds of amphora sherds—of continued trade with the Mediterranean.[8] A section of the riverside wall was rebuilt at this time, while towers were added (c. 350) to the landward wall.[9] These defensive measures fit in with late-fourth-century imperial policy and are paralleled at other walled cities in Britain.

The *Notitia* states that London housed the imperial treasury and the *praepositus Thesaurorum Augustensium* in the last decade of the fourth century. A silver ingot, of the type presented to the army on an imperial accession or anniversary (see Fig. 10), was found within the Tower of London along with two gold coins, one of Honorius and one of Arcadius.[10] Scattered around the Tower as well were several coins running down to 388–402, leading Dominic

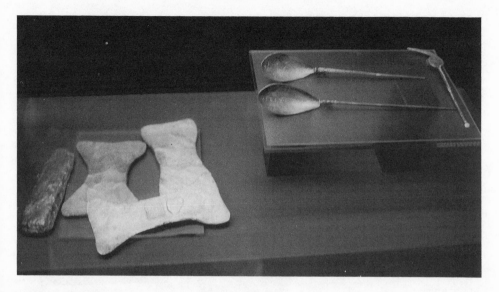

Fig. 10. Part of the late Roman silver hoard found at Canterbury (printed with permission of the Canterbury Heritage Museum)

Perring to postulate that a late Roman salient was built on the Tower site in the last decades of the fourth century, perhaps associated with the campaigns of Stilicho.[11]

But the site that gives the clearest evidence of fifth-century occupation is a masonry building uncovered in Lower Thames Street near Billingsgate (Fig. 11).[12] This large house had underfloor heating and a private bath suite, all of which continued to be used well into the fifth century. A hoard of over two hundred copper coins issued between 388 and 402 were found scattered on the furnace room floor,[13] and under the furnace ashes was found a sherd from a fifth-century amphora imported from the eastern Mediterranean, probably Gaza.[14] The *terminus* of this occupation is marked by broken glass and roof debris, on which was found a circular brooch identical to one found in an early (pagan) Saxon grave at Mitcham, Surrey.

There is little evidence of "Germanic" pottery or *Grubenhäuser* in the city itself,[15] though a "Saxon" cemetery has been identified in the London suburb of Orpington.[16] Anglo-Saxon London (Lundenwic) grew up to the west of the present city and did not become a significant *burg* until quite late. In fact, the *Anglo-Saxon Chronicle* describes London as a place to which the BRITONS fled after defeat in Kent in the 450s.[17] The Roman fort at Cripplegate may have passed from these Britons to become an Anglo-Saxon

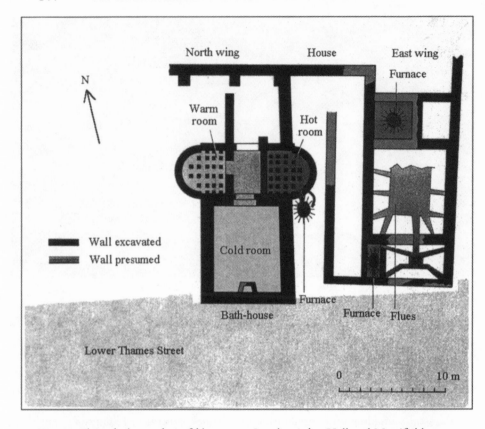

Fig. 11. Plan of a house from fifth-century London (after Hall and Merrifield, *Roman London*, 16)

royal palace.[18] Archaeology is not able to clear up all of the questions posed by London, but it does provide enough evidence to speculate about this last-phase settlement of Britons. Perring sees London as the center of a minor sub-Roman kingdom, a town surrounded by banked ditches constructed to mark the boundaries between it and the sub-Roman communities of Verulamium and Canterbury.[19] Though Roman Britain's largest city appears not to have been a major settlement in the immediate post-Roman years, finds do show sporadic activity in the fifth and early sixth centuries.

COLCHESTER (Camulodunum), Roman Britain's first capital and *colonia*, was on its way to becoming the model provincial city before it too was destroyed by Boudicca. Though rebuilt, Colchester was once again vulnerable to the attacks of seaborne raiders in the fourth and fifth centuries. Excavations at Duncan's Gate and Balkerne Lane have revealed evidence of

Fig. 12. The Balkerne Gate of Roman Colchester

fire destruction and external attacks in the fourth-century town.[20] However, coin finds and graves testify to continuous occupation into the early years of the fifth century.[21] Other fifth-century evidence includes one sunken-floor hut, two cruciform brooches, and parts of military belt buckles.[22] The military buckles could have belonged to any late Roman soldier, but the fact that the hut and graves were found within Colchester's walls suggests that these occupants were present at a time when the Roman restriction against intramural burials no longer existed.[23] The area around the Balkerne Gate, which remains to this day largely intact (see Fig. 12), may yet yield clues about sub-Roman defense and transportation in Colchester, while a recently discovered structure (see the discussion below) promises clues about the city's religious life. While we might expect that Colchester, vulnerable in the East, must have passed into Saxon hands by the end of the fifth century, the city itself has yielded little early Saxon evidence.[24]

The small walled town of CHELMSFORD (Caesaromagus, "Caesar's Plain") also suffered badly from the Boudiccan revolt and could never compete economically with the markets at nearby London and Colchester. The Romans lost interest in developing the small town after the second century, and native Trinovantian influence remained strong in the area. In the fourth century, Chelmsford may have taken on a significant religious role with the construction of a stone temple (see the discussion below). Less is known about Chelmsford's timber structures, traces of which have been found both inside and outside the city walls. One large timber building, destroyed by fire, has been dated to the fifth century because it contained Continental pottery identified stylistically as "Jutish." Locally made sub-Roman pottery has also been recorded both at Chelmsford and at nearby Great Dunmow. "Presumably," writes Rosalind Dunnet, "the bulk of the population continued living in their established homes."[25]

Nearby ST. ALBANS has yielded much more positive evidence of sub-Roman activity. The medieval town that grew up around St. Albans Abbey was the successor of two significant settlements: the Catuvellauni *oppidum* called Verlamion, and the Roman town called Verulamium.[26] A brief Roman military occupation in the area led to the development of the town, which at some point was granted *municipium* status. But this Verulamium, like London and Colchester, soon perished in the flames of the Boudiccan revolt. The town was rebuilt in the Flavian period, and by the fourth century its walls enclosed a forum, a theater, temples, and town houses. Verulamium also produced Britain's first Christian martyr, the soldier Alban, who is thought to have died in the third century.

Verulamium makes one of the strongest cases for the survival of a major Roman town into the fifth and sixth centuries. Sheppard Frere's excavations of Verulamium have revealed a diversity of both public and private activity during the sub-Roman period. One town house in particular reveals the complexity of this activity (Fig. 13).[27] Built c. 380 on a vacant site, the house included twenty-two ground-floor rooms and a colonnade surrounding a garden or courtyard. After a period of use, two extensions were added to the house, complete with a series of high-quality mosaic floors the constant wear of which necessitated frequent replacement. The kitchen floor alone was repaved four times between about 400 and 430, when a hole was cut through it for the placement of a corn-drying oven or small hypocaust. The oven was used so much that it too needed repairs before the house was demolished c. 460. At this stage a large rectangular structure, interpreted as a stone barn or hall, was constructed on the site. After another undetermined period of use, one of the stone buttresses of this building was damaged during the installation of a wooden water pipe, constructed—in the Roman

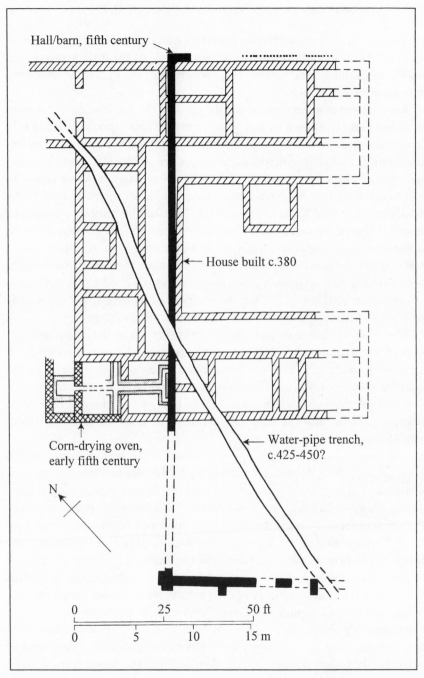

Hall/barn, fifth century

House built c.380

Corn-drying oven,
early fifth century

Water-pipe trench,
c.425-450?

N

| 0 | | 25 | | 50 ft |
| 0 | 5 | 10 | 15 m |

Fig. 13. Plan of a townhouse from sub-Roman Verulamium (after Sheppard Frere, *Verulamium*)

style—with hollowed-out trunks joined by iron collars. Dating is based on associated coins and pottery—of the first decade of the fifth century—and on the continuing stratigraphic sequence, which, the excavator estimates, ran down to A.D. 475+.

Keith Branigan notes that the construction of the sub-Roman water main indicates that (1) Roman hydraulic engineering skills were still alive in sub-Roman Britain, (2) the Roman aqueduct that served Verulamium was still functioning, and (3) municipal authorities were still working for the maintenance of the city c. 450–70.[28] Sherds from eastern Mediterranean amphoras, found on the surface of a timber building constructed after 380, testify to continued trade in this period.[29] The quality mosaic pavements, found in several Verulamium houses, would seem to indicate that the skills of the mosaicist were also still alive in fifth-century Britain. Rosalind Niblett sums up this evidence: "The current picture of late Roman Verulamium is one of widespread occupation, increasingly in timber buildings, amidst areas of open cultivated land; . . . but the standard of living was not necessarily low, witness the new water pipe and the imported amphora."[30]

There are further reasons to be as optimistic about the agrarian economy of Verulamium and its environs. The forum, with its well-worn floor, survived into the fifth century. Branigan takes this as an indicator of the continued occupation of the surrounding villa estates, which needed such markets for their goods. Two cottages in nearby Gadebridge Park were occupied at least into the early fifth century, when animal pens were built as additions.[31]

This survival of a Verulamium community in the fifth century has also been inferred from Constantius's *Life of St. Germanus,* which describes Germanus's visit to the shrine of St. Alban in 429 (see the discussion below). Many scholars have argued for the survival of a "British" population into the sixth century in what has been described as a Saxon-free "Chiltern Zone."[32] According to the *Anglo-Saxon Chronicle,* the area remained in the hands of the Britons until their defeat at the Battle of Bedcanford in 571.[33]

Near continuous archaeological fieldwork is revealing many important clues about late and sub-Roman CANTERBURY (Durovernum Cantiacorum). While decay and demolition were certainly in evidence in many of Canterbury's public buildings, what is interesting is the reuse of these areas for continued economic activity during the tumultuous fifth century. For example, the fourth century saw the demolition of the public baths and the portico of the local temple. But the temple courtyard was still being used in the fifth century, perhaps as a market, and new timber structures were built over the baths complex.[34] Although the southern carriageway at Riding Gate was stopped up at this time, its space was maintained for use as a metalworker's workshop.[35] Other fifth-century structures were built over Roman roads, indicating that urban standards may have been declining in Canterbury, but its sub-Roman occupants were choosing adaptation over desertion.

There is other evidence that at least some of these fifth-century occupants were quite wealthy and Christian. An impressive silver hoard was found outside of the London Gate, and is dated from coin evidence to c. 407–11 or later (Fig. 10).[36] The hoard included silver ingots (late fourth or early fifth century), a gold ring (late fourth), and numerous silver spoons (late fourth) decorated with the Chi-Rho monogram. The spoons in particular offer indisputable evidence of a wealthy Christian community in sub-Roman Canterbury that may have provided the precedent for the Augustinian mission of 597.[37]

Other evidence allows us to extend the sub-Roman occupation at least to the end of the fifth century. In the temple precinct archaeologists uncovered a multiple burial, seemingly a family and their pet dog, with associated jewelry dating stylistically to the mid–fifth century.[38] A. S. Esmonde Cleary points out that this inhumation is in clear violation of the Roman law preventing burial of the dead within town walls.[39] In the Marlowe area, in southeastern Canterbury, excavation revealed timber structures inserted into the shell of an earlier stone building; deposits indicated up to four phases of fifth-century occupation on the site.[40] Nearby, in soil covering a late Roman courtyard, excavators found a Visigothic coin and a firesteel, a metal "match" used to strike flint.[41] The coin, a gold *tremissis* of either Severus III or Zeno, is most likely a Visigothic copy originating in southern Gaul c. 480.[42] Its fragmented condition indicates that it was probably part of a goldsmith's collection, as was the firesteel, which is similar to one found at Portchester and dates by affinity to the mid to late fifth century.

Coin evidence also supports fifth-century continuity in CHICHESTER (Noviomagus Regnorum). Its public baths were still functioning in the 370s, and two houses in Chapel Street show signs of occupation into the next century.[43] Fifth-century numismatic evidence includes a bronze coin of Arcadius[44] and a Visigothic copy of a gold *solidus* of Valentinian III (425–55).[45] There is also numismatic and ceramic evidence of occupation in the late fourth and early fifth centuries at some of the neighboring villas and settlements, including Bignor, Rookery Hill, Thundersbarrow, and Bow Hill.[46] Alec Down has speculated that the strongholds of the sub-Roman *tyranni* may have included "the old *civitas* capitals" like Chichester, "with their strong walls, the forts of the Saxon shore and, in some instances, the large estates where the owners were sufficiently wealthy to maintain armed forces."[47]

This should hold true as well for other walled Roman settlements, like BATH (Aquae Sulis), for which there is ample archaeological and literary evidence for sub-Roman activity. After a defensive wall was built around the religious precinct of Bath in the early fourth century, more and more people began abandoning their extramural settlements and moving inside the walled "city." Having at least eleven major buildings, some quite large and several with underfloor heating and mosaics, Bath was the most thriving of the small towns in late Roman Britain.[48] A recently found hoard of silver coins shows that the wealth spread to the surrounding communities as well.[49]

The flourishing baths complex underwent dramatic changes at the end of the fourth century. The increasing problem of flooding shut down the underfloor heating for long periods, though the numbers of people visiting the springs did not decrease. The precinct of the Temple of Sulis Minerva saw the most drastic changes, perhaps as the result of the rising influence of Christianity in the area.[50] The temple altar was dismantled, and sculpted blocks were torn from the "Gorgon" pediment, then overturned and used to pave the floors. The colonnade in the outer precinct was demolished, and new secular buildings were constructed in its place.

The most complex and significant sequence occurred in the temple's inner paved precinct.[51] The paved floor had been swept regularly until the middle of the fourth century, when an accumulation of earth began to cover it (and a coin of Constans, c. 347–48). A new cobbled floor was then laid on top of the dirt, and again dirt began to accumulate over the worn stones. This pattern was repeated six times until the final collapse of the buildings sealed the sequence with a blanket of masonry rubble. The third level of cobbling sealed a coin of the House of Theodosius (388–402) and related pottery (Oxford color-coated ware and shell-tempered ware), but that leaves three layers of pavement, each of them worn by the passage of feet, extending to a time beyond the last coin issues and datable pottery. The excavators believe that the chronology of this sequence extends occupation of the temple precinct at least to 470, and very likely into the sixth century and beyond.[52] While the pottery experts would like to compress the entire chronology into the late fourth century (squeezing the last three layers into the 390s), most archaeologists agree with Barry Cunliffe (and the coin evidence from here and the sacred spring) that settlement must extend well into the fifth century.[53]

Evidence elsewhere supports the theory that Bath remained populated through the sub-Roman period. Throughout the bath complex the floor slabs, especially beneath the doorways, show considerable wear from the last (fifth-century) phase, indicating that "even though the buildings were now being demolished, the spring continued to be frequented on an impressive scale."[54] While there was much stone robbing in the post-Roman years, not all the buildings were demolished. The reservoir enclosure survived into the early medieval period and became known as the King's Bath.[55] "Elsewhere within the walled area," writes Cunliffe, "there are hints of domestic buildings being used well into the fifth and possibly the sixth centuries."[56] Such "hints" include the Abbeygate Street site, where a Roman building that collapsed in the late fourth century was replaced, after an interval, by a new structure erected on a different alignment, the associated stratigraphy arguing for survival well beyond 410. Excavation has thus lent some credence to the assertion of the *Anglo-Saxon Chronicle* that, at the time of the Battle of Dyrham (c. 577), Bath was a major *civitas* and (perhaps) the residence of a British king.[57]

Late-fourth- and fifth-century domestic buildings also reveal something of the character of DORCHESTER (Durnovaria) and the surrounding area. Late Roman Dorchester produced one of Britain's most distinctive schools for mosaicists, and was the home of a flourishing Christian community (see the discussion below). By c. 420, however, the cemetery in the northwest suburb of Poundbury went out of use, and a substantial agricultural community grew up on the site (the enclosed area equals that of South Cadbury). Features of this post-Roman settlement include fifteen buildings (post-built, beam-slot, combined post-and-beam, and sunken featured structures), seven groups of pits, six grain driers and a threshing floor, four small ditched enclosures, and a substantial ditched enclosure.[58] Additionally, six mausoleums belonging to the late Roman cemetery were either robbed or reused in the post-Roman period, one yielding a Theodosian bronze coin sealed in its wall plaster.[59] This post-Roman settlement seems to have had two phases, spanning (on radiocarbon estimates) from the late fourth to early seventh centuries. Sherds of imported amphoras, quality iron knives, and bone pins tell us something of Poundbury's economic and industrial activities, while the large number of grain driers might suggest the on-site mass processing of grain.[60] The end of sub-Roman Poundbury was sudden, marked by the destruction of drystone and timber structures and the possible slaughter of animals, with radiocarbon estimates suggesting a date in the middle of the seventh century.[61] This would be contemporary with the cemetery evidence for the arrival of the first Saxons in the Dorchester area.

Another *civitas* capital showing strong signs of continuity is EXETER (Isca Dumnoniorum). The forum basilica at Exeter underwent extensive remodeling in the latter part of the fourth century, and the new floor laid in the basilica contained a coin of Valens (c. 367–75).[62] Though grass and weeds were apparently growing in the *palaestra* of the baths,[63] at least one Roman town house was built after the middle of the fourth century, with a water trough laid over a coin of c. 363–67. Adjacent to this large house was a dump of oyster shells and a well-worn coin of Maximus (c. 387–88), indicating probable activity at the site to the beginning of the fifth century.[64]

In the middle of the fifth century, the southern end of the forum and basilica was carefully demolished, and the stones were removed from the site in an orderly manner calling for some organization of manpower.[65] First a large quarry pit, together with several smaller pits, was dug into the *curia* floor to extract clay for bronze-working.[66] Then the site was used as a cemetery, as evidenced by the six excavated inhumation graves that followed the alignment of the Roman buildings. Two of the graves yielded radiocarbon dates placing them in the fifth or sixth centuries, while the rest appeared to belong to the later Saxon minster church.[67]

Paul Bidwell believes that these graves are part of a larger (yet to be fully excavated) Christian cemetery, indicating a fifth-century Christian community at Exeter that he describes as a "proto-monastery."[68] If these Christian graves were succeeded directly by the Saxon church and graveyard, it may signal continuity of occupation at Exeter.[69]

There is an intriguing reference to Exeter in the *Life of St. John the Almsgiver,* written in the early seventh century. A captain sailing from Alexandria with a cargo of corn is blown off course and lands in Britain, where he trades his cargo for Cornish tin (and some bronze *numisma*) and relieves a local famine. This reference has been taken to mean Exeter (or its port at Topsham), the first major Roman port reached by ships rounding the Iberian peninsula.[70] But it could also refer to some other Dumnonian port that had succeeded Exeter in the sub-Roman period. The hillfort at Castle Dore, near Fowey, may have become a new focal-point for the post-Roman inhabitants of Dumnonia. The widespread occurrence of Christian memorial stones with their Ogam script in West Devon and Cornwall suggests Welsh or Irish missionary activity in this area,[71] which was quickly solidifying into a westward-looking "Celtic" kingdom. From written sources we hear that the English established a monastery at Exeter in 670, though Britons remained a significant part of the (perhaps segregated) city population until they were expelled by Aethelstan in the tenth century.[72]

Another *civitas* capital that later became an important English town, WINCHESTER (Venta Belgarum), has shown some signs of Romano-British occupation continuing in the fifth century. A late Roman cemetery at Lankhills, just outside of Winchester's north gate, has yielded an abundance of graves dating to the late fourth or early fifth century.[73] Some of these graves were cut into by sub-Roman structures, two of which appear to have been bedding trenches for plants forming the boundary of a garden.[74] While there was some decay in street and drain maintenance, there were also new pavings (of inferior quality) and new timber structures that encroached on the carriageways.[75] Wacher believes the citizenry began building their houses on top of the paved city streets because they provided a firm, well-drained foundation.[76] "These metallings [road pavings] and structures," comments Esmonde Cleary, "however much they represent a decline in standards, also represent a continuation of population."[77]

Like many *civitas* centers, CAERWENT (Venta Silurum) began as a fort and later developed into a walled town and marketplace. In the middle of the fourth century the town defenses were strengthened with the addition of at least eleven external towers, heptagonal in shape and irregularly spaced, which were built to support *ballistae*.[78] Also at this time both the south and north gates at Caerwent were blocked, seemingly in answer to some external threat.[79] Several Theodosian coin hoards have been found at Caerwent, deposited after buildings had collapsed and possibly (as has been suggested by Richard Reece) as late as the second or third quarter of the fifth century.[80]

Graffiti scratched on the walls of the *curia* in the basilica at Caerwent have been assigned to the fifth century, and the forum remained in use some time after that. Drains were built running through the blocked-up gates, suggesting that the baths were still operating for some time until they collapsed and were replaced by another structure, possibly a church.[81] Though this interpretation has been questioned, four other stone buildings have recently been identified as early medieval and may have belonged to the sixth-century monastery founded by the Irish Saint Tathan.[82] Stylistic analysis of jewelry found in the town confirms occupation and activity during this period.[83]

The excavation of a cemetery just outside the walls of Caerwent revealed further evidence of sub-Roman occupation. Radiocarbon dates taken from the graves show that the people of Caerwent continued to be buried in this cemetery in the fifth and sixth centuries; in fact, the continuity extends to the eighth or ninth century, when the settlement was clearly monastic.[84] One interesting burial contained a Roman coin (c. 335–48) and a late Roman bracelet, yet radiocarbon analysis indicated a date of c. 540–770. "If this is correct," comment Jeremy Knight and Alan Lane, "it implies the continuing use of Roman objects well into the early medieval period."[85]

The *civitas* capital CIRENCESTER (Corinium Dobunnorum) was Roman Britain's "Second City" (after London), and contained flourishing mosaic and sculpture workshops. But the evidence for late Roman Cirencester produces a mixed picture of continued occupation and decay. The floor of the forum was quite worn down, but it was also kept clean, and apparently the market flourished here after the cessation of coins.[86] The Verulamium Gate underwent the refacing of its tower, the rebuilding of the front face of the wall, and the installation of a sluice gate and other flood-prevention work that has been dated on ceramic evidence to the beginning of the fifth century.[87] A roadside ditch beside Ermine Street yielded evidence that the road also remained well-used (and often repaired); at some point, however, grass began to grow on it and two unburied bodies were left to rot in the ditch.[88]

An accumulation of silt and debris in roadside ditches signals that Cirencester began to decline in the middle of the fifth century. At that time, the city population seems to have abandoned their old dwellings and resettled inside the town amphitheater. In the amphitheater, which lies just outside the city walls on the Fosse Way, there is abundant evidence of timber buildings and road and wall repairs dated, from associated coins and (grass-tempered) pottery, to the late fifth century.[89] This has been interpreted as a shrinking city population moving into a smaller and more easily defended area, perhaps to flee disease and epidemic in the city proper. Gaul and Dacia provide ample evidence that Roman amphitheaters were converted into miniature fortified towns.[90] The *ceaster* element in Chesterton, the modern district wherein the amphitheater lies, may refer to this fortified settlement.[91]

Was it, then, the amphitheater of Cirencester, rather than the city itself, that fell to the Saxons in the Battle of Dyrham in 577? Excavation has revealed no signs of violent destruction in the city. "It may be that the population of fifth-century Corinium was no more than a collection of farming families," write Richard Reece and Christopher Catling.[92] "The church no doubt continued, a titular chief or king continued, but few buildings needed to be kept up for human occupation."

GLOUCESTER (Glevum), another British casualty of the Battle of Dyrham, was founded under Nerva (A.D. 96–98) as a *colonia,* with a legionary fortress stationed a mile to the north at Kingsholm. The military presence in Gloucester in the years leading up to 400 seems to have been very high. The late Roman walling of the city was likely part of a scheme to fortify all the

major settlements along the tributaries of the Severn River, to control Irish
or Saxon raids up the Bristol Channel.[93] Gloucester's forum area was in continuous use after the forum itself had been dismantled in the late fourth century, with timber structures replacing stone and evidence of replanning in
the town center in the early fifth century.[94]

Coin evidence associated with the last phase of metaling indicates that the
whole forum may have been resurfaced after 390.[95] A colonnaded stone
structure near the forum was demolished c. 370, only to be replaced by a
timber building that yielded a radiocarbon date of A.D. 430 ± 80.[96] The new
timber structure may have been a sub-Roman market booth, for it contained
a quantity of butcher's bones. Elsewhere, a coin hoard, with several coins of
Honorius and Arcadius, seems to have fallen from the rafters of one building and lay on top of debris.[97] Two or three subsequent occupations overlay
the deposition of *Fel. Temp. Reparatio* imitation coins on Berkeley Street.[98]
A coin of Valens (364–78) was found *beneath* a mosaic on Southgate Street.[99]
Ornamental metalwork, shell-tempered and Oxfordshire wares, and
imported pottery (fragments of North African amphoras) testify to occupation continuing into at least the late fifth century.[100]

A late or post-Roman cemetery at Kingsholm may tell us more about this
community.[101] That there were Christians in this community is indicated by
a sub-Roman timber mausoleum, containing the skeleton of a male with silver belt fittings, found overlying a Roman building and beneath the Saxon
Chapel of St. Mary de Lode.[102] According to the *Anglo-Saxon Chronicle*,
Gloucester fell to the Saxons at the Battle of Dyrham in 577. If this entry is
accurate, the city was then under the control of a king named Conmail. The
late Roman earthwork defenses that surrounded the city would have made
it an attractive residence for a sub-Roman king.[103]

Unlike Gloucester, SILCHESTER (Calleva Atrebatum) is one of the few
Roman cities in Britain that did not evolve into a major medieval and modern town. Thus, the circuit of its Roman walls survives almost completely
intact, and excavation of the now-vacant interior has revealed the most complete plan of any Roman town in Britain. The undisturbed nature of
Silchester's remains gives hope, as well, that we may learn more about the
nature and survival of such towns in the fifth and sixth centuries.

Silchester was the principle center of the northern Atrebates tribe. A
Roman military occupation followed the Claudian conquest in A.D. 43, and
Silchester may have been added to the client kingdom of Cogidubnus.[104]
Ramparts were built around the city, and by the Flavian period Silchester had
become a *civitas* capital. Monumental public buildings and modest timber

houses round out the picture of the thriving early town.

There are numerous signs of new structures and activity in fourth-century Silchester, though the character of occupation was perhaps changing. By 300 the basilica ceased to be used as a public building and was divided by partitions and reorganized as a metal workshop.[105] As late as 320, large-scale renovations were taking place at the baths, and numerous Theodosian coins (including a bronze coin of Arcadius, c. 395–402) attest to activity at the forum.[106] Sometime during the fourth century the walls of the amphitheater were torn down, and the inn and one of the temples contained coins of Valens (364–78).[107] Some of Silchester's town houses were given fourth-century mosaics (associated coins run down to Honorius), and the southeast gate "was deliberately blocked in the Roman or sub-Roman period" in order more easily to control traffic moving in and out of the city.[108] An unusually large number of very worn late Roman coins (including a *siliqua* of Constantine III, c. 407–11), a North African ceramic lamp (c. 395–420), fragments from late Roman glass vessels, and bronze accessories (pins, buckles, a bracelet) signify economic activity continuing at Silchester for much of the fifth century.[109]

If we look at the material evidence for the fifth and sixth centuries in Silchester, apart from the Roman structures, we see a noticeably "Celtic" element asserting itself. Along with Roman metalwork of late-fourth- or early-fifth-century date, there is a relative abundance of pins and penannular brooches whose affinities are Irish and Scottish. Along with this evidence there was found, in a Roman well, a tombstone inscribed with Ogam characters commemorating one EBICATOS in Irish text.[110] This figure has been seen as an Irish pilgrim or mercenary, and his tombstone has been assigned various dates from c. 450 to 700.[111] It is by far the most easterly find of an Ogam inscription in Britain, and contrasts with the early Saxon material found at nearby towns like Winchester and Dorchester-on-Thames. The few Saxon artifacts found at Silchester belong to the seventh century and later.[112]

Fitting into the notion that Silchester was a "Saxon-free zone" during the fifth and sixth centuries is a series of dikes that surround the town, the most substantial of the earthworks is known as Grim's Bank. It was first proposed that Grim's Bank was constructed after the battle of Badon Hill (c. 500) as a boundary between Briton and Saxon lands. This view has now been altered a bit, some preferring a date of c. 450 and seeing the dikes as the boundary of a British kingdom—a sub-Roman *civitas* of sorts—centered on Silchester.[113] This *civitas* likely survived as a center of British power up to the seventh century, when, as an abundance of Saxon finds in the area indicate, the character of the community must have changed. There are, it should be noted, no signs of widespread destruction at Calleva itself.[114] Silchester's transition from British to Saxon control appears to have been both late and nontraumatic.

We can see something of this transition at the Roman town of WALL (Letocetum) in Staffordshire. This small fortified town is one of five situated along Watling Street forming what was likely a chain of *burgi* along the Welsh frontier.[115] Coinage from stray finds and excavations runs down to the end of Roman occupation, and a single bronze bowl bearing a Chi-Rho suggests possible Christian activity.[116] Although no fifth-century artifacts have been found at Wall, there is some literary evidence for sub-Roman occupation. Gildas mentions that there were twenty-eight cities in sub-Roman Britain, though he does not list them; the *Historia Brittonum* does list them, and includes Wall (Cair Luitcoyt) among the likes of London and Dumbarton.[117] "Nennius" (or the original compiler of the *Historia*), writing in Wales in the ninth century, is probably listing ancient settlements thought to have been important—or whose names were still known—in his day.[118] This is verified by a mention of a raid on Wall (Caer Luydcoed) in an early Welsh poem called *Marwnad Cynddylan* (The lament of Cynddylan).[119] Shown to date from the seventh century, the poem describes a raid in which neither the bishop nor "the book-holding monks" were spared, suggesting the presence of an organized Christian community in Wall at that date.[120] The English were clearly in control of the area by the mid–seventh century, when a see was established at nearby Lichfield.[121]

Not much is know about another Roman small town on the Welsh border, WORCESTER. The only Roman structure identified at Worcester is a circular building thought to be a temple or shrine, while traces of timber-framed buildings have been excavated in nearby Sidbury. The only traces of the town's fortifications are northern and eastern sections of a ditch that originally formed a circuit. It seems likely that for the Saxons to have named their settlement Weogornceaster, "Roman walled town of the people called *Weogora*," some form of these defenses must have been standing when they arrived.[122] Worcester has produced some fourth-century coins and pottery and unbroken glass vessels, but the most dramatic sub-Roman discovery is related to a likely Christian presence in the city (see the discussion below).

Nearby WROXETER (Viroconium Cornoviorum) was Roman Britain's fourth largest city, and is relatively well-preserved because no Anglo-Saxon or later town developed on the site. The Cornovii maintained a fortress nearby, on top of the Wrekin, with scattered farmsteads below, but after the Roman conquest a civil settlement grew up around the early legionary fortress built on a plateau overlooking the Severn. After the legions withdrew, Wroxeter became a *civitas* capital, and by the end of the second century defenses were built surrounding a population of several thousand. The emperor Hadrian's visit to Britain resulted in funds to build a forum and basilica complex for Wroxeter, which grew into a prosperous commercial center. Though Wroxeter no longer quartered a legion, the Cornovii continued to raise a militia on their own (some of which was absorbed into the regular army as *Coh. I Cornoviorum*), showing an interest and ability to protect themselves and their town.[123]

Wroxeter is also the Roman site that has yielded the most archaeological evidence for occupation and activity during the sub-Roman period. Philip Barker's meticulous excavations have revealed, in detail, the phases of repair and reconstruction that made Wroxeter a thriving city in the fifth century, while its fellow cities were in sharp decline.

Signs of decline at Wroxeter begin to appear at the beginning of the fourth century, when the forum was destroyed and the main baths suite went out of use (though the *frigidarium* quite possibly continued to be used).[124] The forum was still used as an open market, but civil activity gradually moved to the basilica in the baths complex. This building had been refloored in the late third century, repaired, then refloored three more times up to 375.[125] At this point it ceased to have a public function, and instead was turned into an industrial complex with ramshackle buildings, pits, and a furnace constructed in the interior. Again the floor showed wear, and associated coins date this activity to c. 388–92.

The builder's yard did not last long, however, for it too seems to have been cleared by about 402. At this time the basilica's roof and clerestory were carefully removed, along with all interior walls and columns, leaving an empty shell. The pits in the floor were filled, and some of the tile was used to make a path, presumably to give pedestrians safe passageway through the area.[126] This phase appears to have lasted only a short while after the coin series ends.[127]

For most cities of Roman Britain, this would have been the last evidence of the final chapter of occupation. But at Wroxeter, remarkably, we have evidence that construction resumed in this period, in not one but two subsequent phases. The middle of the fifth century witnessed a major redevelopment on this site (see Fig. 14), most accurately described by the excavators themselves:

Fig. 14. Visible remains of the baths basilica, Wroxeter

Much of the north wall of the basilica was demolished and dug out in places to well below floor level, and tons of rubble were laid down as building platforms. . . . It formed the foundation for a large timber-framed two-storied winged house, perhaps with towers, a verandah and central portico. . . . The building covered about half of the nave and stretched [to about 125 feet long and 52 feet wide]. . . . On its western side, a long thin mortar and rubble platform marked a second building, [extending about 80 feet], which appears to have been something like a *loggia*: solid-walled on the north side and columned on the south. To the east . . . a substantial smaller building was put up against the eastern wall of the basilica. Its structure was most unusual for this phase in that it was built of mortered stone. . . . On the western side [of the former south aisle], five regular platforms of rubble 8 m × 2.5 m . . . carried buildings leaning against the south wall of the basilica . . . but the rest of the aisle was clear of any buildings leaving the entrance to the *frigidarium* accessible. . . . One possible use [of the *frigidarium*] might have been as a small church or chapel or, since some charred grain was found in this room . . . it may have been used as a granary. . . .

On the western portico, a series of buildings was constructed around the main doorway. . . . Each of these buildings was reconstructed several times during the lifetime of [the timber hall]. A further building was constructed at the junction of the west and north porticos.

The east-west street, now saw some remarkable, if not unique, modifications. . . . Both ends of this "gravel street" were revetted and had ramps or steps to provide pedestrian access. . . . North of the gravel street, the southern frontage . . . was covered by a range of timber buildings which seem to have been either shops or residences. Some were placed long side onto the street, others had impressive porticoed facades. Nearly all were rebuilt at least once.[128]

These impressive structures have been described as "the last classically inspired buildings [built] in Britain" before the eighteenth century.[129] But their interpretation is difficult. Though the complex has "the hallmarks of Roman public works, only constructed with timber,"[130] the excavators see it more as a villa than as a public building, perhaps the residence of a *tyrannus* like Vortigern.[131] "Thus we have [at Wroxeter] a powerful character," agrees Graham Webster, "building himself a kind of country mansion in the middle of the city, surrounded with small buildings, which are either stables or . . . houses for his retainers."[132] Alternatively, the smaller timber structures may indeed have been shops lining a covered street, which one archaeologist has likened to a modern shopping mall.[133]

After an unknown period of use, these elaborate structures were deliberately dismantled and removed, and two smaller buildings were constructed at the western end of the basilica. The excavators have suggested 550 for this construction, though no strictly datable materials have been found.[134] Finally, an inhumation burial was dug into the now-abandoned area just south of one of the buildings. Radiocarbon dating of the remains has yielded a date of 610 ± 60.[135]

Associated coinage gives a *terminus post quem* of c. 375–402 for the early phases of the Wroxeter rebuilding, while the radiocarbon determinations give a date of around 600 for the possible abandonment of the site.[136] But can we be more precise about the dating of the extensive rebuilding in the middle phase? A single find of imported pottery, an amphora (probably carrying wine) from Gaza, links Wroxeter with similar finds at London and Cadbury-Congresbury,[137] but a late-fifth- or early-sixth-century date is the only one yet offered. Most intriguing of all is the memorial stone, found just outside the Wroxeter defenses, whose inscription commemorates an Irishman named Cunorix.[138] Kenneth Jackson dated the inscription to the late fifth century, and many have seen this Cunorix as an Irish mercenary hired to protect the city.[139] Margaret Gelling has an alternative theory: "I find it easier to think of Cunorix as a guest, a high-ranking visitor to a British court, whose hosts had sufficient courtesy and just sufficient literacy to give him a memorial in the style appropriate to his nationality. This stone seems to me a strong piece of evidence for the maintenance of a high-status sub-Roman lifestyle at Wroxeter far into the fifth century, probably in peaceful conditions."[140]

What is evident, and not theory, is that sub-Roman Wroxeter was a town worth protecting, with new structures and imported goods worthy of a local lord and his guests. It was not destroyed by violence, but instead carefully dismantled, its British inhabitants likely relocating to a more defensible place, like Berth at Baschurch or their ancestral home, the Wrekin, or else to the new settlement at Shrewsbury.[141]

Like the Welsh border, the North also produced cities, like LINCOLN, that maintained their military character. The Colonia Domitiana Lindensium, or Lindum, succeeded an earlier legionary fortress at Lincoln. Very little is known about the streets and buildings of the *colonia*, which lies beneath the medieval castle and cathedral in the heart of the modern city. (See, however, the still-in-use double archway at Lincoln's north gate: Fig. 15). Thus, most conclusions about sub-Roman Lincoln have been drawn according to what has not been found rather than what has.

Wacher points out that there are remarkably few zoomorphic buckles and fittings of the late Roman army in all of Lincolnshire, and only one in Lincoln itself.[142] There are no early Anglo-Saxon settlements attested in or near Lindum (the closest is some two miles north of the modern city limit), and a sixth-century king of Lindsey had an unmistakably British name—Caedbaed.[143] When an Anglian settlement finally appeared at Lincoln in the late seventh century, Bede tells us that the ruler in the area was a *praefectus Lindocolinae civitatis,* giving the British form (*Lindocolina*) of the city's name.[144]

Excavations at Lincoln have revealed some positive evidence for survival of occupation into the sub-Roman period. Street surfaces within the city were repaired in the fifth century, and stray finds of imported Mediterranean pottery and a pin of "Celtic" design could prolong occupation into the sixth century or later.[145] Evidence of a possible Christian community at Lincoln comes from the courtyard area at the forum. There, beneath the graveyard of a seventh-century Anglian church, lay other burials, which have yielded

Fig. 15. The Newport Arch, Roman Lincoln's north gate

radiocarbon dates centering in the fifth century.[146] It has been suggested that a timber church, destroyed by the construction of the Anglian stone church, was built on this site c. 400, with a sub-Roman cemetery lying close to its walls.[147]

There is no doubt that another northern *colonia,* YORK (Eburacum), enjoyed a special status among Romano-British cities in the third and fourth centuries. This former legionary fortress was used as headquarters for the campaigning emperors Septimius Severus and Constantius Chlorus, both of whom died in the city. York also saw the elevation of Constantine I, and was rewarded with impressive walls and fortifications (see Fig. 3).

Excavations in York have so far concentrated on the military and defenses; we know little about its public and domestic buildings. The best evidence for fifth-century occupation comes from the headquarters building (*principia*) and the legionary bathhouse.[148] The *principia,* in fact, remained intact and in use until it was destroyed by fire in the early seventh century or later.[149] York's early-third-century north gate, the Newport Arch, is to this day intact.[150] A rise in the water level in the late fourth century, however, caused severe flooding in York, resulting in the destruction of much of the wharves and harbor facilities.[151] York probably did not survive as a "center of population," writes James Campbell, but it did survive as a "center of authority."[152] In 601, Pope Gregory the Great instructed Augustine to send to York a bishop, who would become the metropolitan of "that city and province."[153] When the bishop Paulinus arrived in York in c. 625, it was part of the Anglian kingdom of Edwin of Northumbria, who is said to "have brought under his sway all the territories inhabited by the Britons."[154]

A good candidate for Roman Britain's "last city" is CARLISLE (Luguvalium), just inside the northern frontier. Carlisle was elevated to the status of *civitas* capital rather late, perhaps by Caracalla in the third century. By the fourth century, Carlisle was part of the defense system of Hadrian's Wall, possibly even its headquarters.[155] Although excavation has not been extensive here, Carlisle does show some signs of sub-Roman occupation. Excavation at Blackfriars Street has revealed two Roman masonry buildings that were reconstructed in timber and occupied into the early fifth century.[156] After a time these were abandoned and replaced by one "large hall-like building . . . constructed on a completely different alignment, which even ignored the Roman street lines."[157] At Scotch Street, excavators have uncovered a large town house, complete with underfloor heating, that was constructed in the last quarter of the fourth century.[158] Though the hypocaust went out of use by the beginning of the fifth century, the building showed signs of continued use and wear.[159] Evidence of sixth-century occupation is slim, however, despite the fact that Carlisle has long been considered to have been the administrative center of the British kingdom of Rheged.[160]

In light of the preceding survey, a few general remarks can now be made about the towns of sub-Roman Britain, with more discussion on this subject to follow in the next chapter. It should be immediately apparent that nearly every major urban center (*colonia, civitas* capital, *municipium*) in Roman Britain has shown some signs of survival into the fifth century, while some give evidence of sixth-century continuity as well (compare Figs. 6 and 7). This should surprise anyone who has read the literature—both historical and archaeological—for Roman Britain; much of the evidence has seemingly eluded participants in the "urban continuity" debate.[161] With the exception of Wroxeter, however, the evidence has not taken the form of monumental structures. Neither do we see entirely new urban settlements appearing in the fifth or sixth centuries. Sub-Roman Britain should not, then, be characterized as an urban society, certainly not in comparison to the second and third centuries. But what we must lay to rest is the myth that this was a completely rural landscape with no towns, thus making easier the English conquest. Cities, as Gildas would say, were not what they used to be, but they were there, nonetheless; and many more wait to be discovered.[162]

Forts

Some of Roman Britain's most spectacular remains are its fortresses, reminding us that Britannia grew up from a military occupation and struggled against rebellious natives for over a century (much longer if we consider the Caledonians/Picts of the North). Since so many defensive structures remain visible today, we might expect to find evidence of their continued use by sub-Roman Britons. This is indeed the case, as examination of the former legionary fortresses, the forts of Hadrian's Wall and the Saxon Shore, and the numerous smaller forts in Wales and the North (Fig. 16) makes clear.

The legionary fortress at CAERLEON (Isca) was systematically dismantled after its legion was removed c. 260. Thereafter civilian occupation continued in Caerleon until at least 375, and an early Christian tradition in the city is suggested by the literary sources.[163] Sometime after 354, two round-ended buildings were constructed over the *via vicinaria* and the verandah of the barrack blocks (Fig. 17).[164] One building, which was originally 7.2 m × 4.5 m, had "two post holes flanking a *tegula* which had been reused as part of a threshold," stones walls (one of which concealed a late military bronze belt fitting) and partitions, and a floor of well-laid rubble paving.[165] Inserted under the paved floor was a single female inhumation burial, the skeletal remains yielding a radiocarbon date of c. 660–940.[166] "The need for extra buildings in a vernacular style may imply," according to the excavators, "a considerable population for Caerleon during the earlier part of the [medieval] period."[167] Gerald of Wales, writing in the twelfth century, described baths, temples, water conduits, hypocausts, and an amphitheater (Fig. 18), all of which were still standing at Caerleon in his day.[168]

The Roman legionary fortress at CHESTER (Deva) was altered dramatically at the end of the third century, when its barracks were completely demolished. The Chester legion, *legio XX Valeria Victrix,* does not appear in the *Notitia Dignitatum,* and coinage inside the fortress seems to have run out by about 373.[169] Recent excavation has shown, however, that the administrative buildings at the center of the fortress remained in use after the barracks were demolished, and were even refurbished in the fourth century.[170] T. J. Strickland sees fourth-century Chester as "purely an administrative centre, surrounded by acres of [paved] open space, where a field army, when it did eventually come to base, could occasionally bivouac."[171]

It is possible that Chester continued in this administrative role even after the troop withdrawals of the early fifth century. When buildings were destroyed in the third and fourth centuries, their stone was often used for

Fig. 16. Roman forts occupied in sub-Roman Britain

Fig. 17. The barrack blocks at Roman Caerleon

Fig. 18. The Roman amphitheater at Caerleon

street paving, and excavation has shown that these subsequent road surfaces (late fourth or early fifth century) were worn smooth.[172] At the Abbey Green site, excavators uncovered a large (11 m × 5 m) timber-framed building constructed on drystone sleeper walls with a gravel and flagged floor.[173] This building, aligned along the Roman street, apparently underwent several modifications in the fifth and sixth centuries, datable by the presence of amphoras and red color-coated vessels imported from the Mediterranean.[174] Higham sees the imported pottery as a sign that Chester's port was still in operation, a flourishing church in the city causing a demand for wine and oil.[175]

The Laings interpret all of this as evidence that Chester was the sub-Roman civil administrative center of the kingdom of Powys.[176] Although, as yet, the archaeological evidence of sub-Roman occupation in Chester is sparse,[177] the literary evidence amply testifies to a continuing British presence. Bede records two notable events occurring in or near the city at the turn of the seventh century. The first is a council of Welsh church leaders c. 601 called in response to Augustine's demands for British obeisance.[178] After the Britons rejected the new archbishop of Canterbury, Bede records (gleefully) the destruction of a British army, along with 1,200 British monks, at the Battle of Chester (*ad civitatem Legionum*) in 615.[179] "Nennius," a century later, lists Chester (*in urbe Legionis*) as the site of Arthur's ninth battle against the Saxons in the sixth century.[180] Chester has also been suggested as the base from which Saint Germanus set out to win the Alleluia Victory in 429.[181]

While some of the remains of these legionary fortresses can still be seen today, HADRIAN'S WALL is without a doubt the largest and most dramatic military monument that has survived from Roman Britain (Fig. 19). Stretching over seventy miles from coast to coast, the Wall was and is a remarkable engineering feat and testifies to the military genius of the Roman Empire. Although Agricola pushed the legions deep into Scotland after A.D. 70, the legions had to fall back on a makeshift frontier at the Stanegate road. In 122, the emperor Hadrian judged this frontier too vulnerable and ordered the construction of a continuous stone wall with accompanying forts, milecastles, and turrets. Three legions and thousands of non-Roman laborers built Hadrian's Wall, which stood not as a physical limit of Roman influence in Britain, but as an aggressive statement of military might to the tribes to the north that Rome continually sought to suppress.[182]

The notion that the forts along Hadrian's Wall were abandoned following the troop withdrawals of Magnus Maximus, Stilicho, and Constantine III was accepted for a long time. Now it is certain that the Wall was not abandoned, for excavation is revealing plentiful evidence of occupation continuing at the Wall forts after new coinage ceased to arrive in the early fifth century.[183] In fact, archaeologists have recently discovered inside some of the forts new timber structures that indicate occupation into the sixth century and beyond.

The evidence for sub-Roman activity along Hadrian's Wall needs to be assessed by looking first at the forts individually, following their placement from west to east (see Fig. 16). Castlesteads (Camboglanna) is unique among the Wall forts in being built between the Wall and its rear vallum. The sole piece of sub-Roman evidence from Castlesteads is an inscribed stone identified by Ralegh Radford and thought to be of sixth-century date.[184]

The fort of Birdoswald (Banna) was built to guard the Irthing bridge crossing. Recent excavations here have revealed the reuse of Roman military buildings as domestic structures in the fifth century, associated with the latest Romano-British pottery found in northern Britain.[185] Two Roman granaries were, in their final stages, reconstructed and used for human occupation (see Fig. 20). One of these new structures—termed "halls" by the excavators—was a modification of the south granary, while the other,

Fig. 19. Hadrian's Wall at Walltown Crags

built after the north granary had collapsed, partly overlay the granary and partly overlay the adjacent Roman road.[186] Under the floor of the south granary was a fill of earth and rubbish containing the Romano-British pottery (Huntcliff and Crambeck wares, dating to the late fourth to fifth centuries), while a hearth found at one end of this "hall" contained a Roman gold-and-glass earring (later fourth century). Traces of fifth-century British metalwork were also uncovered, and on the other side of the fort an "Anglian" pin and brooch (eighth century) was found in the 1950s.[187]

Chesterholm (Vindolanda) is the sight of several forts, the first timber fort being part of the old Stanegate frontier system. An earthen bank piled against the fort wall suggests the possibility of post-Roman fortifications. Evidence for internal occupation in the sub-Roman period includes an "Anglo-Saxon"-style annular brooch (sixth century?) and a fifth- or sixth-century penannular brooch, both found within the fort.[188] Outside the fort was found an inscribed tombstone (dated late fifth or early sixth century) which commemorates the death of one Brigomaglos.[189] Thus, at Chesterholm we have a curious mixture of Romano-British and Germanic elements within the same community, suggesting the possible presence of Germanic mercenaries.

Housesteads (Vercovicium) is the best-preserved fort on Hadrian's Wall. A seemingly prosperous *vicus,* with numerous shops and temples, grew up

Fig. 20. Foundations of the granary at Birdoswald, Hadrian's Wall

to the south and east of the fort. A defensive earthen bank was apparently built after the fort's stone walls, and evidence of internal occupation includes sixth-century "Anglo-Saxon" pottery and metalwork.[190] It has also been suggested that some of the population of both Housesteads and Chesterholm relocated inside the nearby Iron Age hillfort at Barcombe, which seems to preserve part of the name Vercovicium.[191]

Chesters (Cilurnum) was a bridgehead fort guarding the point where the Wall crosses the North Tyne River. Post-Roman occupation inside the fort is indicated by an "Anglo-Saxon" annular brooch of the sixth or seventh century.[192]

Corbridge (Corstopitum/Coriosopitum), a fort two miles south of the Wall, dates back to the first century. Like Housesteads, a large and prosperous *vicus* grew up around the stone-walled fortress. The main street of the town received its last resurfacing in the latter half of the fourth century (Fig. 21), and a hoard of forty-eight gold coins found in Corbridge dates to this period.[193] Other coin finds (nine coins of Arcadius and Honorius) show that the town was occupied at least to the end of the fourth century.[194] Fifth- and sixth-century finds within the fort include "Anglo-Saxon" pottery and brooches.[195]

Benwell (Condercum) was named by its Roman inhabitants "The Place

Fig. 21. Resurfaced main street at Corbridge, Northumbria

with a Fine View." Sixth-century "Anglo-Saxon" glass and metalwork was found near the fort.[196]

South Shields (Arbeia) is the easternmost fort on the Wall, built to protect supplies entering the mouth of the River Tyne. Around 400, the southwest gate went out of use, and a large ditch was dug in front of it.[197] Subsequent to this, the ditch was filled in, a new approach road was laid, and the gate—by this time in ruins—was replaced by a new gate passage constructed in timber. Associated finds include a gold *solidus* of Magnus Maximus, which has been dated to 388,[198] and an "Anglo-Saxon" spearhead.[199] Outside the fort was a small inhumation cemetery, possibly fifth- or sixth-century.[200]

Other miscellaneous finds from the Wall include an "Anglo-Saxon" spearhead from Carvoran (Magnis), and a hoard of late Roman coins (including one of Honorius) thrown as a votive offering into Coventina's Well at Carrawburgh (Brocolitia).[201]

If, as it thus appears from the physical evidence,[202] the Wall was not completely abandoned when coin payments stopped arriving after 410, what became of the soldiers stationed there? According to David Breeze and Brian Dobson, "we must accept that the soldiers of the Wall returned to the soil from which they had sprung," that is, to the British communities into which they had been born or had married.[203] In support of this view, Michael Jones has pointed out that, from the early third century onward, the assignation of units to Wall forts remained remarkably stable, resulting in a stagnation that may have harmed their military effectiveness while strengthening the soldiers' ties to local communities.[204] Some soldiers undoubtedly remained as paid protectors of the northern *vici*, while others would have gravitated toward the post-Roman political and military powers of the north: Rheged, Strathclyde, and Manau Gododdin.[205]

Kenneth Dark has recently surveyed the fifth- and sixth-century evidence from the Wall and has developed an interesting scenario. He sees the timber halls, inscribed tombstones, and post-Roman defenses as secular high-status British reuse of the Wall forts, perhaps as a continuation or revival of the command of the *dux Britanniarum*.[206] The presence of early Anglo-Saxon weapons within these Romano-British settlements he interprets as a sign that the Britons were hiring Germanic mercenaries (as indeed Gildas says they were doing) while continuing to live in the nearby towns of Corbridge and Carlisle.[207] Michael Jones similarly envisions military occupation continuing along the Wall until at least the mid–fifth century, though in a native British context during their wars against the northern barbarians.[208] In the middle of the sixth century, Procopius recites the story (perhaps heard from Anglo-Saxons in a Frankish embassy to Constantinople) that the Wall had become a barrier between the living and the dead in Britain.[209] This would have had little to do with the political reality of northern Britain, for by then both British and Anglian kingdoms were straddling the Wall in their heroic tug-of-war that captivated historian (Bede) and poet (Aneirin) alike.

Such a tug-of-war likely occurred as well along the SAXON SHORE, though at an earlier date and with neither bard nor historian to record it. Slight evidence, however, has survived in the archaeological record for some of the Saxon Shore forts. At Portchester (Portus Adurni), as at many of the Wall forts, a civilian population grew alongside the military presence. Occupation within the walls was intensive in the fourth century and continued at least into the early fifth century.[210] It is not yet clear whether this fifth-century occupation was the continuation of the military community or a new settlement.[211] Cunliffe's excavations in the 1960s and 1970s revealed what he considered a strong "Germanic" presence at Portchester. Continental pottery, Frankish jewelry, and *Grubenhäuser* were found alongside the Roman finds inside the walls of the fort.[212] Cunliffe interpreted these as clear signs of a settled Germanic detachment (*laeti?*) who maintained some contacts with the Continent and shared space inside the fort with the sub-Roman Britons.[213]

Richborough (Rutupiae, "muddy waters") was once one of Roman Britain's main south-coast ports, welcoming such visitors as Claudius and Count Theodosius. Though it once guarded the southern approach to the Wantsum Channel, which separated the Isle of Thanet from the rest of Kent, changing water levels have now left it some four kilometers from the sea. Excavations in the early part of this century uncovered an exceptional number of Roman coins of the House of Theodosius, which account for 45 percent of all coinage found within the fort.[214] The coins, along with other late Roman military metalwork recovered, indicate that Richborough was one of the last places in Roman Britain to have been held in full military strength.[215]

The walls of nearly all of the Saxon Shore forts remained standing in the post-Roman period and were used to defend subsequent secular and ecclesiastical occupants (see the discussion below). The high walls and corner towers of Burgh Castle (Gariannum/Gariannonum), for example, were later converted by the Normans into a motte-and-bailey castle, and still stand majestically today (Fig. 22), as does most of the wall at Pevensey (Anderitum). So too the *pharos*, or lighthouse, which stands next to the Saxon church inside Dover Castle. Dover (Dubris), a Saxon Shore fort that succeeded an earlier *classis Britannica* fort, has yielded a variety of occupational evidence, including a Roman house with painted floors and walls, timber buildings and huts also of Roman date, and possible *Grubenhäuser.*[216] In the North a series of signal stations, established by Count Theodosius to guard the Yorkshire coast, seem not to have survived seaborne raiding in the early fifth century.[217]

The Welsh coast and Bristol Channel settlements also required protection—probably from Irish raiding—in the early fifth century. Excavation at ABERFFRAW, on Anglesey, revealed what appear to be—because of associated pottery—a late Roman auxiliary fort. Its stone rampart was rebuilt, according to the excavator, possibly as a *ballista* platform, "in the fifth or sixth centuries by the founders of what was to be one of Gwynedd's most successful dynasties."[218] Nancy Edwards does not believe that Aberffraw was a Roman fort, but rather that its construction was wholly the work of the kings of Gwynedd in the fifth century.[219] An inscribed lead coffin, bearing the Alpha and Omega (and possibly the Chi-Rho) symbols, suggests a wealthy Christian community in early post-Roman Anglesey.[220]

Fig. 22. Corner tower of Burgh Castle, on the Saxon Shore

The auxiliary fort at CAERNARVON (Segontium), which underwent extensive internal modifications in the fourth century, appears to have been manned up to about 410 (or that time when payment failed to reach the frontier).[221] Sub-Roman activity is indicated by a new sentry box built in the southeast guardroom of the southwest gateway, and two penannular brooches dating stylistically to the fifth century.[222] An early medieval church was founded just outside of Segontium, at Llanbeblig, and ordered government in this area is indicated by terms like *civis* and *magistratus* inscribed on the sixth-century Penmachno stones.[223]

At BINCHESTER (Vinovia/Vinovium), a fort just south of Hadrian's Wall, occupation continued after the introduction of the latest coins (of Magnentius, 350–53) and of pottery from the Crambeck kilns (conventionally dated post-370).[224] The *praetorium* had an undisturbed rubbish deposit in its yard, suggesting that it decayed naturally and was possibly in use in the fifth century.[225] But there was a change in the character of occupation during this period, as military buildings were put to nonmilitary purposes. By the sixth century, "Anglo-Saxon" burials and artifacts begin to appear.[226]

The *vicus* that grew up inside the Roman fortress at CATTERICK (Cataractonium) shows strong signs of continued occupation in the fifth century. One building had an apse added to its west end in the last decades of the fourth century. "This apsidial building remained in use long enough for occupation material to collect on its floors," write Barry Burnham and John Wacher, "after which it fell into decay, with soil accumulating around its walls and over its floor."[227] Some time later a timber-framed house was built on top of the earlier stone building, its walls on a different alignment; this timber construction must (on stratigraphic grounds) be attributed to the fifth century. Other timber structures share similar structural features and would appear to be of the same phase.[228] "It would appear that a substantial Romano-British settlement still existed at Catterick," write Burnham and Wacher, "sheltered by its massive walls, at least in the first part of the century."[229] But can we extend this "Romano-British" occupation to the late sixth century and the battle of Catraeth? The poems of Taliesin seem to equate Catterick with Catraeth, the seat of King Urien of Rheged and the destination of the warriors in the *Gododdin* of Aneirin.[230] Alcock has questioned this identification of Catterick with the British court of Urien, pointing out the early Saxon material (a *Grubenhäus*, pottery, brooches, and assorted military items) found in and around the *vicus*, which has produced no identifiable "British" items of the sixth and later centuries.[231] While both Alcock and Wacher agree that Catterick is most likely the site of the battle of Catraeth, it is less clear when this settlement passed from British to Anglian hands.

The Roman fort of RAVENGLASS (Glannoventa) in Cumbria has yielded an unusually large amount of late-fourth-century pottery, probably representing several hundred vessels.[232] Pottery and coinage bring the occupation at Ravenglass most likely to the early fifth century, when it may have fitted into a "localized system of defense."[233] Ravenglass has also been suggested as a candidate for the hometown of Saint Patrick, *Glannoventa* possibly being corrupted as *Banna Venta*.[234]

It should not surprise us that Roman fortifications, built to withstand siege, should survive into the sub-Roman period (and beyond) and attract both Britons and Saxons alike. The British occupation of these sites appears mostly to be a continuation of the Romano-British civilian settlements, the *vici*, that invariably surrounded Roman forts. In some cases, however, we see the work of a diligent bishop or abbot finding a safe home for his Christian community behind the high walls of a seemingly abandoned fort (see the discussion below).

Rural Sites

Despite these signs of activity and occupation, Roman forts do not seem to be the most popular defensive option for the sub-Roman Britons. Rather, it is the rural settlements, enclosed by walls and/or making use of natural protection, that have yielded the most evidence of British activity in the later fifth and sixth centuries (Fig. 23). These sites, often given the generic label "hillforts," are entirely pre-Roman in inspiration, and indeed many sub-Roman hillforts had Bronze and Iron Age occupations as well. The following survey considers these hillforts along with other types of rural sites, including the few Roman *villae* that survived Britain's break with the empire.

Somerset is the county with the most abundant evidence of this nature, and GLASTONBURY perhaps is the richest city. Glastonbury has long been the focal point of Arthurian and early Christian tradition. The two features that have received the most attention are Glastonbury Abbey, one of Britain's most magnificent pre-Reformation religious houses, and Glastonbury Tor, an enigmatic terraced hill that rises over five hundred feet above the Somerset plains. The Tor has yielded the strongest evidence for sub-Roman occupa-

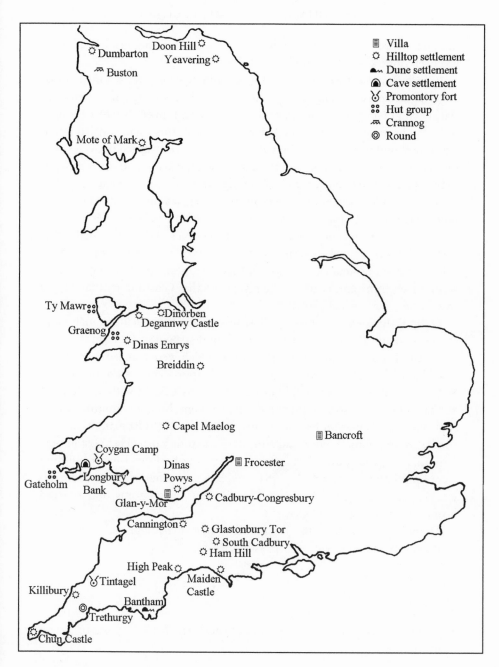

Fig. 23. Rural sites in sub-Roman Britain

tion, but neither area has been fully excavated, and little archaeological work has been done since the 1960s.

Ralegh Radford's excavations at Glastonbury Abbey were aimed at discovering the earliest religious activity on the site. An ancient cemetery of slab-lined graves was found near the remains of a timber structure thought to be the original Church of St. Mary. Along with this small wattled building were found postholes interpreted as the remains of wattled oratories, and the entire area was bounded on the east by a great bank and ditch thought to be a monastic *vallum*. Though no dating evidence was found at the abbey, these features lay beneath later Saxon structures, leading Radford to interpret the site as a "Celtic" monastery, based on Irish parallels.[235] More-recent excavation on the precinct ditch uncovered wooden stakes that yielded radiocarbon determinations centering on the late sixth and seventh centuries.[236] Also found in this area was an eastern Mediterranean copper censer, of late-sixth- or seventh-century date, which suggests that Glastonbury maintained Byzantine ecclesiastical contacts.[237]

Philip Rahtz's excavations on Glastonbury Tor have yielded much more evidence of sub-Roman occupation. He found structures both on the summit of the Tor and on the terrace platforms, which were reached in medieval times by a series of steps cut into the bedrock approaching from the west.[238] Slight remains of wooden buildings were found associated with hundreds of animal bones (representing prepared joints of ham, beef, and mutton), charcoal, and burnt stones. A fenced-in eastern hollow yielded Roman tile, a bone needle, an iron lamp holder, and a mysterious stone cairn. The most important area was the south platform, where traces of a large timber building were found along with two hearths, crucibles and other evidence of metalworking, a dozen pieces of imported Mediterranean amphoras, and a carved bronze head (stylistically "Celtic").

Though the finds from the Tor are rich, their interpretation is rather difficult. Rahtz came up with four possibilities:

1. A pagan shrine.
2. A Christian hermitage.
3. The stronghold of a petty chieftain.
4. A defensive signal station, warning other British settlements of Saxon incursions.

Two north-south aligned graves found on the Tor might support the first explanation, but there is no evidence of a late Roman temple at Glastonbury.[239]

Though the early Christian associations with Glastonbury are many, Rahtz at first ruled out a Celtic monastery or hermitage because the quantity of meat bones seemed contrary to the ascetic lifestyle of "Celtic" monks.[240] Because of the metalworking and Mediterranean imports, Rahtz favored the third interpretation, that the Tor was the fortress of a British chieftain, comparable to the craggy palaces of Dumbarton Rock and Dunadd.[241]

However, others have persisted in preferring the monastic interpretation for the Tor occupation.[242] Evidence of meat eating (i.e., animal bones) has since been found at such monastic sites as Iona and Whithorn, and now Rahtz himself is reconsidering the monastic model.[243] The Tor may then be the earliest attested eremitic monastic site in Britain, and the hermitage may later have been brought under the control of the more accessible abbey.[244] When the new rulers of Wessex began to patronize the abbey in the seventh century, Glastonbury had long been venerated as a Christian holy site.[245]

The hill at SOUTH CADBURY, sometimes called South Cadbury Castle and Cadbury-Camelot, was the site of one of the most publicized (and published) British excavations of the 1960s. Its association with the fabled court of King Arthur was made by two prominent Tudor antiquarians—John Leland and William Camden—in the sixteenth century, disregarding other sites traditionally associated with Arthur (e.g., Celliwic, Caerleon, Winchester) and the fact that "Camelot" was invented by Chrétien de Troyes or his successors in the twelfth and thirteenth centuries.[246] However, when plowing on the hill in the 1950s turned up sherds of late Roman Mediterranean pottery, large-scale excavations soon commenced under the direction of Leslie Alcock, who had recently conducted a precedent-setting excavation of the hillfort at Dinas Powys (see below).

South Cadbury and Dinas Powys, both heavily fortified hilltop settlements, have yielded strong evidence of sixth-century activity. Other factors, however, set South Cadbury apart from the Dinas Powys model. Most obvious is the sheer size of the South Cadbury hill: over five hundred feet high, with steep sides defended by five massive ramparts, enclosing a plateau of about eighteen acres (Fig. 24). Ian Burrow has estimated that it would have taken a force of about 870 men to defend and maintain the ramparts alone, nearly twice the number estimated for the comparably sized Cadbury-Congresbury hillfort (see below).[247] Also of significance is the extended sequence of activity at South Cadbury, noted by Alcock as one of the longest stratified sequences in western Europe.[248] Neolithic activity (beginning about 4500 B.C.) is indicated by pottery, flints, and both human and animal bones.

A native farmstead occupied in the late Bronze Age (eighth century B.C.) fell to Iron Age invaders in the sixth or seventh century B.C., when the first artificial ramparts were constructed. The Iron Age occupation was brought to a violent end shortly after the Roman invasion of A.D. 43, presumably during the campaigns of Vespasian, when the defenses were partly dismantled. Roman occupation (dated by coins, pottery, and military equipment) was slight until the third century, when a Romano-Celtic temple was constructed (out of timber) and frequently visited (coins range in date from 222–35 to 393–402). The defenses were repaired on a massive scale in the later fifth century, and timber structures were constructed in the interior, all associated with Mediterranean imports. After a long period of abandonment beginning c. 600, the fort became the site of a late Saxon *burg* and royal mint during the reign of Aethelred (beginning of the eleventh century), when the gateways were rebuilt in stone. Finally, after Cnut's accession in 1017 the *burg* was abandoned and the hilltop given up to cultivation.

What Alcock terms the "Arthurian" period of occupation, or Cadbury 11 (the fifth and sixth centuries A.D.), is dated by the abundant finds of imported pottery, including fine red bowls, Mediterranean amphoras, and gray bowls and mortars from the Bordeaux region. The quantity of sherds suggests a minimum vessel number comparable to that of Cadbury-Congresbury, and second only to Tintagel.[249] Sealed and scattered pottery was found in the postholes and wall trench of a rectangular structure on the summit of the hill. This building, about 19 m × 10 m, was interpreted by Alcock as the principal building of the fort, probably a feasting hall.[250] Other associated postholes suggest interior divisions and an antechamber. Such halls feature prominently in the poetry of the British Heroic Age, but only a few examples—notably Yeavering and Doon Hill (see below)—have been excavated and published.[251] Alcock, however, suggests that the model for the Cadbury hall was not the Germanic feasting hall but rather the aisled houses of villa complexes in late Roman Britain.[252] Though these were occasionally rebuilt in timber, a better model might be the massive timber building complexes constructed at the baths basilica in sub-Roman Wroxeter. Only one other pottery-dated structure was excavated at Cadbury 11, that of a small (4 m × 2 m) rectangular building near the northern door of the hall, which has been interpreted as a kitchen.[253] Finally, some of the smaller round houses previously attributed to the Iron Age may belong instead to Cadbury 11, with parallels at Cadbury-Congresbury and Buston (see below).[254]

Much of the imported pottery was found in association with the rebuilt defenses and the southwest gate. "The hill-top had been re-fortified with a

Fig. 24. Plateau and ramparts of South Cadbury hillfort

timber fighting platform," writes Alcock, "faced with dressed stone and anchored down with rubble."[255] Stone for the ramparts had been quarried from derelict Roman buildings and was reused unmortared in the non-Roman fashion of dry masonry. The absence of nails suggests wooden pegged joints were used, a somewhat sophisticated carpentry technique.[256] The timber gate tower constructed at the southwest gate was seemingly based on the simple Roman auxiliary-fort gate model, and showed signs of repair in the later sixth century.[257] It likely contained two double-leaved doors, an interior bridge, and possibly a light tower.[258] In all, the defensive circuit spans nearly twelve hundred meters, the same as the perimeter of the Iron Age fort. The size of the Cadbury defenses is without parallel among contemporary hillforts in Britain.

The size of South Cadbury's fortifications and the large quantity of imported pottery discovered there make it and Tintagel the two most significant sub-Roman occupation sites in the Southwest. It should be noted that only 6 percent of the hillfort's summit was excavated by Alcock's team, and future excavation is likely to turn up more of a variety of structural and artifactual evidence.

Less famous is the Somerset hillfort known as CADBURY-CONGRESBURY, or Cadcong, an Iron Age hillfort that was reoccupied in the late or post-Roman period. Around A.D. 400 new earthworks were constructed, including a bank dividing the hillfort into two parts and a linking entrance way.[259] These earthworks included both late Romano-British pottery and fifth- and sixth-century pottery imported from the Mediterranean, putting the reoccupation of Cadcong within the time frame 400–700.[260]

According to its excavators, Cadcong's defensive rampart "is not a major military work, with extensive use of timberframing or revetment (as at South Cadbury); but rather a flat platform on which turf or a light superstructure was piled."[261] However, traces of other defensive structures found at Cadcong, including bastions and watchtowers, argue for a more intensive fortified use. Burrow estimates the manpower needed to defend Cadcong and its inhabitants as between 400 and 650 men.[262]

But Cadcong's defenses are only part of the story. Several domestic buildings were discerned in excavation, as well as a gatehouse and a round house identified by the excavators as a possible shrine or temple.[263] Evidence of metalworking is abundant at Cadcong, which is also one of the sites that has yielded the largest numbers of imported Mediterranean amphoras.[264] By the sixth century, the residents of Cadcong had attained, in the opinion of the excavators, "high status, patronising craft-workers and having access to glass and ceramics from the Anglo-Saxon areas to the East, and from the Eastern Mediterranean."[265]

Still, there is much debate over the exact function of this hilltop settlement. Some of the possibilities are:

1. A regional "fair" site or marketplace, perhaps occupied only seasonally.[266]
2. A court for hosting an itinerant "overking."[267]
3. A monastic enclosure (St. Congar's monastery).[268]

There is no conclusive evidence for any of these possibilities. Until we have a better understanding of the reoccupation of hillforts in general, Cadcong is best left as a "high-status" site.[269]

Other contextual clues may present themselves, however, if we look at sub-Roman Somerset. P. J. Fowler believes that the inhabitants of Cadcong came from nearby Gatcombe, a walled villa and late Roman community.[270] This would parallel what Alcock has suggested for South Cadbury, that its sub-Roman inhabitants had migrated from nearby Ilchester (Lindinis).[271] Cadcong lies at the junction of three tribal kingdoms: the Dobunni, the Durotriges, and the Dumnonii. Given the intensive sub-Roman occupation of hillforts and other settlements in this area, these Britons may have been responsible for the construction of Wansdyke as a defensive border between their *civitates* and the encroaching Saxons.[272] The inhabitants of Cadcong seem to have enjoyed undisturbed peace until the late sixth or early seventh century, when the settlement declined and was finally abandoned.[273]

HAM HILL is one of the largest contour hillforts in Somerset and in Britain, with an oblong plateau enclosed by a circuit of defenses five kilometers in length. However, imprecise and poorly recorded excavations from 1907 to 1930 have only given slight illumination to probable LPRIA, Roman, and sub-Roman occupation. More-recent casual finds have yielded an abundance of Roman material, including pottery and several coin hoards.[274] A twelve-room Roman villa, associated with a coin series running from Carausius (287–93) to Valentinian II (375–92), has been partially excavated and seems to be part of an even larger complex of at least two phases.[275] No sub-Roman structures, however, have been identified.

Excavations of the coastal hillfort at the top of HIGH PEAK in Devon, undertaken in 1871, 1929, and 1961–64, have yielded evidence of Neolithic and sub-Roman occupation. The only structures identified from the sub-Roman fort were a large single ditch, a rampart that formed the crest of the hill, and a small outer rampart on the eastern side of the site.[276] These may represent either a univallate or a bivallate contour hillfort, possibly over-looking a harbor. All three excavations turned up sherds of imported amphoras (dating to c. 475–650 and representing several vessels), found at the crest of the hill, in the large ditch, and in the small rampart outside the ditch.[277] Along with the pottery were found animal bones (mostly ox and pig), a small bronze strap, a shale spindle whorl, and a whetstone. The large amounts of charcoal found in all the ditch fills and in the debris on the inner rampart suggest, to its most recent excavator, that the hillfort met a violent end at the hands of advancing Saxons.[278]

The coastal settlement of TINTAGEL, in Cornwall, may be the link between these British hillforts that have yielded imported Mediterranean pottery. Visible to the visitor today are the picturesque ruins of the Norman castle at Tintagel, which have inspired writers from Geoffrey of Monmouth to Lord Tennyson, who have helped add "King Arthur's Castle" to the tourist's map. More recently, archaeologists and historians have begun to unravel the com-plex history of the site, whose "Dark Age" phase is showing signs of activ-ity on a grander scale than the legends themselves.

Beyond the inner ward of the Norman castle, on the high protruding headland called Tintagel Island, lay the remains of several small rectangular structures made of stone and slate. Radford's excavation of these structures in the 1930s revealed thousands of sherds of imported pottery, then known as "Tintagel ware." Because this pottery dated to the fifth to the seventh cen-turies and was used primarily for the transportation of wine and oil, Radford interpreted the headland settlement as a remote Celtic monastery.

The monastic model for Tintagel was commonly accepted until the 1970s, when Burrow and others began casting doubts on Radford's interpretation of the stone huts, whose number has now grown from thirty to over a hun-dred.[279] Because Tintagel does not appear as a monastery in Cornish hagiog-raphy, and because no early Christian church or cemetery have been found at the castle site, archaeologists now doubt that the stone huts are monastic "cells." Some are likely barracks belonging to the Norman castle, while oth-ers—on both the plateau of the headland and on its terraces (Fig. 25)—are multiperiod, including drystone buildings contemporary with the imported pottery.[280]

A secular interpretation is now replacing the monastic model of the Tintagel settlement. The new models proposed are (1) a fortress or royal seat and (2) an international port of trade. The first model is supported more by linguistic and literary evidence than by archaeology. The name "Tintagel" is thought to derive from the Cornish *tin/din*, "fort," and *tagell*, "neck or constriction."[281] Charles Thomas believes that Tintagel's original identity as a castle or fortress was perpetuated by the Romans, making it the coastal *Durocornovium* (fort of the Cornovii) listed in the *Ravenna Cosmography*.[282] Two inscribed Roman milestones (dating to the third and fourth centuries) have been found in Tintagel, as well as Roman coins and both commercial and locally made pottery of the third and fourth centuries.[283] Whatever role it played during the Roman occupation, later tradition made Tintagel the fortified seat of the rulers of Dumnonia (southwestern Britain), including Mark and Tristan. This tradition, in turn, may have had something to do with the location here of the twelfth- or thirteenth-century Norman castle that Geoffrey of Monmouth linked with Arthur.[284]

The second model holds that Tintagel was a major late and sub-Roman port of trade, perhaps occupied only seasonally. This theory is based primarily on the enormous amount of imported pottery that has been (and still is being) uncovered on the headland, along with other finds, such as a Merovingian ring ornament.[285] More fine pottery and amphoras—over three hundred vessels in all—have been found at Tintagel than at any other site in Britain and Ireland.[286] Slight traces of metalworking found at Tintagel support the widely held view that Cornish tin was traded for the imports.[287] Minor excavation on the headland in the 1980s began to uncover evidence of associated structures, including a possible sub-Roman wharf below the Iron Gate and a court beneath the Norman hall of the inner ward.[288] In the lower ward, on the mainland, excavation revealed two hearths, a well-built oven, a multitude of butchered and cooked bones, and imported glass, pottery, and metalwork, suggesting intensive food preparation and cooking at the site in the late fifth century.[289]

Charles Thomas has recently reevaluated the evidence at Tintagel for English Heritage.[290] He argues that there are too many geographic problems at Tintagel headland—a restricted location, vulnerability to gales and salt-laden spray, meager and shallow soil cover, a limited water supply—to have made it suitable for year-round habitation, so that during the period of its imports (about 450 to 650) it is more likely to have been inhabited only periodically, perhaps solely during the summer months.[291] However, the construction of a ditch-and-rampart line across its only point of landward access, along with the metalworking and ostentatious signs of wealth, make it an ideal candidate for a fortification. Thomas sees Tintagel Island as a stronghold of the post-Roman kings of Dumnonia, but one used only periodically as part of an irregular sequence of dynastic visitations, where food as well as goods required for overseas trade were brought to the king under a system of enforced obligations.[292]

Fig. 25. Sub-Roman structures from the terraces on "Tintagel Island"

Such itinerant kings are well attested in the early medieval world, the theory being that it was easier to take the larger royal households to the food than it was to maintain them in one permanent location.[293]

Even if the settlement on the headland turns out to be thoroughly secular, there is still strong evidence of early Christianity at Tintagel. Thomas led two seasons of excavation at the Tintagel parish churchyard, which is on the mainland not far from the castle. His team uncovered two slate-lined graves, two rock-covered burial mounds, and one memorial pillar; associated imported pottery and a cross on one of the slates identify the site as early Christian (c. 400–600).[294] Near the graves were found traces of open-air fires, the remains of which yielded a (calibrated) radiocarbon date centering on A.D. 403.[295] Thomas suggests that the fire and pottery are the remains of a funeral meal held at the Christian cemetery, a custom common at this time on the Continent.[296] Remains of a low bank of earth and stones surrounding the yard yielded a piece of fine tableware from North Africa, suggesting that an enclosure was added to the cemetery in the later sixth century.[297] Its excavators see Tintagel churchyard as an important burial ground, "contemporary and associated with the post-Roman use of the Island."[298]

The univallate hill-slope enclosure of TRETHURGY is one of many circular walled and ditched fortifications common in southwestern Britain, often referred to as Cornish "rounds." Trethurgy has produced locally made pottery and some fifty sherds from imported amphoras, representing four different styles of vessels, along with sherds of fine tableware from Asia Minor and kitchenware from Gaul.[299] The pottery range suggests a period of occupation throughout the fifth and sixth centuries.[300] Also found was a tin ingot, which lends support to the theory that Cornish tin was exchanged for the Mediterranean and Gaulish imports.[301]

Welsh examples of rural settlements very greatly in size and function. COYGAN CAMP is an Iron Age promontory fort that shows signs of occupation in the Roman and early medieval periods. The fort was defended on its north and west sides by a stone-built rampart with revetments on both sides. Four structures ("huts") have been identified, of both stone and timber construction, but no finds have been associated with them to allow for dating.[302] There is an abundance of finds, however, from other areas of the site. Coins and pottery show that the Roman-period occupation extends from at least the second to the fourth century.[303] Sixth-century occupation is attested by the presence of imported Mediterranean pottery, which came from complete vessels and predates the rampart tumble.[304] Other finds of possible early medieval date include two crucibles, a bronze ingot, a dagger, and three spearheads of non-Roman type. Ewan Campbell believes that the range of finds suggests continuity of occupation from the Roman to early medieval periods, while "the imported pottery indicates that there must have been a high-status site at Coygan in the sixth century."[305]

Literary sources confirm high-status occupation at DEGANNWY CASTLE, whose early medieval fortifications straddle two craggy hilltops overlooking Conwy Bay in Caernarvonshire (Fig. 26). Alcock's excavations between 1961 and 1966 revealed traces of early medieval structures beneath the thirteenth-century castle, especially on the western hill. A drystone wall and two trenches were uncovered on the eastern side of the hill, though this may have enclosed the entire summit. The drystone wall is not closely datable, though datable glass and pottery were found (unstratified) very near it.[306]

Artifactual evidence suggests occupation in the Roman period and a long sequence throughout the medieval period. Late Roman finds include a coin sequence extending from Gallienus (260–68) to Valens (364–78) and pottery of similar date.[307] Early medieval objects include over a dozen sherds from Mediterranean amphoras, datable to the late fifth to mid-sixth century.[308] These were found associated with a fragment of possibly post-Roman glass.

Though coins of the period 330–48 are absent, Roman occupation at Degannwy likely extended from the 260s to the 370s.[309] The imported pottery argues for early-sixth-century occupation, but no material argues for continuity between that occupation and the earlier. Later tradition associates Degannwy Castle with Maelgwn of Gwynedd, one of the *tyranni* denounced by Gildas. Though the tradition is a strong one, it may be rather late.[310] Likewise, an entry in the *Annales Cambriae* for the year 812 states that "[t]he citadel of the Canti [*Decantorum arx*] is struck by lightning and burnt," and this is usually identified with Degannwy.[311]

An even more famous literary association is DINAS EMRYS, "The Fort of Ambrosius," where Merlin makes his dire prophesies to Vortigern. The craggy hillfort of Dinas Emrys lies on one of the principal routes through Snowdonia. Excavations in 1910 and in the 1950s revealed several stone walls and revetted platforms surrounding a small summit. On the summit were found the stone foundations of an oval structure, a square pool or cistern, several postholes (possibly belonging to a palisade), and other structures of indeterminate date and function.

The artifactual evidence ranges from the early Roman to the medieval periods. Roman-period finds include pottery, glass, an iron brooch, and three "Donside" terrets (rein rings from a chariot). Late Roman and early medieval finds include gilt-bronze studs, mortars (late third or fourth century),

Fig. 26. Degannwy Castle, Caernarvonshire

Romano-British pottery (late fourth century), at least seven glass vessels, a two-handled amphora (fifth or sixth century), and a roundel cut from a sherd with a Chi-Rho stamp on it (sixth century).

Dating the periods of occupation at Dinas Emrys has proved to be difficult and controversial. The early material, thought to belong to Iron Age or early Roman occupation, may have been brought to the site at a later date.[312] Late Roman occupation seems certain—because of the abundance of pottery and glass—and probably spans the fourth century. Early medieval occupation is indicated by the imported pottery (fifth to sixth centuries), and both the middle and main ramparts rest on late Roman material.[313]

More questions surround the nature of the pool, discovered in H. N. Savory's excavations in the 1950s. The 1910 excavation sought the legendary sinking tower of Vortigern, but uncovered the remains of a Norman castle instead. When Savory uncovered the pool and found it contained fifth- or sixth-century imported pottery, it was hard not to see it as the pool where Vortigern is confronted by the prophetic boy Ambrosius (called Merlin by Geoffrey of Monmouth) in the *Historia Brittonum*. Radiocarbon dating and a sherd of medieval pottery seem to contradict this, though this material may be intrusive.[314] Even more perplexing is the presence of some thirty-three posts erected within the pool, which must have seen a long and complex sequence of activity.

The picture is a bit clearer at DINAS POWYS, near Cardiff in Glamorganshire, a small hilltop settlement surrounded by crude defensive earthworks (Fig. 27). Leslie Alcock's excavations in the 1950s, extensively documented, made Dinas Powys the classic site of post-Roman Celtic archaeology. In the thirty years since the excavations were first published, Alcock and others have reassessed and reinterpreted the nature of the sub-Roman settlement at Dinas Powys in light of new discoveries at similarly occupied hillforts.

The post-Roman occupation of Dinas Powys does not represent the reuse or refortification of an LPRIA hillfort. Though some Iron Age pottery was discovered at the site, no Iron Age structures were recognized.[315] Excavation did reveal an abundance of Roman-period material, including colored glass and window glass (first to second century), Samian ware (second century), a Roman brick, a La Tène brooch (first century), and tools for the manufacture of shale armlets.[316] Because these objects were not associated with Roman-period structures, Alcock believes that they were brought to the site as "mementos" in the fifth and sixth centuries. Others have questioned Alcock's "mementos theory." Rahtz has suggested that the Roman fine table- and glasswares were hoarded heirlooms that came into use again when pottery and glass became extremely scarce in the late fifth century.[317] The Laings

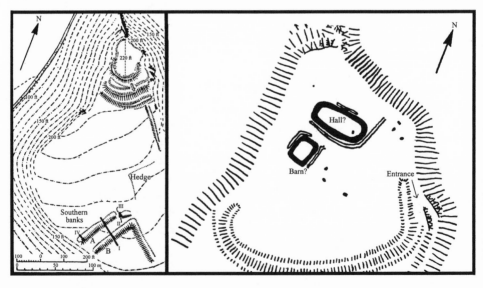

Fig. 27. Dinas Powys contours and structures (after L. Alcock, "Wales," 85)

are convinced that the Romano-British material, because it falls mostly into the first and second centuries, must represent contemporary occupation of some sort.[318] They would even date one of the earthen banks to the early Roman period, which could throw off the chronology of the sub-Roman phases.

Alcock's sub-Roman phase for Dinas Powys—which he labels "Phase 4/ Early Christian"—has three further divisions (A, B, and C) and spans the fifth, sixth, and seventh centuries. Phase 4A (fifth century) is represented by three industrial hearths (with associated metalworking debris), fence holes, one defensive bank and ditch, an incomplete timber structure, a child's grave, and the earliest imported pottery (Phocaean Red Slip Ware, c. 500). Phase 4B (fifth to seventh centuries) showed continued industrial activities, the construction of two stone houses (inferred from two rectangular gullies), and the latest pottery imports (from western Gaul, c. 500–700). Phase 4C (seventh to eighth centuries) began with the construction of a second defensive bank and ditch and ended with the abandonment of the site.

Though Dinas Powys yielded no impressive structures, the quality and quantity of imported pottery and other Early Christian material from Alcock's excavations have made it possible to answer broader questions about economic and industrial aspects of sub-Roman society. Dinas Powys ranks just below Tintagel and Cadbury-Congresbury in the amount of imported pottery it has yielded, which runs from the earliest imports in sub-Roman Britain to the latest. But most remarkable is the wide variety of objects that relate to industrial activity: bronze and iron metalwork, tools for jewelry making, whetstones and querns, glass beads and other raw materials. Accompanying these were objects of likely domestic use, such as Samian tableware, Roman and Germanic glass vessels, carved bone pins, and fine antler combs.

What has perhaps caused the most discussion is the enormous quantity of animal bones discovered at Dinas Powys. Some twelve thousand bones—representing sheep, cattle, and pigs—were uncovered by the excavators, though only a fraction have been studied in detail.[319] Analyses indicate that whole animals were entering the settlement at Dinas Powys and being butchered there.[320] It is not clear, however, whether the inhabitants favored cattle or pig.

Alcock relied heavily on this information about farming economy and industry to formulate his first interpretation of Dinas Powys. He concluded that the early Christian occupation was that of a princely court (*llys*) or stronghold that received tribute in the form of food renders and whose economy depended on animal by-products supplemented by craft industries. Although some have questioned Alcock's use of later Welsh and medieval literary sources to formulate the *"llys* model," no other interpretation of Dinas Powys has gained acceptance. On the contrary, Alcock's model may be gaining more support as other hillfort occupation comes to light. The question, then, is, how does Dinas Powys compare with other fortified sites in Wales and Dumnonia that received imported goods in the sub-Roman period?[321] Esmonde Cleary, expressing support for Alcock's model, points out the problems presented by Dinas Powys: "These [hillforts] . . . were presumably the residences of local rulers. At Dinas Powys the artefactual assemblage included African Red Slip Ware and glass from the Rhineland, which indicates extensive contacts. The site itself was defended and therefore could presumably call upon the labor and resources of a large area round about. Yet the buildings were small and simple. Status must have been proclaimed largely by means which leave us little or no trace."[322]

The means of displaying status, if we are to judge by the evidence of Gildas and the Llandaff Charters, was likely that of clients/retainers and agricultural lands. These leave no archaeological trace, yet are arguably more valuable than lavish buildings and treasure. We may never be able to recover Dinas Powys's true status in the fifth and sixth centuries, but we can—because of its large and varied artifactual assemblage—proclaim it as one of the most important excavated sites of sub-Roman Britain.

More than fifty years of excavation at the multivallate hillfort of DINORBEN in Denbighshire revealed several periods of discontinuous occupation spanning the early Iron Age to the sub-Roman period. Around 260, a large round house was built at the northern end of the site, followed by the construction of small curvilinear huts at the southern end.[323] Associated items include a large number of Roman coins, the latest being two very worn House of Valentinian bronzes from Arles.[324] By the fourth century, Dinorben appears to have become a rural estate, akin to a southern villa, with the round house possibly representing the residence of a Romano-Celtic noble.[325] The round house was succeeded, probably in the early fifth century, by a roughly constructed aisled timber dwelling (identified from a system of postholes) at the northern end, associated with fragments of late Roman flanged bowls of fine pink ware.[326] A sub-Roman reoccupation thus seems likely, though it is not yet possible to trace the continuity between this early fifth-century community and the latest objects from the site, which include several "Anglo-Saxon" ornamental bronze items, a bronze stud (similar to those found at Dinas Powys), and a polychrome glass bead fragment.[327]

Northern Britain has also produced its share of hillforts with early medieval occupation. From DOON HILL in Lothian comes the only completely excavated plan of a northern British hall. Within a polygonal palisaded enclosure lies "hall A," a massive rectangular timber building (70 ft. × 32 ft.) with slightly tapering end bays, two central doors, and a laterally divided central hall with private apartments at each end.[328] It parallels both the large hall at South Cadbury and another northern British hall at Balbridie.[329] "Doon Hill A was certainly an impressive building," writes Alcock, "and taking account of the surrounding palisade, we should see it, in British terms, as a princely *neuadd* [hall] set within the appropriate *llys* [court]."[330]

"Doon Hill might be representative of an archetypal British form," adds Brian Hope-Taylor, "from which 'Yeavering-style' building could directly have been developed, . . . a product of the sixth or possibly the fifth century A.D."[331] But there seems to be a bit of confusion concerning the date of Doon Hill hall A. It was superseded by a second hall—hall B—which was built according to a different plan, one that more closely resembles the hall at Yeavering (see below). The Yeavering hall has been dated c. 640, so Doon Hill hall A must have been built before this time, before the Angles reached Din Eidyn (Edinburgh) in 638.[332] It appears that Doon Hill represents, like Yeavering, a British stronghold taken over by Anglian expansion in the seventh century.[333]

Castle Rock, DUMBARTON—Alt Clut in the British tongue—lies on the north shore of the River Clyde in the heart of the British kingdom of Strathclyde. Bede calls it both *urbs* and *civitas Brettonum munitissima*, and Adomnán insists that King Roderc of Strathclyde "ruled on Clyde Rock."[334] With its twin summits and picturesque castle, this craggy citadel has stimulated much speculation.

Leslie Alcock's excavations at Dumbarton in 1974 and 1975 revealed no coherent defensive plan, but an area on the eastern spur revealed exciting evidence of sub-Roman occupation: the remains of "a dry-stone terrace or fighting platform, laced and revetted with timber beams."[335] Radiocarbon estimates from the oak timbers of the terrace suggest either that it had been built in the sixth century and repaired in the seventh, or that it was a work entirely of the seventh century.[336] Like the ramparts at the Mote of Mark (see below), this structure too was destroyed by fire, probably as a result of a Viking siege in 870.[337]

The artifactual evidence from Dumbarton, however, points to a fifth- and sixth-century date for the occupation. Finds include sherds of amphoras imported from the eastern Aegean and southwest Asia Minor (probably containing wine), Gaulish kitchenware, Merovingian glass, and jewelry-making debris.[338] "This [evidence] points clearly to Alt Clut as one of the dynastic centres of Strathclyde by the time of Rhydderch [Roderc] if not earlier," writes Alcock. "We must think of [Bede's] *civitas Brettonum* in an organizational sense, as an administrative and social center."[339]

Of different character is the MOTE OF MARK, set on a craggy hillock rising above a side estuary of the Solway Firth. Its summit is enclosed by a timber-reinforced stone wall, which was clearly destroyed by fire at some point in the site's history. The enclosed area is approximately 75 m × 35 m, but much of it is covered with rocky outcrops. Excavations in 1913, 1973, and 1979 uncovered an enormous amount of jewelry and metalworking debris, including what may be the first instance of Celtic interlace.[340]

There has been much debate concerning the nature and date of this fort. At first, excavators thought that they had uncovered an Iron Age hillfort reoccupied in the eighth century. The subsequent finds of imported Gaulish pottery and "Germanic" glass indicate occupation in the fifth and sixth centuries, while radiocarbon samples from the rampart show that it too was a post-Roman construction.[341] There is no evidence of Iron Age occupation at the Mote.

More accurate dating thus depends upon the stylistic evidence of the jewelry along with the imported pottery. Lloyd Laing has argued that the brooches and pins as well as the interlace-decorated molds are purely "British" in style and are contemporary with the pottery, giving a sixth-century date to the industrial activity at the Mote.[342] His opponents argue that the interlace is zoomorphic and belongs to a later, seventh-century Anglian phase.[343] Alcock has pointed out that the fortification of hilltops was quite unknown in Anglo-Saxon Northumbria, and thus the ramparts at the Mote of Mark must predate Anglian settlement. He suggests that the site was a British industrial foundation of the sixth century, whose jewelry industry was taken over by the Angles in the seventh.[344] Laing, on the other hand, dates the initial British occupation to the fifth century and the construction of a defensive rampart to the sixth, and believes that the site was abandoned when the Angles arrived in the seventh.[345]

There is also much debate on how to classify the site. The defensive rampart would suggest that the Mote of Mark is a British hillfort. Alcock, who has excavated several of these, sees the Mote as "a princely *llys* [court] with an attendant jeweller."[346] But the profusion of jewelry-making debris suggests that the Mote could have been a purely industrial site, with its own defenses, that continued functioning as such after its ramparts were destroyed by fire and Angles controlled the territory.[347] "They [the Angles] took over the industrial activities of the Mote," writes Alcock, "and no doubt its British craftsmen as well, and exploited them vigorously for the production of elaborate jewelry in an early Anglo-Celtic style."[348]

YEAVERING (Gefrin), in Northumberland, has a similarly mixed character (Fig. 28). Brian Hope-Taylor's excavations revealed a remarkable, though perhaps not unique, settlement type: a northern British fortress that when taken over by Angles becomes an Anglian *villa regia*. The earliest structures at Yeavering—small timber-and-wattle buildings—are identified as "British" type, of fifth- or sixth-century date. Also thought to be British in origin is the double-palisaded Great Enclosure, which later became an elaborate structure associated with the Anglian Great Hall. In its initial phase it consisted of two widely spaced parallel fences attached by two bulbous terminals, each enclosing a rectangular building that may have served as a lookout tower or guard post.[349] Both Hope-Taylor and Alcock believe that this enclosure was originally a place for public gatherings and part of a pre-Anglian royal center of the northern Britons, probably in the kingdom of the Gododdin.[350] "Yeavering's archaeological record clearly testifies to the meeting of two major cultural groups," writes the excavator, "each with diverse strains of influence already within it, at a time probably nearer 550 than 600; and to the vigorous hybrid culture which that produced."[351]

Other structures at Yeavering are more difficult to place, ethnically and chronologically. The enigmatic "building E" was identified by the excavator as "unmistakably" a wooden theater, focused on a stage (which may have carried a throne) and a (carved?) ceremonial pole.[352] "Yeavering-style building," writes Hope-Taylor, "may well have been a response to the special political needs and pretensions of a ruling class . . . [who] would be found not to have been without various enrichments and a certain crude pomp."[353] Datable objects from Yeavering include a silver-inlaid iron buckle of Frankish origin, which likely dates to between c. 570–80 and c. 630–40, and a gold-washed copper-alloy copy of a Merovingian gold *tirens,* probably minted in the 630s or 640s.[354]

The most characteristic rural settlement type in southern Britain during the Roman period, apart from the numerous small farms that have left little archaeological traces, was the villa. These rural estates dominated local agriculture and have left behind numerous examples of their stone structures. But it is widely believed that the villa economy of Britain had disappeared by the fifth century, and that the villas themselves met a violent end, with

Fig. 28. Yeavering Bell, Northumberland

widespread destruction occasionally followed by squatter occupation.

However, Patrick grew up on his father's *villula* in the early fifth century,[355] and we might expect that many of these estates survived—albeit in altered form—in areas less vulnerable to raiding. In the MILTON KEYNES area, both the villa at Bancroft and the *vicus* at nearby Dropshort (Magiovinium) have produced coins of Arcadius.[356] At Bancroft, late Roman and early Saxon pottery overlap each other in the same assemblage.[357]

Two Roman villas at FROCESTER, in Gloucestershire, have produced fifth-century burials, with one of these, Frocester Court villa, producing evidence of sub-Roman timber structures.[358] The stone buildings at Frocester Court were inhabited until the end of the fourth century, though one room had been converted into a stable. In the early fifth century, the villa residents abandoned the stone house and erected at least two timber structures in the courtyard. One building, 14 m × 3 m, appears to have been a hall built on sill beams laid flat (no postholes were found) on a floor of stone and gravel. Around this building and in and under its floor were dozens of sherds of grass-tempered pottery. A second structure, 12 m × 9 m, was erected across part of the courtyard hall and defined by a timber beam slot and internal postholes. Four graves found in the courtyard have also been identified as fifth-century burials. Carolyn Heighway sees Frocester as a significant fifth-century center in Gloucestershire, "perhaps a rural market."[359]

Excavation at GLAN-Y-MOR, on the Bristol Channel, revealed "an unusual Roman building complex consisting of 22 rooms and cellars divided into four ranges built around a central courtyard."[360] Signs of occupation during the Roman period include pottery, iron, glass, and bronze. These artifacts date activity from the late first or early second century to the mid or late fourth century. The building itself probably dates to the late third century and has been identified as "a short-lived *mansio*."[361]

A layer of rubble (containing crushed tile, charcoal, and animal bones) that accumulated subsequent to the partial demolition of this complex indicates reoccupation in possibly five of the rooms. In addition to this reoccupation, the remains of a round-cornered rectangular building (4.7 m × 5.2 m) were found in the southeast corner of the central courtyard. The building had a paved floor and two drains running along its walls.[362] No definitely post-Roman artifacts were found associated with the reoccupations. However, a great quantity of food debris—including cattle, sheep, pig, and dog bones; deer antlers; and limpet and periwinkle shells—were recognized "in post-Roman contexts."[363] Animal bone from one of the reoccupied rooms gave a radiocarbon date of 600–860, while other reoccupied rooms yielded a whetstone and a shale bracelet that are possibly early medieval.[364] "In short," writes Alan Lane, "there is good reason to think that there was early medieval activity in the ruins of a Roman building at Glan-y-mor and possibly traces of a [subsequent] small building or buildings."[365]

The great variety of rural settlements in sub-Roman Britain reflects both Roman models, like the *villa* and the *mansio*, and native models, like the hillfort. Some were created by specifically sub-Roman circumstances. BANTHAM is a rare example of a sub-Roman port or emporium. Bantham Ham at the mouth of the River Avon has, since the eighteenth century, been known as a repository of ancient garbage. Several middens were uncovered by farmers in the nineteenth century, and many of the objects found were collected in 1902 by H. L. Jenkins.[366] In 1953 Aileen Fox identified some of the ceramic finds as sherds of imported pottery dating to the fifth to seventh centuries.[367] A sub-Roman date was then ascribed to this Devon dunes settlement.

Small-scale excavations at the dunes in 1978 revealed more midden material overlying hearths and adjacent hollows, defined by the excavator as areas A, B, C, and D.[368] Area A contained a hearth, stake holes (thought to represent tent supports), a shallow gully, charcoal pipes, shells, slate slabs, animal bones, a knife blade and other iron fragments, part of an enameled brooch, and several sherds of pottery (two of which had been pierced to make whorls). Area B was similarly rich, producing several pits, limpet shells, slate slabs, bone fragments, two hearths, charcoal, seventy stake holes, whetstones, several iron objects, and a single sherd of imported pottery. Area C yielded only bone and shell fragments, charcoal, and mussel shells, while area D contained charcoal deposits, several slate slabs, a group of five stake holes, mussel and limpet shells, and a decorated bone comb.

Analysis of the pottery (twenty-one sherds were found in the most recent excavation) by the excavator identified Roman fine wares and more examples of the imported pottery identified by Fox, the latter representing Mediterranean amphoras and Gaulish kitchenware.[369] Sixty-one iron objects and fragments were uncovered, including a nail, chisel, clamps, and six knife blades (probably once outfitted with wooden shafts). Finely crafted objects found at the site include fragments of a decorated bone comb, two penannular brooches (one bronze and one iron), and a leaded bronze enameled disc brooch. The penannular brooches have been identified as sub- or post-Roman, while the disc brooch is likely of Roman provincial manufacture (second or third century).[370] Finally, a great quantity of marine shells and animal bones were uncovered, the latter representing (in decreasing order) cattle, sheep, goats, pigs, dogs, horses, deer, hares, voles, and various birds and fish.

The large number of artifacts, coupled with slight evidence of structures, has led observers to conclude that Bantham was a temporarily, perhaps seasonally, occupied settlement.[371] A sub-Roman trading post, with occasional but intense use, seems likely because of the location and the Mediterranean imports. The iron fragments, along with a single find of iron slag and eleven whorls, suggest that manufacturing may have occurred alongside, or in relation to, the long-distance trade.

GATEHOLM, a small tidal island in the Broad Sound that was perhaps once a promontory attached to the mainland, has a sub-Roman settlement of mixed Roman and native character. Its eroding cliffs lead up to a flat plateau that is covered with rows of turf-grown walls. These are seemingly the remains of several subrectangular buildings, organized in a more or less homogeneous plan, perhaps protected by a drystone bank. Excavations and occasional finds indicate a long span of occupation.

Activity in the Roman period is indicated by several fragments (thirty-one sherds from twelve to eighteen vessels) of mortars and Samian wares, c. 250–350, and one coin each of Carausius and Tetricius I.[372] Oxford color-coated ware suggests that activity continued to the late fourth century at least, and signs of early medieval occupation include a bronze ringed pin (of sixth- to ninth-century date) and a bronze stag (now lost), the only close parallel that has been found for the stag on the Sutton Hoo whetstone.[373]

Interpretations of the hut settlement at Gateholm have varied. J. L. Davies sees it as a homogeneous but unusual "Roman" settlement that began around 250–300 with perhaps intermittent occupation into the post-Roman period.[374] One sherd of the Oxford ware was incorporated into the cobbling of a building (seen by excavators to be one of the earlier structures), which suggests that it, at least, was not constructed until the very end of the fourth century (and possibly later).[375] Gateholm has also been compared with Tintagel and considered an isolated monastery, but reconsiderations of the nature of Tintagel have weakened this interpretation.[376]

Hut groups are another recurring subcategory of British rural settlements. GRAENOG, in Gwynedd, is the site of three structures that are part of a round-hut group. Sherds of plain Samian pottery and Roman coarse wares have been found over most of the site, dating activity to the second through fourth centuries A.D. After this Roman-period occupation, the structures were reused, and a corn-drying kiln was constructed.[377] A remanent magnetic date from the hearth in one of the huts yielded a date of 500–550.[378]

LONGBURY BANK, resting on a flat-topped limestone ridge in Pembrokeshire, offers a unique settlement type. Several excavations have been carried out on a small cave (Little Hoyle) that runs under the bank, and on an enigmatic vertical shaft that rises to the summit of the ridge. There are no visible structures or earthworks on the summit, but a slight break in the slope running across the promontory suggests a boundary or defense.

Roman pottery was discovered in trenches cut (by modern excavators) into the bank, and two fourth-century Roman coins were found at the nearby manor house of Trefloyne.[379] Excavations in this century and the last have produced a large quantity of imported Mediterranean pottery, as well as a silver trapezoidal plate of possible Byzantine import, and sixty-three fragments from at least fifteen Merovingian glass drinking vessels.[380] Items of local provenance include a bronze penannular brooch, an annular loom weight, shells from various mollusks, and animal bones (mostly cattle).[381] Two samples of charcoal, which yielded radiocarbon dates centering in the fifth or sixth centuries, confirm late Roman activity and occupation in the late fifth through seventh centuries.[382]

Due to the absence of identifiable structures, it has been difficult to interpret the early medieval settlement at Longbury Bank. Some have suggested occupation within the cave, which was possibly the retreat of a hermit from one of the nearby monasteries (Penally or Caldey).[383] A simple chisel-cut cross was found above the floor of the shaft, but its date remains problematic.[384] Most of the imported pottery was found on the summit of the bank, and the site could just as well have been a secular—possibly royal—settlement.[385] "The association with exotic food and drink is clear," write Campbell and Lane, "and the status of those people able to afford such luxuries can be assumed to be high."[386]

Of a more modest nature is the settlement at TY MAWR, a large group of mostly circular stone huts situated on the southern slopes of Holyhead Mountain (Fig. 29). The huts lay below an ancient hillfort and are associated with fields that were enclosed and cultivated by the inhabitants. Much attention has been paid to the prehistoric phase of the hut settlement. Late Roman use of the mountain, perhaps as a naval lookout station, is suggested by traces of a signal tower and by a hoard of twenty-two Theodosian coins, including a clipped *siliqua* of either Arcadius or Honorius.[387] Recent excavation by C. A. Smith indicates possible Roman and early medieval occupation as well. This is centered on two huts, with associated "hearths," and the field that connects them. Radiocarbon readings taken from charcoal found in the two hearths yield dates of 430–770 and 430–775.[388] Post-Roman finds include a large midden of shellfish (mainly limpet) and the charred remains of naked barley and spelt.[389] Though the original round house may have been reoccupied, Smith notes that the two huts showing the most post-Roman use were smaller and more rectangular than the much earlier hut circles.[390]

At BUSTON, in Strathclyde, is an example of the rural settlement type know as a crannog (a single dwelling constructed on an artificial island), found in both Britain and Ireland. This native dwelling showed signs of occupation in both the Roman early medieval periods, with several alterations spanning that time. Radiocarbon samples taken from timber stakes yielded dates of 370 ± 50 A.D. and 520 ± 50 A.D.[391] Decorated wooden objects were preserved in a slumped hollow between the fifth-century house and its seventh-century framework. An Anglo-Saxon gold coin, of a type known only in the Southeast, made its way to the site by about 700.[392]

These rural settlements of sub-Roman Britain obviously vary greatly in size, character, and function. The hillforts had a primarily defensive role, and seem to have been chosen especially for high-status occupation. But the Mediterranean imports that have been used to identify these high-status settlements also found their way, though in fewer numbers, to smaller rural settlements that were seemingly farmsteads, trading posts, and industrial sites. Together these sites yield an abundance of evidence about farming, animal

Fig. 29. Holyhead Mountain *(above)* and the Ty Mawr hut group *(below)*, which rests on its southern slopes

husbandry, and industrial activities in the fifth and sixth centuries.[393] Some also yield important clues about the religious activities of the sub-Roman Britons (see below).

Religious Sites

Many of the sites discussed previously have shown evidence of religious activity. Some sites, however, are especially characterized by such activity, be it pagan or Christian. The final category to be surveyed here is these religious settlements, which include cemeteries, pagan temples, churches, monastic sites, and other significant Christian settlements (Fig. 30).

A cemetery can—but does not always—tell us about the ritual and religious beliefs of its community. Fortunately, archaeologists have discovered several large British cemeteries used in the sub-Roman period that do yield such clues. Over a thousand graves have been examined at POUNDBURY near Dorchester, one of three Christian cemeteries identified in Roman Britain.[394] The majority of the graves were aligned east-west and contained simple wooden coffins without grave goods, though others contained more elaborate stone or lead coffins and a few grave goods. Within some of the coffins at the "main cemetery," bodies were partially preserved by a packing of gypsum plaster.[395] A coin pendant with the Chi-Rho monogram, along with the east-west alignments (which carefully avoid earlier north-south inhumations), strongly suggests that many of these were Christian graves. The Dorchester area has yielded other evidence of early Christians. The villas at Frampton and Hinton St. Mary both contained mosaics bearing such Christian symbols as the Chi-Rho, and presumably these mosaics were part of private chapels. These and stone mausoleums found in the Christian section at Poundbury suggest that Christianity was spreading among the upper classes in the fourth century.

Excavation has revealed another sub-Roman cemetery at BREAN DOWN, in Somerset. Three skeletons yielded calibrated radiocarbon dates of 415–600, 560–660, and 654–786. The skeletons were aligned east-west but were not buried with grave goods. Nearby stones suggest a return to the characteristic pre-Roman slab-lined and cist burials.[396] The east-west alignment and lack of grave goods have supported interpretation of these as Christian burials. A Romano-Celtic temple was also built on the down c. 340, and was demolished c. 390.[397] This was replaced by a small rectangu-

Fig. 30. Excavated religious sites in sub-Roman Britain

lar stone-built structure. One interpretation is that the pagan temple was demolished by the Christian community, who replaced it with a small shrine.[398] But the rectangular structure could just as well have been a subsequent pagan shrine, abandoned sometime after the coming of the Christians.[399]

CANNINGTON, also in Somerset, is the site of one of the largest Roman cemeteries excavated in Britain. The cemetery originally consisted of some two thousand to five thousand graves—only five hundred of which survived to be excavated—and was in use from the second century to the seventh or eighth. The earlier graves were aligned roughly north-south and contained grave goods, while the latter were aligned east-west and lacked grave goods, suggesting an initially pagan and subsequently Christian community. Two explanations have been offered for the size and location of the cemetery. One scenario is that the local Romano-British population migrated to the nearby hillfort and used Cannington as their burial ground.[400] This could have happened in the sub-Roman period, but does not explain the second-century graves, for the hillfort reoccupation is unlikely to have been that early (though a late Roman temple, found on the hilltop, could account for some of the early pagan graves).[401] Another explanation is that Cannington served as a communal burial ground for several communities in Somerset, as was probably the case for Poundbury and the Dorchester area.[402]

Excavations at Beacon Hill on LUNDY ISLAND uncovered a smaller cemetery and stone structures dating back to the Iron Age. Several stone-walled huts were associated with third- and fourth-century pottery, and one fragment belonged to a small red slipped wheel-made bowl, categorized by Charles Thomas as a minor unidentified ware of the early post-Roman period.[403] The cemetery contained thirty cist graves around an unidentified focus, with an enclosure probably dating to the late sixth century.[404] Four inscribed stones were found associated with the graves: two date to the fifth or early sixth century, one to the late fifth or sixth, and one to the seventh.[405] The seventh-century memorial stone contained an inscribed cross, suggesting that by the seventh century the community using this cemetery was Christian.

Limited excavation at PHILLACK in west Cornwall has revealed another small cemetery dated artifactually to the sub-Roman period.[406] The cemetery is enclosed and consists of inhumations in cist graves oriented east-west, which suggests use by a Christian community.[407] Dating evidence includes one sherd from a Phocaean Red Slip Ware bowl (c. 470–550), and a nearby inscribed stone of c. 600.[408] The evidence from Phillack compares to similar burial sites in the Scilly Isles (see below).[409]

SHEPTON MALLET was a small Romano-British settlement, flourishing in the fourth century, situated on the Fosse Way between the larger towns of Bath and Ilchester. Recent excavations have revealed building complexes, cobbled streets, and three small cemeteries. No town defenses, and no apparent planning scheme, meant that these cemeteries could be located close to inhabited buildings, and were perhaps privately owned plots.[410] Most burials were in wooden coffins (only the iron nails survived) set into rock-cut graves, with few surviving grave goods.[411] The largest cemetery contained seventeen inhumations aligned east-west within a ditched enclosure, and included one lead coffin and, in another burial, a silver cross-shaped amulet with a Chi-Rho symbol punched into it.[412] This positive identification of a Christian burial suggests a probable Christian community at Shepton Mallet in the later fourth century. Pottery and coinage take us up to about 400, but it is unclear how long after this the Christian community remained. There are some traces of timber structures cut into the latest levels of Roman buildings, suggesting post-Roman continuity, but dating these structures is not yet possible.[413]

Recent excavation at WELLS Cathedral has revealed a late or sub-Roman stone building standing beside the first Anglo-Saxon church. The building has been tentatively identified as a mausoleum.[414] Later religious activity at the site argues for a Christian identity for this mausoleum, examples of which have appeared at other sub-Roman sites.

A *vicus* or small town developed alongside the Roman fort at ANCASTER, but the character of that settlement is not clear. Outside of the defenses, to the west, excavators uncovered a late Roman cemetery containing over three hundred inhumations. Most used stone-lined graves or wooden coffins aligned east-west, and few contained associated grave goods, leading some to speculate that this was a Christian cemetery.[415] Coins found in one grave date to the 360s, but it is possible that the burials continue into the fifth century.[416] Though no artifacts of this period identified as "Anglo-Saxon" have been found within the town, a cemetery to the southeast has yielded forty cremation urns, common in pagan Saxon cemeteries.[417]

Many sub-Roman burials were associated with pagan temples or Christian shrines, and in some cases a temple was succeeded by a shrine or church on the same site. This appears to have been the case for the small town of CHELMSFORD, which, by the fourth century, had taken on a significant religious role. A Romano-Celtic temple was built just outside the city walls c. 320, in which, states P. J. Drury, "we can see the complete change from the Celtic tradition of worshipping in the open air, to the classical concept of anthropomorphic gods who need houses."[418] The building consists of two concentric octagons, the inner one opening to a semicircular apse on its western wall. "The site," writes Drury, "produced 90 coins more or less equally spread between 310 and 402, ending with issues of Arcadius."[419] Sometime after 402, ritual discontinued at the temple, and a small three-room house was erected against its eastern wall. A subsequent fifth-century phase saw the careful demolition of the temple and the removal of its stones, perhaps, as Drury suggests, to build Chelmsford's first Christian church.[420] The small house remained standing, however, and there is evidence that domestic activity continued at the temple site for some time, probably until the late fifth century.[421]

Another classic example of a Romano-Celtic temple comes from MAIDEN CASTLE in Dorset. Britain's largest Celtic hillfort, Maiden Castle was a political center of the Durotriges tribe before the Roman invasion. It was captured by Vespasian after a bloody massacre of its defenders, and consequently the Durotriges were encouraged to settle in nearby Durnovaria (Dorchester). In the late fourth century, some time after 367, a pagan temple was constructed on the hillfort's plateau.[422] Maiden Castle, with its large ramparts, may then have become an enclosed shrine similar to the temple at Lydney, possibly associated with a sub-Roman cemetery.[423] According to its first excavator, the temple at Maiden Castle had its floor replaced, suggesting "an existence prolonged well into the fifth century."[424] Thereafter, a nearby circular shrine may have replaced the Romano-Celtic temple.[425]

Excavations at the shrine of Apollo at NETTLETON in Wiltshire have revealed much and varied activity in the fourth and fifth centuries. Although the temple had become derelict in the second half of the fourth century, sometime after 370 it was adapted for habitation, and was used as a farmstead until 392 or possibly later.[426] From knife or sword wounds found on skeletons at the site, the excavator believes that the homestead occupants were massacred in a raid on the settlement sometime after 392.[427] Some five hundred Roman coins, ranging in date from 333 to 402, were found along with other objects on the floor of one building, and all had apparently been subjected to fire. One object associated with the coins was a *plumbata* or *martiobarbulus,* a lead-weighted feathered javelin head comparable to those found at Wroxeter (which date to the early fifth century).[428] Glass from this building has been assigned to the late fourth and early fifth centuries, and some of the beads found have been typed "Saxon." Richard Reece, examining the coin evidence from Nettleton, sees occupation at the site continuing well into the fifth century.[429]

There is mixed pagan and Christian evidence from the SCILLY ISLES (Sillina), islets once connected by the now submerged seabed to Cornwall. Both literary and archaeological sources attest that the Scillies were inhabited throughout the Roman period. The emperor Maximus exiled two Priscillianist heretics to Scilly in the fourth century. A Romano-Celtic pagan shrine found on Nor'nour yielded a late Roman treasure trove (including Roman coins of the late fourth century, glass, bronze finger rings, pots, domestic pottery, bronze brooches, and clay goddess figurines from Gaul), suggesting a lingering paganism to the beginning of the fifth century.[430] An early Christian wooden church was replaced by a stone chapel on St. Helen's, and the few graves excavated point to Christian cemeteries in the Scillies.[431] Scattered finds of imported pottery, found at Mary's Hill and Tean, and a Merovingian buckle and girdle hanger found at Tean, indicate commercial activity from the mid–fifth to seventh centuries.[432]

One of the most impressive archaeological sequences was exposed by a rescue excavation in 1977 that uncovered the temple complex on WEST HILL ULEY. Coinage indicates a series of religious structures built on the site beginning in the LPRIA and continuing in the Roman and post-Roman periods. The major feature was a small Romano-Celtic temple consisting of stone-walled concentric rectangles and containing bronze coinage and other votive objects. Coin evidence suggests that the temple was built in the second quarter of the fourth century and demolished c. 400. The dismantling of the buildings was systematic and the removal of the stonework done carefully.[433]

Excavation further disclosed at least three phases of structures succeeding the temple, phases associated with Theodosian coinage and various types of Romano-British pottery. The first of these structures, represented by large post pits and beam slots cut through the demolished remains of the stone temple, has been interpreted as a double-aisled timber basilica (11 m × 9.2 m), probably a church, constructed sometime after the last coins were deposited (c. 402).[434] No apse has been identified, but an attached polygonal structure may have served as a baptistry (with a conjectured altar).[435] In the late fifth or sixth century, a perimeter bank was built around the complex, with two foundations of drystone footings and postholes at the north end possibly representing gate towers with stair turrets.[436]

In the late sixth or early seventh century, the timber basilica was dismantled, and a smaller stone structure was erected over the northeastern corner of the basilica.[437] This rectangular masonry building was later given an apse, and has been interpreted as a two-cell chapel. Associated with the chapel were ten fragments of blue-green window glass, some containing dark red streaks, which have parallels with Anglo-Saxon churches and are thus most likely post-Roman.[438] Also possibly connected with the stone church is a polygonal open-sided structure, south of the church, with mortared stone footings, interpreted as an open "screen" roofed with reused Roman tiles.[439] The incorporation of the pagan altar and a statue of Mercury into the sub-Roman structures' walls lends support to the excavators' interpretation of Uley as a Christian complex that took over a pagan shrine.[440]

Somerset, Wiltshire, and Gloucestershire constitute an area that is the richest in evidence of pagan shrines and temples. In addition to the afore-mentioned temples at Bath, Brean Down, Cadbury-Congresbury, Nettleton, South Cadbury, and Uley, there are those at LAMYATT and PAGANS HILL, which have also yielded some evidence of late or sub-Roman activity. Post-Roman evidence from Pagans Hill includes a seventh-century glass bottle, a windlass made from a piece of Roman pagan sculpture, an iron pale (possibly Anglo-Saxon), and a single sherd of organically tempered pottery.[441] Should this cumulative evidence be treated as proof of a "pagan revival" in sub-Roman Britain, one that was brought to a violent end at the hands of zealous Christians? Broken idols aside, it is more likely that the evidence represents the last gasps of Mediterranean paganism, which died with Julian the Apostate in the rest of the empire but perhaps proved a bit longer-lived in Britain. If Theodosius's edict making Christianity the official religion in the empire had the effect of instantly empowering zealous Christians, we would expect to see much physical evidence of Christianity in the last years of Roman Britain. But, as in the case of Christian churches, such evidence is elusive.

The first, and perhaps strongest, case to be made for a Christian structure in Roman Britain is the fourth-century "basilican church" discovered near the SILCHESTER forum in 1892 (see Fig. 31). This very small building (13 m × 9 m) has been the focus of much attention. Its identification is based on its plan, which is similar to Old St. Peter's in Rome, and on the discovery of a "baptismal font" less than two meters from the main entrance.[442] No significant dating evidence (apart from some third-century pottery sealed beneath the floor) was found during the 1892 and 1961 excavations, though the plan suggests a late-fourth-century erection and some later reconstruction.[443] Only a few Christian objects have been found at Silchester, and none in direct association with the basilica. The Christian community, such as it was, must have been small, though the proximity of the church to the forum suggests that the Christians were not without influence.

By the early fifth century a Christian community was established within the fort of RICHBOROUGH. The foundations of a hexagonal masonry structure identified as a baptismal font were uncovered inside the fort, in the northwest corner, along with artifacts bearing the Chi-Rho.[444] Stephen Johnson sees the Richborough evidence as fitting in with the pattern repeated in other parts of the late empire, "where bishops were glad to establish their congregations within the safety of the now abandoned fort walls."[445]

Recent excavations at one Roman cemetery near the present-day police station have revealed startling evidence of a substantial Christian community in late Roman COLCHESTER.[446] A small pagan cemetery was apparently succeeded by a larger Christian cemetery in the early fourth century. Most of the bodies were in nailed wooden coffins, though some were in lead coffins, hollowed tree trunks, timber vaults, or no coffins at all. To one side of this cemetery excavators found the circuit of a long rectangular stone building, with timber inner partitions, oriented east-west (Fig. 32). It seems to have been constructed between 320 and 340, with later alterations including a rounded apse added at the eastern end. The structural design strongly suggests that this building was a Christian church, though no Christian artifacts have yet been found. The interior did yield, however, hundreds of fourth-century coins, five complete oil lamps, an iron frying pan, and bird and pig bones. The excavator suggests that the latter may have been part of a funerary or other ritual meal.[447]

Another Roman town with strong evidence of early Christian activity is ST. ALBANS (Verulamium), the resting place of Britain's first Christian martyr. When King Offa of Mercia founded St. Albans Abbey in 793, it is likely that he chose a site with previous Christian activity. Excavations at the abbey, which lies just outside of Roman Verulamium, have revealed evidence of near continuous activity from the late Roman period to the "Dissolution of the Monasteries" in the sixteenth century. The earliest level, below the Norman *cellarium* and Anglo-Saxon church, contained several pits, iron nails, charcoal and cremated bones, a silver hand pin, Roman tile and glass, thirty-two Roman coins (all but one or two of fourth-century date), and 252 sherds of Romano-British pottery.[448] The excavators remarked that the striking coin:sherd ratio (1:8) shows that the abbey was no ordinary occupation site. Although there is no conclusive evidence for an early Christian cemetery that might have contained the martyred Alban's remains, the finds suggest "intensive use of the site during the growth of [Alban's] cult in the fourth and fifth centuries."[449] The silver pin is of "Celtic" type and dates by affinity to the sixth or seventh century, while the pottery—"grass- or chaff-tempered"—is of late-fifth- or sixth-century date.[450] Seventh-century "Saxon" material,

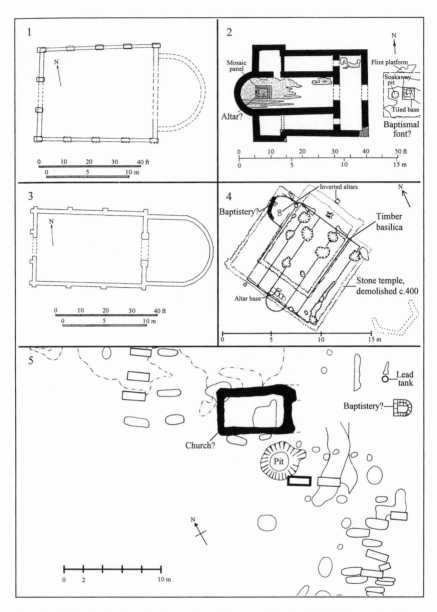

Fig. 31. Plans of churches in late and sub-Roman Britain: (1) Richborough (after P.D.C. Brown and Charles Thomas, in Thomas, *Christianity*, 194), (2) Silchester (after W. H. St. John Hope), (3) St. Pancras, Canterbury (after F. Jenkins and Charles Thomas, in Thomas, *Christianity*, 194), (4) West Hill Uley (after Ann Woodward, Peter Leach, and Peter Salway, in Salway, *Oxford Illustrated History*, 479), and (5) Icklingham, Suffolk (after S. West, J. Plouviez, and Richard Morris, in Morris, *The Church*, 13)

Fig. 32. Foundations of the late Roman basilical "church" at Colchester

together with a reference to St. Alban's shrine in Bede, would suggest that there was some continuity of occupation, perhaps a mixture of pagan and Christian, from the fifth century to the foundation of the Anglo-Saxon abbey by Offa.

There is also good evidence for an early Christian presence in CIRENCESTER. As the administrative capital of the province Britannia Prima, Cirencester was likely the see of a bishop, and it has been suggested that the British bishop missing (but represented by a deacon) at the Council of Arles was from Cirencester.[451] A Christian palindrome, whose letters can be rearranged to form a cross from the words PATER NOSTER, was found carefully scratched into the wall plaster of a house on Victoria Road. It may date from a time when open references to Christianity would have "invited persecution."[452] Excavations at Cirencester's urban cemeteries have not yielded any other clues about this Christian presence. But of the over four hundred skeletons exhumed, most were of fourth- or early-fifth-century date.[453]

Under the refectory of the medieval cathedral at WORCESTER lay two burials probably belonging to the sub-Roman period.[454] Grave one contained a skeleton of a man (age twenty-five to thirty), fragments of very fine spun gold (around the skeleton's neck), a few sherds of Roman pottery, and a single posthole. The bones yielded radiocarbon dates of A.D. 536 (429–643) and A.D. 585 (483–687). The gold thread was woven into a brocade, probably the border of a cloth garment, perhaps a priest's hood or collar. Steven Bassett has shown (through charter evidence) that St. Helen's parish church also originated as a Roman or British church before it became the property of Hwiccan rulers and, subsequently, an Anglo-Saxon see (c. 680).[455] Hwiccan conversions before (and possibly leading to) the creation of the see would then have been the work of British Christians in and around Worcester.

Christianity may provide the evidence bridging the gap between the Roman and sub-Roman communities in CARLISLE. Evidence of an early Christian community consists only of a tombstone and a gold ring with an incised palm branch; but Thomas has argued that, as a *civitas* capital, Carlisle must also have been a bishopric, and perhaps the bishopric of the British saints Ninian and Patrick.[456] When Saint Cuthbert visited Carlisle in the seventh century, he was greeted by a man described as *praepositus civitatis*, and was able to walk along the town walls and see a working fountain (implying that there was still a functioning aqueduct in the city).[457] Burnham and Wacher point out that these are strong signs of continuity: "In this way the Church, as in many other parts of the western empire, would have formed the bridge by which a moderately civilized Romano-British community was maintained and eventually transformed into an English one."[458]

Two long-cist burials were found in early excavations on CALDEY ISLAND, near St. David's Church and the medieval priory respectively.[459] An early Christian Ogam-inscribed stone (ECMW, no. 301) found near the priory could support the later hagiographic evidence of a sixth-century monastery founded on the site by Abbot Pyro.[460] More recently, Ewan Campbell has identified two sherds of imported pottery found in the vicinity of St. David's Church.[461] One is a sherd of Phocaean Red Slip Ware imported from Asia Minor in the mid–fifth or sixth century; the other is a sherd of E ware, probably from a Merovingian jar imported in the seventh century. Campbell believes that these imports belonged to a secular settlement at St. David's associated with the nearby landing place and perhaps the cist burials, and contemporary with the sixth-century monastic (?) foundation at the priory.[462]

Excavations at ARDWALL ISLE, off the Kircudbright coast, have revealed significant evidence of an early medieval Christian community. Charles Thomas has assigned the early medieval activity to three phases.[463] Phase I, which is thought to have begun in the late fifth century, included an unenclosed cemetery with inhumations surrounding a small rock-cut hollow (identified by Thomas as the bottom of a "slab-shrine"). During phase II, perhaps in the seventh century, this cemetery was succeeded by another, whose graves were aligned on the axis of a "corner-post" shrine, with postholes perhaps representing a timber oratory or chapel. Grave markers accompanying the phase II burials included slabs with incised crosses and what appears to be a portable stone altar.[464] Phase III saw further aligned burials and a stone chapel and hut. Thomas interprets much of this evidence as a sign of increasing Irish influence in the area.[465] Was it monastic?

The best evidence—archaeological and literary—for a monastic community in sub-Roman Britain comes from WHITHORN in southwestern Scotland. Bede tells us that the first Christian missionary in Scotland was a bishop named Ninian, a Briton who had studied in Rome. He founded a church in southern Scotland, at a place the English call Hwit-aern, and named it Candida Casa in honor of Saint Martin of Tours. Bede, furthermore, describes this church as made of stone rather than wood, "in a manner to which the Britons were not accustomed."[466]

Although the historicity of Saint Ninian's mission has been in question for some time, archaeology has recently thrown new light upon the very real early Christian community at Whithorn. Peter Hill's extensive excavations, only recently published,[467] have uncovered both an early church and a later monastery that predate the Viking settlement at Whithorn (see Fig. 33).

Phase 1/A of this settlement (late fifth century) is dated by the presence of imported Mediterranean pottery and is characterized by small buildings. At one structure, isolated on the crown of a hill, diggers found the residue of lime that had been imported for whitewashing—as close as archaeology will ever get to Ninian's "shining house" (candida casa).[468] Hill elaborates on these features: "The buildings [of phase 1] were consistently small and were probably rectilinear with bowed sides and straight end walls. The curving ditches may reflect overhanging eaves. No substantial timbers were used and the walls and roof were probably constructed as a single entity of woven wattle."[469]

Phase 1/B (late fifth to mid–sixth century) extended to the last of the Mediterranean imports and saw the growth of the settlement, including a monastic (?) garden.[470] Phase 1/C (c. 550–700) included buildings that were part of a secular settlement that grew up on the fringes of the ecclesiastical site; they yielded broken "wine glasses."[471] Phase 1 ended with a possible disaster—a fire—and the end of contact with the outside world.[472] The period that followed, phase 2 (late sixth century), saw the foundation of a cemetery of lintel graves closely linked with a circular shrine.[473] This has been identified as a monastic oratory, and may have been associated with a small stone chapel.[474] Recently identified was a double circular enclosure that surrounded these early Christian settlements at Whithorn.[475]

According to Hill, "The cumulative evidence of exotic technologies" uncovered at Whithorn—which includes moldboard plows, a mechanical mill, and residue from lime washing and iron smelting—"suggests settlers with skills acquired within the Roman empire."[476] Daphne Brooke builds a model suggesting an offshoot of Saint Martin's monastery Marmoutier, with Gallic hermits bringing Continental technologies to Galloway c. 450.[477] Charles Thomas, who has also excavated in the area, agrees that there must have been Romanized communities along the Galloway coast, perhaps with a sizable enough Christian element in the late fourth century to warrant the provision of a bishop (from Carlisle?) such as Ninian.[478] Further evidence that such communities did exist is the impressive number of inscribed memorial stones from Galloway and Dumfrieshire. One, from Whithorn, was erected by a Christian family (it bore the formula Te Dominum Laudamus) to commemorate the deceased Latinus.[479] Two stones from nearby Kirkmadrine (across Luce Bay) bear Chi-Rho crosses and have been dated to c. 500. One of these commemorates Viventius and Mavorius as sancti et praecipui sacerdotes, indisputable evidence of two priests bearing Latinized names in remote Galloway.[480]

Fig. 33. Excavations at Whithorn, Galloway, in 1988, showing the reconstructed Viking hut *(above, upper left)* and the medieval priory *(below, upper left)*

Though sometimes impressive, this is certainly not a large amount of evidence for Christianity in either Roman or sub-Roman Britain, especially not when compared to Gaul and other parts of the western empire. From the evidence we do possess for Britain, however, we can detect a pattern of religious activity in the late fourth through sixth centuries. Mediterranean pagan cults, typically syncretistic in expressing themselves through "Romano-Celtic" temples, appear to have been strong in Britain in the first half of the fifth century, especially in areas where villas were numerous. Decline set in with the Theodosian emperors, while at the same time Britain's few Christian communities began to grow. The beginning of the fifth century likely witnessed the appearance of many new churches, some at the sites of derelict temples. Only a few of these churches would have copied the basilical model of the Mediterranean; others would have manifested themselves as house chapels (at the remaining villas), open-air shrines, hermitages, and perhaps as other structures that have gone unnoticed or undiscovered. By the sixth century some of these Christian communities would have been organized under a monastic rule, though perhaps these monasteries included laymen as well as clerics. At the close of the sub-Roman period, the written and epigraphic evidences show us nothing but Christian Britons, and we hear nothing more—in the written or the physical testimony—of paganism.

This brief survey of significant settlements in sub-Roman Britain leaves many stones unturned and elicits many unanswered questions. The sites discussed above do, however, give us a well-rounded picture of contemporary society, are representative of urban and rural, secular and ecclesiastical, and span most of Britannia. The archaeological evidence is most silent in parts of eastern England, where the Anglo-Saxon settlement and expansion seems to have begun. This leaves all of Wales, the Southwest, northern Britain, and the major urban centers of the East showing signs of continuity of their Romano-British populations. That this area, the majority of Britain, remained under British control through most of the sixth century, should no longer be in doubt. It only remains to better understand these Britons through a synthesis of the physical and written clues that they left behind.

13

◆

CONTINUITY AND CHANGE

As we move away from discussion of individual sites and begin to look at the society as a whole, questions remain to be asked about the patterns and trends that emerge from the archaeological survey. What do these various towns, hillforts, and churches tell us about the nature of sub-Roman settlement in Britain? Does the evidence suggest a continuity of occupation from the Roman period, or a radical change in the standard of living for the Britons?

"All the major towns were laid low by the repeated battering of enemy rams. . . . It was a sad sight. . . . The Cities of our land are not populated even now as they once were; right to the present they are deserted, in ruins and unkempt."[1] Gildas describes how the barbarians have devastated a once-urban Roman Britain, and effectively dictated the island's rural character in his day and, as it turns out, for most of the medieval period. This model of urban decline has been the traditional one for both historians and archaeologists working on the period. It has dominated historical discussion and set the background for viewing the written evidence. The first archaeologists who studied the cities of Roman Britain were a bit like the narrator of the famous Old English poem "The Ruin":

> Wondrous is this stone-wall, wrecked by fate;
> The city-buildings crumble, the works of the giants decay.[2]

The sprawling urban splendor of the second and third centuries concerned these archaeologists most, and they were willing to concede that by the fifth century the giants were truly gone from Britain.

Much scholarly ink has been spilled recently, however, on the question of the continuity of urban centers from Roman Britain to early medieval (Anglo-Saxon) England.[3] Proponents of continuity have focused on the major Roman towns, optimistically interpreting late coin issues, pottery, and timber structures as evidence of lingering "Romano-British" communities that were taken over by "Germanic" settlers in the sixth century.[4] Excavations in the last twenty-five years at Verulamium, Silchester, and Bath have provided the first strong evidence of fifth-century continuity. Most powerful of all was the fifth-century sequence discovered by Barker at the baths basilica in Wroxeter. These excavations showed that at least one city population remained in sufficient numbers to have constructed new timber residences and shops, the size and quality of which speak well for these urban Britons. Other Romano-British towns, like London, Canterbury, Lincoln, and York, show only slight physical traces of continuity; yet we know, from the written evidence, that a significant population (British? English? mixed?) must have survived as each of them became important ecclesiastical centers and eventually English towns.

There has not been a shortage of critics of continuity either. Leading this group is the archaeologist and numismatist Richard Reece, who has made the radical assertion that the towns of Roman Britain fell into dramatic decline in the third century and ceased to exist as true urban centers by 350.[5] The continuity critics have belittled the evidence as signifying only "isolated instances and survivals" in degenerated "villages" where "desertion" occasionally gave way to "squatter occupation" in derelict Roman structures. They point out the near total collapse of Britain's pottery industry in the early fifth century, and the cessation of new coinage reaching the island after 410.

Most compelling of all, they argue, is the phenomenon called "dark earth" observable at many towns in late Roman Britain. This is usually a layer of dark, sometimes black, soil overlying the rubble of Roman masonry buildings that appear, based on coin evidence, to have gone out of use in the late fourth century, sometimes earlier. Reece and others have interpreted this as wind-blown rubbish and other items decaying inside abandoned town walls. It provides for them a nice archaeological "seal" over Britain's discontinuous urban beginnings.

There are many recent indicators, however, that argue against this picture of dramatic urban collapse in the fourth century. Kenneth Dark discusses micromorphological analyses of "dark earth" that suggest quite the opposite of deserted towns.[6] These tests reveal that the dark soil was made up of various organic materials and industrial and domestic debris more representative of human and animal occupation (stabling?) than desertion. The erosion and decay of nonmasonry structures—turf or mud-walled buildings, wattle-and-daub houses, timber halls—would leave behind the kind of black soil mixed with animal dung, charcoal, and industrial debris revealed by the "dark-earth" analyses. Furthermore, Dark sees this as evidence that there were even *more* buildings in fourth- and fifth-century town than before, with lowstatus city populations crowded around a few remaining highstatus masonry public buildings and town houses.[7] Alternatively, urban elites could—and did (witness Wroxeter)—convert to elaborate timber buildings in the fifth and sixth centuries, seemingly in response to being cut off from imperial stone quarries or at least masonry technology. (Bede claims that stonework was "unknown among the Britons.")[8] These urban timber buildings were sometimes, as at Verulamium, surrounded by open cultivated land,[9] and perhaps, as Philip Dixon suggests, "dark earth" in this case represents the importation of topsoil for landscaped parks and gardens to adorn the town houses.[10]

Separating themselves from the urban-continuity debate are the Celtic archaeologists, who have studied the evidence of hilltop settlements and other fortified enclosures of the fifth and sixth centuries with little or no correlation to contemporary activity in the Roman towns, forts, and villas. Yet this ignores the relationships that did exist between urban and rural centers in late and sub-Roman Britain. Ian Burrow has shown that many of the hillforts in Somerset—though their occupants may have been ousted during the campaigns of the first century—showed evidence of some kind of occupation (or reoccupation) in late Roman Britain.[11] In the sub-Roman period, some urban populations may have moved to these hillforts for greater protection and less upkeep: for example, from Wroxeter to the Wrekin, from Ilchester to South Cadbury, from Dorchester to Poundbury (or Maiden Castle), from Exeter to Castle Dore. These sub-Roman hillforts often had occupations as large and complex as the pre-Roman *oppida,* and, like the *oppida,* may have fulfilled many of the functions of a classical town: political administration, domestic residence, trade, defense, agricultural storage and distribution.

Yet the impression one gets from most archaeological discussions is that sub-Roman Britain was a land of fragmentation and isolation. It is as if those Britons who built the timber gateway and fortifications at South Cadbury were living in a different age and in a different part of the world from those of the Britons who built the timber town houses in fifth-century Wroxeter. The fact is that they were not. The Roman cities of London, Bath, Lincoln, Gloucester, Exeter, Dorchester, Caerleon, Wroxeter, Ilchester, and (possibly) Chester have all yielded sherds of the Mediterranean imports that are so common among the hillforts.[12] Likewise, the "native" settlements at West Hill Uley, Longbury Bank, Gateholm, Degannwy, South Cadbury, Ham Hill, Brent Knoll, Tedbury, Kings Castle, Bathealton, and Cadbury-Congresbury have all yielded Roman coinage of the third to fifth centuries, as well as post-Roman ceramics of both imported and local origin.[13] The written evidence mirrors this, for the Britain of Patrick and Gildas is home to both villas and hillforts, both decurions and warbands.

The continuity debate is partly a semantic one, for continuity means different things to different archaeologists.[14] It is one thing to prove occupation in the fifth or sixth century, quite another to determine its character, its intensity, and its ethnic or religious affiliations. There could not, strictly speaking, have been continuity of Roman urban life in fifth-century Britain. Gone were the imperial administration, the Roman military complex, the supply of new coins and bullion (with the exception of a few stray coins obtained, most likely, from Mediterranean traders), the mass-produced pottery from the state-run factories, the polished stone imported for building, and the large populations that fed off the imperial bureaucracy. This does not mean, however, that urban life came to a dramatic end, that cities ceased to exist. The depleted city populations went on with life pretty much as usual, for coins and pottery continued to circulate, soldiers (native or mercenary) continued to make their presence known, and various local tyrants and magistrates exerted their political influence. Some city dwellers moved to more easily defended hilltop and island settlements; others retreated to shrinking villas. The settlement patterns are complex and enigmatic, not easily provable. The very complexity of this society—which eventually yielded a rich body of hagiographic and heroic legend—demands that it be treated by archaeologists as more than an obscure interlude between the more easily understood Roman and Anglo-Saxon periods.

"The 'British dimension' in fifth-century history," writes Malcolm Todd, "has received far less attention than it deserves."[15] The same could be said of the British dimension in early medieval archaeology, which has been dominated by the quest for signs of the first English settlements. But for every Sutton Hoo, deservedly celebrated for the historical and artistic riches of its royal Anglian tomb, there are thousands of anonymous Britons lying in impoverished Christian graves. Many of these British graves have been found and reported with no pomp and circumstance; many others await the funding of an excavation that promises neither golden jewelry nor princely ship. No one, however, could argue, from the meager fifth-century Saxon cemetery evidence, that this ethnic group controlled any more than small portions of eastern Britain before the late sixth century. Even Bede does not do this, and we should not think that the ninth-century (and later) Anglo-Saxon chroniclers were keeping an accurate political score of the sub-Roman period. That is not to undervalue the influence of Anglo-Saxon artistic styles, manifest in the numerous examples of pottery and jewelry found in the "Celtic" West; but who would claim that the presence of North African dishes in sub-Roman Chester proves that Carthaginians were then living along the Welsh border?

Remembering that it is nigh impossible to prove ethnicity from artifacts, still the fifth and sixth centuries rightly belong to the Britons, regardless of the fact that by the end of the period they had lost much of their *patria*. Only the Britons produced written accounts of their society in the sub-Roman period, and it is their populations—urban and rural—that we can best trace in the archaeological record of continuity. More accurately, there is both continuity and change in the archaeological record, and the barbarian newcomers are only part of that change. This continuity and change is best described by bringing together the written and archaeological evidence, carefully considering the shortcomings of both, and producing a synthesis, a minihistory, of the sub-Roman Britons.

PART IV

◆

SYNTHESIS:

Toward A Picture of Britain in the Fifth and Sixth Centuries

14

◆

THE BRITONS

There is no hope of ever knowing actually what happened for sure [between the years A.D. 200 and 800 in Britain]. We can have ideas and manipulate the material information and the picture we create may be perfectly calm and hopeful, but even if we have judged it to be a good picture, and others have accepted it, this still does not mean that this is actually what happened; it remains our picture, or your picture, or my picture, and should not be confused with reality.[1]

The early years of the fifth century will have been characterized by a continual movement of population: country people moving to the safety of towns or the refortified hillforts of their ancestors; refugees escaping from massacres . . . escaping slaves taking advantage of the confused times; foreign mercenaries hired by townspeople to aid their defense; soldiers making their way home or to a new posting.[2]

The authors of these two passages are both modern scholars of Roman Britain. Both have examined the written and archaeological evidence for the fifth century to reach their respective conclusions about sub-Roman Britain. Yet these two positions could not be more widely divergent. The first position has been called the "reductionist" argument: we can know nothing for certain; therefore nothing happened.[3] The second position has been termed the "positivist" approach: something must have happened, so what can the evidence tell us? Caution and skepticism support the reductionist; curiosity upholds the positivist. Both approaches have their strengths and weaknesses.

I mention these arguments as a preface to saying that this is a "positivist" chapter. While I agree with the reductionists that a historian cannot reproduce or reconstruct past reality, the creation of "my picture" or "your picture" of sub-Roman Britain is nevertheless a worthwhile endeavor. The positivist picture is an attempt to breathe life into the archaeological data and reassemble the vignettes of British society scattered throughout the written sources. It is worthy to construct such models if for nothing else than to promote debate and animate the skeptics. That being said, the positivist picture must be built on a firm foundation of evidence and examples drawn from the written sources, inscriptions, and archaeology of the period. The stronger the evidence, the more attractive the picture.

This chapter is also an attempt at a "synthesis" of the written evidence and archaeological data that heretofore have been treated separately.[4] It is a synthesis concerned with both political and social history, though it makes no attempt to be narrative or all-inclusive. Contemporary society is discussed in some conventional and accessible categories: church and state, the economy, the military, culture and social structure. I hope that this will begin discussion in these areas, for closure to the discussion is out of reach. Simply put, this chapter is an attempt to answer the question raised earlier in the book: Who are the Britons?

Political Association

Students of the *Annales* school, forgive me if I begin my history "from above," that is, by looking at political structures and the elite. Patrick and Gildas were concerned with government in Britain, as were those prominent Britons who celebrated their political titles on inscribed stones. Welsh kings issued charters in the sixth century; local magistrates greeted Saint Germanus in the fifth. Archaeology has yielded less explicit evidence about British rulers, though it sometimes allows us to infer political organization. Overall, evidence for government is fairly accessible—if not always easily understood—and allows for comparison with the known political structures of both Roman Britain and the later fragmented insular kingdoms.

At the opening of the fifth century, Britanniae was a diocese of the Roman Empire whose chief civic official was the *vicarius* in London (who in turn reported to the praetorian prefect in Gaul). The *Notitia Dignitatum* lists several other civic and fiscal posts: the *rationalis summarum,* or comptroller of finances for the diocese; the *praepositus thesaurorum,* or head of the treasury in London; the *procurator gynaecii,* or director of the state weaving mill in the city of Venta; and the *rationalis rei privatae,* or supervisor of the privy purse (i.e., the imperial-owned estates and properties).[5] At the next lower level were the governors of the five British provinces: the governors of Maxima Caesariensis and Valentia bore the title *consularis,* while the other governors were styled *praeses.*[6] Local government was administered through the *civitates* (Gildas numbers them at twenty-eight),[7] which were small territorial units, originally tribal-based, centered on one major urban center, the *civitas* capital, though often containing other urban settlements (*municipii, vici, pagi,* etc.) as well. Each of these "cities" was governed by a council of representatives called the *ordo* or *curia;* its members, the *curiales* or *decuriones,* were drafted from the local aristocracy (*possessores*).

This bureaucratic machine had seen Britain through several restive centuries, and nothing suggests that it was not operating as usual through the first decade of the fifth. We know the names of some of the civil servants serving in these twilight years—the *praeses* Sanctus, the *vicarii* Chrysanthus and Victorinus—and their subsequent positions suggest that a British post was, as usual, just another stepping stone along the political path.[8] Also from these ranks emerged the *municeps* Gratian to make his unsuccessful bid for empire in 406. At the end of the decade, however, the political situation had changed dramatically. In the years 406–7, while Gaul was being devastated by barbarian incursions, three successive usurpers were raised to the purple in Britain. The last of these, Constantine III, apparently granted the wishes of his troops by taking them to Gaul to secure the western frontier. Presumably, he left *his* supporters in command of the civil posts in Britain during his absence. Shortly after his departure, however, Britain itself was devastated by northern invaders, most notably "Saxons."[9] According to Zosimus, the inhabitants of Britain responded by arming themselves to free their cities from attacking barbarians.[10] This was an illegal act, but it did not seem to matter to the Britons, for they had expelled their "magistrates" and set up a government of their own choosing, "no longer submitting to Roman law."[11] In 410 Honorius made this separation official.[12]

The character of the government in Britain after the revolt of 409/410 is not an easy matter to discern. We have no *Notitia Dignitatum* for sub-Roman Britain. Some scholars have taken Zosimus at his (literal) word: the Britons expelled *all* Roman officials from the island, not just the government of Constantine III.[13] Some would even go so far as interpreting these events as a sociopolitical revolution, with dispossessed rebels (*bacaudae*) ousting a pro-imperial establishment.[14] While the *bacaudae* were responsible for fifth-century turmoil in Gaul, nothing in the written sources suggests that rural peasants and slaves took control of Britain.[15] On the contrary, much suggests

that it was not the dispossessed who took over the reins of government in
Britain, but rather the *possessores*. One scenario would have the Britons,
lacking sufficient protection in Constantine's absence, organizing themselves
into *civitas*-based militias to defend life and property. With Constantine's fortunes waning and Honorius in no position to send help, the imperial apparatus would have been seen as unnecessary and therefore would have been
summarily dismissed. However, while there was no longer a need to support
the imperial bureaucracy, there was a need for local defensive support and
for some city maintenance. Those best in position to do this were the members of the curial class, who were at exactly this time being addressed in western legal documents as *possessores*.[16] Zosimus states plainly that the Britons
freed their *civitates* (πολεις) from barbarian attacks, and that it was to the
civitates (πολεις) that Honorius sent his letters.[17] The men who ran the governing of the *civitates* were landed aristocrats at the local level, not transient
civil servants seeking promotion elsewhere, and thus they had the best reason to keep Britain safe and prosperous, at least in their own districts.
Furthermore, no imperial government meant that they no longer had to bil-
let imperial troops,[18] and the only taxes they needed to (or could) collect
would have been those necessary to maintain their own communities.[19]

The *possessores* of sub-Roman Britain undoubtedly came in many shapes
and sizes. *Decuriones*, like Patrick's father, struggled to maintain private
country estates (*villae*) while also seeing to the maintenance of urban centers that served as marketplaces for their produce, *fora* for their assemblies,
and even fortifications in times of danger.[20] A century later, Gildas suggests
that both public and private funds still existed and were employed to construct defenses for the *urbes*.[21] Archaeology shows us some of the successful
endeavors of the *possessores*. At St. Albans they kept the aqueduct working
and laid a new water main,[22] and at Carlisle the town fountain continued to
function into the seventh century.[23] They continued to pave the streets at
Winchester,[24] laid new cobble floors for the inner precinct of the temple at
Bath,[25] provided for a sluice gate and other flood prevention work at
Cirencester,[26] and purchased Mediterranean imports at London and
Wroxeter.[27] They defended their *civitates* with both militias and mercenaries, at least once taking common counsel to tackle a problem affecting more
than a single district of the *patria*.[28] Still, their power and importance was
mostly local. Constantius describes Elafius as "chief man of that region,"[29]
and the Byzantine ship's captain in the *Life of St. John the Almsgiver* deals,
upon landing in Britain, with "the chief man of the town," who offers the
captain both coins and tin in exchange for corn to relieve a local famine.[30]

These men would have given themselves high-sounding Latin titles like *rector, iudex, magistratus,* or simply *civis* of their district.[31] Since their offices had been hereditary under the empire, these titles would likely have been passed down as well.[32]

From a distant perspective, the *possessores* of Britain might not appear to be Roman *curiales* who had simply continued and expanded their powers.[33] They could be seen, and were seen, as "tyrants." Jerome, writing from Judaea shortly after the revolt, declared that "Britain is a province fertile of *tyranni.*"[34] Procopius, writing much later in Constantinople, remarked that after 410 Rome was never able to recover Britain, "but from that time on it remained on its own under τυραννου."[35] The new rulers of Britain were tyrants to these two writers because, cut off from Rome, they seemed illegitimate in some way. Previous usurpers from Britain like Gratian (a *municeps*) and Constantine III—seen retrospectively as unsuccessful and ultimately harmful to the empire—no doubt helped color the opinions of Jerome and Procopius, as Maximus certainly did for Gildas.[36] Philip Dixon, surveying the urban archaeological evidence, similarly observes this connection between *decuriones* and *tyranni:* "The owners, and certainly the controllers, of these fortified [towns] were the *decuriones.* . . . During and after the rebellion of 407, the natural successors to these owners were the usurpers of Zosimus and Procopius, presumably members of the Romanized upper classes who assumed power within their own regions, as the Romanized habits of the group suggest."[37] I would go even further to say that many of the *tyranni* were *decuriones* (Patrick certainly attests to the fact that the latter were still around after 407), not their successors, and that these men were responsible for the British rebellion described by Zosimus. It would not have been the first time in Roman history that usurpation had been made necessary by local emergencies;[38] this time, however, Rome would never recover the rebellious province.

Kenneth Dark has pointed out that one of the biggest problems in interpreting fifth-century Britain is how to get from Roman forms of civil government at the beginning of the century to dynastic kingship at the end.[39] I believe that the *tyrannus* is the key link in this evolution of political forms. Salvian calls the members of the curial class of fifth-century Gaul *tyranni,* and says that they were actually proud of this "title."[40] Gildas states that the *consiliarii* acted in conjunction with the *superbo tyranno,* "the most arrogant tyrant," with a possible inference being that this individual, though of the same ilk as the other members of the council, was the most arrogant of the lot.[41] The name of this tyrant, most now agree, was Vortigern (Vortigernos).[42]

The element *tigernos* was a Common Celtic term meaning "lord," in certain contexts a local lord (*seigneur*) or a king, and *tigernos* was equated in Breton charters with the Latin term *tyrannus*.[43] Gildas knew this and was evidently making a pun on Vortigern's name and political position.[44] To later writers like Bede and the authors of the *Historia Brittonum* and the *Anglo-Saxon Chronicle*, however, this Vortigern is a British *king* as well as a tyrant.[45] Gildas claims that, by the middle of the fifth century in Britain, "kings were anointed" who were cruel and oppressive, only to be deposed at will by their "anointers."[46] "Cruel kings" are most often described by Gildas as *tyranni*, following the precedent of earlier Christian writers who used this term for moral condemnation of any secular ruler.[47] "Kings [*reges*], public officials [*publici*], and private citizens [*privati*]," inhabited the Britain of Gildas's birth.[48] The transition from the *publici* who dominated events at the beginning of the fifth century to the dynastic *reges* who dominated the Britain of Gildas's adulthood (the post-Badon part of his narrative) is best understood by looking at *tyrannus*, a term used in the vernacular to denote the local lord and in Christian Latin to describe any despotic ruler, whether civic or monarchical.

The archaeological evidence shows something of this transition as well. Maintenance of civic amenities in such towns as Verulamium, Cirencester, and Winchester continued in the early decades of the fifth century. While the urban populations receded within the protective walls of these cities, modest timber, turf, and mud-brick structures appeared around the stone mansions of the rich.[49] One of these private residences, a large stone town house in Verulamium, continued to pave its floors and install mosaics up to the middle of the fifth century.[50] Even more impressive is the fifth-century *mansio* at Wroxeter, which has been described as a country mansion inside a city, built in the classical style (though in timber), with several contiguous smaller structures.[51] The construction of a complex of this size would have required enormous resources of both man and material, and the associated structures could have housed a large personal retinue: "The major building . . . is, in plan, more like a *villa*, a Roman suburban or country house, than a public building. We seem to have found here a clear example of the taking-over of a central public site by an individual of wealth and power. He may have been one of the *tyranni* or local rulers who arose in Britain at this time."[52] Such palatial complexes in the hearts of the cities have also been observed in York, London, Cirencester, and Lincoln.[53] It should surprise no one that the *villa* owners in Britain might prefer to move their households within the protective walls of a nearby city, where they likely held curial office.[54]

Another option for these landowners would have been to move their household to fortified rural settlements. These included hilltops, promontories, and other easily defended sites, many of which served as "hillforts" in the pre-Roman Iron Age.[55] After the Claudian invasion and subsequent campaigns, Roman authorities generally resettled the inhabitants of captured hillforts in nearby villages.[56] However, archaeologists have discovered that in some areas, most notably in the North and West, hillforts show signs of near continuous occupation from the LPRIA to the early medieval period.[57] The intensity of such occupation, as seen in the artifactual assemblage, seems to increase from the fourth century onward and overlaps in many areas with the that of the large *villa* estates. Burrow has pointed out that there are many reasons why communities might migrate back to these hillforts, including to defend themselves against attack, to worship at a native shrine, to avoid lowland flooding, and to escape disease in crowded urban centers.[58] Of these reasons, defense against attack may have been most important for fourth-century villagers in Britain, who had seen their imperial protectors mutiny, follow usurpers to the Continent, and generally fail to stop raiding Scots, Picts, and Saxons.[59] These hillforts likely remained temporary refuges in the late Roman period (and therefore show no evidence of elaborate structures), whereas after the Rescript of Honorius they show the first signs of significant defensive reconstruction.[60]

It is less clear who these hillfort inhabitants were. The native tribes who surrendered to or cooperated with the Romans in the first century may have been allowed to continue peacefully to occupy their hilltop settlements. In areas where the dynasties had been destroyed along with the ramparts, humble villagers may have gradually made their way back to uninhabited hillforts and pursued sporadic and limited agriculture.[61] Some hillforts show signs of intense industrial or agricultural activity (metalworking, jewelry making, butchery, weaving),[62] while religious shrines (pagan and/or Christian) are also frequently present.[63] At Cadbury-Congresbury and Tintagel, it has even been suggested that sub-Roman occupation was only seasonal, indicating perhaps a regional "fair" or the court of an itinerant king.[64] The historical sources definitely suggest that by the sixth century some of these hillforts were the residences of dynastic monarchs. Unfortunately, though Gildas, our earliest source, lists five such monarchs and gives us a rough idea of their kingdoms (see Fig. 6), he does not give specific information about their residences.[65] The sub-Roman occupants of these hillforts, then, remain anonymous, consigned to speculative models.[66]

I think it is safe, however, to agree with the archaeologists that sub-Roman "administrative centers" would have included these hillforts, along with the surviving *civitas* capitals and perhaps some of the late Roman forts. As for other sub-Roman political entities, we again tread on dangerously speculative ground. The *civitas,* a Roman "city-state" imposed upon a preexisting tribal territory, seems to have survived in Britain when and if its walled capital could withstand both the postimperial economy and the increasing barbarian raids. Such survival appears strongest in the Southwest, the Midlands, and the North, and weakest in the Southeast, where the first "Anglo-Saxon" political entities formed.[67] London, Chichester, Silchester, Cirencester, Wroxeter, Chester, York, and Carlisle have all been suggested as administrative centers for sub-Roman *civitates*/kingdoms.[68] The larger hillfort settlements such as South Cadbury, Degannwy, and Dumbarton may have performed a similar role.[69] The sub-Roman *civitates* seem also, to some extent, to have reverted to their pre-Roman tribal identities.[70] Gildas mentions "Damnonia" and the Demetae, while inscriptions name an Elmetiacos, an Ordous, a Venedotis *cives,* a *civis* Dunnonia, and the Dobunni.[71] These correspond roughly to pre-Roman tribal entities, which were often large territories subdivided by the Romans.[72] Many of the sub-Roman *civitates* marked off the boundaries of their territory by constructing massive bank-and-ditch earthworks, which may have further acted as defenses against the encroaching Saxons.[73]

The Military

Warfare shaped sub-Roman polities, as it shaped almost every aspect of sub-Roman society. The written sources are unambiguous and unanimous in depicting fifth- and sixth-century Britain as an island plagued by barbarian raids, foreign invasion, civil wars, and the territorial struggles of various groups. Ammianus was the first to describe the attacks of Picts, Scots, and Saxons in the late fourth century; Claudian, Zosimus, Patrick, and the Gallic Chronicles bear witness to the continuing threat of these same groups in the early fifth century. Gildas claims that the Picts and Scots were so threatening that the Britons had to hire Saxon mercenaries to fend them off, only to have the greedy Saxons turn against their employers. The Llandaff Charters and the vernacular poetry reveal that the sixth century was characterized by territorial struggles between the waning power of the Britons and the waxing strength of the Germanic invaders. Archaeologists, however, remain divided over whether the material evidence supports this burn-and-slaughter model or, rather, a more peaceful assimilation of conquerors to the conquered.

For the military structure in Britain around 400, we again have the testimony of the western portion of the *Notitia Dignitatum*. As noted before, the *Notitia* lists three major commands in Britain: the *comes Britanniarum,* the *comes litoris Saxonici,* and the *dux Britanniarum.* These commands reflect the reorganization of the frontier defenses begun by Constantine I and completed, in Britain, by the time of Count Theodosius's campaigns on the island.[74] Unspecified troop withdrawals between 383 and 407 are recorded under Magnus Maximus, Stilicho, and Constantine III. How extensive these withdrawals were and how vulnerable this left Britain we do not know, but there is no reason to believe that the three frontier commands listed in the *Notitia* were not filled by Constantine before his departure in 407. He almost certainly did not remove them to Gaul, though he did fill the posts of the *magistri* above them and took these men with him to the Continent.

The question is, then, what became of the imperial army in Britain after the revolt of 409/10? It is highly unlikely that the "revolutionaries" would have been able or willing to expel armed forces. It is also unlikely that the soldiers stationed in remote frontier posts would have played an active part in expelling governors from the southern *civitates.*[75] Would these soldiers have waited patiently at their posts under the promise that imperial payments would eventually be restored? Such a promise is unlikely given Honorius's letters sent in 410. The remaining army in Britain, whatever its strength, would then have no other choice but gradually to disband itself, with local recruits retiring to their communities and others taking ship for far away homes or other posts where their traditional benefits were still available.[76]

Another possibility, however, is that the soldiers stayed at their posts under new paymasters and that most aspects of military life continued as before, though by the end of the period British armies had completed the slow transition from the Roman to the Heroic. Michael Jones, observing the stagnation of units along Hadrian's Wall, envisions these soldiers as "little more than caretakers and military police, . . . merged into a Celtic social world defined not by empire but by warband and clan."[77] If these soldiers were typical frontier troops, they had families in the community and so would have had a stake in its defense, taking payment in kind, since coinage was increasingly scarce.[78] Dark has now shown from the archaeological evidence that such military continuation did occur at many of the forts along the Wall in the mid–fifth century,[79] and a number of coastal fortifications

show continued activity at this time as well.[80] Honorius told the *civitates* to
arrange their own defense, and naturally the *civitas* leaders would have
turned first to the soldiers in and around their cities. London, Gloucester,
Cirencester, and York show evidence of fifth-century additions or repairs to
their defenses,[81] and evidence from the latter part of the century indicates
that shrinking urban populations moved inside town amphitheaters for security (a phenomenon observable in Gaul and Dacia at this time).[82] Gildas provides written corroboration that the Britain he knows is not without a
variety of fortifications.[83]

Those *civitates* lacking regular soldiers would then have turned to mercenaries. Gildas says that Saxon mercenaries were settled on the eastern side
of the island to fight against the Picts, but regrets that Christians have entered
into a treaty (*foedus*) with pagans.[84] Archaeologists have been quick to interpret the presence of "Germanic" belt buckles, pottery, and *Grubenhäuser*
inside or near Romano-British towns as evidence of Germanic *foederati*
affixed to fifth-century communities.[85] However, we now know that such
"Germanic" belt buckles were worn by both regular soldiers and civic officials in the late empire, and it is dangerous in any case to argue ethnic identity based on the jewelry or pottery used by a community. Derek Welsby has
concluded that there is no evidence to suggest the presence of large groups
of barbarians in Britain before 410, though smaller units had undoubtedly
long been a normal part of the imperial defenses in Britain.[86] By the late fifth
century the archaeological evidence for "Continental" groups increases, but
the relationship between the users of these goods and their neighbors cannot be sufficiently explained.

Another defensive option for the Britons was the rural "enclosed place,"
the hillfort.[87] Gildas states that, in the face of the Saxon threat, the Britons
held out in "the high hills (*montanis . . . praeruptis*), steep (*collibus*), menacing (*minacibus*) and fortified (*vallatis*), to the densest forests (*densissimis
saltibus*), and to the cliffs of the sea coast (*marinisque rupibus*)."[88] Many of
these hilltop settlements, whether continuously occupied or reoccupied, show
signs of extensive fortification in the fifth and sixth centuries. South Cadbury
had five massive ramparts enclosing eighteen acres, a dressed stone wall with
a timber fighting platform, and a timber gate tower with an interior bridge.[89]
Cadbury-Congresbury had a similar timber platform along with earthworks,
bastions, and watchtowers.[90] Drystone and timber defenses were also constructed at Dumbarton, Castle Dore, and Degannwy, while even smaller
homesteads like Dinas Powys used crude earthen banks and ditches.[91] Leslie
Alcock has pointed out that most of these hilltop settlements are located on

the coast or near waterways, but in otherwise inconvenient locations.[92] Given that this is also the area where fifth-century coin hoards are clustered,[93] it is clear that most hilltop occupation in the sub-Roman period is a response to the threat of seaborne barbarian raids.[94] Not only could these hillforts provide protective walls, they could also offer views of the surrounding countryside to forewarn the Britons about impending attacks.

Warfare shaped the lives of the Britons in many ways. But what was sub-Roman warfare like? History and archaeology offer ample testimony to answer this question. Vegetius described, at the beginning of the fifth century, light camouflaged reconnaissance ships that were particular to Britain.[95] We hear no more of this British navy, however, for the army steals most of the subsequent press. Constantius describes the British *milites* as an *exercitus* stationed in a *castra*.[96] Patrick describes the *milites* of Coroticus as *sanguilentos* who wield swords (*gladii*) and live on spoils (*spolii*) and plunder (*rapinae*).[97] Gildas, adding to his description of the town defenses, tells us that the Britons fought with shields (*peltae*), swords (*enses*), and lances (*hastae*), while their opponents hurled barbed spears (*uncinata tela*) that tore them from their walls (*muri*).[98] The kings of Gildas's own day "wage[d] wars, civil and unjust," with their *commanipulares*, rode chariots (*currus*), and fought with *arma speciales*.[99] Archaeologists have uncovered some of these physical objects of war. Belt fittings, spearheads, iron knives, lead-weighted javelin heads (*martiobarbuli*), an iron thrusting spear or lance, an iron crossbow bolt, and a shield boss have all turned up at various sites, and at Dinas Emrys excavators found three Donside terrets, rein rings, from a chariot.[100] Horses had been an important part of warfare for the Britons since Caesar's day, and the early medieval vernacular poetry certainly testifies to the continuing use of cavalry by the British aristocracy.[101] At Tintagel, a graffito etched onto slate depicts a sub-Roman warrior equipped with sword, shield, spear, helmet, and what appears to be a whip.[102] Compared to the Roman and Anglo-Saxon periods, however, weapons finds are scarce. This may have much to do with a newly Christian population of Britons who were giving up the pagan tradition of burial with grave goods.

Religion

The transition from paganism to Christianity in Britain has long been the most pressing religious issue for historians of the period.[103] To what degree was late Roman Britain Christianized? What role did pagan religions play in sub-Roman Britain? Churches, temples, mosaics, burials, inscriptions, and the written accounts of churchmen have all been employed to answer these questions. If a consensus has yet to emerge, it is not because of a lack of evidence. We can, I believe, say more with certainty about the religious life of the Britons than about any other aspect of their society.

"Almost certainly by the time of Gildas," writes James Campbell, "all the Britons were Christian."[104] Though it is unreasonable to assume that "all" the Britons were of any one faith, the written sources would seem to support Campbell's view that pagan religions played no significant role in sub-Roman Britain. Patrick's family had been Christian for three generations, and his only complaint against his fellow Britons is that there were rebel Christians and apostates among them, but not pagans.[105] Similarly, Gildas complains that the Britons had allowed pagan Saxons into their Christian land ("God, the heathen have come into your inheritance"), and that the British kings had broken their vows to God.[106] If paganism was widespread in Britain, Patrick and Gildas would have been all too willing to complain.[107]

Much has been written about a so-called pagan revival in late and sub-Roman Britain.[108] This theory rests almost entirely on an interpretation of physical evidence. There are no written accounts of paganism in Britain after Caesar and Tacitus, and epigraphic evidence is scarce.[109] Formal pagan worship in Roman Britain—in the three forms of imperial cults, indigenous cults, and mystery religions—had been strong primarily in the Romanized South and East. The number of temples and shrines in these areas, especially in urban centers, decreased in the fourth century, and by the end of the century most had gone out of use.[110]

Ritual discontinued at the Romano-Celtic temple at Chelmsford by 402, and the temple was subsequently dismantled to make way for other structures.[111] A similar temple at Brean Down was demolished c. 390,[112] and the complex at West Hill Uley was dismantled in the Theodosian period, its altars and statuary incorporated in subsequent structures at the site.[113] Both the discontinuity of worship and the "desecration" of these temples have been attributed to increasingly influential and zealous Christians. However, there is no direct evidence, literary or physical, that Christians ever engaged in the systematic destruction of paganism in Britain, or even that tensions existed between the two groups.[114] On the contrary, pagan and Christian motifs can often be found together in art from this period, especially in mosaics and silver plate.[115] A more likely scenario is that at many temples worship slowly died out in the fourth century and the structures deteriorated.

The traditional sanctity of many such sites was then recognized by the Christian communities who later established their churches and cemeteries there.[116] The one written account we do possess describing Christian-pagan conflicts in Britain is Pope Gregory's letter to Mellitus.[117] This epistle suggests that successful conversion occurred when clergy adapted pagan temples and rituals to Christian usage in a nonviolent way.[118]

The fourth century began with pagans in the majority, and ended with Christians perhaps pulling up even. Written evidence (slight though it is) attests to Christians in Britain from at least A.D. 200,[119] but the material evidence for the British church is sparse compared to that of other western provinces. This evidence occurs in four forms: churches, villas, cemeteries, and portable objects.[120] Only Silchester, Colchester, Icklingham, and Whithorn have produced buildings that have been convincingly identified as churches.[121] None of these structures is architecturally impressive. The Silchester and Colchester churches are small basilicas (see Fig. 31), while those at Icklingham and Whithorn are simple rectilinear buildings. Baptismal fonts were present near the Silchester and Icklingham churches, and also inside the fort at Richborough, but otherwise the churches of fourth-century Britain bespeak an urban Christianity of modest means.[122]

We get a different picture, however, when we look at the Christian evidence from villas. During the fourth century, the villas at Frampton, Hinton St. Mary, and Lullingstone added extra rooms decorated with explicitly Christian artwork.[123] These apsidal rooms, which had associated antechambers, have been identified as private chapels for the use of the Christian members of the estate. The Lullingstone chapel was not built until c. 385, and continued in use until the villa burned down sometime after c. 420.[124] Thus, by the late fourth century, Christianity had made converts among the landowning elite, and the Christian objects dating to the late fourth and early fifth centuries confirm this increasing affluence. The Chi-Rho and Alpha and Omega symbols appear on numerous silver spoons and plaques, gold disks and finger rings, and pottery.[125] Most of these are items of domestic use. It could be that urban churches are so rare for Roman and sub-Roman Britain because these Christians preferred to worship in house churches and other structures not so easy to identify.

The type of site recently given the most attention by archaeologists is the Christian cemetery. Sites that have graves aligned east-west (with the head pointing west) and that lack grave goods have been identified as possible Christian cemeteries. Associated Christian symbols or epitaphs obviously strengthen the case. Icklingham, Poundbury (Dorchester), Butt Road

(Colchester), Shepton Mallet, Bradley Hill and Brean Down (Somerset), Phillack and Tintagel (Cornwall), St. Paul-in-the-Bail (Lincoln), Ancaster, and Whithorn are the best candidates, while sub-Roman mausoleums have been argued for Wells (Somerset), St. Mary de Lode (Gloucester), and Stone-by-Faversham (Kent).[126] The slight artifactual evidence from these sites tells us but little about the funerary customs of the Britons. At Poundbury, one juvenile skeleton wore a pierced coin pendant displaying an upright Chi-Rho.[127] One burial at Shepton Mallet contained a silver cruciform amulet with a Chi-Rho design punched into it, an item possibly belonging to a priest.[128] At Tintagel, crosses were carved on gravestones, and the site has yielded what appear to be the remains of a ritual funeral meal.[129] The burials themselves took the form of simple inhumations, rock-covered mounds, slab-lined and cist graves (a pre-Roman trait), wood and lead coffins, and stone mausoleums. (Decapitation seems also to have been a not uncommon burial rite in late Roman Britain—seven graves at Lankhills showed evidence of ritual decapitation—which continued in medieval Wales.)[130] Explicitly Christian epitaphs are rare in fourth-century Britain, but in the sub-Roman period there are numerous examples, mostly from Wales and the Southwest.[131] Early Christian inscriptions on crude pillar stones or slabs usually consist of a brief Latin formula (HIC IACET . . .) and the deceased's name, sometimes followed by names of relatives or other identifiers, and are often accompanied by the name inscribed along one edge in Ogam script.[132] Again, the Chi-Rho and Alpha and Omega are the most common Christian symbols in epigraphy, while simple crosses appear with greater frequency from the sixth century on.

New methodologies have recently been employed to identify Christian churches and communities in sub-Roman Britain. Steven Bassett has studied early medieval charters and local topography, looking for evidence of early parish boundaries in Britain.[133] When Roman missionaries came into the seventh-century Anglo-Saxon kingdoms, they found in many areas late and sub-Roman churches, British bishops, and an Anglo-Saxon population at least partially converted by the Britons.[134] The churches of St. Helen's (Worcester), St. Mary de Lode (Gloucester), St. Andrew's (Wroxeter), St. Michael's (Lichfield), and St. Paul-in-the-Bail (Lincoln) have all been proposed as preexisting bishoprics taken over by the Augustinian missionaries—probably on papal advice—to become new English sees.[135] Similarly, other scholars have argued that many of the place-names with the element *eccles* (from the Latin *ecclesia*, "a body of Christians")—such as Eccles (of which there are several), Eccleshall, Eggles, and Eaglesfield—

are either what the Britons were calling their Christian communities (the British form is *egles*) or were so named by Saxons taking over preexisting Christian communities.[136]

So these are several possible Christian communities and churches. But what did these Christians do? For this we are better served by the written sources. Most of our evidence is about the secular clergy, which included *diaconi, pastores* and *ministri, sacerdotes, presbyteri,* and v*episcopi.*[137] Neither Patrick nor Gildas suggests that there was a strict hierarchy in the British church, though there were clearly betters (*meliores*) or elders (*seniores*) and "those beneath them."[138] Pastoral duties to the *parochiae* included administering baptism and confession, serving the Eucharist, confirming oaths, giving alms, performing sacrifices, serving secular rulers, and sometimes pronouncing excommunication. Clerical interactions included the holding of councils, performing consecrations and ordinations, administering penance, and traveling overseas if necessary for church appointments. Celibacy was not required, at least not below the level of bishop, and women appear to have played an active role within the church.[139] Education was of great import, an education that appears to have followed the classical model of grammar, rhetoric, and law, but firmly resting on the foundations of the Bible and the church fathers.[140]

Traditionally, education in early Christian Britain has been associated with monasteries. However, not much is known about the regular clergy of sub-Roman Britain. Constans, son of Constantine III, is the first British monk on record, and a British *antistes et monachus* named Riocatus visited Sidonius Apollinaris in Gaul.[141] Patrick made *monachi et virgines Christi* in Ireland and longed to visit the *fratres* in Gaul, but he speaks not of monastics in Britain.[142] Our chief evidence, then, comes from the writings of Gildas and the early Christian inscriptions, and deals mainly with the sixth century. In general, Gildas describes the monastic movement in Britain as fledgling but gaining ever more enthusiastic supporters, including evidently escapist monarchs like Maelgwn of Gwynedd.[143] In Gildas's day, there are abbots, monks, and nuns following *regulae,* in which they fast, hold vigil, sing psalms, and work in the fields. Yet these British monastics are not completely removed from worldly temptations, and in the "Fragments" Gildas eschews ascetic excesses and severe penances.[144]

The physical evidence of monasticism in Britain is not very strong before the late sixth century. Tintagel, Glastonbury, and Cadbury-Congresbury have all been proposed as monastic sites at one time or another, but interpretations vary. The best evidence comes from Whithorn, which Bede claims is the *Candida Casa* built by bishop Ninian (Saint Nynia).[145] Excavations have revealed a large and varied Christian community from the fifth through the seventh centuries. Lime-washed buildings, Mediterranean pottery, wine glasses, moldboard plows, a mechanical mill, and inscribed stones commemorating Christians with names like Latinus imply a degree of Romanization in southern Scotland and contact with the larger Roman world.[146] Whithorn has been interpreted as a Christian community, probably under a local bishop, that became "monastic" in character by the late sixth century, when a cemetery (with graves centered on a small oratory) and stone chapel were built. Many scholars have pointed out the difficulty in identifying monastic communities in this period, when even the written sources are often unclear whether a Christian community was secular, regular, celibate, or consisted of a mixture of clergy, families, and tenants.[147] Richard Morris has suggested that the first monasteries in Britain, especially in Wales, were founded on or near Roman villas by late Roman aristocratic families converted to ascetic Christianity.[148] Jerome and Augustine record such conversions in the Mediterranean; the Gallic villa owners of Sidonius's generation (and earlier) were attracted to monasticism; and monasteries at Llantwit Major and Llancarfan are depicted as converted villas in Welsh hagiography.[149]

One cannot conclude a discussion of the early British church without mentioning its most infamous export, the heretic Pelagius. What his religious upbringing in late-fourth-century Britain was like we do not know, only that he was undoubtedly Christian and well educated before he left for Rome at the beginning of the fifth century. Pelagius's story is that of the Mediterranean world c. 410, but the spread of his heresy after his disappearance in 418 directly involves Britain. Pelagian bishops were sufficiently influential in the British Isles to worry the pope and warrant the missions of Germanus to Britain and Palladius to Ireland. Claims that Pelagianism played a political role in Britain's separation from Rome and subsequently split the island into factions have never been adequately demonstrated.[150] Pelagian writings did, however, continue to hold the interests of various churchmen in the isles for centuries. Gildas quotes one of these works, the early fifth-century *De Virginitate* (perhaps written by a Briton), and may himself have held some semi-Pelagian views.[151] Wales and Ireland reproduced Pelagian texts and exegesis up to the ninth century, and Pope John II accused the Irish of lapsing back into Pelagianism in the mid–seventh century.[152] If anything, Pelagianism added to the "peculiarity" or "strangeness" of the Celtic churches that drew the ire of writers like Bede, Aldhelm, and Eddius Stephanus.[153]

Economy

Britain may have been peculiar, but it was not entirely isolated in the sub-Roman period. As Pelagianism linked Britain with Gaul and the Mediterranean world, so too did trade. The importation of wine, olive oil, and tablewares in the fifth and sixth centuries is just one indicator that Britain's economy did not collapse when it withdrew from the faltering empire. But what kind of economy survived in independent Britain?

Some would find this an easy question to answer: it was a simple barter, nonmoney economy. This assumes the collapse of a money economy, visible in the numismatic record, c. 410. Theodosian coinage is numerous at many military and civilian sites in Britain, and includes the issues of Honorius and Arcadius in the first decade of the fifth century. The latest coins to appear in large numbers at British sites are those of Constantine III (407–11), which would seem to suggest that shipments from imperial mints stopped coming to Britain when Constantine's usurpation failed and the Britons expelled his administration. Numismatists have shown that Constantine's reign was a time of lawlessness and pessimism for Britain, resulting in the conspicuous clipping and hoarding of coins.[154] But this is not the end of the numismatic record. Coin finds from sub-Roman urban sites include gold, sliver, and bronze issues of Valentinian III (c. 425–55), silver issues of Anthemius (467–72), a *tremissis* of Leo I (457–74), and a Gallic *tremissis* of either Severus III or Zeno (c. 480–93).[155] Patrick mentions *solidi* and *scriptulae,* Gildas *obola* and *denarii,* and in the *Life of St. John the Almsgiver* a Byzantine ship returns from southwestern Britain with *nomismata* and tin.[156] "There was not one end to Roman currency in Britain," comments Anne Robertson; "there were many ends."[157]

The sub-Roman economy was, then, a mixed bag of currency and barter, since political uncertainty and barbarian raids (especially in coastal and riverine areas) did cause many Britons to stash hoards in the years around 410.[158] However, the likelihood is that outdated coins continued to circulate in substantial numbers (enough to show considerable wear) at least for the first few decades after the revolt.[159] With no imperial tax agents or *nummularii* around, clipping and counterfeiting occurred.[160] Gradually, Roman denominations began to lose their meaning in Britain as the shape, weight, and metal of the coin came to determine its value.[161] Bronze coinage was then unloaded on foreign traders, while precious-metal coins were made into pendants or else melted down by goldsmiths to make jewelry and other objects of value to a heroic society.[162]

Political turmoil, however, does not always go hand in hand with economic turmoil. Scholars now agree that many areas of Britain were enjoying wealth and prosperity in the late fourth and early fifth centuries, a time of barbarian raids and usurpers. Villas, the traditional center of agricultural economy, expanded in both numbers and size in the late fourth century.[163] To advertise their prosperity, they added courtyards, chapels, bath suites, wall paintings, and, of course, mosaics, more examples of which can be found in the fourth century than at any other time in Britain.[164] Though some villas were simply country residences, others were large estates, worked by both tenants and slaves, producing agricultural surplus that was sold in city markets. Still others were supported by industrial activity. Traditionally, the abandonment of villas in Britain is thought to have occurred in the first quarter of the fifth century, sometimes succeeded by "squatter occupation."[165] Alternatively, some scholars have argued for tenurial continuity at many villa sites, pointing out the fifth-century replacement of masonry buildings with timber structures and the conversion of some villas to religious, possibly monastic, sites.[166] Patrick gives sufficient testimony that at least some small villas (*villulae*) survived as working estates to the middle of the fifth century.[167]

We know little about industrial activity in the sub-Roman period. Both tin mining and salt production were important industries in the Roman period, and show some signs of continuity into the fifth and sixth centuries.[168] Roger Penhallurick has shown that tin has been extracted from Cornwall continuously over the past four thousand years, while Byzantine sources imply that there was nothing at all unusual about "the Brettanic metal" arriving in Alexandria in the sixth and seventh centuries A.D.[169] The industry we know most about in late Roman Britain, however, is pottery manufacture and its distribution. Again, this is because pottery is ubiquitous and has survived where other products have not. Roman Britain imported fine wares (Red-Glazed or Late Terra Sigillata) from Gaul and amphoras from the Mediterranean, produced fine wares at its own commercial kilns, and made local coarse wares for cooking. The long-distance pottery trade had long since dried up, and fourth-century Britain relied on its own fine-ware production, which in turn is thought to have come to an end in the early fifth century. The Oxfordshire kilns, for example, produced no new types after c. 350, but the industry nevertheless continued to flourish into the late fourth or early fifth century.[170] However, the dating of pottery types usually depends on their association with coins, and thus it is virtually impossible to date with any certainty local wares manufactured after 411. Pottery, like coins, may also have been used for long periods of time after its manufacture date and, when broken, either repaired or put to use as loom weights. Esmonde Cleary has shown that, since the distribution of fine wares centered on the "large towns" of Britain and the coarse wares on the "small towns," the survival of the industry was dependent on the survival of the towns and their markets.[171] So too was the villa-based agricultural economy. However, as more and more cities are yielding evidence of late-fifth- and sixth-century activity, the collapse of the local ceramic industries c. 410 seems less likely. In any case, domestic buildings show frequent signs of industrial activity in the fifth century, and therefore many households and estates probably began producing their own crude wares when better products could not be purchased.

For some Britons, however, fine wares and luxury goods were very much available in the fifth and sixth centuries. In the fourth century, imperial shipments of grain and olive oil from North Africa were sent to Britain to feed the troops, and a parasitic commercial trade of fine wares and other goods entered the island this way.[172] Evidence now indicates that, although these shipments stopped arriving at the frontier by the beginning of the fifth century, shipments of Mediterranean fine wares and amphoras reaching Britain (as well as Ireland) in the later fifth century actually *revived*. The amphoras, which likely contained wine and oil, can be traced to areas all over the eastern Mediterranean, and by the sixth century they are joined by cookware from Gaul.[173] Distribution maps show that, although some cities in Britain received these imports, most finds occur at hillforts and other defended sites along the western seaboard, from the Scillies to Iona.[174] This pottery raises several questions, most of which have not been fully answered. What items were brought in the amphoras? Did the fine ware come as ancillary goods? Was all the pottery merely "space fillers" on ships with obscured motives? What did the Britons exchange for these items? Who controlled such trade? How many trading expeditions does the evidence suggest?

Recent explanations have been offered. Michael Fulford has argued that Britain was the deliberate destination of ships sailing directly from Constantinople or the Aegean, in some twenty to a hundred voyages per year, exchanging luxury items for British tin.[175] This could explain Procopius's information about Britain, as well as the phrase *In tempore Justini consulis* on the Penmachno stone and similar Byzantine phrasing on other inscribed stones from Wales.[176] Dark has suggested that, since such long-distance trade was not usually cost-effective, the ships coming to Britain may also have ferried religious pilgrims and Byzantine diplomats.[177] Trade with Gaul may have seen similar exchanges, given the cross-Channel relationships of several churchmen and the importation of Gallic Christian customs (epigraphic, burial, monastic) into the British church.[178]

Charles Thomas has divided the sites yielding imports into two classes: "primary" sites, where the pottery was first obtained from ships, and "secondary" sites, to which it was subsequently distributed.[179] The distribution of the imports within Britain has been studied at three sites—Tintagel and Cadbury-Congresbury (primary sites), and Dinas Powys (secondary site)—that have yielded the most ceramic remains. A regional and seasonal fair or marketplace, distributing these items of long-distance trade, has been suggested as one possible interpretation of the sites.[180] Recently, however, there seems to be a lot of discussion of the imports as an aspect of the relationship between kings and their clients.[181] In this model, Tintagel and Cadbury-Congresbury become seasonal courts where kings meet with their clients, receiving as enforced obligations local goods (tin, dogs) that could be traded with foreign merchants for luxury items (wine, oil, figs, tableware), some of which the king would retain, and the rest of which would be distributed to his nobles to take back to their (defended) homesteads.[182] At one of these homesteads, Dinas Powys, we see similar exchange at the local level. Whole animals were brought to the site and butchered to fill the lord's larder as part of the tenants' rent, affording the locals the opportunity to purchase or share (through feasting) some of the imported foodstuffs obtained by the lord from his king.[183] Alternatively, "secondary" sites could also include Christian communities like Whithorn and Iona, where wine and oil would be put to liturgical use.

We are, it seems, moving closer to the conventional depiction of a heroic society with these economic models. In examining the archaeological and written evidence, Leslie Alcock has found Britain's economy to display a diversity of industrial activity, including iron smelting, the production of high-quality jewelry, bone pins, and combs, leather working, spinning wool, and weaving.[184] The increasing importance of metalworking is illustrated at many sites, urban and rural. Tintagel and other Cornish sites were smelting tin,[185] and the basilicas at Silchester and Wroxeter were given over to use as metal workshops.[186] The Mote of Mark may have been an entirely industrial settlement, its craftsmen protected by timber-and-stone walls as they produced jewelry and the like in the fifth century.[187] The Bristol Channel region has yielded fifth-century evidence of a thriving tradition of penannular-brooch manufacture.[188] Resident smiths and jewelers have been claimed for high-status sixth-century hillforts like Cadbury-Congresbury, Glastonbury

Tor, and Dumbarton.[189] In the hagiography and vernacular poetry, smiths and jewelers are itinerant craftsmen looking for the most generous patron, secular or ecclesiastical, and are generally held in high esteem. At the other end of the spectrum, it is all too clear in the written sources that slavery and the slave trade were the means by which some of these elites amassed wealth and filled their courts with servants.[190]

Culture and Social Structure

Slavery was a constant in both the Roman world and the heroic society of early medieval Europe. Patrick tells us that men and women, Christians and unbelievers, were capable of becoming *servi* and *ancillae*.[191] That is not to say that sub-Roman Britain was a slave society, in the sense of large numbers of slaves working on great estates and in mines. The economic mechanisms were not in place to handle such large and expensive endeavors. Rather, slaves in sub-Roman Britain would likely have been prisoners of war or non-Britons captured in raids, like those of Coroticus. They would have shared space at the bottom of the social pyramid with the large number of *coloni* or former *coloni* and tenant farmers who go unnoticed in both the written and archaeological records.[192]

Thus, the difficulties in discussing class structure in sub-Roman Britain are almost insurmountable, given the scarcity of evidence. We do see, however, various "social types" among the Britons as they are represented in the historical sources and suggested by the architectural remains. Gildas contrasts slaves (*servi*) with masters (*domini*), and the common people (*vulgus*) with kings (*reges*).[193] Fowler and Dark propose the following list of social types:[194]

1. villa owners or their descendants and retinues
2. urban elite (sub-Roman)
3. upstart indigenous (tribal, dynastic) elite
4. criminals or restless military units
5. social revolutionaries, worker-heroes, etc.
6. power-hungry tenant farmers
7. Christians

This list has some problems. For instance, I do not know where one would find "social revolutionaries" or "worker-heroes" in the historical sources, or why tenant farmers should be termed "power-hungry." However, creating such lists is not a useless endeavor. One could, for example, add "slaves" and "pagans" to such a list, and break down "Christians" into "secular clergy," "regular clergy," and "lay believers." One could even construct social hierarchies, as long as it was acknowledged that such models are likely to be incomplete due to the limitations of our written sources.

These limitations are particularly unfortunate when it comes to discussing the most basic social unit, the family. The ecclesiastical writers are usually more interested in the details of God's family, and women in general are almost invisible.[195] Constantius gives us a glimpse of two families in Britain, though portrayed in the guise of gospel suppliants. In the first, the *vir tribuniciae potestatis* and his wife bring their ten-year-old blind daughter to be healed by Germanus. In the second, Elafius brings his young crippled son to Germanus, accompanied by a "whole province" of concerned individuals.[196] Patrick, alone of these writers, gives us autobiographical details of his family life, though again female family members are conspicuously absent. He first identifies himself by giving his father's and paternal grandfather's names, as well as their positions in the church.[197] In captivity, God protected and comforted him "as a father might his son."[198] Throughout his *Confession*, Patrick speaks warmly of *mei cognati* and *parentes*,[199] but he never explores interrelationships.

Gildas gives us no autobiographical details, but he does describe the generally condemnable familial relationships of his *tyranni*. Constantine of Dumnonia, who may have gained political power through his mother's position, put away "his lawful wife" after "successive adulteries," and also committed "parricide."[200] Aurelius Caninus is "engulfed by . . . parricides, fornications, and adulteries."[201] Vortipor, "bad son of a good king," is found guilty of "the rape of a shameless daughter" and the removal of his wife.[202] Cuneglasus also put his wife aside in favor of "her villainous sister," who had promised God perpetual widowhood.[203] And Maglocunus, who had once been a monk, killed his royal uncle, married illegally, replaced this woman with his nephew's wife, and murdered both his first wife and his nephew.[204] It would be rash, to say the least, to draw general conclusions about marriage and family life in sub-Roman Britain from these examples alone.

With the aid of archaeology, however, we can say something about the domestic arrangements and settlement patterns of the Britons. So far I have discussed settlement in terms of towns, villas, and hillforts. I have noted that many Roman-period towns, both small and large, had private residences showing signs of domestic occupation and industry well into the fifth century at least.[205] Most villas declined early in the fifth century, though some with Christian chapels may have survived as house churches or monasteries. Hillforts show slight activity in the Roman period, with more intense occupation from the late fifth century on. Many of these defensive settlements, however, were entirely new creations of the sub-Roman period. In Wales and Scotland there were also duns (small stone-walled forts) and crannogs (platform lake-dwellings), and in Cornwall the famous "rounds" (small univallate enclosures).[206]

The architectural preferences of the Britons are also very telling. Aside from additions to a few town houses and villas in the early fifth century, masonry all but disappeared in sub-Roman Britain. Bede claims that Saint Ninian built his church at Whithorn out of stone, "which was unusual among the Britons."[207] Scarcity of new-quarried stone and/or skilled masons led to an increasing reliance upon timber-built structures. These buildings ranged from small barns to multistoried mansions and occurred in both urban and rural settings. The most elaborate example is the classically inspired timber complex at Wroxeter, a two-storied *villa* complete with towers, colonnades, shops, and barns.[208] Equally sophisticated are the timber gatehouse and fighting platforms at South Cadbury, which were faced with dressed stone taken from derelict Roman buildings and held together with wooden pegged joints.[209] Timber "halls" are another constant, usually rectilinear with overhanging eaves, sometimes, as at Whithorn, with light walls of woven wattle.[210] "Wattle and daub" and turf predominate among the more modest structures, which are often much harder for excavators to find, because these materials disintegrate so easily.[211]

The timber aisled "hall" is perhaps the most characteristic sub-Roman structure. Hall villas and timber barns occur in late Roman Britain, and perhaps they inspired the hillfort halls of the South and West, such as those at South Cadbury, Tintagel, Dinas Powys, and Dinas Emrys.[212] However, the many examples of northern halls—Catterick, Doon Hill, Yeavering, Balbridie—suggest other than Roman influences. To explain these structures, archaeologists often turn to the royal feasting halls prevalent in both Celtic and Germanic verse of the early medieval period. The impressive size of the excavated halls, their internal divisions, with private "apartments" surrounding a central hall, and the presence of large amounts of ceramics and animal bones all argue forcefully for the interpretation that these structures were indeed used for feasting.[213] The occasion may have been that of a landlord's sharing his prosperity with his tenants, a king's rewarding his warband, or a noble's hosting an itinerant king, the timing coinciding with a religious holiday or a military victory.

"Feast and famine" most accurately describes our image of gastronomy in late antiquity. On the one hand, there were devastating famines and fasting monks; on the other, villa dining and feasting warlords. These extremes are evident in sub-Roman Britain. Patrick, adept at fasting even before he entered the church, tells us that pig's meat (*carnes porcorum*), wild honey (*mel silvestris*), and bread were foods to be found in Britain.[214] Gildas describes fasting, hunting, and "a dreadful and notorious famine" caused by the devastations of the Picts and Scots.[215] But he also attributes to Britain wine and oil, vintage wine (*vinum optimum*), butter, garden vegetables (*horti holeres*), eggs, "British cheese" (*Britannicus formellus*), milk, whey (*tenucla*), buttermilk (*battutum lac*), and Celtic beer (*cervisa*).[216] At various British sites, excavators have found the remains of wheat, barley, spelt, oats, hazelnuts, limpets, oysters, and the cooked bones of butchered cattle, pigs, sheep, and goats, as well as fragments of cooking utensils, corn-drying kilns, plates, silver spoons, iron knives, pitchers, and wine glasses.[217] The large number of olive-oil-carrying amphoras found at Dumbarton suggests to Alcock that the oil in many of these vessels may have been used for the storage of other foods.[218] At South Cadbury, the main activity, as revealed by archaeological evidence, seems to have been the drinking of wine. Of course, the early medieval heroic poems like the *Gododdin* are filled with references to both wine and mead feasts (*gwinfaeth* and *meddfaeth*).[219]

The abundant written and archaeological evidence for feasting should not overshadow grimmer realities. Gildas, for example, vividly describes the devastation caused by disease in fifth-century Britain: "For a deadly plague [*pestifera . . . lues*] swept brutally on the stupid people, and in a short period laid low so many people, with no sword, that the living could not bury all the dead."[220] Occasional outbreaks of plague in various parts of the empire are recorded for the mid–fifth century;[221] a major outbreak of the bubonic plague hit the East in the 540s;[222] and this latter epidemic seems to have made its way to the British Isles in the later sixth and seventh centuries.[223] Many archaeologists have thus turned to disease as an explanation for unburied bodies, the accumulation of debris on city streets, and in general the decline of Romano-British towns. However, Malcolm Todd has surveyed both the written and archaeological evidence for fifth-century Britain and found it unable to support the theory of a catastrophic plague wiping out the urban population of Roman Britain and paving the way for Saxon domination.[224] If we are not entirely to discount Gildas's statement, we may see the combination of famine and disease in the mid–fifth century as partial explanation for population decline in Britain and for the need to bring in foreign mercenaries for defense.

Famine and disease, however, did not leave all Britons impoverished. Constantius says that the Pelagians in Britain "flaunted their wealth in dazzling robes."[225] We know very little about what kinds of clothes the Britons wore. Gildas speaks only of "the habit of a holy abbot," "princely cloaks," and a "royal ring."[226] It is jewelry, not clothing, that survives in the archaeological record (although there is one lucky find, from a Worcester grave, of a spun-gold brocaded collar).[227] Gold and silver finger rings, bone pins and combs, metal belt buckles and fittings, silver amulets, and both annular and penannular brooches have been found at many sub-Roman sites.[228] Of all the Britons' material remains, the brooches can boast the greatest artistic merit, perhaps inspiring the later "interlace" masterpieces of Hiberno-Saxon jewelry. Over one hundred enameled objects from the period 400–700 have also been found in Britain, and from these we can infer that red was the favorite sub-Roman color, followed by yellow, blue, and green; multicolored millefiori enamels also appear occasionally.[229] Gildas criticizes many Britons for ostentatiously showing off their wealth, driving their horse-drawn carriages (*vehicula*), paying too much attention to entertainments (*ludicra*), and "regarding themselves as superior to the rest of men."[230]

How did the Britons regard themselves? How did they regard other peoples? We have finally come to the point where we can answer these questions. Those Britons capable of leaving us written testimony regarded themselves as *Britanni* (or *Brittones*), or as *cives* of a *patria* that was Britain.[231] Some left their identities in stone, displaying the names of their "tribes" or kingdoms within Britain. Many celebrated their titles or status, and one man proudly proclaimed that he was a constant lover of his *patria,* and a preserver of the faith.[232] Patrick longed to visit this *patria,* and Gildas ached for all its sufferings.[233] The greatest of these sufferings—as seen from Ammianus to the Llandaff Charters—were the attacks of the *barbari* and *hostes.* For Patrick these are the Picts and Scots, utterly evil and iniquitous.[234] For Gildas they are also "the ferocious Saxons (name not to be spoken!), hated by man and God."[235] Whatever "peaceful interaction" or "cultural-assimilation" scenarios some scholars have dreamed up to explain the *adventus Saxonum,* the words of Gildas, Aneirin, Aldhelm, Bede, and Eddius Stephanus leave no doubt that fear and hatred dominated most relationships between Britons and *Saxones.*[236] Even those Britons who did not write in

Latin saw themselves as *cives,* or rather *combrogi* (Welsh *cymry*), and the Saxons as "foreigners" (*allmyn*). The Saxons hardly had a better opinion of their neighbors.[237] Though divided politically, the Britons shared a common language[238] and a common faith, and for these reasons they saw themselves as superior to and separate from the pagan Saxons. For this Bede could never forgive them.

CONCLUSION

Many aspects of British society looked much different in the year 600 than they had in the year 400. If sub-Roman Britain was a "heroic society," this means that Romanization in much of Britain was a failure, or at most an ephemeral veneer.[1] On the other hand, one could argue that the survival of Christianity, Latin records, and Roman titles in the sixth century signals the success and continuation of Romanization in Britain.[2] I believe, however, that both of these models are too simplistic. They are attempts to explain the complexities of sub-Roman Britain by casting it in the guise of a better-understood period, usually Roman Britain or Anglo-Saxon England.

The point of this study has been to show that sub-Roman Britain was unique. Britain was the only Roman diocese to separate itself successfully from the imperial government. Of all Rome's former European possessions, Britain alone emerged in the Middle Ages using vernacular languages (English, Welsh, Pictish, and the dialect of Old Irish spoken in western Scotland) not derived from Latin or Greek. That is not to say that the decline of Roman Britain did not share common traits with the rest of the West, for current scholarship is certainly showing us that it did.[3] Nor is it to say that Britain had become an entirely new creation after 410. Rather, what we see is a transformation of Roman institutions and ideas, under the influence of native custom and Christianity. The language of Patrick and Gildas reveals some of the details of this transformation, particularly apparent in such terms as *patria, cives,* and *tyranni*. The inscribed stones further illustrate the point, mixing Latin with Ogam, Celtic names with Latin *formulae,* Roman titles with dynastic pedigrees.

When I argue that sub-Roman Britain was unique, I am not denying that it was part of a continuum of traditions, Mediterranean and insular, or that other areas progressively falling back upon their own resources did not share many of the problems and approaches of Britain. I am simply appealing to historians to recognize it as a singular entity with its own defining characteristics, rather than as a prelude, a transition, or a problem. It is *Britannia,* the *patria* of Patrick, Gildas, and numerous other *cives,* the island home of the *Britanni*. It produced saints and heretics, *decuriones* and kings, Latin letters and vernacular poetry. One has only to look at the example of the British *tyranni* to see the complexity of the society,[4] which archaeology has only begun to help illuminate.

As I see it, sub-Roman Britain has two real problems: a scarcity of source material and a regrettable name. I have endeavored to get the most out of the scant written records and archaeological finds for the period, pointing out both the problems and the rewards of working with this material. Difficult as this was, I find it even more challenging to find an alternative to the label "sub-Roman Britain." Previous attempts such as Dark Age Britain, Arthur's Britain, and Early Christian Britain have uniformly failed to pass the critical tests of the specialists. For this study, I have referred ironically to the period as "an age of tyrants," giving Britain something in common with preclassical Greece. Classicists will probably *not* find this amusing.

It is hard to argue, however, with the language of the Britons themselves, so I offer another label derived from one of their own terms: the Brittonic (or Brythonic, if the vernacular form is to be preferred) Age (or Period). This study began by asking the question, Who were the Britons? It is unlikely that the Celtic-speaking peoples in Britain before the Roman conquest would have identified themselves as Britons. But because Roman writers and governors used this preferred term for the indigenous inhabitants of Britain, some natives, when they adopted Latin, adopted the identification "Briton" as well. In the Roman period, this usage was sporadic and infrequent and had to compete with other identifiers, especially Roman citizenship status.[5] But in the sub-Roman period, *Britto/Brittanus* became the primary term used by those writing in Latin on both sides of the Channel, while *Brython* was eventually adopted as the vernacular equivalent.

Thus, the Brittonic Age is that period, the fifth and sixth centuries, when people who called themselves *and* were called by others "Britons" were the majority population throughout Britain, and in most areas the politically dominant one as well.[6] Politically they were fragmented but autonomous; religiously they were becoming predominantly Christian with a growing enthusiasm for monasticism. They perceived warfare, both internal and against the barbarians, as the greatest threat to their society. Yet despite all their warnings against violence and immorality, neither Patrick nor Gildas could have predicted that, by the eighth century, their *patria* would cease to exist as the single autonomous entity they knew, and would take on the name and culture of the barbarians from the Continent. This process is still not clearly understood, but we can now see that *Britannia* passed through more than just an obscure interlude on its way to becoming England, Scotland, and Wales.

APPENDIX A:
Arthur and Merlin

It would be extremely difficult to write a history of sub-Roman Britain without mentioning the names Arthur and Merlin. These two either dominate books written about the period or else linger in the background with such a presence that the writer feels forced to stop and say, "Look, I know that you're waiting for me to say something about King Arthur, so let me just make it clear where I stand on this issue." Both author and audience know exactly what the issue is. Did Arthur and Merlin really exist? Were they historical persons as well as literary figures?

If you asked these questions to the average premodern citizen of Britain, the answer would most likely have been, "Of course they were real. Arthur was the king of the Britons and Merlin their prophet." English kings, from Henry II to Henry VIII, certainly believed this; chroniclers and poets believed, or at least hoped their audiences would; book publishers from William Caxton to the present have profited from this belief; even a modern statesman and historian like Winston Churchill could remark that "it is all true, or it ought to be." That is not to say that there have not always been skeptics. From the moment Geoffrey of Monmouth published his *History of the Kings of Britain* in 1136, establishing both Arthur's and Merlin's preeminence, there have been critics like William of Newburgh and Gerald of Wales, and when the Tudors tried to promote their "Arthurian" connections, there were skeptical voices heard among the humanist scholars. But until the second half of the twentieth century, the skeptics have never had as much influence as the believers, whose belief in a King Arthur has shaped both history and art.

The modern quest for the historical Arthur began in earnest with a study of the written sources published by R. K. Chambers in 1927.[1] Chambers imagined a Romano-British warrior-king stemming the Saxon tide c. A.D. 500, and his vision found its way into legitimate history via R. G. Collingwood in 1936, who saw Arthur more as a general and cavalry leader of the late empire.[2] While literary scholars like R. S. Loomis began finding archaic Celtic clues in the Arthurian romances and linguists like Kenneth Jackson dissected the names of Arthurian figures and battles, archaeologists began uncovering historical occupations at "Dark Age" settlements, like Tintagel and Glastonbury, linked to the literary Arthur.[3] Soon followed a flood of popular histories with "Arthur" in their titles,[4] which in turn inspired numerous historical novels involving *personae* of the Arthurian drama. Even two well-respected scholars, the archaeologist Leslie Alcock and the historian John Morris, were convinced enough of Arthur's historicity that they gave him center stage in their ambitious histories of the period.[5] These serious works nevertheless provoked a blast from the critics, most notably David Dumville and Charles Thomas,[6] which came to define the prevailing skeptical attitude toward Arthur in current academic circles.[7] Still, such criticism did not prevent subsequent investigations for a historical Arthur,[8] of which the most eloquently argued are the works of Geoffrey Ashe.[9] The search for Merlin has received far less attention, with the most notable study being Nikolai Tolstoy's discovery of a late-sixth-century prototype in the Caledonian wood.[10]

The legitimate evidence used in these investigations can be quickly summarized. The first mention of Arthur is thought to be the offhanded reference in a line from the *Gododdin*—"[Gwawrddur] fed black ravens on the rampart of a fortress / Though he was no Arthur"—sung by the bard Aneirin about the year 600 to commemorate the battle of Catraeth.[11] It is uncertain when this poem was first written down—the oldest extant version is in a thirteenth-century manuscript—and the line referring to Arthur may be a later addition to the poem. The earliest written record of Arthur is in the *Historia Brittonum,* which states that "the warrior Arthur" fought with the kings of the Britons against the Saxons, whom he conquered in twelve incredible battles.[12] The *Annales Cambriae,* attached to the *Historia* in the Harley manuscript, records the date of one of these battles, Badon in 518, and of Arthur's death, at Camlann in 539.[13] Again, both works survive only in later manuscripts, but the *Historia* appears to have been compiled in the early ninth century and the *Annales* in the mid-tenth.[14] Arthur's next major appearance is in the *History* of Geoffrey of Monmouth, who gave "King Arthur" and Merlin worthy, though fictional, careers by mixing the *Historia* and the *Annales* with local traditions and Celtic myth. As Arthur is often said to be a hybrid of historical person and mythological figure, so too does Merlin seem to be an amalgam of early medieval figures. His first appearance is also in a line from the *Gododdin*—"Morien defended / The fair song of Myrddin"—though here it is even more likely that this was a later interpolation.[15] In Geoffrey's Latin poem *Vita Merlini,* Merlin is not associated with Arthur but is rather a prophet living in sixth-century northern Britain. Geoffrey seems to have drawn from two separate traditions. One is the fatherless boy Ambrosius, who prophesies to King Vortigern (a mid-fifth-century historical figure) in the *Historia Brittonum;* Geoffrey simply copies this episode in his *History* and *Prophecies of Merlin* but says that the boy is "Merlin, also called Ambrosius."[16] The second, and perhaps older, tradition is that of the Wildman in the Woods, sometimes the court madman and prophet of King Rhydderch of Strathclyde (a historical late-sixth-century figure). He appears as Myrddin in several Welsh prophetic texts, and as Lailoken (Laloecen) in the twelfth-century *Life of St. Kentigern.* Like Arthur, Merlin then made his way into the medieval French romances, and the rest, as they say, is historical legend. (Or is it "legendary history"?)

This is hardly strong or conclusive evidence with which to build a case, at least a case that will convince modern historians. Dumville once summarized the argument for a historical Arthur as "no smoke without a fire" rhetoric.[17] While this may not be a smart rhetorical strategy, it must be admitted—even by the skeptics—that there has been an awful lot of smoke blowing around the Arthurian tradition. So much similar evidence, circumstantial though it may be, must have some cause, and it is hard to see the "fire" as the tale of one creative medieval bard. This remains a mystery, however, that is perhaps beyond the grasp of the historian.[18] Thomas Charles-Edwards has recently expressed this opinion: "At this stage of the enquiry, one can only say that there may well have been an historical Arthur; that the historian can as yet say nothing of value about him."[19] Admitting this to ourselves will perhaps allow the quests for Arthur and Merlin to continue without the constant griping of academics and, more important, will allow the growth of the legend to continue without the constraints of historical fact. What the historian can contribute, however, is a better understanding of the period and place in which Arthur and Merlin *may have lived* for those who wish to pin down these legendary figures to time and space.

APPENDIX B:
Chronology of Events

	The Empire	The British Isles
A.D. 200	Septimius Severus (A,† 193–211).	Death of Septimus Severus at York (211).
	Caracalla (A, 211–17) extends Roman citizenship to almost all free citizens of the empire.	
	Revolt of Postumus and creation of the Gallic Empire (259/60).	Britain part of the Gallic Empire (260–74).
	Diocletian (A, 284–305) forms the Tetrarchy (293).	Carausius (287–93) and Allectus (293–96) control Britain.
	Constantius I (C, 293–305; A, 305–6).	Constantius defeats Allectus and retakes Britain (296).
A.D. 300	Constantine I ("the Great") (A, 306–37).	Constantius dies at York (306). His son Constantine is proclaimed Augustus by the troops in Britain.
	The Battle of Milvian Bridge (312) and the Edict of Milan (313).	British bishops attend the Council of Arles (314).

† A = Augustius; C = Caesar

This chronology is based on written evidence and similar tables constructed by Michael E. Jones, "Provinces of Iron and Rust: The End of Roman Britain" (Ph.D. diss., University of Texas at Austin, 1985), 291–92; David N. Dumville, "The Chronology of *De excidio Britanniae,* Book I," in *Gildas: New Approaches,* ed. Michael Lapidge and David N. Dumville (Woodbridge, Suffolk: Boydell, 1984), 83; and Peter Salway, *The Oxford Illustrated History of Roman Britain* (Oxford: Oxford University Press, 1993), 539–46. The chronology suggested by Nicholas J. Higham (*The English Conquest: Gildas and Britain in the Fifth Century* [Manchester: Manchester University Press, 1994], 137), which conflates all of the events described by Gildas into the fifth century, lacks sufficient support and is not incorporated here. See, however, my reconstructed chronology of Gildas's narrative in Chapter 3.

Constantine II (A, 337–40).	
Constans (A, 337–50).	The emperor Constans makes an official visit to Britain (343).
Constantius II (A, 337–61).	The usurpation of Magnentius (350–53) results in the cruel suppression of suspected officials in Britain.
Julian II ("the Apostate") (C, 355–60; A, 360–63).	Raiding by Picts and Scots in Britain is reported to the emperor Julian (360).
Valentinian I (A, 364–75).	Ammianus records that Britain was being harassed by Picts, Saxons, Scots, and Attacotti (364).
Valens (A, 364–78).	The *barbarica conspiratio,* which resulted in the death of the count of the Saxon Shore and the capture of the *dux Britanniarum* (367).
	Count Theodosius routs the barbarians in Britain and puts down the rebellion of Valentinus (368).
Gratian (A, 375–83).	
Valentinian II (A, 375–92).	
Theodosius I ("the Great") (A, 379–95).	
Christianity becomes the official religion of the empire (380).	Magnus Maximus defeats the Picts and Scots in the north of Britain (382).
	Magnus Maximus (r. 383–88) is declared emperor of the West by his British troops.
	Magnus Maximus is defeated and killed by the emperor Theodosius (388).
	Victricius of Rouen visits bishops in Britain (c. 396).
	Claudian records that Britain is suffering from "attacks" by

		Saxons, Picts, and Scots (398).
A.D. 400	Honorius (A, 395–423).	Stilicho withdraws troops from Britain for the defense of Italy (401 or 402).
	Arcadius (A, 395–408).	
	Constantine III (407–11).	The army in Britain elects a series of usurpers: Marcus, Gratian, and Constantine (406–7).
		Constantine III crosses to Gaul with troops from Britain (407).
	Assassination of Stilicho (408)	Britain is devastated by Saxon incursions (408 or 410).[1]
		The Britons revolt from the empire and set up independent rule (409). The Romans can no longer hold on to Britain, which is henceforth ruled by "tyrants."[2]
	Alaric's Visigoths sack Rome (410).	The emperor Honorius sends a rescript to the cities of Britain urging them to see to their own defense (410).
	Valentinian III (A, 425–55).	Saint Germanus of Auxerre visits Britain to combat the Pelagian heresy (429).
		Some Britons send a letter to Agitius (Aetius), *ter consul,* asking for aid against the barbarians (c. 430–54).[3]
		Palladius is named first bishop of Ireland (431), succeeded sometime afterward by Patrick.
		Witnesses in Gaul observe that some portion of Britain has fallen into the hands of the Saxons (c. 441).
		Plague infects Britain and much of Europe (c. 443–c. 450).

	Saint Germanus makes a second visit to Britain (c. 445).[4]
Odovacer deposes the emperor Romulus Augustulus (476), and the emperor Julius Nepos is murdered (480), marking the official end of the Roman Empire in the West.	Britons convene a *consilium* and decide to hire Saxon mercenaries. The *superbus tyrannus* settles the Saxons in northeastern Britain, from which they rebel. The British survivors turn to Ambrosius Aurelianus, who leads them to a series of victories over the Saxons (c. 455–c. 485).
	The Battle of Mount Badon and slaughter of the Saxons. The birth of Gildas (c. 485).
A.D. 500	The birth of Saint Columba (521).
	Gildas writes the *De excidio Britanniae* (c. 529)
	Bubonic plague devastates Constantinople, eventually reaching to Britain and Ireland (542–49).
	Saint Columba establishes a monastery on Iona and begins his mission among the Picts (563–65).
	The Battle of Dyrham. The British towns of Gloucester, Cirencester, and Bath fall to the Saxons (577).
	The Battle of Catraeth. A British war band from Din Eidyn is wiped out by the Saxons (c. 590).
	Papal missionaries led by Augustine arrive at Canterbury. The death of Saint Columba at Iona (597).
A.D. 600	

LIST OF ABBREVIATIONS

BAR	British Archaeological Reports
BBCS	*Bulletin of the Board of Celtic Studies*
CBA	Council for British Archaeology
CIIC	MacAlister, *Corpus Inscriptionum Insularum Celticarum*
CMCS	*Cambridge/Cambrian Medieval Celtic Studies*
ECMS	*Early Christian Monuments of Scotland*, ed. Allen and Anderson
ECMW	*Early Christian Monuments of Wales*, ed. Nash-Williams
EH	Bede, *Ecclesiastical History of the English People*
HB	*Historia Brittonum*
HF	Gregory of Tours, *Historia Francorum*
HMSO	Her Majesty's Stationery Office
LPRIA	late pre-Roman Iron Age
MGH	*Monumenta Germaniae Historica*
PL	*Patrologia Latina*
PLRE	*The Prosopography of the Later Roman Empire*, ed. Martindale et al.
RIB	*Roman Inscriptions of Britain*
RIC	*Roman Imperial Coinage*
TLL	*Thesaurus Linguae Latinae*

NOTES

Introduction

1. Leo Sherley-Price, trans., *Bede: A History of the English Church and People* (Harmondsworth, Middlesex: Penguin, 1955), 38: "At the present time there are in Britain . . . four nations—English, British, Scots, and Picts." Bede believed that in his time the Angles, the Saxons, and other Germanic-speaking peoples in Britain recognized a common "English" identity. See Patrick Wormald, "Bede, the *Bretwaldas*, and the Origins of the *Gens Anglorum*," in *Ideal and Reality in Frankish and Anglo-Saxon Society*, ed. Patrick Wormald et al. (Oxford: Blackwell, 1983), 99–129.

The present study focuses on the BRITONS, whom the English labeled "Welsh" (*Wealas*). For the PICTS, see F. T. Wainwright, ed., *The Problem of the Picts* (Perth: Melven Press, 1955); Isabel Henderson, *The Picts* (New York: Praeger, 1967); J.G.P. Friell and W. G. Watson, eds., *Pictish Studies: Settlement, Burial, and Art in Dark Age Northern Britain*, BAR British Series, no. 125 (Oxford: Tempvs Reparatvm, 1984); Anna Ritchie, *The Picts* (Edinburgh: HMSO, 1989); Elizabeth Sutherland, *In Search of the Picts: A Celtic Dark Age Nation* (London: Constable, 1994); W. A. Cummins, *The Age of the Picts* (Stroud, Gloucestershire: Alan Sutton, 1995); and Eric H. Nicoll, ed., *A Pictish Panorama: The Story of the Picts and a Pictish Bibliography* (Belgavies, Angus: Pinkfoot Press for the Pictish Arts Society, 1995). For the origins of the SCOTS, see Maire De Paor and Liam De Paor, *Early Christian Ireland* (New York: Praeger, 1958); John Bannerman, *Studies in the History of Dalriada* (Edinburgh: Scottish Academic Press, 1974); Nancy Edwards, *The Archaeology of Early Medieval Ireland* (London: Batsford, 1990); Lloyd Laing and Jennifer Laing, *The Picts and the Scots* (Gloucester: Alan Sutton, 1993); and Dáibhí O Cróinín, *Early Medieval Ireland, 400–1200* (London: Longman, 1995). Works on the origins of the ANGLO-SAXONS are too numerous to list here; a few good recent surveys are James Campbell, ed., *The Anglo-Saxons* (Ithaca, N.Y.: Cornell University Press, 1982); J.N.L. Myres, *The English Settlements* (Oxford: Clarendon Press, 1986); Steven Bassett, ed., *The Origins of the Anglo-Saxon Kingdoms* (Leicester: Leicester University Press, 1989); and Martin G. Welch, *Discovering Anglo-Saxon England* (University Park: Pennsylvania State University Press, 1992).

2. See Appendix A below.

3. See, for example, Philip Dixon, "'The Cities Are Not Populated As Once They Were,'" in *The City in Late Antiquity*, ed. John Rich (London: Routledge, 1992), 145–60 ("the transition between the Roman province and the English successor kingdoms" [146]), and David N. Dumville, "The Idea of Government in Sub-Roman Britain," in *After Empire: Towards an Ethnology of Europe's Barbarians*, ed. Giorgio Ausenda (Woodbridge, Suffolk: Boydell, 1995), 177–216 ("The period of transition from Roman control in Britain to the barbarisation of the whole former Imperial diocese" [177]).

4. See, for example, A. S. Esmonde Cleary, *The Ending of Roman Britain* (London: Batsford, 1989), xi: "[We can see] a discernible post-Roman but non-Saxon interlude over most of the

country of half a century at least; much more in the west. Of interest as a society in its own right, it also has far-reaching consequences for the vexed question of continuity from Roman Britain to Anglo-Saxon England."

There is also a trend to understand sub-Roman Britain—or, more accurately, the end of Roman Britain—by concentrating on the context of events happening elsewhere in the empire. See, for example, Ian N. Wood, "The End of Roman Britain: Continental Evidence and Parallels," in *Gildas: New Approaches,* ed. Michael Lapidge and David N. Dumville (Woodbridge, Suffolk: Boydell, 1984), 1–26, and Martin Millet, *Roman Britain* (London: Batsford/English Heritage, 1995), 132.

5. E.g., Walter Goffart, *The Narrators of Barbarian History (*A.D. *550–800)* (Princeton: Princeton University Press, 1988), 169: "Gildas is . . . the famous narrator of the British 'dark age,' that is, the period between the Roman evacuation and Gregory the Great's mission to the English."

6. I have discussed the historiography of sub-Roman Britain in detail elsewhere; see Christopher A. Snyder, "'The Tyrants of Tintagel': The Terminology and Archaeology of Sub-Roman Britain (A.D. 400–600)" (Ph.D. diss., Emory University, 1994), 1–15. Also of use is the (now dated) historiographical essay by Susanne Haselgrove, "Romano-Saxon Attitudes," in *The End of Roman Britain,* BAR British Series 71, ed. P. J. Casey (Oxford: Tempvs Reparatvm, 1979).

7. Bede, *Ecclesiastical History of the English People;* hereafter *EH.*

8. Gildas, *De excidio Britanniae* (The ruin of Britain); hereafter *De excidio.*

9. For a full discussion of all the written sources, see Chapter 4.

10. Saint Patrick, *Epistola ad Coroticum* (Letter to Coroticus) and *Confessio* (Declaration); hereafter *Epistola* and *Confessio.*

11. Constantius, *Vita Sancti Germani;* hereafter *Vita.*

12. *Chronica Gallica a CCCCLII* and *Chronica Gallica a DXI,* in *Monumenta Germaniae Historica* (hereafter *MGH*), vol. 9, bk. 1 of *Chronica Minora,* ed. Theodor Mommsen, 617–66; hereafter *Gallic Chronicle of 452* and *Gallic Chronicle of 511.*

13. Ammianus, *Res Gestae;* hereafter Ammianus.

14. *Notitia Dignitatum Occidentis;* hereafter *Notitia.*

15. Collected in the twelfth-century MS *Liber Landavensis* (The book of Llan Dâv).

16. Nennius, *Historia Brittonum;* hereafter *HB.*

17. Versions exist in numerous MSS; hereafter referred to as *Anglo-Saxon Chronicle,* followed by the MS title.

18. The inscriptions are described in several collections; see Chapter 4.

19. Since the publication of John Morris's *Age of Arthur: A History of the British Isles from 350 to 650* (New York: Scribner's, 1973), only two purely historical works—both limited to the fifth century—have appeared: E. A. Thompson, *St. Germanus of Auxerre and the End of Roman Britain* (Woodbridge, Suffolk: Boydell, 1984), and Nicholas J. Higham, *The English Conquest: Gildas and Britain in the Fifth Century* (Manchester: Manchester University Press, 1994). See Snyder, "'Tyrants of Tintagel,'" 4–5.

20. See, for example, C. J. Arnold, *Roman Britain to Saxon England* (Bloomington: Indiana University Press, 1984).

21. Among the most notable: Ian Burrow, *Hillfort and Hill-Top Settlement in Somerset in the First to Eighth Centuries* A.D., BAR British Series 91 (Oxford: Tempvs Reparatvm, 1981); Charles Thomas, ed., *A Provisional List of Imported Pottery in Post-Roman Western Britain and Ireland* (Truro: Institute of Cornish Studies, 1981); Leslie Alcock, *Economy, Society, and Warfare Among the Britons and Saxons* (Cardiff: University of Wales Press, 1987); Nancy Edwards and Alan Lane, eds., *Early Medieval Settlements in Wales,* A.D. *400–1100* (Cardiff: University of Wales Press, 1988); idem, *The Early Church in Wales and the West,* Oxbow Monograph, no. 16 (Oxford: Oxbow, 1992); Lynette Olson, *Early Monasteries in Cornwall*

(Woodbridge, Suffolk: Boydell, 1989); and Kenneth Rainsbury Dark, *Discovery by Design: The Identification of Secular Elite Settlements in Western Britain, A.D. 400–700*, BAR British Series, no. 237 (Oxford: Tempvs Reparatvm, 1994). See Chapter 11.

22. For the dangers of combining these disciplines, see F. T. Wainwright, *Archaeology and Place-Names and History* (London: Routledge & Kegan Paul, 1962).

23. The definitions for some of these terms are not as obvious as my translations here in parentheses suggest. For full treatment, see the discussion under individual terms in Part II.

24. For a more detailed discussion, see Chapter 9.

25. *Epistola*, 6; *De excidio*, 27.

26. For a useful definition (though one to which I have not consistently adhered), see Dark, *Discovery*, 3–5.

27. See Chapter 11.

28. See Chapter 13.

29. See Chapter 14.

30. The phrase is Sheppard Frere's, who used it to describe the obscure archaeological reports brought to life by Alan Sorrell in his fascinating reconstruction drawings; see Sorrell, *Roman Towns in Britain* (London: Batsford, 1976), 7.

31. See the Conclusion.

Chapter 1

1. See, for example, Martin Millet, *The Romanization of Britain* (Cambridge: Cambridge University Press, 1990), and Michael E. Jones, "The Failure of Romanization in Britain," *Proceedings of the Harvard Celtic Colloquium* 7 (1987): 126–45.

2. A chronology of these persons and events can be found in Appendix B.

3. Marcus Aurelius Mausaeus Carausius in A.H.M. Jones, J. R. Martindale, and J. Morris, *The Prosopography of the Later Roman Empire, vol. 1, A.D. 260–395* (Cambridge: Cambridge University Press, 1970), 180–81; hereafter *PLRE*, 1, followed by the page number. Gaius Allectus in *PLRE*, 1:45.

4. Aurelius Victor, *Liber de Caesaribus*, 39.20 (trans. Stanley Ireland, in *Roman Britain: A Sourcebook* [London: Routledge, 1986], 126): "[Carausius] was put in charge of fitting out a fleet and repelling the Germans, who infested the seas"; Eutropius, 9.21: "[H]e had undertaken the task of policing the sea in the region of Belgica and Armorica, which was then swarming with Franks and Saxons." These early references to the Saxons portray them as a threat—along with other Germanic peoples, notably the Franks—in the English Channel and, presumably (because Carausius exercised control over both coasts), to both British and Gallic coastal settlements where they gathered their booty.

5. Peter Salway, *Roman Britain* (Oxford: Clarendon Press, 1981), 289.

6. See ibid., 297; Sheppard Frere, *Britannia: A History of Roman Britain*, 3d ed. (London: Routledge & Kegan Paul, 1987), 327; and P. J. Casey, *Carausius and Allectus: The British Usurpers* (New Haven: Yale University Press, 1995), 58, 65. Salway believes that Carausius's British propaganda "implies, or tries to suggest, the existence of a general body of opinion that had awaited some such relief from unspecified troubles."

7. Eutropius, 9.22.2. See also *Panegyric on Constantius Caesar* (delivered A.D. 297), 8.13–20, in *XII Panegyrici Latini*, ed. R.A.B. Mynors (Oxford: Clarendon Press, 1964). All panegyrics cited below (except those of Claudian) are from Mynors's edition and are identified by their name, followed by Mynors's number (1–12), chapter, and line (if specified).

8. *Panegyric on Constantius*, 8.11; *Panegyric on Constantine*, 6.7.1–2. See also *Laterculus Veronensis* (A.D. 300), in *Geographi Latini Minores*, ed. Alexander Riese (Hildesheim: G. Olms, 1964), 128. None of these terms refers to a specific tribe; they are, instead, rather broad

ethnographic labels employed by Roman literati. "Picts" seems to denote a confederation that included *Caledonii* and other tribes who lived in Scotland north of the Forth-Clyde valley.

9. Crocus, *Rex Alamannorum*, in *PLRE*, 1:233.

10. Aurelius Victor, *Liber de Caesaribus*, 40.2–4; Eutropius, 10.1.3 and 2.2; Zosimus, 2.8.2 and 9.1.

11. P. J. Casey, "Constantine the Great in Britain: The Evidence of the Coinage at the London Mint," in *Collectanea Londiniensia*, London and Middlesex Archaeological Society Special Paper, no. 2, ed. J. Bird, H. Chapman, and J. Clark (London: London and Middlesex Archaeological Society, 1978), 181–93. See also Eusebius, *De vita Constantini*, 1.8 and 25.

12. These posts are listed in the *Notitia*; see the discussion in Chapter 4.

13. On the origins of the Saxon Shore forts, see Salway, *Roman Britain*, 320–21; idem, *The Oxford Illustrated History of Roman Britain* (Oxford: Oxford University Press, 1993), 182, 299, 332; Stephen Johnson, *The Roman Forts of the Saxon Shore* (London: Paul Elek, 1976); idem, *Later Roman Britain* (London: Paladin, 1980), 98ff.; D. E. Johnston, ed., *The Saxon Shore*, CBA Research Report, no. 18 (London: CBA, 1977); Valerie A. Maxfield, ed., *The Saxon Shore: A Handbook* (Exeter: Department of History and Archaeology, University of Exeter, 1989); and Esmonde Cleary, *Ending*, 52ff.

14. The title of count first appears in the *Notitia*, and though some of the Shore forts date back to the early third century, they did not become a unified system under a single command until much later. The term *litus Saxonicum* may only date to Stilicho's reforms at the end of the fourth century. See Ian N. Wood, "The Channel from the Fourth to the Seventh Centuries A.D.," *in Maritime Celts, Frisians, and Saxons*, CBA Research Report, no. 71, ed. Sean McGrail (London: CBA, 1990), 93–97.

15. Julius Firmicus Maternus, *De Errore Profanum Religionum*, 28.6; Libanius, *Oration*, 59.141. Ammianus Marcellinus's account of the visit is in one of his lost books, though he does mention it elsewhere (Ammianus, 20.1.1) in connection with the *areani* (frontier spies) in Britain. Constans's coinage of that year shows him on a warship steered by Victory. See Johnson, *Later Roman Britain*, 120–21, and Salway, *Illustrated History*, 244.

16. Gratianus I in *PLRE*, 1:400; Ammianus, 30.7.3.

17. Flavius Magnus Magnentius in *PLRE*, 1:532. Magnentius is said to have had a British father.

18. Paulus "Catena" 4 in *PLRE*, 1:683–84; Ammianus, 14.5.6–8.

19. Julian, *Letter to the Athenians*, 279D; Ammianus, 18.2.3; Libanius, *Oration*, 18.82–83; Eunapius, frag. 12; Zosimus, 3.5.2. See Salway, *Roman Britain*, 359–60.

20. Ammianus, 20.1.

21. Flavius Lupicinus 6 in *PLRE*, 1:520–21.

22. Ammianus, 26.4.5. It would seem that this is the first specific mention in the sources of a Saxon attack on Britain; see, however, Philip Bartholomew, "Fourth-Century Saxons," *Britannia* 15 (1984): 169–85.

23. Jerome, *Adversus Jovinianum*, 2.7.48: "atticotos, gentem Britannicam, humanis vesci carnibus." See Salway, *Roman Britain*, 269.

24. Ammianus, 27.8 and 28.3: "barbarica conspiratio."

25. Ibid., 28.3.8. Ammianus calls them Arcani, and says that Theodosius later removed them from their posts because they had been bribed to give Roman military plans to the barbarians. They must also have failed to report the movements of the barbarians along the frontier in 367.

26. Fullofaudes in *PLRE*, 1:375.

27. Nectaridus in ibid., 621.

28. See J. C. Mann, "The Historical Development of the Saxon Shore," in *The Saxon Shore*, ed. Maxfield, 1–11 ("There cannot be any serious doubt that the maritimum tractus lay in Britain: the name is either a 'polite' literary form of the uncouth and uneuphonious litus

Saxonicum or, less probably, it is an earlier name for the same command" [8]).

29. Ammianus, 27.8.2. The text is confusing and incomplete here. Valentinian first sent Severus, the *comes domesticorum*, but he was soon recalled. Then one Jovinus set out for Britain but returned to gather a larger force. Rumors caused even greater alarm, necessitating that the command go to Theodosius.

30. Flavius Theodosius 3 in *PLRE*, 1:902–4.

31. The panegyrics praise Theodosius's victories over Picts, Scots, and Saxons; see Pacatus, *Panegyric on Theodosius*, 2.5.2.; Claudian, *Panegyric on the Third Consulship of Honorius*, in *Claudian*, ed. and trans. Maurice Platnauer (Cambridge: Harvard University Press, Loeb Classical Library, 1922), 1:51–56; and idem, *Panegyric on the Fourth Consulship of Honorius*, in ibid., 1:24–33.

32. Valentinus 5 in *PLRE*, 1:935; Johnson, *Later Roman Britain*, 122–23.

33. See Salway, *Roman Britain*, 392–96, 411; idem, *Illustrated History*, 276–78; Frere, *Britannia* (1987), 200; and Bartholomew, "Fourth-Century Saxons," 185. The origin and location of Valentia remain problematic, all evidence deriving from a brief mention by Ammianus and another in the Notitia. Salway believes that the province consisted of lands recovered from dissident Romans (such as Valentinus), not necessarily from lands taken by the barbarians; Bartholomew sees Valentia simply as Maxima Caesariensis renamed.

34. On the extent of the devastation and restoration in 367–68, see Salway, *Roman Britain*, 383–91; Johnson, *Later Roman Britain*, 122–26; and Esmonde Cleary, *Ending*, 45–46.

35. Salway, *Roman Britain*, 383–84; Johnson, *Later Roman Britain*, 127–30.

36. Magnus Maximus 39 in *PLRE*, 1:588. See also P. J. Casey, "Magnus Maximus in Britain," in *The End of Roman Britain*, 66–79.

37. Welsh tradition claims Maximus as the founder of the dynasty of the kings of Dyfed, and he becomes the hero of the medieval tale "The Dream of Macsen Wledig" (which incorporates parts of the legend of Constantine the Great and Helena) in the Welsh collection known as the *Mabinogion*. See Rachel Bromwich, ed. and trans., *Trioedd Ynys Prydein: The Welsh Triads* (Cardiff: University of Wales Press, 1978), 454, and John F. Matthews, "Macsen, Maximus, and Constantine," *Welsh History Review* 11 (1983): 431–48. Maximus is also linked with the disputed migration of Cunedda to Gwynedd and the settlement of Irish tribal protectorates (the Deisi) in southern Wales, both of which movements were aimed at controlling Irish infiltration in Wales. See David N. Dumville, "Sub-Roman Britain: History and Legend," *History* 62 (1977): 181–82, and Johnson, *Later Roman Britain*, 83, 131. If there is truth behind any of this, a command as ranking comes would have put Maximus in a better position to have dealings in Wales. See Salway, *Roman Britain*, 404: "[Maximus] may have been responsible for establishing loyal men in posts of authority in Wales that later became hereditary, possibly to counter the Irish raiding."

38. *Gallic Chronicle of 452*, sub anno 382; Zosimus, 4.35.2–6 and 37.1–3. Orosius (7.34.9–10) suggests that Maximus was an unwilling usurper.

39. Saint Ambrose served Maximus in negotiations with Valentinian II, and Maximus and his wife actively sought the friendship of Saint Martin of Tours. But Martin rebuked the pretender for using the army in an attempt to hunt down the Priscillianist heretics (Maximus became the first Christian emperor to order the execution of a heretic). See John F. Matthews, *Western Aristocracies and Imperial Court, A.D. 364–425* (Oxford: Clarendon Press, 1975), and idem, "Macsen," 431.

40. Sozomen, 7.13; Orosius, 7.35.3–4. Many of Maximus's British troops must have perished or been relocated after the war with Theodosius. On the theory that some of these Britons settled in Brittany (Armorica), see Nora K. Chadwick, *Early Brittany* (Cardiff: University of Wales Press, 1969), and Patrick Galliou and Michael Jones, *The Bretons* (Oxford: Blackwell, 1991), 131.

41. Orosius, 7.35.4 (trans. Ireland, in *Roman Britain*, 161); Ambrose, *Epistolae*, 40.23;

Prosper Tiro, *Chronicon*, sub anno 1191 (A.D. 388). Theodosius permitted Maximus's wife and daughter to live quietly in retirement.

42. *De excidio*, 15.2.

43. Claudian, *Against Eutropius*, 1.391–93.

44. Claudian, *On the Consulship of Stilicho*, 2.247–55.

45. Claudian, *Gothic War*, in Claudian, ed. and trans. Maurice Platnauer (Cambridge, Mass.,: Harvard University Press, Loeb Classical Library, 1922), 2:416–18; all further translations of Claudian's Gothic War are taken from this edition unless otherwise noted. See Salway, *Roman Britain*, 423–24.

46. Salway, *Roman Britain*, 425.

47. Ibid., 312, 380; Frere, *Britannia* (1987), 342.

48. Johnson, *Later Roman Britain*, 123.

49. Ammianus, 29.4.7.

50. Johnson, *Later Roman Britain*, 125–26; Salway, *Roman Britain*, 386–88; Thomas Burns, *A History of the Ostrogoths* (Bloomington: Indiana University Press, 1984), 11ff. For a detailed discussion of these finds, see S. C. Hawkes and G. C. Dunning, "Soldiers and Settlers in Britain, Fourth to Fifth Century," *Medieval Archaeology* 5 (1961): 1–70 (though this work is dated and not widely accepted); and C. J. Simpson, "Belt-Buckles and Strap-Ends of the Later Roman Empire," *Britannia* 7 (1976): 192–223.

51. Salway, *Roman Britain*, 418. The presence of Anglo-Saxon federates in fourth-century Britain is a critical point in the misguided argument for "continuity" between Roman Britain and Anglo-Saxon England. Esmonde Cleary (*Ending*, 191–204) is doubtful of a federate presence and of such an argument's underlying assumption: that if we find Saxon federates in fourth-century Britain, these must have been the ones assuming power with the collapse of the Roman system in the fifth century: "Such 'continuity' between Roman Britain and Anglo-Saxon England hardly deserves the name. We would be better employed trying to find and trace the processes of contact between Briton and Saxon" (204).

52. This theory is fully developed by Richard M. Reece, "Town and Country: The End of Roman Britain," *World Archaeology* 12 (1980): 77–92.

53. Johnson, *Later Roman Britain*, 123–25; Salway, *Roman Britain*, 387–89.

54. Millet, *Romanization of Britain*, 149–51.

55. Ibid., 221.

56. Malcolm Todd, "The Cities of Roman Britain: After Wheeler," in *Roman Towns: The Wheeler Inheritance: A Review of 50 Years' Research*, CBA Research Report, no. 93, ed. Stephen J. Greep (York: CBA, 1993), 5–10, esp. 8.

57. See Jeremy Evans, "From the End of Roman Britain to the Celtic West," *Oxford Journal of Archaeology* 9 (1990): 98: "A fundamental shift in values occurred here, from status defined by property ownership to status defined by control of persons (generally peasants)."

58. Jerome, *Epistolae*, 133.9.14 (my translation).

Chapter 2

1. For a recent detailed discussion of these events, see Thomas S. Burns, *Barbarians Within the Gates of Rome: A Study of Roman Military Policy and the Barbarians, ca. 375–425* (Bloomington: Indian University Press, 1994).

2. Claudian, *Against Eutropius*, 1.391–93.

3. Claudian, *On the Consulship of Stilicho*, 2.247–55.

4. See Mollie Miller, "Stilicho's Pictish War," *Britannia* 6 (1975): 144–45. Miller believes that Gildas's account of a "second Pictish war" (*De excidio*, 16–18) is likely Stilicho's campaign.

5. Claudian, *Gothic War,* 416–18: "There also came the legion set to guard the furthest Britons, the legion that curbs the savage Scot and scans the lifeless patterns tattooed on the dying Picts" (trans. Stanley Ireland, *Roman Britain: A Sourcebook* [London: Routledge, 1986], 165).

6. Miller, "Stilicho's Pictish War," 144: "It appears . . . that Stilicho's Pictish war occurred in 398; that measures about fortifications were ordered in 399; and that 'the legion' was ordered overseas in 401."

7. *De excidio,* 18.3 (trans. Winterbottom).

8. Zosimus, 6.3.1; Prosper Tiro, *Chronicon,* 1230.

9. Zosimus, 6.3.1 (trans. Ireland): "Such was the slaughter they inflicted that they inspired terror even among the forces in Britain, who were then forced through fear the barbarians might move against them into electing usurpers."

10. Marcus 2 in J. R. Martindale, *The Prosopography of the Later Roman Empire, vol. 2,* A.D. *395–527* (Cambridge: Cambridge University Press, 1980), 719–20; hereafter *PLRE,* 2, followed by the page number.

11. Zosimus, 6.2: "The troops in Britain mutinied and enthroned Marcus, obeying him as emperor there, but when he would not accede to their demands, they killed him." Nothing more is known about Marcus. Cf. Olympiodorus, frag. 12; Sozomen, 9.11.

12. Gratianus 3 in *PLRE,* 2:518–19.

13. Orosius, 7.40.4 (trans. Ireland): "While these tribes were rampaging through Gaul, in Britain Gratian, a civilian official on the island [municeps eiusdem insulae], was illegally made emperor and killed." Cf. Sozomen, 9.11.

14. Zosimus, 6.2.

15. Ibid.; Orosius, 7.40.4; Sozomen, 9.11.

16. Constantinus 21 in *PLRE,* 2:316–17. On Constantine, in general, see François Paschoud, ed., *Zosime: Histoire nouvelle* (Paris: Les Belles Lettres, 1989), vol. 3, pt. 2, 17–68; Ronald T. Ridley, trans., *Zosimus: New History* (Sydney: Australia Association for Byzantine Studies, 1982), 225–26; and Emilienne Demougeot, "Constantin III, l'empereur d'Arles," in *Hommage a André Dupont* (Montpellier: Federation Historique du Languedoc, 1974), 83–125.

17. Orosius, 7.40.4 (trans. Ireland): "In his [Gratian's] place Constantine was elected from the lowest ranks of the military, solely on the basis of the hope engendered by his name, and not because of any valour he had." Sozomen, 9.11: "When he [Gratian] too was put to death after no more than four months, they next chose Constantine, thinking that since he bore this name, he would gain firm control of the empire." The sources conflict with regard to the origins of Constantine. Orosius and the Latin tradition claim that he was an unknown soldier, while the Greek tradition derived from Olympiodorus states that he was "a not obscure man" (Procopius, *De Bello Vandalico,* 3.2.31, trans. Dewing). It is probable that Constantine held, at least, an important military post in Britain. See Burns, *Barbarians.*

18. Constans 1 in *PLRE,* 2:310; Julianus 7 in *PLRE,* 2:638. See Paschoud, *Zosime,* vol. 3 pt. 2, 31–32; Ridley, *Zosimus,* 225 n. 8; and Michael E. Jones, "Provinces of Iron and Rust: The End of Roman Britain" (Ph.D. diss., University of Texas at Austin, 1985), 279. In his coinage issued from Gaul, Constantine used the names Flavius Claudius Constantinus and represented himself as both Augustus and colleague of the House of Theodosius; see J.P.C. Kent, "The End of Roman Britain: The Literary and Numismatic Evidence Reviewed," in *The End of Roman Britain,* BAR British Series, no. 71, ed. P. J. Casey (Oxford: Tempvs Reparatvm, 1979), 18 n. 20; Philip Grierson and Melinda Mays, *Catalogue of Late Roman Coins in the Dumbarton Oaks Collection and in the Whittemore Collection: From Arcadius and Honorius to the Accession of Anastasius* (Washington, D.C.: Dumbarton Oaks, 1992), 214–17; and Burns, *Barbarians.*

19. Zosimus, 6.2.2. Cf. Olympiodorus, frag. 12.

20. See Ridley, *Zosimus,* 226 n. 11; Gregory of Tours, *Historia Francorum,* 2.9; hereafter *HF.*

21. Zosimus, 6.2.2: "[H]e thus seemed to have secure possession of the empire." Orosius (7.40.4), however, holds a different view of Constantine's successes: "There [in Gaul] he was frequently tricked by worthless pacts with the barbarians and was the cause of great harm to the state."

22. Zosimus, 6.2.3.

23. Zosimus, 6.2.4.

24. Edobichus in *PLRE*, 2:386. The sources in which he appears give various spellings of this Frankish name. Gerontius 5 in *PLRE*, 2:508.

25. Zosimus, 6.2.4–5. Constantine's magistri continued to harass the retreating Sarus, who had to give his booty to the bacaudae in order to cross the Alps safely into Italy.

26. Zosimus, 6.2.6. These events were unfolding at the end of 407 and the beginning of 408. Zosimus gets a bit confused here (6.3) and redescribes the barbarian invasion of 406.

27. Zosimus, 6.4. Constans was originally a monk (ex monacho Caesarem factum). According to Renatus Frigeridus (in *HF*, 2.9), Constans was, like his father, "also a tyrant" (idemque tyranno) (trans. Lewis Thorpe, in Gregory of Tours, *History of the Franks* [New York: Penguin, 1974]).

28. Zosimus, 6.4.2.

29. The aristocrats included the grandfather of Sidonius Apollinaris. Zosimus, 6.4.2, 6.13.1; Sidonius, *Epistola*, 3.12. See also Ridley, *Zosimus*, 227 n. 22.

30. Zosimus, 6.5.1; HF, 2.9. Constans angered the indigenous Spanish troops by giving over the protection of the Spanish provinces to British troops—the Honoriaci. See Ridley, *Zosimus*, 227–28 n. 26.

31. Olympiodorus, frag. 16; Zosimus, 5.43, 6.1, and 6.5.2. Zosimus implies that these men were killed by Constantine; Orosius (7.40.5–8) places the blame on the Honoriaci. Ridley (*Zosimus*, 225 n. 3) points out that it would have been far more sensible to keep them alive to bargain with Honorius.

32. Zosimus, 5.43.

33. Honorius had earlier (5.31.5) planned to send Alaric against Constantine, but Stilicho's death in 408 caused a switch in his policy; see Ridley, *Zosimus*, 225 n. 8. Zosimus, 5.43.2 (trans. Ireland): "Honorius gave in to the request and sent Constantine the imperial apparel." Constantine proclaimed—on a Greek inscription from Trier—that he and Honorius jointly held the consulship in the West in 409, and he minted his own coins (both solidi and siliquae) portraying himself as Augustus. See Matthews, *Western Aristocracies*, 310, and P. J. Casey, *Roman Coinage in Britain* (Aylesbury: Shire Archaeology, 1980), 46–48.

34. Zosimus, 6.1.

35. HF, 2.9. Frigeridus includes the additional commentary that Constantine, undisturbed by the news from Honorius, resumed "his daily round of over-drinking and over-eating" (trans. Thorpe). For the possibility that this was a racial slur aimed at the British usurper, see Jones, "Failure of Romanization," 133 n. 25. Alternatively, it may simply have rehearsed a common stereotype associated with the tyrants of ancient Greece. Zosimus (6.5.2) mentions the new magister, Justus, but does not give Constantine's motives for replacing Gerontius. See Paschoud, *Zosime*, vol. 3, pt. 2, 9 n. 122; Ridley, *Zosimus*, 228 n. 28.

36. Frigeridus in HF, 2.9; Olympiodorus, frag. 16; Sozomen, 9.13; Orosius, 7.42.4; Prosper Tiro, *Chronicon*, 1243. Olympiodorus claims that Maximus was the son of Gerontius and a former member of the domestici.

37. Zosimus, 6.5.2. This is a skewed account of the invasion of Spain by the Vandals in 409 (Hydatius, 42; Salvian, 6.12; Orosius, 7.38–40; Sozomen, 9.12; Olympiodorus, frag. 30). For some restored clarity, see Paschoud, *Zosime*, vol. 3, pt. 2, 9 n. 122; Ridley, *Zosimus*, 228 n. 29.

38. Zosimus, 6.5.2–3; *Gallic Chronicle of 452*, 281.17. Zosimus sometimes uses the phrase "Celtic peoples of Gaul," possibly implying the inhabitants of Armorica (Brittany). Paschoud (*Zosime*, vol. 3, pt. 2, p. 9 and n. 123) points out Zosimus's imprecise language, and does not

further define these quelques-unes des populations de la Gaul.

39. Zosimus, 6.6.1. The "revolt" here must refer to the rebellion of the inhabitants of Britain against Constantine and Rome, not the actions of the three usurpers. See Paschoud, *Zosime*, vol. 3, pt. 2, 9 n. 123.

40. Zosimus, 6.13.1; Olympiodorus, frag. 16; Sozomen, 9.11–12; Frigeridus in *HF*, 2.9. Decimus Rusticus had been master of the offices.

41. Frigeridus in *HF*, 2.9.

42. Olympiodorus, frag. 16. See Ridley, *Zosimus*, 225–26 n. 8.

43. Frigeridus in *HF*, 2.9.

44. Olympiodorus, frag. 16; Sozomen, 9.12–13; Orosius, 7.42.4; Prosper Tiro, *Chronicon*, 1243; Marcellinus, *Chronicon*, 411 (2.70).

45. Orosius, 7.42.4.

46. The account is in Sozomen, 11.13. Most of Gerontius's troops deserted to Honorius's army, and when those he left in Spain heard the news, they besieged Gerontius in his fortified house. For a discussion of Gerontius's dramatic final days, in which he took the life of his wife as well as his own, see Jones, "Provinces," 280–81.

47. Sozomen, 9.14; Frigeridus in *HF*, 2.9.

48. See Ralph W. Mathisen, *Ecclesiastical Factionalism and Religious Controversy in Fifth-Century Gaul* (Washington, D.C.: Catholic University of America Press, 1989), 32.

49. Olympiodorus, frag. 16; Sozomen, 9.15; Orosius, 7.42.3; Hydatius, *Chronicon*, 50.

50. Frigeridus in *HF*, 2.9.

51. Ibid.

52. Zosimus, 5.43.1: "the (τυραννος) Constantine"; 6.1.1: "Constantine, who had usurped power (τυραννησαντος)"; 6.3.1: "the (τυραννων) . . . Marcus, Gratian, and Constantine"; 6.6.1: "the usurpation (ετυραννει) of Constantine." Frigeridus in *HF*, 2.9: "Constantine, who had become a tyrant" (Constantinus, adsumpta tyrannide); "The tyrant Constantine summoned his son Constans, who was also a tyrant" (Accito Constantinus tyrannus . . . Constante filio idemque tyranno); "Decimus Rusticus, the prefect of the tyrants" (praefectus tyrannorum Decimus Rusticus). Sozomen, 9.11.2–3: "they next chose Constantine . . . for the tyranny (τυραννιδα)." *Gallic Chronicle of 452*, A.D. 408: "the (tyrannus) Constantine." Orosius, 7.42.1–4: "of the tyrants . . . Constantine (and) his son Constans" (tyrannorum . . . Constantem Constantini filium). See Jones, "Failure of Romanization," 133, and Anthony Birley, *The People of Roman Britain* (Berkeley and Los Angeles: University of California Press, 1980), 160–61.

53. Zosimus, 6.3.1.

54. The passage is under Honorius XVI (410): "Britanniae Saxonum incursione devastatae" (The British provinces were devastated by an incursion of Saxons). The dating of this event is hotly debated, and cases have been made for 408, 409, 410, and 411. See E. A. Thompson, "Britain, A.D. 406–410," *Britannia* 8 (1977): 303–18; Mollie Miller, "The Last British Entry in the 'Gallic Chronicles,'" *Britannia* 9 (1978): 315–18; Philip Bartholomew, "Fifth-Century Facts," *Britannia* 13 (1982): 261–70; Steven Muhlberger, "The Gallic Chronicle of 452 and Its Authority for British Events," *Britannia* 14 (1983): 23–33; Wood, "End of Roman Britain"; and esp. Michael E. Jones and John Casey, "The Gallic Chronicle Restored: A Chronology for the Anglo-Saxon Invasions and the End of Roman Britain," *Britannia* 19 (1988): 367–97.

55. R. W. Burgess, "The Dark Ages Return to Fifth-Century Britain: The 'Restored' Gallic Chronicle Exploded," *Britannia* 21 (1990): 185–95, though I would not go as far as Burgess in saying that this entry "is unlikely to have any historical value whatsoever" (191). See also Michael E. Jones and John Casey, "The Gallic Chronicle Exploded?" *Britannia* 22 (1991): 212–15.

56. Zosimus, 6.5 (trans. Ridley). Cf. Procopius, *De Bello Vandalico*, 1.2.38. The "barbarians over the Rhine" who were harassing Britain and Armorica are generally thought to be

"Saxons," that is, Anglian, Saxon, Jutish, and Frankish pirates who regularly patrolled the English Channel and the rivers of western Gaul.

57. Procopius, *De Bello Vandalico*, 1.2.31 and 38 (trans. Dewing).

58. *Narratio de imperatoribus domus Valentinianae et Theodosianae (MGH, Chronica Minora*, bk. 1, 629, my translation): "Britaniae Romano nomini in perpetuum sublatae." That the author chose to add the phrase in perpetuum shows that, in the period 423–50 (between the deaths of Honorius and Theodosius II), when the *Narratio* was written, Rome had no hope of recovering Britain. See Steven Muhlberger, *The Fifth-Century Chroniclers: Prosper, Hydatius, and the Chronicler of 452* (Leeds: Francis Cairns, 1990), 194.

59. *EH*, 1.11: "Rome fell to the Goths in the 1164th year after its foundation, and Roman rule came to an end in Britain," and 5.24: "In the year 409, Rome was taken by the Goths, and thenceforward Roman rule came to an end in Britain." *HB*, 28 (trans. Morris): "Hitherto the Romans had ruled the British for 409 years. But the British overthrew the rule of the Romans." *Anglo-Saxon Chronicle* (A, Parker Chronicle), sub anno 409: "In this year the Goths took the city of Rome by storm, and never afterward did the Romans rule in Britain." Wood, "End of Roman Britain," 2, states that Bede's account "was not . . . dependent of Procopius here . . . [and] would appear to suggest the existence of a Western tradition recording the emergence of an independent Britain ca 410, thus corroborating Procopius's." Cf. Jones, "Provinces," 278–79.

60. J.N.L. Myres, "Pelagius and the End of Roman Rule in Britain," *Journal of Roman Studies* 50 (1960): 21–36. John Morris ("Pelagian Literature," *Journal of Theological Studies*, n.s., 16 [1965]: 26–60) constructs a similar Pelagian model for the end of Roman Britain.

61. Pelagius's ideas did not become widespread even in the Mediterranean world until after 410, and therefore could not have played a significant role in British politics c. 409. See Salway, *Roman Britain*, 443, and Charles Thomas, *Christianity in Roman Britain to A.D. 500* (London: Batsford, 1981), 57–60.

62. Thompson's theory is best articulated in his "Britain, A.D. 406–410." See also E. A. Thompson, "Peasant Revolts in Late Roman Gaul and Spain," *Past and Present* 2 (1952): 11–23, and idem, "Fifth-Century Facts?"

63. The basis for Thompson's theory is Zosimus's remark (6.5.3) that the provincials in Armorica and Gaul were imitating the Britons in rebelling. Thompson's theory is criticized in Salway, *Roman Britain*, 444–45.

64. Wood, "End of Roman Britain," 4–5: "We are not dealing with a simple class-conflict of honestiores and humiliores but with a situation complicated by local rivalry and factionalism." See also Raymond Van Dam, *Leadership and Community in Late Antique Gaul* (Berkeley and Los Angeles: University of California Press, 1985), 34–48.

65. Zosimus, 6.5.3.

66. Wood, "End of Roman Britain," 5; Salway, *Roman Britain*, 441.

67. See Jones, "Provinces," 278 n. 19, and Esmonde Cleary, *Ending*, 138.

68. Zosimus, 6.5.3 (trans. Ridley).

69. E.g., *De excidio*, 4.1, 5.1, 15.1 (trans. Winterbottom).

70. Salway (*Oxford Illustrated History of Roman Britain*, 307–8) sees them as "strangers" whose "local involvement was probably minimal." The Gallic nobility, in contrast, was capable of supplying its own civil servants, who often rose to the highest provincial posts in the West (e.g., Ausonius, Victorinus, Apollinaris, Decimus Rusticus).

71. This does not, however, imply the total disbandment of the army in Britain; see ibid., 308–11; Nicholas J. Higham, *The Northern Counties to A.D. 1000* (London: Longman, 1986), 241; and Chapter 15 in this volume.

72. Zosimus, 6.10.2 (trans. Ridley).

73. See Martin Biddle, "Towns," in *The Archaeology of Anglo-Saxon England*, ed. David M. Wilson (London: Methuen, 1976), 99–150, esp. 104. Biddle believes that Honorius was

simply giving the British civitates a directive to exercise their legitimate military authority.

74. The suggestion was first made by Gothofredus (1587–1652), in his commentary on the Theodosian Code, and was taken up by Mendelssohn in his edition of Zosimus. More recently it has been argued by A.L.F. Rivet and Colin Smith, *The Place-Names of Roman Britain* (Princeton: Princeton University Press, 1979), 102, and Bartholomew, "Fifth-Century Facts."

75. E. A. Thompson, "Zosimus 6.10.2 and the Letters of Honorius," *Classical Quarterly* 32 (1982): 445–62. Cf. idem, "Britain, A.D. 406–410," and idem, "Fifth-Century Facts?"

76. Thompson, "Zosimus," 447–48.

77. *De excidio*, 18.1 (trans. Winterbottom). See Thompson, "Zosimus," 449.

78. Paschoud (*Zosime*, vol. 3, pt. 2, 57–60) discusses both sides of this debate and sides (cautiously) with Thompson.

79. Jones, "Provinces," p. 278 and n. 19. Admittedly, Zosimus's confusing narrative requires an alternative chronology.

Chapter 3

1. See, for example, Leslie Alcock, *Arthur's Britain* (New York: Penguin, 1971); John Morris, *The Age of Arthur* (New York: Scribner's, 1973); and Appendix A in this volume.

2. Dumville, "Sub-Roman Britain." Dumville believes that Patrick and Gildas are reliable sources because they are contemporary with many of the events they describe; however, the "Celtic" material—including the *Historia Brittonum*—derives mostly from the eighth century and later. Cf. Ian N. Wood, "The Fall of the Western Empire and the End of Roman Britain," *Britannia* 18 (1987): 251–62 ("If we wish to learn about sub-Roman Britain there is little we can do, other than investigate the cultural and social worlds of Patrick and Gildas" [260]).

3. See, for example, Arnold, *Roman Britain;* Esmonde Cleary, *Ending;* and Lloyd Laing and Jennifer Laing, *Celtic Britain and Ireland, a.d. 200–800: The Myth of the Dark Ages* (New York: St. Martin's, 1990). Leslie Alcock, however, has taken the "new archaeologists" to task for their eagerness to accept Dumville's strictures as permission to throw out all historical evidence. See Ian C. G. Burrow, review of *Economy, Society, and Warfare,* by Leslie Alcock, *Antiquity* 61 (1987): 494–95.

4. Jones Casey, "Gallic Chronicle Restored."

5. By R. W. Burgess. See Burgess, "Dark Ages Return."

6. See Thompson, *St. Germanus,* and Wood, "End of Roman Britain."

7. Wendy Davies, *An Early Welsh Microcosm: Studies in the Llandaff Charters* (London: Royal Historical Society, 1978). See discussion of the Llandaff Charters later in Chapter 3.

8. See John C. Rolfe, introduction to *Ammianus Marcellinus,* 3 vols. (Cambridge, Mass.: Harvard University Press, Loeb Classical Library, 1935), x, xlii.

9. Ammianus, 14.9.1.

10. See Rolfe, Ammianus, xiii.

11. Ammianus, 28.3.7.

12. See E. A. Thompson, "Ammianus Marcellinus and Britain," *Nottingham Medieval Studies* 34 (1990): 1–15.

13. The standard edition is Otto Seeck, ed., *Notitia Dignitatum* (Frankfurt: Minerva, 1962).

14. A.H.M. Jones, *The Later Roman Empire, 284–602* (Norman: University of Oklahoma Press, 1964), vol. 3, app. 2. See also Frere, *Britannia* (1987), 217–24, 360–61; J. H. Ward, "The British Sections of the *Notitia:* An Alternative Interpretation," *Britannia* 4 (1973): 253–63; Roger Goodburn and Philip Bartholomew, eds., *Aspects of the "Notitia Dignitatum,"* BAR Supplemental Series, no. 15 (Oxford: Tempvs Reparatvm, 1976); David J. Breeze and Brian Dobson, *Hadrian's Wall* (London: Penguin, 1976), chap. 7 and app. 4; Rivet and Smith,

Place-Names of Roman Britain, 216–25; Salway, *Roman Britain,* 336; and Mann, "Historical Development of the Saxon Shore," 1–11.

15. Rivet and Smith, *Place-Names of Roman Britain,* 217.

16. The shore "settled by Saxons" or "attacked by Saxons"? For a discussion of this question, see J.G.F. Hind, "*Litus Saxonicum*—the Meaning of 'Saxon Shore,'" in *Roman Frontier Studies, 1979: Papers Presented to the Twelfth International Congress of Roman Frontier Studies,* BAR International Series 71, ed. W. S. Hanson and L.J.F. Keppie (Oxford: Tempvs Reparatvm, 1980), 1:317–24; and Chapters 10 and 14 in this volume.

17. The *Notitia* is especially helpful with the structures along Hadrian's Wall. See Kenneth Rainsbury Dark, "A Sub-Roman Re-Defense of Hadrian's Wall?" *Britannia* 23 (1992): 111–20.

18. Olympiodorus 1 in *PLRE,* 2:798–99.

19. John F. Matthews, "Olympiodorus of Thebes and the History of the West (407–425)," *Journal of Roman Studies* 60 (1970): 79.

20. See Karl Muller, ed., *Fragmenta Historicum Graecorum,* vol. 4 (Paris: Ambrosio, 1851); vol. 5 (1870). The fragments are translated in R. C. Blockley, *The Fragmentary Classicising Historians of the Later Roman Empire: Eunapius, Olympiodorus, Priscus, and Malchus* (Liverpool: Francis Cairns, 1983). Sozomen and Zosimus (see the discussion later in Chapter 3) also make much use of Olympiodorus.

21. Matthews, "Olympiodorus," 85–86.

22. Thompson, "Zosimus," 460.

23. Orosius in *PLRE,* 2:813.

24. Orosius, 7.40.4, 7.42.1–4. The original may be found in *Adversum Paganos,* ed. C. Zangemeister (Hildesheim: G. Olmse, 1967). An English translation has been done by I. W. Raymond, *Seven Books of History Against the Pagans* (New York: Columbia University Press, 1936).

25. See Thompson, "Zosimus," 460.

26. *PLRE,* 2:485–86. See also Philip Wynn, "Frigeridus, the British Tyrants, and the Early-Fifth-Century Barbarian Invasions of Gaul and Spain," *Athenaeum* (forthcoming).

27. The original may be found in *Gregor von Tours: Zehn Bücher Geschichten,* ed. and trans. Rudolf Buchner, 2 vols. (Berlin: Rutten & Loening, 1967). An English translation has been done by Lewis Thorpe: Gregory of Tours, *History of the Franks* (New York: Penguin, 1974).

28. *HF,* 2.9. Frigeridus's accounts of Constantine and Constans are perhaps included by Gregory in his *History* because of the tyrants' relations with the barbarians, especially through their Frankish *magister* Edobech (Edobinchus).

29. Salamanes Hermeias Sozomenus 2 in *PLRE,* 2:1023–24.

30. Sozomen, 9.11. The original may be found in *Sozomenus Kirchengeschichte,* ed. Joseph Bidez (Berlin: Akadamie-Verlag, 1960). An English translation has been done by Edward Walford, *The Ecclesiastical History of Sozomen* (London: Bohn, 1855). Problems with dating are addressed by Charlotte Roueche, "Theodosius II, the Cities, and the Date of the 'Church History' of Sozomen," *Journal of Theological Studies* 37 (1986): 130–32.

31. Thompson, "Zosimus," 459.

32. Zosimus 6 in *PLRE,* 2:1206.

33. Zosimus, *Historia Nova,* chaps. 5 and 6. The original may be found in *Historia Nova,* ed. Ludwig Mendelssohn (Leipzig: Teubner, 1887), and in *Zosime: Histoire Nouvelle,* 3 vols., ed., with detailed commentary and a French translation, by François Paschoud (Paris: Les Belles Lettres, 1989). An English translation has been done by Ronald T. Ridley, *Zosimus: New History* (Sydney: Australian Association for Byzantine Studies, 1982).

34. Zosimus survives in a single manuscript, the *Vaticanus Graecus* 156.

35. Nor is Zosimus idealized even by his modern defenders; see Thompson, "Zosimus," 446: "Zosimus has an unsurpassable claim to be regarded as the worst of all extant Greek historians of the Roman Empire."

36. See the discussion in the previous chapter. Gildas perhaps provides independent evidence for the rescript.

37. R. T. Ridley, "Zosimus the Historian," *Byzantinische Zeitschrift* 65 (1972): 292–93.

38. Procopius's works are edited and translated by H. B. Dewing, *Procopius,* 6 vols. (Cambridge, Mass.: Harvard University Press, Loeb Classical Library, 1914–40). For the most recent biography and textual criticism, see Averil Cameron, *Procopius and the Sixth Century* (London: Duckworth, 1985).

39. *Anekdota,* 19.13 (trans. Dewing): "And he [Justinian] never ceased pouring out great gifts of money to all the barbarians, both those of the East and those of the West and those of the North and to the South, as far as the inhabitants of Britain."

40. *De Bellis,* 1.2.38, 3.1.17, 3.2.31–38, 5.24.36, 6.6.28, 6.15.1–26, 8.20.1–10, 8.20.42–55.

41. J. O. Ward, "Procopius' Bellum Gothicum II.6.28: The Problem of Contacts Between Justinian I and Britain," *Byzantion* 38 (1968): 460–71.

42. Cameron, *Procopius,* 215. See *De Bellis,* 4.20.10.

43. E. A. Thompson, "Procopius on Brittia and Britannia," *Classical Quarterly* 30 (1980): 498–507.

44. Cameron, *Procopius,* 216.

45. Both chronicles are edited by Theodor Mommsen, in *MGH,* vol. 9, bk. 1 of *Chronica Minora,* 617–66.

46. British Library Additional Manuscript 16974. Mommsen based his edition on this copy. For a discussion of the manuscript tradition, see Jones and Casey, "Gallic Chronicle Restored," 367–68, and Wood, "End of Roman Britain," 17–18.

47. Jones and Casey, "Gallic Chronicle Restored," 367; Wood, "End of Roman Britain," 18. Ian Wood has also suggested that the *Chronicle of 452* was written by Faustus of Riez, which would make it in some sense a British text; see his comments in *After Empire,* ed. Ausenda, 205.

48. Wood, "End of Roman Britain," 18.

49. Ibid. Also, while regnal dates are given in the *Chronicle of 452* down to the death of Theodosius II (450), there is no indication how long Valentinian III and Marcian reigned, suggesting that the author was writing before the murder of Valentinian in 455.

50. Jones and Casey, "Gallic Chronicle Restored," 374–76. This Carolingian interpolation resulted in the triple dating scheme of the *Chronicle of 452.*

51. See, for example, J. B. Bury, *History of the Later Roman Empire* (London: Macmillan, 1889), 200; idem, *History of the Later Roman Empire,* 2d ed. (London: Dover, 1923); Frere, *Britannia* (1987), 373; Miller, "The Last British Entry"; Todd, *Roman Britain,* 240; Salway, *Roman Britain,* 433–34; Thompson, "Zosimus," 306; Bartholomew, "Fifth-Century Facts"; and Muhlberger, "Gallic Chronicle of 452," 25–27.

52. Jones and Casey, "Gallic Chronicle Restored," 379–96.

53. Ibid., 392, 396.

54. Burgess, "Dark Ages Return." But see also the authors' response: Jones and Casey, "Gallic Chronicle Exploded?"

55. This is mostly overreaction. For example, Burgess actually confirms Jones and Casey's date of 441 for the second British entry in the *Chronicle of 452,* but he maintains that these "Gallic observations" may not "reflect anything of what was actually going on in Britain at the time" ("Dark Ages Return," 192). Cf. Muhlberger, *Fifth-Century Chroniclers,* 179: "[The chronicler of 452] simply invoked the name of Britain to supplement his picture of a defeated empire in the process of disintegration."

56. Wood, "End of Roman Britain," 17.

57. Ibid., 18; Mommsen, *Chronica Minora,* bk. 1, 617; Jones and Casey, "Gallic Chronicle Restored," 396.

58. Constantius, *Vita Sancti Germani.* The original may be found in *Scriptores Rerum Merovingicarum,* ed. Wilhelm Levison, vol. 7 of *MGH.* An English translation has been done

by F. R. Hoare, *The Life of St. Germanus,* in *The Western Fathers* (New York: Sheed & Ward, 1954). See also the edition by Rene Borius, *Constance de Lyon: Vie de Saint Germain d'Auxerre* (Paris: Les Editions du Cerf, 1965). Citations used here are from Borius's edition.

59. Constantius 10 in *PLRE,* 2:320. Constantius's verse was inscribed on the walls of a church in Lyon. See ibid., and Wood, "End of Roman Britain," 9.

60. Wood ("End of Roman Britain," 9) sees the *Vita* as "a handbook for bishops" facing the problems (especially famine) caused by the barbarian expansion in Gaul; both Patiens and Constantius were notable in this respect.

61. Prosper Tiro, *Chronicon,* a. 429 (in *MGH,* vol. 9, bk. 1 of *Chronica Minora,* ed. Mommsen, 472; my translation): "Agricola Pelagianus, Severiani episcopi Pelagiani filius, ecclesias Brittaniae dogmatis sui insinuatione corrumpit, sed ad insinuationem Palladii diaconi papa Caelestinus Germanum Autisidorensem episcopum vice sua mittit et deturbatis hereticis Britannos ad catholicam fidem dirigit."

62. Constantius, *Vita,* 3.12 (trans. Hoare): "Eodem tempore ex Brittaniis directa legatio Gallicanis episcopis nuntiavit Pelagianam perversitatem in locis suis late populos occupasse et quam primum fidei catholicae debere succurri. Ob quam causam synodus numerosa collecta est, omniumquae iudicio duo praeclara religionis lumina universorum precibus ambiuntur, Germanus ac Lupus apostolici sacerdotes, terram corporibus, caelum meritis possidentes."

63. See Thompson, *St. Germanus,* 7, and Wood, "End of Roman Britain," 10. Constantius neglects to tell us who composed the British deputation (*legatio*)—priests, bishops, laity?— who sent them, and what area of Britain they represented (only the vague *in locis suis*).

64. *Vita,* 3.14. Cf. Thompson, *St. Germanus,* 19, and Wood, "End of Roman Britain," 10.

65. *Vita,* 3.15: "vir tribuniciae potestatis" (my translation). For discussion, see Chapter 10.

66. See Wood, "End of Roman Britain," 12–14.

67. Constantius attributes a *ducatus culmen* to Germanus in chapter 1, but interpreting *dux* in a purely military sense may be problematic; see ibid., 11. See also, however, Thompson, *St. Germanus,* 62 n. 29, who follows A.H.M. Jones in believing that Germanus had served as *dux tractus Armoricani et Nervicani* in his early days.

68. Most notably Nora K. Chadwick, *Poetry and Letters in Early Christian Gaul* (London: Bowes & Bowes, 1955), 255–56.

69. Wood ("End of Roman Britain," 14) points out that the second visit is corroborated in the *Vita Genouefae.* See also Thompson, *St. Germanus,* 4.

70. Ralph W. Mathisen, "The Last Year of Saint Germanus of Auxerre," *Analecta Bollandiana* 99 (1981): 158–59.

71. E. A. Thompson, "A Chronological Note on St. Germanus of Auxerre," *Analecta Bollandiana* 75 (1957): 135–38; idem, *St. Germanus,* 55–70.

72. Wood, "End of Roman Britain," 14–17.

73. *Vita,* 5.25 (trans. Hoare): "Interea ex Brittaniis nuntiatur Pelagianam perversitatem iterato paucis auctoribus dilatari rursusque ad beatissimum virum preces sacerdotum omnium deferuntur, ut causam Dei, quam prius obtinuerat, tutaretur."

74. Ibid., 5.26. For discussion, see Chapter 10.

75. Ibid., 5.27: "ut in illis locis etiam nunc fides intemerata perduret."

76. E.g., *EH,* 2.19. See David N. Dumville, "Late-Seventh- or Eighth-Century Evidence for the British Transmission of Pelagius," *CMCS* 10 (1985): 39–52.

For contrasting views on Germanus's success battling Pelagianism in Britain, see Wood, "End of Roman Britain," 17, and R. A Markus, "Pelagianism: Britain and the Continent," *Journal of Ecclesiastical History* 37 (1986): 191–204. Markus argues that Pelagianism was recognized as heresy in Britain only after a minority had introduced Augustinianism, but despite Germanus's support of the latter, some of Pelagius's views survived in the Celtic churches because they were not seen therein as heretical.

77. The earliest manuscript containing Patrick's writings is the ninth-century *Book of Armagh,*

which carries a scribal colophon datable to 807. The definitive modern critical edition of Patrick is that of Ludwig Bieler, "Libri Epistolarum Sancti Patricii Episcopi," in *Classica et Mediaevalia* 11 (1950): 1–150, and 12 (1951): 81–214. A good Latin text with English translation is A.B.E. Hood's *St. Patrick: His Writings and Muirchu's "Life"* (London: Phillimore, 1978). An English translation with extensive commentary is provided by R.P.C. Hanson, *The Life and Writings of the Historical St. Patrick* (New York: Seabury Press, 1983). Unless stated otherwise, citations and translations used here are from Hood's edition.

78. The earliest Latin biography of Patrick is Muirchu's *Vita Sancti Patricii,* written in the late seventh century, an incomplete version of which is also included in the *Book of Armagh.* See Ludwig Bieler and Fergus Kelly, eds., *The Patrician Texts in the Book of Armagh* (Dublin: Institute for Advanced Studies, 1979). The complete Latin edition, along with later *Lives,* can be found in Bieler, *Four Latin Lives of St. Patrick* (Dublin: Institute for Advanced Studies, 1971). For a recent Latin edition with English translation, see Hood, *St. Patrick.* Other early medieval writings about or attributed to Patrick can be found (in translation) in Liam de Paor, *Saint Patrick's World: The Christian Culture of Ireland's Apostolic Age* (Notre Dame, Ind.: University of Notre Dame Press, 1993).

79. Thomas (*Christianity in Roman Britain,* 310–13) suggests we look along the western portion of Hadrian's Wall near Birdoswald (Banna).

80. Presumably these raiders were Irish; however, they may have been Britons—like Coroticus—operating in both Britain and Ireland. See Charles Thomas, review of *Saint Patrick,* by David N. Dumville et al., *English Historical Review* 111, no. 441 (1996): 402–3.

81. *Confessio,* 26–27. It seems that a close friend of Patrick's had betrayed an unnamed boyhood sin that Patrick had confided to him, and some thirty years later this was being charged against him by enemies in Britain who wanted to ruin his career. This brings up the important question whether the British church initiated, or at least supported, Patrick's mission in Ireland. See Hanson, *Life and Writings,* 97.

82. The table of contents in Muirchu's seventh-century *Life of Patrick* (the *Book of Armagh* text) describes Coroticus as "king of Alclut" (*regem Aloo*), that is, the citadel of Dumbarton Rock in Strathclyde. Most historians have accepted this identification of Coroticus with a historical king of Strathclyde who flourished, according to some genealogies, c. 465–75; see Thomas, *Christianity in Roman Britain,* 341–43, and Hanson, *Life and Writings,* 24. E. A. Thompson has put forward a theory that Coroticus and his warband were Britons living in Ireland; see Thompson, "St. Patrick and Coroticus," *Journal of Theological Studies,* n.s., 31 (1980): 12–27, and idem, *Who Was Saint Patrick?* (New York: St. Martin's, 1985), 126–37. It remains an interesting possibility, but has not yet been adequately proved.

83. However, this may be a reflection of the term *tyrannus,* which was used in Britain after 410 to describe various types of rulers. See Hanson, *Life and Writings,* 7, 65, and the discussion in Chapter 9 in this volume.

84. See David N. Dumville, "The Floruit of St. Patrick: Common and Less Common Ground," in David N. Dumville et al., *Saint Patrick, a.d. 493–1993* (Woodbridge, Suffolk: Boydell, 1993), 13–18.

85. The date given by Gregory of Tours. Some scholars now prefer a later date of 503 or 507/8.

86. Ludwig Bieler, "Der Bibeltext des Heiligen Patrick," *Biblica* 28 (1947): 31–58 and 236–63.

87. This tradition is based upon Prosper's *Chronicon,* which states that, in the year 431, "Palladius, ordained by Pope Celestine, was sent as first bishop to those Irish believing in Christ" (Ad Scottos in Christum credentes ordinatus a papa Caelestino Palladius primus episcopus mittitur) (my translation). Prosper's work was apparently known in Ireland, and the Irish saw 432 as the next possible date for the arrival of their saint.

88. J. B. Bury, *The Life of St. Patrick and His Place in History* (London: Macmillan, 1905).

For a critique of this scheme, see Thomas, *Christianity in Roman Britain,* 314–16.

89. T. F. O'Rahilly, *The Two Patricks: A Lecture on the History of Christianity in Fifth-Century Ireland* (Dublin: Institute for Advanced Studies, 1942).

90. James Carney, *The Problem of St. Patrick* (Dublin: Institute for Advanced Studies, 1961).

91. John Morris, "The Dates of the Celtic Saints," *Journal of Theological Studies,* n.s., 17 (1966): 369–72; see also Morris's introduction in Hood, *St. Patrick,* 1–16. R.P.C. Hanson, *St. Patrick: His Origins and Career* (Oxford: Clarendon Press, 1968), 178–88; idem, "The Date of Patrick," *Bulletin of the John Rylands University Library* 61 (1978–79): 60–77; idem, *Life and Writings,* 18–35.

92. Thomas, *Christianity in Roman Britain,* 318–27.

93. Dumville et al., *Saint Patrick,* 57.

94. Thompson, *Who Was Saint Patrick?* 175. There is, at this moment, no consensus of scholarly opinion; see Michael E. Jones, *The End of Roman Britain* (Ithaca, N.Y.: Cornell University Press, 1996), 112–13. Jones prefers the earlier, traditional chronology; Wood ("End of Roman Britain," 6 n. 40) and Patrick Wormald (personal communication, 1992) are sure that Patrick's career extended considerably into the second half of the fifth century.

95. For the theological merit of Patrick's works, see Noel Dermot O' Donoghue, *Aristocracy of Soul: Patrick of Ireland* (Wilmington, Del.: Michael Glazier, 1987), a study that focuses on Patrick's mysticism.

96. Christine Mohrmann, *The Latin of St. Patrick* (Dublin: Institute for Advanced Studies, 1961).

97. See Dumville et al., *Saint Patrick,* 25.

98. David R. Howlett, *"Liber Epistolarum Sancti Patricii Episcopi": The Book of Letters of Saint Patrick the Bishop* (Dublin: Four Courts Press, 1994), 115: "[T]he modern scholars' picture of Patrick—a naive and barely literate rustic struggling to express himself in a language he could not master—is a grotesque misrepresentation of the thought and praise of a writer who was more than competent." Howlett's study includes full Latin (based on Bieler) and English editions of the *Epistola* and *Confessio*—arranged to illustrate Patrick's biblical style—as well as a new proposed structure for the *Confessio.*

99. See David R. Howlett, *The Celtic Latin Tradition of Biblical Style* (Portland, Ore.: Four Courts Press, 1995), and my review in *Arthuriana.*

100. Peter Dronke, "St. Patrick's Reading," *CMCS* 1 (1981): 21–38.

101. The first date given for the battle, 516, was recorded in the *Annales Cambriae,* compiled (at the earliest) in the late eighth century. Alcock (*Arthur's Britain,* 53–55) amends this date to 490 to reconcile the annals' date for the death of Maelgwn; Morris (*Age of Arthur,* 37f.) opts for 495; Dumville ("Gildas and Maelgwn: Problems of Dating," in *Gildas: New Approaches,* ed. Lapidge and Dumville, 51–59) cautions against relying on these later annals and genealogies for Gildas's dates. See also Mollie Miller, "Relative and Absolute Publication Dates of Gildas's *De Excidio* in Medieval Scholarship," *BBCS* 26 (1974–76): 169–74.

102. Columbanus, *Epistola,* 1.7; *EH,* 1.22. See Richard Sharpe, "Gildas as a Father of the Church," in *Gildas: New Approaches,* ed. Lapidge and Dumville, 191–206.

103. The *Vita S. Gildasii* I, written by a monk of Ruis (in Brittany) in the eleventh century, and the *Vita S. Gildae* II, written by Caradoc of Llancarfan in the middle of the twelfth; both are included in *MGH,* vol. 13, bk. 3 of *Chronica Minora,* ed. Mommsen, 91–110. See also Hugh Williams, ed. and trans., *Gildas,* 2 vols. (London: Cymmrodorian, 1899–1901).

104. Owen Chadwick ("Gildas and the Monastic Order," *Journal of Theological Studies,* n.s., 5 [1954]: 78–80) was the first to question the assumption that Gildas was a monk, suggesting instead that he was a deacon, a view now supported by, among others, David Dumville ("Idea of Government," 192). This question is explored in detail by Michael W. Herren, "Gildas and Early British Monasticism," in *Britain, 400–600: Language and History,* Anglistische Forschungen 205, ed. Alfred Bammesberger and Alfred Wollmann (Heidelberg:

C. Winter, 1990), 67–77, and Neil Wright, "Gildas's Reading: A Survey," *Sacris Erudiri* 32 (1991): 121–62, esp. 159–61. Herren believes that Gildas aspired to be a monk (*sanctus*) but was probably a deacon; Wright suggests that Gildas was a priest or a deacon when he wrote the *De excidio,* and perhaps became a monk later in life.

105. A. W. Wade-Evans, ed. and trans., *Vitae Sanctorum Britanniae et Genealogiae* (Cardiff: University of Wales Press, 1944); H. Marsille, "Saint Gildas et l'abbaye de Rhuys," *Bulletin Mensuel de la Société Polymathique du Morbihan* 101 (1973): 8–29.

106. The earliest extant manuscript is Cotton Vitellius A vi in the British Library, an eleventh-century manuscript that was badly damaged by fire in 1731. The undamaged book, however, was copied by Polydore Virgil in 1525 and Josselin in 1568. The first modern critical edition is *De excidio et conquesta Britanniae,* in *MGH,* vol. 13, bk. 3 of *Chronica Minora,* ed. Mommsen, 1–85. The most recent version (with English translation) is edited by Michael Winterbottom in *Gildas: The Ruin of Britain and Other Works* (London: Phillimore, 1978). Unless stated otherwise, citations and translations used here are from Winterbottom's edition.

107. Much modern commentary has ignored this fact. See, however, Rex Gardner, "The New Testament Motivation of Gildas and His Friends," *Transactions of the Cymmrodorion, 1994,* n.s., 1 (1995): 5–26, and Howlett, *Celtic Latin Tradition,* 72–73. Howlett believes that Gildas's epistle may be an imitation of Patrick's.

108. Howlett (*Celtic Latin Tradition,* 74) postulates an alternative structure for the *De excidio* that breaks these parts into smaller units.

109. Robert W. Hanning, *The Vision of History in Early Britain from Gildas to Geoffrey of Monmouth* (New York: Columbia University Press, 1966), 46–48; Goffart, *Narrators of Barbarian History,* 170; Jones, *End of Roman Britain,* 121; Neil Wright, "Gildas' Prose Style and Its Origins," in *Gildas: New Approaches,* ed. Lapidge and Dumville, 107ff.; and Higham, *English Conquest,* 7–34. See also Dodie A. Brooks, "Gildas' *De Excidio:* Its Revolutionary Meaning and Purpose," *Studia Celtica* 18 (1983): 1–10. Rex Gardner has further illustrated how Gildas used passages in the New Testament—especially Stephen's speech in Acts, chapter 7—as models for his "historical" preface; see Gardner, "New Testament," 5, and idem, "Gildas' New Testament Models," *CMCS* 30 (1995): 1–12.

110. *De excidio,* 20.1. Bede (*EH,* 1.13) corrects Gildas's spelling (*Agitius*) to *Aetius.* If this equation (*Agitius* = *Aetius*) is correct, it constitutes a rare chronological clue from Gildas: Aetius was *ter consuli* in the years 446 to 454. See David N. Dumville, "The Chronology of *De Excidio Britanniae,* Book I," in *Gildas: New Approaches,* ed. Lapidge and Dumville, 67–68, 83; and contra, see P. J. Casey and Michael E. Jones, "The Date of the Letter of the Britons to Aetius," *BBCS* 37 (1990): 281–90.

111. *De excidio,* 23 (trans. Winterbottom). The name Vortigernus appears in two early MSS of the *De excidio* (twelfth and thirteenth centuries), as well as the *Vita Gildasii* I, in place of *superbo tyranno;* in Bede he appears as Vertigernus and Vurtigernus. See Dumville, "Sub-Roman Britain," 183–84. Since "Vortigern" is almost certainly a British name or title meaning "overlord," Gildas may have been making a play on the words *superbo tyranno.* See Kenneth Jackson, "*Varia:* II. Gildas and the Names of the British Princes," *CMCS* 3 (1982): 36ff., and the discussion in Chapter 9 in this volume.

112. *De excidio,* 26.1 (trans. Winterbottom).

113. Many attempts have been made to identify these tyrants and locate their kingdoms; see, for example, Alcock, *Arthur's Britain,* 121ff. Jackson ("*Varia:* II," 31) has demonstrated the masterful ways with which Gildas plays upon the meanings of these British names, especially in distorting *Cun-* (Latin *Caninus*)—a popular element in royal names that to the British meant "loyal or brave 'hound'"—to take on the (biblically) pejorative meaning "dog" or "whelp."

114. Alcock, *Arthur's Britain,* 29.

115. Little has been written about the authenticity of these two works, but both have been included in the latest edition of Gildas (Winterbottom's). See Sharpe, "Gildas," 193–202.

116. The *Fragmenta* derive from two sources: a late-ninth-century collection of patristic passages now in Cambridge (Corpus Christi College, MS 279), and an Irish collection of c. 700 called the *Hibernensis*. They are edited by Mommsen, in *Chronica Minora,* bk. 3, 86–88, and by Winterbottom, in *Gildas.* Citations here are from Winterbottom's edition.

117. See Sharpe, "Gildas," 196–97, and David N. Dumville, "Gildas and Uinniau," in *Gildas: New Approaches,* ed. Lapidge and Dumville, 207.

118. Herren ("Gildas," 70) believes that the *Fragmenta* show that Gildas eschewed both ascetic excesses and severe penances.

119. "The Preface of Gildas on Penance," in *The Irish Penitentials,* Scriptores Latini Hiberniae, vol. 5, ed. Ludwig Bieler (Dublin: Institute for Advanced Studies, 1963). Bieler's edition and translation are included in Winterbottom, *Gildas.* Citations here are from Winterbottom's edition.

120. Sharpe, "Gildas," 201.

121. See, for example, François Kerlouegan, "Le Latin du *De excidio Britanniae* de Gildas," in *Christianity in Britain, 300–700,* ed. M. W. Barley and R.P.C. Hanson (Leicester: Leicester University Press, 1968), 151–76; Miller, "Publication Dates of Gildas's *De Excidio*"; idem, "Starting to Write History: Gildas, Bede, and Nennius," *Welsh History Review* 8 (1977): 456–65; Thomas David O'Sullivan, *The "De Excidio" of Gildas: Its Authenticity and Date* (Leiden: E. J. Brill, 1978); E. A. Thompson, "Gildas and the History of Britain," *Britannia* 10 (1979): 203–26; Nicholas J. Higham, *The English Conquest: Gildas and Britain in the Fifth Century* (Manchester: Manchester University Press, 1994); and Jones, *End of Roman Britain,* 43–53, 121–130.

But the most significant contribution to the study of Gildas is the collection of conference papers edited by Michael Lapidge and David N. Dumville, *Gildas: New Approaches* (Woodbridge, Suffolk: Boydell, 1984). Here, Lapidge ("Gildas's Education and the Latin Culture of Sub-Roman Britain," 27–50) argues that Gildas's Latin reveals an education more proper to the fifth than to the sixth century; Dumville ("Gildas and Maelgwn: Problems of Dating," 51–59, and "The Chronology of *De Excidio Britanniae,* Book I," 61–84) proposes "a chronological table of Gildas's narrative" that estimates Gildas's *floruit* at c. 500–45; and Neil Wright ("Gildas's Geographical Perspective: Some Problems," 85–106) argues (against Miller and Thompson) that Gildas's narrative refers to "Britain as a whole," rather than to just the north or to any one area of the island. These and the rest of the papers are remarkable in their clarity and freshness, and their provocative new models will surely set the tone for Gildasian scholarship for many years to come. See Thomas Charles-Edwards, review of *Gildas: New Approaches, CMCS* 12 (1986): 120.

122. These are discussed in Dumville, "Gildas and Maelgwn," and idem, "Chronology of *De Excidio.*"

123. See Chapter 2.

124. See Chapter 3.

125. For recent discussion of the letter to Aetius, see Michael E. Jones, "The Appeal to Aetius in Gildas," *Nottingham Medieval Studies* 32 (1988): 141–55; Casey and Jones, "Date of the Letter of the Britons to Aetius"; Higham, *English Conquest,* 118–45; and Appendix B in this volume.

126. Dumville, "Chronology of *De Excidio,*" 83.

127. The *Annales Cambriae,* for example, give the date 516 for the Battle of Badon and 570 as Gildas's *obit.*

128. Michael Lapidge ("Gildas's Education") believes that Gildas's Latinity is more analogous to fifth-century writers; Michael Herren ("Gildas and Early British Monasticism") argues, on the basis of Gildas's limited references to insular monasticism, for a c. 500 date for the *De excidio* and a c. 530–40 date for the *Fragmenta*; and Thomas O'Sullivan (*"De Excidio" of Gildas*) suggests the period 515–20 for Gildas's literary career.

Most recently, Nicholas Higham (*Rome, Britain, and the Anglo-Saxons* [London: Seaby, 1992] and *English Conquest*) has argued for a wholly fifth-century Gildas, dating the *De excidio* to 479–84 on the basis of Gildas's Latinity and a reassessment of the date of the Appeal to Aetius. But even if Higham is right about the Appeal, that it dates to the period 425–35 instead of 446–54, his proposed chronology (*English Conquest*, 137) ignores Gildas's more subtle chronological clues. A reconstructed chronology that includes such clues would look something like this:

c. 430	The Appeal to Aetius.
+25 yrs.?	"Meanwhile," a "dreadful famine," then "a period of truce" after the Picts and Scots went home, which led to an age of "luxury" but also "civil war" and "plague."
c. 455	A council was convened, and the Saxons were invited to Britain as federates.
+10 yrs.?	"For a long time" the Saxons were satisfied with their increased payments.
c. 465	Saxon rebellion, the beginning of the "War of the Saxon Federates."
+10 yrs.?	"After a time" of coast-to-coast slaughter and devastation of "town and country," the rebels returned "home."
c. 475	Ambrosius Aurelianus led the "wretched survivors" to victory over the Saxons.
10 yrs.?	A period in which victories were traded by both sides.
c. 485	The year of the siege of Badon Hill and of Gildas's birth.
+44 yrs.	"One month of the forty-fourth year since then has already passed."
c. 529	Gildas writes the *De excidio*, as a contemporary of Ambrosius's grandchildren.

This dating scheme gives a Gildas whose primary education belongs to the fifth century and whose adult life belongs to the sixth. Thus it has the advantage of being something of a compromise between the "fifth-century" and "sixth-century" Gildasian schools, and may fit in with current thinking. See, for example, Jones, *End of Roman Britain*, 46: "Literary and linguistic considerations thus suggest that Gildas was probably educated in the later fifth century and composed the *De Excidio* at the beginning of the sixth century."

129. Wright ("Gildas's Reading," 158), while acknowledging that this could place Gildas's literary career in the 490s or early 500s, warns that "too much emphasis should not be placed on what is ultimately an *argumentum ex silentio*."

130. For recent support of Dumville's dating scheme, see Kenneth Rainsbury Dark, *Civitas to Kingdom: British Political Continuity, 300–800* (Leicester: Leicester University Press, 1993), 258–60. Columbanus seems to know Gildas as a sixth-century figure and is certainly familiar with the *De excidio* and the *Fragmenta,* perhaps quoting from the latter a correspondence between Gildas and "Vennianus," a sixth-century cleric working in Ireland. See Sharpe, "Gildas as a Father of the Church," 197: "That the [*Fragmenta*] belongs to the sixth century is without doubt—Columbanus's evidence guarantees the date."

131. See, for example, Thompson, "Gildas," 203–26.

132. Higham, *English Conquest*, 90–117; Dark, *Civitas*, 260–66.

133. François Kerlouégan, *Le "De excidio Britanniae" de Gildas: Les destinées de la culture latine dans l'île de Bretagne au VIe siecle* (Paris: Publications de la Sorbonne, 1987). See the review by Michael Lapidge in CMCS 17 (1989): 75–78. Lapidge, "Gildas's Education," 27–50. Neil Wright, "Gildas's Prose Style and Its Origins," in *Gildas: New Approaches*, ed. Lapidge and Dumville, 107–28.

134. Neil Wright ("Gildas's Reading," 124–52) has compiled a very useful *index scriptorum* that includes passages where Gildas is quoting, imitating, or echoing other Latin works.

135. See Lapidge, review of *Le "De excidio,"* by Kerlouégan, 76; idem, "Gildas's Education"; and Chapter 10.

136. National Library of Wales MS 17110E. The bulk of this book was written in Llandaff c. 1125–50. For a fuller description of the MS, see E. D. Jones, "The Book of Llandaff," *National Library of Wales Journal* 4 (1945–46): 123–57. The modern critical edition is by J. G. Evans (with J. Rhys), *The Text of the Book of Llan Dâv* (Oxford, 1893; reprint, Aberystwyth: National Library of Wales, 1979).

137. Wendy Davies's studies of the Llandaff Charters include: "The Church in Wales," in *Christianity in Britain,* ed. Barley and Hanson, 131–50; "*Unciae:* Land Measurement in the Liber Landavensis," *Agrarian History Review* 21 (1973): 115–17; "Land and Power in Early Medieval Wales," *Past and Present* 8 (1978): 323ff.; and *An Early Welsh Microcosm: Studies in the Llandaff Charters* (London: Royal Historical Society, 1978). Davies is also responsible for a new critical edition of the charters—*The Llandaff Charters* (Aberystwyth: National Library of Wales, 1979).

138. Davies deduces, from the language of the charters, that large Roman estates (*agri*) continued in use in southeast Wales until the early eighth century, when they were divided into smaller, single-focus estates (*villae/trefs*). See also Higham, *Rome, Britain, and the Anglo-Saxons,* 92.

139. E.g., Patrick Sims-Williams, review of *The Llandaff Charters,* by Wendy Davies, *Journal of Ecclesiastical History* 33 (1982): 128: "It is questionable whether *Liber Landavensis* can legitimately be used as an indicator of social and economic change, since problems about the nature of recording are so manifold." See also Alcock, *Economy,* 94–95, and Dark, *Civitas.*

140. Davies, *Early Welsh Microcosm,* 5–6. For a discussion of the chronology of the charters, see also Myfanwy Lloyd Jones, *Society and Settlement in Wales and the Marches (500 b.c. to a.d. 1100),* BAR British Series 121 (Oxford: Tempvs Reparatvm, 1984), vol. 2, app. 23.

141. Davies did herself begin such a study for the Oxford O'Donnell Lectures in 1983, comparing the political terminology of the Llandaff Charters with that in other early medieval Celtic material; see Davies, *Patterns of Power in Early Wales* (Oxford: Clarendon Press, 1990).

142. See Jones, "Failure of Romanization," 130–31, and J. C. Mann, "Epigraphic Consciousness," *Journal of Roman Studies* 75 (1985): 204–6.

143. See Anthony Birley, *The People of Roman Britain* (Berkeley and Los Angeles: University of California Press, 1980).

144. R. G. Collingwood and R. P. Wright, *The Roman Inscriptions of Britain,* vol. 1 (Oxford: Oxford University Press, 1965); hereafter *RIB.* Volume 2 is currently being published in fascicules (1 through 8 have appeared so far). An index to volume 1 has been compiled by Roger Goodburn and Helen Waugh: *Roman Inscriptions of Britain I: Inscriptions on Stone: Epigraphic Indexes* (Gloucester: Sutton, 1983). The most recent finds are usually published in *The Journal of Roman Studies* and *Britannia.* See also M. C. Greenstock, ed., *Some Inscriptions from Roman Britain,* 2d ed. (Hatfield, Hertfordshire: London Association of Classical Teachers, 1971).

145. General problems in dating Roman inscriptions are discussed by A.L.F. Rivet, "Notes on Roman Epigraphy," in *Some Inscriptions from Roman Britain,* ed. Greenstock, xiii.

146. Elisabeth Okasha, *Corpus of Early Christian Inscribed Stones of Southwest Britain* (Leicester: Leicester University Press, 1993). V. E. Nash-Williams, *The Early Christian Monuments of Wales* (Cardiff: University of Wales Press, 1950); hereafter *ECMW.* J. Romilly Allen and Joseph Anderson, eds., *Early Christian Monuments of Scotland* (Edinburgh: Society of Antiquarians of Scotland, 1903), hereafter *ECMS.* See also R.A.S. MacAlister, *Corpus Inscriptionum Insularum Celticarum,* vol. 1 (Dublin: Stationery Office, 1945), hereafter *CIIC;* P. C. Bartrum, *Early Welsh Genealogical Tracts* (Cardiff: University of Wales Press, 1966); Stewart Cruden, *Early Christian and Pictish Monuments* (London: HMSO, 1964); Elisabeth Okasha, "The Non-Ogam Inscriptions of Pictland," *CMCS* (1985): 43–69; and Charles Thomas, *And Shall These Mute Stones Speak? Post-Roman Inscriptions in Western Britain*

(Cardiff: University of Wales Press, 1994). Recent finds have been published in Jeremy K. Knight et al., "New Finds of Early Christian Monuments," *Archaeologia Cambrensis* 126 (1977): 60–73, and Kenneth Rainsbury Dark, *The Inscribed Stones of Dyfed* (Llandysul, Dyfed: Gomer, 1992).

147. For the most recent discussion of Ogam (variants include "ogom," "Ogham"), see Damian McManus, *A Guide to Ogam* (Maynooth: An Sagart, 1991).

148. See *ECMW,* 3.

149. For a discussion of the language and dating of these inscriptions, see Jones, *Society and Settlement in Wales,* vol. 2, app. 10; Jeremy K. Knight, "*In Tempore Iustini Consulis:* Contacts Between the British and Gaulish Churches Before Augustine," in *Collectanea Historica: Essays in Memory of Stuart Rigold,* ed. Alex Detsicas (Gloucester: Sutton, 1981)," 54–62, and Dark, *Civitas.*

150. Bieler, *Irish Penitentials.* The earliest of these works is "The First Synod of St. Patrick," recording an event that Bieler dates to 457. The following works likely date to the sixth or early seventh century: "The Preface of Gildas on Penance," "The Synod of North Britain," "The Synod of the Grove of Victory," "Excerpts from a Book of David," and "The Penitential of Finnian."

151. For critical editions and translations of these texts, see Ifor Williams, ed., *Canu Aneirin* (Cardiff: University of Wales, 1938); Kenneth Jackson, trans. *The Gododdin: The Oldest Scottish Poem* (Edinburgh: Edinburgh University Press, 1969); A.O.H. Jarman, ed., *Aneirin: Y Gododdin* (Llandysul, Dyfed: Gomer Press, 1988); and Ifor Williams, ed., and J. E. Caerwyn Williams, trans., *The Poems of Taliesin* (Dublin: Institute for Advanced Studies, 1968). For their use in writing history, see Dumville, "Sub-Roman Britain," 178–79; idem, "Early Welsh Poetry: Problems of Historicity," in *Early Welsh Poetry: Studies in the Book of Aneirin,* ed. B. F. Roberts (Aberystwyth: National Library of Wales, 1988), 1–16; and Davies, *Patterns of Power.* See also Jenny Rowland, "Warfare and Horses in the *Gododdin* and the Problem of Catraeth," *CMCS* 30 (1995): 13–40 ("One of the few remaining tenets of faith amidst all doubts raised about the *Gododdin* in the past few years is that the poem at least preserves a reasonably accurate picture of the heroic way of life of the northern Britons in the sixth century" [13]).

152. A new critical edition of the *Historia* is currently being prepared by David Dumville. The standard edition is by Mommsen, in *MGH,* vol. 13, bk. 3 of *Chronica Minora.* The edition used here is *Nennius: British History and the Welsh Annals,* ed. and trans. John Morris (London: Phillimore, 1980). For detailed discussion of dating and authorship, see the following articles by David Dumville: "'Nennius' and the *Historia Brittonum,*" *Studia Celtica* 10–11 (1975–76): 78–95; "Some Aspects of the Chronology of the *Historia Brittonum,*" *BBCS* 25 (1972–74), 439–45; "Sub-Roman Britain," 176ff.; and "The Historical Value of the *Historia Brittonum,*" *Arthurian Literature* 6 (1986): 1–26. Dumville dates the original text to 829/30 and believes that the "Nennian Preface" was added later, in a subsequent recension.

153. The *Annales* are included in *Nennius,* ed. Morris. For study of the dating and sources of the annals, see Kathleen Hughes, "The Welsh Latin Chronicles: *Annales Cambriae* and Related Texts," *Proceedings of the British Academy* 59 (1973): 233–58; Mollie Miller, "Date-Guessing and Dyfed," *Studia Celtica* 12 (1977): 33–61; Dumville, "Sub-Roman Britain," 176 ff.; and Alcock, *Arthur's Britain,* 39–40, 45–55.

154. See Bartrum, *Early Welsh Genealogical Tracts,* and Wade-Evans, *Vitae Sanctorum Britanniae et Genealogiae.* For discussion of the problems in using this material, see Morris, "Dates of the Celtic Saints," and Dumville, "Sub-Roman Britain," 175ff.

155. Dumville, "Sub-Roman Britain."

Chapter 4

1. The most notable examples are Leslie Alcock, *Arthur's Britain,* and John Morris, *The Age of Arthur,* both of which use later material as well.

2. See the discussion in Thomas, *Christianity in Roman Britain,* 244–51.

3. E.g., Thomas, *Christianity in Roman Britain;* Alcock, *Economy;* Laing and Laing, *Celtic Britain and Ireland;* Higham, *Rome, Britain, and the Anglo-Saxons.*

4. The phrase *insula Albionum,* "isle of the *Albiones,*" first appears in Avienus, *Ora Maritima* (fourth century A.D.), which is based on a *periplus* composed by an anonymous Greek of Marseille in the sixth century B.C. "Albion" also appears in the works of Pseudo-Aristotle, Pseudo-Agathemerus, Marcian, Stephanus, Eustathius, and Pliny. See C.F.C. Hawkes, *Pytheas: Europe and the Greek Explorers,* Eighth J. L. Myres Memorial Lecture (Oxford: Oxford University Press, 1977), and Rivet and Smith, *Place-Names of Roman Britain,* 39.

5. Ρρεττανια appears in Eustathius, Diodorus Siculus, Marcian, and Ptolemy. Both forms appear in book 1 of Strabo's *Geography.* See Rivet and Smith, *Place-Names of Roman Britain,* 39.

6. Procopius (in *De Bellis and the Anekdota*) uniquely distinguishes between βρεττανια (vars. βρεταυια, βριτανια) and an island called βριττια. See Rivet and Smith, *Place-Names of Roman Britain,* 39, 82–83, and Thompson, "Procopius on Brittia and Britannia."

7. Caesar, *De Bello Civili,* 1.54.1; idem, *De Bello Gallico,* 2.4.7, 2.14.3, 3.8.1, 3.9.9, 4.20.1, 4.21.3, 4.22.5, 4.23.2, 4.27.2, 4.28.1, 4.30.1, 4.37.1, 4.38.1, 5.2.3, 5.6.5, 5.8.2, 5.22.4, 6.13.11, 7.76.1. Cf. Catullus, *Carmina,* 29.4; Tacitus, *Agricola,* 11.4; and Ammianus, 26.4.5.

8. *Thesaurus Linguae Latinae* (Leipzig: B. G. Teubner, 1900–), s.v. *Britanni, Britannia, and Britannicus;* hereafter TLL. See also R. E. Latham, *The Dictionary of Medieval Latin from British Sources* (London: Oxford University Press, 1975), s.v. *Britannia, Britannicus, and Britannus;* and Rivet and Smith, *Place-Names of Roman Britain,* 39–46. The adjective *Britannicus* is often accompanied by the words *oceanus or mare,* signifying the English Channel, and Gildas (*De Poenitentia,* 1) mentions "British cheese" (*Britannico formello*). Rivet and Smith (*Place-Names of Roman Britain,* 40) point out that, at least in Tacitus, the adjective *Britannicus* always means "of Britain," never "of Britons."

9. This was likely done to reduce the number of legions under the sway of any one provincial governor. Herodian (3.8) attributes this to Septimius Severus in 197 (though it may not have occurred until the reign of Caracalla), and Cassius Dio (55.23.2) records their names (confirmed by inscriptions). See Rivet and Smith, *Place-Names of Roman Britain,* 46; Salway, *Oxford Illustrated History of Roman Britain,* 171; and Frere, *Britannia* (1987), 162.

10. These provincial names first appear in the Verona List of 312–14. Ammianus, the *Notitia,* and Polemius Silvius record a fifth province, *Valentia* (*Valentiana* in Polemius). See discussion in Chapter 2.

11. The Greek writers tended to stay with the singular, even after the partition, or used the adjectival form. Olympiodorus, however, uses both the singular and the plural: frags. 13.1 (*Brettanias*) and 13.2 (*Brettania*).

12. *Nomina Provinciarum Omnium (Laterculus Veronensis),* chap. 7, in *Geographi Latini Minores,* ed. Riese.

13. *Codex Theodosianus,* ed., Theodor Mommsen, Paul Meyer, and Paul Kruger (Hildesheim: Weidmann, 1990), 11.7.2 (319 Nov. 20): "IDEM A. A.D. PACATIANUM VIC(ARIUM) BRITTANIARUM" (To Pacatianus, vicar of the Britains).

14. Polemius Silvius, *Laterculus,* 2.11.1–6, in *MGH,* vol. 9., bk. 1 of *Chronica Minora,* ed. Mommsen.

15. See, for example, the use of the singular in *Expositio Totius Mundi et Gentium* (c. 350), in *Geographi Latini Minores,* 68; *Dimensuratio Provinciarum (Epitome Totius Orbis)* (c. 400), in ibid., 30; and Julius Honorius, *Cosmographia* (fifth century), in ibid., 15–18. The

dimensions of the island are given in the *Dimensuratio,* and *Britannia* is said to be bounded by the *Oceanus Atlanticus* and the *Oceanus Britannicus* (var. *Brittannicus*). In his geographic work, Rufius Festus (fl. 365) uses both singular and plural forms: see *Breviarium,* 3 and 6.

For a contemporary adjectival geographic form, see *Divisio Orbis Terrarum* (c. 400, also in the *Geographi Latini Minores*), 7: *insulae Britannicae* (variant *Britanicae*), "the British island"; and Eunapius Sardianus, *Historia,* frag. 12: *Brettanike nesos,* "the Brettanic island."

16. In the *Panegyrici Latini,* there are about nineteen occurrences of *Britannia* in the singular, and only two in the plural.

17. Claudian, *On the Consulship of Stilicho,* 2.247. He refers to Britain a total of six times in his poems, all in the singular. In doing so, his rhetorical models are probably prediocesan writers like Pliny and Tacitus.

18. See the following examples in Harold Mattingly et al., eds., *Roman Imperial Coinage* (London: Spink, 1923–), hereafter *RIC,* and idem, *Roman Imperial Coinage,* 2d ed. (London: Spink, 1984–), hereafter *RIC²: RIC²,* 515, rev. ARMENIA CAPTA; *RIC,* 148B, rev. IUDAEA DEVICTA; *RIC,* 12b, rev. DACIA; *RIC,* 429, rev. SARMATIA DEVICTA; *RIC,* 278a, rev. GERMANIA CAPTA; *RIC,* 49, rev. ALAMANNIA DEVICTA. See Thomas S. Burns and Bernhard H. Overbeck, *Rome and the Germans As Seen in Coinage: Catalog for the Exhibition* (Atlanta, Ga.: Emory University, 1987), 1–14. These geographical personifications are common and always in the singular. One inhabitant of Roman Britain even personified his home as a goddess: "To holy Britannia [*Britanniae sanctae*] Publius Nikomedes, freedman of our Emperors, [set this up]" (RIB, no. 643, on a column from York).

19. Ammianus, 27.8.1 and 10, 27.9.1.

20. Ibid., 28.3.4.

21. Ibid., 29.1.44. See also the list of *vicarii* in *PLRE,* 2.

22. Ammianus, 14.5.6.

23. Ibid., 27.8.4.

24. *Notitia,* OC. 29.1 and 5; 28.1 and 12; 5.142.

25. Ibid., 29.

26. Frere, *Britannia* (1987), 225 n. 31, points out that the heading of chapter 29, *Comes Britanniae,* is corrected to *comitis Britanniarum* in line 4 of that same chapter.

27. Aurelius Victor, *Liber de Caesaribus,* 24.2–4, 4.2, 20.18, 20.27, 39.21, 40.2; idem, *Epitome de Caesaribus,* 20.4, 41.2, 47.7.

28. Eutropius, *Breviarum ab Urbe Condita,* ed. C. Santini (Leipzig: Teubner, 1979), 7.13.2–3 (s. and pl.), 14.4 (s.), 19.1 (s. twice), 8.19.1 (s.), 9.21.1 (pl.), 22.1 (pl.), 22.2 (pl. twice), 10.1.3 (s.), 2.2 (s.). There is no clear reason—chronological or geographical—why Eutropius chooses the endings that he does. E.g., *Carausius in Britaniis rebellaret* (9.22.2), while Constantius *obiit in Britannia* (10.1.3). Rivet and Smith (*Place-Names of Roman Britain,* 65) point out that some MSS give variants that change the plural to the singular.

29. *Scriptores Historiae Augustae,* ed. Ernestes Hohl (Leipzig: Teubner, 1971): Hadrian, 11.2 (s.), 12.1 (s.); Commodus, 13.5 (s.); Pertinax, 2.1 (s.), 3.6 (s.), 3.8 (s.); Albinus, 13.7 (pl.); Severus, 6.10 (pl.); 18.2 (s.), 19.1 (s.), 22.4 (s.), 24.1 (s.); Severus, Alexander, 59.6 (s.); Probus, 18.5 (pl.), 18.8 (pl.); Carus, Carinus, and Numerianus, 16.2 (pl.). Unfortunately, the various forms do not correspond with the dates of the subject matter. See Rivet and Smith, *Place-Names of Roman Britain,* 69 n. 4.

30. *Acta Concilii Arelatensis,* in *Concilia Galliae,* Corpus Christianorum, Series Latina, no. 148, ed. C. Munier (Turnhout: Typographi Brepols, 1963). To complicate things further, this may be a reference to Britain as an ecclesiastical province: see David N. Dumville, "British Missionary Activity in Ireland," in Dumville et al., *Saint Patrick,* 137.

31. Orosius, 1.2.75–82, 7.40.4. Orosius uses the singular and the plural equally in this work, while the singular is preferred in the *Descriptio Terrarum.*

32. Victricius Rotamagensis, *De Laude Sanctorum,* 1.24, 1.31, 1.39.

33. Prosper Tiro, *Chronicon*, 1301, *sub anno* 429. Prosper uses the singular four times, the plural only once.

34. Sulpicius Severus, *Chronica*, ed. C. Halm (Vienna, 1866; reprint 1966), 2.51.3–4, 2.41.3, 2.49.5.

35. Jerome, *Epistulae*, 58.3.7 (s.), 60.4.12 (s.), 133.9.13 (s., *Britanni* most likely being a corruption of *Britannia*), 77.10.22 (s.), 146.1.14 (pl.); *Commentarii in Isaiam*, 18.66.20 (pl.); *Commentarii in Prophetas Minores (In Sophianum)*, 2.341 (pl.); *Tractus Lix in Psalmos*, 95.156 (s.), 135.40 (s.); *Altercatio Luciferiani et Orthodoxi*, 15.177.25 (pl.); *Continuatio de Eusebii*, 248.8 (s.). Sometimes (e.g., *Epistulae*, 146.1.14) Britain appears in the plural along with other dioceses, like Gaul and Spain, while external nations, like Persia and India, remain singular. At other times (e.g., *Tractatus*, 95.156), Jerome puts Britain in the singular along with remote lands, like India.

36. For the passages and discussion, see Chapter 4.

37. *Vita*, 3.12.1, 5.25.1. Borius (*Constance de Lyon*, 144–45) points out that the various manuscripts are inconsistent in their spelling—one or two *t*s, one or two *n*s—but the plural is signified in each case.

38. Patrick is also consistent in referring to Gaul in the plural: *Epistola*, 14 (*Gallorum*); *Confessio*, 43 (*Gallias*).

39. Muirchu, *Vita*, 1.1 (pl. twice), 1.9 (pl. twice), 1.27 (s.). In chapter 1, which is a borrowing from the beginning of Patrick's *Confessio*, Muirchu writes that Patrick was *"Brito natione, in Britannis natus"* (of British nationality, born in the Britains) and that he fled Ireland *"ad Britanias"* (to the Britains). Similarly, in chapter 9, Muirchu states that Palladius died *"in Britannis"* (in the Britains), after which Patrick *"pervenit Brittanias"* (arrived in the Britains). In chapter 27, however, Muirchu speaks of the time when unbelief covered *"tota Britannia"* (all of Britain), perhaps a geographic reference.

40. *De excidio*, 1.14.

41. *De excidio*, 3.1.

42. Ibid., 4.1–4.

43. Ibid., 7.

44. Ibid., 10.1.

45. Ibid., 13.1, 14.1.

46. Dumville, "Idea of Government," 183: "[F]or Gildas *Britannia insula* is a concept which has geographical and political meaning."

47. Wright, "Gildas's Geographical Perspective: Some Problems," 85–105.

48. Ibid., 87ff. Bede, for example, in *EH*, 1.12, uses the phrase *Brittania in parte Brettonum* (Britain, in the area of the Britons) to limit his meaning to the area of the Roman diocese, excluding the lands of the Picts and the Scots.

49. Ibid., 102

50. Patrick Sims-Williams, "Gildas and the Anglo-Saxons," *CMCS* 6 (1983): 5–15. Higham, *English Conquest*, 94–95: "His perspective was not 'regional.'. . . His concern was with the entire *ecclesia* of the Britons—so the total community. . . . It was this geographical and social concept of *Britannia* and *patria* which interested him, . . . that same 'fatherland' . . . concerning which he was wont to generalize." Jones, *End of Roman Britain*, 121: "[Gildas's] horizon in the historical section is probably best judged as including all Britain: it is not restricted to any particular region."

51. Aponius, *Explanationis in Canticum Canticorum Libri XII*, ed. H. Bottino and J. Martini (Rome, 1843), 12.237.

52. Cassiodorus, *Chronica*, in *MGH*, vol. 11, bk. 2 of *Chronica Minora*, ed. Mommsen, 893 (A.D. 211).

53. Jordanes, *Getica*, 1.8–2.15 (s., twice), 2.260 (s., twice), 297 (pl.), 308 (s.).

54. Venantius Honorius Clementianus Fortunatus, *Carmina*, in *MGH*, vol. 4, ed. F. Leo, 8.3.155.

55. Gregorius Magnus, *Moralia in Job,* 27.11.66; *Registrum Epistularum,* 11.36.1, 39.28.

56. Isidorus Hispalensis, *Etymologiae,* in *Patrologia Latina* (hereafter *PL*), ed. Jacques Paul Migne (Paris: Excudebat Migne, 1844–80), vol. 82: 14.6.2–6 (s., five times), 16.4.3 (s.), 16.22.3 (s.).

57. For example: *EH,* 1.1, 1.3, 1.7, 2.5.

58. See ibid., 1.4–21.

59. For example, in 1.21 he is discussing Saint Germanus in Britain and using Constantius—who uses the plural—for his information. Then, in 1.22, he switches to a discussion of the Britons' civil wars, for which he uses Gildas's account, and there finds only the singular form. Rivet and Smith (*Place-Names of Roman Britain,* 57) noticed a similar switching of forms—from *Brettones* to *Brittanni*—when Bede is specifically quoting ancient authorities. This same pattern, where *Britannia* is concerned, can be seen in his *De Temporum Ratione Liber.*

60. As well as in the *EH,* this can be seen in his persistent use of the singular in *De Temporibus Liber,* 7.5, 7.12, 22.57, 22.68; *De Temporum Ratione Liber,* 15.41, 31.55, 31.62, 33.87, 66.1041; *In Regum Librum XXX Questiones,* 25.19; *De Templo Libri II,* 2.1041; *In Marci Evangelium Espositio,* 4.15.1680; *Retractio in Actus Apostolorum,* 19.13; and *Homeliarum Evangelii Libri II,* 1.13.107, 1.13.128.

Chapter 5

1. See *TLL,* s.v. *Patria,* and *A Glossary of Later Latin to 600 a.d.,* comp. Alexander Souter (Oxford: Clarendon Press, 1949), s.v. *Patria.*

2. Suzanne Teillet, *Des Goths à la nation gothique: Les origines de l'idee de nation en occident du Ve au VIIe siecle* (Paris: Les Belles Lettres, 1984). Further discussion of *patria* in late antiquity can be found in François Paschoud, *Roma aeterna: Etudes sur le patriotisme romain dans l'Occident latin a l'Epoque des Grandes Invasions* (Rome: Institut Suisse, 1967), 11–13; and Kerlouégan, *Le "De excidio,"* 528, 558–60.

3. Teillet, *Des Goths,* 28.

4. See Ioannes Viansino, *Ammiani Marcellini Rerum Gestarum Lexicon* (Hildesheim: Olms-Weidmann, 1985), 249; hereafter *Ammianus Lexicon.*

5. Ammianus, 14.6.7, attributing (perhaps wrongly) the sentiment to the lyric poet Simonides. Cf. ibid., 20.4.16, where Julian speaks of the "charm of your *patria*" to his troops in contrast to the "strange places . . . beyond the Alps" (trans. Rolfe).

6. Ibid., 17.11.4.

7. Teillet, *Des Goths,* 74–79.

8. Hugh G. Evelyn White, ed. and trans., *Ausonius,* 2 vols. (Cambridge, Mass.: Harvard University Press, Loeb Classical Library, 1919). For the latest biographical and textual commentary, see Hagith S. Sivan, *Ausonius of Bordeaux: Genesis of a Gallic Aristocracy* (London: Routledge, 1993). Unfortunately, Sivan says very little about Ausonius's provincial loyalties as discerned from his language.

9. Ausonius, *Ordo,* chap. 20 (Bordeaux), line 40. See Sivan, *Ausonius of Bordeaux,* 3.

10. Ausonius, *Ordo,* 20.2 and 8.

11. Ibid., 38. The translation is White's.

12. Teillet, *Des Goths,* 75–76. Ausonius also reminds us (*Ordo,* 20.41) that while his cradle (*cunae*) lay in Bordeaux, his curule chair (*sela curulis*) lay in Rome.

13. Teillet, *Des Goths,* 76. Ausonius prefers the poetic singular in the poems, but uses the official plural in his prose works addressed to Gratian.

14. Ibid.

15. Maurice Lavarenne, ed., *Prudence: Contre Symmaque et Peristephanon,* 2 vols. (Paris: Les Belles Lettres, 1963). While Rome is *Urbs patria* (*Contre Symmaque,* 2.612), Prudentius

repeatedly employs *noster* (*Peristephanon*, 1.116, 4.1, 4.96 and 100, 13.3) to refer to Calagurris, and similarly applies the poetic adjective *Hiberus* to geographic features throughout Hispania.

16. Prudentius, *Peristephanon*, 1.4, 13.3.

17. Emanuele Castorina, ed., *Claudio Rutilio Namaziano: De Reditu* (Firenze: Sansoni, 1967).

18. Rutilius, 1.63.

19. Ibid., 1.20, 25, 32, 161, 209, 551.

20. Ibid., 1.20 and 209. See Teillet, *Des Goths*, 79.

21. Teillet, *Des Goths*, 198–202. See, for example, Sidonius, *Epistolae*, 1.7.4, 2.1.4. In *Carmina*, 9.309–11, Sidonius lists several *poetis . . . nostrum . . . solum* (poets of our soil), and these men (whom he names) come from all parts of Gaul.

22. Sidonius prefers the singular *Gallia* in the *Poems* and *Letters*, but uses the plural form *Galliae* when discussing administrative matters (e.g., *Epistolae*, 1.7.5, 1.11.6, 3.12.5).

23. See the discussion of *Britannia* in the previous chapter. Teillet (*Des Goths*, 201–2) sees an increasing *unité de territoire* among the provinces of Gaul and Spain, corresponding roughly to the diocese. This seems not, however, to have been the case for Italy: see Arnobius Iunior (writing in the time of Pope Leo I), *Commentarii in Psalmos*, 104.60: "sub una lingua [Latina] diversae sunt patriae Bruttiorum, Lucanorum, Apulorum, Calabrorum, Picentum, Tuscorum."

24. Ambrosius, *Expositio Evangelii Secundum Lucam*, 3.603, 7.2364, 10.108; Arnobius Iunior, *Commentarii in Psalmos*, 21.38; Augustine, *Quaestionum in Heptateuchum Libri Septem*, bk. 1 (Genesis), 156.2070; idem, *In Iohannis Evangelium Tractatus*, 16.1.10, 28.5.22; idem, *Enarrationes in Psalmos*, 38.22.36; Jerome, *Tractatuum in Psalmos Series Altera*, 88.150; Prosper Tiro, *Expositio Psalmorum*, 136.9.

25. E.g., Jerome, *Epistulae*, 123.7, 123.14 ("*in patriam revertitur*"), 82.10.117 ("*quis enim monachorum exul patriae non exul est mundi?*"), 53.8.461 ("*populi redeuntis in patriam*"); idem, *Chronicon*, 1405; Ambrose, *Expositio Evangelii Secundum Lucam*, 7.2364 ("*etenim qui se a christo separat exul est patriae*"); Augustine, *De Beata Vita*, 1.21 ("*a sua patria peregrinari audent*"). See Teillet, *Des Goths*, 80 n. 292.

26. See, for example, Augustine, *Confessionum Libri Tredecim*, 9.11.29.

27. *Epistulae*, 122.4.15.

28. Augustine, *Confessionum Libri Tredecim*, 12.16.6: "Hierusalem patriam meam, Hierusalem matrem meam." See also Augustine's prayer in *Soliloquiorum Libri Duo*, in *PL*, vol. 32, p. 871, line 54: "exaudi, exaudi, exaudi me, deus meus, domine meus, rex meus, pater meus, causa mea, spes mea, res mea, honor meus, domus mea, *patria mea*, salus mea, lux mea, vita mea."

29. Constantius, *Vita*, 7.41–2.

30. *Vita Honorati*, 17–19: "quae ad huc terra, quae natio in monasterio illius cives suos non habet. . . . congregatio . . . ex diversa terrarum parte collecta . . . omnes . . . in illo sibi patriam ac propinquos et omnia simul redditat conputantes."

31. Faustus, *Vita Maximi*, in *PL*, 3.636: "ambiebant illum diversae patriae, sed vel maxime proxima eremi civitas . . . quae inter locum hunc et insulam (ut nosti) interiacet."

32. *Epistola*, 1; *Confessio*, 36 and 43. It has been suggested (by Michael E. Jones and Thomas F. X. Noble in a personal communication) that this alliterative phrase is a standard hagiographic topos. It does occur in the *Vita Sancti Hilarii Episcopi Arelatensis*, written c. 476–96, but I have not found it in this form occurring in sources predating (and therefore possibly influencing) Patrick.

33. *Epistola*, 11.

34. See David N. Dumville, "Coroticus," in Dumville et al., *Saint Patrick*, 109 and 121.

35. *Confessio*, 17.

36. *Confessio*, 36 and 43.

37. See Thompson, *Who Was Saint Patrick?* 110–11. We need not, however, go as far as Thompson in believing that *patria* does not equal *Britanniae* because "the idea of nationality did not exist . . . at a provincial level." It is clear that although modern nationalism certainly did not exist, imperial, provincial, tribal, and civic loyalties in the later Roman Empire were very complex and need detailed consideration.

38. Wright, "Gildas's Geographical Perspective," 102. See also the discussion of *Britannia* in the previous chapter.

39. *De excidio,* 1.1, 2.1.

40. Ibid., 4.2–4.

41. Ibid., 15, 67.5–6.

42. It is not as clear, however, whether Gildas considered the Scottish Highlands and islands—inhabited by Picts and Scots—as part of his *patria.* The question is whether *insula Britannia,* a geographical concept, and *patria Britannia,* a political (or ethnic?) concept, are synonymous for Gildas. For the author of the *Historia Brittonum,* who drew from Gildas for this section (chap. 9) of his work, geography and politics are seemingly inseparable: "The *Brittones* once occupied and ruled it [*Britannia*] all from sea to sea" (trans. Morris).

43. Ibid., 17.1.

44. Ibid., 18.1, 23.1.

45. Ibid., 23.4 (*insula* and *patria* are here obviously synonymous), 25.1.

46. Ibid., 26.2, 26.4, 27.1, 30.1, 64.1, 62.2, 67.6. Kerlouegan (*Le "De excidio,"* 195 n. 8) notes twenty-two occurrences of the term patria in the *De excidio.*

47. See Higham, *English Conquest,* 146: "The political context in which [Gildas] wrote was . . . universal: the 'damages and inflictions' of the 'fatherland' were not specific to one small British community but . . . [to] the entire people—the body of cives, the *patria* and *Britannia* herself."

48. Kerlouegan, *Le "De excidio,"* 528 (my translation). Kerlouégan (560–61) suggests that Gildas's concept of *patria* is closer to that of Cicero (a single province) than to that of Prudentius and Rutilius (the whole empire). Cf. Jones, *End of Roman Britain,* 121: "Gildas's concept of *patria* involves more than the orthodox Roman idea of one's native province and includes the entire Roman diocese and even beyond. In the *De excidio, patria, Britannia,* and *insula* seem essentially interchangeable."

49. *ECMW,* no. 139. Nash-Williams (107–9) categorizes the inscription as a metrical epitaph (in two barbarous hexameters), common to the fifth and sixth centuries, whose descriptive phrases are clichés that can be found in early-sixth-century examples from Rome and Gaul. He also supports the association of this Paulinus with the Welsh saint of that name, who was a teacher of Saint David (d. 588?) and who attended the "Synod of Llanddewi-Brefi" (in 545) as an old man. Cf. Patrick Sims-Williams, "Gildas and Vernacular Poetry," in *Gildas: New Approaches,* ed. Lapidge and Dumville, 170–71.

50. But "patriotism" may not be too strong a word to describe Gildas's sentiments; see the comments of Ian Wood in *After Empire,* ed. Ausenda, 211: "There is already patriotism in fifth-century writers [e.g., Sidonius]."

51. E.g., *HB,* 27 (trans. Morris): "That is why *Britannia* has been occupied by *extraneis gentibus,* and the cives driven out, until God shall give them help." All three of these authors express unabashed hopes that the Britons will take back their island from the English. For Nennius and Geoffrey, see Jones, *End of Roman Britain,* 130–143, and Christopher A. Snyder, "Celtic Continuity in the Middle Ages," *Medieval Perspectives* 11 (1996), 164–78. For the *Armes,* see the commentary by Ifor Williams and Rachel Bromwich in *Armes Prydein: The Prophecy of Britain from the Book of Taliesin,* ed. Williams, trans. Bromwich (Dublin: Institute for Advanced Studies, 1972), esp. xxvi, and David N. Dumville, "Brittany and 'Armes Prydein Vawr,'" *Etudes Celtiques* 20 (1983): 145–59.

Chapter 6

1. For an anthropologist's view of this problem, see Malcolm Chapman, *The Celts: The Construction of a Myth* (New York: St. Martin's, 1992).

2. In two entirely independent studies of the place-names and geography of Roman Britain, A.L.F. Rivet and Colin Smith (*Place-Names of Roman Britain*, 10–29) and Barri Jones and David Mattingly (*An Atlas of Roman Britain* [Oxford: Blackwell, 1990], 42) have demonstrated that the Celtic Brythonic (or Brittonic) remained the dominant spoken language in Britain throughout the Roman period, with the exception of the *coloniae* and the villa-owning gentry. Most of the towns retained their British names, as did the rivers and other natural features. Even Roman forts were known by British, rather than Roman, names.

3. Avienius, *Ora Maritima*, 94–134 (*insula Albionum*), written in the fourth century A.D. but based on a *periplus* written by an anonymous citizen of Massilia in the sixth century B.C. Later references to *Albiones* occur in Pliny, *Natural History*, 4.111 (*[Navi]albione*), and Stephanus of Byzantium (*Albionius*). See Rivet and Smith, *Place-Names of Roman Britain*, 39.

4. For reasons of meter, both *Brettanos* and *Britannus* were sometimes used by poets as an adjective, "British." Latin examples can be found in Grattius Faliscus, *Cynegetica*, 178 (*"catulis Britannis"*); Propertius, *Elegiae*, 2.1.76 (*"esseda Britanna"*); Ammianus, 30.7.3 (*"Brittanum . . . exercitum,"* var. *"Brittanicum"*); and Sidonius, *Carmina*, 7.370 (*"salum . . . Britanum"*). The adjectival form, *Brit(t)annica, us, um*, usually means "of Britain" and is often found in association with *mare* or *oceanus*: e.g., Tertullian, *De Cultu Feminarum*, 1.6.8; Jerome, *Commentarii in Isaiam*, 11.40.219. For *Britannica* likely referring to "the British people," however, see Jerome, *Adversus Jovinianum*, 2.7.48: *"atticotos, gentem Britannicam."*

5. See *TLL*, s.v. *Britanni*. The *TLL* gives a list of literary sources using *Britanni* that includes Caesar, Lucretius, Catullus, Vergil, Horace, Ovid, Seneca, Lucan, Pliny, Martial, Tacitus, and Suetonius. The Coh. III Britannorum is recorded in an inscription from Eining (*Corpus Inscriptionum Latinarum* [Berlin: G. Reinder], 3.5935) and again in the *Notitia* (OC. 35.25).

6. Martial, 11.21.9 (*"veteres bracae Britonis pauperis"*). See *TLL*, s.v. *Britto*, and Latham, *Dictionary of Medieval Latin*, s.v. *Brito*. *Brettones* is the normal form for Bede, except when he is quoting ancient authorities, in which case he uses *Brittanni*. Cf. Rivet and Smith, *Place-Names of Roman Britain*, 40, 57.

7. Ammianus, 28.3.1 and 28.1.21. Cf. 20.9.9 (*"apud Britannos"*), 22.3.3 (*'in Brittannos"*), 26.4.5 (*"Britannos . . . vexavere"*), 30.7.9 (*"Britannos . . . hostium non ferentes"*).

8. *Scriptores Historiae Augustae*, Hadrian, 5.2 (*"Brittanni"*), 16.3 (*"per Brittanos,"* quoting a poem); Antonius Pius, 5.4 (*"Brittannos . . . et Germanos et Dacros"*); Marcus, 8.8 (*"adversus Brittannos"*); Commodus, 8.4 (*"Brittanni . . . voluerint"*); Severus, 23.3 (*"Brittannis relinquo"*); Gordian, 3.7 (*"ducenti[s] mixtis Brittanni[s]"*); Firmus, Saturninus, Proculus, and Bonosus, 14.1 (*"origine Brittannus"*).

9. The form *Brit(t)an(n)i* also appears in the following fourth- and fifth-century secular works: Avienius, *Descriptio Orbis Terrae*, 118, 749; Claudian, *Carmina*, 5.149, 15.19, 24.149, 26.416; Eutropius, *Breviarium*, 6.17.4 (*Brittani*), 7.13.2 (*Britanni*); Vegetius Renatus, *Epitoma Rei Militaris*, 4.37 (*Britanni*, vars. *Brittanni, Britani, Brittani, Britanii*). The attitude of the secular Latin historians toward the Britons is comparable to that of their Greek counterparts, Zosimus and Procopius: Britain is remote, an island of exiles (Zosimus, 1.68.3) and spirits (Procopius, *De Bello Gothico*, 4.20.42ff.), its inhabitants beleaguered (Zosimus, 6.5.3; Procopius, *De Bello Gothico*, 1.24.36).

10. Jerome, *Commentarii in Isaiam*, 18.20.104 (*"de Britannis, Hispanis, Gallis"*); *Epistulae*, 46.10.1 (*"nostro Britannus,"* i.e., Pelagius); *In Hieremiam Prophetam Libri VI*, 3.15 (*"Scotticae gentis de Brittanorum vicinia"*); *Interpretatio Chronicae Eusebii*, A.D. 46; A.D. 207.

11. Orosius, 5.22.7, 6.9.5, 6.10.1 (*"a Britannis reversus"*).

12. Sulpicius Severus, *Chronica,* 2.41.3. In 2.51.3 a certain Instantius is deported to an island beyond the *Britanniae.*

13. Prudentius, *Liber Peristefanon,* 13.103: "Gallos fovet, inbuit Britannos, / praesidet hesperiae, Christum serit ultimis hiberis."

14. Sidonius, *Carmina,* 7.89: "Victricia Caesar signa Caledonios transvexit ad usque Britannos."

15. Augustine, *Epistulae,* 186.1.9 (*"qui pelagius terenti dicitur, Brittonem fuisse cognominatum"*); Arnobius Iunior, *Commentarii in Psalmos,* 147.25 (*"nec ipsos Indos lateat a parte orientis nec ipsos Britones a parte occidentis"*); Prosper Tiro, *Chronicon,* 763 (*Brittanos,* vars. *Brittannos, Brittandos*); 1301 (*Brittanos,* var. *Brittanos*); 1252 (*Britto,* vars. *Brito, Bruto,* referring to Pelagius).

16. I.e., those whom we now call Bretons living in Bretagne (Brittany). See Thomas, *Christianity in Roman Britain,* 51–52.

17. Sidonius, *Epistulae,* 1.7.5, 3.9.2. On Riothamus, see the discussion of *Reges* in Chapter 8.

18. *HF,* 2.18 (*Brittani*); Jordanes, *Getica,* 45.237 (*Brittones*).

19. For a recent study of the problem, see Patrick Galliou and Michael Jones, *The Bretons* (Oxford: Blackwell, 1991), 128ff. See also Dermot Fahy, "When Did Britons Become Bretons? A Note on the Foundation of Brittany," *Welsh History Review* 2 (1964–65): 111–24.

20. *De excidio,* 25.1.

21. *De Bello Gothico,* 8.20.

22. See Thompson, "Procopius on Brittia and Brittania"; Cameron, *Procopius,* 215; Galliou and Jones, *Bretons,* 130–33; and the discussion in Chapter 4.

23. See *HB,* 27 ("They are the Armorican British, and they never came back, even to the present day"); Geoffrey of Monmouth, *Historia regum Britanniae,* 5.14; and the *Dream of Macsen Wledig* (in the *Mabinogi*).

24. Galliou and Jones (*Bretons,* 131–33) summarize these.

25. *Concilium Turonense (a.d. 567),* 179.91: "Adicimus etiam, ne quis Brittanum aut Romanum in Armorico sine metropolis aut comprovincialium voluntate vel literis episcopum ordinare praesumat."

26. See Thompson, "Procopius on Brittia and Brittania," 504: "This canon of the Council of Tours [567] also shows . . . that British newcomer and Roman native had not yet fused [in Armorica]."

27. Constantius, *Vita,* 3.17.1.

28. The sole exception being the *Alani,* who were occupying part of Italy (*Vita,* 4.28.6). Constantius never uses the term *Romani.*

29. The inhabitants of Gaul are simply *plebs or provinciales,* not Gauls or Armoricans. See Thompson, *St. Germanus,* 8ff.

30. For an argument that the intended audiences of both the *Epistola* and the *Confessio* were most likely Britons, see Dumville et al., *Saint Patrick,* 27, 108ff.

31. For discussion of these terms, see Chapter 7.

32. Patrick does use the term *Romani*—though not in a British context—and its meaning is somewhat problematic; see the discussion in Chapter 7.

33. For the evidence that Patrick was a Briton from Britanniae, see Chapter 4.

34. See Chapter 7.

35. Gildas, *De excidio,* 6.2 and 20.1.

36. Ibid., 5.1, 17.3, 25.3. See also Wood, "End of Roman Britain," 22 n. 163: "Gildas always depicts the Romans as outsiders." For the popular colloquial phrase "King(s) of the Romans," see Stephen Fanning, "Emperors and Empires in Fifth-Century Gaul," in *Fifth-Century Gaul: A Crisis of Identity?* ed. John F. Drinkwater and Hugh Elton (Cambridge: Cambridge University Press, 1992), 288–97.

37. Dumville, "Idea of Government," 185: "[F]or a century before Gildas's day [the Romans] had been completely out of the picture."

38. Jones, *End of Roman Britain,* 123.

39. See Myres, "Pelagius," 21–36; Morris, "Pelagian Literature," 26–60; Wood, "End of Roman Britain," 4–5; Jones, "Failure of Romanization," 137; and idem, *End of Roman Britain,* 129. The phrase is Jones's.

40. James Campbell, "The Lost Centuries," in *The Anglo-Saxons,* ed. James Campbell (Ithaca, N.Y.: Cornell University Press, 1982), 22: "Almost certainly by the time of Gildas all the Britons were Christian." Many scholars have disagreed, but no thorough study has yet been produced.

41. Kurt Hunter-Mann, "When (and What) Was the End of Roman Britain?" in *Theoretical Roman Archaeology: First Conference Proceedings,* ed. Eleanor Scott (Aldershot, Hampshire: Avebury, 1993), 67–78 ("Even in the fourth century, it is not clear to what degree Romano-Britons saw themselves as Roman, rather than British with Roman influences, or even as tribal, with only superficial diocesan and imperial loyalties" [74]). British tribal allegiance is frequently declared on inscribed stones from the Roman period: see *RIB,* vol. 1, passim.

42. *De excidio,* 28.1 and 31.1.

43. *ECMW,* nos. 87, 126, and 103; see also the discussion on p. 14.

44. See Davies, *Patterns of Power,* 18–19. The vernacular poetry ascribed to Taliesin and Aneirin, as well as the Latin *Annales Cambriae,* are filled with phrases like "the men of Gwent" (*gwyr Guenti*) and "the men of Brycheiniog" (*viri Broceniauc*). In the earliest of the Llandaff Charters (sixth century?), however, there is no mention either of *Britanni* or tribes, but rather of smaller *unciae, villae,* and *territoriae.*

45. The *TLL* gives many examples of *Britannus* and *Britto* occurring in Roman inscriptions (e.g., *Corpus Inscriptionum Latinarum,* 6.3301.6; 13.1981; 9.5357; 13.8208; 11.3104; 7.1094; 6.3594; 8.1950; 8.3962), but most come from Continental inscriptions. For insular examples, see *Some Inscriptions from Roman Britain,* ed. Greenstock, no. 46; *RIB,* nos. 88, 2152, and 2335.

46. See, for example, *RIB,* no. 2152: "*Brittones . . .* gladly, willingly, and deservedly paid the vow." This inscription is on an altar base found in Canterbury.

47. For *Britanus* used as a personal name on the Continent, see the sixth-century Count Britanus of Javols in *HF,* 4.39.

48. Fernand Benoit, *Sarcophages paléochrétiens d'Arles et de Marseille, Gallia,* Suppl. 5 (Paris: Centre National de la Recherche Scientifique, 1954), no. 98. The inscription uses a version of the *Hic iacet* formula, which suggests a mid-fifth-century date. Cf. Knight, "*In Tempore,*" 57.

49. *Concilium Turonense I (a.d. 461),* 148, line 125. See Thomas, *Christianity in Roman Britain,* 51, and Galliou and Jones, *Bretons,* 131.

50. Gennadius, *De Scriptoribus Ecclesiasticis,* 56. One MS has *Britannorum episcopus,* another *Britto.* See Rivet and Smith, *Place-Names of Roman Britain,* 66; Morris, "Pelagian Literature," 34–36.

51. Avitus of Vienne (*Epistolae,* 4.1) writes, "Faustum ortu Britannum, habitaculo Regiensem." Cf. Sidonius, *Epistolae,* 9.9.

52. *Inscriptionum Christianorum Hispaniae,* 305. See Charles Thomas, *The Early Christian Archaeology of North Britain* (London: Oxford University Press, 1971), 108, fig. 50; idem, *Christianity in Roman Britain,* 52.

53. E.g., Jerome, *Epistulae,* 46.10.1 ("*nostro Britannus*"); Augustine, *Epistulae,* 186.1.1 ("*Pelagium . . . Britonem fuisse cognominatum*"); Prosper Tiro, *Chronicon,* 1.1252 ("*Pelagius Britto*"); Gennadius, *De Scriptoribus Ecclesiasticis* (Corbie MS only). See Jones, "Failure of Romanizaton," 133, and John Ferguson, *Pelagius: A Historical and Theological Study* (Cambridge: W. Heffer & Sons, 1956), 45.

54. Ausonius, *Epigrammata,* 107–12 (trans. Hugh G. Evelyn White).

55. White, *Ausonius,* 2:214–15 n. 1.

56. Rutlius, *De Reditu Suo,* 1.500. See Birley, *People of Roman Britain,* 11, 56–57; Jones, "Failure of Romanization," 132–33; and H. D. Rankin, *Celts and the Classical World* (London: Areopagitica Press, 1987), 212.

57. For confirmation that this was a common stereotype—not just a conception popular only among the literati—compare with the evidence of the Vindolanda writing tablets: Robin Birley, *The Roman Documents from Vindolanda* (Greenhead: Roman Army Museum Publications, 1990), 26–28. On tablet no. 1985/32 (dated A.D. 90–95), some soldier stationed along Hadrian's Wall refers derisively to the natives as *Brittunculi,* "wretched little Britons." Birley (28): "[I]t is delightful to find at long last what the Romans called the British." Two centuries later this Roman attitude toward the Britons had not changed, even though the latter were now Roman citizens. Game boards from both Rome and Trier, dating from the period of the Tetrarchy, bear the following legend: "The Parthians have been killed, the Britons [BRITT(O)] vanquished, play Romans!" See M. McCormick, *Eternal Victory* (Cambridge, 1986), 34.

58. E.g., in the poems of Aneirin and Taliesin, and in the *Armes Prydein.*

59. Gerald preferred the term *Kambria* over *Wallia* for "Wales." See Robert Bartlett, *Gerald of Wales, 1146–1223* (Oxford: Clarendon Press, 1982), p. 51 and n.112. But while *Kambria* derives ultimately from the Welsh *Cymru,* it too is a Latinized version of an English word, "Camber"/"Cumber."

Chapter 7

1. A. N. Sherwin-White, *The Roman Citizenship* (Oxford: Clarendon Press, 1939; 2d ed., 1973), traces this history from Latium to the late empire.

2. See *TLL,* s.v. *Civis.* Common alternative forms, orthographic abbreviations, and misspellings include *ceus, ceivis, civeis, cibis, civvis, cevis,* and *cis.*

3. *Ammianus Lexicon,* 236.

4. Ammianus, 27.3.3, 27.9.8, 27.9.9.

5. Ibid., 19.2.14 (Amidae), 31.6.3 (Hadrianopolis), 25.9.1 and 25.9.12 (Nisibis), 28.6.6 and 28.6.16 (Leptis).

6. Ibid., 19.10.3, 23.5.3, 28.6.28.

7. See Sivan, *Ausonius of Bordeaux,* 3.

8. Ausonius, *Ordo Urbium Nobilium,* 20.39–41. Trans. Hugh G. Evelyn White.

9. Sivan (*Ausonius of Bordeaux,* 3) interprets the poem as explicit proof of Ausonius's "dual citizenship," but does not elaborate on her reasons for doing so.

10. E.g., Deut. 15.3–4: "a peregrino et advena exiges civem et propinquum repetendi." Cf. Lev. 21.1, 24.16, 24.22; Num. 15.29; Deut. 1.16; Eph. 2.19. Also, as is often the case in the secular sources, intimacy with the *civis* is established by using possessives (*mei, tuo, suis, suorum*); see 4 Ezra 9.47, 10.2; Lev. 21.1, 24.18, 25.13; Judg. 14.17; 2 Macc. 5.6. Secular terms associated with *civis* in the Vulgate include *locus* (Judg. 14.10), *urbs* (2 Kings 23.17), *terra Beniamin* (Jer. 37.11), *Iudaei* (2 Macc. 9.18), *patria* (2 Macc. 5.9, 13.14), *civitas* (2 Macc. 5.5, 13.14), and *regio* (Luke 15.14). Of course, the Roman citizenship of Paul features prominently in the account of his arrest: *civis Romanus* appears twice, alternating with *Romanus* (Acts 22.26–29).

11. Ambrose, *De Abraham,* 2.62.21: "unde apostolus ad fideles viros et cives Hierusalem illius, quae in caelo est, et ecclesiae filios dicit: ergo iam non estis advenae atque peregrini, sed estis cives sanctorum et domestici dei."

12. E.g., Augustine, *De civitate Dei,* 1.35, 5.16. This is discussed by Sherwin-White, *Roman Citizenship,* 461–62.

13. *De civitate Dei,* 5.17. Trans. Sherwin-White.

14. Ibid., 1.4.1 (Troy); *Confessio,* 8.2.13 (Rome), 8.6.10 (Milan), 8.6.22 (*civis noster,* referring to a fellow African); *Epistulae,* 177.15.14 (Hippo).

15. *Confessio,* 4.15.40. Cf. 9.13.52 (*"civium meorum in aeterna hierusalem"*); 10.4.20 (*"civium meorum et me cum peregrinorum"*); *In Iohannis Epistulam ad Parthos Tractatus* 10.23 (*"invenisti christianum; invenisti civem hierusalem; invenisti civem angelorum; invenisti in via suspirantem peregrinum"*).

16. *Epistulae,* 55.6.12.

17. Teillet, *Des Goths,* 558 n. 154.

18. Thompson, *St. Germanus,* 8–9. The only exception is *Vita,* 27.15, where the Britons are called *plebem* in one manuscript but *populum* in another.

19. *Epistola,* 1–2.

20. See Hood, *St. Patrick,* 55; Hanson, *Life and Writings,* 58–59; Dumville et al., *Saint Patrick,* 118.

21. Those who interpret *civibus meis* as "Romans" include Hanson, *Life and Writings,* 59–61; Wood, "End of Roman Britain," 22; and Thompson, *Who Was Saint Patrick?* 130–31. Contra, see Jones, *End of Roman Britain,* 114: "The implied sting in Patrick's rebuke has been traditionally taken to mean that Coroticus must have regarded himself as a Roman. I disagree. The implied sting is that Coroticus considered himself to be a good Briton. Patrick suggests that no self-respecting Briton would consort with Picts and Scots, his people's traditional enemies."

22. Thompson, *Who Was Saint Patrick?* 130; Hanson, *Life and Writings,* 59–61: "Patrick indicates that he would like to call Coroticus and his men 'fellow citizens' and 'Romans' . . . the first because they had inherited a tradition of civilization from the Roman Empire, the second because they were the heirs of Roman order." See also, however, Jones, *End of Roman Britain,* 114: "What would be the point of distinguishing between fellow Romans and fellow Holy Romans in a Christian Roman Empire?"

23. *Epistola,* 11.

24. Hanson, *Life and Writings,* 67.

25. See Chapter 4.

26. *Epistola,* 2, 12, and 15.

27. *Confessio,* 42: "et de genere nostro qui ibi nati sunt nescimus numerum eorum." Thompson (*Who Was Saint Patrick?* 110) translates this as "of those who were born there [in Ireland] of our nationality we do not known their number," and elsewhere (n. 8) as "those of our race," which he interprets as "Britons." Hanson (*Life and Writings,* 110) gives the translation "and I cannot reckon the number from those of our race who have been born there," and states later (111) that "'those of our race' in all probability refers to people of British stock in Ireland." Thanks to Michael E. Jones for pointing this passage out to me.

28. Ralph Mathisen, personal communication.

29. See Morris, *Age of Arthur,* 18; Thomas, *Christianity in Roman Britain,* 330; and note 21, above.

30. For a discussion of the locus of Coroticus, see Chapter 3. While Strathclyde is outside of imperial dominion, both Miller ("Bede's Use of Gildas," *English Historical Review* 90 [1975]: 244 n. 1) and Jones (*End of Roman Britain,* 114) have pointed out a tendency in early medieval Welsh, Irish, and Scottish sources to see a common group of "Britons" in territory extending north of the late imperial border and into Strathclyde.

31. Jones, *End of Roman Britain,* 113–15. See also idem, "Failure of Romanization," 135: "All of [Patrick's] references to Rome are in the narrow religious context of the Christian church. When Patrick mentions his fellow citizens he means the Britons. Romans simply equal

Christians." Dumville ("Coroticus," in *Saint Patrick,* 108–9, 118) translates *sancti Romani* as "the Roman saints," but also takes the entire phrase as referring to "Christians."

32. *Epistola,* 14; *Confessio,* 43; *Dicta,* 3.

33. *Epistola,* 5 and 7. See Dumville et al., *Saint Patrick,* 119.

34. Dumville et al., *Saint Patrick,* 127.

35. *Epistola,* 21. See Thompson, *Who Was Saint Patrick?* 130, and Dumville et al., *Saint Patrick,* 118.

36. *Epistola,* 10. See Dumville et al., *Saint Patrick,* 121: "Patrick assumes that his christian audience ('in Christo Jesu Domino *nostro*') will know what a decurion is or was." Patrick is clearly proud of his family's status, defined here in Roman terms, and perhaps he is intentionally using the phrase *nobilitatem meam* as a play on his name *Patricius.*

37. *Epistola,* 2 (*civibus meis*), 10 (*Domino nostro*), 11 (*mei* and *sua patria*). Cf. *Confessio,* 42 (*genere nostro*).

38. Hanson, *Life and Writings,* 59–61: "'Romans' was a word specially used for citizens of the former Western Roman Empire who either survived in independent enclaves among the invading barbarians or who, though under barbarian rule, retained their own culture, language, and system of law." Unfortunately, Hanson remains vague about how he sees the status of Coroticus.

39. See Peter Dronke, "St. Patrick's Reading," *CMCS* 1 (1981): 21–38.

40. Augustine, *Confessio,* 8.6.22. This man, Ponticianus, was a fellow provincial; later, Augustine has to specify that he was also a Christian.

41. Ibid., 9.13.52.

42. *De excidio,* 4.1.

43. Ibid., 7, 15.3.

44. Ibid., 19.3, 20.3.

45. Ibid., 25.2, 25.3.

46. Ibid., 26.1, 28.1.

47. Ibid., 4.1, 4.4, 19.2, 19.3.

48. Ibid., 32.1.

49. Wright, "Gildas's Geographical Perspective," 102.

50. See Jones, *End of Roman Britain,* 122: "The use of *cives* by Gildas and Patrick, in fact, seems similar in a number of ways. It is tempting to view both Patrick and Gildas, with an eye to Roman and Byzantine perceptions of a permanent break between Britain and Rome in roughly 410, as expressing a nascent, precocious British sense of nationality."

51. *ECMW,* no. 103. Nash-Williams notes that similar inscriptions bearing names of civic antecedents have been found in Italy, North Africa, and Gaul, dating from the mid–fourth to the mid–sixth centuries.

52. Ibid., no. 33. Jackson (*Language and History,* 118) regards this evidence and that of Gildas as referring to Roman citizenship: "[I]t is evident that the free Britons of the first half of the sixth century, even in the Highland Zone, still regarded themselves as Roman citizens."

53. See *ECMW,* 92 n. 5.

54. Morris, *Age of Arthur,* 41, 98: "*Cymry* was the name adopted by the native population in the former Roman diocese, after Britain ceased to be Roman. Their descendants were called Welshmen by the English." Cf. Thomas, *Christianity in Roman Britain,* 257: "[C]ombrogi— '(those) with (the same) border [*bro*]: fellow-countrymen'—this must have been a common intra-national name." See also Jackson, *Language and History,* 9–10, 445, 653, and Thomas, *Celtic Britain,* 47.

55. E.g., Cumbria, Cumberland, Comberton, Comber Mere, Cumberworth. See Thomas, *Christianity in Roman Britain,* 257–58.

56. See Dark, *Civitas,* 257: "[T]he modern Welsh name *Cymry* may, therefore, recall an identity as independent sub-Roman citizens, of a single British nation, whose only precedent was

Roman Britain." Dark draws an analogy with the Byzantine *romaioi*.

57. See *HB*, 27: "That is why *Brittannia* has been occupied by foreigners, and the *cives* driven out [to Armorica], until God shall give them help." *Cymry* first appears in a praise poem to Cadwallon, probably composed about 633: "Ar wynep Kymry Cadwallawn was." The author of the *Armes Prydein* (c. 930) uses *Kymry* (or its mutated form *Gymry*) some sixteen times, *Brython* (or its mutated form *Vrython*) only thrice. In the *Brut y Tywysogyon*, *Kymry* first appears in the entry for the years 1113–16, eventually replacing *Brytanyeit*, which last appears in the entry for 1196–97. In the early vernacular poetry, the *cives* are "nobles" (*mynawc*), in contrast with the *gentes,* the pagan Saxons; see Thomas Charles-Edwards, "The Authenticity of the *Gododdin:* An Historian's View," in *Astudiaethau ar yr Hengerdd: Studies in Old Welsh Poetry,* ed. Rachel Bromwich and R. F. Jones (Cardiff: Gwasg Prifysgol Cymru, 1978), 44–71.

58. Dumville, "Idea of Government," 199.

59. See Gildas, *De excidio,* 1.1, 2.1; *HB,* 9, 27, and 42; *Armes,* passim; and Geoffrey of Monmouth, *Historia regum Britanniae,* 1.2, 7.3, 12.17, 12.19, and the *explicit.*

60. *HB,* 42 (*"et postea gens nostra surget"*); *Armes,* lines 12 (*"Atporyon uyd Brython pan dyorfyn"*) and 178 (*"rydrychafwynt Gymry kadyr qyweithyd"*).

Chapter 8

1. The Germanic languages seem to have developed two words for "king," representing two different regal functions. For example, Gothic has the cognate *reiks,* applied to the military leader, and *thiudans,* referring to the traditional, or ceremonial, king (these distinct functions were observed by Tacitus, though he does not give the vernacular terminology). Latin writers during the migration period saw the former as the more important function, and thus used the term *rex* to describe most barbarian kings. See Edward James, "The Origins of Barbarian Kingdoms: The Continental Evidence," in *Origins of Anglo-Saxon Kingdoms,* ed. Bassett, 43.

2. Since the Republican authors knew Greek political terminology quite well, they often used the term *tyrannus* to describe some Hellenistic rulers; see Chapter 9. Republicans like Cicero might also use *rex* and *regnum* as a sting against would-be Roman monarchs like Caesar.

3. Fanning, "Emperors and Empires," 290–95. The quote is from Orosius (2.4.13), who himself calls several emperors *rex.*

4. Caesar, *Gallic Wars; Res Gestae,* 32. Native coinage in Britain, most of which was produced between the invasions of Caesar and Claudius, is a mixture of Celtic La Tène and classical *oikoumene* styles. See Rankin, *Celts and the Classical World,* 213–14; R. D. Van Arsdale, *Celtic Coinage of Britain* (London: Spink, 1989); and Melinda Mays, *Celtic Coinage: Britain and Beyond: The Eleventh Oxford Symposium on Coinage and Monetary History,* BAR British Series 222 (Oxford: Tempvs Reparatvm, 1992).

5. Cogidubnus styled himself both "king" and "imperial legate"; see *RIB,* no. 91 (CLAVD*COGIDVBNI*R).

6. Dumville ("Idea of Government," 179) argues that Roman government had ceased in the upland regions of Britain in the third century, allowing the survival—or resurgence—of native government in those areas.

7. Sidonius, *Epistolae,* 3.9.1–2.

8. Jordanes, *Getica,* 45.237. The Bituriges were a Celtic people of Aquitania. Jordanes's claim that Britons were settled in central Gaul to oppose Euric is confirmed by Sidonius (*Epistolae,* 1.7.5), who places the *Britanni* "north of the Loire [*Liger*]."

9. Jordanes, *Getica,* 45.238. Cf. Sidonius, *Epistolae,* 3.9.

10. *HF,* 2.18.

11. See Geoffrey Ashe, *The Discovery of King Arthur* (New York: Doubleday, 1985), 97–98. Ashe states that he and Leon Fleuriot prefer to see *Riothamus* as a noun and title meaning "supreme king," while Kenneth Jackson ("*Varia*: II," 38 n. 44) prefers to interpret it as an adjective and a personal name meaning "supremely royal." Patrick Galliou and Michael Jones (*Bretons,* 131) seemingly follow Fleuriot, interpreting it as "a Celtic name or title signifying supreme king or leader."

12. See Galliou and Jones, *Bretons,* 131–32. Those who have taken Riothamus to be a Breton include Morris, *Age of Arthur,* 90, and Hugh Elton, "Defense in Fifth-Century Gaul," in *Fifth-Century Gaul,* ed. Drinkwater and Elton, 173. The settlement of Britons in the Armorican peninsula is similar to the *adventus Saxonum* in Britain: both are undeniable events that, due to the lack of contemporary accounts, have never been sufficiently explained. Precise chronology is impossible, and the migration was likely a gradual process taking place between the late fourth and early seventh centuries. See Galliou and Jones, *Bretons,* 128–33; Leon Fleuriot, *Les origines de la Bretagne* (Paris: Payot, 1980); Nora K. Chadwick, "Colonization of Brittany from Celtic Britain," *Proceedings of the British Academy* 51 (1965): 235–99; and Chapter 6 in this volume.

13. Most notably, Fleuriot, *Les origines;* Geoffrey Ashe, "A Certain Very Ancient Book," *Speculum* 56 (1981): 301–23; Campbell, *Anglo-Saxons;* and Wood, "End of Roman Britain," 21–22. Fleuriot believes that Riothamus may be equated with Gildas's Ambrosius Aurelianus.

14. If *Riothamus* is not itself a title, the title "king of the Britons" recorded by Jordanes may be an accurate reflection of how Riothamus was viewed by his own people. Sidonius appeals to Riothamus to "bring the opponents face to face and impartially unravel their contentions," and to give the claimant "a fair and equitable hearing." Sidonius seems to be describing formal arbitration functions that Gildas later ascribes to his British kings. See *De excidio,* 27, and the discussion below.

15. Fleuriot (*Les origines*) and Morris (*Age of Arthur,* 251) see Riothamus as a king who had authority on *both* sides of the Channel. Celtic hagiography claims this for several British kings. Wood ("Fall of the Western Empire," 261) sees Riothamus not as king but as a general: "Riothamus crossed from Britain to the continent . . . with a considerable body of men. . . . [He] is perhaps best seen as a general who left Britain because he wanted to serve the imperial cause. . . . He and his men could thus be the successors to the British pro-Roman party of the first half of the century."

Again, as Fanning has shown, one man's "emperor" was quite often another man's "king." The emperor Julian was raised on a shield by his Germanic soldiers and proclaimed *rex.* Maximus is variously titled both *rex* (Sulpicius Severus, *Vita Martini,* 20.2; Venantius Fortunatus, *Vita Martini,* 2.1.59 and passim; *ECMW,* no. 182) and *imperator,* and clearly the Briton(s) who composed "The Dream of Macsen Wledig" regarded Maximus as a king or prince.

16. Riothamus made quite an impression on Sidonius; see Jeremy DuQuesnay Adams, "Sidonius and Riothamus," *Arthurian Literature* 12 (1993): 157–64. Adams argues (160) further that the "level of vocabulary and that of the whole letter [Sidonius, *Epistolae,* 3.9] suggest either that Riothamus had had the benefit of a rather genteel education, or that members of his staff had."

17. *Epistola,* 6.

18. *Confessio,* 41.

19. Most historians have preferred the Strathclyde Coroticus because Patrick says he has dealings with the Picts and because the unknown author of Muirchu's table of contents in *The Book of Armagh* calls Coroticus "king of Aloo" (i.e., *Alclut,* the Strathclyde citadel of Dumbarton Rock). See Thomas, *Christianity in Roman Britain,* 341.

20. See the discussion in Chapter 9.

21. *De excidio*, 21.4. Trans. Winterbottom.

22. Ibid., 21.2.

23. Ibid., 26.2–3: "et ob hoc reges, publici, privati, sacerdotes, ecclesiastici, suum quique ordinem servarunt."

24. Ibid., 27. The Avranches MS reads "Habet etenim Britannia reges sed tyrannos" (In fact, Britain has kings, but also tyrants). For this reading, see B. S. Bachrach, "Gildas, Vortigern, and Constitutionality in Sub-Roman Britain," *Nottingham Medieval Studies* 32 (1988): 126–40, esp. 128.

25. *De excidio*, 31.1, 33.2–5.

26. Ibid., 28.1, 29.3, 34.2, 64.1.

27. E.g., ibid., 27 (*"Reges habet Britannia, sed tyrannos"*); 37.3 (*"contumacibus superbisque huius aetatis principus"*). Kerlouegan (*Le "De excidio,"* 561) gives the following breakdown of terms used by Gildas to describe British kings: *rex* (5), *tyrannus* (15), and *princeps* (1). *Rex* (twice) and *tyrannus* (once) are also used by Gildas to describe Roman emperors. For Gildas's use of *tyrannus,* see the discussion in Chapter 9.

28. See Jackson, "*Varia:* II." Three of these names contain the Celtic element *cun*, "hound," a noble attribute, and in all five cases Gildas associates these men with beasts (lioness, lion whelp, leopard, bear, dragon). Jackson shows that Gildas is rather ingeniously punning by taking what the kings themselves thought of as attributes of power and might (e.g., *Cunoglastos,* "Gray Wolf") and turning them in Latin, through their biblical connotations, into sarcastic insults (*Cuneglasus,* "Tawny Butcher").

29. Paul Schaffner, "Britain's *Iudices,*" in *Gildas: New Approaches,* ed. Lapidge and Dumville, 151–56. Contra, see Bachrach ("Gildas"), who believes Gildas used separate, though sometimes overlapping, definitions for *rex* and *tyrannus.* On the contemporary Gothic institutions of judgeship and kingship, see Peter Heather, *Goths and Romans, 332–489* (Oxford: Clarendon Press, 1991), 98: "The Goths would seem to have been using *rex* (Gothic *reiks*) with the original Celtic sense of 'leader of men' (their number not specified) rather than as 'monarch' or 'overall leader.' Hence the judge occupied a position superior to that of the ordinary nobility." While Gildas may be using rex in this "original Celtic sense" of "leader of men," he does not single out judges who are above kings, but rather kings who act as judges.

30. For an example of simony practiced by the *tyranni,* see *De excidio,* 67.2.

31. See *Ammianus Lexicon,* 503–5, and Fanning, "Emperors and Empires," 292. For example, the former soldier Ammianus (16.12.23–26) writes in great detail about the military formations of the Alamannic nobility—*reges, regales, reguli,* and *subreguli*—but is concerned only with their valor, not with how they rule their own people.

32. Even when they were trying to be more precise for political reasons, the choice of phrase was usually dictated by scripture. For example, Edward James ("Origins of Barbarian Kingdoms," 43) describes how Saint Ambrose addressed the Visigothic ruler Athanaric—who preferred that the Romans call him "judge" rather than "king"—as *iudex regum,* "judge of kings."

33. See Judith McClure, "Bede's Old Testament Kings," in *Ideal and Reality in Frankish and Anglo-Saxon Society,* ed. Wormald et al., 76–98.

34. *De Gubernatione Dei,* 4.1–5.

35. *Epistola,* 19.

36. Jones, *End of Roman Britain,* 121; Wood, "End of Roman Britain," 1; Michael Winterbottom, "The Preface of Gildas' *De Excidio,*" *Transactions of the Cymmrodorion Society* (1974–75): 277–87; Wright, "Gildas's Prose Style," 107; Hanning, *Vision of History,* 46–48; and Higham, *English Conquest,* 67ff.

37. *De excidio,* 21.4. Gildas's description of "anointing" kings is undoubtedly derived from biblical accounts. The Vulgate contains some 85 references to "anointing," 72 from the Old

Testament and 13 in the New Testament. Though anointing accompanies religious and healing rituals, most often in the Old Testament the term *ungo/ungere* refers to the anointing of kings, either by God or by priests. Gildas's statement that British kings were anointed "not in God's name, but as being crueller than the rest" (*De excidio*, 21.4, trans. Winterbottom), is given to contrast these despotic rulers with Old Testament kings like David and Solomon, who sought the unction of God. The anointing of Mekhisedeck is depicted in a contemporary (sixth-century) mosaic in S. Apollinare in Classis, Ravenna. Did the British church formally anoint native kings in the absence of legitimate Roman rulers?

38. *Epistola*, 18: "As for lying oath-breakers (*Mendacibus periuris*), their lot will be in the lake of everlasting fire" (quoting Rev. 21.8); *De excidio*, 27: "[The *reges*] constantly swear false oaths [*crebro iurantes, sed periurantes*]; they make vows [*voventes*], but almost at once tell lies [*mentientes*]; . . . they hang around the altars swearing oaths [*iurando*]—then shortly afterwards scorn them."

39. See Hanning, *Vision of History*; R. William Leckie Jr., *The Passage of Dominion: Geoffrey of Monmouth and the Periodization of Insular History in the Twelfth Century* (Toronto: Toronto University Press, 1981).

40. Gildas (*De excidio*, 64.1) speaks of the *regibus patriae*, a paradox of division and uniformity.

41. Davies (*Early Welsh Microcosm*, 17–18, 65–107) has, from the earliest charters, identified the following sixth/seventh-century kings: Erb (c. 525–55), Peibio ap Erb (c. 555–85), Cinuin and Gwyddgi ap Peibio (c. 585–615), all of the Ergyng dynasty of southeast Wales; King Iddon (c. 595–600), who took lands from the Saxons; Kings Tewdrig (c. 555–625) and Meurig (c. 585–665) of the Gwent/Glywysing dynasty; King Aergol (c. 500) of Dyfed; and a King Constantine (c. 580), whose kingdom lay across the Wye. See Fig. 4.

42. Ibid., 93. See Davies, *Patterns of Power*, 32: "From at least the early sixth century Welsh politics were dominated by kings (the *reges* of the Latin texts and 'territorial rulers' of the [vernacular poetry]), who—in the earlier centuries—were clearly associated with territorial kingdoms." That is, in Wales the idea that kings ruled territory (in the abstract sense, *regnum*), as opposed to people, predominates. This contrasts with Continental evidence from the migration period—perhaps because the Welsh dynasties were not uprooted by the Romans and merely expanded their *regna* after 410—and with contemporary English practice. Cf. Davies, *Patterns of Power*, 16–17: "This strongly territorial framework to rule contrasts with English practice at the same period, for in England it was usual to define rule in relation to groups of people. . . . Of course, in Wales rulers did rule people as well as territory, but it is the idea of the territory that predominates . . . in vernacular [terms like] . . . *gwlad* . . . used to express the notion 'sphere of rule,' although a sphere which has a territorial dimension."

43. Davies, *Early Welsh Microcosm*, 103–5: "Since a king was nearly always present when lay grants were made, and recorded in the witness list . . . the essential point seems to be that most grants were made in public meetings at which a king was present."

44. *De excidio*, 27 and 66.

45. Davies, *Early Welsh Microcosm*, 102. In the *De excidio*, Gildas calls Vortipor "son of a good king" (31.1), says that Maglocunus dispatched his "uncle the king" (33.4), and accuses Constantine of killing "two princes" (28.1–2).

46. See especially *Y Gododdin*; *Canu Taliesin*; and the "Stanzas of the Graves" from *The Black Book of Carmarthen*.

47. *ECMW*, no. 13.

48. See Peter C. Bartrum, *A Welsh Classical Dictionary* (Aberystwyth: National Library of Wales, 1993), 75. The Welsh genealogies list Cadfan as the son of Iago, who died (according to the *Annales Cambriae*) in 613, the year of the Battle of Chester. Cadfan, who perhaps began his reign that year, is also listed as the father of Cadwallon.

49. *ECMW*, p. 57 and n. 3: "The magniloquent phraseology of the inscription plainly echoes the formal language of the imperial Byzantine court, which was copied by the courts of the barbarian kings." Cf. Alcock, *Economy*, 64. Contact between Britain and the Byzantine world in the fifth and sixth centuries is confirmed by the presence of imported pottery, and is suggested by the inscription IN TEMPORE IUSTINI CONSULIS on the Penmachno Stone (*ECMW*, no. 104), dated c. 540. See Michael G. Fulford, "Byzantium and Britain," *Medieval Archaeology* 33 (1989): 1–5, esp. 5; P. K. Johnstone, "A Consular Chronology of Dark Age Britain," *Antiquity* 36 (1962): 102–9, esp. 102; and the discussion in Chapter 14 in this volume.

50. The rulers of Gwynedd include Maelgwn (Maglocunus) and Cadwallon. See N. J. Higham, "Medieval 'Overkingship' in Wales: The Earliest Evidence," *Welsh History Review* 16 (1992): 154–59 ("Gildas's recognition of [Maglocunus's] military superiority must imply a political superiority over the [other British] kings" [155]).

51. *ECMW*, no. 138.

52. See Thomas, *Celtic Britain*, 70.

53. See ibid., 77.

54. See Jackson, "*Varia*: II," 37–38. Of course, as Jackson points out, these names were likely given at infancy to members of the nobility or aristocracy, and so we should not expect that all of these individuals became monarchs.

55. See Graham Webster, *The Cornovii* (London: Duckworth, 1975), 114; Margaret Gelling, *The West Midlands in the Early Middle Ages* (Leicester: Leicester University Press, 1992), 21–27; and Jackson, *Language and History*. Jackson dates the Cunorix stone to A.D. 460–75.

56. Thomas, *Celtic Britain*, 77.

57. *ECMW*, no. 272. Nash-Williams suggests that this is the Latin name Caelestis. Cf. Dark, *Civitas*, 76–77, who dates the monument to the fifth century and sees it as evidence for the survival of a dynasty among the Ordovices.

58. These are discussed further in Chapter 14.

Chapter 9

1. See *Glossary of Later Latin*, comp. Souter; Charles Du Cange, et al., *Glossarium Mediae et Infimae Latinitatis*, vol. 8 (Paris: Librairie des Sciences et des Arts, 1938), 220–21; Nicholas Du Mortier, *Etymologi Sacrae Graeceo-Latinae* (Rome: Jacobi Komarech Bohemi, 1703).

2. See, for example, Acts 19.9–10 (*"scola Tyranni"*); Jerome, *Apologia Adversus Libros Rufini*, 1.1.1 ("Rufinus Tyrannius"); and *RIB*, no. 6 ("Titus Egnatius *Tyranus* is cursed"), on a lead curse plate from London.

3. See Antony Andrewes, *The Greek Tyrants* (New York: Harper & Row, 1963), 21–22, and idem, *The Greeks* (New York: W. W. Norton, 1967), 57. The term first appears in a poem by Archilochus (frag. 25) describing the kingdom/tyranny of Gyges of Lydia. The medieval jurist Bartolus of Sassoferrato believed that "tyrant" "derived from the Greek word *tyrus*, in Latin *fortis* (strong) or *angustia* (oppression)." See Bartolus, *On the Tyrant*, in *Il "De Tyranno" di Bartolo da Sassaferrato (1314–57)*, ed. Diego Quaglioni (Florence: Leo S. Olschki, 1983), chap. 1. He bases his argument on an observation by Isidore of Seville (*Etymologiarum sive Originum libri XX*, 9.3): "[P]owerful kings were called tyrants" (trans. Quaglioni).

4. Aeschylus and Sophocles, for example, use it as a synonym that is not at all derogatory. See Andrewes, *Greek Tyrants*, 22. Arguing contra this view is Christopher Tuplin, "Imperial Tyranny: Some Reflections on a Classical Greek Political Metaphor," in *CRUX: Essays in Greek History Presented to G.E.M. de Ste. Croix on His 75th Birthday*, ed. P. A. Cartledge et al. (London: Duckworth, 1985), 348–75.

5. Solon is the first to use τυραννος in this way, but it is Thucydides (1.13.1 and 17) who

comes closest to providing a concrete definition: kings are hereditary and have fixed privileges; tyrants are not hereditary, and their privilege has no limit. See Andrewes, *Greek Tyrants*, 28.

6. See Andrewes, *Greek Tyrants*, 28–30.

7. See J. Roger Dunkle, "The Rhetorical Tyrant in Roman Historiography: Sallust, Livy, and Tacitus," *Classical World* 65 (1971): 12–20.

8. See Fanning, "Emperors and Empires," and Chapter 8.

9. Both Caligula and Domitian are known to have put such writers to death. See Dunkle, "Rhetorical Tyrant," 14. Appianus of Alexandria was allegedly put to death by Commodus for calling the emperor τύραννος to his face. His martyrdom is recorded on *POxy*. 33, in Herbert Musurillo, *Acts of the Pagan Martyrs* (Oxford: Clarendon Press, 1954), 65–70 and 214–20. In his speech to Commodus, Appianus uses Plato's distinction between kings and tyrants. See Ramsay MacMullen, "The Roman Concept Robber-Pretender," *Revue Internationale des Droits de l'Antiquité*, 3d ser., 10 (1963): 321–25.

10. *Scriptores Historiae Augustae*, trans. David Magie (Cambridge, Mass.: Harvard University Press, 1932), vol. 3, "The Thirty Pretenders" (by Trebellius Pollio), 64 n. 1.

11. *Historia Augusta*, 1.1, 2.4, 3.1.6, 5.4, 6.5.

12. Alan E. Wardman, "Usurpers and Internal Conflicts in the Fourth Century A.D.," *Historia* 33 (1984): 225.

13. See *Ammianus Lexicon*.

14. Ammianus, 15.5.24, 27.6.2. The latter reference implies that the tyrant is Maximus; see Rolfe, *Ammianus*, vol. 3, 36 n. 2, and *Ammianus Lexicon*.

15. Ammianus, 16.8.10, 15.9.6.

16. Ibid., 15.8.6 and 17.5.13, 27.5.1 and 27.4.1.

17. E.g., Tertullian, *Ad Martyras*, 4.7; *Ad Nationes*, 1.18.37; *Apologeticum*, 2.75–76, 46.61, 50.31 and 36; *Ad Marcionem*, 2.358.11; *De Anima*, 46.29; *De Ieiunio Adversus Phsycicos*, 283.10.

18. The only instance in the New Testament, Acts 19.9–10, is an enigmatic passage in which Paul and his disciples "argued daily in the hall of Tyrannus [*scola Tyranni*]" in Ephesus. Jerome gave his nemesis Rufinus the epithet Tyrannius, perhaps in reference to this Ephesian tyrant; see Jerome, *Apologia Adversus Libros Rufini*, 1.1.1 (*"et vestris et multorum litteris, didici obici mihi in schola tyranni"*). For Tyrannus as a personal name in the Hellenistic period, see 2 Macc. 4.40 (*"duce quodam Tyranno"*).

19. 1 Kings/III Reg. 16.19–20; Job 15.20–21; Wisd. of Sol. 16.4; 2 Macc. 7.26–27.

20. E.g., *"neque rex neque tyrannus"* (Wisd. of Sol. 12.13–14); *"nobiles tyrannosque et principes"* (Ezek. 23.23); *"primus de regis principibus ac tyrannis"* (Est. 6.8–9); *"non accipit personas principum nec cognovit tyrannum"* (Job 34.19); *"de regibus . . . et tyranni"* (Hab. 1.10); *"de semine regio et tyrannorum pueros"* (Dan. 1.3–4); and *"duces et tyrannos et praefectos"* (Dan. 3.2 and 3.3). See also the neutral references to "the strong arm of the tyrants" (Job 35.9); "the command of the tyrants" (Wisd. of Sol. 14.17); "tyrants who sat enthroned" (Sir. 11.5); "provinces, nations and tyrants" (1 Macc. 1.4–5); and "Aretas the Arab tyrant" (2 Mac. 5.8). The only undeniably negative instances occur in the account of the Maccabaean revolt: "the fury of a cruel tyrant" (2 Mac. 4.25) and "the cruel tyrant" (2 Mac. 7.27).

21. Ambrose, *De Abraham*, 2.4.16; *De Patriarchis*, 7.32.5; *De Tobia*, 4.12.13 and 11.38.17; *Expositio Evangelii Secundum Lucam*, 4.366 and 5.995. Jerome, *Liber Quaestionum Hebraicarum in Genesim*, 16, line 12; *Liber Interpretationis Hebraicorum Nominum*, 9, line 4; 36, line 7; 71, line 28; *Commentarius in Ecclesiasten*, 3.22.358; *Commentarii in Isaiam*, 18.66.139; *In Hieremiam Prophetam Libri VI*, 4.4; *Commentarii in Ezechielem*, 6.18.335, 6.20.1349, 7.23.955, 7.23.999, 9.28.122, 14.47.1317; *Commentarii in Danielem*, 1.1.42, 1.1.45, 1.3.476, 3.11.1168; *Commentarii in Prophetas Minores (In Osee)*, 2.10.55; (*In Michaeam*) 1.2.170, 1.3.59, 2.7.175, 2.7.510; (*In Abucac*) 1.1.138, 1.1.152, 1.1.276, 1.1.286,

1.1.367, 1.1.370, 1.1.384, 1.1.431, 2.3.983; (*In Sophoniam*) 3.100; *Commentarii in Evangelium Matthaei*, 2.472, 3.644. Jerome also speaks of tyranny in a very general way throughout his *Epistulae*.

22. E.g., *Adversus Iovinianum*, 2.11.2 (*"Diogenes tyrannos"*); *Dialogi Contra Pelagianos Libri III*, 3.19.1 (*"tyrannidis Heracliani"*); *De Viris Inlustribus*, 121.53.2 (*"Maximo tyranno"*); *Eusebii Caesariensis Chronicon—Hieronymi Continuatio*, 244.20 (*"procopius, qui aput constantinopolim tyrannidem invaserat"*).

23. *Eusebii Caesariensis Chronicon—Hieronymi Continuatio*, 246.8 ("Valentinianus in Brittania, antequam tyrannidem invaderet, oppressus"); *Epistulae*, 133.9.19 ("Neque enim Britanni fertilis provincia tyrannorum, et Scythiae gentes, omnesque usque ad Oceanum per circuitum barbarae nationes Moysen prophetasque cognoverant").

24. See, for example, Augustine, *Sermones*, 30.41.141 ("si vis te tyranni esse victorem, christum invoca imperatorem"); *Enarrationes in Psalmos*, 42.3.33 ("et nunc habes quod agas; elige consilium, regem admitte, tyrannum exclude"); *De Magistro*, 9.96 ("nam idem persius omnibus poenis, quas tyrannorum vel crudelitas excogitavit vel cupiditas pendit").

25. *De civitate Dei*, 2.21.56 (trans. McCracken).

26. Ibid., 3.16.25 and 39, 5.25.14, 5.26.15.

27. "Per me reges regnant et tyranni per me tenent terram." Augustine liked this passage so much that he quoted it in two separate works: *De civitate Dei* (5.19.41) and *De Natura Bona* (32.870.18).

28. The more learned medieval authors were occasionally able to look back to the earlier traditions. Gregory the Great (*Moralium Libri*, 12.38), who defined five types of tyrants, stated that "a tyrant, in the strict sense, is one who rules a commonwealth unlawfully." Bartolus of Sassoferrato (*On the Tyrant*, chap. 2) follows Gregory's "strict sense" definition: "Just as a king or a Roman emperor is strictly a legitimate, true, and universal ruler, so if anyone wishes to occupy that office unlawfully he is called a tyrant in the strict sense."

29. Concerning the debt owed to Eunapius and Olympiodorus by such writers as Sozomen and Zosimus, see R. C. Blockley, *The Fragmentary Classicising Historians of the Later Roman Empire: Eunapius, Olympiodorus, Priscus, and Malchus* (Liverpool: Francis Cairns, 1981). For the British usurpers, the influence of Olympiodorus is strongest.

30. Zosimus, 6.35. See Matthews, "Macsen," 435. Pacatus (*Panegyric on Theodosius*, chap. 31) snidely comments that Maximus was a mere "menial and hanger-on" (*neglegentissimus vernula . . . statuarius lixa*) in the household of Theodosius.

31. *Gallic Chronicle of 452, sub anno* 382; Zosimus, 6.35; Gildas, *De excidio*, 13. Orosius (7.34.9–10) adds that Maximus "was created emperor by the army in Britain almost against his will."

32. Sozomen, 7.13.

33. *De excidio*, 13.

34. See the discussion in Chapter 1.

35. Forms of *tyrannus* (or τυραννος) are used to describe Maximus by the following writers: SECULAR: Ammianus, 27.6.2 (*tyrannidis*, in a context implying Maximus); Pacatus, *Panegyric on Theodosius*, 12.23.3 (*tyrannus*); Zosimus, 4.46.3 (τυραννιδος).ECCLESIASTICAL: Socrates, *Historia Ecclesiastica*, 5.11 (τυραννου); Orosius, 7.34.9 (*"per tyrannidem"*); the *Gallic Chronicle of 452*, a. 379 (*"Maximus tyrannus in Brittania a militibus constituitur"*); Sozomen, 7.13 (τυραννου); Prosper Tiro, *Chronicon*, 1191, a. 388 (*"Maximus tyrannus"*); Gildas, *De excidio*, 13.1 (*"tyrannico . . . Maximum"*); and Gregory of Tours, *Historia Francorum*, 1.43 (*"Maximus . . . per tyrannidem oppraessis Brittanis"*) and 2.9 (*"Victuris, fili Maximi tyranni"*), derived from Orosius and the lost *Historia* of Sulpicius Alexander.

36. *Vita Sancti Martini*, 20.1; *Dialogues*, I (2,VI and 2,VII) and II (III) 11–3.

37. *Vita Martini*, 4.4. It may be worth noting that, technically, Julian was a usurper of imperial power, as was Constantine the Great; both men turned successful usurpations into reigns

with the appearance of legitimacy. See Wardman, "Usurpers," 232–33.

38. *Dialogues,* I (2,VI). Trans. F. R. Hoare, "The Dialogues of Sulpicius Severus," in *Western Fathers,* 110. The last line is reminiscent of the view of Pericles (Thucydides, 2.63–64), that an empire, like a tyranny, is worth holding if it is a really good one. See also *Dialogues,* II (III) 11: "The Emperor Maximus, in other respects undoubtedly a good man" (Hoare, "Dialogues," 133). It seems that Severus and Martin were, at first, impressed by Maximus because he established his capital in Gaul and attempted to secure there both the administration of the western empire and orthodoxy in the western church. The latter was then being threatened by the Priscillianists, and it is only after Maximus sentences Priscillian to death at Trier (against Martin's orders) that the emperor becomes an enemy of the saint.

39. Orosius, 7.34.9. Trans. Ireland, *Roman Britain,* 158.

40. See Muhlberger, *Fifth-Century Chroniclers,* 190.

41. Sivan, *Ausonius of Bordeaux,* 145: "Gauls had always appreciated the presence of royalty in their land. This attitude explains, in part at least, the relative ease with which Magnus Maximus . . . gained Gallic support. . . . His eager Catholicism found a ready echo in the breasts of the Gallic bishops, and . . . [his] regime was praised, albeit with some reservations, by one Aquitanian noble, Sulpicius Severus. Gallic expressions of protest against Maximus were only uttered when he was safely out of the way for good."

42. Ausonius, *Ordo,* 9 (Aquileia): "Maximus, armigeri quondam sub nomine lixa . . . Rutupinum . . . latronem." Ausonius's language is reminiscent of that of his friend Pacatus. See Sivan, *Ausonius of Bordeaux,* 164.

43. Sozomen, 7.13.10.

44. Paulinus, *Vita Sancti Ambrosii,* chap. 19, referring to the assassination of Gratian. Trans. F. R. Hoare, "The Life of Saint Ambrose," in *Western Fathers,* 163.

45. Zosimus, 6.3.1.

46. Olympiodorus, frag. 12; Sozomen, 9.11.2; Zosimus, 6.3.1 and 6.2. Sozomen calls Marcus specifically τυραννος, while Zosimus includes him in the list of "tyrants" (τυραννου).

47. Orosius, 7.40.4. Cf. Olympiodorus, frag. 12; Sozomen, 9.11; and Zosimus, 6.2. Only Zosimus includes Gratian in his list of "tyrants" (τυραννου), though Sozomen remarks later, while speaking of Constantine's elevation, that "it was for this reason [i.e., their names] they [the troops] appear to have chosen the others [Marcus and Gratian] too for usurpation (τυραννιδα)."

48. Zosimus, 6.2. Wardman ("Usurpers," 225–27) discusses the importance of such visible "tokens of one's imperial dignity" in rallying support for the usurper.

49. Sozomen, 9.11.

50. Orosius, 7.40.4.

51. Ibid., 6.40.4.

52. Renatus Profuturus Frigeridus in *HF,* 2.9. These stereotypical attributes of the tyrant as one who indulges all of his "appetites" are an important part of the "philosophical" definition used by Plato, Cicero, et al.

53. Olympiodorus, frag. 16; Sozomen, 9.11.2; Orosius, 7.42.1–4; Frigeridus in *HF,* 2.9; Zosimus, 5.43.

54. Frigeridus in *HF,* 2.9.

55. Ibid.; Olympiodorus, frags. 12 and 16; Zosimus, 6.1–2.

56. Orosius, 7.42.1.

57. See *Codex Theodosianus,* 15.14.14 (March 416), which repeals all acts of "the tyrants and the barbarians." Ambrose had remarked earlier (*De Officiis,* 1.244) that it was considered a serious offense merely to possess the imago of a *tyrannus.* See Wardman, "Usurpers," 227. The opinions of the written sources may not, however, reflect the actual climate in the provinces. Constantine undoubtedly had the support of much of the Gallic aristocracy, whom he rewarded with promotions to the Gallic prefecture (setting a precedent that would be his

greatest legacy), and received military support from many of the barbarian tribes settled inside the provinces. See Matthews, *Western Aristocracies,* 314, 333. Constantine also enjoyed a cordial relationship with many Gallic bishops and with the city of Arles, which supplanted Trier as the new provincial capital. See Mathisen, *Ecclesiastical Factionalism,* 32ff.

58. Jerome, *Epistola,* 133.9.14.

59. Procopius, *Bellum Vandalicum,* 3.2.31–38. Trans. Dewing. Morris (*Age of Arthur,* 48) believes that Procopius was using τυραννου to describe the illegitimate emperors raised in Britain (i.e., Marcus, Gratian, Constantine III, and, perhaps, the parents of Ambrosius Aurelianus).

60. It may be significant that Procopius here calls Constantine "king." Did Procopius consider the unnamed τυραννου who came after Constantine to be kings?

61. *Epistola,* 2.

62. Ibid., 6.

63. Muirchu certainly believed that Patrick was calling this man a "tyrant." See the *Vita,* 1.29: *"Corictic, infausti crudelisque tyrrani"* (Coroticus, an ill-starred and cruel tyrant).

64. *Epistola,* 2, 6, and 12.

65. Ibid., 21 and 19. Patrick asks that this letter be read "in front of all the people (*plebibus*) and in the presence of Coroticus himself." His language, evoking Old Testament imagery, seems to elevate Coroticus to royal status, where his actions, especially, will be held accountable to God.

66. Morris, *Age of Arthur,* 18; Hood, *St. Patrick,* 17; Thomas, *Christianity in Roman Britain,* 343.

67. Thompson, *Who Was Saint Patrick?* 137; Jones, *End of Roman Britain,* 113.

68. Hanson, *Life and Writings,* 64–65; cf. 7.

69. Morris, *Age of Arthur,* 18–19.

70. *Epistola,* 2. See also the discussion in Chapter 7.

71. One exception is Prudentius (*In Symmachum,* 2.696), who calls Alaric "the Gothic tyrant." See Wardman, "Usurpers," 232. Alaric is admittedly an exceptional individual, having operated under Roman orders before (at least symbolically) usurping imperial authority in Rome itself.

72. Along with *milites,* Patrick (*Epistola,* 12) uses the term *latrunculi* to describe Coroticus's soldiers. MacMullen ("Roman Concept Robber-Pretender," 323–24) has shown that *latrones* and *latrunculi* are commonly associated with (or even synonyms for) *tyranni* in late Roman sources (e.g., in Ammianus and the *Historia Augusta*), setting "the robber apart from the external, and so to speak, official enemies of the state, *latrones* as opposed to *hostes.*"

73. *De excidio,* 2.

74. Ibid., 4.3. This passage, showing Gildas's knowledge and use of an ambiguous statement by Jerome (*Epistula,* 13.9), is discussed briefly in Wright, "Gildas's Prose Style," 108–9.

75. *De excidio,* 9.

76. In fact, this passage in the *De excidio* is an imitation of a passage in Rufinus's *Historia Ecclesiastica* (8.2.4), where Gildas replaces Rufinus's *imperii Diocletani* with *Diocletani tyranni.* See Wright, "Gildas's Reading," 148.

77. *De excidio,* 13.1.

78. Ibid., 13.2. The second reference is to Gratian, who was a Christian and therefore, in Gildas's opinion, deserving to be called *imperator legitimus,* unlike Diocletian, a persecutor of Christians and therefore a *tyrannus.*

79. See Winterbottom, *Gildas,* 149 n. 13.2; Lapidge, "Gildas's Education," 39; Dumville, "Chronology of De Excidio," 63; and Wright, "Gildas's Prose Style," 110–11.

80. See Thompson, "Gildas and the History of Britain."

81. *De excidio,* 14.

82. Wright, "Gildas's Prose Style," 110.

83. Gildas twice adds "tyrant" to Severus's description of Maximus: *De excidio*, 13.2, using Severus's *Vita Sancti Martini*, 20.2; and *De excidio*, 13.1, using Severus's *Dialogi*, 2.6.2. See Wright, "Gildas's Reading," 151.

84. *De excidio*, 23.1.

85. Ibid., 23.4.

86. *Uortigerno* in MS A (Avranches MS 162, twelfth century), *Gurthigerno* in MS X (thirteenth century). For a discussion of the textual history of the *De excidio*, see Dumville, "Sub-Roman Britain," 183–85. Cf. D. P. Kirby, "Vortigern," *BBCS* 23 (1968–70): 37–59.

87. Bede, *De Temporum Ratione*, 66 (*Vertigernus*); *EH*, 1.14 and 2.5 (*Vurtigern*); *HB*, 31ff. (*Guorthigirnus*); *Anglo-Saxon Chronicle* (Parker and Laud Chronicles), *sa* 449 (*Wyrtgeorn*). *Gwrytheyrn* appears to be the early Welsh form. See Dumville, "Sub-Roman Britain," 183–85.

88. See Dumville, "Sub-Roman Britain," 186–87. The name *Guarthigern* appears on the ninth-century "Pillar of Eliseg" (*ECMW*, no. 182), along with "King" Maximus and Saint Germanus!

89. See the discussion of *consilium* in Chapter 10.

90. Those who see the *superbus tyrannus* as having powers of a high king (or even emperor) include Morris, *Age of Arthur*, 49; Peter Berresford Ellis, *Celt and Saxon: The Struggle for Britain* (London: Constable, 1993), 31; Alcock, *Arthur's Britain*, 320; Frere, *Britannia* (1987), 374; and Ashe, *Discovery*, 53. Dumville ("Chronology of *De Excidio*," 70–71) believes that Gildas is talking about one large kingdom, with repercussions for all of *Britannia*, and ("Idea of Government," 198) that Gildas's analogy of the pharaoh and the princes of Zoan may indeed indicate an overkingship for the *superbus tyrannus*. Bede (*EH*, 1.14–15) also implies that "their King Vortigern" (*suo rege Vurtigerno*) had authority over all the Britons; the *Anglo-Saxon Chronicle* (Parker Chronicle), *sa* 449, calls Vortigern "King of the Britons" (G. N. Garmonsway, ed. and trans., *The Anglo-Saxon Chronicle* [London: Everyman, 1953]); and the *HB* (xxvii and 31) states that "the unholy Vortigern" "ruled in Britain" (trans. Morris). Clearly, in the eighth and ninth centuries this tyrant was regarded as a prominent king.

91. *De excidio*, 23.4.

92. See Higham, *English Conquest*, 38–39: "There are no grounds whatever within the text to imagine that 'Vortigern' was king only over part of Britain. He was presumably, therefore, a man whose rule Gildas was content to portray as universal. It necessarily included that east coast of Britain, where the Saxons were about to be established, and Gildas may well have been correct in portraying it as all-encompassing."

93. *De excidio*, 23.1. Gildas always speaks of the *consilium* as if it were a separate and formal body or event. For example, in chapter 2 he mentions, in his long list of topics, that he will talk "about a council" (*de consilio*); here there is no mention of the *tyrannus*.

94. Compare with Gildas's use of *superbus* to describe the soldiers of the *tyranni* (*De excidio*, 27: "*sanguinarios superbos parricidas commanipulares*") and the *principes* (37.3: "*contumacibus superbisque huius aetatis principibus*").

95. *De civitate Dei*, 3.16.25 and 39.

96. The "Pillar of Eliseg" makes Vortigern the son-in-law of Maximus.

97. A thirteenth-century MS of the *De excidio* (Cambridge University Library MS Ff. I. 27) reads "*tyranno Gurthingerno Britannorum duce*" (the tyrant Vortigern, duke of the Britons). See Bachrach, "Gildas," 138.

98. Alcock, *Economy*, 290.

99. *De excidio*, 21.4.

100. Ibid., 25.3: "Ambrosio Aureliano viro modesto, qui solus forte Romanae gentis."

101. Ibid., 26.2.

102. Ibid., 27.1. Note that in this chapter and elsewhere Gildas, like Patrick, also uses such terms as *latrones* (to describe those who serve the tyrants), which are typically associated with *tyranni* in late Roman sources; see MacMullen, "Roman Concept Robber-Pretender," 323–34.

103. *De excidio*, 28.1, 31.1, 34.1.

104. Ibid., 75.3.

105. See Kerlouegan, *Le "De excidio,"* 560–63. Kerlouegan points out that Gildas often uses the terms *tyrannus* and *princeps* as synonyms for *rex*, but *tyrannus*, unlike *rex*, is always used in a pejorative sense.

106. Higham, *Northern Counties*, 251.

107. For example, Maximus is called *Maximus Brittanniae* and *Maximi Regis* on the "Pillar of Eliseg." I am suggesting a phenomenon similar to that of calling emperors *rex*, shown to have been quite popular by Fanning ("Emperors and Empires," passim).

108. *De excidio*, 66.4: "[T]hey [the *sacerdotes*] canvass posts in the church more vigorously than the kingdom of heaven; they get them and keep them like tyrants [*tyrannico ritu*], and bring to them no luster of lawful behaviour."

109. See Alcock, *Economy*, 290: "[T]he kings of Gildas' own day were *tyranni* in his eyes either because they were the creation of usurpers like Maximus and Vortigern, or because they had seized by force their small territories." I believe that there were many factors that contributed to Gildas's judgment of a ruler as *tyrannus*, including (but not limited to) the unrestrained use of force, the breaking of oaths and promises made to God or His priests, homicide and regicide, illicit or lewd behavior, and associating with criminals or other *tyranni*.

110. Davies, *Patterns of Power*, 11. Gildas's use of the words *crudelis* and *superbus* to describe the behavior of the *tyranni* has a long literary precedent. Dunkle ("Rhetorical Tyrant") has shown that these terms were the traditional insults hurled at tyrants, citing examples from Cicero (*Thirteenth Philippic*, 18), Livy (*History*, 3.44.4, 2.56.7, 21.57.14, 24.5.3–6), and Tacitus (*Annals*, 1.4.11–12). Even a respected Roman leader could be tarnished by association with the term, as in this description of Constantius III by Olympiodorus (frag. 23): "On his progresses Constantius went with downcast eyes and sullen countenance. He was a man with large eyes, long neck, and broad head, who bent far over toward the neck of the horse carrying him and glanced here and there out of the corners of his eyes so that he showed to all, as the saying goes, 'an appearance worthy of a tyrant.'"

111. Vortipor, whom Gildas called *tyrannus*, is styled *protector* on a monument dated c. 540–50. See *ECMW*, no. 138, and the discussion later in Chapter 9.

112. Andrewes, *Greek Tyrants*, 23.

113. Thucydides, 6.59.3.

114. Andrewes, *Greek Tyrants*, 23–24.

115. Ibid., 24–25.

116. Hanson, *Life and Writings*, 64–65.

117. Dark, *Civitas*, 63. See also Kerlouegan, *Le "De excidio,"* 562.

118. *De excidio*, 4.3.

119. Jackson, "*Varia*: II," 36–38.

120. Many have interpreted "Vortigern" as a title meaning something akin to "high king." See, for example, Frere, *Britannia* (1987), 361; Alcock, *Arthur's Britain*, 103; Ashe, *Discovery*, 38; and Ellis, *Celt and Saxon*, 31. Jackson ("*Varia*: II," 36ff.), however, has argued persuasively that it is simply a personal name.

121. Jackson, "*Varia*: II," 40.

122. See ibid., 30–35, and Chapter 8 in this volume.

123. A possible Gallic parallel to Vortigern is the Seronatus frequently attacked by Sidonius Appolinaris (see, for example, *Epistulae*, 2.1). Sidonius describes Seronatus, who was either praetorian prefect in Gaul or *vicarius*, as acting "like a tyrant" (*ut tyrannus*) and giving orders in council (the *Concilium Septem Provinciarum*) amidst "counsellors" (*consilio*) (trans. Anderson).

124. See Thomas Charles-Edwards, "Native Political Organization in Roman Britain and the Origins of MW *Brenhin*," in *Antiquitates Indo-Germanicae*, ed. M. Mayrhofer et al. (Innsbruck, 1974), 35–45, esp. 37.

125. Jarman, *Aneirin,* 196; Williams, *Armes Prydein,* passim.

126. See Charles Thomas, *Britain and Ireland in Early Christian Times* (London: Thames & Hudson, 1971), 27; Eric Hamp, "*Varia.* XVIII. *Mech Deyrn,*" *Etudes Celtiques* 21 (1984): 139; Wendy Davies, *Small Worlds: The Village Community in Early Medieval Brittany* (London: Duckworth, 1988), 138; and Galliou and Jones, *Bretons,* 164. The Irish term occurs in a seventh-century poem, and all of these terms may carry the meaning of "first among equals."

127. See Hamp, "Varia. XVIII," 139. The *mach/mech* element is similar to Old Irish *mass,* "fine noble," and comes from British *maglo* > Welsh *Mael(gwn),* Latin *magnus.*

128. See, for example, Davies, *Small Worlds.*

129. J.G.T. Sheringham, "Les machtierns: Quelques témoignages gallois et cornouaillois," *Memoires de la Société d'Histoire et d'Archéologie de Bretagne* 58 (1981): 61–72.

130. See also Jackson, *Language and History,* 398 and 446. Common Celtic *tegos,* "house" x> Old Welsh *tig,* Middle and Modern Welsh *ty,* Old Cornish *ti,* Old Breton *tig,* and Middle Breton *ti.* Apparently there would have been an intermediate (Celtic) *tigos,* and seemingly a derivative of this *tegos/tigos* was the Common Celtic *tegernos,* "lord," which had an early by-form in *tig;* for example, the Gallo-Latin Thigernum Castrum(Thiers), the Old Irish *tigernae,* and the numerous British personal names (Bivatigirni, Catotigirni, Tigerni, Tigernomalus, Vurtigernus) that have preserved the *tig* element in sub-Roman writings and inscriptions.

131. Jones (*End of Roman Britain,* 147) points out that the *curiales* of Roman Britain were chosen, for the most part, from the tribal aristocracies.

132. Salvian, *De Gubernatione Dei,* 5.18 (trans. J. F. O'Sullivan, *The Writings of Salvian* [Washington, D.C.: Catholic University of America Press, 1962]): "Quae enim sunt non mod urbes sed etiam municipia atque vici, ubi non quot curiales fuerint, tot tyranni sunt? Quamquam forte hoc nomine gratulentur quia potens et honoratum esse videatur." See also ibid., 4.20, where Salvian complains about the "tyranny" of such men, those who are attacked by name in Sidonius's letters.

133. One further link between tyrants and cities is provided by Sidonius, who refers to the inhabitants of Lyon as *tyrannopolitarum,* "tyrant-governed citizens" (*Epistulae,* 5.8.3). W. B. Anderson (*Sidonius Appolinaris: Poems and Letters,* ed. and trans. W. B. Anderson [Cambridge, Mass.: Harvard University Press, Loeb Classical Library, 1936], 2:198 n.1) suggests that the original may have read *tyrannopolitanorum,* a possible pun on *Constantinopolitanorum.*

134. Sheringham, "Les machtierns," 71. He gives as example a charter from Quimper, dated 1058–84: "Consul Hoellus . . . in hostes suos scilicet Cornubie tyrannos bellum pararet."

135. Galliou and Jones, *Bretons,* 165: "[Machtierns] seem to reflect an earlier age, one that possibly goes back to the earliest days after the migrations." This is certainly the case for the *plebs* (Breton *plou*), the "parish" or administrative unit in which the machtierns exercised their authority (machtierns were sometimes called *princeps plebis*).

136. Aurélien de Courson, *Cartulaire de l'abbaye de Redon en Bretagne* (Paris: Imprimerie Impérial, 1863), 675. Variants for *machtierni* include *tiarni, tiranni,* and *principes.* See also Davies, *Small Worlds,* 138.

137. De Courson, *Cartulaire,* no. 267 (pp. 216–17). This is the only charter where the form *tyrannus* appears. See Sheringham, "Les machtierns," 66 n. 22, 71.

138. See Galliou and Jones, *Bretons,* 164.

139. This is especially clear in the Welsh tradition and continues throughout the Middle Ages. For example, in the *Brut y Tywysogyon,* the term *tir* refers to "land," as in *tir y Brytannyeit,* "the land of the Britons" (*sub anno* 1100–1102), while *teyrnas* signifies "kingdom," as in *deyrnas y Brytanyeit,* "the kingdom of the Britons" (*sub anno* 1196–97).

140. TIGERNI appears on early Christian monuments from Lundy Island (Lundy I in Okasha, *Corpus*) and Henfynyw, Wales (*ECMW,* no. 108), while TEGERNOMALI appears on a stone from Cubert (Cubert, in Okasha, *Corpus*). Compare this to the appearance of *Tyranus* as a

Roman *cognomen,* discussed above, to the Old Welsh names *Guorthegirnus* and *Categirn,* and to the Old Breton names *Gurtiern, Gurdiern, Ritern, Uuiutihern, Tiarnmael,* and *Tiarnoc,* which appear in the Redon cartulary and contemporary records. See Jackson, *Language and History,* 446–47.

141. See Galliou and Jones, *Bretons,* 164. A female machtiern, the *tiranissa* Aourken, was a ninth-generation tyrant; see de Courson, *Cartulaire,* no. 257 (p. 208). Compare with the female *tyranna* in the *Historia Augusta,* 2.31.10.

Chapter 10

1. Ammianus, 27.8.1 and 28.8.8.

2. For example, some small forces manned the signal stations, like Scarborough, along the northeast coast, and soldiers were stationed in the forts and landing places along the western coast of Wales and Cumbria. Evidence also suggests that the *comitatenses* were normally billeted in the cities and towns of the interior, and some scholars believe that barbarian *laeti* or *foederati* were also used to guard some cities. See Esmonde Cleary, *Ending,* 50–56; R.S.O. Tomlin, "Notitia Dignitatum Omnium, Tam Civilium Quam Militarium," in *Aspects of the "Notitia Dignitatum,"* ed. Goodburn and Bartholomew; and Chapter 12 in this volume.

3. Claudian, *Gothic War,* 416–18.

4. Olympiodorus, frag. 12; Orosius, 7.40.4; Zosimus, 6.2.

5. Zosimus, 6.5.3. Paschoud (*Zosime,* vol. 3, pt. 2, 9) translates this phrase "les autorites romaines," and observes that Zosimus uses αρχουτας to mean "officers in general" (208). See also the discussion in Chapter 2.

6. Constantius, *Vita Germani,* 3.17–18. An *exercitus provinciae* is recorded on a Roman inscription (*RIB,* no. 1051) found in Jarrow churchyard.

7. Constantius, *Vita Germani,* 3.18. See also Thomas F. X. Noble and Thomas Head, eds., *Soldiers of Christ: Saints and Saints' Lives from Late Antiquity and the Early Middle Ages* (University Park: Pennsylvania State University Press, 1995), 90.

8. Thompson, *St. Germanus,* 39–46.

9. For a defense of this episode, see Michael E. Jones, "The Historicity of the Alleluja Victory," *Albion* 18 (1986): 363–73, and idem, "Saint Germanus and the *Adventus Saxonum,*" *Haskins Society Journal* 2 (1990): 1–11.

10. *Epistola,* 2, 5, 12, 13, and 19.

11. Although the *milites* are not "pirates" in the technical sense, as defined by Roman law. See Jennifer McKnight, "When Is a Pirate Not a Pirate? When He Is Ashore: A Reconsideration of 'Piracy' in the Early Irish Seas and Its Possible Implications" (paper presented at the annual conference of the Celtic Studies Association of North America, April 1994).

12. See the remarks of J. B. Bury in Thompson, *Who Was Saint Patrick?* 139–40: "The continuity of the rule of Coroticus with the military organization of the Empire is strongly suggested by the circumstance that his power was maintained by 'soldiers.'. . . His soldiers may well be the successors of the Roman troops who defended the north of Britain." Thompson likewise believes it unlikely that a Roman writer like Patrick would describe "a random collection of civilian outlaws" as soldiers, and views Coroticus as a sub-Roman officer who became a "tyrant." Bury and Thompson have offered an attractive explanation of the status of Coroticus and his men, but the evidence as we have it can go no further in support of this.

13. *De excidio,* 14.

14. Ibid., 18–19. Kerlouegan (*Le "De excidio,"* 135) shows that the term *latrunculus* had a precise juridical meaning (as in Ulpian, *Digest,* 49.15.24); Lapidge (review of *Le "De*

excidio," 77) believes this implies a legal training for Gildas. Note that Patrick (*Epistola,* 12) also uses this term, which was commonly associated with tyrants. On the *exemplaria,* see Wood, "End of Roman Britain," 21 n. 153.

15. *De excidio,* 23.5.

16. Ibid. Wood ("End of Roman Britain," 21) interprets *annona* as evidence that Vortigern was depending on imperial practice in hiring the Saxons. In his translation, Winterbottom (*Gildas,* 150n, note for 23.5) maintains that *annonae, epimenia,* and *hospites* are all "late Roman technical terms for the billeting of federate allies." Lapidge ("Gildas's Education," 37ff.) explains that Gildas's precision in using such technical terms comes from his training at the hands of a *rhetor.* See *De excidio,* 92.3: *"foedere hostes . . . foederati."* Note that these specific terms had been used for the billeting of *regular* army units since at least the reign of Valentinian I. Gildas's knowledge of these military terms may have come from contacts beyond that with a rhetorician. Perhaps he had read some such "weapons manuals" as he claims the Romans left behind. For an archaeologist's appraisal of these terms, and what they mean for the *adventus Saxonum,* see S. C. Hawkes, "The South-East After the Romans: The Saxon Settlement," in *Saxon Shore,* ed. Maxfield, 78–95, esp. 87. The archaeological evidence is summed up by Martin G. Welch, "The Archaeological Evidence for Federate Settlement in Britain Within the Fifth Century," in *L'armée romaine et les barbares du IIIe au VIIe siécle,* ed. Françoise Vallet and Michel Kazanski (Rouen: Musée des Antiquités Nationales, 1994), 269–77.

17. See Higham, *English Conquest,* 40–42. However, it is less likely that the Britons "had little or no coinage" to pay the Saxons than that the Saxons did not want coin payments in a land with a deteriorating money economy. For extensive discussion of late Roman military rationing, see Walter Goffart, *Barbarians and Romans, a.d. 418–584: The Techniques of Accommodation* (Princeton: Princeton University Press, 1980).

18. See Bachrach, "Gildas," 135: "[T]here seems to be no reason to assume that Gildas erred when he indicated that the infrastructure in Britain for collecting the military *annona* was still viable in the mid-fifth century."

19. *De excidio,* 25.1. The terrain that Gildas describes is exactly where archaeologists have uncovered the remains of fortified settlements of the fifth and sixth centuries. See Chapters 12 and 14.

20. Ibid., 25.2 to 26.1.

21. Ibid., 27. Cf. 40.2: *"regi Israhel istorum conmanipulari."* The rare term *commanipulares,* literally "of the same *manipulus,"* again suggests familiarity with military terminology, though Marius Mercator (in the preface to *Commonitorium Adversum Haeresim Pelagii*) uses it in the general sense of "companions." See Kerlouégan, Le *"De excidio,"* 94–95, 281.

22. *De excidio,* 28.2, 29.1, 33.4, 32.1, 33.2.

23. Contra Higham (*English Conquest,* passim), who sees many veiled references to Saxons and Saxon domination in Gildas's biblical metaphors. See Christopher A. Snyder, review of *The English Conquest,* by Nicholas J. Higham, *Arthuriana* 6, no. 3(1996): 69–71.

24. See, for example, no. 123 in Davies, *Early Welsh Microcosm,* 167.

25. *De excidio,* 27.

26. See Davies, *Patterns of Power,* 22–24.

27. Ibid., 18.

28. See Tomlin, "Notitia Dignitatum Omnium," 189ff.; Jones, *Later Roman Empire,* 1:101 and 373ff.; and Ramsay MacMullen, *Soldier and Civilian in the Later Roman Empire* (Cambridge, Mass.: Harvard University Press, 1963), chap. 3.

29. Orosius, 7.40.4.

30. See *TLL,* s.v. *Municeps.* Ammianus (22.9.10, 25.9.3, 28.6.21, 29.2.27) always uses *municeps* to refer, in general, to a "townsman."

31. Zosimus, 6.5.3.

32. *Vita*, 3.14: *"conspicui divitiis, veste fulgentes."* See Wood, "End of Roman Britain," 10.

33. *Vita*, 3.15.

34. Wood, "End of Roman Britain," 10 n. 81. Sidonius, *Epistolae*, 1.3.2 (a *tribunus et notarius*), 1.11.5 (probably a *vicarius* who seized the Gallic prefecture), 4.24.1, 7.11(10).2 (another *tribunus et notarius*). All of these *viri*, as far as I can tell from Sidonius's descriptions, were civil servants, not military tribunes.

35. Thompson, *St. Germanus*, 6: "Constantius seems to be making an attempt to be precise: he seems to wish his readers to understand that, although the man was not what his readers in Gaul would take to be a tribune, yet he was something of that kind, something like a tribune. The implication appears to be that Constantius knew the nature of the man's authority and is trying to explain it. He is giving the nearest Roman equivalent of the man's office." See also 11–12.

36. This stone, from Rialton, has been dated sixth to eighth century; see Okasha, *Corpus*, 222. *Tribunus* appears as a name in the genealogy of the sixth-century kings of Demetia; see Morris, *Age of Arthur*, 125.

37. *Vita*, 5.26.

38. See chap. 10 of Leontius's *Life of St. John the Almsgiver*, in *Three Byzantine Saints*, ed. and trans. Elizabeth Dawes and Norman H. Baynes (London: Mowbrays, 1977). An anonymous editor fused the earlier *Life* by John Moschus and Sophronius with a supplement by Leontius, bishop of Neapolis, sometime after A.D. 641. The Britain episode is in Leontius's supplement. For a skeptical view on using the *Life* as a historical source, however, see Jeremy Knight in P. F. Wilkinson et al., "Excavations at Hen Gastell, Briton Ferry, West Glamorgan, 1991–92," *Medieval Archaeology* 39 (1995): p. 45 and n. 122.

39. See Thompson, *St. Germanus*, 12. Higham (*Rome, Britain, and the Anglo-Saxons*, 75) points out that Constantius, Gildas, and Bede all use the term *regio* to refer to a "region" where important political and military events occur: "It may well have designated the expanded estates of one aristocratic family, who were well on their way to usurping many of the prerogatives of empire."

40. *Confessio*, 1. See the comments by Hanson, *Life and Writings*, 77: "His mention of an estate, and (*Letter* 10) of the many servants on his father's estate and this claim to noble birth assure us that Patrick came from the upper class of native British society and must have been brought up in wealth and comfort."

41. *Epistola*, 10.

42. *Confessio*, 37. For this reading of *munera*, see Frere, *Britannia* (1987), 366.

43. See, for example, Hanson, "Date of Patrick," 70ff, and Timothy E. Powell, "Christianity or Solar Monotheism: The Early Religious Beliefs of St. Patrick," *Journal of Ecclesiastical History* 43, no. 4 (1992): 531–40.

44. See *TLL*, s.v. *Decurio*. The general usage was often adopted by Christian writers, who described Joseph as a *decurio* of Arimathea (e.g., Augustine, *De Consensu Evangelistarum*, 3.59.20; Bede, *In Marci Evangelium Expositio*, 4.15.1629).

45. See, for example, *RIB*, nos. 596, 748, 1039, 1269, 1445, 1453, 1527, 1561, 1870, and 1991.

46. Ammianus, 20.4.20, 28.6.10.

47. E.g., Powell, "Christianity." Patrick claims that he was not leading a Christian life before his captivity; thus Calpornius appears to have been unconcerned about his duties to the church. For discussion of this decurion/deacon problem, see Hanson, *Life and Writings*, 22–23, 67, 77; Thomas, *Christianity in Roman Britain*, 307–14; Thompson, *Who Was Saint Patrick?* 8–9, 139; and Jones, *End of Roman Britain*, 117–118. Jones points out that Patrick does not say that Calpornius was simultaneously deacon and decurion.

48. Salvian, *De Gubernatione Dei*, 5.18 and 21–23.

49. "Roman law" (Zosimus, 6.5.2) should perhaps be read as "imperial mandates," for it

is unlikely that Roman law disappeared immediately and entirely after 409, despite Gildas's assertion (*De excidio*, 13.1) that it had disappeared from Britain in the time of Magnus Maximus.

50. Thompson, *Who Was Saint Patrick?* 9. If British decurions had such a reputation for graft, it is unlikely that Patrick would have so conspicuously bragged that his father was a decurion.

51. A sub-Roman weight, found at Bath, has been seen as evidence for the continuation of tax collection; see Dark, *Discovery by Design*, 9 n. 123.

52. *De excidio*, 1.14.

53. Winterbottom, *Gildas*, 148n (note for 1.14). Higham (*Rome, Britain, and the Anglo-Saxons*, 84; *English Conquest*, 151ff.) similarly sees Gildas's juxtaposition of the terms *rectores* and *speculatores* as implying the persistence of a Romanized government with distinguishable functions.

54. In Ammianus, *rector* is used of emperors (16.12.13), provincial governors (19.13.2), military officers (14.2.15), barbarian client kings (17.13.30), a ship's captain (22.8.22), and a horse's rider (16.12.22). See *Ammianus Lexicon*, 464.

55. *RIB*, no. 103.

56. See, for example, the use of *rector* in Commodianus, 980.21.39 (for a bishop); Augustine, *Cass. Var.*, 5.21.2 (for God); Ambrose, *De Isaac Vel Anima*, 8.64.22 (for Christ). See also Souter, *Glossary of Later Latin*, s.v. *Rector*.

57. *De excidio*, 6.1 and 14.1 (trans. Winterbottom).

58. Ammianus, 16.9.3, 16.12.19, 26.6.6.

59. E.g., *RIB*, no. 19: "*speculator* of the II Legion Augusta Antoniana, . . . set up by the *speculatores* of the legion." This inscription is on a column found in London.

60. See, for example, Tertullian, *Apologeticum*, 45.26 (God); Augustine, *De civitate Dei*, 1.9.76 (Christ and bishops); and Columbanus, *First Letter to Gregory the Great*, para. 1 (the pope). See also Howlett, *Celtic Latin Tradition*, 84.

61. Contra Nicholas J. Higham ("Gildas, Roman Walls, and British Dykes," *CMCS* 22 [1991]: 11–12), who believes that Gildas uses *speculatores* in the technical sense, for *limitatenses*: "[H]is *speculatores* were Roman-style soldiers."

62. Contra Higham, *English Conquest*, 39.

63. See *TLL*, s.v. *Consilium*.

64. The diocesan assembly of Viennensis, attendance at which was made compulsory by an edict of Honorius (in 418). See Ernest Carette, *Droit Romain: Les assemblies provinciales de la Gaule romaine* (Paris: A. Picard, 1895), 460–63; J.A.O. Larsen, *Representative Government in Greek and Roman History* (Berkeley and Los Angeles: University of California Press, 1955), 126, 142ff., 152, 161; and M. Heinzelmann, "The 'Affair' of Hilary of Arles (445) and Gallo-Roman Identity in the Fifth Century," in *Fifth-Century Gaul*, ed. Drinkwater and Elton, 245–46. At Vienne, provincial governors, *honorati* (former imperial officeholders living in the diocese), and *curiales* were all required to attend.

65. See *Ammianus Lexicon*, 300–301.

66. See, for example, Sidonius, *Epistulae*, 1.3.3 and 5.10.2. The specific assembly that Sidonius alludes to is the Council of the Seven Provinces (Concilium Septem Provinciarum), which met in Arles annually beginning in 418.

67. *De excidio*, 23.2 (quoting Isa. 19.11), 69.2; *Fragmenta*, 6.

68. *De excidio*, 22.3 ("*Initur namque consilium*").

69. Evans, "From the End of Roman Britain," 99: "Whatever the nature of Gildas' council it seems likely that it was related to the traditional Roman form of government by *ordo* and magistrates."

70. Lapidge, "Gildas's Education," 46–47. For example, Gildas describes a written law code (*regula recti iudicii*), witnesses (*testes*), and the presentation of judicial evidence (*respondeant*

and *comprobetur*) in technical language that indicates familiarity with the procedure of Roman law courts. Cf. Higham, *Rome, Britain, and the Anglo-Saxons,* 84.

71. *De excidio,* 27 (trans. Winterbottom). Here, *impios* modifies *iudices* as *tyrannos* modifies *reges.*

72. Schaffner, "Britain's *Iudices,*" 151–53.

73. See ibid., 153, and *TLL,* s.v. *Iudex.*

74. Ammianus, 14.9.3, 15.7.1, 18.6.12. The Gothic king Athanaric is called *iudex* twice (27.5.6 and 31.3.4). See *Ammianus Lexicon,* 779–80. Ambrose (*De Spiritu Sancto,* prologue, 17) characterizes the judge of the Tervingi as a "judge of kings" (*iudex regum*), placing him in a position above the ordinary nobility (the *reges*). See Heather, *Goths and Romans,* 98.

75. Schaffner, "Britain's *Iudices,*" 154–55. For example, in the Vulgate *iudex* is used for a judge proper (Job 12.17), a provincial governor (Est. 3.12; Dan. 3.2), a member of a governing council (1 Esd. 2.17), *reges* (Wisd. of Sol. 9.7), and *principes* (Macc. 3.9).

76. *De excidio,* 63 (quoting Wisd. of Sol. 6.2–11). Cf. 51, 62.2, 62.7. Schaffner does not comment on the term *arbitraturi* or address the question of "function" versus "office."

77. See Davies, *Early Welsh Microcosm,* 108. These terms all appear on charters issued between A.D. 500 and 600. Later charters use, as well, terms like *seniores* and *optimates. Meliores* also appears in Gildas (*Fragmenta,* 2), where it indicates the "better" or stricter monks.

78. Ibid., 109.

79. Ibid., 111ff., 43–46. These appear mostly in the later charters.

80. *ECMW,* no. 138. Dated stylistically and with reference to Gildas's Vortipor.

81. The Ogam seems to give the Irish spelling of his name, while the Latin transliterates the British spelling. See Thomas, *Christianity in Roman Britain,* 245; Dumville, "Gildas and Maelgwn," 56–57; Jackson, *Language and History,* 169–70, 175–77, 749. A Guortepir also seems to figure in various versions of an Irish saga describing the emigration of his ancestral tribe from Ireland to Demetia (Dyfed). See Alcock, *Economy,* 53.

82. The full official title—*protector lateris divini Augusti nostri*—appears in an inscription (*Eph. Epigr.,* v. 121, no. 4). When the praetorian troops were disbanded by Constantine in 312, he gave their rank and duties to the *protectores et domestici,* who were commanded by the *comites domesticorum.* See Rolfe, introduction to *Ammianus Marcellinus,* x, xlii–xliii.

83. E.g., Ammianus, 14.7.12, 14.10.2, 15.5.22. Antoninus is called *protector* of the governor of Mesopotamia (18.5.1).

84. Ibid., 14.9.1. See Rolfe, introduction to *Ammianus Marcellinus,* x, xlii–xliii.

85. See Jones, *Later Roman Empire,* 636–40; Campbell, *Anglo-Saxons,* 21; Alcock, *Economy,* 53 and 93; and Sims-Williams, "Gildas and Vernacular Poetry," 171 and 192. Apparently one son of a German noble was given the title.

86. Evans ("From the End of Roman Britain," 99) regards Vortipor as a royal descendant of a fifth-century Roman unit commander. See also *ECMW,* 107; Miller, "Date-Guessing and Dyfed"; and Morris, *Age of Arthur,* 125–27. A tenth-century genealogy of the kings of Demetia (in Harleian MS 3859) lists Vortipor and the title *protector.* Morris's interpretation of this confusing genealogy has Agricola, a military *tribunus,* as Vortipor's father. Alcock (*Economy,* 53 and 93) believes that Vortipor's Irish family were established in Dyfed as *foederati* in the 380s, their leader (Eochiad) assuming the title *protector.*

87. See Davies, *Patterns of Power,* 11.

88. See *ECMW,* 107 n. 5.

89. See Rachel Bromwich, *Trioedd Ynys Prydein* (1978), 454. In the *Triads,* Maximus carries the title *gwledic,* which, like its Breton counterpart *gloedic,* was originally applied to the leader of a local, native militia. Bromwich suggests that *protector* may well have been the Roman equivalent of *gwledic.*

90. *ECMW,* no. 103. See the discussion in Chapter 7.

91. See *ECMW,* 93 n. 2.

92. Ibid., 92–93. There were no true urban centers in Roman Gwynedd, only fortifications, of which Segontium was the most substantial.

93. Alcock, *Economy,* 290. He adds that these individuals, seen as *magistratus* to their fellow Britons, may have appeared as *cyninges* to the Saxons who took the towns of Cirencester, Gloucester, and Bath and slew their "kings" Conmail, Condidan, and Farinmail (recorded in the *Anglo-Saxon Chronicle* under the year 577).

94. See *TLL,* s.v. *Magistratus.*

95. Ammianus, 31.6.2. See *Ammianus Lexicon,* 49.

96. Zosimus, 6.5.3. See also Paschoud's comments on the term in the index (*Zosime,* vol. 3, pt. 2, 208).

97. Vulgate Luke 12.11 (*"magistratus et potestates"*); Jth. 2.7 (*"duces et magistrtus virtutis Assyriorum"*); Luke 22.4 (*"cum principibus sacerdotum, et magistratibus"*); Jerome, *Commentaria in Ezechielem,* 7.23 (*"duces et magistratus"*). Note the mix of Mesopotamian, Greek, and Roman administrative terms used to describe Nebuchadnezzar's government in Vulgate Dan. 3.2: *satrapas, magistratus, et iudices, duces, et tyrannos, et praefectos, omnesque principes regionem.*

98. *Epistola,* 10.

99. See Thomas, *Christianity in Roman Britain,* 242: "The glosses of Roman citizenship [on inscribed stones], Roman *praenomina* and *nomina,* and progressively more inappropriate (if jealously guarded) Roman titles, together with a century or more of Imperial recognition in their caste, can hardly have disposed them to do other than to continue ruling, in their own names."

100. *De excidio,* 36.1.

101. See Lapidge, "Gildas's Education," 48, 50. Lapidge believes that it would have been inappropriate for Gildas to use the adjective *elegans* to describe a monk, but quite appropriate to describe an orator or author thus.

102. Ibid. On the survival of classical education—especially grammar and rhetoric—in the sixth-century Welsh and Irish monasteries, see Pierre Riche, *Education and Culture in the Barbarian West,* trans. John J. Contreni (Columbia: University of South Carolina Press, 1976), 307–14.

103. *Confessio,* 13 (trans. Winterbottom): "So then, be amazed, you . . . *dominicati rethorici. . . .* Who raised me up, a fool, from the midst of those who seem to be wise and learned in the law and powerful in speaking [*sapientes et legis periti et potentes in sermone*]?" Patrick hesitates (chap. 9) to write in his rustic style because he is afraid that the Latinists in Britain will mock him. See Davies, "Church in Wales," 137. Whereas Gildas seems to have studied under both a *grammaticus* and a *rhetor,* Patrick is constantly reminding his readers that his Latin education was interrupted by his captivity at age 16. See Hanson, "Date of Patrick," 65: "It is clear that the stage of education which he missed was the school of the *rhetor,* where he would have learnt both rhetoric and some law."

104. *De excidio,* 34.6, 35.3, 43.1. For the reading of *praecones* and *parasiti* as bards, see Hermann Moisl, "A Sixth-Century Reference to the British *Bardd,*" *BBCS* 29 (1980–82), 269–73; Sims-Williams, "Gildas and Vernacular Poetry," 174–75; J.E.C. Williams, "Gildas, Maelgwn, and the Bards," in *Welsh Society and Nationhood,* ed. R. R. Davies et al. (Cardiff: University of Wales Press, 1984), 19–37; and Michael Richter, *The Formation of the Medieval West: Studies in the Oral Culture of the Barbarians* (New York: St. Martin's Press, 1994), 206–7. Posidonius (in Athenaeus, *Deipnosophistae,* 6.49) uses the term *parasitoi* explicitly to describe ancient Celtic bards; see J. J. Tierney, "The Celtic Ethnography of Posidonius," *Proceedings of the Royal Irish Academy* 60C (1959–60): 189–275. Though Gildas's parasites may have simply been the king's flattering courtiers, we know from later sources that Maelgwn did have bards at his court.

105. *ECMW*, no. 92. Cf. Gildas, *De Poenitentia*, 18: "not in the spirit of an accuser, but of a physician [*medentis*]."

106. See *ECMW*, 90 n. 2.

107. For the view that political factionalism lay behind much of these theological disputes, see Myres, "Pelagius," 21–36; Morris, "Pelagian Literature," 26–60; Wood, "Fall of the Western Empire," 261. Myres's theory linking Pelagianism with British independence has been gradually discarded by most (see Thomas, *Christianity in Roman Britain*, 53–60), though it has recently been revived in a watered-down form by Wood.

108. See Rivet and Smith, *Place-Names of Roman Britain*, 49–50; Esmonde Cleary, *Ending*, 47–48; Thomas, *Christianity in Roman Britain*, 133, 197.

109. See A.H.M. Jones, "The Western Church in the Fifth and Sixth Centuries," in *Christianity in Britain*, ed. Barley and Hanson, 16; Esmonde Cleary, *Ending*, 34ff.; Thomas, *Christianity in Roman Britain*, 197–201; and Hanson, *Saint Patrick*, 32–34. Of the many bishops present at the Council of Rimini (A.D. 359), it is recorded that "three only from Britain" accepted imperial funds, implying that there were more British bishops present who had not.

110. *De Laude Sanctorum*, 1.24–39, in *PL*, 20:443–58.

111. See comments by Thomas, *Christianity in Roman Britain*, 198–200.

112. Gennadius of Marseilles (*De Scriptoribus Ecclesiasticis*, 56) calls Fastidius *Britannorum episcopus;* Sidonius Appolinaris (*Epistolae*, 9.9) addresses Faustus as *domino papae* and mentions writings that Riochatus is carrying "to your Britons [*Britannis tuis*] on your behalf"; *Concilium Turonense* I (A.D. 461), 148, line 125: "Mansuetus episcopus Britannorum interfui et subscripsi."

113. Prosper Tiro, *Chronicon, sub anno* 429, 1301: "Agricola Pelagianus Severiani Pelagiani episcopi filius ecclesias Britanniae dogmatis sui insinuatione corrupit."

114. Markus ("Pelagianism," 203) argues that both Severianus and Agricola were from Britain.

115. Prosper Tiro, *Chronicon, sub anno* 429. The translation is from Thomas, *Christianity in Roman Britain*, 60. Cf. "The First Synod of St. Patrick" (Bieler, *Irish Penitentials*, 58–59), chap. 33: "A cleric who comes [to Ireland] from the Britons [*de Britanis*] without a letter, even though he lives in a community [*in plebe*], is not allowed to minister." Bieler (*Irish Penitentials*, 59 n. 9) sees this as a provision against the infiltration of semi-Pelagianism.

116. *Vita Germani*, 3.12. Gildas (*De excidio*, 15.1 and 17.1) also mentions *legati* who are sent to ask Rome for military aid. *Legatus/legati*, in late Roman parlance, could denote political, ecclesiastical, or military "envoys"; see *TLL*, s.v. *Legato (Legatvm)*.

117. See Alcock, *Arthur's Britain*, 133; Thompson, *St. Germanus*, 20ff.

118. Prosper Tiro, *Contra Collatorem*, 21, in *PL*, 51:271; idem, *Chronicon, sub anno* 431, 1307. See Thompson, *St. Germanus*, 29.

119. On the fate of Palladius and his mission to Ireland, see Dumville et al., *Saint Patrick*, 59–88; Thompson, *Who Was Saint Patrick?* 161ff.; Hanson, *Life and Writings*, 119; and Morris's introduction in Hood, *St. Patrick*, 4–5. Muirchu, in his seventh-century *Life* of Patrick, claims (chap. 8) that Palladius died leaving Ireland after a brief and unsuccessful mission.

120. This view, inferred from Patrick's own comments about the British church, is held by Thompson (*Who Was Saint Patrick?* 66–76), Hanson (*Life and Writings*, 30), Thomas (*Christianity in Roman Britain*, 332–33), and Morris (introduction in Hood, *St. Patrick*, 6).

121. *Epistola*, 1.

122. See, e.g., *Epistola*, 1 and 12, and *Confessio*, 1, 13, 26, 27, 29, 32, and 37.

123. *Confessio*, 26.

124. Ibid., 13. See Hanson, *Life and Writings*, 84–85; Thomas, *Christianity in Roman Britain*, 339.

125. E.g., *De excidio*, 65.1, 66.6, 69.1, 67.1, 108.3.

126. *Fragmenta*, 5, 6, and 7; *De Poenitentia*, 24.

127. *De excidio*, 68, 106–9. See also Davies, "Church in Wales," 140 n. 96.

128. *EH*, 1.27.

129. Ibid., 2.2. See Thomas, *Christianity in Roman Britain*, 267–68.

130. See Davies, *Early Welsh Microcosm*, 149 n. 1.

131. Ibid., 147.

132. Ibid., 146–48.

133. F. C. Burkitt and L.C.G. Clarke, "Roman Pewter Bowl from the Isle of Ely," *Proceedings of the Cambridge Antiquarian Society* 31 (1931): 66–72; Thomas, *Christianity in Roman Britain*, 125.

134. See K. A. Steer, "Two Unrecorded Early Christian Stones," *Proceedings of the Society of Antiquaries of Scotland* 101 (1972): 127–29; Thomas, *Christianity in Roman Britain*, 291.

135. Thomas, *Christianity in Roman Britain*, 267: "the *sacerdotes*—almost certainly meaning 'bishops' as contrasted with *presbyteres*, 'priests'—on very late fifth-century or early sixth-century stones from south-west Scotland and north-west Wales."

136. *ECMW*, no. 33. See also the comments by Nash-Williams (ibid., 63): "*Sacerdos* was commonly, but not invariably, used of a bishop." This usage is also found in North Africa, and its equivalent was used in the Greek East.

137. Ibid., no. 83.

138. See Thomas, *Celtic Britain*, 99, and the discussion of Whithorn in Chapter 12 in this volume.

139. *De excidio*, 66 (trans. Winterbottom).

140. Davies ("Church in Wales," 140–41) gives the relevant passages in the *De excidio* in the notes. We can add Gildas's testimony (*De excidio*, 67.4) to the act of ordination (*ordinant*) in Britain. A "cleric's wife" (*clericus . . . et uxor eius*) and British clerics traveling to Ireland are recorded in "The First Synod of St. Patrick" (Bieler, *Irish Penitentials*, 54–59), chaps. 6 and 33.

141. *De excidio*, 67.5 (*parochiam*), 74.2 (*Christianos*), 110.3 (*congregationis*).

142. See *TLL*, s.v. *Paroecia*.

143. See, for example, Augustine, *Epistulae*, 209.2.2 (*"ad parochiam Hipponiensis ecclesiae pertinebat"*); Gennadius, *De Viris Illustribus*, 109.2.1 (*"episcopum, in cuius paroecia"*); Sulpicius Severus, *Dialogues*, 1.8.2 (discussing the *paroechia* of the Bishop of Jerusalem; see also Hoare, *Western Fathers*, 77 n. 1).

144. Caesarius Arelatensis, *Sermones Caesarii uel ex aliis Fontibus Hausti*, 1.1–2, 2.2, 2.22, 13.1 (titled *Sermo in parochiis necessarius*).

145. For the role that villa chapels may have played in the formation of parishes, see Thomas, *Christianity in Roman Britain*, 158ff., and John Percival, "Fifth-Century Villas: New Life or Death Postponed?" in *Fifth-Century Gaul*, ed. Drinkwater and Elton, 160–61. Much new work is being done on the (British) origins of Anglo-Saxon parishes; see Steven Bassett, "Church and Diocese in the West Midlands: The Transition from British to Anglo-Saxon Control," in *Pastoral Care Before the Parish*, ed. John Blair and Richard Sharpe (Leicester: Leicester University Press, 1992), 13–40; idem, "Churches in Worcester Before and After the Conversion of the Anglo-Saxons," *Antiquaries Journal* 69 (1989): 225–56; and Dark, *Civitas*.

146. *Confessio*, 1.

147. See Davies, *Early Welsh Microcosm*, 126.

148. Ibid., 124–28.

149. "Excerpts from a Book of David" (Bieler, *Irish Penitentials*, 70–71), chaps. 10 and 11.

150. *ECMW*, no. 77.

151. *ECMW*, no. 78.

152. Orosius, 7.40.7 (*"ex monacho Caesarem factum"*); Olympiodorus, frags. 12 and 16.

153. In his *Letter to Demetrias* (see Birley, *People of Roman Britain*, 154).

154. *Confessio*, 41, 42, 43, 49; *Epistola*, 12. On the question whether Patrick was a monk, see Hanson, *Life and Writings*, 49–51.

155. *De excidio,* 26.3–4, 28.1, 34.1–2, 34.2, 65.1, 65.2.

156. Columbanus, *Epistola,* 1.6–7. See Sharpe, "Gildas as a Father of the Church," 196ff., and Michael Winterbottom, "Columbanus and Gildas," *Vigiliae Christianae* 30 (1976): 310–17.

157. On the use of the *De Poenitentia* for writing sixth-century British history, see Lapidge, "Gildas's Education," 37. Columbanus and Vinnian also wrote penitentials.

158. Sharpe, "Gildas as a Father of the Church," 197–99. Cf. John Ryan, *Irish Monasticism: Origins and Early Development* (Dublin: Institute for Advanced Studies, 1931), 157.

159. Lapidge ("Gildas's Education," 37) points out that Gildas's language in the "Penitential" shows that Roman terms for weights and measures (e.g., *himina romana,* "a Roman half-pint") are still being used in Britain. See also the discussion in Chapter 14.

160. Charters 72a, 73a, 77, 121, and 127b. See Davies, *Early Welsh Microcosm,* 134–36.

161. Davies, *Early Welsh Microcosm,* 122.

162. Ibid., 124–25.

163. *ECMW,* no. 78.

164. See John MacQueen, *St. Nynia,* (Edinburgh: Polygon, 1990), 20–21, 82–83, and Chapter 12 in this volume. Bede (*EH,* 3.4) believed that Ninian founded *Candida Casa* (Whithorn) in imitation of the famous monastic community of Saint Martin of Tours, Marmoutier.

165. For British examples, see "The Preface of Gildas on Penance," "The Synod of North Britain," "The Synod of the Grove of Victory," and "Excerpts from the Book of David," in Bieler, *Irish Penitentials.*

166. "Synod of the Grove of Victory" (Bieler, *Irish Penitentials,* 68–69), chap. 9: *"votum perfectionis fuerit homo."*

167. Thomas, *Christianity in Roman Britain,* 348ff. Thomas claims that monasticism was not common until the end of the sixth century, but I think that Gildas gives ample evidence that monasticism was a prominent part of the British church in his day. For example, Gildas (*De excidio,* 34.1, 35.2) does not see it as extraordinary or difficult for Maglocunus to step down from his throne to become a monk, then return again.

168. In Constantius: bishops leading an army into battle (*Vita Germani,* 3.17–8). In Patrick: the excommunication of a ruler (*Epistola,* 5). In Gildas: kings swearing oaths at the altar (*De excidio,* 27), a king taking monastic vows (34.1), and priests purchasing their offices from tyrants (67.2).

Chapter 11

1. R. G. Collingwood and J.N.L. Myres, *Roman Britain and the English Settlements* (Oxford: Clarendon Press, 1936); John S. Wacher, *The Towns of Roman Britain* (Berkeley and Los Angeles: University of California Press, 1974); Frere, *Britannia;* Alcock, *Arthur's Britain.*

2. See Leslie Alcock, "The Activities of Potentates in Celtic Britain, A.D. 500–800: A Positivist Approach," in *Power and Politics in Early Medieval Britain and Ireland,* ed. S. T. Driscoll and M. R. Nieke (Edinburgh: Edinburgh University Press, 1988), 22. Cf. Richard Hodges, *The Anglo-Saxon Achievement: Archaeology and the Beginnings of English Society* (London: Duckworth, 1989), 22, who portrays sub-Roman Britain as "A Prehistoric Episode" preceding the "Anglo-Saxon Achievement." A semireductionist approach is taken by Esmonde Cleary in *The Ending of Roman Britain* (1989).

3. This problem has recently been discussed by archaeologists in the collection of articles edited by Stephen Shennan, *Archaeological Approaches to Cultural Identity* (London: Unwin Hyman, 1989).

4. Wainwright, *Archaeology,* 111.

5. This theory is explored in depth in Laing and Laing, *Celtic Britain and Ireland*. See also Salway, *Oxford Illustrated History of Roman Britain*, 298 (fig.), 328–29, 332 (fig.), and Julian D. Richards, "An Archaeology of Anglo-Saxon England," in *After Empire*, ed. Ausenda, 51–74, esp. 57.

6. See, for example, Niall M. Sharples, *Maiden Castle* (London: Batsford/English Heritage, 1991), 130: "They are known as Romano-Celtic temples because they are believed to represent a fusion of Celtic and classical religions."

7. My view is, however, that the Germanic migrations to Britain involved small numbers (of mostly warriors) until the latter sixth century, and that the overwhelming majority of the population in Britannia throughout the sub-Roman period were ethnically Romano-British. This seems to be the prevailing scholarly attitude; see, for example, Jones, *End of Roman Britain*, 27–32, who estimates the total population of the Anglo-Saxon migration between A.D. 410 and 550 at ten to twenty thousand. The chief evidence for early Anglo-Saxon population in Britain is a few excavated cremation cemeteries (e.g., Dorchester-on-Thames, Milton Regis, Mucking), whose burials were associated with datable metalwork (especially brooches). For a recent study, see Horst Wolfgang Böhme, "Das Ende der Römerherrschaft in Britannien und die Angelsächsische Besiedlung Englands im 5. Jahrhundert," *Jahrbuch des Romisch-Germanischen Zentralmuseums Mainz* 33 (1986): 469–574.

8. I have more fully discussed currency in late and sub-Roman Britain elsewhere: see Snyder, *Sub-Roman Britain* (A.D. 400–600): *A Gazetteer of Sites*, BAR British Series, no. 247 (Oxford: Tempvs Reparatvm, 1996), 6–8.

9. There are several general studies of coinage in Roman Britain. See, for example, Casey, *Roman Coinage in Britain*, and Richard Reece, *Coinage in Roman Britain* (London: Seaby, 1987).

10. See Casey, "Constantine the Great in Britain," and Anne S. Robertson, *Roman Imperial Coins in the Hunter Coin Cabinet, University of Glasgow*, vol. 5, *Diocletian (Reform) to Zeno* (Oxford: Oxford University Press, 1982), xx, 428. The London mint issued gold *solidi* for Maximus.

11. See Kent, "End of Roman Britain," 21; Reece, *Coinage in Roman Britain*, 23; Esmonde Cleary, *Ending*, 93, 138–39; and Grierson and Mays, *Catalogue of Late Roman Coins*, 39–47, 138, 207–9, 214–18.

12. See George C. Boon, "Counterfeit Coins in Roman Britain," in *Coins and the Archaeologist*, ed. P. J. Casey and Richard Reece (London: Seaby, 1987), 102–88, and Mark Blackburn, "Three Silver Coins in the Names of Valentinian III (425–55) and Anthemius (467–72) from Chatham Lines, Kent," *Numismatic Chronicle* 148 (1988): 169–74. Coin hoards, however, may tell a different story. In June 1997 a late Roman hoard was discovered at Patching, West Sussex, which contained three official gold issues of Valentinian III in addition to both gold and silver Visigothic imitations. The latest coin in the hoard dates to c. 461 (pers. comm., Dr. Sally White, July 1997).

13. See C.H.V. Sutherland, "Coinage in Britain in the Fifth and Sixth Centuries," in *Dark-Age Britain: Studies Presented to E. T. Leeds*, ed. D. B. Harden (London: Methuen, 1956), 5; Richard M. Reece, "The Use of Roman Coinage," *Oxford Journal of Archaeology* 3 (1984): 205; Boon, "Counterfeit Coins in Roman Britain," 145; idem, "Byzantine and Other Exotic Ancient Bronze Coins from Exeter," in *Exeter Archaeological Reports*, vol. 4, *Roman Finds from Exeter*, ed. Neil Holbrook and Paul T. Bidwell (Exeter: University of Exeter Press, 1991); idem, "Theodosian Coins from North and South Wales," *BBCS* 33 (1986): 429–35; and Dark, *Civitas*, 200ff.

14. See Dark, *Civitas*, 201–3; Reece, "Use of Roman Coinage"; and Cécile Morrison, "The Re-Use of Obsolete Coins: The Case of Roman Imperial Bronzes Revived in the Late Fifth Century," in *Studies in Numismatic Method Presented to Philip Grierson*, ed. C.N.L. Brooke et al. (Cambridge: Cambridge University Press, 1983), 95–111.

15. Patrick mentions (*Epistola,* 14; *Confessio,* 50) both *solidi* and *scriptulae;* Gildas states (*De excidio,* 66.3–5) that the priests of his day have not contributed a single *obolum* to the poor, yet they "grieve if they lose a single *denarius;* if they gain one, they cheer up"; and Leontius's *Life of St. John the Almsgiver* (chap. 10) includes an account of a Byzantine ship returning from southwestern Britain, laden with *nomismates* and tin. See Dark, *Civitas,* 203, and Roger D. Penhallurick, *Tin in Antiquity* (London: Institute of Metals, 1986), 245.

16. See Vivien G. Swan, *Pottery in Roman Britain,* 4th rev. ed. (Aylesbury: Shire, 1988), and idem, *The Pottery Kilns of Roman Britain* (London: HMSO, 1984).

17. See the discussion under Wroxeter and St. Albans in Chapter 12.

18. See the discussion under Tintagel in Chapter 12.

19. See C. A. Ralegh Radford, "Imported Pottery Found at Tintagel, Cornwall," in *Dark-Age Britain,* ed. Harden, 59–67, and Charles Thomas, "Imported Pottery in Dark-Age Western Britain," *Medieval Archaeology* 3 (1959): 89–111.

20. John W. Hayes, *Late Roman Pottery* (London: British School at Rome, 1972); idem, *A Supplement to Late Roman Pottery* (London: British School at Rome, 1980); John Dore and Kevin Greene, eds., *Roman Pottery Studies in Britain and Beyond,* BAR Supplemental Series, no. 30 (Oxford: Tempvs Reparatvm, 1977); and D.P.S. Peacock, *Amphorae and the Roman Economy* (London: Longman, 1986).

21. Thomas, *Provisional List.* See also idem, "Imported Late-Roman Mediterranean Pottery in Ireland and Western Britain: Chronologies and Implications," *Proceedings of the Royal Irish Academy* 76C (1976): 245–56; idem, "The Context of Tintagel: A New Model for the Diffusion of Post-Roman Mediterranean Imports," *Cornish Archaeology* 27 (1990): 7–25; idem, "'Gallici Nautae de Galliarum Provinciis': A Sixth/Seventh Century Trade with Gaul, Reconsidered," *Medieval Archaeology* 34 (1990): 1–26; and the descriptive catalog of imports in *Early Medieval Settlements,* ed. Edwards and Lane.

22. See Kenneth Rainsbury Dark, "High Status Sites, Kingship, and State Formation in Post-Roman Western Britain, A.D. 400–700" (Ph.D. thesis, Cambridge University, 1989), 129: "[I]t is sadly true that no two modern surveys of the settlement archaeology of the period have managed to agree on a common corpus of sites."

Chapter 12

1. The most significant recent works include Alcock, *Economy, Society, and Warfare Among the Britons and Saxons* (1987); Esmonde Cleary, *The Ending of Roman Britain* (1989); Laing and Laing, *Celtic Britain and Ireland* (1990); Higham, *Rome, Britain, and the Anglo-Saxons* (1992); and Dark, *Civitas to Kingdom* (1993).

2. The best regional survey is *Early Medieval Settlements,* ed. Edwards and Lane, though discussion under individual sites is brief. This is true as well for the wider-ranging survey by Dark, *Discovery by Design,* excellent in its coverage of secular settlements but purposely excluding religious sites and cemeteries. For the most comprehensive catalog of sites and data, including a full bibliography of excavation reports, see Snyder, *Sub-Roman Britain,* and the electronic version, "A Gazetteer of Sub-Roman Britain (A.D. 400–600): The British Sites," *Internet Archaeology* <http://intarch.york.ac.uk> 3 (summer 1997). Both versions of the gazetteer, however, include only brief narrative discussion under individual sites.

3. Simon James, *The World of the Celts* (London: Thames & Hudson, 1993), 48 and 129. There is much debate over whether such developments in Iron Age Britain were brought about by invasion, immigration, cultural trade, or simply native innovation. The debate is taken up in the following works: John Collis, ed., *The Iron Age in Britain: A Review* (Sheffield: University of Sheffield Press, 1977); idem, *Oppida: Earliest Towns North of the Alps* (Sheffield:

University of Sheffield Press, 1984); Valery Rigby, "The Iron Age: Continuity or Invasion?" in *Archaeology in Britain Since 1945*, ed. I. Longworth and J. Cherry (London: British Museum, 1986), 52–72; Venceslas Kruta et al., eds., *The Celts* (London: Thames & Hudson, 1991); and Barry Cunliffe, *Iron Age Communities in Britain*, 3d ed. (London: Routledge, 1991).

4. See the concise account of the city's early history in Jenny Hall and Ralph Merrifield, *Roman London* (London: HMSO, 1986), 8–16.

5. See Rivet and Smith, *Place-Names of Roman Britain*, 396–98.

6. Gustav Milne, *From Roman Basilica to Medieval Market* (London: HMSO, 1992), 29.

7. Gustav Milne, *The Port of Roman London* (London: Batsford, 1995), 33.

8. Ibid.; Thomas, *Provisional List*, 14 and 16; John Morris, *Londinium: London in the Roman Empire* (London: Weidenfeld & Nicolson, 1982), 329–30.

9. Hall and Merrifield, *Roman London*, 14.

10. Ibid.; K. S. Painter, "A Roman Silver Ingot," British Museum Occasional Paper, no. 35 (London: British Museum Department of Greek and Roman Antiquities, Acquisitions 1976, 1981).

11. Dominic Perring, *Roman London* (London: Seaby, 1991), 127; Ralph Merrifield, *London, City of the Romans* (London: Batsford, 1983), 226.

12. Perring, *Roman London*, 128; Hall and Merrifield, *Roman London*, 14–16.

13. Theodosian bronze coinage including, presumably, the Honorius AE 4 issued between 395 and 402. These were the last copper/bronze issues to reach Britain.

14. Peter Marsden, *Roman London* (London: Thames & Hudson, 1980), 180–81; Thomas, *Provisional List*, 16.

15. There is one lone fifth-century example of a sunken-floored structure, built *within* the shell of a Roman building, at Pudding Lane; see Perring, *Roman London*, 128.

16. Susann Palmer, *Excavation of the Roman and Saxon Site at Orpington* (London Borough of Bromley: Libraries Department, 1984), 19. These inhumations were found immediately outside the walls of a Roman bath/house complex that had been abandoned c. 400.

17. *Anglo-Saxon Chronicle* (The Laud [Peterborough] Chronicle), *sub anno* 456 (trans. Garmonsway): "In this year Hengest and Aesc fought against the Britons . . . and slew four companies; and the Britons then forsook Kent and fled to London in great terror."

18. Biddle, "Towns," 106.

19. Perring, *Roman London*, 129–30.

20. Philip Crummy, *Colchester Archaeological Report 3: Excavations at Lion Walk, Balkerne Lane, and Middleborough* (Colchester: Archaeological Trust, 1984), 18. Early (1853 and 1927–29) excavations at Duncan's Gate detected much charcoal, scorched stone, and gray soil indicating three successive fires. The middle fire layer sealed a damaged bronze coin with legible diademed head, a symbol that occurs from 307 onward.

21. David T. Clarke, *Roman Colchester* (Colchester: Colchester Borough Council, 1980), 48. Twelve coins issued between 388 and 402 were recorded but not cataloged.

22. See Rosalind Dunnett, *The Trinovantes* (London: Duckworth, 1975), 137, and Philip Crummy, *Colchester Archaeological Report 1: Aspects of Anglo-Saxon and Norman Colchester*, CBA Research Report, no. 39 (London: CBA, 1981), 23.

23. Such graves, usually identified as "early Saxon," have also been found within the town walls at Winchester, Portchester, and Dorchester-on-Thames. See Crummy, *Colchester Report 1*, 22.

24. See Dunnett, *Trinovantes*, 144 and fig. 44.

25. Ibid., 142.

26. See Wacher, *Towns of Roman Britain*, 202ff., and Rivet and Smith, *Place-Names of Roman Britain*, 497–99.

27. The Insula XXVII townhouse is discussed in detail in Sheppard Frere, *Verulamium*

Excavations (1972–84), 3 vols. (London: Society of Antiquaries, 1972–83). See also Laing and Laing, *Celtic Britain and Ireland*, 74–75; Keith Branigan, *The Catuvellauni* (Gloucester: Sutton, 1985), 191; and Esmonde Cleary, *Ending*, 148–51. The coins (from all *insulae*) are discussed in Reece, "The Coins," in Frere, *Verulamium*, 3:3–17.

28. Branigan, *Catuvellauni*, 196. Cf. Esmonde Cleary, *Ending*, 151: "The survival of Roman hydraulic techniques to such a late date is worthy of note." Frere (*Verulamium*, 2:226) estimates the dates based on the stratification of the associated structures discussed earlier in Chapter 12. The only coins found beneath the pipe trench were one of Constantius II (c. 337–41), one of Constans (c. 341–46), and one small barbarous copy, *Fel. Temp. Reparatio* (horseman) type.

29. See Andrew Selkirk, "Verulamium," *Current Archaeology* 120 (1990): 410–17; Rosalind Niblett, "'Verulamium' Since the Wheelers," in *Roman Towns: The Wheeler Inheritance: A Review of 50 Years' Research*, CBA Research Report, no. 93, ed. S. J. Greep (York: CBA, 1993), 78–92, esp. 89; and Dark, *Civitas*, 88.

30. Niblett, "'Verulamium,'" 90–91.

31. Keith Branigan, *Town and Country: The Archaeology of Verulamium and the Roman Chilterns* (Bourne End, Buckinghamshire: Spurbooks, 1973), 136.

32. This idea has been argued by R.E.M. Wheeler (1934), K. R. Davis (1982), and Sheppard Frere (1966). For discussion, see Laing and Laing, *Celtic Britain and Ireland*, 74–75.

33. *Anglo-Saxon Chronicle* (Parker and Laud Chronicles), *sub anno* 571.

34. Paul Bennett, "Canterbury," in *Saxon Shore*, ed. Maxfield, 118–29, esp. 128; Dodie A. Brooks, "The Case for Continuity in Fifth-Century Canterbury Re-Examined," *Oxford Journal of Archaeology* 7 (1988): 99–114, esp. 103.

35. P. Blockley, "Excavations at Ridingate," *Archaeologia Cantiana* 100 (1984): 205–9.

36. C. M. Johns and T. W. Potter, "The Canterbury Late Roman Treasure," *Antiquaries Journal* 55 (1985): 313–52. The dates of the coins range from 360 to 404, but two coins of Honorius and one of Maximus were clipped. If the Canterbury hoard compares to those studied by Andrew Burnett ("Clipped *Siliquae* and the End of Roman Britain," *Britannia* 15 [1984]: 163–68), the clipping perhaps took place during the reign of Constantine III (407–11), though it could have occurred later. Johns and Potter state "that the hoard was not deposited before the second decade of the fifth century." Grierson and Mays (*Catalogue of Late Roman Coins*, 18) accept this *terminus post quem*.

37. For the influence that preexisting communities of Christian Britons had on the conversion of the Anglo-Saxons and on the reestablishment of episcopal dioceses in Anglo-Saxon England, see Bassett, "Church and Diocese," 13–40. See also idem, "Churches in Worcester," 230: "[The placement of English sees in Roman towns was] a clear acknowledgement of the extent to which Romano-British tribal capitals and other central places had remained politically (or often economically) important."

38. Bennett, "Canterbury," 128.

39. Esmonde Cleary, *Ending*, 151: "Roman civic norms were no longer being adhered to at Canterbury."

40. Ibid.

41. J.P.C. Kent et al., "A Visigothic Gold Tremiss and a Fifth-Century Firesteel from the Marlowe Theatre Site, Canterbury," *Antiquaries Journal* 53 (1983): 371–73.

42. Ibid., 372; Blackburn, "Three Silver Coins," 173–74.

43. Alec Down, *Roman Chichester* (Chichester: Phillimore, 1988), 101; Laing and Laing, *Celtic Britain and Ireland*, 78.

44. Down (*Roman Chichester*, 103) suggests a date of 408 for this coin. However, the coin has the reverse legend VICTORIA AUG, which is only found on the Arcadius AE 4 (*RIC*, 187/63c) struck in 383. See Grierson and Mays, *Catalogue of Late Roman Coins*, 102–3.

45. Down, *Roman Chichester*, 103. The *solidus* is in mint condition and may never have cir-

culated, and Down suggests that it was held as "bullion" by a trader waiting to pay for imported goods. See also Blackburn, "Three Silver Coins," 173–74.

46. Martin G. Welch, *Early Anglo-Saxon Sussex,* BAR, no. 112 (Oxford: Tempvs Reparatvm, 1983), 14–15; idem, "Late Romans and Saxons in Sussex," *Britannia* 2 (1971): 232–37. Evidence includes coins ranging in date from A.D. 97 to 395, and crude handmade pottery termed "Thundersbarrow ware." These wares appear to have replaced the mass-produced pottery that was no longer available by the beginning of the fifth century.

47. Down, *Roman Chichester,* 101.

48. Barry C. Burnham and John Wacher, *The "Small Towns" of Roman Britain* (London: Batsford, 1990), 174.

49. A. M. Burnett, "The Newton Mills, Bath, Treasure Trove," in *Coin Hoards from Roman Britain,* ed. A. M. Burnett and Roger Bland (London: British Museum, 1987), 193–98. A hoard of 255 silver *siliquae* was found in 1983 at Newton Mills Park near Bath. The coins range from one Trier *siliqua* of Constans (c. 347–48) to 62 Trier *siliquae* of Magnus Maximus (383–88). Because the hoard lacks later issues of Maximus and his son Falvius Victor (elevated 387), Burnett (p. 194) suggests a deposition date of about 385, before the end of Maximus's minting of *siliquae* at Trier.

50. Burnham and Wacher, *"Small Towns" of Roman Britain,* 175; Barry Cunliffe, *Roman Bath Discovered* (London: Routledge & Kegan Paul, 1984), 211.

51. The original account is in Barry Cunliffe and Peter Davenport, *The Temple of Sulis Minerva at Bath,* vol. 1, *The Site* (Oxford: Oxford University Committee for Archaeology, 1985), 74ff. The excavators point out the time and care with which this sequence, in particular, was excavated. For discussion, see also Barry Cunliffe, *The City of Bath* (Gloucester: Sutton, 1986), 43–48; Esmonde Cleary, *Ending,* 155–57; Burnham and Wacher, *"Small Towns" of Roman Britain,* 175; and Laing and Laing, *Celtic Britain and Ireland,* 76.

52. Cunliffe and Davenport, *Temple of Sulis Minerva,* 1:11: "[E]xcavation of the temple has demonstrated conclusively that substantial parts of the Roman structure remained standing for some considerable time, possibly into the seventh or eighth century, while surrounding ground-surfaces were sporadically repaired."

53. See Esmonde Cleary, *Ending,* 157 ("The pottery experts seem to be over-compressing the sequence"); Laing and Laing, *Celtic Britain and Ireland,* 76 ("a very late [post-Roman] repaving of the temple precinct floor"); Burnham and Wacher, *"Small Towns" of Roman Britain,* 175 ("even on conservative estimates [the sequence] must have continued well into the fifth century if not beyond").

54. Cunliffe and Davenport, *Temple of Sulis Minerva,* 1:11.

55. Ibid.; Cunliffe, *Roman Bath,* 209: "During period 5 we see the attempts of the late or sub-Roman population to keep the old building in use."

56. Cunliffe, *City of Bath,* 48.

57. *Anglo-Saxon Chronicle* (F Lat), *sub anno* 577 (trans. Garmonsway): "In this year Cuthwine and Ceawlin fought against the Britons and slew three kings, Coinmail, Condidan, and Farinmail, at the place which is called Dyrham; and they captured *tres civitates,* Gloucester, Cirencester, and Bath."

58. C.J.S. Green, *Excavations at Poundbury, Dorchester, Dorset, 1966–1982,* vol. 1, *The Settlements,* Dorset Natural History and Archaeological Society Monograph, no. 7 (Dorchester: Dorset Natural History and Archaeological Society, 1988), 70–71; Esmonde Cleary, *Ending,* 178–79.

59. Green, *Excavations,* 83; D. E. Farwell and T. L. Molleson, *Excavations at Poundbury, 1966–1980,* vol. 2, *The Cemeteries,* Dorset Natural History and Archaeological Society Monograph, no. 11 (Dorchester: Dorset Natural History and Archaeological Society, 1993), 89.

60. Philip Rahtz has interpreted this second-phase settlement at Poundbury as a monastery; see Dark, *Discovery by Design,* 46.

61. Green, *Excavations,* 153.

62. Paul T. Bidwell, *Roman Exeter: Fortress and Town* (Exeter: Exeter Museums Service, 1980), 86.

63. Wacher, *Towns of Roman Britain,* 334.

64. Holbrook and Bidwell, *Exeter Archaeological Reports,* 4:13.

65. Bidwell, *Roman Exeter,* 86.

66. Ibid.; Esmonde Cleary, *Ending,* 152.

67. Bidwell, *Roman Exeter,* 86.

68. Ibid., 87. See also Dixon, "'The Cities Are Not Populated As Once They Were,'" esp. 147.

69. Susan Pearce, *The Kingdom of Dumnonia* (Padstow, Cornwall: Lodenek Press, 1978), 43: "The post-400 graveyard [at Exeter] testifies to the existence of a continuing community."

70. Wacher, *Towns of Roman Britain,* 334–35.

71. Ibid., 335; Johnson, *Later Roman Britain,* 201–2.

72. Willibald, *Life of Saint Boniface;* William of Malmesbury, *Chronicle of the Kings of England,* trans. J. A. Giles (London: Henry G. Bohn, 1847), chap. 6: "This city [Aethelstan], which had cleansed by purging it of its contaminated race." See also Wacher, *Towns of Roman Britain,* 335: "Certainly Britons continued to live peacefully in Exeter with Saxons until the early ninth century, when [the Britons] were expelled from the town."

73. Giles Clarke, *The Roman Cemetery at Lankhills,* Winchester Studies, no. 3: Pre-Roman and Roman Winchester, pt. 2 (Oxford: Clarendon Press, 1979), 5, 105–7, 238. The graves contained one coin of Valentinian I (364–75), one bronze coin from the house of Theodosius (c. 388–402), and two or three sherds of coarse pottery dated to the end of the fourth century.

74. J. L. MacDonald, "Features 24, 25, and 26," in Clarke, *Roman Cemetery,* 107.

75. Martin Biddle, "The Study of Winchester: Archaeology and History in a British Town," *Proceedings of the British Academy* 69 (1983): 93–135, esp. 111–13.

76. Wacher, *Towns of Roman Britain,* 288.

77. Esmonde Cleary, *Ending,* 132.

78. Wacher, *Towns of Roman Britain,* 388.

79. Ibid., 189; Esmonde Cleary, *Ending,* 145–46. Though there is evidence of gate blocking in other towns, such as Colchester and Lincoln, it is not clear from the evidence whether this is in response to an external threat or the internal breakdown of security.

80. Richard M. Reece, "Numerical Aspects of Roman Coin Hoards in Britain," in Casey and Reece, eds., *Coins and the Archaeologist,* 92; Jeremy K. Knight and Alan Lane, "Caerwent," in *Early Medieval Settlements,* ed. Edwards and Lane, 35–38.

81. Wacher, *Towns of Roman Britain,* 389.

82. Ibid.; Laing and Laing, *Celtic Britain and Ireland,* 108; Wendy Davies, *Wales in the Early Middle Ages* (Leicester: Leicester University Press, 1982), 24–25, 57.

83. Laing and Laing, *Celtic Britain and Ireland,* 108.

84. Wendy Davies, "Roman Settlements and Post-Roman Estates in South-East Wales," in *End of Roman Britain,* ed. Casey, 153–73, esp. 154; Heather James, "Early Medieval Cemeteries in Wales," in *Early Church in Wales,* ed. Edwards and Lane, 90–103, esp. 96 and 103.

85. Knight and Lane, "Caerwent," 37. Needless to say, this would have far-reaching implications for the traditional identification of Roman and sub-Roman sites in Britain.

86. John S. Wacher, "Late Roman Developments," in *Studies in the Archaeology and History of Cirencester,* BAR, no. 30, ed. Alan McWhirr (Oxford: Tempvs Reparatvm, 1976), 15–18; Richard M. Reece and Christopher Catling, *Cirencester: The Development and Buildings of a Cotswold Town,* BAR, no. 12 (Oxford: Tempvs Reparatvm, 1975), 9.

87. Wacher, "Late Roman Developments," 15. Within the mortar of the masonry was embed-

ded a piece of color-coated pottery of the late fourth century.

88. Ibid., 16. The Laings (*Celtic Britain and Ireland,* 76) point out that one of these bodies was found associated with medieval pottery.

89. Wacher, "Late Roman Developments," 17 n. 11. Wacher quotes a personal communication with "Dr. Richard Reece," but does not describe the coins.

90. Ibid., 17.

91. Alan McWhirr et al., eds., *Cirencester Excavations II: Romano-British Cemeteries at Cirencester* (Cirencester: Excavations Committee, 1982), 27.

92. Reece and Catling, *Cirencester,* 9.

93. H. R. Hurst, *Gloucester: The Roman and Later Defenses* (Gloucester: Archaeological Publications, 1986), 123–24.

94. H. R. Hurst, "Excavations, 1968–71," *Antiquaries Journal* 52 (1972): 24–69, esp. 58; C. M. Heighway et al., "Excavations at 1 Westgate Street, Gloucester," *Medieval Archaeology* 23 (1979): 159–213, esp. 159.

95. Heighway et al., "Excavations at 1 Westgate Street," 165.

96. Ibid., 163.

97. Laing and Laing, *Celtic Britain and Ireland,* 76.

98. Ibid.; H. R. Hurst, "Excavations at Gloucester, 1971–3, Second Interim Report, Part II," *Antiquaries Journal* 54 (1974): 8–52, esp. 23. *Fel. Temp. Reparatio* coins were introduced in 348. Imitations, which occur predominantly in Britain, belong to the third quarter of the fourth century. See Grierson and Mays, *Catalogue of Late Roman Coins,* 71, and R. J. Brickstock, *Copies of the Fel. Temp. Reparatio Coinage in Britain,* BAR Series, no. 176 (Oxford: Tempvs Reparatvm, 1987), 112–17.

99. Jones, *Society and Settlement in Wales,* 1:66.

100. The Romano-British pottery at Gloucester was not locally made—the shell-tempered ware came from the Midlands, the Oxfordshire ware from the upper Thames valley—which supports the view that Gloucester's forum remained an active marketplace in the sub-Roman period. See Heighway et al., "Excavations at 1 Westgate Street," 171.

101. H. R. Hurst, "Excavations at Gloucester, Third Interim Report: Kingsholm, 1965–75," *Antiquaries Journal* 55 (1975): 267–94.

102. R. Bryant, "Excavations at the Church of St. Mary de Lode, Gloucester," *Bulletin of the CBA Churches Committee* 13 (1980): 15–18; Carolyn Heighway, *Anglo-Saxon Gloucestershire* (Gloucester: Sutton, 1987), 10–11; Richard Morris, *The Church in British Archaeology,* CBA Report, no. 47 (London: CBA, 1983), 26; idem, *Churches in the Landscape,* (London: Dent, 1989), 35.

103. See Bassett, "Churches in Worcester," 243.

104. See Wacher, *Towns of Roman Britain,* 256–60.

105. Michael G. Fulford, "Silchester," *Current Archaeology* 82 (1982): 326–31, esp. 328.

106. George C. Boon, *Silchester: The Roman Town of Calleva* (London: David & Charles, 1974), 72.

107. Ibid.; Michael G. Fulford, *The Silchester Amphitheatre: Excavations of 1979–85,* Britannia Monograph Series, no. 10 (London: Society for the Promotion of Roman Studies, 1989).

108. Boon, *Silchester,* 73; Michael G. Fulford, *Silchester Defenses, 1974–80,* Britannia Monograph Series, no. 5 (London: Society for the Promotion of Roman Studies, 1984), 237.

109. George C. Boon, "The Latest Objects from Silchester, Hampshire," *Medieval Archaeology* 3 (1959): 79–88.

110. Boon, *Silchester,* 77–78. It is perhaps significant that this inscription is not accompanied by Latin text, as are most Christian Ogam inscriptions. For the debate over the authenticity of this inscription, see Michael G. Fulford and Bruce Sellwood, "The Silchester Ogham Stone: A Reconsideration," *Antiquity* 54 (1980): 95–99; George C. Boon, "The Silchester Ogham,"

Antiquity 54 (1980): 122–23; and Dark, *Civitas,* 150.

111. Boon, *Silchester,* 77–78; idem, *The Roman Town "Calleva Atrebatum" at Silchester, Hampshire* (Reading: Calleva Museum, 1983), 8.

112. Boon, *Silchester,* 77; Laing and Laing, *Celtic Britain and Ireland,* 75.

113. See Boon, *Silchester,* 78–80; Laing and Laing, *Celtic Britain and Ireland,* 75; Wacher, *Towns of Roman Britain,* 276 and 419; Esmonde Cleary, *Ending,* 198; and Dark, *Civitas,* 101, 150–51. However, as Dark has pointed out (*Civitas,* 151), the Silchester dikes have not yet been securely dated.

114. Boon, *Roman Town,* 8.

115. Graham Webster, "A Roman System of Fortified Posts Along Watling Street, Britain," in *Roman Frontier Studies, 1967,* ed. Shimon Applebaum (Tel Aviv: University of Tel Aviv Press, 1971), 38–45. See also Burnham and Wacher, *"Small Towns" of Roman Britain,* 276.

116. Graham Webster, *Wall Roman Site* (London: English Heritage, 1985), 8; Burnham and Wacher, *"Small Towns" of Roman Britain,* 278.

117. *Historia Britonum,* 66a.

118. Webster, *Wall,* 9. The Laings (*Celtic Britain and Ireland,* 79), stating that Wall is the only (Roman?) town in the list that was not a cantonal capital, assume Nennius must have had special knowledge to prompt him to include it.

119. Webster, *Wall,* 9–10: "Here may be preserved in poetic form the memory of a clash between the Celtic pagan west and the remnants of the Romano-British Christian community in that twilight period in the fifth and sixth centuries before the advent of the Saxon settlers." The attackers need not, however, have been pagan.

120. See Basset, "Church and Diocese," 13–40, and Jenny Rowland, *Early Welsh Saga Poetry: A Study and Edition of the Englynion* (Cambridge: D. S. Brewer, 1990).

121. *EH,* 4.3. Basset ("Church and Diocese," 34–35) has shown that there was a British see (and possibly a monastery) at sub-Roman Wall, which was succeeded by St. Michael's Church in the adjacent settlement of Lichfield. This could explain Eddius Stephanus's statement (Eddius, *Life of Wilfrid,* chap. 15) that Lichfield was "a suitable place" to establish the see of the Mercians in 669. The see was given to the Irish-schooled Chad, who was consecrated (first) by schismatic *British* bishops (and thus a good choice for an area still heavily populated by Britons).

122. Bassett, "Churches in Worcester," 243.

123. Wacher, *Towns of Roman Britain,* 373. Wacher points out that finds of lead-weighted javelins (*martiobarbuli*) indicate that "the regular army were passing through Wroxeter in the very late fourth or early fifth century."

124. Ibid.; Roger White, "Excavations on the Site of the Baths Basilica," in *From Roman "Viroconium" to Medieval Wroxeter,* ed. Philip Barker (Worcester: West Mercian Archaeological Consultants, 1990), 5.

125. Laing and Laing, *Celtic Britain and Ireland,* 79.

126. Roger White, "Excavations," 6.

127. Ibid. White suggests 420–50, though he takes for granted the collapse of Britain's money economy at this time.

128. Ibid.

129. Philip Barker, ed., *Wroxeter Roman City Excavations, 1960–80,* 18.

130. Michael Wood, *In Search of the Dark Ages* (New York: Facts on File, 1987), 47.

131. Roger White, "Excavations," 7. Cf. Esmonde Cleary, *Ending,* 153: "The main phase of timber buildings is interpreted by the excavator as the residence and compound of a fifth-century notable."

132. Webster, *Cornovii,* 117. This model, however, does not explain the relationship between the "villa" and the rest of the city, which seems to have shared in the renewed prosperity. Mike Corbishley (*Town Life in Roman Britain* [London: Harrap, 1981], 47) notes the sig-

nificance of the rebuilding of both public and private buildings in fifth-century Wroxeter.

133. Dixon, "'The Cities Are Not Populated As Once They Were,'" 147.

134. Roger White, "Excavations," 7. See also Dixon, "'The Cities Are Not Populated As Once They Were,'" 147.

135. Esmonde Cleary, *Ending*, 152.

136. White ("Excavations," 7) states that "there is no evidence for a sack of the town by Anglo-Saxons, who moved into this area in the later 6th or early 7th century." Julie Crickmore (*Romano-British Urban Settlements in the West Midlands*, BAR British Series, no. 127 [Oxford: Tempvs Reparatvm, 1984], 96) believes that the organized construction and abandonment at Wroxeter "suggest . . . some form of controlling authority."

137. Thomas, *Provisional List*, 16.

138. Graham Webster and Philip Barker, *Wroxeter Roman City* (London: English Heritage, 1991), 28. The full Latin inscription reads CUNORIX MAQUS MAQUI COLONI, "Hound King, son of the Son of the Holly."

139. E.g., Webster, *Cornovii*, 114, and Wacher, *Towns of Roman Britain*, 374.

140. Gelling, *West Midlands in the Early Middle Ages*, 26–27

141. See Dark, *Civitas*, p. 79 and n. 43; and Barker, ed., *Wroxeter Roman City*, 18.

142. Wacher, *Towns of Roman Britain*, 136–37.

143. Todd, *The Coritani* (Gloucester: Sutton, 1991), 140; Laing and Laing, *Celtic Britain and Ireland*, 76–77; Pauline Stafford, *The East Midlands in the Early Middle Ages* (Leicester: Leicester University Press, 1985), 87. Caedbaed (*Catuboduos*) appears in a genealogy of Aldfrith, an eighth-century English king of Lindsey.

144. *EH*, 2.16. Wacher, *Towns of Roman Britain*, 137: "We might wonder if the colonial territorium became one of the protected reserves which seem to have occurred in parts of Britain during the earliest part of the Anglo-Saxon period, when an equilibrium was reached between the Romano-British inhabitants of the area and the incoming settlers." Cf. Stafford, *East Midlands*, 87.

145. Laing and Laing, *Celtic Britain and Ireland*, 76–77; Thomas, *Provisional List*, 14.

146. B. Gilmour, "The Anglo-Saxon Church at St. Paul-in-the-Bail, Lincoln," *Medieval Archaeology* 23 (1979): 214–18.

147. Esmonde Cleary, *Ending*, 152; Todd, *Coritani*, 140. Stafford (*East Midlands*, 87) suggests that this sub-Roman Christian community buried their dead on the site of a then-ruined fourth-century church.

148. Margaret L. Faull, "Settlement and Society in North-East England in the Fifth Century," in *Settlement and Society in the Roman North*, ed. P. R. Wilson et al. (Bradford, West Yorkshire: Yorkshire Archaeological Society, 1984), 49–52.

149. Derek A. Welsby, *The Roman Military Defense of the British Provinces in Its Later Phases*, BAR British Series, no. 101 (Oxford: Tempvs Reparatvm, 1982), 131.

150. Patrick Ottaway, *Archaeology in British Towns: From Emperor Claudius to the Black Death* (London: Routledge, 1992), 97.

151. Wacher, *Towns of Roman Britain*, 176; Laing and Laing, *Celtic Britain and Ireland*, 72.

152. James Campbell, "The Lost Centuries," in *Anglo-Saxons*, ed. Campbell, 39.

153. *EH*, 1.29.

154. Ibid., 2.9ff. Cf. *Anglo-Saxon Chronicle* (The Laud Chronicle), *sub anno* 626.

155. Dark, "Sub-Roman Re-Defense," 112–13.

156. M. R. McCarthy, *A Roman, Anglian, and Medieval Site at Blackfriars Street* (Kendal, Cumbria: Cumberland and Westmorland Antiquarian and Archaeological Society, 1990), 45, 103, 369–72. These reconstructions are associated with thirty-eight coins dating after 364 and ending with a coin of Arcadius.

157. Burnham and Wacher, *"Small Towns" of Roman Britain*, 58.

158. G. D. Keevill et al., "A Solidus of Valentinian II from Scotch Street, Carlisle," *Britannia*

20 (1989): 254–55. Two coins dating 341–46 and 364–75 were hidden between the floor slabs of the townhouse.

159. A *solidus* of Valentinian II was found in the mud infill of the partly waterlogged cellar of the townhouse. The *solidus* (*RIC*, 9.90a) bears the obverse legend D N VALENTINIANVS P F AVG, and was minted between 388 and 392. See Keevill et al., "Solidus of Valentinian II," 254: "The *solidus* suggests that the hypocaust fell from use at the end of the fourth or early fifth century. The room continued in use for a layer of *opus signium* 0.1 m thick sealed the slab floor with a further two floor levels above. There are, therefore, strong grounds for believing that this building continued well into the fifth century." Cf. M. R. McCarthy et al., "Carlisle," *Current Archaeology* 116 (1989): 300: "This high-status building clearly continued in use for some considerable time into the fifth century."

160. Nicholas J. Higham and Barri Jones, *The Carvetii* (Gloucester: Sutton, 1985), 133; Higham, *Northern Counties,* 263.

161. See the discussion in Chapter 13.

162. The Wroxeter excavations have shown to many archaeologists that the classical methods of excavating Roman towns may be overlooking—indeed destroying—evidence of timber and earth structures perhaps more typical (but not always more crude than their masonry counterparts) of fourth- and fifth-century towns.

163. Gildas (*De excidio,* 10.2) says that the British martyrs Aaron and Julius were "citizens of Caerleon" (*Legionum urbis cives*).

164. D. R. Evans and V. M. Metcalf, *Roman Gates, Caerleon,* Oxbow Monograph, no. 15 (Oxford: Oxbow, 1992), 75: "The buildings have a *terminus post quem* of c. A.D. 354, but a far later date is almost certain."

165. Ibid., 56.

166. Ibid., 75; Alan Lane, "Caerleon," in *Early Medieval Settlements,* ed. Edwards and Lane, 34.

167. Evans and Metcalf, *Roman Gates,* 75.

168. See Davies, *Wales,* 14.

169. J. C. McPeake, "The End of the Affair," in *New Evidence for Roman Chester,* ed. T. J. Strickland and P. J. Davey (Liverpool: Liverpool University Press, 1978), 43; Lloyd Laing and Jennifer Laing, *The Dark Ages of West Cheshire,* Council Monograph Series, no. 6 (Chester: City Council, 1986), 42; Esmonde Cleary, *Ending,* 57.

170. T. J. Strickland, "Chester," *Current Archaeology* 84 (1982): 6–12, esp. 6.

171. Ibid., 6.

172. McPeake, "End of the Affair," 41.

173. Ibid., 43; Nicholas J. Higham, *The Origins of Cheshire* (New York: Manchester University Press, 1993), 65.

174. Thomas, "Provisional List," 25. These pottery finds occurred too late for inclusion in Thomas's list, though he does reproduce the excavators' description and identification of the sherds.

175. Higham, *Origins,* 66.

176. Laing and Laing, *West Cheshire,* 42.

177. Simon Ward, *Excavations at Chester: Roman Headquarters Building to Medieval Row* (Chester: City Council, 1988), 26.

178. *EH,* 2.2.

179. Ibid. This is corroborated by the *Annales Cambriae,* 613. The Laings see Bede's use of *civitas* as implying a thriving settlement. Cf. Higham, *Origins,* 85.

180. *Historia Britonum,* 56. See also Rivet and Smith, *Place-Names of Roman Britain,* 337.

181. Laing and Laing, *West Cheshire,* 27.

182. The Wall also served as a delineation between barbarian and Roman in the process of Romanization in Britain; see Michael E. Jones, "Geographical-Psychological Frontiers in Sub-

Roman Britain," in *Shifting Frontiers in Late Antiquity,* ed. Ralph W. Mathisen and Hagith S. Sivan (Aldershot: Variorum, 1996), 45–58.

183. Breeze and Dobson, *Hadrian's Wall,* 232: "It is certainly clear that the Wall was not abandoned as a result of these troop withdrawals."

184. *RIB,* no. 2331. See also Dark, "Sub-Roman Re-Defense," p. 112 and n. 10.

185. Andrew Selkirk and Tony Wilmott, "Birdoswald: Dark-Age Halls in a Roman Fort," *Current Archaeology* 116 (1989): 288–91; Dark, "Sub-Roman Re-Defense," 112, 119–20; Laing and Laing, *Celtic Britain and Ireland,* 119.

186. Selkirk and Wilmott, "Birdoswald," 290.

187. Ibid., 291.

188. Sheppard Frere et al., "Roman Britain in 1987," *Britannia* 19 (1988): 416–84, esp. 436–37; Dark, "Sub-Roman Re-Defense," 111–12, 119–20.

189. *CIIC,* 1.428. See Breeze and Dobson, *Hadrian's Wall,* 233, and A. R. Burn, *The Romans in Britain: An Anthology of Inscriptions* (Columbia: University of South Carolina Press, 1969), 177.

190. J. G. Crow, *Housesteads Roman Fort* (London: English Heritage, 1989), 49; Dark, "Sub-Roman Re-Defense," 119–20.

191. Crow, *Housesteads Roman Fort,* 49–50.

192. Dark, "Sub-Roman Re-Defense," 112, 119.

193. See Keevill et al., "Solidus of Valentinian II," 255. This hoard contained 4 coins of Valentinian I, 2 of Valens, 16 of Gratian, 8 of Valentinian II, 5 of Theodosius I, and 13 of Magnus Maximus.

194. J. N. Dore, *Corbridge Roman Site* (London: English Heritage, 1989), 27; Breeze and Dobson, *Hadrian's Wall,* 233.

195. Dark, "Sub-Roman Re-Defense," 113, 115, 120.

196. Ibid., 119.

197. Paul T. Bidwell and Stephen Speak, "South Shields," *Current Archaeology* 116 (1989): 283–87.

198. *RIC,* 9.2b (London mint). See Keevill et al., "Solidus of Valentinian II," 255.

199. Dark, "Sub-Roman Re-Defense," 112, 119.

200. Ibid.; Stephen Johnson, *Hadrian's Wall* (London: Batsford/English Heritage, 1989), 115; Breeze and Dobson, *Hadrian's Wall,* 231.

201. Dark, "Sub-Roman Re-Defense," 112, 119; Breeze and Dobson, *Hadrian's Wall,* 233.

202. Pollen analyses have also shown that rapid reforestation (a sign of radical change in land use) did not occur along the Wall in the fifth century; see Judith Turner, "Some Pollen Evidence for the Environment of North Britain: 1000 B.C. to A.D. 1000," in *Settlement in North Britain: 100 b.c. to a.d. 1000,* ed. J. Chapman and H. Mytum, BAR British Series 118 (Oxford: Tempvs Reparatvm, 1983), 3–27, and Jones, "Geographical-Psychological Frontiers," 50–51.

203. Breeze and Dobson, *Hadrian's Wall,* 234.

204. Jones, "Geographical-Psychological Frontiers," 48.

205. Robin Birley, *Civilians on the Roman Frontier* (Newcastle: Graham, 1973), 60.

206. Dark, "Sub-Roman Re-Defense," 115, 118.

207. Ibid., 115.

208. See Jones, "Geographical-Psychological Frontiers," 50–55, who develops five such plausible scenarios for the fate of the Wall troops.

209. Procopius, *Wars,* 8.20.42–46. See the discussion in Jones, "Geographical-Psychological Frontiers," 54–55.

210. Julian Munby, "Portchester," in *Saxon Shore,* ed. Maxfield, 160–62; Barry Cunliffe, *Excavations at Portchester Castle,* vol. 2, *Saxon,* Society of Antiquaries Research Report, no. 33 (London: Society of Antiquaries, 1976), 301.

211. See Munby, "Portchester," 162: "It is difficult to say whether a civilian population took

over an abandoned fort, or whether a military militia together with their families formed a continuing military garrison. Certainly the fort was occupied up to the end of Roman Britain and [possibly] beyond."

212. Barry Cunliffe, *The Regni* (London: Duckworth, 1973), 132.

213. Ibid.; Cunliffe, *Excavations at Portchester,* 2:301.

214. T.F.C Blagg, "Richborough," in *Saxon Shore,* ed. Maxfield, 140–45; Welsby, *Roman Military,* 131; Grierson and Mays, *Catalogue of Late Roman Coins,* 26. Sixty thousand Roman coins were recorded from the 1922–38 excavations, the majority of which were bronze.

215. Blagg, "Richborough," 145.

216. Brian Philp, *The Excavations of the Roman Forts of the Classis Britannica at Dover, 1970–1977,* Kent Monograph Series 3 (Dover, 1981); Stephen Johnson, "Dover," in *Saxon Shore,* ed. Maxfield, 145–50.

217. P. J. Casey ("The End of Fort Garrisons on Hadrian's Wall: A Hypothetical Model," in *L'armée romaine et les barbares du IIIe au VIIe siécle,* ed. Françoise Vallet and Michel Kazanski [Rouen: Musée des Antiquités Nationales, 1994], 264–66) surveys the evidence of violent destruction at the Goldsborough, Huntcliff, and Filey signal stations and attributes it to seaborne Pictish raids.

218. Richard B. White, "Excavations at Aberffraw, Anglesey, 1973 and 1974," *BBCS* 28 (1979): 319–42, esp. 341.

219. Nancy Edwards, "Aberffraw," in *Early Medieval Settlements,* ed. Edwards and Lane, 18–21. See also Laing and Laing, *Celtic Britain and Ireland,* 108, and Davies, *Wales,* 24.

220. *ECMW,* no. 27. Found at nearby Llangeinwen (five miles from Aberffraw), the side plates of the lead coffin bear the inscriptions CAMVLORIS H (ic?) O (ssa?) I (acent?), "Here lie the bones of Camulorix," and CAMVLORIS, "Camulorix." Nash-Williams states that such coffins are common among Christian inhumations in Britain and Gaul from the fourth century onward, and dates this specimen to the fifth century. "Camulorix" seems to have been a popular name in sub-Roman Wales; cf. *ECMW,* nos. 349 and 403.

221. Esmonde Cleary, *Ending,* 54; Welsby, *Roman Military,* 128. According to Boon ("Theodosian Coins," 429 n. 4), the clipped *siliqua* found at Caernarvon most likely belongs to Theodosius. Cf. J. L. Davies, "Segontium, Caernarfon," in *Early Medieval Settlements,* ed. Edwards and Lane, 115–16: "The practice of clipping *siliquae,* although confined to Britain, is more likely to be attributed to the decade 410–20 than in a post 430 era (pers. comm. Dr. J.P.C. Kent)."

222. Lloyd Laing, "Segontium and the Roman Occupation of Wales," in *Studies in Celtic Survival,* BAR, no. 37, ed. Lloyd Laing (Oxford: Tempvs Reparatvm, 1977), 57–60.

223. Ibid., 57–59; Davies, *Wales,* 24, 82.

224. I. M. Ferris and R. F. Jones, "Excavations at Binchester, 1976–9," in *Roman Frontier Studies, 1979,* ed. Hanson and Keppie, 233–54; Esmonde Cleary, *Ending,* 143.

225. Welsby (*Roman Military,* 131) postulates sub-Roman activity here.

226. Dark, "Sub-Roman Re-Defense," 112, 119–20.

227. Burnham and Wacher, *"Small Towns" of Roman Britain,* 116–17.

228. Ibid.; B. R. Hartley and R. Leon Fitts, *The Brigantes* (Gloucester: Sutton, 1988), 115.

229. Burnham and Wacher, *"Small Towns" of Roman Britain,* 117.

230. Higham, *Northern Counties,* 263, 273.

231. Leslie Alcock, "Gwyr y Gogledd: An Archaeological Appraisal," *Archaeologia Cambrensis* 132 (1983): 15–17; idem, *Economy,* 250–54.

232. T. W. Potter, *Romans in North-West England* (Kendal, Cumbria: T. Wilson, 1979), 45.

233. Ibid., 366.

234. Higham and Jones, *Carvetii,* 128.

235. C. A. Ralegh Radford, "Glastonbury Abbey," in *The Quest for Arthur's Britain,* ed. Geoffrey Ashe (New York: Paladin, 1971), 104–7. Radford was also led to this conclusion

by the existence, in the twelfth century, of the shrines of saints Indracht and Patrick near the abbey's old church: "St. Indracht and St. Patrick are Celtic saints, and it is difficult to believe that their cult was introduced at Glastonbury after the Saxon conquest of Somerset in the middle of the seventh century."

236. P. Ellis, "Excavations at Silver Street, Glastonbury, 1978," *PSANHS* 126 (1982): 17–31.

237. See Philip Rahtz, "Pagan and Christian by the Severn Sea," in *The Archaeology and History of Glastonbury Abbey: Essays in Honor of the Ninetieth Birthday of C. A. Ralegh Radford*, ed. Leslie Abrams and James P. Carley (Woodbridge, Suffolk: Boydell, 1991), 33; and Dark, *Discovery by Design*, 46.

238. Philip Rahtz, "Glastonbury Tor," in *Quest for Arthur's Britain*, ed. Ashe, 115.

239. Twenty miles away, at Pagans Hill, there is a late Roman temple comparable to those identified at Maiden Castle and Lydney.

240. Rahtz, "Glastonbury Tor," 120.

241. Ibid., 120–21.

242. E.g., Alcock, *Economy*, 190, and Dark, *Discovery by Design*, 46.

243. Rahtz, "Pagan and Christian," 32–33.

244. Dark (*Discovery by Design*, 46), sees the tor as "an island hermitage."

245. William of Malmesbury, in the twelfth century, described Glastonbury Abbey as the oldest church in all of England. In William's day, the Glastonbury monks claimed that the old church was built by missionaries from Gaul in the second century. William also writes that the Irish tradition at Glastonbury was very strong. Several shrines in the abbey contained the relics of Irish saints, including Patrick, who by tradition established a rule for the community about 460. The chapel at nearby Beckery (Bec Eriu) had an early cult of Saint Brigid, and claimed to possess this Irish saint's relics. The name Bec Eriu, "Little Ireland," makes the Irish connection explicit. Plausibly, Irish monastics could have frequented Glastonbury in the sixth century, before the arrival of the West Saxons.

246. Alcock, *Economy*, 172–73.

247. Ian C. G. Burrow, *Hillfort and Hill-Top Settlement in Somerset in the First to Eighth Centuries a.d.*, BAR British Series, no. 91 (Oxford: Tempvs Reparatvm, 1981), 157. Burrow based this estimate on the *Burghal Hidage* evidence of four men to every 5_ yards of rampart.

248. Alcock, *Economy*, 186.

249. Ibid., 190; Leslie Alcock, et al., *Cadbury Castle, Somerset: The Early Medieval Archaeology* (Cardiff: University of Wales Press, 1995), 118. While over 160 sherds of imported pottery have been found, no locally made pottery has been recognized.

250. Alcock, *Economy*, 182.

251. See Brian Hope-Taylor, *Yeavering: An Anglo-British Centre of Early Northumbria* (London: HMSO, 1977); idem, "Balbridie . . . and Doon Hill," *Current Archaeology* 72 (1980): 18–19; and Nicholas Reynolds, "Dark Age Timber Halls and the Background to Excavation at Balbridie," *Scottish Archaeological Forum* 10 (1980): 41–60.

252. Alcock, *Economy*, 206–7.

253. Ibid., 207.

254. Ibid., 200–201.

255. Ibid., 182.

256. Ibid., 193, 196. Nailed timber ramparts—*murrus gallicus*—are most common in Iron Age western Europe, and were also used in the Pictish forts of Burghead and Dundurn.

257. Ibid., 182–83.

258. Ibid., 197.

259. Philip Rahtz et al., *Cadbury Congresbury, 1968–73: A Late/Post-Roman Hilltop Settlement in Somerset*, BAR British Series, no. 223 (Oxford: Tempvs Reparatvm, 1992), 2.

260. Ibid.; Laing and Laing, *Celtic Britain and Ireland*, 106; Alcock, *Economy*, 165: "Congresbury shows no signs of a hiatus, and the Roman pottery continued in use alongside

the [Mediterranean] imports" of the fifth and sixth centuries.

261. Rahtz et al., *Cadbury Congresbury,* 231.

262. Burrow, *Hillfort,* 157.

263. Rahtz et al., *Cadbury Congresbury,* 233. Dark (*Discovery by Design,* 52) does not believe that the round house was a pagan shrine.

264. Alcock, *Economy,* 160; Fulford, "Byzantium and Britain," 1–5. Cadbury-Congresbury is second only to Tintagel in imported wares.

265. Rahtz et al., *Cadbury Congresbury,* 2.

266. Ibid., 249.

267. Ibid., 250.

268. Alcock, *Economy,* 183. *Congar's burgh* becomes *Congresbury.*

269. Rahtz et al., *Cadbury Congresbury,* 250.

270. Fowler in ibid., 249.

271. Alcock, *Economy,* 212.

272. Rahtz et al., *Cadbury Congresbury,* 251.

273. Ibid., 2 and 251. "It cannot be claimed that it was declining fortunes in the west which ceased to attract distant traders and led to an end to the importation of pottery, glass and other goods; the causes are more likely to lie in the changing fortunes of the Mediterranean" (251).

274. These are recorded by Burrow, *Hillfort,* 268–77. The coins, however, are not cataloged.

275. Ibid., 268. See also R. H. Leech, "Romano-British Rural Settlement in South Somerset and North Dorset" (Ph.D. thesis, University of Bristol, 1977), 119–21.

276. S.H.M. Pollard, "Neolithic and Dark Age Settlements on High Peak, Sidmouth, Devon," *Proceedings of the Devonshire Archaeological Society* 23 (1966): 35–59, esp. 42.

277. Ibid., 35.

278. Ibid., 57. See also Dark, *Discovery by Design,* 87.

279. Ian C. G. Burrow, "Tintagel: Some Problems," *Scottish Archaeological Forum* 5 (1973): 99–103; Thomas, *Celtic Britain,* 73; Kenneth Rainsbury Dark, "The Plan and Interpretation of Tintagel," *CMCS* 9 (1985): 1–17.

280. See Kenneth Rainsbury Dark, review of *Tintagel: Arthur and Archaeology,* by Charles Thomas, *CMCS* 28 (1994): 103–4.

281. Thomas, *Celtic Britain,* 71; O. J. Padel, "Tintagel: An Alternative View," in *Provisional List,* ed. Thomas, 28–29.

282. Thomas, *Celtic Britain,* 75; Rivet and Smith, *Place-Names of Roman Britain,* 350.

283. Charles Thomas, *Tintagel: Arthur and Archaeology* (London: Batsford/English Heritage, 1993), 13 and 84. Ten bronze coins, ranging from Tetricus I to Constantine II, were found in a drawstring leather purse. The pottery, dating to the fourth century, consisted of sherds of Oxford red color-coated ware as well as sherds from locally made jars and bowls.

284. Thomas, *Celtic Britain,* 75–76.

285. See Dark, *Discovery by Design,* 80–86. Dark theorizes that the Mediterranean imports may have passed through Frankish middlemen on the way to Tintagel.

286. Malcolm Todd, *The South West to a.d. 1000* (London: Longman, 1987), 163; Thomas, *Tintagel,* 71. Indeed, the number of finds from Tintagel is greater than the total of all the sherds of "Tintagel ware" found at all sites in Britain and Ireland combined.

287. Thomas, *Tintagel,* 94–95. Cornwall was a major supplier of tin for the Roman Empire. That it remained a sought-after commodity in the post-Roman world is affirmed by the account, in the sixth-century *Life of St. John the Almsgiver,* of the Byzantine ship returning from Britain loaded with tin. Cf. Penhallurick, *Tin in Antiquity,* 245.

288. Charles Thomas, ed., *Tintagel Papers,* Cornish Studies 16 (Redruth: Institute of Cornish Studies, 1988), 46, 54.

289. Ibid., 19; C. D. Morris, Jacqueline A. Nowakowski, and Charles Thomas, "Tintagel,

Cornwall: The 1990 Excavations," *Antiquity* 64 (1990): 843–49. One of the clay hearths yielded an archaeomagnetic date of A.D. 450–500 (at a 68 percent confidence level).

290. See Thomas, *Tintagel*.

291. Ibid., 85–86. Dark (review of *Tintagel*, 104) dismisses this evidence for seasonal habitation.

292. Thomas, *Tintagel*, 87. Cf. Dark, *Civitas*, 91–94.

293. See Thomas, *Tintagel*, 88, and Thomas Charles-Edwards, "Early Medieval Kingships in the British Isles," in *The Origin of Anglo-Saxon Kingdoms*, ed. Steven Bassett (Leicester: Leicester University Press, 1989), 28ff.

294. Jaqueline A. Nowakowski and Charles Thomas, *Excavations at Tintagel Parish Churchyard: Interim Report, Spring 1990* (Truro: Institute of Cornish Studies, 1990), 2; Thomas, *Tintagel*, 103. Pottery finds include sherds of Bi, Bii, Biv, and Bv amphoras.

295. Thomas, *Tintagel*, 103. If one adds a century to this date, to allow for the tree to mature (that from which the firewood was taken), this gives a date of c. 503 for the fire.

296. Ibid. The "arc crosses" carved on the Tintagel tombstones may also have been a Continental borrowing.

297. Ibid., 105.

298. Nowakowski and Thomas, *Excavations at Tintagel*, 2.

299. The ceramic imports represented PRSW, Bi, Bii, Biv, Bmisc, and E ware. See Pearce, *Dumnonia*, 49; Thomas, *Provisional List*, passim; Dark, *Discovery by Design*, 86.

300. Pearce, *Dumnonia*, 49.

301. Thomas, *Tintagel*, 96. A crude stone furnace containing a block of smelted tin was found at another Cornish fortification, Chun Castle, which has also produced sherds of imported pottery.

302. Ewan Campbell, "Coygan Camp," in *Early Medieval Settlements*, ed. Edwards and Lane, 44–46.

303. Ibid., 45–46. The "counterfeiter's coin hoard" suggests the presence of a forger's workshop in the later third century. See also G. J. Wainwright, *Coygan Camp* (Cardiff: Cambrian Archaeological Association, 1967), 70–71, 157–58, and Laing and Laing, *Celtic Britain and Ireland*, 114.

304. Campbell, "Coygan Camp," 45–46. The pottery includes one sherd of Bi and five sherds of PRSW.

305. Ibid., 46.

306. Alan Lane, "Degannwy Castle," in *Early Medieval Settlements*, ed. Edwards and Lane, 50–53.

307. Ibid. 51; Laing and Laing, *Celtic Britain*, 114. The pottery was calcite-gritted material and a "Dinorben bowl."

308. Lane, "Degannwy Castle," 51, 124; Thomas, *Provisional List*, 11, 18. One sherd was Bi, the rest were Bmisc.

309. See J. L. Davies's dating schemes in Lane, "Degannwy Castle," 52.

310. Alcock (*Economy*) maintains the association, while Dumville ("Gildas and Maelgwn") believes the evidence—from the *Annales Cambriae*—is no earlier than the tenth century.

311. See, for example, Morris, *Nennius*, 47, and Lane, "Degannwy Castle," 52.

312. Ewan Campbell and J. L. Davies in Campbell, "Dinas Emrys," in *Early Medieval Settlements*, ed. Edwards and Lane, 54–57; Lloyd Laing and Jennifer Laing, "Scottish and Irish Metalwork and the *Conspiratio Barbarica*," *Proceedings of the Society of Antiquaries of Scotland* 116 (1986): 211–21, esp. 213.

313. Campbell, "Dinas Emrys," 56; Laing and Laing, *Celtic Britain*, 57–58.

314. Campbell, "Dinas Emrys," 57.

315. Alcock, *Economy*, 7.

316. Ibid., 20–22.

317. Ibid., 23 n.4.

318. Laing and Laing, *Celtic Britain and Ireland,* 55–57.

319. Dr. I. W. Cornwall analyzed 1,677 bones in the 1950s, and Roberta Gilchrist analyzed another 5,576 bones in 1987. See Alcock, *Economy,* 67–82.

320. Roberta Gilchrist, "A Re-Appraisal of Dinas Powys," *Medieval Archaeology* 32 (1988): 50–62, esp. 59.

321. Gilchrist ("Re-Appraisal," 61) questions Alcock's assumption that Dinas Powys was engaged in long-distance trade, preferring to see the princely stronghold engaged in "local exchange of animals primarily for their by-products."

322. Esmonde Cleary, *Ending,* 179.

323. Willoughby Gardner and H. N. Savory, *Dinorben: A Hillfort Occupied in Early Iron Age and Roman Times* (Cardiff: National Museum of Wales, 1964), 95–96; Dark, *Discovery by Design,* 52.

324. George C. Boon, "The Coins," in Gardner and Savory, *Dinorben,* 114–30, esp. 126.

325. Gardner and Savory, *Dinorben,* 95–96.

326. Ibid., 99 and 205.

327. Ibid., 99, 162, 188–89; Dark, *Discovery by Design,* 76.

328. Alcock, "Gwyr y Gogledd," 9; Alcock, *Economy,* 244.

329. Reynolds, "Dark Age Timber Halls."

330. Alcock, *Economy,* 244.

331. Hope-Taylor, "Balbridie . . . and Doon Hill."

332. See Alcock, *Economy,* 244f.

333. Alcock ("Activities of Potentates," 28) cites evidence that the hall (which?) at Doon Hill was destroyed by fire.

334. See Alcock, *Economy,* 162, and idem, "Activities of Potentates," 31.

335. Alcock, *Economy,* 235.

336. Ibid., 235–36.

337. Ibid., 235; Alcock, "Activities of Potentates," 28.

338. Alcock, *Economy,* fig. 16.3; Thomas, *Provisional List,* 9–11, 20. The sherds were from Bi, Bii, and E ware.

339. Alcock, *Economy,* 236.

340. Lloyd Laing, "The Mote of Mark and the Origins of Celtic Interlace," *Antiquity* 49 (1975): 98–108.

341. Radiocarbon calibrations failed to give a more precise date. See Alcock, *Economy,* 241.

342. Laing, "Mote of Mark"; Laing and Laing, *Celtic Britain and Ireland,* 58.

343. James Graham-Campbell et al., "The Mote of Mark and Celtic Interlace," *Antiquity* 50 (1976): 48–53.

344. Alcock, *Economy,* 241.

345. Laing and Laing, *Celtic Britain and Ireland,* 58–59.

346. Alcock, *Economy,* 241.

347. David Longley, "The Date of the Mote of Mark," *Antiquity* 56 (1982): 132–34.

348. Alcock, *Economy,* 241. Alcock also points out (239) the superstitious awe with which Celtic smiths and craftsmen were regarded in Irish myth, where they often possess their own defended homesteads.

349. Leslie Alcock, "The North Britons, the Picts, and the Scots," in *End of Roman Britain,* ed. Casey, 134–42, esp. 136.

350. Hope-Taylor, *Yeavering;* Alcock, "Gwyr y Gogledd," 6; idem, *Economy,* 242–43.

351. Hope-Taylor, *Yeavering,* 267.

352. Ibid., 242 and fig. 57.

353. Ibid., 271.

354. Leslie Alcock, *Bede, Eddius, and the Forts of the North Britons,* Jarrow Lecture (Jarrow:

St. Paul's Church, 1988), 7–8.

355. *Confessio,* 1. See Kenneth Rainsbury Dark, "Saint Patrick's *Uillula* and the Fifth-Century Occupation of Romano-British Villas," in Dumville et al., *Saint Patrick,* 19–24.

356. R. J. Zeepvat et al., *Roman Milton Keynes* (Aylesbury: Buckinghamshire Archaeological Society, 1987), 10.

357. P. T. Marney, *Roman and Belgic Pottery from Excavations in Milton Keynes, 1972–82* (Aylesbury: Buckinghamshire Archaeological Society, 1989), 54.

358. Heighway, *Anglo-Saxon Gloucestershire,* 3–5, 12; Dark, *Civitas,* 50.

359. Ibid., 12.

360. Alan Lane, "Glan-Y-Mor," in *Early Medieval Settlements,* ed. Edwards and Lane, 76–78.

361. Ibid., 77–78; E. Evans et al., "A Third-Century Maritime Establishment at Cold Knap, Barry, South Glamorgan," *Britannia* 16 (1985): 57–125, esp. 94 and 103.

362. Lane, "Glan-Y-Mor," 77; Evans et al., "Third-Century Maritime Establishment," 63–68, 90.

363. Lane, "Glan-Y-Mor," 77; Evans et al., "Third-Century Maritime Establishment," 122; G. Dowdell, "Glan-y-Mor, Barry," in *Glamorgan County History,* ed. H. N. Savory (Cardiff: University of Wales Press, 1988), 2:344–45.

364. Lane, "Glan-Y-Mor," 77; Evans et al., "Third-Century Maritime Establishment," 108.

365. Lane, "Glan-Y-Mor," 78.

366. H. L. Jenkins, "Ancient Camp at the Mouth of the River Avon," *Devon Cornwall Notes Queries* 2 (1902): 20–23.

367. Aileen Fox, "Some Evidence for a Dark Age Trading Site at Bantham, Near Thurlestone, South Devon," *Antiquaries Journal* 35 (1955): 55–67.

368. R. J. Silvester, "An Excavation on the Post-Roman Site at Bantham, South Devon," *Proceedings of the Devon Archaeological Society* 39 (1981): 89–118.

369. Ibid., 105–6.

370. Ibid., 103, 105.

371. Ibid., 114–16.

372. Dating by Ewan Campbell and J. L. Davies in Alan Lane, "Gateholm," in *Early Medieval Settlements,* ed. Edwards and Lane, 72–75, esp. 74.

373. Ibid., 74.

374. J. L. Davies in Ibid.

375. Ibid., 74–75: "Consequently, it would seem likely that some of the settlement, if not all of it, is of early medieval date." Cf. T. C. Lethbridge and H. E. David, "Excavation of a House-Site on Gateholm, Pembrokeshire," *Archaeologia Cambrensis* 85 (1930): 366–74, esp. 374, and J. L. Davies et al., "The Hut Settlement on Gateholm, Pembrokeshire," *Archaeologia Cambrensis* 120 (1971): 102–10, esp. 104 and 106.

376. Lane, "Gateholm," 75.

377. Richard S. Kelly, "Recent Research on the Hut Group Settlements of North-West Wales," in *Conquest, Co-Existence, and Change,* ed. Barry C. Burnham and J. L. Davies (Lampeter, Dyfed: St. David's University College, 1990), 102–11, esp. 104.

378. Ibid.; Richard S. Kelly, "Graenog," in *Early Medieval Settlements,* ed. Edwards and Lane, 79–80.

379. Ewan Campbell, "Longbury Bank," in *Early Medieval Settlements,* ed. Edwards and Lane, 88–90.

380. Ibid., 88 and app. 1. The pottery finds include one PRSW dish; one Bi, one or two Bii, one Biv, and one or two Bmisc amphoras; a mortarium and a plate of D ware; and five E ware vessels. Campbell ("Longbury Bank," 88) describes one of these glass vessels as "from a cone-beaker with opaque white marvered trails identical to a vessel from Dinas Powys." See also Ewan Campbell and Alan Lane, "Excavations at Longbury Bank, Dyfed," *Medieval Archaeology* 37 (1993): 15–77, esp. 15 and 21.

381. Campbell and Lane, "Excavations at Longbury Bank," 15 and 21.

382. Ibid.; Campbell, "Longbury Bank," 89.

383. Alcock in Campbell, "Longbury Bank," 89.

384. Campbell, "Longbury Bank," 88; H. S. Green, "Excavations at Little Hoyle (Longbury Bank), Wales, in 1984," in *Studies in the Upper Paleolithic of Britain and N.W. Europe*, BAR, no. 296, ed. D. A. Roe (Oxford: Tempvs Reparatvm, 1986), 99–119.

385. Campbell, "Longbury Bank," 89.

386. Campbell and Lane, "Excavations at Longbury Bank," 62. The authors (15) interpret Longbury as an "undefended high status secular site."

387. Dark, *Discovery by Design*, 98; Boon, "Theodosian Coins," 434–35. The hoard was discovered at Holyhead Mountain Tower. The clipped *siliqua* bears the reverse legend VIRTVS ROMANORVM, which would place it in the date range 392–408.

388. Nancy Edwards, "Ty Mawr," in *Early Medieval Settlements*, ed. Edwards and Lane, 118–20; Kelly, "Recent Research," 104. Kelly gives the range A.D. 420–710.

389. Kelly, "Recent Research," 104.

390. Ibid., 120; C. A. Smith, "Excavations at the Ty Mawr Hut-Circles, Holyhead, Anglesey: Part II," *Archaeologia Cambrensis* 134 (1985): 11–52, esp. 38.

391. Anne Crone, "Buiston Crannog," *Current Archaeology* 127 (1991): 295–97.

392. Laing and Laing, *Celtic Britain and Ireland*, 49.

393. See the discussion in Chapter 14.

394. Esmonde Cleary, *Ending*, 125.

395. Ann Woodward, *English Heritage Book of Shrines and Sacrifice* (London: Batsford/English Heritage, 1992), 88. At the Crown Buildings site, excavators found bits of clothing and a plait of red hair preserved by the plaster.

396. Martin Bell, *Brean Down Excavations, 1983–87* (London: English Heritage, 1990), 80.

397. A. M. Ap Simon, "The Roman Temple on Brean Down, Somerset," *Proceedings of the University of Bristol Spelaeological Society* 10 (1964–65): 195–258, esp. 232–33. Three coins sealed in the original floor are of Constantine II and date to c. 330–37. The latest coins from the temple area are eighteen struck between 364 and 375 and three struck between 383 and 395. One worn Theodosian coin was sealed by a fall of stones from the wall.

398. Bell, *Brean Down*, 82.

399. Esmonde Cleary, *Ending*, 184.

400. Robin Hanley, *Villages in Roman Britain* (Aylesbury: Shire Archaeology, 1987), 55: "In Somerset there appears to have been a widespread transference of village settlements back into the local iron age hillforts."

401. Laing and Laing, *Celtic Britain and Ireland*, 72.

402. Esmonde Cleary, *Ending*, 184.

403. Charles Thomas et al., "Lundy, 1969," *Current Archaeology* 16 (1969): 139; Thomas, *Provisional List*, 25.

404. Thomas et al., "Lundy, 1969," 140–42.

405. Ibid., 139.

406. See Pearce, *Dumnonia*, 66–67.

407. Charles Thomas, "Christians, Chapels, Churches, and Charters," *Landscape History* 11 (1989): 19–26, esp. 22.

408. Ibid. Thomas also records an enigmatic "architectural fragment . . . of the fifth century."

409. Ibid.

410. Peter Leach, *Shepton Mallet: Romano-Britons and Early Christians in Somerset* (Birmingham: Birmingham University Field Archaeology Unit, 19991), 19. Thanks to Deborah Crawford for sharing this report with me.

411. Ibid., 24.

412. Ibid. Leach points out that this "is one of the most positive identifications ever made in Roman Britain of a Christian burial," and suggests that the amulet may have belonged to a priest.

413. Ibid., 27.

414. See Wardwick Rodwell, *Wells Cathedral: Excavations and Discoveries* (Wells: Friends of Wells Cathedral, 1979), and Richard Morris, *The Church in British Archaeology,* CBA Report, no. 47 (London: CBA, 1983), 26–28.

415. Burnham and Wacher, *"Small Towns" of Roman Britain,* 239–40; Laing and Laing, *Celtic Britain and Ireland,* 79.

416. David M. Wilson, "An Early Christian Cemetery at Ancaster," in *Christianity in Britain,* ed. Barley and Hanson, 197–200; Laing and Laing, *Celtic Britain and Ireland,* 79.

417. Burnham and Wacher, *"Small Towns" of Roman Britain,* 240. The excavator's claim that these cremations date to "the period prior to A.D. 450" must, however, be taken with some suspicion.

418. P. J. Drury, "Chelmsford," *Current Archaeology* 41 (1974): 166–76, esp. 168.

419. Ibid.

420. Ibid., 169.

421. Ibid.; Wacher, *Towns of Roman Britain,* 200; Warwick Rodwell and Trevor Rowley, eds., *The "Small Towns" of Roman Britain,* BAR, no. 15 (Oxford: Tempvs Reparatvm, 1975), 172. Domestic activity is indicated by pits full of rubbish, a collapsed oven, fragments of a bone comb, and a polychrome bead.

422. R.E.M. Wheeler, *Maiden Castle, Dorset* (Oxford: Oxford University Press, 1943), 334–35; Sharples, *Maiden Castle,* 130. Four gold *solidi* (Theodosian) and a finger ring were found immediately outside the temple entrance, while a hoard of seventy coins (mostly Constantinian) were found in a pot on the surface of the fourth-century road south of the temple. Inside the temple, another hoard of coins (running to 367) was found sealed under the plain mosaic floor.

423. Dark, *Discovery by Design,* 51 n. 199.

424. Wheeler, *Maiden Castle,* 78.

425. Sharples, *Maiden Castle,* 130.

426. W. J. Wedlake, *The Excavation of the Shrine of Apollo at Nettleton, Wiltshire, 1956–71* (London: Society of Antiquaries, 1982), 82.

427. Ibid., 86–87.

428. Ibid., 109–10.

429. Reece, in ibid., 117: "At the end of the fourth century there are enough coins of the House of Theodosius and, more surprisingly, copies of such coins to be reasonably sure that some substantial occupation continued up to, and beyond, the year 400." Wedlake (109) is even more optimistic: "There is no apparent reason why this occupation should not have continued well beyond the date of the latest currency (A.D. 402) into the fifth and sixth centuries." See also Dark, *Discovery by Design,* 50.

430. Charles Thomas, *Exploration of a Drowned Landscape: Archaeology and History of the Isles of Scilly* (London: Batsford, 1985), 173.

431. Ibid., 187; Susan M. Pearce, *The Archaeology of South West Britain* (London: Collins, 1981), 188.

432. See Dark, *Discovery by Design,* 80.

433. Ann Ellison, *Excavations at West Hill Uley, 1977: The Romano-British Temple: Interim Report* (Bristol: Committee for Rescue Archaeology in Avon, Gloucestershire, and Somerset, 1978); idem, *Excavations at West Hill Uley, 1977–79: A Native, Roman, and Christian Ritual Complex of the First Millennium a.d.: Second Interim Report* (Bristol: Committee for Rescue Archaeology in Avon, Gloucestershire, and Somerset, 1980).

434. Ann Woodward and Peter Leach, *The Uley Shrines: Excavation of a Ritual Complex on*

West Hill, Uley, Gloucestershire, 1977–79 (London: English Heritage/British Museum, 1993), 318ff.

435. Ibid., 322.

436. Ibid., 321.

437. Ibid., 324ff.

438. Ibid., 189.

439. Ibid., 327.

440. Ibid., passim, and Ann Ellison, "Natives, Romans, and Christians on West Hill, Uley: An Interim Report on the Excavation of a Ritual Complex of the First Millennium A.D.," in *Temples, Churches, and Religion in Roman Britain,* ed. Warwick Rodwell, BAR British Series, no. 77 (Oxford: Tempvs Reparatvm, 1980), passim.

441. See Dark, *Discovery by Design,* 51.

442. Boon, *Silchester,* 72–73, 181–83. Though the basilical plan is also similar to some mystery-cult temples in Rome, the Silchester structure is different in that it contains a transept in front of the apse. Boon thus concludes (175): "This is the one particular element of the design which enables us to identify the building beyond doubt as a church."

443. Ibid., 173, 177–78; Boon, *Roman Town,* 4.

444. Blagg, "Richborough," 145.

445. Johnson, *Later Roman Britain,* 193.

446. See Philip Crummy, "A Roman Church in Colchester," *Current Archaeology* 120 (1990): 406–8.

447. Ibid., 408.

448. Martin Biddle and Birthe Kjølbye-Biddle, *The Origins of Saint Albans Abbey: Excavations in the Cloister, 1982–1983* (St. Albans, Hertfordshire: St. Albans Abbey Research Committee, 1984), 12.

449. Ibid., 13.

450. Ibid.

451. See Wacher, *Towns of Roman Britain,* 311, and Thomas, *Christianity in Roman Britain,* 133.

452. Wacher, *Towns of Roman Britain,* 311.

453. McWhirr et al., *Cirencester Excavations II,* 27; McWhirr, "Cirencester—'Corinum Dobunnorum,'" in *Roman Towns,* ed. Greep, 48. McWhirr believes that one of these cemeteries may have been in use well into the fifth or even the sixth century.

454. See Philip Barker et al., "Two Burials Under the Refectory at Worcester Cathedral," *Medieval Archaeology* 18 (1974): 146–51.

455. Bassett, "Churches in Worcester," 238–40; idem, "Church and Diocese," 24ff.

456. Thomas, *Christianity in Roman Britain,* chap. 13. This would appear even more likely if Carlisle was the capital of the late-formed province of Valentia. See also Burnham and Wacher, *"Small Towns" of Roman Britain,* 52, 58.

457. *Vita Sancti Cuthberti,* 4, written by an anonymous monk of Lindisfarne c. 700. Cf. Burnham and Wacher, *"Small Towns" of Roman Britain,* 51.

458. Burnham and Wacher, *"Small Towns" of Roman Britain,* 58.

459. G. E. Evans, "Caldey Island: Discovery of Stone-Lined Graves," *Transactions of the Carmarthenshire Antiquarian Society* 12 (1918): 43; A. L. Leach, "Ancient Graves on the Isle of Caldey," *Archaeologia Cambrensis* (1918): 174–75.

460. Ewan Campbell, "New Finds of Post-Roman Imported Pottery and Glass from South Wales," *Archaeologia Cambrensis* 138 (1989): 59–66, esp. 61.

461. Ibid., 59–60.

462. Ibid., 61.

463. Charles Thomas, "An Early Christian Cemetery and Chapel in Ardwall Isle, Kircudbright," *Medieval Archaeology* 11 (1967): 127. See also Morris, *Church in British Archaeology,* 51.

464. Thomas, "An Early Christian Cemetery," 158–62.

465. Ibid., 169, 174.

466. *EH*, 3.4. For discussion on the career of Ninian, see Thomas, *Christianity in Roman Britain*, chap. 11; MacQueen, *St. Nynia;* idem, "The Literary Sources for the Life of St. Ninian," in *Galloway: Land and Lordship*, ed. R. D. Oram and Geoffrey P. Stell (Edinburgh: School of Scottish Studies, 1991), 17–25; and Daphne Brooke, *Wild Men and Holy Places: St. Ninian, Whithorn, and the Medieval Realm of Galloway* (Edinburgh: Canongate Press, 1994).

467. The interim reports will be succeeded by Peter Hill, *Whithorn and Saint Ninian* (forthcoming).

468. Peter Hill, *Whithorn 4: Excavations, 1990–91, Interim Report* (Whithorn: Whithorn Trust, 1992), 4.

469. Ibid., 7.

470. Peter Hill, *Whithorn 2: Excavations, 1984–87, Interim Report* (Whithorn: Whithorn Trust, 1988), 5.

471. Ibid., 9. These glass fragments were from imported cone beakers.

472. Hill, *Whithorn 4*, 7.

473. Ibid., 8.

474. Higham and Jones, *Carvetii*, 130.

475. Brooke, *Wild Men*, 16.

476. Hill, *Whithorn 4*, 8.

477. Brooke, *Wild Men*, 18ff.

478. Thomas, *Celtic Britain*, 97. See also Hill, *Whithorn 2*, 4: "None of our sources credit St. Ninian with the conversion of Galloway and we must safely conclude that he was chosen as bishop by a Christian community already in existence."

479. Thomas, *Celtic Britain*, 99.

480. Ibid.; Richard D. Oram, *A Journey Through Time 1: The Christian Heritage of Wigtownshire* (Whithorn: Whithorn Trust, 1987), 12–13; Higham and Jones, *Carvetii*, 128. Other inscribed stones, dating from the sixth to the twelfth century, have been found at Kirkmadrine and St. Ninian's Cave, a popular early medieval pilgrimage stop.

Chapter 13

1. Gildas, *De excidio*, 24.3 and 26.2.

2. "The Ruin" (eighth century), trans. Kevin Crossley-Holland, in *The Anglo-Saxon World: An Anthology* (Oxford: Oxford University Press, 1984).

3. See Dark, *Civitas*, 13ff.

4. See, for example, Wacher, *Towns of Roman Britain*, chap. 10; Biddle, "Towns," 103–12, and Frere, *Britannia* (1987), 247–49, 368–70.

5. Reece, "Town and Country." See also idem, "The End of Roman Britain—Revisited," *Scottish Archaeological Review* 2 (1983): 149–53; idem, "The End of the City in Roman Britain," in *The City in Late Antiquity,* ed. John Rich (London: Routledge, 1992), 136–44; Jeremy Evans, "Towns and the End of Roman Britain in Northern England," *Scottish Archaeological Review* 2 (1983): 144–49; idem, "From the End of Roman Britain," 91–103; and Dodie A. Brooks, "A Review of the Evidence for Continuity in British Towns in the Fifth and Sixth Centuries," *Oxford Journal of Archaeology* 5, no. 1 (1986): 77–102, and Esmonde Cleary, *Ending*, 132–34 and 145–53. Critics like Brooks and Esmonde Cleary prefer to see a more gradual decline of Romano-British towns, with extinction soon after 400.

6. Dark, *Civitas,* 15ff.

7. Ibid., 17. See, however, J. L. Davies and D. P. Kirby, review of *Civitas to Kingdom,* by

Kenneth Rainsbury Dark, *CMCS* 29 (1995): 70–72.

8. *EH*, 3.4.

9. See Niblett, "'Verulamium,'" 90–91.

10. Dixon, "'The Cities Are Not Populated As Once They Were,'" 156.

11. Burrow, *Hillfort*.

12. See Thomas, *Provisional List*.

13. For a discussion of the Roman material from hilltop sites in Somerset, see Burrow, *Hillfort*, 11–48.

14. See Burnham and Wacher, *"Small Towns" of Roman Britain*, 316–19, and Biddle, "Towns," 103. Martin Biddle wisely observes that the continuity question "might have been rephrased to ask whether occupation had been continuous even if non-urban in character."

15. Malcolm Todd, "After the Romans," in *The Making of Britain: The Dark Ages*, ed. Lesley M. Smith (London: Macmillan, 1984), 32–33.

Chapter 14

1. Richard M. Reece, *My Roman Britain*, Cotswold Studies 3 (Cirencester: Cotswold Studies, 1988), pages (purposely) unnumbered.

2. Lindsay Allason-Jones, *Women in Roman Britain* (London: British Museum Publications, 1989), 190.

3. For definition and discussion of the "positivist" and "reductionist" positions, see Alcock, "Activities of Potentates," 22–46, and Burrow, review of *Economy*, 494–95.

4. Wainwright (*Archaeology*, 126) prefers the term "coordination," which, he stresses, "can proceed effectively only from a thorough understanding of the nature of the different kinds of evidence involved and . . . the techniques used."

5. *Notitia*, OC. 11.20, 11.37, 11.60 (there are actually three known Ventas in Britain), 12.15. See also Esmonde Cleary, *Ending*, 47–50.

6. *Notitia*, OC. 1.75, 1.118.

7. *De excidio*, 3.1–2: "*Brittannia insula* . . . is ornamented with twenty eight *civitates* and a number of *castella*." The *Historia Brittonum* (66a) also gives the number twenty-eight. Ptolemy had recorded thirty-eight cities in Britain south of Hadrian's Wall, and Winterbottom (*Gildas*, 148) believes that a scribal error has changed "xxxviii" to "xxviii."

8. Ausonius (*Parentalia*, 18) dedicates a poem to his Gallic kinsman Flavius Sanctus, "*praeses* [of] the Rutupian land (Britain)." Socrates (*Hist. Eccl.*, 7.12.1) describes the political career of Chrysanthus, "Vicar of the British Isles." Rutilius Namatianus (*De Reditu Suo*, 493–502) praises the abilities of his friend and fellow Gaul Victorinus, writing in 417: "[T]hat warlike British land [*ferox arva Britannus*] remembered the restraint of his power when he had been vicar; all men in that country recall his stay with the highest regard." See Birley, *People of Roman Britain*, 55–56.

9. *Gallic Chronicle of 452*, under Honorius XVI: "The British provinces were devastated by an incursion of Saxons." This occurred sometime between 408 and 411; see Jones and Casey, "Gallic Chronicle Restored," 367–97, and the discussion in Chapter 2 in this volume. Zosimus (6.5), however, states that it was barbarians "over the Rhine" that were threatening the inhabitants of both Britain and Gaul.

10. Zosimus, 6.5.3.

11. Ibid., 6.5.2 to 6.6.1. Zosimus adds that "the whole of Armorica and other Gallic provinces" imitated the Britons, freeing themselves in the same way.

12. Ibid., 6.10.2: "Honorius sent letters to the *poleis* in Britain, urging them to fend for themselves." *Narratio de Imperatoribus* (410): "The Britains were taken away from Rome

forever." Gildas, *De excidio*, 18.1: "The Romans informed the *patria* that they could not go on being bothered with troublesome expeditions. . . . The Britons should stand alone, get used to arms, fight bravely, and defend with all their powers their land."

13. See Thompson, "Zosimus," 455, and Jones, "Provinces," 278 n.19, 279. Defining who was a "Roman" official would not, however, have been an easy task.

14. See Thompson, *St. Germanus*, 34–35, and Wood, "End of Roman Britain," 3–5.

15. Such a cataclysmic event would surely not have escaped the notice of Patrick or Gildas. If, as Wood ("End of Roman Britain," 3ff.) suggests, we broaden the definition of *bacaudae* to include disgruntled landowners, local magistrates, and peasants, the bacaudic theory may partly explain what was going on in Britain.

16. *Codex Theodosianus*, 2.28.5 (A.D. 409): "*honorati et possessores per Africam.*" Larsen (*Representative Government,* 153) also points out that, in the edict of Honorius concerning the assembly of the diocese of Viennensis (A.D. 418), "the members are referred to as *honorati, possessores,* and *iudices* in such a way that *possessores* clearly refer to *curiales.*" John F. Drinkwater ("The Bacaudae of Fifth-Century Gaul," in *Fifth-Century Gaul,* ed. Drinkwater and Elton, 216) suggests that disaffected members of the curial class may have played a part in the Armorican revolts of the early fifth century.

17. Zosimus, 6.5.3 and 6.10.2.

18. Esmonde Cleary (*Ending,* 64) has pointed out that the fortified *civitas* capitals in Britain would have acted as bases for the comitatensian troops and as store bases. Gildas (*De excidio,* 23) writes that the Saxon mercenaries expected *hospites, annonae,* and *epimenia,* terms used for the regular billeting of troops.

19. Thompson (*Who Was Saint Patrick?* 9) believes that the city councillors lingered on for many years in Britain, continuing to collect taxes, not to forward to the imperial authorities, but to maintain their own interests. Jeremy Adams has suggested that the *bacaudae* uprisings themselves may have been "regionally organized response," led not by slaves and brigands but rather by "local elite committed to their peoples' security"; see Adams, "Sidonius and Riothamus," 163, following Van Dam, *Leadership,* 34–48.

20. Patrick speaks proudly of his noble status (*Epistola,* 10: "*nobilitatem meam*"), and tells us that his father owned a small estate (*villula*), yet belonged to a nearby *vicus* (*Confessio,* 1). See Dark, "Saint Patrick's *Uillula,*" 19–24. Archaeologists have observed for some time the phenomenon of urban fortification in the late empire, which occurred in Britain even more so than in Gaul. By the fourth century, most of the *civitas* capitals and many of the smaller towns shrank to a more easily defensible size and received stone walls, projecting towers, and wide ditches. See Esmonde Cleary, *Ending,* 22, 63–64.

21. *De excidio,* 18.2: "*sumptu publico privatoque.*" See Higham, "Gildas, Roman Walls, and British Dykes," 11: "Gildas's comment concerning the use of public and private resources . . . may imply that the pairing of public and private resources mirrored the normal methods of resourcing large-scale public works within the society in which he himself lived."

22. See Branigan, *Catuvellauni,* 196.

23. *Vita Sancti Cuthberti,* chap. 4.

24. Biddle, "Study of Winchester," 111–13.

25. Cunliffe and Davenport, *Temple of Sulis Minerva,* 74ff.

26. Wacher, "Late Roman Developments," 15.

27. Thomas, *Provisional List;* Snyder, *Sub-Roman Britain,* 16–17, 43–44.

28. Gildas's *consilium* (*De excidio,* 22–23) met to decide on a solution to the problem of the Picts raiding in the north. The decision was to hire Saxon mercenaries and settle them "on the east side of the island." Clearly this council involved potentates from more than one *civitas.*

29. *Vita Germani,* 5.26. Knight ("*In Tempore,*" 56) and Frere (*Britannia* [1987], 362) believe Constantius may be using *regionis* with the specific connotation of *civitas.*

30. Leontius, *Life of St. John the Almsgiver,* chap. 10: "[C]hoose as you wish, either one *nomisma* for each bushel or a return freight of tin."

31. These terms are discussed in Chapters 7 and 10.

32. Patrick (*Confessio*, 37) was expected to take up the curial duties (*munera*) of his father, who tried to persuade him to stay in Britain; Patrick (*Epistola*, 10), however, gave up his noble status (*nobilitatem meam*) to be a "slave in Christ."

33. Perring, *Roman London*, 129: "Cities remained symbols of authority for post-Roman communities, whose rulers maintained them to justify their own power."

34. *Epistola*, 133.9.14.

35. *Bellum Vandalicum*, 3.2.38.

36. See Dumville, "Idea of Government," 187: "If all present authority was illegitimate, it was because of the origins of its power in rebellion against Rome and because of the current unjust exercise of its authority." Dumville (183) goes so far as to see the sub-Roman tyrants as "British emperors," with kings like Voteporix Protector "in a place of honor at the hand of a *rex Romanorum* in Britain."

37. Dixon, "'The Cities Are Not Populated As Once They Were,'" 156. Cf. Markus, "Pelagianism," 193: "The only prominent man who turns up [in Constantius's account of Germanus's second visit to Britain] is the Elafius, *regionis illius primus. . . .* perhaps he was something like one of Procopius' *tyrannoi*."

38. See Matthews, "Macsen," 431: "At various times in the fourth century, as, more obviously, in the third, usurpation had met needs for local defence and financial and legal administration when legitimate emperors were too distant and too harassed to attend to them." Cf. Wardman, "Usurpers," 228: "[Usurpation] was also a way of making a political challenge to governments which could seem too remote from local interests and provincial malaise."

39. Dark, "High Status Sites," 10. Cf. Ian C. G. Burrow, "Dark Age Devon: The Landscape, A.D. 400–1100," in *Archaeology of the Devon Landscape*, ed. Peter Beacham et al. (Exeter: County Planning Department, 1980), 63: "At some time the Romanized government of the *civitas*, based on a council of locally important men, was replaced by a monarchy."

40. Salvian, *De Gubernatione Dei*, 5.18. See Thompson, *St. Germanus*, 33, and Wood, "End of Roman Britain," 4.

41. *De excidio*, 23.1

42. See Dumville, "Sub-Roman Britain," 183–85. Dumville considers Vortigern "an overlord of some sort, who had a general control over military matters for the territories of a group of southern *civitates*."

43. See Kerlouegan, *Le "De excidio*," 562; Sheringham, "Les machtierns," 66–71; and Davies, *Small Worlds*, 138. Davies (*Patterns of Power*, 12–14) shows that in the sixth century the Welsh form *teryn* signified a "lesser ruler," as in *arbenhic teryned*, "ruler of rulers." Thus Vortigern (Welsh *Gwrtheyrn*, "overruler") is called by Gildas the *superbus tyrannus*, which could be translated as "the most arrogant of the local rulers."

44. See Jackson, "*Varia*: II," 36–40.

45. *EH*, 14; *Anglo-Saxon Chronicle* (Parker Chronicle), *sub anno* 449; *HB*, 37, 45.

46. *De excidio*, 21.4: "Ungebantur reges non per deum sed qui ceteris crudeliores exstarent, et paulo post ab unctoribus non pro veri examinatione trucidabantur aliies electis trucioribus." This comes in Gildas's narrative immediately after the Appeal to Aetius *ter consuli* (A.D. 446). See Higham, *Northern Counties*, 251: "Gildas makes it clear that the role of kingship evolved only slowly, with the 'anointers'—probably the war-bands—making and unmaking kings almost at will."

47. *De excidio*, 27: "Reges habet Britannia, sed tyrannos." See Schaffner, "Britain's *Iudices*," 154, and the discussion in Chapter 9 in this volume.

48. *De excidio*, 26.2. This occurs in the narrative immediately after the Siege of Badon Hill, dated conventionally to c. 500, which Gildas claims occurred the year of his birth. For the idea that the *publici* may have constituted a sub-Roman bureaucracy, see Dark, *Discovery by Design*, 7, and Higham, *English Conquest*, 151ff.

49. Dark, *Civitas,* 15ff.

50. Frere, *Verulamium,* 319; Branigan, *Catuvellauni,* 191; Laing and Laing, *Celtic Britain and Ireland,* 74–75. This house, with over twenty-two rooms and a colonnaded courtyard, was constructed after c. 380, with two extensions and a series of mosaics added much later.

51. Roger White, "Excavations," 4–7.

52. Ibid., 7. Cf. Webster, *Cornovii,* 117: "Thus we have a powerful character, building himself a kind of country mansion in the middle of the city, surrounded with small buildings, which are either stables or . . . houses for his retainers."

53. Dark, *Civitas,* 20–21; Frere, *Britannia* (1987), 190, 199.

54. Patrick's father, who owned a *villula* and belonged to a *vicus,* is a good illustration of this, though keeping his estate cost him his son; see *Confessio,* 1; *Epistola,* 10. Down (*Roman Chichester,* 101) argues that the strongholds of the *tyranni* included "the old *civitas* capitals with their strong walls, the forts of the Saxon shore and, in some instances, the large estates where the owners were sufficiently wealthy to maintain armed forces." Philip Dixon ("Life After Wroxeter: The Final Phases of Roman Towns," in *From Roman Town to Norman Castle: Essays in Honor of Philip Barker,* ed. Aubrey Burl [Birmingham: Birmingham University Press, 1988], 37) points out that "no fewer than 17 of the 22 major Roman towns have [English] names which emphasize their defenses (3 in *byrig* and 14 in *ceastre*). Towns struck the Anglo-Saxon, then as fortresses, and perhaps as *royal* fortresses."

55. Gildas says that the beleaguered Britons "based themselves on the mountains, caves, heaths, and thorny thickets" (*De excidio,* 20.2), while some of the survivors "were caught in the mountains and butchered" (25.1).

56. A good example is Maiden Castle, which was stormed by Vespasian's army and whose survivors were resettled in nearby Dorchester (Durnovaria).

57. See Dark, *Civitas,* 40ff.; Burrow, *Hillfort,* 5–6 and chaps. 6 and 7.

58. Burrow, *Hillfort,* 149.

59. See Ammianus, 20.1, 27.8, 28.3, and Orosius, 7.34.9.

60. See the discussion of South Cadbury and Dinas Powys in Chapter 12.

61. This seems especially to have been the case in Somerset; see Hanley, *Villages,* 55.

62. See Alcock, "Activities of Potentates," 25.

63. Dark, *Civitas,* 40; Burrow, *Hillfort,* 160–66.

64. Rahtz et al., *Cadbury Congresbury,* 249–50; Thomas, *Tintagel,* 86–87.

65. Gildas's "siege of *Badonici montis*" implies a fortification at Mount Badon, and he places Cuneglasus at the *receptaculi ursi,* "Bear's Stronghold," which is a Latin translation of *Din Eirth,* Dinarth, near Llandudno. See Jackson, "*Varia* II: Gildas," 34. The later sources are more specific than Gildas: Bede calls Dumbarton *civitas Brettonum munitissima,* while his contemporary Adomnán claims that Dumbarton is the seat of the British king Roderc; the *Gododdin* tells of King Mynyddog Mwyanfawr and his great hall at *Din Eidyn* (Edinburgh); and the *Historia Brittonum* relates how Vortigern built a fortress in the mountains of Snowdon and gave it to the boy Emrys, hence the name of the sub-Roman hillfort Dinas Emrys.

66. For the most convincing of such models, see Dark, *Civitas,* passim, and Burrow, *Hillfort,* 152ff.

67. Gildas (*De excidio,* 10.2) speaks of "the unhappy partition with the barbarians" that denied some Britons access to Verulamium and Caerleon. Archaeological finds of "Germanic" artifacts confirms Bede's testimony that the first Anglo-Saxon kingdoms were in the Southeast.

68. London (Perring, *Roman London,* 129); Chichester (Cunliffe, *Regni,* 132); Silchester (Boon, *Roman Town,* 8); Cirencester (Reece and Catling, *Cirencester,* 9); Wroxeter (Roger White, "Excavations," 7); Chester (Laing and Laing, *West Cheshire,* 28); York (Campbell, *Anglo-Saxons,* 39); Carlisle (Higham and Jones, *Carvetii,* 133). See also Bassett, "Churches in Worcester," 230: "[The placement of English sees in Roman towns was] a clear acknowledgement of the extent to which Romano-British tribal capitals and other central places had remained politically . . . important."

69. Bede calls Dumbarton the *civitas* of Strathclyde. See Alcock, "Gwyr y Gogledd," 4ff.

70. Lloyd Laing, *Settlement Types in Post-Roman Scotland,* BAR, no. 13 (Oxford: Tempvs Reparatvm, 1975), 35: "The origins of the early British kingdoms of the post-Roman period must be sought in the tribal structure of the Roman Iron Age."

71. *De excidio,* 28 and 31; *ECMW,* nos. 87, 126, and 103; *Inscriptiones Latinae Christianae Veteres,* ed. Ernestus Diehl (Berlin: Weidmann, 1961), 1.185; *CIIC,* 1.428.

72. For example, Dumnonia, the land of the Dumnonii, encompassed all of Devon, Cornwall, and part of Somerset, but was divided into two *civitates* by the Romans. The sub-Roman *civitas* seems to have reverted to its larger tribal size.

73. Grim's Bank (Silchester), Bokerly Dyke (Dorset), and Wansdyke (Wiltshire) are three notable examples. See Boon, *Silchester,* 77–80; Perring, *Roman London,* 129; Rahtz et al., *Cadbury Congresbury,* 251; Higham, *Rome, Britain, and the Anglo-Saxons,* 93–95; and Dark, *Civitas,* 150. Gildas, in his confused account of the construction of walls across Britain (*De excidio,* 16 and 18), may actually have been thinking about the construction of these dikes. See Higham, "Gildas, Roman Walls, and British Dykes," 13: "Gildas and his audience were familiar with the construction of linear barriers [dikes]."

74. In 368; see Ammianus, 27.8. It is likely that part of Count Theodosius's initiative included the additional fortification of Britain's walled towns (Ammianus, 28.2), a phenomenon archaeologists have observed at many sites.

75. See Higham, *Northern Counties,* 241.

76. Welsby (*Roman Military,* 130) believes that Britons, recruited through the local/hereditary system, would have made up the bulk of the soldiers who remained in Britain when Constantine left for Gaul.

77. Jones, "Geographical-Psychological Frontiers," 48.

78. There is some evidence that silver ingots were used by British communities to pay troops after new coins failed to arrive from the Continent. See Welsby, *Roman Military,* 127; Johns and Potter, "Canterbury Late Roman Treasure," 328; and Hall and Merrifield, *Roman London,* 14.

79. Dark, "Sub-Roman Re-Defense." See also the discussion in Chapter 12.

80. The Saxon Shore: Richborough yielded an abundance of early fifth-century coins and housed a fifth-century church (Welsby, *Roman Military,* 125, 131); the defenses at Pevensy and Portchester show some reuse and a lingering British presence (Cunliffe, *Regni,* 132–33, and *Excavations at Portchester,* 2:301–2). Wales: the Roman auxiliary fort at Aberffraw (on Anglesey) had its stone rampart rebuilt, possibly as a *ballista* platform (White, "Excavations at Aberffraw," 341); a new sentry box was built in a guardroom at the Roman fort of Segontium (Laing, "Segontium," 57); a disused Roman fort at Pen Llystyn was reused as a palisaded enclosure (Edwards and Lane, *Early Medieval Settlements,* 102–4).

81. A salient was constructed at the Tower of London c. 402; see Perring, *Roman London,* 127. The late Roman walling and earthwork defenses at Gloucester and Worcester seem to be part of a scheme to fortify every major settlement along the tributaries of the Severn River against Irish or Saxon raids; see Hurst, *Gloucester,* 123–24, and Bassett, "Churches in Worcester," 243. The Verulamium Gate at Cirencester began the refacing of its tower and the rebuilding of the front face of its wall c. 410; see Wacher, "Late Roman Developments," 15. The *principia* at York remained intact and in use until it was destroyed by fire in the seventh century; see Welsby, *Roman Military,* 131.

82. Cirencester, for example, has yielded abundant evidence of late-fifth-century timber buildings and road and wall repairs within its extramural amphitheater. The *ceaster* element in Chesterton may be what the later Anglo-Saxon settlers called this amphitheater settlement. See McWhirr et al., *Cirencester Excavations II,* 27; and Wacher, "Late Roman Developments," 17.

83. *De excidio,* 3.2: "*Brittannia . . .* is ornamented with twenty-eight cities [*civitatibus*]

and a number of castles [*castellis*], and well equipped with fortifications [*munitionibus*]—walls [*murorum*], castellated towers [*turrium serratarum*], gates [*portarum*] and houses [*domorum*], whose sturdily built roofs reared menacingly skyward."

84. Ibid., 23; 92.3: "We greatly desire that the enemies [*hostes*] of the church be our enemies also, with no kind of alliance [*foedere*], and that her friends and protectors be not only our allies [*foederati*] but our fathers and masters too."

85. The presence of fifth-century *foederati* or *laeti* has been claimed, for example, for Colchester (Dunnett, *Trinovantes*, 137–38), Portchester (Cunliffe, *Regni*, 132), and several sites along Hadrian's Wall (Dark, "Sub-Roman Re-Defense," 115–16).

86. Welsby, *Roman Military*, 162–64. Ammianus (29.4.7) records the transfer of the Alamannic king Fraomarius to Britain (in 372) with the rank of *tribunus* to command a *numerus* of Alamanni.

87. There are several good surveys of hillfort occupation in this period, though all of these studies are regional. See, for example, Elizabeth A. and Leslie Alcock, "Catalogue of Fortified Sites in Wales and Dumnonia, c. A.D. 400–800," in Alcock, *Economy*, 168–71; Burrow, *Hillfort;* Edwards and Lane, eds., *Early Medieval Settlements;* Laing, *Settlement Types;* Elizabeth A. Alcock, "Appendix: Defended Settlements, Fifth to Seventh Centuries A.D.," in *Twenty-Five Years of Medieval Archaeology*, ed. David A. Hinton (Sheffield: Department of Prehistory and Archaeology, University of Sheffield, 1983), 58–59; and idem, "Appendix: Enclosed Places, A.D. 500–800," in *Power and Politics*, ed. Driscoll and Nieke, 40–46.

88. *De excidio*, 25.1. See Alcock, "Activities of Potentates," 31.

89. See Alcock et al., *Cadbury Castle*, and the discussion in Chapter 12 in this volume.

90. See Rahtz et al., *Cadbury Congresbury*, 231–33.

91. See Alcock, "Gwyr y Gogledd," 2ff.; C. A. Ralegh Radford, "Romance and Reality in Cornwall," in *Quest for Arthur's Britain*, ed. Ashe, 74–75; Lane, "Degannwy Castle," 51–52; and Leslie Alcock, *Dinas Powys: An Iron Age, Dark Age, and Early Medieval Settlement in Glamorgan* (Cardiff: University of Wales Press, 1963).

92. Alcock, "Activities of Potentates," 24–27.

93. See Anne S. Robertson, "Romano-British Coin Hoards: Their Numismatic, Archaeological, and Historical Significance," in *Coins and the Archaeologist*, ed. Casey and Reece, 33–34.

94. In the *Confessio*, Patrick speaks of sea-borne raids by the Scots. Constantius (*Vita Germani*, 17–18) describes an attack by Picts and Saxons in a river valley. Gildas (*De excidio*, 16 and 19) writes that the Picts and Scots came, "relying on their oars . . . and on the winds swelling their sails," in "coracles that carried them across the sea-valleys," while the Saxons came "in three keels, as they call their warships" (23.3).

95. Vegetius, *Epitoma Rei Militaris*. Bachrach ("Gildas," 136) points out that, when Vegetius's work was redacted c. 450, the editor did not amend this passage, implying that Britain was still thought to possess a navy.

96. *Vita*, 17–18.

97. *Epistola*, 2, 3, and 13.

98. *De excidio*, 18.1, 19.2. Gildas always uses *ensis* for "sword."

99. Ibid., 27, 32.1–2.

100. Knight and Lane, "Caerwent," 35–38; Campbell, "Coygan Camp," 44–46; idem, "Dinas Emrys," 54–57; Burrow, *Hillfort*, 273; Alcock et al., *South Cadbury*, 118.

101. Vindolanda tablet 85/32 refers to the native British cavalry, which, together with their Celtic counterparts in Gaul and Spain, were frequently drafted as units into the Roman army. The question remains whether the cavalry of sub-Roman Britain were light or heavy (*cataphractarii*). According to the *Notitia*, two active regiments of heavy-armored cavalry were stationed in Britain. Arguing persuasively for the latter is Rowland, "Warfare and Horses in the *Gododdin*," 22ff.

102. See Thomas, *Tintagel,* and Dark, *Discovery by Design,* fig. 2.

103. See Esmonde Cleary, *Ending,* 116ff.

104. Campbell, *Anglo-Saxons,* 22.

105. See *Epistola,* 2, 15, and 19, and *Confessio,* 1–2.

106. *De excidio,* 24.2, 27–36.

107. When Gildas refers to native paganism (specifically nature worship; *De excidio,* 4.2–3), he speaks of it as a practice of long-past days. See Martin Henig, *Religion in Roman Britain* (London: Batsford, 1984), 224: "Ancient errors, the veneration of idols, belong for [Gildas] to a very distant past."

108. See, most recently, Dorothy Watts, *Christians and Pagans in Roman Britain* (London: Routledge, 1991). See also W.H.C. Frend, "Pagans, Christians, and 'the Barbarian Conspiracy' of A.D. 367 in Roman Britain," *Britannia* 23 (1992): 121–31, and Rahtz, "Pagan and Christian," 7ff. Dark (*Civitas,* 32ff.) argues convincingly that there was no pagan revival in fourth-century Britain, then (55ff.) inexplicably argues that Christian militants were rebelling against the pagan elite and destroying their temples! See Davies and Kirby, review of *Civitas to Kingdom,* 70–72.

109. I do not, however, see any evidence that pagan writings were "suppressed" by Christians in Britain, as many have claimed. The most valuable epigraphic evidence is that of the lead curse tablets (*defixiones*) found in large numbers at many Romano-British sites. See, for example, R.S.O. Tomlin, "The Curse Tablets," in *The Temple of Sulis Minerva at Bath,* vol. 2, ed. Barry Cunliffe (Oxford: University Committee for Archaeology, 1988), 59–277.

110. See Esmonde Cleary, *Ending,* 119–20.

111. Drury, "Chelmsford," 168–69.

112. Bell, *Brean Down,* 82.

113. Ellison, *Excavations at West Hill Uley—Second Interim Report,* 313ff.

114. No evidence, only the opinions of some excavators. *Contra* Dark, *Civitas,* 38–39, 55ff. See Esmonde Cleary, *Ending,* 119–20, and Thomas, *Christianity in Roman Britain,* 133–36.

115. Chi-Rhos and figures from Greco-Roman myth can be seen coexisting in villa mosaics from Frampton and Hinton St. Mary, and on objects from the silver hoards of Water Newton and Mildenhall. See Frend, "Pagans, Christians," 122–23, and Jones, *End of Roman Britain,* 177: "Absorption rather than destruction of pagan traditions [by Christians in Roman Britain] seems indicated."

116. As has been suggested for West Hill Uley, Cannington, Brean Down, South Cadbury, Nettleton, and Lamyatt Beacon. See Dark, *Civitas,* 60–62, and discussion of the individual sites in Snyder, *Sub-Roman Britain.*

117. *EH,* 1.30 (quoting a letter sent c. 601 by Gregory to Bishop Milletus): "[T]he temples of the idols of that country should on no account be destroyed. . . . the temples themselves are to be aspersed with holy water, altars set up, and relics enclosed in them."

118. Cf. Henig, *Religion in Roman Britain,* 226: "[Pope Gregory's advice on temple conversion] seems to have been common practice for a long time, to judge from the Christianization of the Chedworth spring as early as the fourth century. Furthermore, churches were probably built on temple land at Witham in Essex, Icklingham in Suffolk and West Hill, Uley in Gloucestershire amongst other places during the late fourth and fifth centuries A.D."

119. Both Tertullian and Origen offhandedly mention Christians in Britain. Tertullian's statement (in *Adversus Judaeos*) that Christianity was even reaching the non-Romanized parts of Britain may imply early missionary activity among the northern tribes or the Picts. See Thomas, *Christianity in Roman Britain,* 42–43, and Howlett, *Celtic Latin Tradition,* 55.

120. Esmonde Cleary, *Ending,* 124.

121. See ibid.; Dark, *Civitas,* 35–37; and the discussion in Chapter 12 in this volume.

122. Large circular lead tanks bearing the Chi-Rho, such as that found at Icklingham, may have been used for baptisms or ablutions.

123. Chi-Rhos were featured prominently in the mosaics at Frampton and Hinton St. Mary (behind a beardless Christ) and in wall paintings at Lullingstone. See Esmonde Cleary, *Ending,* 110, 124–25.

124. See David S. Neal, *Lullingstone Roman Villa* (London: English Heritage, 1991), 27; Watts, *Christians and Pagans,* 100; and Alec Detsicas, *The Cantiaci* (Gloucester: Sutton, 1983), 182.

125. See Esmonde Cleary, *Ending,* 127–28, and Thomas, *Christianity in Roman Britain,* 96–142. Christian "hoards" have been found at Mildenhall, Canterbury, and Water Newton.

126. See Dark, *Civitas,* 36; Esmonde Cleary, *Ending,* 125–26; Morris, *Churches in the Landscape,* 33–35; and Watts, *Christians and Pagans.*

127. See Esmonde Cleary, *Ending,* 125.

128. See Leach, *Shepton Mallet,* 24.

129. See Thomas, *Tintagel,* 103–5.

130. See Malcolm Todd, "*Famosa Pestis* and Britain in the Fifth Century," *Britannia* 8 (1977): 319–25, esp. 324 n. 19; Barker, ed., *Wroxeter Roman City,* 15; Ottaway, *Archaeology in British Towns,* 109; and Frederick Suppe, "The Cultural Significance of Decapitation in High Medieval Wales and the Marches," *BBCS* (1989): 147–60.

131. For discussion of these early Christian inscriptions, see *ECMW;* Okasha, *Corpus;* Thomas, *These Mute Stones;* and Chapter 3 in this volume.

132. For a recent discussion of Ogam (and possible Irish influence) on early Christian inscriptions in Britain, see Dark, *Civitas,* 267ff.

133. Bassett, "Church and Diocese" ; idem, "Churches in Worcester"; idem, "In Search of the Origins of Anglo-Saxon Kingdoms," in *Origins of Anglo-Saxon Kingdoms,* ed. Bassett, 3–27.

134. See Bassett, "Church and Diocese," 39: "[The Britons] converted the immigrants . . . [and] left the missionaries from Canterbury and Iona with little left to do here—and Bede with little to report, especially since he notoriously disliked the British churches and wrote them out of his *Ecclesiastical History* as much as he could." Cf. Dark, *Civitas,* 65, who accepts these conclusions.

135. Bassett and Dark both suggest that a list of Romano-British *civitates,* similar to the *Notitia Galliarum,* was used both by Gildas (who mentions Britain's twenty-eight *civitates*) and by Pope Gregory, who instructed Augustine and company to make use of these preexisting "administrative centers."

136. See Stafford, *East Midlands,* 89, and Thomas, *Christianity in Roman Britain,* 147, 262–65. Thomas is "inclined to see most, perhaps all, of these Eccles- sites originating in sub-Roman British Christian communities," but points out that *eccles* means "Christian community" but not necessarily "Christian church."

137. See the discussion in Chapter 10.

138. Gildas, *Fragmenta,* 6.

139. Women participated mostly as well-respected "widows" and "religious sisters." However, Gallic bishops complained in the early sixth century that British priests in Armorica were allowing women to assist in the Eucharist as "fellow hostesses" (*conhospitas*); see the *Letter to Louocatus and Catihernus* in Howlett, *Celtic Latin Tradition,* 66–72.

140. Patrick complains (*Confessio,* 9), "I have not studied like others, who have successfully imbibed both law and Holy Scripture." See Lapidge, "Gildas's Education"; Howlett, *Celtic Latin Tradition,* 78; and the discussion in Chapters 3 and 10 in this volume.

141. Orosius, 7.40.7; Sidonius, *Epistola,* 9.9.6.

142. *Epistola,* 12; *Confessio,* 43.

143. *Fragmenta,* 3: "They prefer fasting to charity, vigils to justice, . . . the cell [*clausulam*] to the church [*ecclesiae*]." See Herren, "Gildas and Early British Monasticism," 67–77, and Thomas, *Christianity in Roman Britain,* 348ff.

144. Gildas (*Fragmenta*, 3) even forgives monks who "possess horse and carriage [*pecora et vehicula*] because it is the custom of the *patria*." See Herren, "Gildas and Early British Monasticism," 70.

145. *EH*, 3.4. See MacQueen, *St. Nynia*.

146. See Hill, *Whithorn* (interim reports 2–4); Higham and Jones, *Carvetii*, 130; and the discussion in Chapter 12 in this volume.

147. Morris, *Churches in the Landscape*, 104: "Around 500 a *monasterium* might have been defined by the behavior of its members, but not by the form or disposition of its structures." See also Davies, *Early Welsh Microcosm*, 121ff., and the essays in Blair and Sharpe, *Pastoral Care Before the Parish*.

148. Morris, *Churches in the Landscape*, 100–102.

149. See Dark, *Civitas*, 59; idem, "Saint Patrick's *Uillula*," 19–24; and Heinzelmann, "'Affair' of Hilary of Arles," 145.

150. J.N.L. Myres ("Pelagius") was the first to propose that Pelagian independents sparked the revolt of 409/10. Ian Wood ("Fall of the Western Empire") sees, at the time of Germanus's visits, two parties in Britain with differing views on imperial authority—Pelagian independents and orthodox Romanists, who appeal to Aetius in 446. But Pelagianism could never have played a significant role in Britain as early as 409, and if Pelagians subsequently held political power, surely Patrick and Gildas would have complained. Neither of them even mentions Pelagianism, and even Constantius does not associate the heresy with British politics.

151. *De excidio*, 38.2: "As one of us well says, . . ." Rex Gardner ("Gildas' New Testament Models," *CMCS* 30 [1995]: 11) sees in *De excidio*, 69–72, evidence of semi-Pelagian views, "with 'faith only' [Augustinianism] as a new-fangled heresy to be resisted."

152. See Wendy Davies, "The Myth of the Celtic Church," in *Early Church in Wales*, ed. Edwards and Lane, 18; Markus, "Pelagianism"; Dumville, "Late-Seventh- or Eighth-Century Evidence for the British Transmission of Pelagius," *CMCS* 10 (1985): 39–52; Kathleen Hughes, *Church and Society in Ireland* (London: Variorum, 1987), 71–72; and Morris, "Pelagian Literature," 26–60.

153. See Snyder, "Celtic Continuity in the Middle Ages," 167, 170–71. Wendy Davies ("Myth of the Celtic Church") has shown that the plural "Celtic churches" is probably the more accurate identifier.

154. See Burnett, "Clipped Siliquae," 163–68; Robertson, "Romano-British Coin Hoards," 13–37; Reece, *Coinage in Roman Britain*, 45; and Snyder, *Sub-Roman Britain*, 7–8.

155. See Blackburn, "Three Silver Coins," 169–74, and Snyder, *Sub-Roman Britain*, 14, 15, 17, and 43.

156. *Epistola*, 14; *Confessio*, 50; *De excidio*, 66.3–5; *Life of St. John the Almsgiver*, 10.

157. Robertson, "Romano-British Coin Hoards," 22.

158. See ibid., 33–34, and especially the map of hoard clusters.

159. See Reece, "Use of Roman Coinage," 205.

160. See Boon, "Counterfeit Coins in Roman Britain," 102–88.

161. See Dark, *Civitas*, 201.

162. So-called *Hacksilber* probably met a similar fate. Note that many jewelry finds, beginning already in the fourth century, occur in multiple units of Roman weights. See discussion in Snyder, *Sub-Roman Britain*, 8.

163. See Dark, *Civitas*, 25ff.; Esmonde Cleary, *Ending*, 108; Burrow, *Hillfort*, 14; and Cunliffe, *Regni*, 129.

164. See Dark, *Civitas*, 26–27; Millet, *Romanization of Britain*, 175; and Zeepvat et al., *Roman Milton Keynes*, 10.

165. See Esmonde Cleary, *Ending*, 158, and John Percival, *The Roman Villa* (London: Batsford, 1976), 171–82.

166. See Dark, "Saint Patrick's *Uillula*," 19–24; Higham, *Rome, Britain, and the Anglo-*

Saxons, 116ff; and Susan M. Pearce, "Estates and Church Sites in Dorset and Gloucestershire: The Emergence of a Christian Society," in *The Early Church in Western Britain and Ireland,* BAR British Series, no. 102, ed. Susan M. Pearce (Oxford: Tempvs Reparatvm, 1982), 117–38. For some parallels in Gaul, see Percival, "Fifth-Century Villas," 156–64.

167. *Confessio,* 1.

168. The best evidence for salt production comes from Droitwich (Latin *Salinae,* OE *Saltwic*), where ash and charcoal residues from brine-boiling pits yielded calibrated radiocarbon dates of A.D. 435 ± 95 and A.D. 630 ± 30; see Derek Hurst, "Major Saxon Discoveries at Droitwich," *Current Archaeology* 126 (1991): 252–55, and Snyder, *Sub-Roman Britain,* 40.

169. Penhallurick, *Tin in Antiquity,* xi, 10, 237. In addition to the evidence from the *Life of St. John the Almsgiver,* there is a short Greek treatise on alchemy by Stephanos of Alexandria (fl. 610–41), which lists "the Celtic nard, the Atlantic Sea, the Brettanic metal."

170. Crickmore, *Romano-British Urban Settlements,* 86. Dark (*Discovery by Design,* 93) believes that the New Forest and West Midlands kilns also continued for some time after 400, and cites fifth-century examples of Black Burnished Ware1 and shell, calcite, and limestone-tempered, wares.

171. Esmonde Cleary, *Ending,* 85–91.

172. See Ibid., 12.

173. See Thomas, *Provisional List,* and the discussion of types in Snyder, *Sub-Roman Britain,* 8–9.

174. Though the pottery has been classified and cataloged, no detailed studies of distribution and trade routes have yet been made. See, however, the maps in Thomas, *Tintagel,* 97; idem, *Christianity,* 272 and 250; and idem, *Celtic Britain,* 59.

175. Fulford, "Byzantium and Britain." Cf. Dark, *Discovery by Design,* 12: "[The imported pottery suggests] constant contact over a period of decades, or even a century or more." Thomas (*Celtic Britain,* 58–59) adds wool, hunting dogs, and pewter to the list of what the Britons had to offer, while Hunter-Mann ("When [and What] was the End of Roman Britain?" 76) suggests that salt was one of the raw materials traded by the Britons.

176. See Fulford, "Byzantium and Britain," 5; Ward, "Procopius' Bellum Gothicum"; and Johnstone, "Consular Chronology of Dark Age Britain," 102. Knight (*"In Tempore,"* 62) and Thomas (*Christianity in Roman Britain,* 272), however, prefer a Gallic origin for the consular dating.

177. Dark, *Civitas,* 209–13. Procopius writes (*Anekdota,* 19.13) that Justinian "never ceased pouring out great gifts of money to all the barbarians, . . . as far as the inhabitants of Britain [βρεττανίαις]." Elsewhere (*Bellum Gothicum,* 2.6.28), he has Belisarius offer "the whole of Britain [βρεττανίαν]" to the Goths in exchange for Sicily. On Procopius and Britain, see Thompson, "Procopius on Brittia and Britannia"; Ward, "Procopius' Bellum Gothicum"; and the discussion in Chapter 3 in this volume.

178. On the wide impact of this trade with Gaul, see Thomas, *Christianity in Roman Britain,* 271–74, 347–55, and idem, "Gallici Nautae," 1–26. For British churchmen in fifth-century Gaul, see the discussion in Chapters 6 and 10. On the influence of Gallic epigraphic traditions in Britain, see Knight, *"In Tempore,"* 54–62.

179. Thomas, *Early Christian Archaeology,* 24–25. Cf. Burrow, *Hillfort,* 169ff.

180. See Rahtz et al., *Cadbury Congresbury,* 249, and Gilchrist, "Re-Appraisal."

181. See, for example, Dark, *Civitas,* 207, and Thomas, *Tintagel,* 87–88.

182. See Thomas, *Tintagel,* 87–88, and Rahtz et al., *Cadbury Congresbury,* 250.

183. See Dark, *Civitas,* 207, and Gilchrist, "Re-Appraisal," 59–61.

184. Alcock, "Activities of Potentates," 25.

185. Thomas, *Tintagel,* 94–96.

186. Fulford, "Silchester," 328; Roger White, "Excavations," 5.

187. Longley, "Date of the Mote of Mark," 132–34.

188. Lloyd Laing, "The Beginnings of 'Dark Age' Celtic Art," in *Britain, 400–600*, ed. Bammesberger and Wollmann, 44–45.

189. See Burrow, *Hillfort*, 171, and Alcock, "Gwyr y Gogledd," 4.

190. Patrick, *Epistola*, 15 and 19: "[F]reeborn men have been sold, Christians reduced to slavery—and what is more, as slaves of the utterly iniquitous, evil and apostate Picts. . . . Coroticus and his villains . . . allot poor baptised women as prizes, for the sake of a miserable temporal kingdom."

191. Ibid., 12 and 15.

192. See, however, the role of these classes in the Llandaff Charters: Davies, *Early Welsh Microcosm*, 43ff.

193. *Fragmenta*, 3.

194. In Rahtz et al., *Cadbury Congresbury*, 248.

195. The penitentials, however, occasionally give us glimpses of family life and sexual habits; see Bieler, *Irish Penitentials*, passim. The "bride price," or "groom's gift," (*dos*) is mentioned in "The First Synod St. Patrick" (chap. 22) and "The Penitential of Finnian" (chap. 44). Various forms of fornication and sodomy, male homosexuality, nocturnal emissions, and love potions are condemned in "The Synod of the Grove of Victory" (chap. 8), "Excerpts from a Book of David" (chaps. 5, 8, and 9), and "The Penitential of Finnian" (chaps. 2, 3, and 18).

196. *Vita Germani*, 3.15 and 5.26–27.

197. *Confessio*, 1.

198. Ibid., 2.

199. E.g., ibid., 6, 23, and 43, and *Epistola*, 10.

200. *De excidio*, 28. See Bachrach, "Gildas," 130.

201. *De excidio*, 30.

202. Ibid., 31.

203. Ibid., 32.

204. Ibid., 33–35.

205. See the discussion in Chapter 12.

206. See Laing, *Settlement Types*, and Dark, *Discovery by Design*.

207. *EH*, 3.4. A small stone chapel and oratory were discovered by excavators at Whithorn; see Higham and Jones, *Carvetii*, 133.

208. See Roger White, "Excavations," 6–7.

209. See Alcock, *Economy*, 182, 193, and 196.

210. See Hill, *Whithorn 4*, 7.

211. Dark (*Civitas*, 15–17) argues that the "dark earth" so common among late Roman cities in Britain is the disintegrated remains of these simple dwellings.

212. See Dark, *Civitas*, 178–80 and 209; Richard Hingley, *Rural Settlement in Roman Britain* (London: Seaby, 1989), 39–45 and 48–50; and Alcock, *Economy*, 206–7.

213. See Dark, *Civitas*, 206–9; and Alcock, *Economy*, 206 and 243–44.

214. *Confessio*, 17 and 19; *Epistola*, 5.

215. *Fragmenta*, 2; *De excidio*, 19.3–4 and 20.2. Cf. Leontius, *Life of St. John the Almsgiver*, chap. 10: "a great famine raging there [in southwestern Britain]."

216. *De excidio*, 7 and 31.1; *De Poenitentia*, 1, 2, and 22. Cf. "Excerpts from a Book of David" (in Bieler, *Irish Penitentials*, 70–73), chaps. 1 and 11: "wine or strong drink" (*vinum aut siceram*), "pease porridge" (*leguminis talimpulo*), and "a half-pint of beer" (*cervissa*). On the popularity of this "Celtic beer" in Britain, see the account of food supplies left by a Roman soldier at Vindolanda in Alan K. Bowman, *The Roman Writing Tablets from Vindolanda* (London: British Museum Publications, 1983), 25, 31–32, and 36. *Cervesa* appears twice on this list, which records that some fifty liters of beer were consumed.

217. See Kelly, "Recent Research," 104; Alcock, "Activities of Potentates," 25; Holbrook and Bidwell, *Exeter Archaeological Reports*, 4:13; Thomas, *Provisional List;* and Johns and

Potter, "Canterbury Late Roman Treasure," 335.

218. Alcock et al., *Cadbury Castle*, 84. The olive-oil-carrying amphoras (Bii) outnumbered their wine-carrying counterparts (Bi) by nine to two.

219. Ibid., 119.

220. *De excidio*, 22.2.

221. Hydatius (*Continuatio Chronicorum Hieronymianorum*, 126) says that a plague broke out in the year 443 and "spread throughout almost the whole world." Marcellinus Comes (*Chronicon*, 8) describes a plague that hit Constantinople in 445–46. Gregory of Tours (*HF*, 2.18) writes that "a great pestilence caused the death of many people" in Gaul c. 465. It should be noted that Gregory also testifies to the seriousness of epidemic dysentery in the sixth century.

222. This plague, which devastated Constantinople and the eastern provinces in 542 (and affected the emperor Justinian), is described by Procopius, John of Ephesus, and Evagrius; see Averil Cameron, *The Mediterranean World in Late Antiquity, a.d. 395–600* (London: Routledge, 1993), 111, 127–28, 164.

223. The Irish annals contain many entries describing casualties of the "Yellow Plague," starting in the year 544. The *Annals of Tigernach* record plagues devastating Ireland in 549 (causing the deaths of Saints Finnian of Clonard and Ciaran of Clonmacnoise) and 664. Bede (*EH*, 3.27) says that this second plague decimated southern Britain and Northumbria as well as Ireland. Adomnán (*Life of Saint Columba*, 2.46) writes that plague devastated Britain and Ireland twice in his time (c. 664–68 and c. 680–86), sparing only Dalriada and Pictland (both areas where Columba had established monasteries). See Richard Sharpe, trans., *Adomnán of Iona, "Life of St. Columba"* (London: Penguin, 1995), 348 n. 346, and Lisa M. Bitel, *Isle of the Saints: Monastic Settlement and Christian Community in Early Ireland* (Ithaca, N.Y.: Cornell University Press, 1990), 191.

224. Todd, *"Famosa Pestis,"* 319–25.

225. *Vita Germani*, 3.14 (*"conspicui divitiis, veste fulgentes"*).

226. *De excidio*, 28.1–2 (*amphibalo, pallia*), 29.3 (*"regium anulum"*).

227. See Barker et al., "Two Burials," 146–51. The spun-gold threads, found around the neck of one skeleton, were woven into a brocade, probably the border of a cloth garment. A tunic collar and a priest's vestment have been suggested.

228. See Alcock, "Activities of Potentates," 25.

229. See J. D. Bateson, *Enamel-Working in Iron Age, Roman, and Sub-Roman Britain*, BAR British Series, no. 93 (Oxford: Tempvs Reparatvm, 1981), 59–65.

230. *Fragmenta*, 2; *De excidio*, 66.4. Regarding another luxury, Cunliffe (in Cunliffe and Davenport, *Temple of Sulis Minerva*, 1:11 and 185) believes that the hot springs at Bath continued to receive visitors throughout the sub-Roman period, so much so that the buildings and floors needed repairing.

231. See Chapters 6 and 7.

232. *ECMW*, no. 139.

233. *Confessio*, 43; *De excidio*, 1 (*"condolentis patriae"*).

234. *Epistola*, 2 and 15.

235. *De excidio*, 23.1.

236. See, for example, *EH*, 2.20: "[Cadwallon] was set upon exterminating the entire English race in Britain"; and Eddius, *Life of Wilfrid*, 17: "various places which the British clergy had deserted, when fleeing from the hostile sword wielded by the warriors of our nation." In "The Synod of the Grove of Victory" (in Bieler, *Irish Penitentials*, 69), chap. 4, a penance of thirteen years is given to those "who afford guidance to the barbarians." See Snyder, "Celtic Continuity in the Middle Ages"; and David N. Dumville, *Britons and Anglo-Saxons in the Early Middle Ages* (Aldershot: Variorum, 1993), ix: "In the middle ages [the distinction between Britons and English] was a fundamental of political life, which the historian ignores at his peril."

237. See Snyder, "Celtic Continuity in the Middle Ages," 166–67, and the comments by John Hines in *After Empire,* ed., Ausenda, 214: "[The Old English word *walh*] shows a very clear contempt and a sense of the very low status of those who were regarded as Welsh." The Old English word *wealh* (pl. *wealas*) originally meant "a Celtic-speaking person"; on the Continent it was extended by other Germanic speakers to Romanized (i.e., Latin-speaking) peoples in and around Gaul. On the Continent *welsch* came to have pejorative connotations, and in Britain *wealas* (i.e., Welsh) came to mean specifically "slaves" or "foreigners." See Margaret L. Faull, "The Semantic Development of Old English *Wealh,*" *Leeds Studies in English* 8 (1975): 20–37, and Dafydd Jenkins, "*Gwalch:* Welsh," CMCS 19 (1990): 55–67.

238. See Johnson, *Later Roman Britain,* 54, 221, and Salway, *Oxford Illustrated History of Roman Britain,* 339.

Conclusion

1. Leslie Alcock (*Arthur's Britain*) was the first fully to develop the "heroic-society" model for sub-Roman Britain. For contrasting views of the extent of Romanization in Britain, see Millet, *Romanization of Britain,* and Jones, "Failure of Romanization."

2. This position has been argued by Dark, *Civitas,* 172ff.; Higham, *Rome, Britain, and the Anglo-Saxons,* 69–107; and Esmonde Cleary, *Ending,* 131–87.

3. See Wood, "End of Roman Britain," 1–25; Esmonde Cleary, *Ending,* x; and Dark, *Civitas.*

4. See Dumville, "Idea of Government," 178: "Even the history of that . . . sub-Roman generation must have been complex in terms of attitudes and political history."

5. This is particularly illustrated by the epigraphic evidence; see Greenstock, *Some Inscriptions from Roman Britain.*

6. See Dark, *Discovery by Design,* 5: "The Anglo-Saxons, even until A.D. 600, seem to have controlled less than half of the island, while in A.D. 500 it was certainly they, and not the 'Celtic' Britons, who represented a 'fringe' on the 'edge' of the island."

Appendix A

1. E. K. Chambers, *Arthur of Britain* (London: Sidgwick, 1927).

2. Collingwood and Myres, *Roman Britain and the English Settlements.*

3. See R. S. Loomis, *Celtic Myth and Arthurian Romance* (New York: Columbia University Press, 1927); idem, *Wales and the Arthurian Legend* (Cardiff: University of Wales Press, 1956); Kenneth Jackson, "The Arthur of History," in *Arthurian Literature in the Middle Ages,* ed. R. S. Loomis (Oxford: Clarendon Press, 1959); Ashe, *Quest for Arthur's Britain;* and C. A. Ralegh Radford and Michael J. Swanton, *Arthurian Sites in the West* (Exeter: University of Exeter Press, 1975).

4. See, for example, Geoffrey Ashe, *From Caesar to Arthur* (London: Collins, 1960); R. W. Barber, *King Arthur in Legend and History* (London: Cardinal, 1973); Elizabeth Jenkins, *The Mystery of King Arthur* (New York: Coward, McCann & Geoghegan, 1975); and Jean Markale, *King Arthur: King of Kings,* trans. Christine Hauch (London: Gordon & Cremonesi, 1977).

5. Alcock, *Arthur's Britain;* Morris, *Age of Arthur.*

6. Dumville, "Sub-Roman Britain," 188: "The fact of the matter is that there is no historical evidence about Arthur; we must reject him from our histories and, above all, from the titles of our books." Thomas, *Christianity in Roman Britain,* 245: "Any sane person would

agree [with Dumville]. These enticing Will-of-the-wisps have too long dominated, and deflected, useful advances in our study."

7. For a very recent and extreme example, see Higham, *English Conquest,* 211: "There was, therefore, no heroic age fit for the deeds of a King Arthur. . . . Not only did Arthur himself not exist but the age which led to his invention was no less fictional."

8. These vary greatly in quality. See, for example, Robert Dunning, *Arthur: King in the West* (Gloucester: Sutton, 1988); Graham Fife, *Arthur the King* (London: BBC, 1990); Graham Phillips and Martin Keatman, *King Arthur: The True Story* (London: Random House, 1992); C. Scott Littleton and Linda A. Malcor, *From Scythia to Camelot* (New York: Garland, 1994); and Frank D. Reno, *The Historic King Arthur* (Jefferson, N.C.: McFarland, 1996). In some of these, history and fiction are often blurred. See, especially, Norma L. Goodrich, *Merlin* (New York: Franklin Watts, 1987); idem, *Arthur* (New York: Franklin Watts, 1989); and Tom Clare, *King Arthur and the Riders of Rheged* (Kendal, Cumbria: Rheged Books, 1992).

9. See Ashe, "Certain Very Ancient Book," and idem, *Discovery.*

10. Nikolai Tolstoy, *The Quest for Merlin* (Boston: Little, Brown, 1985). See also A.O.H. Jarman, "Early Stages in the Development of the Myrddin Legend," in *Astudiaethau,* ed. Bromwich and Jones, 326–49.

11. Jarman, *Aneirin,* lines 971–72.

12. Morris, *Nennius.*

13. Ibid.

14. See Dumville, "Sub-Roman Britain," 176–77, and idem, "Historical Value of the *Historia Brittonum.*"

15. See Jarman, *Aneirin,* 107–8. The poem seems to have been written down by (at least) two scribes. Scribe A includes this line about Myrddin (though he spells it *mirdyn*), while scribe B does not. Kenneth Jackson sees it as a later interpolation, translating the phrase as "the blessed inspiration of Merlin," in a general sense meaning "Welsh poetry."

16. Lewis Thorpe, trans., *Geoffrey of Monmouth: History of the Kings of Britain* (New York: Penguin, 1966), 6.19.

17. Dumville, "Sub-Roman Britain," 187.

18. Geoffrey Ashe may even be going in this direction; see Ashe, "The Origins of the Arthurian Legends," *Arthuriana* 5, no. 3 (1995): 1–24 ("A more fruitful approach is to ask, not 'Did Arthur exist?' but 'How did the Arthurian legend originate; what facts is it rooted in?' To do so is to acknowledge that this is a literary problem rather than a historical one" [3]).

19. Thomas Charles-Edwards, "The Arthur of History," in *The Arthur of the Welsh: The Arthurian Legend in Medieval Welsh Literature,* ed. Rachel Bromwich et al. (Cardiff: University of Wales Press, 1991), 15–32.

Appendix B

1. This is recorded in the *Gallic Chronicle of 452.* For arguments concerning the date, see Thompson, "Britain, A.D. 406–410"; Miller, "Last British Entry"; Bartholomew, "Fifth-Century Facts"; Muhlberger, "Gallic Chronicle of 452"; Wood, "End of Roman Britain," 1–25; and esp. Jones and Casey, "Gallic Chronicle Restored," 367–97.

2. For the debated significance of this date, see Thompson, "Zosimus," 216, and Cameron, *Procopius,* 213–14.

3. Gildas's "Agitius" could be either Aegidius or Aetius, but only Aetius was consul three times, his third consulship beginning in 446. Bede, in copying this passage from Gildas, gives the form Aetius. However, there are no less than eight men named Flavius Aetius listed in *PLRE* 2, two of whom—the *magister militum* of the West and the *comes domesticorum stabulorum* of the East—held consulships and were exact contemporaries. See Jones, "Appeal to

Aetius in Gildas," and Casey and Jones, "Date of the Letter of the Britons to Aetius." Casey and Jones argue that Gildas, in writing *ter consuli,* was only trying to indicate that the Britons were writing to the *magister* Aetius—"the one who held three consulships"—and thus was not intending any specific date for the letter at all. This leaves us with an alternative range of dates for the letter, the years in which Aetius held office as *magister* and was active in Gaul. Higham (*English Conquest,* 120–41) suggests c. 425–35 to place the appeal before the Saxon devastation of c. 441 recorded in the *Gallic Chronicle,* which maintains the integrity of Gildas's relative chronology of the *adventus Saxonum.* Casey ("The End of Fort Garrisons," 264–65) is more precise, preferring the date 429, and suggests that the appeal came from Brittany, where Aetius was frequently active.

4. For the date of Germanus's second visit, I have followed the argument of Mathisen, "Last Year of Saint Germanus," 58–59. See also Thompson, "Chronological Note," 135–38; idem, *St. Germanus,* 55–70; and Wood, "End of Roman Britain," 14–17.

BIBLIOGRAPHY

I. Bibliographies, Collections, and Dictionaries

Allen, J. Romilly, and Joseph Anderson. *Early Christian Monuments of Scotland.* Edinburgh: Society of Antiquarians of Scotland, 1903.

Bartrum, P. C. *Early Welsh Genealogical Tracts.* Cardiff: University of Wales Press, 1966.

———. *A Welsh Classical Dictionary.* Aberystwyth: National Library of Wales, 1993.

Benoit, Fernand. *Sarcophages paléochrétiens d'Arles et de Marseille, Gallia.* Paris: Centre National de la Recherche Scientifique, 1954.

Bowman, Alan K., and J. David Thomas. *Vindolanda: The Latin Writing-Tablets.* London: Society for the Promotion of Roman Studies, 1983.

Burn, A. R. *The Romans in Britain: An Anthology of Inscriptions.* Columbia: University of South Carolina Press, 1969.

Collingwood, R. G., and R. P. Wright, eds. *Roman Inscriptions of Britain.* Vol. 1. Oxford: Oxford University Press, 1965.

Corpus Inscriptionum Latinarum. Berlin: G. Reinder.

Diehl, Ernestus, ed. *Inscriptiones Latinae Christianae Veteres.* Berlin: Weidmann, 1961.

Du Cange, Charles, et al. *Glossarium Mediae et Infimae Latinitatis.* 10 vols. Paris: Librairie des Sciences et des Arts, 1938.

Du Mortier, Nicholas. *Etymologiae Sacrae Graeceo-Latinae.* Rome: Jacobi Komarech Bohemi, 1703.

Goodburn, Roger, and Helen Waugh. *Roman Inscriptions of Britain I: Inscriptions on Stone: Epigraphic Indexes.* Gloucester: Sutton, 1983.

Greenstock, M. C., ed. *Some Inscriptions from Roman Britain.* 2d ed. Hatfield, Hertfordshire: London Association of Classical Teachers, 1971.

Grierson, Philip, and Melinda Mays. *Catalogue of Late Roman Coins in the Dumbarton Oaks Collection and in the Whittemore Collection: From Arcadius and Honorius to the Accession of Anastasius.* Washington, D.C.: Dumbarton Oaks, 1992.

Ireland, Stanley. *Roman Britain: A Sourcebook.* London: Routledge, 1986.

Jones, A.H.M., J. R. Martindale, and J. Morris. *The Prosopography of the Later Roman Empire.* Vol. 1, A.D. 260–395. Cambridge: Cambridge University Press, 1971.

Koch, John T., ed. *The Celtic Heroic Age: Literary Sources*. Malden, Mass.: Celtic Studies Publications, 1994; 2d ed., 1995.

Lapidge, Michael, and Richard Sharpe. *A Bibliography of Celtic-Latin Literature, 400–1200*. Dublin: Royal Irish Academy, 1985.

Latham, R. E. *The Dictionary of Medieval Latin from British Sources*. London: Oxford University Press, 1975.

MacAlister, R.A.S. *Corpus Inscriptionum Insularum Celticarum*. Vol. 1. Dublin: Stationery Office, 1945.

Mann, J. C., ed. *The Northern Frontier in Britain from Hadrian to Honorius: Literary and Epigraphic Sources*. Newcastle upon Tyne: Museum of Antiquities, 1969.

Martindale, J. R. *The Prosopography of the Later Roman Empire*. Vol. 2, *a.d. 395–527*. Cambridge: Cambridge University Press, 1980.

Mattingly, Harold, et al., eds. *Roman Imperial Coinage*. 10 vols. London: Spink, 1923–; 2d ed. 1984–.

Migne, Jacques Paul. *Patrologia Latina*. 221 vols. Paris: Excudebat Migne, 1844–80.

Mommsen, Theodor, et al., eds. *Monumenta Germaniae Historica*. Berlin: Weidmann, 1826–.

Moore, R. W. *The Romans in Britain: A Selection of Latin Texts Edited with a Commentary*. London: Methuen, 1938.

Nash-Williams, V. E. *The Early Christian Monuments of Wales*. Cardiff: University of Wales Press, 1950.

Noble, Thomas F. X., and Thomas Head, eds. *Soldiers of Christ: Saints and Saints' Lives from Late Antiquity and the Early Middle Ages*. University Park: Pennsylvania State University Press, 1995.

Okasha, Elisabeth. *Corpus of Early Christian Inscribed Stones of Southwestern Britain*. Leicester: Leicester University Press, 1993.

Robertson, Anne S. *Roman Imperial Coins in the Hunter Coin Cabinet, University of Glasgow*. Oxford: Oxford University Press, 1982.

Souter, Alexander, comp. *A Glossary of Later Latin to 600 a.d.* Oxford: Clarendon Press, 1949.

Thesaurus Linguae Latinae. 10 vols. Leipzig: Teubner, 1900–.

Viansino, Ioannes. *Ammiani Mercellini Rerum Gestarum Lexicon*. Hildesheim: Olms-Weidmann, 1985.

Whitelock, Dorothy, ed. *English Historical Documents, c. 500–1042*. New York: Oxford University Press, 1955.

II. Primary Sources

Acta Concilii Arelatensis. In *Concilia Galliae*, Corpus Christianorum, Series Latina, no. 148, ed. C. Munier. Turnhout: Typographi Brepols, 1963.

Adomnán of Iona. *Adomnán of Iona, "Life of St. Columba."* Translated by Richard Sharpe. London: Penguin, 1995.

Ammianus Marcellinus. Translated by John C. Rolfe. 3 vols. Cambridge, Mass.: Harvard University Press, Loeb Classical Library, 1935–40.

Aneirin. *Canu Aneirin*. Edited by Ifor Williams. Cardiff: University of Wales Press, 1938.

——. *Aneirin: Y Gododdin*. Edited and translated by A.O.H. Jarman. Llandysul, Dyfed: Gomer, 1988.

The Anglo-Saxon Chronicle. Edited and translated by G. N. Garmonsway. London: Everyman, 1953.

Aponius. *Explanationis in Canticum Canticorum Libri XII*. Edited by H. Bottino and J. Martini. Rome, 1843.

Armes Prydein: The Prophecy of Britain from the Book of Taliesin. Edited by Ifor Williams, translated by Rachel Bromwich. Dublin: Institute for Advanced Studies, 1972.

Augustine of Hippo. *The City of God Against the Pagans*. Translated by George E. McCracken. 7 vols. Cambridge, Mass.: Harvard University Press, Loeb Classical Library, 1957.

Ausonius. Translated by Hugh G. Evelyn White. 2 vols. Cambridge, Mass.: Harvard University Press, Loeb Classical Library, 1919.

Bartolus of Sassoferrato. *De Tyranno*. Edited by Diego Quaglioni. *Il "De Tyranno" di Bartolo da Sassoferrato (1314–57)* . Florence: Leo S. Olschki, 1983.

Bede. *Baedae: Opera Historica*. Translated by J. E. King. 2 vols. Cambridge, Mass.: Harvard University Press, Loeb Classical Library, 1930.

——. *Bede: A History of the English Church and People*. Translated by Leo Sherley-Price. Harmondsworth, Middlesex: Penguin, 1955.

Brut y Tywysogyon, or "The Chronicle of the Princes." Edited and translated by Thomas Jones. Cardiff: University of Wales Press, 1955.

Claudian. Edited and translated by Maurice Platnauer. 2 vols. Cambridge, Mass.: Harvard University Press, Loeb Classical Library, 1922.

Codex Theodosianus. Edited by Theodor Mommsen, Paul Meyer, and Paul Kruger. 2 vols. Hildesheim: Weidmann, 1990.

Constantius. *Vita Sancti Germani*. Edited by Wilhelm Levison. In *Scriptores Rerum Merovingicarum*, vol. 7 of *Monumenta Germaniae Historica*. Berlin: Weidmann, 1920.

——. *Vita Sancti Germani*. Edited, with a French translation, by Rene Borius. In *Constance de Lyon: Vie de Saint Germain d'Auxerre*. Paris: Les Editions du Cerf, 1965.

Eutropius. *Breviarum ab Urbe Condita*. Edited by C. Santini. Leipzig: Teubner, 1979.

Fragmenta Historicum Graecorum. Edited by Karl Muller. Vols. 4 and 5. Paris: Ambrosio, 1851 and 1870.

Geoffrey of Monmouth. *Geoffrey of Monmouth: History of the Kings of Britain*. Translated by Lewis Thorpe. New York: Penguin, 1966.

Geographi Latini Minores. Edited by Alexander Riese. Hildesheim: G. Olms, 1964.

Gildas. *Gildas*. Edited and translated by Hugh Williams. 2 vols. London: Cymmrodorian, 1899–1901.

——. *Gildas: The Ruin of Britain and Other Works*. Edited and translated by Michael Winterbottom. Totowa, N.J.: Rowman & Littlefield, 1978.

The Gododdin: The Oldest Scottish Poem. Translated by Kenneth Jackson.

Edinburgh: Edinburgh University Press, 1969.

Gregory of Tours. *Historia Francorum.* Edited, with a German translation, by Rudolf Buchner. In *Gregor von Tours: Zehn Bücher Geschichten.* 2 vols. Berlin: Rutten & Loening, 1955.

———. *History of the Franks.* Translated by Lewis Thorpe. New York: Penguin, 1974.

The Irish Penitentials. Scriptores Latini Hiberniae, vol. 5, edited by Ludwig Bieler. Dublin: Institute for Advanced Studies, 1963.

Leontius. *The Life of St. John the Almsgiver.* In *Three Byzantine Saints,* translated by Elizabeth Dawes and Norman H. Baynes. London: Mowbrays, 1977.

Liber Landavensis: The Text of the Book of Llan Dâv. Edited by J. G. Evans. Oxford, 1893; Aberystwyth: National Library of Wales, 1979.

Lives of the Welsh Saints. Edited by Gilbert H. Doble. Cardiff: University of Wales Press, 1984.

The Llandaff Charters. Edited by Wendy Davies. Aberystwyth: National Library of Wales, 1979.

Muirchú. *Vita Sancti Patricii.* In *Four Latin Lives of St. Patrick,* ed. Ludwig Bieler. Dublin: Institute for Advanced Studies, 1971.

Nennius: British History and the Welsh Annals. Edited and translated by John Morris. London: Phillimore, 1980.

Notitia Dignitatum. Edited by Otto Seeck. Frankfurt: Minerva, 1962.

Orosius. *Adversum Paganos.* Edited by C. Zangemeister. Hildesheim: G. Olmse, 1967.

———. *Seven Books of History Against the Pagans.* Translated by I. W. Raymond. New York: Columbia University Press, 1936.

The Patrician Texts in the Book of Armagh. Edited and translated by Ludwig Bieler and Fergus Kelly. Dublin: Institute for Advanced Studies, 1979.

Patrick, Saint. *Epistola* and *Confessio.* Edited and translated by A.B.E. Hood. In *St. Patrick: His Writings and Muirchu's "Life."* London: Phillimore, 1978.

———. *Epistola* and *Confessio.* Translated by R.P.C. Hanson. In *The Life and Writings of the Historical St. Patrick.* New York: Seabury, 1983.

———. "Libri Epistolarum Sancti Patricii Episcopi." Edited by Ludwig Bieler. *Classica et Mediaevalia* 11 (1950): 1–150, and 12 (1951): 81–214.

Procopius. *Anekdota.* Translated by H. B. Dewing. Cambridge, Mass.: Harvard University Press, Loeb Classical Library, 1925.

———. *History of the Wars.* Translated by H. B. Dewing. Cambridge, Mass.: Harvard University Press, Loeb Classical Library, 1919.

Prosper of Aquitaine. *Chronicon.* In bk. 1 of *Chronica Minora,* vol. 9 of *Monumenta Germaniae Historica,* edited by Theodor Mommsen. Berlin: Weidmann, 1892.

Prudentius. *Prudence: Contre Symmaque et Peristephanon.* Edited and translated by Maurice Lavarenne. 2 vols. Paris: Les Belles Lettres, 1963.

Redon Cartulary. Edited by Aurélien de Courson. In *Cartulaire de l'abbaye de Redon en Bretagne.* Paris: Imprimerie Impérial, 1863.

"The Ruin" (eighth century). Translated by Kevin Crossley-Holland. In *The Anglo-Saxon World: An Anthology.* Oxford: Oxford University Press, 1984.

Rutilius Namatianus. *De Reditu Suo.* In *Claudio Rutilio Namaziano: De Reditu,* edited by Emanuele Castorina. Firenze: Sansoni, 1967.

Salvian. *Salvien de Marseille: Oeuvres.* Edited, with a French translation, by Georges Lagarrigue. 2 vols. Paris: Les Editions du Cerf, 1971.

———. *The Writings of Salvian.* Translated by J. F. O'Sullivan. Washington, D.C.: Catholic University of America Press, 1962.

Scriptores Historiae Augustae. Edited by Ernestus Hohl. 3 vols. Leipzig: Teubner, 1971.

Scriptores Historiae Augustae. Translated by David Magie. Cambridge, Mass.: Harvard University Press, 1932.

Sidonius. *Sidonius Appolinaris: Poems and Letters.* Edited and translated by W. B. Anderson. 2 vols. Cambridge, Mass.: Harvard University Press, Loeb Classical Library, 1936.

Sozomen. *The Ecclesiastical History of Sozomen.* Translated by Edward Walford. London: Bohn, 1855.

———. *Sozomenus Kirchengeschichte.* Edited by Joseph Bidez. Berlin: Akadamie-Verlag, 1960.

Sulpicius Severus. *Vita Sancti Martini.* Edited, with a French translation, by Jacques Fontaine. In *Sulpice Severe: Vie de Saint Martin.* Paris: Les Edition du Cerf, 1967.

Taliesin. *The Poems of Taliesin.* Edited by Ifor Williams, translated by J. E. Caerwyn Williams. Dublin: Institute for Advanced Studies, 1968.

Trioedd Ynys Prydein: The Welsh Triads. Edited and translated by Rachel Bromwich. Cardiff: University of Wales Press, 1961; 2d ed., 1978.

Vitae Sanctorum Britanniae et Genealogiae. Edited and translated by A. W. Wade-Evans. Cardiff: University of Wales Press, 1944.

The Western Fathers. Translated by F. R. Hoare. New York: Sheed & Ward, 1954.

William of Malmesbury. *Chronicle of the Kings of England.* Translated by J. A. Giles. London: Henry G. Bohn, 1847.

XII Panegyrici Latini. Edited by R.A.B. Mynors. Oxford: Clarendon Press, 1964.

Zosimus. *Historia Nova.* Edited by Ludwig Mendelssohn. Leipzig: Teubner, 1887.

———. *Historia Nova.* Edited, with a French translation, by François Paschoud. In *Zosime: Histoire nouvelle.* 3 vols. Paris: Les Belles Lettres, 1989.

———. *Zosimus: New History.* Translated by Ronald T. Ridley. Sydney: Australian Association for Byzantine Studies, 1982.

III. Secondary Sources

Abrams, Leslie, and James P. Carley, eds. *The Archaeology and History of Glastonbury Abbey: Essays in Honor of the Ninetieth Birthday of C. A. Ralegh Radford.* Woodbridge, Suffolk: Boydell, 1991.

Adams, Jeremy DuQuesnay. "Sidonius and Riothamus." *Arthurian Literature* 12 (1993): 157–64.

Alcock, Elizabeth A. "Appendix: Defended Settlements, Fifth to Seventh Centuries A.D." In *Twenty-Five Years of Medieval Archaeology,* edited by David A.

Hinton, 58–59. Sheffield: Department of Prehistory and Archaeology, University of Sheffield, 1983.

———. "Appendix: Enclosed Places, A.D. 500–800." In *Power and Politics in Early Medieval Britain and Ireland,* edited by S. T. Driscoll and M. R. Nieke, 40–46. Edinburgh: Edinburgh University Press, 1988.

Alcock, Leslie. "The Activities of Potentates in Celtic Britain, A.D. 500–800: A Positivist Approach." In *Power and Politics in Early Medieval Britain and Ireland,* edited by S. T. Driscoll and M. R. Nieke, 22–46. Edinburgh: Edinburgh University Press, 1988.

———. "The Archaeology of Celtic Britain, Fifth to Twelfth Centuries A.D." In *Twenty-Five Years of Medieval Archaeology,* edited by David A. Hinton, 48–66. Sheffield: Department of Prehistory and Archaeology, University of Sheffield, 1983.

———. *Arthur's Britain.* New York: Penguin, 1971.

———. *Bede, Eddius, and the Forts of the North Britons.* Jarrow Lecture. Jarrow: St. Paul's Church, 1988.

———. "'By South Cadbury Is That Camelot . . .'" *Antiquity* 41 (1967): 50–53.

———. *"By South Cadbury Is That Camelot."* London: Thames & Hudson, 1972.

———. "Cadbury Castle, 1967." *Antiquity* 43 (1968): 52–56.

———. "The Cadbury Castle Sequence in the First Millennium B.C." *BBCS* 28 (1980): 656–718.

———. "Cadbury-Camelot: A Fifteen-Year Perspective." *Proceedings of the British Academy* 68 (1982): 355–88.

———. *Dinas Powys: An Iron Age, Dark Age, and Early Medieval Settlement in Glamorgan.* Cardiff: University of Wales Press, 1963.

———. *Economy, Society, and Warfare Among the Britons and Saxons.* Cardiff: University of Wales Press, 1987.

———. "Excavations at Cadbury-Camelot, 1966–70." *Antiquity* 46 (1972): 29–38.

———. "Excavations at South Cadbury Castle, 1967: A Summary Report." *Antiquities Journal* 48 (1968): 6–17.

———. "Excavations at South Cadbury Castle, 1968: A Summary Report." *Antiquities Journal* 49 (1969): 30–40.

———. "Excavations at South Cadbury Castle, 1969: A Summary Report." *Antiquities Journal* 50 (1970): 14–25.

———. "Excavations at South Cadbury Castle, 1970: A Summary Report." *Antiquities Journal* 51 (1971): 1–7.

———. "Gwyr y Gogledd: An Archaeological Appraisal." *Archaeologia Cambrensis* 132 (1983): 1–18.

———. "The North Britons, the Picts, and the Scots." In *The End of Roman Britain,* BAR British Series, no. 71, edited by P. J. Casey, 134–42. Oxford: Tempvs Reparatvm, 1979.

———. *"Populi Bestiales Pictorum Feroci Animo*: A Survey of Pictish Settlement Archaeology." In *Roman Frontier Studies, 1979: Papers Presented to the Twelfth International Congress of Roman Frontier Studies,* BAR International Series 71, edited by W. S. Hanson and L.J.F. Keppie, 1:61–95. Oxford: Tempvs Reparatvm, 1980.

―――. "A Reconnaissance Excavation at South Cadbury Castle, Somerset." *Antiquities Journal* 47 (1967): 70–76.

―――. "Refortified or Newly Fortified? The Chronology of Dinas Powys." *Antiquity* 54 (1980): 231–32.

―――. "South Cadbury Excavations, 1968." *Antiquity* 43 (1969): 52–56.

―――. "South Cadbury Excavations, 1969." *Antiquity* 44 (1970): 46–49.

―――. "A Survey of Pictish Settlement Archaeology." In *Pictish Studies: Settlement, Burial, and Art in Dark Age Northern Britain,* BAR British Series, no. 125, edited by J.G.P. Friell and W. G. Watson, 7–41. Oxford: Tempvs Reparatvm, 1984.

―――. "Wales in the Arthurian Age." In *The Quest for Arthur's Britain*, ed. Geoffrey Ashe, 79–95. St. Albans: Paladin Press, 1971.

―――. "Was There an Irish Sea Culture–Province in the Dark Ages?" In *The Irish Sea Province in Archaeology and History,* edited by Donald Moore, 55–65. Cardiff: Cambrian Archaeological Association, 1970.

Alcock, Leslie, and Geoffrey Ashe. "Cadbury: Is It Camelot?" In *The Quest for Arthur's Britain,* edited by Geoffrey Ashe, 123–47. St. Albans: Paladin Press, 1971.

Alcock, Leslie, et al. *Cadbury Castle, Somerset: The Early Medieval Archaeology.* Cardiff: University of Wales Press, 1995.

Allason-Jones, Lindsay. *Women in Roman Britain.* London: British Museum Publications, 1989.

Andrewes, Antony. *The Greeks.* New York: W. W. Norton, 1967.

―――. *The Greek Tyrants.* New York: Harper & Row, 1963.

Applebaum, Shimon. "Land Tenure and Politics in Fifth-Century Britain." In *The Romano-British Countryside: Studies in Rural Settlement and Economy,* edited by David Miles, BAR British Series, no. 103:433–49. Oxford: Tempvs Reparatvm, 1982.

Arnold, C. J. "The End of Roman Britain: Some Discussion." In *The Romano-British Countryside: Studies in Rural Settlement and Economy,* edited by David Miles, BAR British Series, no. 103:451–59. Oxford: Tempvs Reparatvm, 1982.

―――. *Roman Britain to Saxon England.* Bloomington: Indiana University Press, 1984.

Ashe, Geoffrey. *Avalonian Quest.* London: Fontana, 1984.

―――. "A Certain Very Ancient Book." *Speculum* 56 (1981): 301–23.

―――. *The Discovery of King Arthur.* New York: Doubleday, 1985.

―――. "The Origins of the Arthurian Legends." *Arthuriana* 5, no. 3 (1995): 1–24.

―――, ed. *The Quest for Arthur's Britain.* St. Albans: Paladin, 1971.

Askew, Gilbert. *The Coinage of Roman Britain.* 2d ed. London: Seaby, 1980.

Atkinson, Donald. *Report on Excavations at Wroxeter.* Oxford: Oxford University Press, 1942.

Ausenda, Giorgio, ed. *After Empire: Towards an Ethnology of Europe's Barbarians.* Woodbridge, Suffolk: Boydell, 1995.

Bachrach, B. S. "Gildas, Vortigern, and Constitutionality in Sub-Roman Britain." *Nottingham Medieval Studies* 32 (1988): 126–40.

Baldwin, B. "Olympiodorus of Thebes." *L'Antiquité Classique* 49 (1980): 212–31.

Bammesberger, Alfred, and Alfred Wollmann, eds. *Britain, 400–600: Language and*

History. Anglistische Forschungen, no. 205. Heidelberg: C. Winter, 1990.

Barker, Philip. "Excavations at the Baths Basilica at Wroxeter, 1966–74: Interim Report." *Britannia* 6 (1975): 106–17.

———. *Excavations on the Site of the Baths Basilica, at Wroxeter, 1966–73.* Birmingham, 1973.

———, ed. *From Roman "Virconium" to Medieval Wroxeter.* Worcester, Hereford and Worcester: West Mercian Archaeological Consultants, 1990.

———. *Wroxeter Roman City Excavations, 1960–80.*

Barker, Philip, et al. "Two Burials Under the Refectory at Worcester Cathedral." *Medieval Archaeology* 18 (1974): 146–51.

Barley, M. W., and R.P.C. Hanson, eds. *Christianity in Britain, 300–700.* Leicester: Leicester University Press, 1968.

Bartholomew, Philip. "Fifth-Century Facts." *Britannia* 13 (1982): 261–70.

———. "Fourth-Century Saxons." *Britannia* 15 (1984): 169–85.

Bartlett, Robert. *Gerald of Wales, 1146–1223.* Oxford: Clarendon Press, 1982.

Bassett, Steven. "Church and Diocese in the West Midlands: The Transition from British to Anglo-Saxon Control." In *Pastoral Care Before the Parish,* edited by John Blair and Richard Sharpe, 13–40. Leicester: Leicester University Press, 1992.

———. "Churches in Worcester Before and After the Conversion of the Anglo-Saxons." *Antiquarians Journal* 69 (1989): 225–56.

———. "In Search of the Origins of Anglo-Saxon Kingdoms." In *The Origins of Anglo-Saxon Kingdoms,* edited by Steven Bassett, 3–27. Leicester: Leicester University Press, 1989.

———, ed. *The Origins of the Anglo-Saxon Kingdoms.* Leicester: Leicester University Press, 1989.

Bateson, J. D. *Enamel-Working in Iron Age, Roman, and Sub-Roman Britain.* BAR British Series, no. 93. Oxford: Tempvs Reparatvm, 1981.

Beacham, Peter, et al., eds. *Archaeology of the Devon Landscape.* Exeter: County Planning Department, 1980.

Bell, Martin. *Brean Down Excavations, 1983–87.* London: English Heritage, 1990.

Biddle, Martin. "The Study of Winchester: Archaeology and History in a British Town." *Proceedings of the British Academy* 69 (1983): 93–135.

———. "Towns." In *The Archaeology of Anglo-Saxon England,* edited by David M. Wilson, 99–150. London: Methuen, 1976.

Biddle, Martin, and Birthe Kjølbye-Biddle. *The Origins of Saint Albans Abbey: Excavations in the Cloister, 1982–1983.* St. Albans, Hertfordshire: St. Albans Abbey Research Committee, 1984.

Bidwell, Paul T. *Roman Exeter: Fortress and Town.* Exeter: Exeter Museums Service, 1980.

———. *The Roman Fort of Vindolanda at Chesterholm, Northumberland.* London: Historic Buildings and Monuments Commission, 1985.

Bidwell, Paul T., and Stephen Speak. "South Shields." *Current Archaeology* 116 (1989): 283–87.

Bieler, Ludwig. "Der Bibeltext des Heiligen Patrick." *Biblica* 28 (1947): 31–58 and 236–63.

Birley, Anthony R. *The "Fasti" of Roman Britain*. Oxford: Clarendon Press, 1981.
————. *The People of Roman Britain*. Berkeley and Los Angeles: University of California Press, 1980.
Birley, Robin. *Civilians on the Roman Frontier*. Newcastle: Graham, 1973.
————. *The Roman Documents from Vindolanda*. Greenhead: Roman Army Museum Publications, 1990.
————. "Vindolanda." *Current Archaeology* 116 (1989): 275–79.
Bitel, Lisa M. *Isle of the Saints: Monastic Settlement and Christian Community in Early Ireland*. Ithaca, N.Y.: Cornell University Press, 1990.
Blackburn, Mark. "Three Silver Coins in the Names of Valentinian III (425–55) and Anthemius (467–72) from Chatham Lines, Kent." *Numismatic Chronicle* 148 (1988): 169–74.
Blagg, T.F.C., and A. C. King, eds. *Military and Civilian in Roman Britain*. BAR British Series, no. 136. Oxford: Tempvs Reparatvm, 1984.
Blair, John, and Richard Sharpe, eds. *Pastoral Care Before the Parish*. Leicester: Leicester University Press, 1992.
Blockley, P. "Excavations at Ridingate." *Archaeologia Cantiana* 100 (1984): 205–9.
Blockley, R. C. *The Fragmentary Classicising Historians of the Later Roman Empire: Eunapius, Olympiodorus, Priscus, and Malchus*. Liverpool: Francis Cairns, 1983.
Böhme, Horst Wolfgang. "Das Ende der Römerherrschaft in Britannien und die Angelsächsische Besiedlung Englands im 5. Jahrhundert." *Jahrbuch des Romisch-Germanischen Zentralmuseums Mainz* 33 (1986): 469–574.
Boon, George C. "Counterfeit Coins in Roman Britain." In *Coins and the Archaeologist*, by P. J. Casey and Richard M. Reece, 2d ed., 102–88. London: Seaby, 1988.
————. "The Latest Objects from Silchester, Hampshire." *Medieval Archaeology* 3 (1959): 79–88.
————. *The Roman Town "Calleva Atrebatum" at Silchester, Hampshire*. Reading: Calleva Museum, 1983.
————. *Silchester: The Roman Town of Calleva*. London: David & Charles, 1974.
————. "The Silchester Ogham." *Antiquity* 54 (1980): 122–23.
————. "Theodosian Coins from North and South Wales." *BBCS* 33 (1986): 429–35.
Bowen, E. G. "Britain and the British Seas." In *The Irish Sea Province in Archaeology and History*, edited by Donald Moore, 13–28. Cardiff: Cambrian Archaeological Association, 1970.
Bowman, Alan K. *The Roman Writing Tablets from Vindolanda*. London: British Museum Publications, 1983.
Branigan, Keith. *The Catuvellauni*. Gloucester: Sutton, 1985.
————. *Town and Country: The Archaeology of Verulamium and the Roman Chilterns*. Bourne End, Buckinghamshire: Spurbooks, 1973.
Breeze, David J. *The Northern Frontiers of Roman Britain*. New York: St. Martin's, 1982.
Breeze, David J., and Brian Dobson. *Hadrian's Wall*. London: Penguin, 1976; 3d ed., 1987.

————. "Roman Military Deployment in North England." *Britannia* 16 (1985): 1–19.

Brickstock, R. J. *Copies of the Fel. Temp. Reparatio Coinage in Britain.* BAR Series, no. 176. Oxford: Tempvs Reparatvm, 1987.

Britnell, W. J. "Capel Maelog, Llandrindod Wells, Powys: Excavations, 1984–87." *Medieval Archaeology* 34 (1990): 27–96.

Bromwich, Rachel, and R. F. Jones, eds. *Astudiaethau ar yr Hengerdd: Studies in Old Welsh Poetry.* Cardiff: Gwasg Prifysgol Cymru, 1978.

Bromwich, Rachel, et al., eds. *The Arthur of the Welsh: The Arthurian Legend in Medieval Welsh Literature.* Cardiff: University of Wales Press, 1991.

Brooke, C.N.L., et al., eds. *Studies in Numismatic Method Presented to Philip Grierson.* Cambridge: Cambridge University Press, 1983.

Brooke, Daphne. *Wild Men and Holy Places: St. Ninian, Whithorn, and the Medieval Realm of Galloway.* Edinburgh: Canongate Press, 1994.

Brooks, Dodie A. "The Case for Continuity in Fifth-Century Canterbury Re-Examined." *Oxford Journal of Archaeology* 7 (1988): 99–114.

————. "Gildas' *De Excidio*: Its Revolutionary Meaning and Purpose." *Studia Celtica* 18 (1983): 1–10.

————. "A Review of the Evidence for Continuity in British Towns in the Fifth and Sixth Centuries." *Oxford Journal of Archaeology* 5, no. 1 (1986): 77–102.

Bryant, R. "Excavations at the Church of St. Mary de Lode, Gloucester." *Bulletin of the CBA Churches Committee* 13 (1980): 15–18.

Burgess, R. W. "The Dark Ages Return to Fifth-Century Britain: The 'Restored' Gallic Chronicle Exploded." *Britannia* 21 (1990): 185–95.

Burkitt, F. C., and L.C.G. Clarke. "Roman Pewter Bowl from the Isle of Ely." *Proceedings of the Cambridge Antiquarian Society* 31 (1931): 66–72.

Burl, Aubrey, ed. *From Roman Town to Norman Castle: Essays in Honor of Philip Barker.* Birmingham: Birmingham University Press, 1988.

Burnett, A. M. "The Newton Mills, Bath, Treasure Trove." In *Coin Hoards from Roman Britain,* ed. A. M. Burnett and Roger Bland, 193–98. London: British Museum, 1987.

Burnett, Andrew. "Clipped *Siliquae* and the End of Roman Britain." *Britannia* 15 (1984): 163–68.

Burnham, Barry C., and John Wacher. *The "Small Towns" of Roman Britain.* London: Batsford, 1990.

Burnham, Barry C., and J. L. Davies, eds. *Conquest, Co-Existence, and Change.* Lampeter, Dyfed: St. David's University College, 1990.

Burns, Thomas S. *Barbarians Within the Gates of Rome: A Study of Roman Military Policy and the Barbarians, ca. 375–425.* Bloomington: Indiana University Press, 1994.

————. *A History of the Ostrogoths.* Bloomington: Indiana University Press, 1984.

Burns, Thomas S., and Bernhard H. Overbeck. *Rome and the Germans As Seen in Coinage: Catalog for the Exhibition.* Atlanta, Ga.: Emory University, 1987.

Burrow, Ian C. G. "Dark Age Devon: The Landscape, A.D. 400–1100." In *Archaeology of the Devon Landscape,* edited by Peter Beacham et al. Exeter: County Planning Department, 1980.

———. *Hillfort and Hill-Top Settlement in Somerset in the First to Eighth Centuries a.d.* BAR British Series, no. 91. Oxford: Tempvs Reparatvm, 1981.

———. Review of *Economy, Society, and Warfare,* by Leslie Alcock. *Antiquity* 61 (1987): 494–95.

———. "Tintagel: Some Problems." *Scottish Archaeological Forum* 5 (1973): 99–103.

Bury, J. B. *History of the Later Roman Empire.* London: Macmillan, 1889; 2d ed., London: Dover, 1923.

———. *The Life of St. Patrick and His Place in History.* London: Macmillan, 1905.

Cameron, Averil. *The Mediterranean World in Late Antiquity, a.d. 395–600.* London: Routledge, 1993.

———. *Procopius and the Sixth Century.* London: Duckworth, 1985.

Cameron, Averil, and Amélie Kuhrt, eds. *Images of Women in Antiquity.* Detroit: Wayne State University Press, 1983.

Campbell, Ewan. "Coygan Camp." In *Early Medieval Settlements in Wales, a.d. 400–1100,* edited by Nancy Edwards and Alan Lane, 44–46. Cardiff: University of Wales Press, 1988.

———. "Dinas Emrys." In *Early Medieval Settlements in Wales, a.d. 400–1100,* edited by Nancy Edwards and Alan Lane, 54–57. Cardiff: University of Wales Press, 1988.

———. "Longbury Bank." In *Early Medieval Settlements in Wales, a.d. 400–1100,* edited by Nancy Edwards and Alan Lane, 88–90. Cardiff: University of Wales Press, 1988.

———. "New Finds of Post-Roman Imported Pottery and Glass from South Wales." *Archaeologia Cambrensis* 138 (1989): 59–66.

Campbell, Ewan, and Alan Lane. "Excavations at Longbury Bank, Dyfed." *Medieval Archaeology* 37 (1993): 15–77.

Campbell, James, ed. *The Anglo-Saxons.* Ithaca, N.Y.: Cornell University Press, 1982.

Carette, Ernest. *Droit romain: Les assemblies provinciales de la Gaule romaine.* Paris: A. Picard, 1895.

Carney, James. *The Problem of St. Patrick.* Dublin: Institute for Advanced Studies, 1961.

Casey, P. J. *Carausius and Allectus: The British Usurpers.* London: Batsford, 1994; New Haven: Yale University Press, 1995.

———. "Constantine the Great in Britain: The Evidence of the Coinage at the London Mint." In *Collectanea Londiniensia,* London and Middlesex Archaeological Society Special Paper, no. 2, edited by J. Bird, H. Chapman, and J. Clark, 181–93. London: London and Middlesex Archaeological Society, 1978.

———. "The End of Fort Garrisons on Hadrian's Wall: A Hypothetical Model." In *L'armée romaine et les barbares du IIIe au VIIe siécle,* edited by Françoise Vallet and Michel Kazanski, 259–68. Rouen: Musée des Antiquités Nationales, 1994.

———. *Roman Coinage in Britain.* Aylesbury: Shire Archaeology, 1980.

———, ed. *The End of Roman Britain.* BAR British Series, no. 71. Oxford: Tempvs Reparatvm, 1979.

Casey, P. J., and Michael E. Jones. "The Date of the Letter of the Britons to Aetius." *BBCS* 37 (1990): 281–90.

Casey, P. J., and Richard M. Reece. *Coins and the Archaeologist.* 2d ed. London: Seaby, 1988.

Chadwick, Nora K. *The British Heroic Age.* Cardiff: University of Wales Press, 1976.

———. "Colonization of Brittany from Celtic Britain." *Proceedings of the British Academy* 51 (1965): 235–99.

———. *Early Brittany.* Cardiff: University of Wales Press, 1969.

———. *Poetry and Letters in Early Christian Gaul.* London: Bowes & Bowes, 1955.

Chadwick, Owen. "Gildas and the Monastic Order." *Journal of Theological Studies,* n.s., 5 (1954): 78–80.

Chapman, Malcolm. *The Celts: The Construction of a Myth.* New York: St. Martin's, 1992.

Charles-Edwards, Thomas. "The Arthur of History." In *The Arthur of the Welsh: The Arthurian Legend in Medieval Welsh Literature,* edited by Rachel Bromwich et al., 15–32. Cardiff: University of Wales Press, 1991.

———. "The Authenticity of the *Gododdin*: An Historian's View." In *Astudiaethau ar yr Hengerdd: Studies in Old Welsh Poetry,* ed. Rachel Bromwich and R. F. Jones, 44–71. Cardiff: Gwasg Prifysgol Cymru, 1978.

———. "Native Political Organization in Roman Britain and the Origins of MW *Brenhin*." In *Antiquitates Indo-Germanicae,* ed. M. Mayrhofer et al., 35–45. Innsbruck, 1974.

———. Review of *Gildas: New Approaches,* edited by Michael Lapidge and David N. Dumville. *CMCS* 12 (1986): 120.

———. "Some Celtic Kinship Terms." *BBCS* 24 (1971): 105–22.

Clarke, David T. *Roman Colchester.* Colchester: Colchester Borough Council, 1980.

Clarke, Giles. *The Roman Cemetery at Lankhills.* Winchester Studies, no. 3: Pre-Roman and Roman Winchester, pt. 2. Oxford: Clarendon Press, 1979.

Collingwood, R. G. *The Archaeology of Roman Britain.* New York: Dial Press, 1930.

Collingwood, R. G., and J.N.L. Myres. *Roman Britain and the English Settlements.* Oxford: Clarendon Press, 1936.

Corbishley, Mike. *Town Life in Roman Britain.* London: Harrap, 1981.

Crickmore, Julie. *Romano-British Urban Settlements in the West Midlands.* BAR British Series, no. 127. Oxford: Tempvs Reparatvm, 1984.

Crone, Anne. "Buiston Crannog." *Current Archaeology* 127 (1991): 295–97.

Crow, J. G. *Housesteads Roman Fort.* London: English Heritage, 1989.

Cruden, Stewart. *Early Christian and Pictish Monuments.* London: HMSO, 1964.

Crummy, Philip. *Colchester Archaeological Report 1: Aspects of Anglo-Saxon and Norman Colchester.* CBA Research Report, no. 39. London: CBA, 1981.

———. *Colchester Archaeological Report 3: Excavations at Lion Walk, Balkerne Lane, and Middleborough.* Colchester: Archaeological Trust, 1984.

———. "A Roman Church in Colchester." *Current Archaeology* 120 (1990): 406–8.

Cummins, W. A. *The Age of the Picts.* Stroud, Gloucestershire: Alan Sutton, 1995.

Cunliffe, Barry. *The Celtic World.* New York: Crown, 1986.

————. *The City of Bath*. Gloucester: Sutton, 1986.

————. *Excavations at Portchester Castle*. Vol. 1, *Roman*. Society of Antiquaries Research Report, no. 32. London: Society of Antiquaries, 1975.

————. *Excavations at Portchester Castle*. Vol. 2, *Saxon*. Society of Antiquaries Research Report, no. 33. London: Society of Antiquaries, 1976.

————. "Images of Britannia." *Antiquity* 58 (1984): 175–78.

————. *Iron Age Britain*. London: Batsford/English Heritage, 1995.

————. *The Regni*. London: Duckworth, 1973.

————. *Roman Bath Discovered*. London: Routledge & Kegan Paul, 1971; rev. ed., 1984.

Cunliffe, Barry, and Peter Davenport. *The Temple of Sulis Minerva at Bath*. Vol. 1, *The Site*. Oxford: University Committee for Archaeology, 1985.

Daniels, C. M. "Excavation at Wallsend and the Fourth-Century Barracks on Hadrian's Wall." In *Roman Frontier Studies, 1979: Papers Presented to the Twelfth International Congress of Roman Frontier Studies*, BAR International Series 71, edited by W. S. Hanson and L.J.F. Keppie, 1:173–93. Oxford: Tempvs Reparatvm, 1980.

Dark, Kenneth Rainsbury. "Celtic Monastic Archaeology: Fifth to Eighth Centuries." *Monastic Studies* 14 (1983): 17–30.

————. *Civitas to Kingdom: British Political Continuity, 300–800*. Leicester: Leicester University Press, 1993.

————. *Discovery by Design: The Identification of Secular Elite Settlements in Western Britain, a.d. 400–700*. BAR British Series, no. 237. Oxford: Tempvs Reparatvm, 1994.

————. "High Status Sites, Kingship, and State Formation in Post-Roman Western Britain, A.D. 400–700." Ph.D. thesis, Cambridge University, 1989.

————. *The Inscribed Stones of Dyfed*. Llandysul, Dyfed: Gomer Press, 1992.

————. "The Plan and Interpretation of Tintagel." *CMCS* 9 (1985): 1–17.

————. Review of *Tintagel: Arthur and Archaeology*, by Charles Thomas. *CMCS* 28 (1994): 103–4.

————. "Saint Patrick's *Uillula* and the Fifth-Century Occupation of Romano-British Villas." In *Saint Patrick, a.d. 493–1993*, by David N. Dumville et al., 19–24. Woodbridge, Suffolk: Boydell, 1993.

————. "A Sub-Roman Re-Defense of Hadrian's Wall?" *Britannia* 23 (1992): 111–20.

Darling, M. J. "The Caistor-by-Norwich 'Massacre' Reconsidered." *Britannia* 18 (1987): 263–72.

Davies, J. L., and D. P. Kirby. Review of *Civitas to Kingdom*, by Kenneth Rainsbury Dark. *CMCS* 29 (1995): 70–72.

Davies, J. L., et al. "The Hut Settlement on Gateholm, Pembrokeshire." *Archaeologia Cambrensis* 120 (1971): 102–10.

Davies, K. Rutherford. *Britons and Saxons. The Chiltern Region*. Chichester: Phillimore, 1982.

Davies, R. R., et al. *Welsh Society and Nationhood*. Cardiff: University of Wales Press, 1984.

Davies, Wendy. "Celtic Women in the Early Middle Ages." In *Images of Women in*

Antiquity, edited by Averil Cameron and Amélie Kuhrt, 145–66. Detroit: Wayne State University Press, 1983.

———. *An Early Welsh Microcosm: Studies in the Llandaff Charters.* London: Royal Historical Society, 1978.

———. "A Historian's View of Celtic Archaeology." In *Twenty-Five Years of Medieval Archaeology,* edited by David A. Hinton, 67–73. Sheffield: Department of Prehistory and Archaeology, University of Sheffield, 1983.

———. "Land and Power in Early Medieval Wales." *Past and Present* 8 (1978): 323ff.

———. "The Myth of the Celtic Church." In *The Early Church in Wales and the West,* Oxbow Monograph, no. 16, edited by Nancy Edwards and Alan Lane, 12–21. Oxford: Oxbow, 1992.

———. *Patterns of Power in Early Wales.* Oxford: Clarendon Press, 1990.

———. *Small Worlds: The Village Community in Early Medieval Brittany.* London: Duckworth, 1988.

———. "*Unciae*: Land Measurement in the Liber Landavensis." *Agrarian History Review* 21 (1973): 115–17.

———. *Wales in the Early Middle Ages.* Leicester: Leicester University Press, 1982.

De La Bedoyere, Guy. *The Buildings of Roman Britain.* London: Batsford, 1991.

———. *The Finds of Roman Britain.* London: Batsford, 1989.

Demougeot, Emilienne. "Constantin III, l'empereur d'Arles." In *Hommage a André Dupont,* 83–125. Montpellier: Federation Historique du Languedoc, 1974.

———. *De l'unité a la division de l'empire Romain: 395–410.* Paris, 1951.

De Paor, Liam. *Saint Patrick's World: The Christian Culture of Ireland's Apostolic Age.* Notre Dame, Ind.: University of Notre Dame Press, 1993.

Detsicas, Alec. *The Cantiaci.* Gloucester: Sutton, 1983.

———, ed. *Collectanea Historica: Essays in Memory of Stuart Rigold.* Gloucester: Sutton, 1981.

Dixon, Philip. "'The Cities Are Not Populated As Once They Were.'" In *The City in Late Antiquity,* edited by John Rich, 145–60. London: Routledge, 1992.

———. "Life After Wroxeter: The Final Phases of Roman Towns." In *From Roman Town to Norman Castle: Essays in Honor of Philip Barker,* edited by Aubrey Burl, 30–39. Birmingham: Birmingham University Press, 1988.

Dore, J. N. *Corbridge Roman Site.* London: English Heritage, 1989.

Dore, John, and Kevin Greene, eds. *Roman Pottery Studies in Britain and Beyond.* BAR Supplemental Series, no. 30. Oxford: Tempvs Reparatvm, 1977.

Dowdell, G. "Glan-y-Mor, Barry." In *Glamorgan County History,* edited by H. N. Savory, 2:344–45. Cardiff: University of Wales Press, 1988.

Down, Alec. *Roman Chichester.* Chichester: Phillimore, 1988.

Drinkwater, John F. "The Bacaudae of Fifth-Century Gaul." In *Fifth-Century Gaul: A Crisis of Identity?* edited by John F. Drinkwater and Hugh Elton, 208–17. Cambridge: Cambridge University Press, 1992.

Drinkwater, John F., and Hugh Elton, eds. *Fifth-Century Gaul: A Crisis of Identity?* Cambridge, England: University Press, 1992.

Driscoll, S. T., and M. R. Nieke, eds. *Power and Politics in Early Medieval Britain and Ireland.* Edinburgh: Edinburgh University Press, 1988.

Dronke, Peter. "St. Patrick's Reading." *CMCS* 1 (1981): 21–38.

Drury, P. J. "Chelmsford." *Current Archaeology* 41 (1974): 166–76.

Dumville, David N. *Britons and Anglo-Saxons in the Early Middle Ages.* Aldershot: Variorum, 1993.

———. "Brittany and 'Armes Prydein Vawr.'" *Etudes Celtiques* 20 (1983): 145–59.

———. "The Chronology of *De Excidio Britanniae,* Book I." In *Gildas: New Approaches,* edited by Michael Lapidge and David N. Dumville, 61–84. Woodbridge, Suffolk: Boydell, 1984.

———. "Early Welsh Poetry: Problems of Historicity." In *Early Welsh Poetry: Studies in the Book of Aneirin,* edited by B. F. Roberts, 1–16. Aberystwyth: National Library of Wales, 1988.

———. "Gildas and Maelgwn: Problems of Dating." In *Gildas: New Approaches,* edited by Michael Lapidge and David N. Dumville, 51–59. Woodbridge, Suffolk: Boydell, 1984.

———. "Gildas and Uinniau." In *Gildas: New Approaches,* edited by Michael Lapidge and David N. Dumville, 207–14. Woodbridge, Suffolk: Boydell, 1984.

———. "The Historical Value of the *Historia Brittonum.*" *Arthurian Literature* 6 (1986): 1–26.

———. *Histories and Pseudo-Histories of the Insular Middle Ages.* Aldershot: Variorum, 1990.

———. "The Idea of Government in Sub-Roman Britain." In *After Empire: Towards an Ethnology of Europe's Barbarians,* edited by Giorgio Ausenda, 177–216. Woodbridge, Suffolk: Boydell, 1995.

———. "Late-Seventh- or Eighth-Century Evidence for the British Transmission of Pelagius." *CMCS* 10 (1985): 39–52.

———. "'Nennius' and the *Historia Brittonum.*" *Studia Celtica* 10–11 (1975–76): 78–95.

———. "Some Aspects of the Chronology of the *Historia Brittonum.*" *BBCS* 25 (1972–74): 439–45.

———. "Sub-Roman Britain: History and Legend." *History* 62 (1977): 173–92.

Dumville, David N., et al. *Saint Patrick, a.d. 493–1993.* Woodbridge, Suffolk: Boydell, 1993.

Dunkle, J. Roger. "The Rhetorical Tyrant in Roman Historiography: Sallust, Livy, and Tacitus." *Classical World* 65 (1971): 12–20.

Dunnett, Rosalind. *The Trinovantes.* London: Duckworth, 1975.

Edwards, Nancy, and Alan Lane, eds. *Early Medieval Settlements in Wales, a.d. 400–1100.* Cardiff: University of Wales Press, 1988.

———. *The Early Church in Wales and the West.* Oxbow Monograph, no. 16. Oxford: Oxbow, 1992.

Ellis, P. "Excavations at Silver Street, Glastonbury, 1978." *PSANHS* 126 (1982): 17–31.

Ellis, Peter Berresford. *Celt and Saxon: The Struggle for Britain, a.d. 410–937.* London: Constable, 1993.

———. *The Celtic Empire.* Durham, N.C.: Carolina Academic Press, 1990.

Ellison, Ann. *Excavations at West Hill Uley, 1977: The Romano-British Temple:*

Interim Report. Bristol: Committee for Rescue Archaeology in Avon, Gloucestershire, and Somerset, 1978.

———. *Excavations at West Hill Uley, 1977–79: A Native, Roman, and Christian Ritual Complex of the First Millennium a.d.: Second Interim Report.* Bristol: Committee for Rescue Archaeology in Avon, Gloucestershire, and Somerset, 1980.

———. "Natives, Romans, and Christians on West Hill, Uley: An Interim Report on the Excavation of a Ritual Complex of the First Millennium A.D." In *Temples, Churches, and Religion in Roman Britain,* BAR British Series, no. 77, ed. Warwick Rodwell. Oxford: Tempvs Reparatvm, 1980.

Esmonde Cleary, A. S. "Changing Constraints on the Landscape, A.D. 400–600." In *Landscape and Settlement in Britain, a.d. 400–1066,* edited by Della Hooke and Simon Burnell, 11–26. Exeter: University of Exeter Press, 1995.

———. *The Ending of Roman Britain.* London: Batsford, 1989.

———. *Extra-Mural Areas of Romano-British Towns.* BAR British Series, no. 169. Oxford: Tempvs Reparatvm, 1987.

Evans, D. R., and V. M. Metcalf. *Roman Gates, Caerleon.* Oxbow Monograph, no. 15. Oxford: Oxbow, 1992.

Evans, E., et al. "A Third-Century Maritime Establishment at Cold Knap, Barry, South Glamorgan." *Britannia* 16 (1985): 57–125.

Evans, Jeremy. "From the End of Roman Britain to the Celtic West." *Oxford Journal of Archaeology* 9 (1990): 91–103.

———. "Towns and the End of Roman Britain in Northern England." *Scottish Archaeological Review* 2 (1983): 144–49.

Evison, Vera I. *The Fifth-Century Invasions South of the Thames.* London: Athlone Press, 1965.

———, ed. *Angles, Saxons, and Jutes.* Oxford: Clarendon Press, 1981.

Fahy, Dermot. "When Did Britons Become Bretons? A Note on the Foundation of Brittany." *Welsh History Review* 2 (1964–65): 111–24.

Fanning, Steven. "Emperors and Empires in Fifth-Century Gaul." In *Fifth-Century Gaul: A Crisis of Identity?* edited by John Drinkwater and Hugh Elton, 288–97. Cambridge: Cambridge University Press, 1992.

Farwell, D. E., and T. L. Molleson. *Excavations at Poundbury, 1966–1980.* Vol. 2, *The Cemeteries.* Dorset Natural History and Archaeological Society Monograph, no. 11. Dorchester: Dorset Natural History and Archaeological Society, 1993.

Faull, Margaret L. "British Survival in Anglo-Saxon Northumbria." In *Studies in Celtic Survival,* BAR, no. 37, edited by Lloyd Laing, 1–56. Oxford: Tempvs Reparatvm, 1977.

———. "British Survival in Anglo-Saxon Yorkshire." Ph.D. thesis, Leeds University, 1979.

———. "The Semantic Development of Old English *Wealh.*" *Leeds Studies in English* 8 (1975): 20–37.

———. "Settlement and Society in North-East England in the Fifth Century." In *Settlement and Society in the Roman North,* edited by P. R. Wilson et al., 49–52. Bradford, West Yorkshire: Yorkshire Archaeological Society, 1984.

Ferguson, John. *Pelagius: A Historical and Theological Study.* Cambridge: W. Heffer & Sons, 1956.

Firey, A. "Cross-Examining the Witness: Recent Research in Celtic Monastic History." *Monastic Studies* 14 (1983): 17–30.

Fleuriot, Leon. *Les origines de la Bretagne.* Paris: Payot, 1980.

Fox, Aileen. "Some Evidence for a Dark Age Trading Site at Bantham, Near Thurlestone, South Devon." *Antiquaries Journal* 35 (1955): 55–67.

Frend, W.H.C. "Pagans, Christians, and 'the Barbarian Conspiracy' of A.D. 367 in Roman Britain." *Britannia* 23 (1992): 121–31.

Frere, Sheppard. *Britannia: A History of Roman Britain.* London: Routledge & Kegan Paul, 1967; 2d ed., 1978; 3d ed., 1987.

———. *Verulamium Excavations (1972–84).* 3 vols. London: Society of Antiquaries, 1983.

Frere, Sheppard, and J.K.S. St. Joseph. *Roman Britain from the Air.* Cambridge: Cambridge University Press, 1983.

Frere, Sheppard, et al. "Roman Britain in 1987." *Britannia* 19 (1988): 416–84.

Friell, J.G.P., and W. G. Watson, eds. *Pictish Studies: Settlement, Burial, and Art in Dark Age Northern Britain.* BAR British Series, no. 125. Oxford: Tempvs Reparatvm, 1984.

Fulford, Michael G. "Byzantium and Britain." *Medieval Archaeology* 33 (1989): 1–5.

———. "Excavations on the Sites of the Amphitheatre and Forum-Basilica at Silchester, Hampshire: An Interim Report." *Antiquaries Journal* 65 (1985): 39–81.

———. *Guide to the Silchester Excavations: The Forum Basilica, 1982–84.* Reading: Reading University Press, 1985.

———. *The Silchester Amphitheatre: Excavations of 1979–85.* Britannia Monograph Series, no. 10. London: Society for the Promotion of Roman Studies, 1989.

———. "Silchester." *Current Archaeology* 82 (1982): 326–31.

———. *Silchester Defenses, 1974–80.* Britannia Monograph Series, no. 5. London: Society for the Promotion of Roman Studies, 1984.

Fulford, Michael G., and Bruce Sellwood. "The Silchester Ogham Stone: A Reconsideration." *Antiquity* 54 (1980): 95–99.

Galliou, Patrick, and Michael Jones. *The Bretons.* Oxford: Blackwell, 1991.

Gardner, Jane. *Being a Roman Citizen.* London: Routledge, 1993.

Gardner, Rex. "Gildas' New Testament Models." *CMCS* 30 (1995): 1–12.

———. "The New Testament Motivation of Gildas and His Friends." *Transactions of the Cymmrodorion, 1994,* n.s., 1 (1995): 5–26.

Gardner, Willoughby, and H. N. Savory. *Dinorben: A Hillfort Occupied in Early Iron Age and Roman Times.* Cardiff: National Museum of Wales, 1964.

Gelling, Margaret. *The West Midlands in the Early Middle Ages.* Leicester: Leicester University Press, 1992.

Gilchrist, Roberta. "A Re-Appraisal of Dinas Powys." *Medieval Archaeology* 32 (1988): 50–62.

Gilmour, B. "The Anglo-Saxon Church at St. Paul-in-the-Bail, Lincoln." *Medieval Archaeology* 23 (1979): 214–18.

Goffart, Walter. *Barbarians and Romans, a.d. 418–584: The Techniques of Accommodation.* Princeton: Princeton University Press, 1980.

———. *The Narrators of Barbarian History (a.d. 550–800).* Princeton: Princeton University Press, 1988.

Goodburn, Roger, and Philip Bartholomew, eds. *Aspects of the "Notitia Dignitatum."* BAR Supplemental Series, no. 15. Oxford: Tempvs Reparatvm, 1976.

Graham-Campbell, James, et al. "The Mote of Mark and Celtic Interlace." *Antiquity* 50 (1976): 48–53.

Grant, Eric, ed. *Central Places, Archaeology, and History.* Sheffield: Department of Archaeology and Prehistory, University of Sheffield, 1986.

Green, C.J.S. *Excavations at Poundbury, Dorchester, Dorset, 1966–1982.* Vol. 1, *The Settlements.* Dorset Natural History and Archaeological Society Monograph, no. 7. Dorchester: Dorset Natural History and Archaeological Society, 1988.

Green, H. S. "Excavations at Little Hoyle (Longbury Bank), Wales, in 1984." In *Studies in the Upper Paleolithic of Britain and N.W. Europe,* BAR, no. 296, ed. D. A. Roe, 99–119. Oxford: Tempvs Reparatvm, 1986.

Greenhalgh, Michael. *The Survival of Roman Antiquities in the Middle Ages.* London: Duckworth, 1989.

Greep, Stephen J., ed. *Roman Towns: The Wheeler Inheritance: A Review of 50 Years' Research.* CBA Research Report, no. 93. York: CBA, 1993.

Guilbert, Graeme, ed. *Hill-Fort Studies: Essays for A.H.A. Hogg.* Leicester: Leicester University Press, 1981.

Hall, Jenny, and Ralph Merrifield. *Roman London.* London: HMSO, 1986.

Hamp, Eric. "*Varia. XVIII. Mech Deyrn.*" *Etudes Celtiques* 21 (1984): 139.

Hanley, Robin. *Villages in Roman Britain.* Aylesbury: Shire Archaeology, 1987.

Hanning, Robert W. *The Vision of History in Early Britain from Gildas to Geoffrey of Monmouth.* New York: Columbia University Press, 1966.

Hanson, R.P.C. "The Date of Patrick." *Bulletin of the John Rylands University Library* 61 (1978–79): 60–77.

———. *St. Patrick: His Origins and Career.* Oxford: Clarendon Press, 1968.

Hanson, W. S., and L.J.F. Keppie. *Roman Frontier Studies, 1979: Papers Presented to the Twelfth International Congress of Roman Frontier Studies.* BAR International Series 71. 3 vols. Oxford: Tempvs Reparatvm, 1980.

Harden, D. B., ed. *Dark-Age Britain: Studies Presented to E. T. Leeds.* London: Methuen, 1956.

Hartley, B. R., and R. Leon Fitts. *The Brigantes.* Gloucester: Sutton, 1988.

Haselgrove, Susanne. "Romano-Saxon Attitudes." In *The End of Roman Britain,* BAR British Series, no. 71, edited by P. J. Casey, 4–13. Oxford: Tempvs Reparatvm, 1979.

Hawkes, C.F.C. *Pytheas: Europe and the Greek Explorers.* Eighth J. L. Myres Memorial Lecture. Oxford: Oxford University Press, 1977.

Hawkes, S. C., and G. C. Dunning. "Soldiers and Settlers in Britain, Fourth to Fifth Century." *Medieval Archaeology* 5 (1961): 1–70.

Hayes, John W. *Late Roman Pottery.* London: British School at Rome, 1972.

———. *A Supplement to Late Roman Pottery*. London: British School at Rome, 1980.

Heather, Peter. *Goths and Romans, 332–489*. Oxford: Clarendon Press, 1991.

Heighway, C. M., et al. "Excavations at 1 Westgate Street, Gloucester." *Medieval Archaeology* 23 (1979): 159–213.

Heighway, Carolyn. *Anglo-Saxon Gloucestershire*. Gloucester: Sutton, 1987.

Heinzelmann, M. "The 'Affair' of Hilary of Arles (445) and Gallo-Roman Identity in the Fifth Century." In *Fifth-Century Gaul: A Crisis of Identity?* edited by John Drinkwater and Hugh Elton, 245–46. Cambridge: Cambridge University Press, 1992.

Henderson, Isabel. *The Picts*. New York: Praeger, 1967.

Henig, Martin. *Religion in Roman Britain*. London: Batsford, 1984.

Herren, Michael W. "Gildas and Early British Monasticism." In *Britain, 400–600*, Anglistische Forschungen 205, edited by Alfred Bammesberger and Alfred Wollmann, 65–78. Heidelberg: C. Winter, 1990.

Higgitt, John. *Early Medieval Sculpture in Britain and Ireland*. BAR British Series, no. 152. Oxford: Tempvs Reparatvm, 1986.

Higham, Nicholas J. *The English Conquest: Gildas and Britain in the Fifth Century*. Manchester: Manchester University Press, 1994.

———. "Gildas, Roman Walls, and British Dykes." *CMCS* 22 (1991): 1–14.

———. *The Kingdom of Northumbria, a.d. 350–1100*. Gloucester: Sutton, 1993.

———. "Medieval 'Overkingship' in Wales: The Earliest Evidence." *Welsh History Review* 16 (1992): 154–59.

———. *The Northern Counties to a.d. 1000*. London: Longman, 1986.

———. *The Origins of Cheshire*. New York: Manchester University Press, 1993.

———. *Rome, Britain, and the Anglo-Saxons*. London: Seaby, 1992.

Higham, Nicholas J., and Barri Jones. *The Carvetii*. Gloucester: Sutton, 1985.

Hill, Peter. *Whithorn 2: Excavations, 1984–87, Interim Report*. Whithorn: Whithorn Trust, 1988.

———. *Whithorn 3: Excavations, 1988–90, Interim Report*. Whithorn: Whithorn Trust, 1990.

———. *Whithorn 4: Excavations, 1990–91, Interim Report*. Whithorn: Whithorn Trust, 1992.

Hills, Catherine. Review of *Rome, Britain, and the Anglo-Saxons,* by Nicholas J. Higham. *Antiquity* 66 (1992): 988–99.

Hind, J.G.F. "*Litus Saxonicum*—the Meaning of 'Saxon Shore.'" In *Roman Frontier Studies, 1979: Papers Presented to the Twelfth International Congress of Roman Frontier Studies*, BAR International Series 71, edited by W. S. Hanson and L.J.F. Keppie, 1:317–24. Oxford: Tempvs Reparatvm, 1980.

Hines, John. "The Anglo-Saxons Reviewed." *Medieval Archaeology* 37 (1993): 314–18.

———. "Philology, Archaeology, and the *Adventus Saxonum vel Anglorum*." In *Britain, 400–600*, edited by Alfred Bammesberger and Alfred Wollmann, 17–36. Heidelberg: C. Winter, 1990.

Hingley, Richard. *Rural Settlement in Roman Britain*. London: Seaby, 1989.

Hinton, David A., ed. *Twenty-Five Years of Medieval Archaeology*. Sheffield:

Department of Prehistory and Archaeology, University of Sheffield, 1983.

Hodges, Richard. *The Anglo-Saxon Achievement: Archaeology and the Beginnings of English Society.* London: Duckworth, 1989.

Holbrook, Neil, and Paul T. Bidwell, eds. *Exeter Archaeological Reports.* Vol. 4, *Roman Finds from Exeter.* Exeter: University of Exeter Press, 1991.

Hooke, Della, and Simon Burnell, eds. *Landscape and Settlement in Britain, a.d. 400–1066.* Exeter: University of Exeter Press, 1995.

Hope-Taylor, Brian. "Balbridie . . . and Doon Hill." *Current Archaeology* 72 (1980): 18–19.

——. *Yeavering: An Anglo-British Centre of Early Northumbria.* London: HMSO, 1977.

Howlett, David R. *The Celtic Latin Tradition of Biblical Style.* Portland, Ore.: Four Courts Press, 1995.

——. *"Liber Epistolarum Sancti Patricii Episcopi": The Book of Letters of Saint Patrick the Bishop.* Dublin: Four Courts Press, 1994.

Hughes, Kathleen. *Celtic Britain in the Early Middle Ages: Studies in Scottish and Welsh Sources.* Edited by David N. Dumville. Woodbridge, Suffolk: Boydell, 1980.

——. *Church and Society in Ireland.* London: Variorum, 1987.

——. "The Welsh Latin Chronicles: *Annales Cambriae* and Related Texts." *Proceedings of the British Academy* 59 (1973): 233–58.

Hunter-Mann, Kurt. "When (and What) Was the End of Roman Britain?" In *Theoretical Roman Archaeology: First Conference Proceedings,* edited by Eleanor Scott, 67–78. Aldershot: Avebury, 1993.

Hurst, Derek. "Major Saxon Discoveries at Droitwich." *Current Archaeology* 126 (1991): 252–55.

Hurst, H. R. "Excavations, 1968–71." *Antiquaries Journal* 52 (1972): 24–69.

——. "Excavations at Gloucester, 1971–3, Second Interim Report, Part II." *Antiquaries Journal* 54 (1974): 8–52.

——. "Excavations at Gloucester, Third Interim Report: Kingsholm, 1965–75." *Antiquaries Journal* 55 (1975): 267–94.

——. *Gloucester: The Roman and Later Defenses.* Gloucester: Archaeological Publications, 1986.

Jackson, Kenneth. *Language and History in Early Britain.* Edinburgh: Edinburgh University Press, 1953; Dublin: Four Courts Press, 1994.

——. "*Varia*: II. Gildas and the Names of the British Princes." *CMCS* 3 (1982): 30–40.

James, Edward. "The Origins of Barbarian Kingdoms: The Continental Evidence." In *The Origins of Anglo-Saxon Kingdoms,* edited by Steven Bassett. Leicester: Leicester University Press, 1989.

James, Simon. *The World of the Celts.* London: Thames & Hudson, 1993.

Jarman, A.O.H. "Early Stages in the Development of the Myrddin Legend." In *Astudiaethau ar yr Hengerdd: Studies in Old Welsh Poetry,* ed. Rachel Bromwich and R. F. Jones, 326–49. Cardiff: Gwasg Prifysgol Cymru, 1978.

Jenkins, Dafydd. "*Gwalch*: Welsh." *CMCS* 19 (1990): 55–67.

Jenkins, H. L. "Ancient Camp at the Mouth of the River Avon." *Devon Cornwall Notes Queries* 2 (1902): 20–23.

Johns, C. M., and T. W. Potter. "The Canterbury Late Roman Treasure." *Antiquaries Journal* 55 (1985): 313–52.

Johns, Catherine. *The Jewellery of Roman Britain: Celtic and Classical Traditions.* Ann Arbor: University of Michigan Press, 1996.

Johnson, Stephen. *Hadrian's Wall.* London: Batsford/English Heritage, 1989.

———. *The Roman Forts of the Saxon Shore.* London: Paul Elek, 1976.

———. *Later Roman Britain.* London: Paladin, 1980.

Johnston, D. E., ed. *The Saxon Shore.* CBA Research Report, no. 18. London: CBA, 1977.

Johnstone, P. K. "A Consular Chronology of Dark Age Britain." *Antiquity* 36 (1962): 102–9.

Jones, A.H.M. *The Later Roman Empire, 284–602.* 3 vols. Norman: University of Oklahoma Press, 1964.

———. "The Western Church in the Fifth and Sixth Centuries." In *Christianity in Britain, 300–700,* edited by M. W. Barley and R.P.C. Hanson. Leicester: Leicester University Press, 1968.

Jones, Barri, and David Mattingly. *An Atlas of Roman Britain.* Oxford: Blackwell, 1990.

Jones, E. D. "The Book of Llandaff." *National Library of Wales Journal* 4 (1945–46): 123–57.

Jones, Michael E. "The Appeal to Aetius in Gildas." *Nottingham Medieval Studies* 32 (1988): 141–55.

———. *The End of Roman Britain.* Ithaca, N.Y.: Cornell University Press, 1996.

———. "The Failure of Romanization in Celtic Britain." *Proceedings of the Harvard Celtic Colloquium* 7 (1987): 126–45.

———. "Geographical-Psychological Frontiers in Sub-Roman Britain." In *Shifting Frontiers in Late Antiquity,* edited by Ralph W. Mathisen and Hagith S. Sivan, 45–58. Aldershot: Variorum, 1996.

———. "The Historicity of the Alleluja Victory." *Albion* 18 (1986): 363–73.

———. "Provinces of Iron and Rust: The End of Roman Britain." Ph.D. diss., University of Texas at Austin, 1985.

———. Review of *Who Was Saint Patrick?* by E. A. Thompson. *Albion* 19 (1987): 209–10.

———. "Saint Germanus and the *Adventus Saxonum.*" *Haskins Society Journal* 2 (1990): 1–11.

Jones, Michael E., and John Casey. "The Gallic Chronicle Exploded?" *Britannia* 22 (1991): 212–15.

———. "The Gallic Chronicle Restored: A Chronology for the Anglo-Saxon Invasions and the End of Roman Britain." *Britannia* 19 (1988): 367–97.

Jones, Myfanwy Lloyd. *Society and Settlement in Wales and the Marches (500 b.c. to a.d. 1100).* BAR British Series, no. 121. 2 vols. Oxford: Tempvs Reparatvm, 1984.

Keevill, G. D., et al. "A Solidus of Valentinian II from Scotch Street, Carlisle." *Britannia* 20 (1989): 254–55.

Kelly, Richard S. "Recent Research on the Hut Group Settlements of North-West Wales." In *Conquest, Co-Existence, and Change,* edited by Barry C.

Burnham and J. L. Davies, 102–11. Lampeter, Dyfed: St. David's University College, 1990.

Kent, J.P.C. "The End of Roman Britain: The Literary and Numismatic Evidence Reviewed." In *The End of Roman Britain,* BAR British Series, no. 71, edited by P. J. Casey, 15–27. Oxford: Tempvs Reparatvm, 1979.

———. "A Visigothic Gold Tremiss and a Fifth-Century Firesteel from the Marlowe Theatre Site, Canterbury." *Antiquaries Journal* 53 (1983): 371–73.

Kerlouégan, François. *Le "De excidio Britanniae" de Gildas: Les destinées de la culture latine dans l'île de Bretagne au VIe siecle.* Paris: Publications de la Sorbonne, 1987.

———. "Le Latin du *De excidio Britanniae* de Gildas." In *Christianity in Britain, 300–700,* edited by M. W. Barley and R.P.C. Hanson, 151–76. Leicester: Leicester University Press, 1968.

Kirby, D. P. "Vortigern." *BBCS* 23 (1968–70): 37–59.

Knight, Jeremy K. "*In Tempore Iustini Consulis:* Contacts Between the British and Gaulish Churches Before Augustine." In *Collectanea Historica: Essays in Memory of Stuart Rigold,* edited by Alex Detsicas, 54–62. Gloucester: Sutton, 1981.

Knight, Jeremy K., and Alan Lane. "Caerwent." In *Early Medieval Settlements in Wales, a.d. 400–1100,* edited by Nancy Edwards and Alan Lane, 35–38. Cardiff: University of Wales Press, 1988

Knight, Jeremy K., et al. "New Finds of Early Christian Monuments." *Archaeologia Cambrensis* 126 (1977): 60–73.

Laing, Lloyd. "The Beginnings of 'Dark Age' Celtic Art." In *Britain, 400–600,* edited by Alfred Bammesberger and Alfred Wollmann, 37–50. Heidelberg: C. Winter, 1990.

———. "The Mote of Mark and the Origins of Celtic Interlace." *Antiquity* 49 (1975): 98–108.

———. "Segontium and the Roman Occupation of Wales." In *Studies in Celtic Survival,* BAR, no. 37, ed. Lloyd Laing, 57–60. Oxford: Tempvs Reparatvm, 1977.

———. *Settlement Types in Post-Roman Scotland.* BAR, no. 13. Oxford: Tempvs Reparatvm, 1975.

———, ed. *Studies in Celtic Survival.* BAR, no. 37. Oxford: Tempvs Reparatvm, 1977.

Laing, Lloyd, and Jennifer Laing. *Celtic Britain and Ireland, a.d. 200–800: The Myth of the Dark Ages.* New York: St. Martin's, 1990.

———. *The Dark Ages of West Cheshire.* Council Monograph Series, no. 6. Chester: City Council, 1986.

———. *A Guide to the Dark Age Remains in Britain.* London: Constable, 1979.

———. "Scottish and Irish Metalwork and the *Conspiratio Barbarica,*" *Proceedings of the Society of Antiquaries of Scotland* 116 (1986): 211–21.

Lane, Alan. "Degannwy Castle." In *Early Medieval Settlements in Wales, a.d. 400–1100,* edited by Nancy Edwards and Alan Lane, 50–53. Cardiff: University of Wales Press, 1988.

Lapidge, Michael. "Gildas's Education and the Latin Culture of Sub-Roman

Britain." In *Gildas: New Approaches*, edited by Michael Lapidge and David N. Dumville, 27–50. Woodbridge, Suffolk: Boydell, 1984.

———. Review of *Le "De excidio Britanniae" de Gildas*, by François Kerlouegan. *CMCS* 17 (1989): 75–78.

Lapidge, Michael, and David N. Dumville, eds. *Gildas: New Approaches*. Woodbridge, Suffolk: Boydell, 1984.

Larsen, J.A.O. *Representative Government in Greek and Roman History*. Berkeley and Los Angeles: University of California Press, 1955.

Leach, A. L. "Ancient Graves on the Isle of Caldey." *Archaeologia Cambrensis* (1918): 174–75.

Leach, Peter. *Shepton Mallet: Romano-Britons and Early Christians in Somerset*. Birmingham: Birmingham University Field Archaeology Unit, 1991.

Leckie, R. William, Jr. *The Passage of Dominion: Geoffrey of Monmouth and the Periodization of Insular History in the Twelfth Century*. Toronto: University of Toronto Press, 1981.

Leech, R. H. "Romano-British Rural Settlement in South Somerset and North Dorset." Ph.D. thesis, University of Bristol, 1977.

Lethbridge, T. C., and H. E. David. "Excavation of a House-Site on Gateholm, Pembrokeshire." *Archaeologia Cambrensis* 85 (1930): 366–74

Longley, David. "The Date of the Mote of Mark." *Antiquity* 56 (1982): 132–34.

MacMullen, Ramsay. "The Roman Concept Robber-Pretender." *Revue Internationale des Droits de l'Antiquité*, 3d ser., 10 (1963): 321–25.

———. *Soldier and Civilian in the Later Roman Empire*. Cambridge, Mass.: Harvard University Press, 1963.

MacQuarrie, Alan. "Early Christian Religious Houses in Scotland: Foundation and Function." In *Pastoral Care Before the Parish*, edited by John Blair and Richard Sharpe, 110–33. Leicester: Leicester University Press, 1992.

———. *Iona Through the Ages*. Isle of Coll, Argyll: Society of West Highland and Island Historical Research, 1983.

MacQueen, John. "The Literary Sources for the Life of St. Ninian." In *Galloway: Land and Lordship*, edited by R. D. Oram and Geoffrey P. Stell, 17–25. Edinburgh: School of Scottish Studies, 1991.

———. *St. Nynia*. Edinburgh: Polygon, 1990.

Mango, Marlia Mundell, et al. "A Sixth-Century Mediterranean Bucket from Bromeswell Parish, Suffolk." *Antiquity* 63 (1988): 295–311.

Mann, J. C. "Epigraphic Consciousness." *Journal of Roman Studies* 75 (1985): 204–6.

———. "The Historical Development of the Saxon Shore" In *The Saxon Shore: A Handbook*, ed. Valerie A. Maxfield, 1–11. Exeter: Department of History and Archaeology, University of Exeter, 1989.

Markus, R. A. "Pelagianism: Britain and the Continent." *Journal of Ecclesiastical History* 37 (1986): 191–204.

Marney, P. T. *Roman and Belgic Pottery from Excavations in Milton Keynes, 1972–82*. Aylesbury: Buckinghamshire Archaeological Society, 1989.

Marsden, Peter. *Roman London*. London: Thames & Hudson, 1980.

Marsille, H. "Saint Gildas et l'abbaye de Rhuys." *Bulletin Mensuel de la Société*

Polymathique du Morbihan 101 (1973): 8–29.

Mathisen, Ralph W. *Ecclesiastical Factionalism and Religious Controversy in Fifth-Century Gaul.* Washington, D.C.: Catholic University of America Press, 1989.

———. "The Last Year of Saint Germanus of Auxerre." *Analecta Bollandiana* 99 (1981): 151–59.

Mathisen, Ralph W., and Hagith S. Sivan, eds. *Shifting Frontiers in Late Antiquity.* Aldershot: Variorum, 1996.

Matthews, John F. "Macsen, Maximus, and Constantine." *Welsh History Review* 11 (1983): 431–48.

———. "Olympiodorus of Thebes and the History of the West (407–425)." *Journal of Roman Studies* 60 (1970): 79–97.

———. *Western Aristocracies and Imperial Court, a.d. 364–425.* Oxford: Clarendon Press, 1975.

Maxfield, Valerie A., ed. *The Saxon Shore: A Handbook.* Exeter: Department of History and Archaeology, University of Exeter, 1989.

Maxfield, Valerie A., and M. J. Dobson. *Roman Frontier Studies, 1989.* Exeter: University of Exeter Press, 1991.

Mays, Melinda. *Celtic Coinage: Britain and Beyond: The Eleventh Oxford Symposium on Coinage and Monetary History.* BAR British Series, no. 222. Oxford Tempvs Reparatvm, 1992.

McCarthy, M. R. *A Roman, Anglian, and Medieval Site at Blackfriars Street.* Kendal, Cumbria: Cumberland and Westmorland Antiquarian and Archaeological Society, 1990.

McCarthy, M. R., et al. "Carlisle." *Current Archaeology* 116 (1989): 298–302.

McClure, Judith. "Bede's Old Testament Kings." In *Ideal and Reality in Frankish and Anglo-Saxon Society,* edited by Patrick Wormald et al., 76–98. Oxford: Blackwell, 1983.

McGrail, Sean, ed. *Maritime Celts, Frisians, and Saxons.* CBA Research Report, no. 71. London: CBA, 1990.

McKnight, Jennifer. "When Is a Pirate Not a Pirate? When He Is Ashore: A Reconsideration of 'Piracy' in the Early Irish Seas and Its Possible Implications." Paper presented at the annual conference of the Celtic Studies Association of North America, April 1994.

McManus, Damian. *A Guide to Ogam.* Maynooth: An Sagart, 1991.

McPeake, J. C. "The End of the Affair." In *New Evidence for Roman Chester,* edited by T. J. Strickland and P. J. Davey. Liverpool: Liverpool University Press, 1978.

McWhirr, Alan. "Cirencester—'Corinum Dobunnorum.'" In *Roman Towns: The Wheeler Inheritance: A Review of 50 Years' Research,* CBA Research Report, no. 93, edited by S. J. Greep, 46–49. York: CBA, 1993.

McWhirr, Alan, ed. *Studies in the Archaeology and History of Cirencester.* BAR, no. 30. Oxford: Tempvs Reparatvm, 1976.

McWhirr, Alan, et al., eds. *Cirencester Excavations II: Romano-British Cemeteries at Cirencester.* Cirencester: Excavations Committee, 1982.

Megaw, J.V.S., and M. R. "Ancient Celts and Modern Ethnicity." *Antiquity* 70, no. 267 (1996): 175–81.

Merrifield, Ralph. *London, City of the Romans*. London: Batsford, 1983.

Miles, David, ed. *The Romano-British Countryside: Studies in Rural Settlement and Economy*. BAR British Series, no. 103. Oxford: Tempvs Reparatvm, 1982.

Miller, Mollie. "Bede's Use of Gildas." *English Historical Review* 90 (1975): 241–61.

———. "Date-Guessing and Dyfed." *Studia Celtica* 12 (1977): 33–61.

———. "Historicity and the Pedigrees of the North Countrymen." *BBCS* 26 (1975): 255–80.

———. "The Last British Entry in the 'Gallic Chronicles.'" *Britannia* 9 (1978): 315–18.

———. "Relative and Absolute Publication Dates of Gildas's *De Excidio* in Medieval Scholarship." *BBCS* 26 (1974–76): 169–74.

———. "Starting to Write History: Gildas, Bede, and Nennius." *Welsh History Review* 8 (1977): 456–65.

———. "Stilicho's Pictish War." *Britannia* 6 (1975): 141–45.

Millet, Martin. *Roman Britain*. London: Batsford/English Heritage, 1995.

———. *The Romanization of Britain*. Cambridge: Cambridge University Press, 1990.

Milne, Gustav. *From Roman Basilica to Medieval Market*. London: HMSO, 1992.

———. *The Port of Roman London*. London: Batsford, 1995.

Mohrmann, Christine. *The Latin of St. Patrick*. Dublin: Institute for Advanced Studies, 1961.

Moisl, Hermann. "A Sixth-Century Reference to the British *Bardd*," *BBCS* 29 (1980–82), 269–73.

Momigliano, Arnaldo. *Alien Wisdom: The Limits of Hellenization*. Cambridge: Cambridge University Press, 1975.

Moore, Donald, ed. *The Irish Sea Province in Archaeology and History*. Cardiff: Cambrian Archaeological Association, 1970.

Morris, C. D. "Tintagel Castle Excavations 1990." Unpublished interim statement, University of Durham, 1990.

———. "Tintagel Island, 1990: An Interim Report." *Cornish Archaeology* 30 (1991): 260–62.

Morris, C. D., Jaqueline A. Nowakowski, and Charles Thomas. "Tintagel, Cornwall: The 1990 Excavations." *Antiquity* 64 (1990): 843–49.

Morris, John. *The Age of Arthur: A History of the British Isles from 350 to 650*. New York: Scribner's, 1973.

———. "The Dates of the Celtic Saints." *Journal of Theological Studies*, n.s., 17 (1966): 342–91.

———. *Londinium: London in the Roman Empire*. London: Weidenfield & Nicolson, 1982.

———. "Pelagian Literature." *Journal of Theological Studies*, n.s., 16 (1965): 26–60.

Morris, Richard. *Churches in the Landscape*. London: Dent, 1989.

———. *The Church in British Archaeology*. CBA Report, no. 47. London: CBA, 1983.

Morrisson, Cécile. "The Re-Use of Obsolete Coins: The Case of Roman Imperial Bronzes Revived in the Late Fifth Century." In *Studies in Numismatic*

Method Presented to Philip Grierson, ed. C.N.L. Brooke et al., 95–111. Cambridge: Cambridge University Press, 1983.

Muhlberger, Steven. *The Fifth-Century Chroniclers: Prosper, Hydatius, and the Chronicler of 452.* Leeds: Francis Cairns, 1990.

———. "The Gallic Chronicle of 452 and Its Authority for British Events." *Britannia* 14 (1983): 23–33.

Musset, Lucien. *The Germanic Invasions.* Translated by Edward James and Columba James. University Park: Pennsylvania State University Press, 1975.

Myres, J.N.L. *The English Settlements.* Oxford: Clarendon Press, 1986.

———. "Pelagius and the End of Roman Rule in Britain." *Journal of Roman Studies* 50 (1960): 21–36.

Neal, David S. *Lullingstone Roman Villa.* London: English Heritage, 1991.

Niblett, Rosalind. "'Verulamium' Since the Wheelers." In *Roman Towns: The Wheeler Inheritance: A Review of 50 Years' Research,* CBA Research Report, no. 93, edited by Stephen J. Greep, 78–92. York: CBA, 1993.

Nicoll, Eric H., ed. *A Pictish Panorama: The Story of the Picts and a Pictish Bibliography.* Belgavies, Angus: Pinkfoot Press for the Pictish Arts Society, 1995.

Nolte, Nancy W. Review of *The English Conquest,* by Nicholas J. Higham. *Albion* 27, no. 3 (1995): 455–56.

Nowakowski, Jaqueline A., and Charles Thomas. *Excavations at Tintagel Parish Churchyard: Interim Report, Spring 1990.* Truro: Institute of Cornish Studies, 1990.

———. *Grave News from Tintagel. An Account of a Second Season of Archaeological Excavation at Tintagel Churchyard, Cornwall.* Truro: Institute of Cornish Studies, 1992.

O'Donoghue, Noel Dermot. *Aristocracy of Soul: Patrick of Ireland.* Wilmington, Del.: Michael Glazier, 1987.

Okasha, Elisabeth. "The Non-Ogam Inscriptions of Pictland." *CMCS* (1985): 43–69.

Olson, Lynette. *Early Monasteries in Cornwall.* Woodbridge, Suffolk: Boydell, 1989.

O'Rahilly, T. F. *The Two Patricks: A Lecture on the History of Christianity in Fifth-Century Ireland.* Dublin: Institute for Advanced Studies, 1942.

Oram, Richard D. *A Journey Through Time 1: The Christian Heritage of Wigtownshire.* Whithorn: Whithorn Trust, 1987.

———. *A Journey Through Time 2: The Archaeology of Wigtownshire.* Whithorn: Whithorn Trust, 1987.

Oram, Richard D., and Geoffrey P. Stell. *Galloway: Land and Lordship.* Edinburgh: School of Scottish Studies, 1991.

O'Sullivan, Thomas David. *The "De Excidio" of Gildas: Its Authenticity and Date.* Leiden: E. J. Brill, 1978.

Ottaway, Patrick. *Archaeology in British Towns: From Emperor Claudius to the Black Death.* London: Routledge, 1992.

Padel, O. J. "Tintagel: An Alternative View." In *A Provisional List of Imported Pottery in Post-Roman Western Britain and Ireland,* edited by Charles

Thomas, 28–29. Truro: Institute of Cornish Studies, 1981.

Palmer, Susann. *Excavation of the Roman and Saxon Site at Orpington*. London Borough of Bromley: Libraries Department, 1984.

Paschoud, François. *Roma aeterna: Etudes sur le patriotisme romain dans l'Occident latin a l'Epoque des Grandes Invasions*. Rome: Institut Suisse, 1967.

Peacock, D.P.S. *Amphorae and the Roman Economy*. London: Longman, 1986.

Pearce, Susan M. *The Archaeology of South West Britain*. London: Collins, 1981.

———. "Estates and Church Sites in Dorset and Gloucestershire: The Emergence of a Christian Society." In *The Early Church in Western Britain and Ireland*, BAR British Series, no. 102, edited by Susan M. Pearce, 117–38. Oxford: Tempvs Reparatvm, 1982.

———. *The Kingdom of Dumnonia*. Padstow, Cornwall: Lodenek Press, 1978.

———, ed. *The Early Church in Western Britain and Ireland*. BAR British Series, no. 102. Oxford: Tempvs Reparatvm, 1982.

Penhallurick, Roger D. *Tin in Antiquity*. London: Institute of Metals, 1986.

Percival, John. "Fifth-Century Villas: New Life or Death Postponed?" In *Fifth-Century Gaul: A Crisis of Identity?* edited by John Drinkwater and Hugh Elton, 156–64. Cambridge: Cambridge University Press, 1992.

———. *The Roman Villa*. London: Batsford, 1976.

Perring, Dominic. *Roman London*. London: Seaby, 1991.

Philp, Brian. *The Excavations of the Roman Forts of the Classis Britannica at Dover, 1970–1977*. Kent Monograph Series 3. Dover, 1981.

Pierce, G. O. *The Place-Names of Dinas Powys Hundred*. Cardiff: University of Wales Press, 1968.

Pollard, S.H.M. "Neolithic and Dark Age Settlements on High Peak, Sidmouth, Devon." *Proceedings of the Devonshire Archaeological Society* 23 (1966): 35–59.

Potter, T. W. *Romans in North-West England*. Kendal, Cumbria: T. Wilson, 1979.

Powell, Timothy E. "Christianity or Solar Monotheism: The Early Religious Beliefs of St. Patrick." *Journal of Ecclesiastical History* 43, no. 4 (1992): 531–40.

Priolo, Gary P. "From Roman Britain to Norman England: Continuity and Change, c. A.D. 284–1066." M.A. thesis, Old Dominion University, 1990.

Pryce, Huw. "Pastoral Care in Early Medieval Wales." In *Pastoral Care Before the Parish*, edited by John Blair and Richard Sharpe, 41–62. Leicester: Leicester University Press, 1992.

Radford, C. A. Ralegh. "Glastonbury Abbey." In *The Quest for Arthur's Britain*, edited by Geoffrey Ashe, 97–110. New York: Paladin, 1971.

———. "Imported Pottery Found at Tintagel, Cornwall." In *Dark-Age Britain*, edited by D. B. Harden, 59–67. London: Methuen, 1956.

———. "Romance and Reality in Cornwall." In *The Quest for Arthur's Britain*, edited by Geoffrey Ashe, 59–77. New York: Paladin, 1971.

———. *Tintagel Castle*. London: Historic Buildings and Monuments Commission, 1939.

Radford, C. A. Ralegh, and Michael J. Swanton. *Arthurian Sites in the West*. Exeter: University of Exeter Press, 1975.

Rahtz, Philip. "Excavations on Glastonbury Tor, Somerset, 1964–66."

Archaeological Journal 127 (1970): 1–81.

———. "Glastonbury Tor." In *The Quest for Arthur's Britain,* edited by Geoffrey Ashe, 111–22. New York: Paladin Press, 1971.

Rahtz, Philip, et al. *Cadbury Congresbury, 1968–73: A Late/Post-Roman Hilltop Settlement in Somerset.* BAR British Series, no. 223. Oxford: Tempvs Reparatvm, 1992.

Ramm, Herman. *The Parisi.* London: Duckworth, 1978.

Rankin, H. D. *Celts and the Classical World.* London: Areopagitica Press, 1987.

Reece, Richard M. *Coinage in Roman Britain.* London: Seaby, 1987.

———. "The End of Roman Britain—Revisited." *Scottish Archaeological Review* 2 (1983): 149–53.

———. "The End of the City in Roman Britain." In *The City in Late Antiquity,* edited by John Rich, 136–44. London: Routledge, 1992.

———. *My Roman Britain.* Cotswold Studies 3. Cirencester: Cotswold Studies, 1988.

———. "Numerical Aspects of Roman Coin Hoards in Britain." In *Coins and the Archaeologist,* edited by P. J. Casey and Richard M. Reece, 78–94. London: Seaby, 1988.

———. "Town and Country: The End of Roman Britain." *World Archaeology* 12 (1980): 77–92.

———. "The Use of Roman Coinage." *Oxford Journal of Archaeology* 3 (1984): 197–210.

Reece, Richard M., and Christopher Catling. *Cirencester: The Development and Buildings of a Cotswold Town.* BAR, no. 12. Oxford: Tempvs Reparatvm, 1975.

Renfrew, Colin. *Archaeology and Language.* London: Cape, 1987.

Renfrew, Colin, and S. J. Shennan, eds. *Ranking Resource and Exchange.* Cambridge: Cambridge University Press, 1982.

Reynolds, Nicholas. "Dark Age Timber Halls and the Background to Excavation at Balbridie." *Scottish Archaeological Forum* 10 (1980): 41–60.

Rich, John, ed. *The City in Late Antiquity.* London: Routledge, 1992.

Richards, Julian D. "An Archaeology of Anglo-Saxon England." In *After Empire: Towards an Ethnology of Europe's Barbarians,* edited by Giorgio Ausenda, 51–74. Woodbridge, Suffolk: Boydell, 1995.

Riche, Pierre. *Education and Culture in the Barbarian West.* Translated by John J. Contreni. Columbia: University of South Carolina Press, 1976.

Richter, Michael. *The Formation of the Medieval West: Studies in the Oral Culture of the Barbarians.* New York: St. Martin's, 1994.

Ridley, R. T. "Zosimus the Historian." *Byzantinische Zeitschrift* (1972): 277–303.

Ritchie, Anna. *The Picts.* Edinburgh: HMSO, 1989.

Rivet, A.L.F., ed. *The Roman Villa in Britain.* New York: Praeger, 1969.

Rivet, A.L.F., and Colin Smith. *The Place-Names of Roman Britain.* Princeton: Princeton University Press, 1979.

Roberts, B. F., ed. *Early Welsh Poetry: Studies in the Book of Aneirin.* Aberystwyth: National Library of Wales, 1988.

Robertson, Anne S. "Romano-British Coin Hoards: Their Numismatic, Archaeological, and Historical Significance." In *Coins and the Archaeologist,* edited by P. J. Casey and Richard M. Reece, 13–37. London: Seaby, 1988.

Rodwell, Wardwick. *Wells Cathedral: Excavations and Discoveries.* Wells: Friends of Wells Cathedral, 1979.

Rodwell, Warwick, and Trevor Rowley, eds. *The "Small Towns" of Roman Britain.* BAR, no. 15. Oxford: Tempvs Reparatvm, 1975.

Roueche, Charlotte. "Theodosius II, the Cities, and the Date of the 'Church History' of Sozomen." *Journal of Theological Studies* 37 (1986): 130–32.

Rowland, Jenny. *Early Welsh Saga Poetry: A Study and Edition of the Englynion.* Cambridge: D. S. Brewer, 1990.

———. "Warfare and Horses in the *Gododdin* and the Problem of Catraeth." *CMCS* 30 (1995): 13–40.

Ryan, John. *Irish Monasticism: Origins and Early Development.* Dublin: Institute for Advanced Studies, 1931.

Salway, Peter. *The Frontier People of Roman Britain.* Cambridge: Cambridge University Press, 1965.

———. *The Oxford Illustrated History of Roman Britain.* Oxford: Oxford University Press, 1993.

———. *Roman Britain.* Oxford: Clarendon Press, 1981.

Schaffner, Paul. "Britain's *Iudices.*" In *Gildas: New Approaches,* edited by Michael Lapidge and David N. Dumville, 151–56. Woodbridge, Suffolk: Boydell, 1984.

Scott, Eleanor, ed. *Theoretical Roman Archaeology: First Conference Proceedings.* Aldershot: Avebury, 1993.

Scull, Christopher. "Post-Roman Phase I at Yeavering: A Re-Consideration." *Medieval Archaeology* 35 (1991): 51–63.

Selkirk, Andrew. "Verulamium." *Current Archaeology* 120 (1990): 410–17.

Selkirk, Andrew, and Tony Wilmott. "Birdoswald: Dark-Age Halls in a Roman Fort." *Current Archaeology* 116 (1989): 288–91.

Sharpe, Richard. "Gildas as a Father of the Church." In *Gildas: New Approaches,* edited by Michael Lapidge and David N. Dumville, 191–206. Woodbridge, Suffolk: Boydell, 1984.

Sharples, Niall M. *Maiden Castle.* London: Batsford/English Heritage, 1991.

Shennan, Stephen, ed. *Archaeological Approaches to Cultural Identity.* London: Unwin Hyman, 1989.

Sheringham, J.G.T. "Les machtierns: Quelques témoignages gallois and cornouaillais." *Memoires de la Société d'Histoire et d'Archéologie de Bretagne* 58 (1981): 61–72.

Sherwin-White, A. N. *The Roman Citizenship.* 2d ed. Oxford: Clarendon Press, 1973.

Silvester, R. J. "An Excavation on the Post-Roman Site at Bantham, South Devon." *Proceedings of the Devon Archaeological Society* 39 (1981): 89–118.

Simon, A. M. Ap. "The Roman Temple on Brean Down, Somerset." *Proceedings of the University of Bristol Spelaeological Society* 10 (1964–65): 195–258.

Simpson, C. J. "Belt-Buckles and Strap-Ends of the Later Roman Empire." *Britannia* 7 (1976): 192–223.

Sims-Williams, Patrick. "Gildas and the Anglo-Saxons." *CMCS* 6 (1983): 1–30.

———. "Gildas and Vernacular Poetry." In *Gildas: New Approaches*, edited by Michael Lapidge and David N. Dumville, 169–90. Woodbridge, Suffolk: Boydell, 1984.

———. Review of *The Llandaff Charters*, by Wendy Davies. *Journal of Ecclesiastical History* 33 (1982): 124–29.

———. "The Visionary Celt: The Construction of an Ethnic Preconception." *CMCS* 11 (1986): 71–96.

Sivan, Hagith S. *Ausonius of Bordeaux: Genesis of a Gallic Aristocracy*. London: Routledge, 1993.

Smith, C. A. "Excavations at the Ty Mawr Hut-Circles, Holyhead, Anglesey: Part II." *Archaeologia Cambrensis* 134 (1985): 11–52.

Smith, Lesley M., ed. *The Making of Britain: The Dark Ages*. London: Macmillan, 1984.

Smyth, Alfred P. *Warlords and Holy Men: Scotland, A.D. 80–1000*. London: Edward Arnold, 1984.

Snyder, Christopher A. "Celtic Continuity in the Middle Ages." *Medieval Perspectives* 11 (1996), 164–78.

———. "A Gazetteer of Sub-Roman Britain (A.D. 400–600): The British Sites." *Internet Archaeology* (http://intarch.york.ac.uk) 3 (summer 1997).

———. Review of *Archaeology in British Towns*, by Patrick Ottaway. *Bryn Mawr Classical Review* 8.2(1997), 175–77.

———. Review of *The Celtic Latin Tradition of Biblical Style*, by David R. Howlett. *Arthuriana* 6, no. 3 (1996): 78–80.

———. Review of *The English Conquest*, by Nicholas J. Higham. *Arthuriana* 6, no. 3 (1996): 69–71.

———. Review of *The Formation of the Medieval West*, by Michael Richter. *Journal of Interdisciplinary History* 27, no. 2 (1996): 285–86.

———. Review of *Roman Britain: A Sourcebook*, by Stanley Ireland. *Bryn Mawr Classical Review* (forthcoming).

———. *Sub-Roman Britain (A.D. 400–600): A Gazetteer of Sites*. BAR British Series, no. 247. Oxford: Tempvs Reparatvm, 1996.

———. "Sub-Roman Britain: An Introduction." In *The ORB (On-line Resource Book for Medieval Studies) Encyclopedia*, edited by Carolyn Schriber et al. (http://orb.rhodes.edu), 1996.

———. "'The Tyrants of Tintagel': The Terminology and Archaeology of Sub-Roman Britain (A.D. 400–600)." Ph.D. diss., Emory University, 1994.

Sorrell, Alan. *Roman Towns in Britain*. London: Batsford, 1976.

Stafford, Pauline. *The East Midlands in the Early Middle Ages*. Leicester: Leicester University Press, 1985.

Steer, K. A. "Two Unrecorded Early Christian Stones." *Proceedings of the Society of Antiquaries of Scotland* 101 (1972): 127–29.

Stevenson, J. B. "The Beginnings of Literacy in Ireland." *Proceedings of the Irish Academy* 89C (1989): 127–65.

Strickland, T. J. "Chester." *Current Archaeology* 84 (1982): 6–12.

Suppe, Frederick. "The Cultural Significance of Decapitation in High Medieval

Wales and the Marches." *BBCS* (1989): 147–60.

Sutherland, C.H.V. "Coinage in Britain in the Fifth and Sixth Centuries." In *Dark-Age Britain: Studies Presented to E. T. Leeds,* ed. D. B. Harden. London: Methuen, 1956.

Sutherland, Elizabeth. *In Search of the Picts: A Celtic Dark Age Nation.* London: Constable, 1994.

Swan, Vivien G. *Pottery in Roman Britain.* 4th rev. ed. Aylesbury: Shire, 1988.

———. *The Pottery Kilns of Roman Britain.* London: HMSO, 1984.

Teillet, Suzanne. *Des Goths à la nation gothique: Les origines de l'idee de nation en occident du Ve au VIIe siecle.* Paris: Les Belles Lettres, 1984.

Thomas, Charles. *And Shall These Mute Stones Speak? Post-Roman Inscriptions in Western Britain.* Cardiff: University of Wales Press, 1994.

———. *Celtic Britain.* London: Thames & Hudson, 1986.

———. *Christianity in Roman Britain to a.d. 500.* London: Batsford, 1981.

———. "Christians, Chapels, Churches, and Charters." *Landscape History* 11 (1989): 19–26.

———. "The Context of Tintagel. A New Model for the Diffusion of Post-Roman Mediterranean Imports." *Cornish Archaeology* 27 (1990): 7–25.

———. *The Early Christian Archaeology of North Britain.* London: Oxford University Press, 1971.

———. "An Early Christian Cemetery and Chapel in Ardwall Isle, Kircudbright," *Medieval Archaeology* 11 (1967): 127–88.

———. "The Early Church in Wales and the West: Concluding Remarks." In *The Early Church in Wales and the West,* Oxbow Monograph, no. 16, edited by Nancy Edwards and Alan Lane, 145–49. Oxford: Oxbow, 1992.

———. "East and West: Tintagel, Early Mediterranean Imports, and the Insular Church." In *The Early Church in Western Britain and Ireland,* BAR British Series, no. 102, edited by Susan M. Pearce, 17–34. Oxford: Tempvs Reparatvm, 1982.

———. *Exploration of a Drowned Landscape: Archaeology and History of the Isles of Scilly.* London: Batsford, 1985.

———. "'Gallici Nautae de Galliarum Provinciis': A Sixth/Seventh Century Trade with Gaul, Reconsidered." *Medieval Archaeology* 34 (1990): 1–26.

———. "Imported Late-Roman Mediterranean Pottery in Ireland and Western Britain: Chronologies and Implications." *Proceedings of the Royal Irish Academy* 76C (1976): 245–56.

———. "Imported Pottery in Dark-Age Western Britain." *Medieval Archaeology* 3 (1959): 89–111.

———. "Irish Colonists in South-West Britain." *World Archaeology* 5 (1973): 5–13.

———. Review of *Saint Patrick,* by David N. Dumville. *English Historical Review* 111, no. 441 (1996): 402–3.

———. *Tintagel: Arthur and Archaeology.* London: Batsford/English Heritage, 1993.

———. "Tintagel Castle." *Antiquity* 62 (1988): 421–34.

———. "Tintagel, Cornwall: The 1990 Excavations." *Antiquity* 64 (1990): 843–49.

———, ed. *A Provisional List of Imported Pottery in Post-Roman Western Britain and Ireland*. Truro: Institute of Cornish Studies, 1981.

———, ed. *Tintagel Papers*. Cornish Studies 16. Redruth: Institute of Cornish Studies, 1988.

Thomas, Charles, et al. "Lundy, 1969." *Current Archaeology* 16 (1969): 138–42.

Thompson, E. A. "Ammianus Marcellinus and Britain." *Nottingham Medieval Studies* 34 (1990): 1–15.

———. "Britain, A.D. 406–410." *Britannia* 8 (1977): 303–18.

———. "A Chronological Note on St. Germanus of Auxerre." *Analecta Bollandiana* 75 (1957): 135–38.

———. "Fifth-Century Facts?" *Britannia* 14 (1983): 272–74.

———. "Gildas and the History of Britain." *Britannia* 10 (1979): 203–26.

———. "Peasant Revolts in Late Roman Gaul and Spain," *Past and Present* 2 (1952): 11–23.

———. "Procopius on Brittia and Brittania." *Classical Quarterly* 30 (1980): 498–507.

———. *St. Germanus of Auxerre and the End of Roman Britain*. Woodbridge, Suffolk: Boydell, 1984.

———. "St. Patrick and Coroticus." *Journal of Theological Studies,* n.s., 31 (1980): 12–27.

———. *Who Was Saint Patrick?* New York: St. Martin's, 1985.

———. "Zosimus 6.10.2 and the Letters of Honorius." *Classical Quarterly* 32 (1982): 445–62.

Tierney, J. J. "The Celtic Ethnography of Posidonius." *Proceedings of the Royal Irish Academy* 60C (1959–60): 189–275.

Todd, Malcolm. "After the Romans." In *The Making of Britain: The Dark Ages,* edited by Lesley M. Smith. London: Macmillan, 1984.

———. "The Cities of Roman Britain: After Wheeler." In *Roman Towns: The Wheeler Inheritance: A Review of 50 Years' Research,* CBA Research Report, no. 93, edited by Stephen J. Greep, 5–10. York: CBA, 1993.

———. *The Coritani*. Gloucester: Sutton, 1991.

———. "*Famosa Pestis* and Britain in the Fifth Century." *Britannia* 8 (1977): 319–25.

———. *Roman Britain*. Atlantic Highlands, N.J.: Humanities Press, 1981.

———. *The South West to a.d. 1000*. London: Longman, 1987.

———, ed. *Research on Roman Britain, 1960–89*. Britannia Monograph Series, no. 11. London: Britannia, 1989.

Tolkien, J.R.R. et al. *Angles and Britons*. Cardiff: University of Wales Press, 1963.

Tomlin, R.S.O. "The Curse Tablets." In *The Temple of Sulis Minerva at Bath,* edited by Barry Cunliffe, 2:59–277. Oxford: University Committee for Archaeology, 1988.

———. "Notitia Dignitatum Omnium, Tam Civilium Quam Militarium." In *Aspects of the "Notitia Dignitatum,"* BAR Supplemental Series, no. 15, edited by Roger Goodburn and Philip Bartholomew, 189–210. Oxford: Tempvs Reparatvm, 1976.

Tuplin, Christopher. "Imperial Tyranny: Some Reflections on a Classical Greek Political Metaphor." In *CRUX: Essays in Greek History Presented to*

G.E.M. de Ste. Croix on His 75th Birthday, ed. P. A. Cartledge et al., 348–75. London: Duckworth, 1985.

Turner, Judith. "Some Pollen Evidence for the Environment of North Britain: 1000 B.C. to A.D. 1000." In *Settlement in North Britain: 100 b.c. to a.d. 1000,* ed. J. Chapman and H. Mytum, BAR British Series 118, 3–27. Oxford: Tempvs Reparatvm, 1983.

Vallet, Françoise, and Michel Kazanski, eds. *L'armée romaine et les barbares du IIIe au VIIe siécle.* Rouen: Musée des Antiquités Nationales, 1994.

Van Arsdale, R. D. *Celtic Coinage of Britain.* London: Spink, 1989.

Van Dam, Raymond. *Leadership and Community in Late Antique Gaul.* Berkeley and Los Angeles: University of California Press, 1985.

Wacher, John S. *The Civitas Capitals of Roman Britain.* Leicester: Leicester University Press, 1966.

———. "Late Roman Developments." In *Studies in the Archaeology and History of Cirencester,* BAR, no. 30, edited by Alan McWhirr, 15–18. Oxford: Tempvs Reparatvm, 1976.

———. *Roman Britain.* London: Dent, 1978.

———. *The Towns of Roman Britain.* Berkeley and Los Angeles: University of California Press, 1974.

———, ed. *The Roman World.* 2 vols. London: Routledge, 1987.

Wainwright, F. T. *Archaeology and Place-Names and History.* London: Routledge & Kegan Paul, 1962.

———, ed. *The Problem of the Picts.* Perth: Melven Press, 1955.

Wainwright, G. J. *Coygan Camp.* Cardiff: Cambrian Archaeological Association, 1967.

Ward, J. H. "The British Sections of the Notitia: An Alternative Interpretation." *Britannia* 4 (1973): 253–63.

Ward, J. O. "Procopius' Bellum Gothicum II.6.28: The Problem of Contacts Between Justinian I and Britain." *Byzantion* 38 (1968): 460–71.

Ward, Simon. *Excavations at Chester: Roman Headquarters Building to Medieval Row.* Chester: City Council, 1988.

Wardman, Alan E. "Usurpers and Internal Conflicts in the Fourth Century A.D." *Historia* 33 (1984): 220–37.

Watts, Dorothy. *Christians and Pagans in Roman Britain.* London: Routledge, 1991.

Webster, Graham. *The Cornovii.* London: Duckworth, 1975.

———. "A Roman System of Fortified Posts Along Watling Street, Britain." In *Roman Frontier Studies, 1967,* ed. Shimon Applebaum, 38–45. Tel Aviv: University of Tel Aviv Press, 1971.

———. *Wall Roman Site.* London: English Heritage, 1985.

———. "Wroxeter (Viroconium)." In *Fortress into City,* 120–44. London: Batsford, 1988.

Webster, Graham, and Philip Barker. *Wroxeter Roman City.* London: English Heritage, 1991.

Wedlake, W. J. *The Excavation of the Shrine of Apollo at Nettleton, Wiltshire, 1956–71.* London: Society of Antiquaries, 1982.

Welch, Martin G. "The Archaeological Evidence for Federate Settlement in Britain

Within the Fifth Century." In *L'armée romaine et les barbares du IIIe au VIIe siécle*, edited by Françoise Vallet and Michel Kazanski, 269–77. Rouen: Musée des Antiquités Nationales, 1994.

———. *Discovering Anglo-Saxon England*. University Park: Pennsylvania State University Press, 1992.

———. *Early Anglo-Saxon Sussex*. BAR, no. 112, 14–15. Oxford: Tempvs Reparatvm, 1983.

———. "Late Romans and Saxons in Sussex." Britannia 2 (1971): 232–37.

Wellard, James. *In Search of Unknown Britain*. London: Constable, 1983.

Welsby, Derek A. *The Roman Military Defense of the British Provinces in Its Later Phases*. BAR British Series, no. 101. Oxford: Tempvs Reparatvm, 1982.

Wheeler, R.E.M. *Maiden Castle, Dorset*. Oxford: Oxford University Press, 1943.

White, Richard B. "Excavations at Aberffraw, Anglesey, 1973 and 1974." *BBCS* 28 (1979): 319–42.

White, Roger. "Excavations on the Site of the Baths Basilica." In *From Roman "Virconium" to Medieval Wroxeter,* edited by Philip Barker, 3–7. Worcester: West Mercian Archaeological Consultants, 1990.

Whittock, Martyn J. *The Origins of England, 410–600*. London: Croom Helm, 1986.

Wilkinson, P. F., et al. "Excavations at Hen Gastell, Briton Ferry, West Glamorgan, 1991–92." *Medieval Archaeology* 39 (1995): 1–50.

Williams, J.E.C. "Gildas, Maelgwn, and the Bards." In *Welsh Society and Nationhood,* edited by R. R. Davies et al., 19–37. Cardiff: University of Wales Press, 1984.

Wilson, David M. "Medieval Britain in 1970: Pre-Conquest." *Medieval Archaeology* 15 (1971): 124–35.

———, ed. *The Archaeology of Anglo-Saxon England*. London: Methuen, 1976.

Wilson, P. R., et al., eds. *Settlement and Society in the Roman North*. Bradford, West Yorkshire: Yorkshire Archaeological Society, 1984.

Winterbottom, Michael. "Columbanus and Gildas." *Vigiliae Christianae* 30 (1976): 310–17.

———. "Notes on the Text of Gildas." *Journal of Theological Studies,* n.s., 27 (1976): 132–40.

———. "The Preface of Gildas' *De Excidio*." *Transactions of the Cymmrodorion Society* (1974–75): 277–87.

Wood, Ian N. "The Channel from the Fourth to the Seventh Centuries A.D." In *Maritime Celts, Frisians, and Saxons,* CBA Research Report, no. 71, edited by Sean McGrail, 93–97. London: CBA, 1990.

———. "The End of Roman Britain: Continental Evidence and Parallels." In *Gildas: New Approaches,* edited by Michael Lapidge and David N. Dumville, 1–25. Woodbridge, Suffolk: Boydell, 1984.

———. "The Fall of the Western Empire and the End of Roman Britain." *Britannia* 18 (1987): 251–62.

———. Review of *The Ending of Roman Britain,* by A. S. Esmonde Cleary. *Britannia* 22 (1991): 313–15.

Wood, Michael. *In Search of the Dark Ages*. New York: Facts on File, 1987.

Woodward, Ann. *English Heritage Book of Shrines and Sacrifice*. London: Batsford/English Heritage, 1992.

Woodward, Ann, and Peter Leach. *The Uley Shrines: Excavation of a Ritual Complex on West Hill, Uley, Gloucestershire, 1977–79*. London: English Heritage/British Museum, 1993.

Wormald, Patrick, et al., eds. *Ideal and Reality in Frankish and Anglo-Saxon Society*. Oxford: Blackwell, 1983.

Wright, Neil. "Gildas's Geographical Perspective: Some Problems." In *Gildas: New Approaches*, edited by Michael Lapidge and David N. Dumville, 85–106. Woodbridge, Suffolk: Boydell, 1984.

———. "Gildas's Prose Style and Its Origins." In *Gildas: New Approaches*, edited by Michael Lapidge and David N. Dumville, 107–28. Woodbridge, Suffolk: Boydell, 1984.

———. "Gildas's Reading: A Survey." *Sacris Erudiri* 32 (1991): 121–62.

Wynn, Philip. "Frigeridus, the British Tyrants, and the Early-Fifth-Century Barbarian Invasions of Gaul and Spain." *Athenaeum* (forthcoming)

Yule, Brian. "The Dark Earth and Late Roman London." *Antiquity* 64 (1990): 620–28.

Zeepvat, R. J., et al. *Roman Milton Keynes*. Aylesbury: Buckinghamshire Archaeological Society, 1987.

INDEX

abba, 124–26
abbots, 45, 122, 125, 126, 176, 239
Aberdaron, 126
Aberffraw, 174, 328, 342
Abraham, 36, 61
Adomnán, 193, 341
adventus Saxonum, 249, 297, 309, 352
advocatus, 33, 34
Aegean Sea, 135, 194, 243
Aeschylus, 105, 300
Aethelred, 180
Aethelstan, 153, 322
Aetius, 44, 69, 259, 279–81, 340, 346, 351
Africa, 13, 61, 78, 96, 192, 243, 294, 295, 315, 339
Age of the Saints, 120, 125
Age of Tyrants (Greek), 91, 105
Agricola, 4, 82, 168, 276, 284
Agricola, the Pelagian, 38, 121, 314
Alamanni, 14, 21, 117, 298, 343
Alans, 18, 69, 291
Alaric, 18, 20, 21, 24, 34, 95, 259, 270, 304
Alban, Saint and martyr, 38, 146, 148, 209, 212
Albion, 51, 284, 290
Albiones, 67, 284, 290
Aldhelm, 240, 249
Alexandria, 135, 152, 242, 301, 347
Allectus, 5, 257, 265
Alleluia Victory, 39, 111, 168
Alps, 13, 19, 21, 270, 287
Alypius, 52
Ambrose, Saint, 61, 62, 75, 85, 94, 97, 267, 288, 293, 298, 301, 303, 311, 312
Ambrosius Aurelianus, 44, 69, 78, 104, 112, 118, 188, 189, 254, 260, 281, 297, 304

Ammianus Marcellinus, xv, 10, 12–14, 30, 31, 52, 59, 67, 74, 85, 86, 93, 94, 101, 104, 110, 114–19, 132, 232, 249, 258, 264, 266–68, 273, 284, 285, 287, 290, 293, 298, 301, 302, 304, 308–13, 341–43
amphitheaters, 154, 156, 164, 167, 234, 342
Ancaster, 205, 238
Aneirin, 48, 113, 173, 175, 249, 254, 292, 293, 351
Angles, xiii, 35, 193–95, 263
Anglesey, 79, 87, 174, 342
Anglian, 161–63, 169, 173, 176, 193–95, 221, 272
Anglo-Saxon Chronicle, xvi, 48, 102, 143, 148, 151, 155, 230, 264, 272, 305, 313, 319–21, 340
Anglo-Saxonists, xiv
Annales Cambriae, 48, 188, 254, 278, 280, 292, 299, 326, 331
Annales school, 226
annona, 14, 112, 115, 134, 309, 339
anointing, 84–86, 104, 120, 230, 298, 299, 340
Anthemius, 82, 83, 241
Antioch, 31
Antonine Wall, 4
Apollinaris, 272
Apollo, 206
Aponius, 56, 286
aqueducts, 148, 212, 228
Aquileia, 13, 74, 303
Aquitania, 38, 53, 60, 61, 296, 303
Arbogast, 13
Arcadius, 18, 134, 142, 149, 155, 156, 170, 196, 200, 206, 241, 259, 320, 325
Archedice, 105
archiepiscopus, 122

Ardwall Isle, 213
areani, 11, 110, 266
Arelate, 21
Aristotle, xviii, 91, 93, 95
Arles, 53, 70, 192, 304, 311
Armenians, 60
Armes Prydein Vawr, 65, 106, 289, 293, 296
Armorica, 22, 23, 67–69, 72, 83, 107, 265, 267, 270–72, 276, 291, 296, 297, 338, 339, 345
Arnobius, 67, 288, 291
Arthur, King, xiii, 30, 50, 80, 168, 176, 179, 180, 184, 185, 252–55, 350, 351
Asia Minor, 187, 194, 213
Athens, 91, 93, 105
Atrebates, 155
Attacotti, 10, 11, 258
Audetus, 87
Augustine, archbishop of Canterbury, xiii, 122, 134, 149, 163, 167, 238
Augustine, bishop of Hippo, xviii, 36, 43, 59, 61, 62, 64, 67, 74–76, 78, 79, 85, 86, 94, 95, 99, 100, 103, 105, 124, 240, 260, 288, 291, 292, 294, 295, 302, 310, 311, 315, 345
Aurelius Caninus, 44, 85, 246
Aurelius Victor, 53, 117, 265, 266, 285
Ausonius of Bordeaux, 60, 61, 63, 65, 70–72, 74, 97, 272, 287, 293, 303, 338
Auvergne, 61
Avon River, 197

bacaudae, 23, 227, 270, 339
Badon Hill, 43–45, 64, 84, 112, 156, 230, 254, 260, 280, 281, 340, 341
Balbridie, 193, 247
ballistae, 15, 153, 174, 342
Bancroft, 196
Bannavem Taburniae, 40, 114
Bantham, 197, 198
baptismal fonts, 208, 209, 237
baptistry, 207
"barbarian conspiracy," 10, 31, 132, 258, 266
Barcombe, 170
bards, xiv, 48, 110, 119, 124, 173, 254, 255, 313
Barmouth, 87
barns, 146, 247

βασιλευς, 91, 105
basilicas, 15, 142, 152, 153, 156, 158–60, 180, 207, 208, 211, 216, 218, 237, 244, 336
Bath, 150, 151, 205, 208, 218, 220, 228, 260, 311, 313, 321, 349
  Abbeygate Street, 151
Bathealton, 220
baths, 143, 148–53, 156, 158, 159, 162, 164, 180, 218, 242, 319
Bedcanford, Battle of (A.D. 571), 148
Bede, xiv, xv, xvi, 22, 29, 48, 56, 57, 67, 86, 102, 122, 161, 167, 173, 193, 194, 212, 213, 219, 221, 230, 239, 240, 247, 249, 264, 272, 279, 286, 287, 290, 305, 310, 316, 326, 341, 342, 345, 349, 351
beer, 248, 348
Belisarius, 34, 35, 347
belt buckles, 14, 133, 145, 234, 249
Benwell, 170
Beowulf, xiii
Berth at Baschurch, 161
Bethlehem, 61
Bignor, 149
Binchester, 175
Birdoswald, 168, 170, 277
birds, 198, 209
bishops, 24, 38–42, 45, 46, 67, 68, 70, 76, 87, 95, 111, 114, 116, 117, 120–23, 125, 126, 157, 163, 167, 176, 209, 212–14, 238–40, 257–59, 276, 277, 303, 304, 310, 311, 314–16, 324, 337, 345
Bituriges, 82, 296
Bivatigirnus, 79, 106, 122
Bodafon, 122
Bordeaux, 60, 74, 75, 180, 287, 303
Boudicca, 4, 82, 142, 144–46
Boulogne, 5, 19
Bourges, 83
Bow Hill, 149
Bracara, 33
bracelets, 154, 156, 197
Bradley Hill, 238
bread, 248
Brean Down, 202, 208, 236, 238, 344
Brent Knoll, 220
Breton, 43, 64, 68, 70, 83, 106, 107, 230, 291, 307, 308, 312
Brettania, 34, 284

βρεττανια, 24, 51, 284
βρεττανος, 51, 67
Bretto, 67, 122, 193, 194, 286, 287, 290, 341
Brigomaglos, 169
Bristol Channel, 155, 174, 197, 244
Britanni, 51, 66, 68, 121, 252
Britannia, xiii, 5, 6, 12, 18, 32, 35, 36, 50–58, 61, 63, 64, 67–69, 84, 101, 104, 113, 123, 142, 164, 216, 226, 251, 252, 271, 284–89, 291, 298, 314, 317, 340
Britannia Inferior, 52
Britannia Prima, 5, 52, 115, 212
Britannia Secunda, 5, 52
Britannia Superior, 5, 52, 142
Britannus, 51, 67, 70–72, 284, 290, 292, 338
British church, the, xv, 40, 45, 119–21, 124–27, 212, 237, 239, 240, 244, 277, 299, 314, 316, 345, 347
Britons, ix, x, xiv, xv, xviii, 3, 4, 13, 18, 22, 23, 25, 29, 35, 38, 44, 48, 49, 51, 63, 66–69, 70–72, 76–80, 82–84, 86, 96, 101, 103, 107–9, 111–13, 115, 116, 121, 122, 125, 131, 133, 134, 136–38, 143, 144, 148, 152, 163, 164, 167, 172, 173, 176, 183, 195, 202, 213, 216–21, 225–27, 232, 234–36, 238, 241, 243, 245–47, 249, 252–54, 259, 260, 263, 267, 269, 272, 277, 283, 284, 286, 287, 289, 290–97, 305, 307, 309, 313, 314, 319–22, 324, 338, 339, 341, 342, 345, 347, 350
Brittany, 35, 43, 68, 105, 106, 108, 267, 270, 278, 291, 352
Brittia, 35, 284
"British cheese," 248, 284
Britto, 67, 70, 72
Brittonic, 65, 68, 82, 87, 106, 108, 252, 290
Broad Sound, 198
Bronze Age, 138, 176, 180, 241
Bruttium, 24
Brython, 72, 80, 252, 290, 296
Burgh Castle, 173, 174
Burgundians, 23, 83
Buston, 180, 200
butter, 248
Byzacena, 135

Cadbury-Congresbury, 160, 179, 180, 182, 183, 191, 208, 220, 231, 234, 239, 244, 330
Cadfan, king of Gwynedd, 87, 299
Cadwaladr, 80
Caedbaed, 161, 325
Caelextis Monedorix, 87
Caerleon, 164, 166, 167, 179, 220, 326, 341
Caernarvon, 79, 119, 175, 328
Caernarvonshire, 79, 122, 125, 188, 189
Caerwent, 153
Caesar, Julius, 51, 52, 67, 82, 92, 138, 236
Caesarea, 34
Caesarius of Arles, 124
Caesaromagus, 145
Caldey Island, 199, 213
    St. David's Church, 213
Caledonians, 67, 164, 266
Calgacus, 82
Calpornius, father of St. Patrick, 40, 114, 115, 119, 124, 310
Camden, William, 179
Camelot, 179
Camlann, Battle of, 254
Camulodunum, 142, 144
Cannington, 204, 344
Canterbury, xiii, 122, 134, 138, 143, 144, 148, 149, 210, 218, 260, 292, 320, 345
    London Gate, 149
    Marlowe, 149
    Riding Gate, 149
    St. Pancras, 210
Cantiorix, 79, 118
Caracalla, 4, 73, 163, 257, 284
Caradoc of Llancarfan, 278
Caratacus, 4, 82
Carausius, 5, 6, 183, 198, 257, 265, 285
Cardiff, 190
Cardigan, 83
Carlisle, 163, 172, 212, 214, 228, 232, 336, 341
    Blackfriars Street, 163
    Scotch Street, 163
Carmarthenshire, 64, 118
Carolingians, 108
Carrawburgh, 172
carriages, 249
Carthage, 135, 221
Cartimandua, 82

Carvoran, 172
Cassian, John, 46
Cassiodorus, 56, 91, 286
Castell Dwyran, 118
Castle Dore, 152, 220, 234
Castlesteads, 168
Catraeth, Battle of, 175, 176, 254, 260
Cattegirn, 106
Catterick, 175, 247
Catuvellauni, 146
cavalry, 8, 14, 235, 253, 343
Caxton, William, 253
Celestine, Pope, 38, 42, 121, 277
Celliwic, 179
Celtic, xiv, xviii, xix, 4, 23, 30, 47, 66, 81,
    83, 87, 92, 105–8, 133, 138, 152,
    156, 161, 178, 179, 184, 190, 192,
    195, 202, 205–7, 209, 216, 219,
    221, 230, 233, 236, 240, 247, 248,
    251–54, 270, 273, 276, 282, 290,
    296–98, 307, 308, 313, 317, 324,
    329, 332, 343, 347, 348, 350
Celticists, xiv, 106
Celts, 66, 96
cemeteries, xvi, 125, 143, 151–53, 155,
    162, 172, 178, 184, 187, 202,
    204–7, 209, 212–14, 221, 237, 240,
    317, 318, 336
chariots, xiv, 112, 188, 235
Chelmsford, 145, 146, 205, 206, 236
Chester, 154, 164, 167, 220, 221, 232,
    299, 341
    Abbey Green, 167
Chester, Battle of (A.D. 615), 168
Chesterholm, 169, 170
Chesters, 170
Chesterton, 154, 342
Chichester, 149, 232, 341
Chilterns, 148
Chi-Rho, 149, 157, 174, 189, 202, 205,
    209, 214, 237, 238, 344, 345
chisels, 198
Chrétien de Troyes, 179
Chrysanthus, 227, 338
Churchill, Winston, 253
Cicero, 59, 74, 289, 296, 303, 306
Cirencester, 115, 120, 154, 212, 228, 230,
    232, 234, 260, 313, 321, 341, 342
    Verulamium Gate, 154, 342
    Victoria Road, 212
cist graves, 202, 204, 213, 238

cives, xiii, xvii, xix, 41, 47, 51, 56, 60, 63,
    64, 68–70, 72–80, 100, 104, 105,
    111, 112, 175, 229, 232, 249–51,
    288, 289, 293–96, 326
Civilis, 12
civitas capitals, 15, 120, 150, 152–55,
    158, 163, 212, 227, 232, 339, 341
civitates, 103, 183, 227, 228, 232–34,
    273, 321, 338, 340, 342, 345
clamps, 198
classis Britannica, 5, 174
Claudian, 13, 18, 52, 61, 111, 155, 232,
    258, 265, 267–69, 285, 290, 308
Claudius, 4, 52, 82, 142, 173, 231, 296
Clodius Albinus, 4
Clovis, 41
Cnut, 180
Codex Iustinianus, 117
Codrus, 60
coffins, 174, 202, 205, 209, 238, 328
Cogidubnus, 82, 155, 296
coins, xiv, xvi, xvii, 5, 8, 13, 14, 17, 52,
    82, 133–36, 142, 143, 148, 150,
    154–58, 160, 164, 168, 170, 172,
    173, 175, 176, 180, 185, 188, 192,
    196, 199, 200, 205–7, 209, 218,
    220, 228, 233, 241, 242, 266, 269,
    270, 296, 309, 317, 319–21, 323,
    325–28, 330, 334, 335, 342
    clipping, 241, 320, 328
    counterfeit, 134, 241, 331
    hoards, 143, 149, 150, 153, 155, 170,
        172, 183, 200, 235, 241, 320, 321,
        327, 331, 334, 335, 344–46
Colchester, 4, 138, 142, 144–46, 209,
    211, 237, 238, 322, 343
    Balkerne Gate, 144, 145
coloniae, 144, 154, 161–63, 290, 325
Columba, Saint, 260
Columbanus, Saint, 43, 45, 126, 278, 281,
    311, 316
combrogi, 79, 80, 250
combs, 36, 47, 136, 151, 170, 183, 191,
    198, 244, 249, 335
comes Britanniarum, 8, 12, 32, 53, 110,
    233
comes litoris Saxonici, 8, 32, 53, 110,
    233, 258
comes rei militaris, 10, 12
comitatenses, 8, 32, 110, 308, 339
Commodianus, 59, 311

Congar, Saint, 183, 330
Conmail, 155, 313
consiliarii, 116, 229
consilium, 44, 84, 102, 103, 112, 116, 117, 260, 302, 305, 311, 339
Constans, son of Constantine III, 19, 20, 21, 22, 33, 98, 102, 125, 239, 270, 271, 274
Constans I, 4, 8, 10, 150, 258, 266, 320, 321
Constantine I, 4, 6, 8, 12, 14, 16, 19, 31, 85, 117, 120, 162, 233, 257, 267
Constantine II, 8, 258, 330, 334
Constantine III, xvii, 6, 19–24, 32, 33, 83, 95, 97–100, 102, 103, 111, 118, 125, 134, 156, 168, 227–29, 233, 239, 241, 246, 259, 269–71, 274, 302–4, 312, 320, 342
Constantine of Dumnonia, 44, 70, 78, 104, 299
Constantinople, 33–35, 59, 173, 229, 243, 260, 349
Constantius I, 4, 6, 162, 257, 285
Constantius II, 8, 10, 258, 320
Constantius III, 21, 306
Constantius of Lyon, ii, xv, 5, 6, 8, 21, 29, 30, 37–40, 50, 54, 56, 62, 68, 69, 76, 82, 111, 113, 114, 121, 124, 125, 127, 148, 228, 235, 246, 249, 264, 275, 276, 287, 288, 291, 308, 310, 316, 339, 340, 343, 346
consularis, 113, 227
Conwy Bay, 188
Corbridge, 170–72
Cornish, 106, 152, 184, 185, 244, 307, 330, 331
Cornish rounds, 39, 42, 98, 175, 187, 247
Cornovii, 157, 158, 185
Cornwall, 79, 87, 108, 135, 152, 184, 204, 207, 238, 242, 247, 330, 342
Coroticus, xv, 40, 42, 62, 76, 77, 83, 86, 99, 100, 111, 114, 235, 245, 264, 277, 294, 295, 297, 304, 308, 348
Council of Ariminum, 67
Council of Arles (A.D. 314), 53, 120, 212, 257
Council of Rimini (A.D. 359), 314
Council of Tours (A.D. 461), 70, 121
Count Theodosius, 12, 31, 67, 96, 173, 174, 233, 258, 342
Coventina's Well, 172

cows, 191, 197–99, 248
Coygan Camp, 187, 188
crannogs, 200, 247
Crocus, 8, 266
crucibles, 178, 187
Cumbria, 12, 176, 295, 308
Cunedda, 267
Cuneglasus, 44, 78, 85, 246, 298, 341
Cunomorus (King Mark), 87
Cunorix, 87, 161, 300
curiales, 107, 114, 227, 229, 307, 311, 339
Cuthbert, Saint, 212
Cymry, 72, 79, 80, 250, 295, 296
Cynan, 80
Cynwyl Gaeo, 64
Cyprian, 43
Cyprus, 135

Dacia, 154, 234
daggers, 187
Dalmatia, 79
Danube River, 96
dark earth, 219, 348
David, King, 85
De Virginitate, 240
deacons, 38, 40, 42, 114, 115, 121, 124, 125, 212, 239, 278, 310
decapitation, 238
Decimus Rusticus, 21, 22, 98, 271, 272
decurion, 15, 40, 77, 107, 114, 115, 119, 220, 295, 310, 311
decuriones, 15, 40, 77, 107, 113, 114, 116, 227–9, 252, 310, 311
deer, 197, 198
Degannwy, 188, 189, 220, 232, 234
Deisi, 267
Demetae, 44, 70, 79, 118, 232
Denbighshire, 192
Devon, 79, 87, 152, 183, 197, 342
Dicalydones, 11
Didymus, 20
Din Eidyn (Edinburgh), 193, 260, 341
Dinas Emrys, 188, 189, 235, 247, 341
Dinas Powys, 179, 190–92, 234, 244, 247, 332, 333, 341
Dinorben, 192, 331
Diocletian, 5, 8, 52, 101, 102, 142, 257, 304
Dionysius of Syracuse, 93
Dissolution of the Monasteries, 209
Dobunni, 183, 232

dogs, 101, 149, 197, 198, 244, 279, 347
Doon Hill, 180, 193, 247, 332
Dorchester, 151, 152, 202, 204, 206, 220, 237, 341
 Poundbury, 151, 202, 204, 220, 237, 238
Dorchester-on-Thames, 156, 317, 319
Dorian War, 60
Dorset, 45, 206, 342
Dover, 173
Dropshort, 196
Dumbarton, 99, 157, 179, 193, 232, 234, 245, 248, 277, 297, 341, 342
Dumfrieshire, 214
Dumnonia, 44, 70, 72, 87, 152, 185, 192, 246, 342
Dumnonii, 79, 183, 342
Dunadd, 179
duns, 247
Durotriges, 183, 206
dux Britanniarum, 8, 11, 53, 110, 172, 233, 258
Dyfed, 118, 267, 299, 312
Dyfrig, 122
Dyrham, Battle of (A.D. 577), 151, 154, 155, 260, 321

Eaglesfield, 238
Eccles, 238
Eccleshall, 238
Eddius Stephanus, 240, 249, 324
Edict of Milan (A.D. 313), 257
Edobinchus, 19, 21, 274
Edwin, king of Northumbria, 163
Eggles, 238
eggs, 248
Egypt, 31, 33
Elafius, 39, 114, 228, 246, 340
Elmet, 70, 232
enamel, 197, 198, 249
England, xiv, 133, 216, 218, 251, 252, 268, 299, 320, 329
English Channel, 5, 6, 19, 22, 37, 252, 265, 272, 284, 297
Ennodius, 46
Ephesus, 59, 301, 349
epigraphy, x, 48, 56, 64, 70, 82, 87, 88, 110, 116, 118, 122, 125, 216, 236, 238, 244, 344, 347, 350
epimenia, 14, 112, 309, 339

episcopus, 70, 120–24, 127, 239, 276, 277, 291, 292, 314, 315
Ermine Street, 154
Etruscans, 82
Eugenius, 95
Eugippius, 74
Eunapius, 34, 95, 266, 285, 302
Euric, 82, 83, 296
Eutropius, 53, 265, 266, 285, 290
Exeter, 152, 220, 322
 Topsham, 152

famine, 86, 152, 228, 248, 249, 276, 281, 348
Fastidius, Pelagian bishop, 70, 121, 314
fasting, 126, 248, 345
Faustus of Riez, 70, 121, 125, 275
federates, 14, 15, 112, 116, 268, 281, 309
figs, 244
Firth of Forth, ix, 266
fish, 198, 200
Flavia Caesariensis, 5, 52
Flavians, 146, 155
foederati, 14, 112, 133, 234, 308, 309, 312, 343
foedus, 112, 115, 234
fora, 15, 142, 146, 148, 152–56, 158, 161, 208, 323
Fosse Way, 154, 205
Fowey, 152
Frampton, 202, 237, 344, 345
Francia, 68
Franks, 5, 11–13, 19, 21, 33, 35, 41, 69, 76, 173, 195, 265, 270, 272, 274, 330
French, 68, 254
Frocester, 196
Frontinus, 67
Fullofaudes, 11, 266

Gadebridge Park, 148
Galilee, 61
Gallic Chronicles, xv, 30, 35–37, 54, 232
 Chronicle of 452, 22, 35–37, 96, 264, 267, 270, 271, 275, 302, 338, 351
 Chronicle of 511, 29, 35–37, 264
Gallic Empire, 4, 257
Gallienus, 93, 188
Galloway (Scotland), 214, 215, 337
Gatcombe, 183

Gateholm, 198, 199, 220
Gaul, xix, 5, 6, 11–13, 18–23, 31–34,
    36–38, 52, 60, 62, 68–70, 76, 77, 82,
    83, 96–98, 101, 106–8, 111, 113,
    116, 118, 121, 124, 125, 134, 135,
    138, 149, 154, 187, 191, 194, 198,
    207, 216, 226, 227, 229, 233, 234,
    239, 241–43, 259, 269, 270, 272,
    276, 286, 288, 289, 291, 295, 296,
    303, 306, 310, 328, 329, 338, 339,
    342, 343, 347, 349, 350, 352
Gaza, 33, 135, 143, 160
genealogies, 30, 42, 45, 48, 83, 99, 100,
    277, 278, 299, 310, 312, 325
Gennadius of Marseilles, 70, 314
Geoffrey of Monmouth, 65, 72, 80, 86,
    102, 184, 185, 189, 253, 254, 289,
    291, 296
Geographi, 52, 265, 284, 285
Gerald of Wales, 72, 164, 253, 293
Germanic, xviii, 8, 14, 110, 133, 143,
    169, 172, 173, 180, 191, 194, 218,
    232, 234, 247, 263, 265, 296, 297,
    317, 341, 350
Germans, 66, 265
Germanus of Auxerre, Saint, xv, 29, 30,
    37–40, 42, 62, 68, 69, 111, 113, 114,
    121, 148, 168, 226, 240, 246, 259,
    276, 287, 305, 308, 340, 346, 352
Germany, 21
Gerontius, 19–23, 98, 270, 271
Gildas, x, xv, xvii, xviii, 13, 18, 23–25,
    29, 30, 43–46, 48, 50, 51, 55–58, 63,
    64, 68, 69, 72, 78–81, 83–86, 89, 90,
    95–97, 99, 101–8, 111–13, 115–19,
    121–27, 157, 163, 172, 188, 192,
    217, 220, 226–29, 231, 232, 234–36,
    239–41, 245, 246, 248, 249, 251,
    252, 257, 260, 264, 268, 273, 275,
    279–81, 284, 286, 287, 289, 291,
    292, 295–300, 302, 304–6, 309–16,
    318, 326, 337–46, 351
Glamorganshire, 190
Glan-y-mor, 197
glass, 143, 156, 157, 169, 172, 182, 185,
    188–92, 194, 197, 199, 206–9, 214,
    240, 248, 330, 333, 337
Glastonbury, 176, 178, 179, 239, 244,
    253, 329
    Glastonbury Abbey, 176, 178, 179
    Glastonbury Tor, 176, 178, 179, 244

Gloucester, 220, 234, 260, 321, 342
    Kingsholm, 154, 155
    St. Mary de Lode, 155, 238
Gloucestershire, 196, 197, 208, 344, 347
goats, 198, 248
Gododdin, 106, 175, 248, 254, 299, 341,
    343
Goths, 35, 76, 272, 347
Graenog, 199
grain, 5, 10, 134, 151, 159, 243
    barley, 200, 248
    oats, 248
    spelt, 200, 248
    wheat, 248
grammaticus, 119, 313
granaries, 159, 168–70
Gratian, British tyrant, 19, 53, 95, 97, 99,
    102, 113, 227, 229, 259, 269, 271,
    287, 303, 304, 327
Gratian, the Elder, 10
Gratian I, 13, 97, 258, 266, 304
Great Dunmow, 146
Greece, xvii, 90, 91, 252, 270
Gregory of Tours, 33, 68, 83, 95, 96, 269,
    270, 277, 302, 349
Gregory the Great, Pope, 56, 122, 163,
    237, 264, 287, 302
Grim's Bank, 156, 342
Grubenhäuser, 133, 143, 173–75, 234
Gwynedd, 70, 79, 87, 118, 174, 188, 199,
    239, 267, 300, 313

Hadrian, 4, 10, 12, 13, 18, 158, 168, 233
Hadrian's Wall, 4, 8, 9, 32, 47, 100, 110,
    163, 164, 168–70, 172, 173, 175,
    233, 274, 277, 293, 327, 338, 343
Hadrianopolis, 119
hagiography, 30, 40, 43, 45, 68, 120, 125,
    184, 213, 221, 240, 245, 288, 297
halls, xiii, xvi, 10, 63, 68, 86, 101, 107,
    137, 146, 160, 163, 168, 169, 172,
    180, 185, 193, 196, 219, 247, 301,
    332, 341
Ham Hill, 183, 220
hares, 198
hazelnuts, 248
hearths, 169, 178, 185, 191, 197–200,
    331
Helena, Saint, mother of Constantine I, 267
helmets, 235
Hengest and Horsa, 50

Henry II, king of England, 253
Henry VIII, king of England, 253
Hercules, 93
Herodotus, 93
Heroic Age (British), xviii, 80, 89, 110,
    180, 233, 241, 244
Hiberni, 8
High Peak, 183
Highlands, xiv, 289
hillforts, xvi, xviii, 138, 152, 170, 176,
    179, 181–84, 188, 190, 192–94, 197,
    200, 204, 206, 217, 219, 220, 225,
    231, 232, 234, 235, 243, 244, 246,
    247, 334, 341, 343
Hinton St. Mary, 202, 237, 344, 345
Hippias, 105
Historia Augusta, 53, 67, 91, 93, 94, 96,
    301, 304, 308
Historia Brittonum, 48, 157, 189, 230,
    254, 264, 273, 289, 338, 341
Holyhead, 200, 201, 334
honestiores, 272
honey, 248
Honoriaci, 270
Honorius, 3, 13, 18–21, 24, 25, 35, 98,
    119, 134, 142, 155, 156, 170, 172,
    200, 227, 228, 233, 234, 241, 259,
    270–72, 311, 319, 320, 338, 339
horses, ii, 198, 235, 249, 306, 311, 346
Housesteads, 169, 170
humiliores, 272
Huns, 33
hunting, 248, 347
huts, 133, 145, 150, 174, 184, 187, 192,
    199–201, 204, 213, 215
Hwicca, 212
Hydatius, 61, 270, 271, 349
hypocausts, 143, 146, 150, 163, 164, 326

Iarnhitin, 107
Icklingham, 210, 237, 344
Ilchester, 183, 205, 220
imperator, 22, 86, 93, 96, 97, 102, 297,
    302, 304
inscriptions, x, xiv, xvi, 14, 35, 47, 51, 67,
    70, 72, 79, 82, 87, 108, 110, 114,
    118, 119, 125, 126, 152, 172, 226,
    232, 236, 238, 239, 282–84, 292,
    295, 307, 323, 328, 345
interlace (Celtic), 194, 249
Iona, 179, 243, 244, 260, 345

Ireland, x, xv, 10, 40, 41, 42, 51, 63, 117,
    121, 122, 124, 125, 135, 185, 200,
    239, 240, 243, 259, 260, 277, 281,
    286, 294, 312, 314, 315, 329, 330, 349
Irish, xv, 8, 14, 40, 42, 45, 47, 48, 62, 76,
    77, 81, 83, 106, 121, 122, 133, 152,
    153, 155, 156, 161, 174, 178, 213,
    240, 251, 267, 277, 280, 294, 307,
    308, 312, 313, 324, 329, 332, 342,
    345
Irish annals, 41, 349
iron, xvi, 13, 20, 148, 151, 178, 188, 191,
    195, 197, 198, 205, 208, 209, 214,
    235, 244, 248, 334
Iron Age, 138, 170, 176, 180, 182, 187,
    189, 190, 192, 194, 204, 231, 318,
    329, 342
Irthing River, 168
Isidore of Seville, 56, 300
Isle of Ely, 122
Isle of Thanet, 173
Isocrates, 105
Israel, 44, 61, 65
Italy, 18–22, 24, 31, 59, 69, 259, 270,
    288, 291, 295
iudices, 44, 84, 85, 117, 229, 298, 312,
    313, 339
Iuriucus, 87

Jerome, Saint, 10, 16, 21, 36, 41, 44, 46,
    53, 55, 59, 61, 62, 67, 71, 72, 85,
    90, 94, 98, 99, 101, 108, 124, 125,
    229, 240, 266, 268, 286, 288, 290,
    292, 300–302, 304, 313
Jerusalem, 21, 59, 61, 62, 75, 315
Jesus, 61
jewelry, 133–36, 149, 153, 173, 191, 194,
    221, 231, 234, 241, 244, 249, 346
  armlets, 190
  brooches, 133, 143, 145, 156, 169,
    170, 175, 188, 190, 194, 197–99,
    207, 244, 249, 317
John II, Pope, 240
Jordanes, 56, 68, 82, 83, 91, 286, 291,
    296, 297
Josephus, 94
Jovinus, 21, 22, 267
Jovius, 20
judges, 44, 84, 86, 87, 110, 117, 298
Julian II, 10, 31, 59, 96, 120, 208, 258,
    266, 287, 297, 302

Julian, son of Constantine III, 19, 21, 269
Julius Nepos, 260
Justinian I, 19, 34, 35, 275, 347, 349
Justinianus, 19
Justus, 20, 270
Jutes, 146, 272

Kent, 106, 142, 143, 173, 238, 319
Kentigern, Saint, 106, 254
kilns, 134, 175, 199, 242, 248, 347
kings, xiii–xv, xvii, 23, 43, 44, 64, 69,
    81–92, 95, 99, 101, 103, 104, 108,
    110, 112, 117, 120, 174, 185, 187,
    226, 229, 235, 236, 244, 245,
    252–54, 267, 296–301, 304–6,
    310–13, 316, 321, 340
Kings Castle, 220
Kircudbright, 213
Kirkmadrine, 123, 214, 337
knives, 197, 198, 206, 235, 248

La Tène, 190, 296
laeti, 14, 15, 173, 308, 343
Lailoken, 254
Lamyatt, 208, 344
Land's End, 87
late pre-Roman Iron Age (LPRIA), 138,
    183, 190, 207, 231
Latinus, 74, 214, 240
leather, 244, 330
Leland, John, 179
Liber Landavensis, 46, 122, 124, 264, 282
Lichfield, 157, 238, 324
    St. Michael's, 238
Life of St. Honoratus, 62
Life of St. John the Almsgiver, 114, 152,
    228, 241, 310, 318, 330, 339,
    346–48
Life of St. Kentigern, 254
Life of St. Maximus, 62
limes, 14, 15, 17, 347
limitanei, 8, 32
limpets, 197, 198, 200, 248
Lincoln, 120, 161, 162, 218, 220, 230,
    238, 322
    Newport Arch, 162
    St. Paul-in-the-Bail, 238
Lincolnshire, 161
Lindsey, 161, 325
Little Hoyle, 199
litus Saxonicum, 8, 266
Livy, 59, 92, 306

Llan-Arth, 126
Llanbeblig, 175
Llancarfan, 240
Llandaff Charters, xv, 30, 46, 47, 70, 86,
    89, 112, 117, 122, 126, 192, 232,
    249, 282, 292, 348
Llanddowror, 126
Llandeilo Fawr, 126
Llandinabo, 126
Llangadwaldr, 87
Llangian, 119
Llantrisant, 79, 122
Llantwit Major, 240
llys, 107, 191–94
Loire River, 67, 296
London, xi, 5, 6, 8, 10, 12, 15, 32, 120,
    134, 138, 142–44, 146, 154, 157,
    160, 218, 220, 226, 228, 230, 232,
    234, 300, 311, 317, 327, 341
    Billingsgate, 143
    Cripplegate, 143
    Tower of London, 142, 143, 342
Longbury Bank, 199, 220
Lothian, 193
Luce Bay, 214
Lullingstone, 237, 345
Lundy Island, 204, 307
Lupicinus, 10, 266
Lupus, companion of St. Germanus, 38,
    39, 276
Lydia, 91, 105, 300
Lydney, 206, 329

Mabinogi, 267, 291
machtiern, 106–8, 307, 308
Maelgwn (Maglocunus), king of
    Gwynedd, 44, 85, 104, 119, 125,
    188, 239, 246, 278, 299, 300, 316
magister equitum, 10, 117
magister militum, 13, 18, 19, 21, 31, 98,
    118, 233, 274, 351
magistrates, xiv, 22, 23, 107, 111, 113,
    115, 117, 220, 226, 227, 311, 339
magistratus, 48, 113, 118, 175, 229, 313
Maglos, 79, 118, 119
Magnentius, 10, 31, 175, 258, 266
Magnus Maximus, 6, 12–14, 16, 19, 45,
    68, 83, 93, 94–8, 100–104, 111, 115,
    118, 134, 152, 168, 172, 207, 229,
    233, 258, 267, 268, 270, 297,
    301–3, 305, 306, 311, 312, 317,
    320, 321, 327

Maiden Castle, 206, 220, 329, 341
Maiozamalcha, 59
Manau Gododdin, 172, 195
mansio, 61, 160, 197, 230, 247, 341
Mansuetus, 70, 121, 314
Marcian, 275
Marcus, 19, 95, 97, 99, 102, 259, 269,
    271, 303, 304
Mark, King, 185
Marmoutier, 214, 316
Martial, 59, 67, 290
Martin of Tours, Saint, 15, 39, 41, 96,
    213, 214, 267, 297, 302, 303, 316
Martinus, 119
martiobarbuli, 206, 235
Marwnad Cynddylan, 157
mausolea, 151, 155, 202, 205, 238
Mavorius, 123, 214
Maxima Caesariensis, 52, 142, 227, 267
Maximianus, 5
Maximus, dependent of Gerontius, 20, 98
Maximus, philosopher, 59
mead, 248
medicus, 48, 119
Mellitus, archbishop of Canterbury, 237
Melus, 119
Mens Scryfys, 87
Mercury, 208
Merlin, xiii, 188, 189, 252–55, 351
Merovingian, 185, 194, 195, 199, 207,
    213
Mertola, 70
Mesopotamia, 31, 312, 313
metalwork, xiii, xvii, 14, 149, 155, 156,
    169, 170, 172, 173, 178, 179, 182,
    185, 191, 194, 231, 244, 317
Meurig, 87, 299
Milan, 13, 69, 294
Mildenhall, 344, 345
Miletus, 59
milites, 77, 78, 86, 99, 111, 112, 235,
    304, 308
milk, 248
Milton Keynes, 196
Milton Regis, 317
Mincio River, 22
ministri, 124, 239
Mitcham, 143
moldboard plows, 214, 240
monachi, xvii, 124–26, 239, 270, 288, 315
monasteries, xiv, 43, 120, 122, 124, 126,

    152, 153, 178, 183, 184, 199, 216,
    239, 240, 247, 313, 349
monasticism, xviii, 41, 109, 125–27, 202,
    239, 252, 280, 316
monks, xiv, xvi, xvii, 43, 45, 48, 119, 125,
    126, 157, 167, 179, 239, 246, 248,
    270, 278, 279, 312, 313, 315, 316,
    329, 336, 346
mosaics, 8, 148, 150, 156, 202, 230, 236,
    242, 341, 344, 345
Mote of Mark, 193–95, 244
Mucking, 317
Muirchú, 54, 55, 83, 277, 286, 297, 304,
    314
municeps, 19, 97, 113, 114, 227, 229,
    269, 309
municipium, 146, 163, 227
munificentia, 112
Myrddin, 254, 351

nails, xvi, 182, 198, 205, 209
Narratio de imperatoribus, 22, 272
Nebiogastes, 19
Nectaridus, 11, 266
Nennius, xvi, 48, 65, 80, 86, 102, 157,
    168, 264, 289, 324
Neolithic period, 179, 183
Nerva, 31, 154
Nettleton, 206, 208, 344
New Testament, 61, 75, 85, 279, 299, 301
Nicolas, British bishop, 122
Ninian (Nynia), Saint, 126, 212–14, 240,
    247, 316, 337
Nisibis, 31, 59, 293
Noricum, 39
Norman, 173, 184, 185, 189, 209
North Sea, 4
Northumberland, 195, 196
Northumbria, xiv, 163, 171, 194, 349
Notitia Dignitatum, xv, 14, 15, 31, 32, 53,
    110, 113, 142, 164, 226, 227, 233,
    264, 266, 267, 273, 274, 284, 285,
    290, 338, 343, 345
nuns, 239

Octavian "Augustus," 92
Odovacer, 260
Offa, king of Mercia, 209, 212
Ogam, 47, 118, 152, 156, 213, 238, 251,
    283, 312, 323, 345
oil lamps, 209

Old Latin bible, 41, 43, 46
Old St. Peter's (Rome), 208
Old Testament, 41, 44, 61, 75, 85, 86, 94, 117, 299, 304
olive oil, 241, 243, 248
Olympiad, 36
Olympiodorus of Thebes, 24, 33, 34, 91, 95, 98, 101, 111, 269–71, 274, 284, 302, 303, 306, 308, 315
oppida, 138, 146, 220
oratories, 119, 213, 214, 240, 348
ordo, 114, 124, 227, 311
Ordovices, 70, 232
Orosius, xv, 13, 19, 33, 46, 53, 67, 95–98, 102, 104, 111, 113, 267, 269, 270, 271, 274, 285, 291, 296, 302, 303, 308, 309, 315, 341, 345
Orpington, 143
Ostrogoths, 14
ovens, 60, 103, 146, 185, 212, 335
Ovid, 74, 290
oysters, 152, 248

paganism, xix, 33, 34, 70, 79, 85, 96, 100, 124, 143, 178, 202, 204–9, 212, 216, 231, 234–37, 246, 250, 296, 324, 330, 344
Pagans Hill, 208, 329
pagi, 15, 227
Palladius, 38, 42, 121, 240, 259, 277, 286, 314
panegyrics, 8, 18, 52, 265, 267
Pannonia, 13, 31
parochia, 122–24, 239, 315
Passio Sancti Leodegarii, 91
Pastor Hermas, 43
pastores, 123, 124, 239
Patiens, bishop of Lyon, 38, 276
patria, xvii, xix, 41, 51, 55–64, 73, 74, 76–80, 84, 85, 103, 104, 221, 228, 249, 251, 252, 286–9, 293, 295, 299, 339, 346, 349
Patrick, Saint, x, xiii, xv, xvii, xviii, 29, 30, 40–43, 45, 48, 51, 54–58, 62–65, 69, 72, 76–79, 83, 86, 95, 99, 100, 104, 108, 111, 114, 116, 119, 121, 124, 125, 127, 176, 196, 212, 220, 226, 228, 229, 232, 235, 236, 239, 241, 242, 245, 246, 248, 249, 251, 252, 259, 264, 273, 276–79, 286, 288, 291, 294, 295, 297, 304, 305,

308–11, 313–16, 318, 329, 339–41, 343, 345, 346, 348
Paul the Deacon, x
Paul, Saint, 75
Paulinus, 64, 122
Paulinus, archbishop of York, 163
Paulus Catena, 10, 52
Peebles, 122
Pelagianism, 23, 36, 38, 39, 53, 70, 113, 121, 124, 126, 240, 241, 249, 259, 272, 276, 314, 346
Pelagius, 36, 38, 39, 67, 70, 72, 125, 240, 272, 276, 290–92
Pembrokeshire, 199
Penally, 126, 199
penance, 97, 239, 280, 349
penitentials, xiv, 45, 48, 125, 126, 316, 348
Penmachno Stone, 79, 118, 175, 243, 300
Persians, 31, 59
Pevensey, 173
Phillack, 204, 238
Phocaea, 135
Photius, 33
Picti, x, 6, 12, 69, 328, 329
Picts, x, xiii, xiv, xv, 6, 10, 11, 13, 18, 32, 39, 44, 53, 63, 76–78, 84, 96, 99, 111, 116, 164, 231, 232, 234, 248, 249, 251, 258, 260, 263, 266–69, 281, 286, 289, 294, 297, 339, 343, 344, 348
pigs, 184, 191, 197, 198, 209, 248
pilgrimage, 61, 337
Pindar, 105
pins, 249
plague, 23, 44, 86, 102, 248, 259, 260, 281, 349
Plato, xviii, 91–95, 105, 301, 303
Plautus, 59, 74
Pliny the Elder, 59, 74, 284, 285, 290
plumbata, 206
πολεις, 228
Polemius Silvius, 52, 284
Pompey the Great, 59, 94
Porphyry, 55, 63, 101
Portchester, 149, 173, 319, 342, 343
Portugal, 70
positivist approach, 132, 225, 226, 338
possessores, 15, 115, 227–29, 339
Postumus, 257
Potitus, grandfather of St. Patrick, 40, 124

pottery, ix, xvi, xvii, 133–36, 143, 146, 148, 150, 154, 155, 157, 160, 161, 167–70, 173–76, 179, 180, 182–85, 187–91, 194, 196–200, 204, 207–9, 212–14, 218, 220, 221, 234, 237, 240, 242–44, 300, 321–23, 326, 329–31, 333, 347
  amphoras, 134, 135, 142, 143, 148, 151, 155, 160, 167, 178, 180, 182, 184, 185, 187, 188, 189, 193, 198, 242, 243, 248, 331, 333, 349
  Black Burnished ware, 347
  Crambeck ware, 169, 175
  E ware, 213, 331, 332
  Huntcliff ware, 169
  Oxford color-coated ware, 150, 198, 199
  Oxfordshire ware, 242
  Phocaean Red Slip Ware, 191, 204, 213
  Samian ware, 135, 190, 191, 198, 199
  Thundersbarrow ware, 321
Powys, 102, 167
praepositus, 142, 212, 226
praeses, 6, 113, 115, 227, 338
Prasutagus, 82
presbyter, 48, 70, 98, 114, 122–25, 239, 315
priests, xv, 21, 33, 38, 40, 42, 44, 63, 79, 84, 99, 104, 119, 120, 122–25, 212, 214, 238, 276, 279, 299, 306, 315, 316, 318, 335, 345, 349
primicerius notariorum, 32
princeps, 85, 94, 96, 104, 108, 117, 298, 306, 307
Principate, Roman, xvii, 5
Priscillianists, 207, 267, 303
Procopius, 22, 34, 68, 95, 98, 173, 229, 243, 269, 271, 272, 275, 284, 290, 304, 327, 340, 347, 349
Procopius (the tyrant), 93, 94
procurator, 97, 142, 226
Prosper of Aquitaine, 38, 42, 53, 67, 72, 95, 96, 102, 121, 127, 268, 269, 270, 271, 276, 277, 286, 288, 291, 292, 302, 314
protector, 13, 31, 47, 118, 306, 312, 343
Prudentius, 46, 60, 67, 287–89, 291, 304
Pyro, Abbot, 213

querns, 191

rationalis rei privatae, 226
rationalis summarum, 226
Ravenglass, 176
Ravenna, 21, 62, 299
Ravenna Cosmography, 185
rector, 6, 24, 55, 111, 115, 229, 311
Redon, 107, 308
reductionist approach, 30, 132, 225, 316, 338
reges, xvii, 14, 44, 47, 69, 80, 82–87, 92, 94, 96, 104, 108, 110, 117, 230, 245, 288, 296–99, 301, 302, 306, 312, 340
Renatus Profuturus Frigeridus, 20, 33, 95, 98, 270, 271, 274, 303
Rescript of Honorius, 24, 34, 45, 119, 134, 231
Rheged, 163, 172, 175
rhetor, 119, 121
Rhine River, 18, 20, 22, 23, 97, 118, 192, 271, 338
Richborough, 12, 97, 173, 209, 210, 237, 342
Rigalobranus, 87
Riocatus, 239
Riothamus, 68, 82, 83, 291, 297, 339
Ritigern, 106
River Clyde, ix, 193, 266
roads (Roman), 4, 8, 45, 50, 56, 59, 61, 63, 64, 70, 72, 110, 118, 124, 131, 132, 138, 140, 142, 149, 153, 154, 161, 163, 167–70, 172, 205, 228, 248, 335, 339, 342
Roderc (Rhydderch), king of Strathclyde, 193, 194, 254, 341
Romanists, xiv, 346
Romanitas, xix, 89, 119
Romanization, 4, 5, 52, 58, 68, 106, 214, 229, 236, 240, 251, 311, 326, 340, 344, 350
Romano-British, 15, 46, 133, 153, 162, 168, 169, 172, 175, 176, 182, 189, 191, 204, 205, 207, 209, 212, 216, 218, 234, 248, 253, 317, 320, 323–25, 337, 341, 344, 345
Romulus Augustulus, 260
Rookery Hill, 149
round houses, 180, 182, 192, 200, 330
Ruffiac, 107
Rufinus, 46, 300, 301, 304

"The Ruin," 218, 337
Rusticus Julianus, 93
Rutilius Namatianus, 60, 63, 65, 71, 288, 289, 338

sacerdos, 44, 48, 56, 64, 79, 122–25, 214, 239, 276, 298, 306, 313, 315
Sallust, 92
Salonae, 79
salt, 185, 234, 242, 347
Salvian of Marseilles, 44, 86, 107, 108, 115, 229, 270, 307, 310, 340
Sanctinus, 123
Sanctus, 227
Saragossa, 20
Sarmatians, 60
Sarus, 19, 270
Saxon Shore, 8, 12, 32, 68, 164, 173, 174, 266, 342
Saxons, x, xiii, xix, 8, 10–13, 18, 20, 22, 35–37, 39, 44, 64, 68, 69, 77, 84, 87, 102, 103, 111, 112, 133, 137, 143, 145, 152, 154, 155, 157, 168, 173, 176, 178, 183, 184, 227, 231, 232, 236, 239, 248, 249, 253, 254, 258–60, 263, 265, 267, 271, 272, 274, 281, 296, 299, 305, 309, 313, 320, 322, 325, 329, 338, 343, 350
Scilly Isles, ix, 204, 207, 243
  Mary's Hill, 207
  Nor'nour, 207
  St. Helen's, 207
  Tean, 207
Scipio, 94
Scotland, x, xiii, 4, 18, 47, 67, 122, 168, 213, 240, 247, 251, 252, 266, 315
Scots, x, xiii, xv, 10, 11, 13, 44, 63, 77, 78, 84, 96, 99, 116, 231, 232, 248, 249, 258, 263, 267, 281, 286, 289, 294, 343
Scotti, x, 8, 69, 121, 290
Second Council of Tours (A.D. 567), 68
seigneur, 92, 107, 230
Selgovae, 14
Senacus, 125
Seneca, 59, 74, 290
Seneca the Elder, 59, 74
Septimius Severus, 4, 5, 162, 257, 284
Serenianus, 60

Severianus, Pelagian bishop, 38, 121, 276, 314
Severinus, Saint, 39
Severn River, 155, 158, 342
Severus III, 149, 241
Severus, companion of St. Germanus, 39
sheep, 191, 197, 198, 248
Shepton Mallet, 205, 238
shields, 235, 297
shrines, 38, 148, 157, 178, 182, 204–8, 212–14, 216, 231, 236, 329, 330
Sicily, 35, 347
Sidbury, 157
Sidonius Apollinaris, 38, 46, 61, 64, 67, 70, 82, 83, 91, 113, 116, 239, 240, 270, 288–92, 296, 297, 306, 307, 310, 311, 314, 339, 345
signal stations, 174, 178, 200, 308, 328
Silchester, 138, 155–57, 208, 210, 218, 232, 237, 244, 341, 342
Silvanus, 93
Silvius Bonus, 52, 70, 71
slavery, xvii, 40, 68, 82, 99, 111, 120, 225, 227, 242, 245, 246, 339, 340, 348, 350
Snowdonia, 188
Solomon, King, 85, 299
Solon, 93, 300
Solway Firth, 194
Somerset, 176, 182, 183, 202, 204, 208, 219, 238, 329, 334, 338, 341, 342
Sophocles, 105, 300
South Cadbury, 151, 179, 181, 182, 183, 193, 208, 220, 232, 234, 247, 248, 341, 344
South Shields, 172
Sozomen, xv, 33, 91, 95–97, 267, 269, 270, 271, 274, 302, 303
Spain, 19–23, 33, 52, 59, 60, 62, 96, 111, 270, 271, 286, 288, 343
Sparta, 91
spears, 112, 172, 188, 235
speculatores, 115, 116, 311
spindle whorls, 184, 198
St. Albans, 138, 142, 146, 209, 228, 318
St. Albans Abbey, 146, 209
Staffordshire, 157
Stanegate, 168, 169
Stilicho, 13, 18, 19, 21, 32, 111, 143, 168, 233, 259, 266, 269, 270
Stoicism, 59, 95

Stone Age, 138
Stone-by-Faversham, 238
Stourton, 87
Strathclyde, 42, 77, 83, 172, 193, 194,
    200, 254, 277, 294, 297, 342
Sueves, 18
Sulla, 92
Sulpicius Alexander, 33, 302
Sulpicius Severus, 46, 53, 67, 95, 96, 102,
    286, 291, 297, 303, 305, 315
Surrey, 143
Sutton Hoo, xiv, 199, 221
swords, 16, 60, 112, 206, 235, 248, 343,
    349
Symmachus, 31

Tacitus, 4, 31, 52, 59, 67, 68, 72, 83, 86,
    92, 236, 284, 285, 290, 296, 306
Taliesin, 48, 106, 113, 175, 292, 293, 299
Tarquin, 95, 103
Tathan, Saint, 153
Tedbury, 220
Teilo, 122
temples, xiii, 119, 133, 146, 148–50, 156,
    157, 164, 169, 178, 180, 182, 202,
    204–8, 216, 228, 236, 237, 317,
    321, 329, 334–36, 344
Tennyson, Alfred, 184
Tertullian, 94, 290, 301, 311, 344
Tetrarchy, 5, 257, 293
Tetricius I, 198
Tetricus, 330
Thames River, 138, 142, 323
theaters, 92, 146, 195
Theodosian Code, 52, 273
Theodosius I, 13, 18, 208, 258, 268, 327
Theodosius II, 33, 36, 272, 275
Thrace, 31
Thucydides, 93, 300, 303, 306
Thundersbarrow, 149
Tiberius Gracchus, 92
Tigernmaglus, 106
tigernos, 105, 106, 230
tin, 5, 152, 185, 187, 228, 241, 242, 244,
    318, 330, 331, 339
Tintagel, 135, 180, 182, 184–87, 191,
    199, 231, 235, 238, 239, 244, 247,
    253, 318, 330, 331
Tolosanus, 70
Toulouse, 118
townhouses, xvi, 24, 146, 147, 152, 156,

    163, 219, 220, 230, 247, 319, 326
Tractus Armoricanus et Nervicanus, 68
Trefloyne, 199
Trethurgy, 187
tribune, 14, 38, 113, 114, 246, 276, 310,
    312, 343
Trier, 13, 101, 270, 293, 303, 304, 321
Trinovantes, 146
Tristan, 185
Ty Mawr, 200, 201
Tyne River, 170, 172
tyranni, xvii, xviii, xix, 16, 44, 51, 70, 79,
    83–85, 90–108, 110, 112, 116, 117,
    149, 160, 188, 229, 230, 246, 251,
    252, 260, 270, 271, 277, 279, 296,
    298, 300–308, 312, 313, 340, 341
τυραννος, xvii, 91, 93, 97, 99, 105, 229,
    271, 300, 301–4
tyranny, ix, 20, 41, 91–94, 96, 97, 99,
    100, 101, 105, 303
tyrants, ii, ix, xv, xvii, xviii, 16–19, 22, 34,
    44, 55, 63, 64, 70, 71, 77, 78, 81,
    83–85, 90–108, 110–12, 115, 117,
    118, 123, 220, 229, 230, 252, 259,
    270, 271, 274, 279, 298, 300–309,
    316, 340

Uley. See West Hill Uley
Urien, king of Rheged, 175
Ursicinus, 31, 117
usurpers, xvii, 4, 10, 13, 16, 18–21, 33,
    34, 90–98, 100, 101, 103, 104, 106,
    113, 227, 229, 231, 241, 242, 258,
    259, 267, 269–71, 302, 303, 306,
    340

Valens, 31, 60, 152, 155, 156, 188, 258,
    327
Valentia, 12, 31, 32, 227, 267, 284, 336
Valentinian I, 10, 11, 94, 258, 309, 322,
    327
Valentinian II, 183, 258, 267, 326, 327
Valentinian III, 36, 149, 241, 259, 275
Valentinus, 12, 258, 267
Valerian, 93
Vandals, 13, 18, 270
vegetables, 248
Venantius Fortunatus, 56, 297
Veracius, 125
Verenianus, 20
Verona List, 52, 284

Verturiones, 11
Verulamium, 39, 135, 142, 144, 146–48,
    209, 218, 219, 230, 341
Vespasian, 180, 206, 341
vicarius, 6, 12, 15, 24, 32, 53, 113, 115,
    142, 226, 284, 306, 310
vici, 53, 169, 170, 172, 175, 176, 196,
    205, 227, 307, 339, 341
Victorinus, 71, 227, 272, 338
Victricius of Rouen, 53, 120, 258
Vikings, 193, 213, 215
villas, xiii, xiv, 4, 8, 15, 16, 40, 46, 63,
    114, 148, 149, 160, 176, 180, 183,
    192, 195–97, 202, 216, 219, 220,
    228, 230, 231, 237, 240, 242, 243,
    245–48, 282, 290, 292, 315, 324,
    334, 339, 341, 344
Vinnian, 45, 126, 316
Virgil, 46, 59
Visigoths, 14, 18, 20, 21, 59, 82, 149,
    259, 298
Viventius, 123, 214
voles, 198
Vortigern, 50, 102, 106, 160, 188, 189,
    229, 254, 279, 305, 306, 309, 340,
    341
Vortipor, 44, 70, 85, 87, 104, 118, 246,
    299, 306, 312
Votadini, 14
Vulgate bible, 41, 43, 46, 61, 75, 94, 293,
    298, 312, 313

Wales, xi, xiii, xiv, xvi, 13, 14, 30, 43, 46,
    47, 70, 72, 79, 86, 87, 108, 112,
    117–19, 122, 126, 157, 164, 192,
    216, 238, 240, 243, 247, 252, 253,
    282, 293, 299, 307, 308, 315, 328,
    336, 342
Wall, 157
Wallenses, 72
Walltown Crags, 169
Wansdyke, 183, 342
Wantsum Channel, 173
warbands, 110, 112, 113, 220, 247
Water Newton, 344, 345
Watling Street, 157
weapons, 84, 111, 136, 172, 235, 309

Wells, 205, 238
Welsh, xiii, xvi, 4, 8, 43, 48, 70, 79, 83,
    87, 102, 106, 107, 112, 117, 122,
    152, 157, 161, 167, 174, 187, 192,
    221, 226, 240, 250, 251, 254, 263,
    267, 289, 293–95, 299, 305, 307,
    308, 313, 340, 350, 351
Welsh Bicknor, 126
Wessex, 48, 179
West Country, 45
West Hill Uley, 207, 208, 210, 220, 236,
    344
Western Isles, the, xiv, 10
whetstones, 184, 191, 197–99
whey, 248
Whithorn, 123, 126, 179, 213–15,
    237–39, 244, 247, 315, 316, 348
William of Malmesbury, 322, 329
William of Newburgh, 253
Wiltshire, 206, 208, 342
Winchester, 138, 153, 156, 179, 228, 230,
    319
    Lankhills, 153, 238
wine, xiv, 160, 167, 184, 194, 214, 240,
    241, 243, 244, 248, 348, 349
wool, 244, 347
Worcester, 157, 212, 238, 249, 342
    St. Helen's, 212, 238
Wrekin, the, 158, 161, 220
Wroxeter, 87, 135, 157–61, 163, 180,
    206, 218–20, 228, 230, 232, 238,
    244, 247, 318, 324–26, 341
    St. Andrew's, 238

Xenophon, 91

Yeavering, 180, 193, 195, 196, 247
York, 5, 8, 9, 120, 162, 218, 230, 232,
    234, 257, 279, 285, 297, 341, 342
Yorkshire, 70, 174

Zeno, 149, 241
Zosimus, xv, 18–20, 22–25, 33, 34, 91,
    95, 97, 98, 111, 113, 115, 119, 227,
    229, 232, 266, 267, 269–74, 290,
    302, 303, 308–10, 313, 338, 339